A SYNOPSIS OF THE GOSPELS

A SYNOPSIS OF THE GOSPELS

H. F. D. SPARKS

Part I. The Synoptic Gospels with the Johannine Parallels

Part II. The Gospel according to St John with the Synoptic Parallels

A
SYNOPSIS OF THE GOSPELS

H. F. D. SPARKS, D.D., F.B.A.

Formerly Oriel Professor of the Interpretation of Holy Scripture
in the University of Oxford

ADAM AND CHARLES BLACK

LONDON

PART I
FIRST PUBLISHED 1964
SECOND EDITION 1970
REPRINTED 1976

PART II
FIRST PUBLISHED 1974

COMBINED VOLUME
FIRST PUBLISHED 1977

A. AND C. BLACK LTD.
35 BEDFORD ROW   LONDON WC1R 4JH

© 1964, 1970, 1974, 1977 HEDLEY FREDERICK DAVIS SPARKS

ISBN 0 7136 1738 1

Reproduced and printed by photolithography and bound in
Great Britain at The Pitman Press, Bath

PUBLISHER'S NOTE

The two parts of this work were originally published separately, the first edition of Part I in 1964, and Part II in 1974. In this 'combined volume' edition, for various reasons readily intelligible to any habitual user of the *Synopsis*, the original page-numbers of the separate parts have been retained, with only very minor adjustments affecting the Introductions and Tables of Contents at the beginning of each part, and the Indexes at the end. No serious confusion is likely to result, so long as it is remembered that the two parts, though now published together in a single volume, are still distinct and are to be used separately.

INTRODUCTION

THE primary aim of this Synopsis is to enable the Greekless student of the gospels to read through any one of them continuously, in the English of the Revised Version, with the parallel passages in the other three printed in parallel columns alongside.

As is well known, the first three gospels share very much more in common with one another, both as regards subject-matter and the arrangement of that subject-matter, than they do, either individually or collectively, with the fourth. That is why we call them 'The Synoptic Gospels', why we recognize that there is a specifically 'Synoptic Problem' to solve, and why, in consequence, the majority of the synopses of the gospels in use to-day concentrate on exhibiting the relationship between these gospels only, and either pay scant attention to the fourth or else ignore it completely. But that there is a relationship between all four gospels, as well as between the first three, is incontrovertible: in other words, there is a 'Four Gospel Problem' to solve, and not merely a 'Synoptic Problem'; and the most recent gospel scholarship has shown itself well aware of this problem and has concerned itself not a little with its solution.

This means that any synopsis of the gospels that is to be of more than limited value to the modern student must include the fourth gospel on equal terms with the other three. But that is more easily said than done. The obvious way to do it is to treat all four exactly alike—*i.e.*, first to set out opposite one another the parallel passages which occur in all four gospels, and then sandwich in between them in the appropriate places the material that is in fact found between them in each separate gospel. A simple diagram should make this plain ('| | | | | | |' represents the presence of material, '————' its absence):

Matt.	Mark	Luke	John
|||||||||||||	|||||||||||||	|||||||||||||	|||||||||||||
||||||||||||	————	————	————
||||||||||||	|||||||||||||	||||||||||||	|||||||||||
————	————	||||||||||||	————
|||||||||||||	|||||||||||||	||||||||||||	|||||||||||||
||||||||||||	||||||||||||	————	||||||||||||
|||||||||||||	||||||||||||	||||||||||	||||||||||||

But the execution of such a plan, when it comes to the setting out of the actual material, is nothing like so simple, nor can the result be as satisfactory, as the above diagram might suggest. So long as we apply the plan to the Synoptics only, no serious complications arise. The amount of material shared in common by the Synoptics is very large indeed: a high proportion of it occurs in the same order in each of them: the 'fixed points', therefore, are many; and the result is that the 'sandwich' material for the most part falls naturally into place without posing the editor any problems about what order he is going to put it in. But as soon as John is added a radically different picture emerges.

The amount of material shared in common by all four gospels is relatively small: very little of even this small amount occurs in the same order: the 'fixed points' are therefore few; and the result is that in the arrangement of the 'sandwich' material the widest possible discretion is left to the editor. Even where the 'fixed points' are fairly close together there is still considerable latitude. For example, two incidents which are shared in common by all four gospels, and which occur in the same order in all four, are The Feeding of the Five Thousand (Matt. 14 13–21 ‖ Mark 6 30–44 ‖ Luke 9 10–17 ‖ John 6 1–14) and Peter's Confession (Matt. 16 13–20 ‖ Mark 8 27–30 ‖ Luke 9 18–21 ‖ John 6 66–69). In the Synoptics the complete series of incidents at this point works out as follows:

Matt.	Mark	Luke
The Feeding of the Five Thousand	The Feeding of the Five Thousand	The Feeding of the Five Thousand
Jesus walks on the Water	Jesus walks on the Water	———
Healings in Gennesaret	Healings in Gennesaret	———
A Question from the Scribes	A Question from the Scribes	———
The Canaanitish Woman	The Syro-Phoenician Woman	———
Healings by the Sea	The Healing of a Deaf-Mute	———
The Four Thousand	The Four Thousand	———
A Request for a Sign	A Request for a Sign	———
The Leaven of the Pharisees	The Leaven of the Pharisees	———
	The Healing of a Blind Man	———
———		
Peter's Confession	Peter's Confession	Peter's Confession

Here, it will be observed, there is no 'sandwich' material at all in Luke: the eight 'sandwich' incidents in Matt. and nine in Mark arrange themselves naturally in parallel throughout; and the editor has no problem. In John, however, there are two 'sandwich' incidents, and the sequence runs like this:

John

The Feeding of the Five Thousand
Jesus walks on the Water
In the Synagogue at Capernaum
Peter's Confession

The first 'sandwich' incident in John ('Jesus walks on the Water') is obviously parallel with the same incident in Matt. and Mark; but 'In the Synagogue at Capernaum' has no parallel. Where, then, if all four gospels are to be in parallel, should the editor place it in relation to the incidents in Matt. and Mark? Should it go before 'Healings in Gennesaret'? Or after it? Or should the two be printed in parallel (on the ground that Capernaum was situated in the Gennesaret district, and that John expressly states that the incident in the synagogue took place 'on the morrow' after The Feeding of the Five Thousand)? On the other hand, John distinctly implies that Peter's Confession followed straight after the synagogue incident, and that the two are intimately and causally connected. Should the editor, therefore, reserve 'In the Synagogue at Capernaum' until after 'The Healing of a Blind Man' in Mark, and put it immediately before Peter's Confession, in order to maintain and emphasize this Johannine connection, in spite of the statement that it took place 'on the morrow' after the Feeding?

This kind of problem is repeated on a larger scale elsewhere. In fact it reaches such proportions that the inclusion of John must inevitably become an embarrassment to any editor who tries to construct a synopsis in this way; and, even if he is apparently successful, it is very doubtful whether the result can ever be regarded as a really satisfactory tool for the student, inasmuch as the ordering of so much of the contents must of necessity depend on the subjective judgement of one particular editor. Another editor might well prefer a quite different arrangement and with equal justification.

In constructing this Synopsis it has accordingly been thought best to cut the Gordian knot by presenting the material in two distinct parts. Part I contains the text of the Synoptic Gospels with

the Johannine parallels, Part II the text of John with the Synoptic parallels. By this means it is hoped that the primary aim of enabling each of the four gospels to be read through continuously together with the parallels in the other three has been achieved with the minimum of editorial idiosyncrasy.

This does not, of course, eliminate entirely the necessity for some subjective judgements on the part of the editor. If it be asked, upon what principles, in this instance, the editor's subjective judgements are founded, the answer is: (1) upon what seems to be the natural logical or chronological order of the material, and (2) upon the commonly accepted order of the four gospels. Thus, in Part I, 'The Lucan Prologue' stands at the very beginning as § 1, simply because it is a prologue (of the first three gospels, Luke alone has a prologue), and the Matthaean Nativity Narrative (§§ 2–6) precedes the Lucan (§§ 7–15) because it is customary to arrange the gospels in the order, Matthew-Mark-Luke-John.

And so, in Part I, this is the order in which the texts of the four are presented in parallel—or, if we prefer it, horizontally. There are in the Synopsis four columns throughout, one for each gospel. These columns are always of the same relative width where there are parallels printed (e.g., § 113). Where there are no parallels printed, the column or columns with nothing in them contract (in order not to waste space) and the corresponding columns or column of text expand (e.g., §§ 114, 115, and 122). The only exception occurs in those few cases where there is a parallel in the same gospel to print as well as parallels in other gospels, or where it has been thought advisable to print a parallel from outside the gospels altogether. In these cases, five, or even six, columns may be required (e.g., §§ 66, 67, and 68); but in these cases the same conventions about the relative width of columns, and contraction and expansion, apply. However, although a parallel in the same gospel means in practice an additional column at that point, theoretically the additional column is nothing more than a sub-division of the original single column allocated to the gospel. To mark this distinction, columns containing parallels from the same gospel are separated by only a dotted line, instead of the standard 'rule' used to separate one gospel column from another (see again §§ 67 and 68). At the other extreme, a 'heavy rule' is used to separate the Synoptic columns from the John column, in order to remind the reader that this last column differs from the Synoptic columns in not offering a continuous text.

Thus, to read through a Synoptic gospel with the parallels, the student starts at the beginning (p. 3 of Part I for Matt., p. 11 for Mark, and p. 3 for Luke) and follows on from section to section. Whenever he comes to a section that does not continue the text of his gospel, he looks at the headline at the top of the page, and there he will find where to look for the continuation. For example, if he starts reading Luke in § 1 on p. 3, he will find that this section takes him only as far as verse 4 of the first chapter, but a glance at the headline will show him at once that for verse 5 he must turn to p. 6: he can then read continuously from Luke 1 5, in § 7 on p. 6, to Luke 4 30, in § 24 on p. 20; and so on, through §§ 26–31 on pp. 21 to 25, to where the Lucan text is resumed again in § 52 on p. 37. If, at any time, he wants to refer back, because the text of his gospel does not appear in the preceding section, he will find also in the headline a reference backwards to the page at which the text broke off —e.g., if he is concerned with Luke 5 12–16, in §52 on p. 37, and wants to look back to Luke 5 11, he will be directed by the headline to § 31 on p. 25.

To read through John with the Synoptic parallels, the student turns to Part II. There he will find the order of the Synoptic and Johannine columns reversed: the text of John, as the text to be read through continuously, now occupies the first column on the left-hand side of the page, with the Synoptic parallels arranged (still in the traditional order, Matthew-Mark-Luke) on the right-hand side of the 'heavy rule'.

It will be noted that in both parts two sizes of type have been used. The larger (normal) size has been used for the text of each of the four gospels that is to be read through continuously: it has also been used for any parallels in the other gospels that occur in the same context. Use of the smaller size is confined to the parallels, and it indicates that the context of any parallel so printed is different.

It will be noted further (and this is a special feature of this Synopsis) that in setting out the parallels great care has been taken to ensure that identical or alternative words and phrases are printed *exactly* parallel. Naturally, this results in a very large number of gaps in any passage which has a parallel, and in very much more total space being required than if the parallels had been printed simply as they stand without regard to correspondences in detail. But convenience in use should more than compensate for extra length. As the parallels have been set out, the student has all the material arranged in such a way that he can see at once which words and phrases in a passage occur in more than one gospel and which do not, and he has no need to search through up to (perhaps) twenty or so lines of text in the

neighbourhood in order to discover what may, or may not, be relevant.

Another special feature of this Synopsis is the references. Very occasionally a reference consists of just the chapter and verse numbers—*e.g.*, in Part I, §16, '11 10' appears in the Matthew column and '7 27' in the Luke column opposite Mark 1 2, and similarly in Part II, §2: in these cases attention is drawn to what is in fact a parallel, though for one reason or another it has not been printed in full. But usually the chapter and verse numbers are preceded by '*cp.*' (= 'compare'): these are in no sense parallels, but references proper; and they are of several kinds. Sometimes they draw attention to similar or comparable incidents or situations, as when Jesus is accused of blasphemy (Part I, §§ 59 and 242: Part II, § 47), or when He is said to have 'gone up into a mountain' and 'prayed' (see, for example, the references in Part I, § 114). Sometimes the point of comparison is theological rather than factual, as when Jesus is referred to as a 'prophet' (*e.g.*, Part I , § 194: Part II, § 42), or when what is popularly known as a 'universalistic' note is struck (*e.g.*, Part I, § 53: Part II, § 45); and under this head should probably also be included those *motifs* which run through all the gospel material, such as the exhibition of 'fear' or 'amazement' by the bystanders after a miracle has been wrought (*e.g.*, Part I, § 59; Part II, § 33). At other times a reference may apply only to a single word or phrase, especially to words or phrases characteristic of the different evangelists: examples here are 'the holy city' as a synonym for Jerusalem (Matt. 4 5 and 27 53, but not elsewhere), 'the apostles' as a synonym for 'the twelve' (five times in Luke, once in Matthew, once in Mark, but never in John: see Part I, § 177), 'there shall be the weeping and gnashing of teeth' (six times in Matt., once in Luke, but not elsewhere: see Part I, § 103), and the fourth evangelist's regular description of the miracles or 'mighty works' of Jesus as 'signs' (John 2 11, 23; etc.) and his repeated use of 'the hour cometh' (John 4 21, 23; etc.). The student is thus provided with what is virtually a miniature concordance to gospel usage; and he should find this of great help in learning to appreciate the stylistic peculiarities and theological preferences of the evangelists—a subject on which great stress is normally laid in modern study of the gospels. If his interests do not happen to tend that way, he can, of course, ignore the references completely. But in any case, he will soon discover from experience what sorts of references are worth pursuing from his own particular point of view, and what sorts are not, and treat them accordingly.

Wherever possible the division of the material into sections follows the paragraph divisions in the Revised Version. The exceptions are those comparatively rare instances where two or more gospels appear in parallel in the Synopsis but the Revised Version paragraphing differs between one gospel and another. Thus, in the Revised Version, Matt. 9 18–26 (The Healing of Jairus's Daughter and The Woman with an Issue of Blood) is given one paragraph only, but the parallels at Mark 5 21–43 and Luke 8 40–56 are each given three paragraphs: in the Synopsis there is a single section (Part I, § 108).

The supplying of titles for sections in a work of this kind is always something of a problem. There are some titles which are so inseparably linked with their sections by custom that to attempt to change them would seem almost indecent (*e.g.*, 'The Feeding of the Five Thousand'). On the other hand, there are many sections which have no generally agreed title, and some of these are so devoid of any obviously outstanding characteristic that to find any appropriate title at all is well-nigh impossible (*e.g.*, Part I, § 151). And even when titles that are suitable in themselves have been found, there is the further probability that they will not mix happily with the titles of adjacent sections laid down by custom. It is hoped that the titles chosen will not be found unduly bizarre or uneven. When they seem unusual, there may well be a reason. For instance, Part I, § 254 bears the title 'The Penitent Malefactor', instead of the more usual 'The Penitent Thief': the reason is that the Revised Version text of the section refers to 'malefactors' and not to 'thieves'.

Finally, it may be asked, why has the Revised Version of 1881 been printed as the English text and not the more modern Revised Standard Version of 1946 or the New English Bible of 1961?

The simplest answer to this question may be given by quoting from the Revisers' own preface. The Revisers' commission, it will be remembered, was not to produce a new version, but to revise the Authorized Version, and, in doing so, 'to introduce as few alterations as possible . . . consistently with faithfulness'. One of the things they found amiss with the AV was what they stigmatized as 'a studied variety of rendering, even in the same chapter and context': this, they maintained, 'produced a degree of inconsistency that cannot be reconciled with the principle of faithfulness'; and they went on to confess to having had no hesitation in such cases in introducing alterations 'even though the sense might not seem to the general reader to be materially affected'. They explained this point as follows:

'When a particular word is found to recur with characteristic frequency in any one of the Sacred Writers, it is obviously desirable to adopt for it some uniform rendering. Again, where, as in the case of the first three Evangelists, precisely the same clauses or sentences are found in more than one of the Gospels, it is no less necessary to translate them in every place in the same way. These two principles may be illustrated by reference to a word that perpetually recurs in St. Mark's Gospel, and that may be translated either "straightway", "forthwith", or "immediately". Let it be supposed that the first rendering is chosen, and that the word, in accordance with the first of the above principles, is in that Gospel uniformly translated "straightway". Let it be further supposed that one of the passages of St. Mark in which it is so translated is found, word for word, in one of the other Gospels, but that there the rendering of the Authorised Version happens to be "forthwith" or "immediately". That rendering must be changed on the second of the above principles; and yet such a change would not have been made but for this concurrence of two sound principles, and the consequent necessity of making a change on grounds extraneous to the passage itself.'

The importance of this approach, if we are choosing a version to serve as the basis for a Synopsis, is obvious. Yet the translators of the NEB deliberately repudiate it.

'We have not felt obliged (as did the Revisers of 1881)', they wrote in their Introduction, 'to make an effort to render the same Greek word everywhere by the same English word. We have in this respect returned to the wholesome practice of King James's men, who (as they expressly state in their preface) recognized no such obligation.'

And the most cursory study of the NEB makes the truth of this statement only too plain. For example, γραμματεύς occurs in the Greek gospels 59 times: in the RV it is uniformly translated 'scribe' (following the AV); but in the NEB it is variously translated 'lawyer' (30 times), 'doctor of the law' (23 times), 'teacher' (4 times), and 'teacher of the law' (twice)—and the variants are to be found even in passages that are parallel (e.g., Matt. 7 29 ‖ Mark 1 22 and Mark 11 18 ‖ Luke 19 47). Conversely (and the translators make no mention of this in their Introduction), the same English not infrequently does duty for different Greek: thus, 'lawyer' renders not only γραμματεύς (sometimes), but also νομικός (always—and both in parallel at Matt. 23 13 ‖ Luke 11 52 and Mark 12 28 ‖ Luke 10 25), while 'Jesus was at Bethany' renders both 'τοῦ δὲ Ἰησοῦ γενομένου ἐν Βηθανίᾳ' at Matt. 26 6 and 'καὶ ὄντος αὐτοῦ ἐν Βηθανίᾳ' in the parallel at Mark 14 3. Clearly, to construct a Synopsis on the basis of such a version, whatever be that version's merits for other purposes, would be irresponsible and culpably misleading.

By way of contrast with the NEB, which is a completely fresh translation, the Revised Standard Version is a revision—a revision, moreover, of the American Standard Version of 1901, which was in turn a very slight revision of the Revised Version itself. It might therefore be supposed that, standing in such a direct line of descent, the RSV must necessarily be superior to the RV, and that it consequently has greater claims to serve as the basis for a modern Synopsis than the RV could possibly have.

Oddly enough, this very natural supposition is not borne out by the facts. Take, for instance, a single sentence from Part I, § 108. In the RV the parallels are:

Mark 5 29	**Luke 8 44**
And straightway the fountain of her blood was dried up.	And immediately the issue of her blood stanched.

This represents in the Greek:

Mark 5 29	**Luke 8 44**
καὶ εὐθὺς ἐξηράνθη ἡ πηγὴ τοῦ αἵματος αὐτῆς.	καὶ παραχρῆμα ἔστη ἡ ῥύσις τοῦ αἵματος αὐτῆς.

The RSV gives:

Mark 5 29	**Luke 8 44**
And immediately the hemorrhage ceased.	And immediately her flow of blood ceased.

Here we note that according to the RSV rendering the only difference between Mark and Luke is 'hemorrhage' in Mark and 'flow of blood' in Luke: this reflects the difference in the Greek between

πηγὴ τοῦ αἵματος and ῥύσις τοῦ αἵματος, and corresponds to the difference in the RV between 'fountain of her blood' and 'issue of her blood'. But there are two other differences in the Greek, both of which are reflected in the RV, but of which the RSV takes no account at all—viz., εὐθύς in Mark (RV 'straightway') as against παραχρῆμα in Luke (RV 'immediately') and ἐξηράνθη in Mark (RV 'was dried up') as against ἔστη in Luke (RV 'stanched'). And furthermore, the RSV's translation of ἡ πηγὴ τοῦ αἵματος αὐτῆς in Mark by 'the hemorrhage' passes over the word αὐτῆς (='her') altogether, and so creates the impression that there is an additional difference between Mark and Luke at this point, when in fact there is not.

If readability and conformity with modern idiom be regarded as the sole criteria for a version, there can be no doubt that the RSV has the advantage over the RV here: 'hemorrhage' is obviously a more meaningful and idiomatic expression than 'fountain of blood', and 'ceased' is even more obviously more modern than 'stanched'; and from this point of view the RSV's ignoring of the differences in the Greek between εὐθύς and παραχρῆμα, and between ἐξηράνθη and ἔστη, is a mere trifle, not to mention its passing over of αὐτῆς in Mark. Yet from the point of view of an editor of a Synopsis readability and conformity with modern idiom are by no means the sole criteria. What an editor of a Synopsis requires from a version above all else is the clear and unambiguous reflection in English of the agreements and disagreements between the gospels as they exist in Greek. Compared with that the stylistic merits of a version are a secondary consideration. In the present passage, therefore, from the point of view of an editor of a Synopsis, the RV is patently preferable: all the differences in the Greek are clearly reflected in the RV, whereas in the RSV they are not; and one might press the argument even farther and claim that for the student even the RV's 'fountain of blood' and 'was dried up' have the advantage over the RSV's 'hemorrhage' and 'ceased' in that they are both more exact renderings of the Greek.

It was precisely this 'mechanically exact, literal, word-for-word translation' (which makes the RV such a satisfactory basis for a Synopsis), that those responsible for the RSV especially wished to avoid. In a pamphlet entitled *An Introduction to the Revised Standard Version of the New Testament*, published in 1946 by Members of the Revision Committee, Dr. Luther A. Weigle, the Chairman of the Committee, gave three reasons why the revision had been undertaken. The first of these reasons he stated thus:

'1. The English Revised Version of 1881 and its variant, the American Standard Version of 1901, lost some of the beauty and force which made the King James Version a classic example of English literature. They are mechanically exact, literal, word-for-word translations, which follow the order of the Greek words, so far as this is possible, rather than the order which is natural to English. Charles H. Spurgeon, the English preacher of the closing nineteenth century, put it tersely when he remarked that the Revised New Testament was "strong in Greek, weak in English". "The Revisers in their scrupulous and conscientious desire to be perfectly true to the Greek have . . . been too unmindful of the claims of their own language", was the comment of Dean Perowne. "They have sometimes been too literal, construing instead of translating; they have inverted the natural order of words in English in order to follow the Greek; and they have carried the translation of the article, and of the tenses, beyond their legitimate limits." A well-balanced and generally favorable article in the *Edinburgh Review* for July, 1881, concluded by saying: "The revisers were not appointed to prepare an interlinear translation for incompetent school-boys." These criticisms, which were made when the English Revised Version was published, apply as well to the American Standard Version. These versions convey the meaning of the Scriptures more accurately than the King James Version, but they have lost much of its beauty and power.'

In other words, we are dealing in this matter with two incompatibles. The characteristics which commend a version for use in a Synopsis are not those which commend it for popular reading, and *vice versa*. The RV displays the former characteristics, the RSV (we may assume) the latter.

Lest, however, it be thought that the case for the RV as against the RSV depends entirely on the evidence of a single gospel passage, supported by a few chance remarks from one of the members of the American Revision Committee, it may be as well to add some further illustrative detail.

First, some more instances of inconsistency in translation in parallels—*i.e.*, instances where either the same Greek is translated differently in the RSV or different Greek is translated similarly: (1) At Matt. 14 13 ‖ Mark 6 32 ‖ Luke 9 10 κατ᾽ἰδίαν is rendered by the RSV 'apart' in Matthew and Luke, but 'by themselves' in Mark: the RV has 'apart' in all three instances. (2) At Matt. 26 11 ‖ Mark 14 7 ‖ John 12 8 ἐμὲ δὲ οὐ πάντοτε ἔχετε is rendered by the RSV 'but you do not always have me' in John, but as 'but you will not always have me' in Matthew and Mark: the RV has 'but me ye have not always' in all three instances. (3) πῶς ἐρεῖς at Matt. 7 4 and πῶς δύναται λέγειν in the parallel at Luke 6 42 are both rendered by the RSV 'how can you say?': the RV differentiates between 'how wilt thou say?' and 'how canst thou say?' (4) ἀμὴν λέγω ὑμῖν is regularly rendered by the RSV

'Truly I say to you' and ἀληθῶς λέγω ὑμῖν in the parallels 'Truly I tell you' (*i.e.*, a differentiation is made, but the words which differ are translated the same and those which are the same are translated differently): in the RV the renderings are 'Verily I say unto you' and 'Of a truth I say unto you' (the difference, that is, is located precisely where it belongs).

From the point of view of the general reader such inconsistencies may be dismissed as mere trifles, for which the RSV translators may well have had very good reasons. In the third of the instances just quoted, for example, their rendering 'how can you say?' for two different Greek expressions may well have been prompted by stylistic considerations—the literal rendering in Matthew ('how will you say?') perhaps seemed stilted, and so something like what anyone would normally say was substituted for it. And stylistic considerations are doubtless also the justification for the many other more idiomatic renderings in the RSV that so frequently replace 'mechanically exact, literal, word-for-word' renderings in the RV. Yet for the student, idiomatic renderings are a secondary consideration, and he will get the feel of the gospels much better, learn more about their language, and come to appreciate their characteristic turns of phrase much more readily from, say, 'sons of the bridechamber' as a rendering than from 'wedding guests', and from 'And his lord commended the unrighteous steward because he had done wisely' than from 'The master commended the dishonest steward for his prudence'—especially when, as in the last example, the RV adds a marginal note to the effect that 'the unrighteous steward' is in 'Gr. *the steward of unrighteousness*'.

The RSV gives no marginal note to its 'dishonest steward'. And marginal notes are on the whole much fewer in the RSV than in the RV (and fewer still in the NEB). Once again this is a loss for the student. For example, at Mark 9 41, in the passage about giving to drink a cup of water 'because ye are Christ's', the RV adds to 'because ye are' the note 'Gr. *in name that ye are*', thus making it plain that its rendering is a free one. The RSV renders 'because you bear the name of Christ' with no note; and with this we may compare the 'because you are followers of the Messiah' of the NEB, likewise without a note.

One other deviation of the RSV (and the NEB) from the practice of the RV also deserves mention in this connection. It is the disuse of italics. When words stood in their translation, which were not represented in the Greek but had been supplied, either to make sense or to bring out the sense, the Revisers continued the convention (well established through the various editions of the AV) of printing the words supplied in italics. As a result, what was not in the original stood out clearly from what was. In any case such a convention is useful; and it is particularly useful in parallels. Thus, in the RV we have:

Matt. 11 8	Luke 7 25
But what went ye out for to see? a man clothed in soft *raiment*? Behold, they that wear soft *raiment* are in king's houses.	But what went ye out to see? a man clothed in soft raiment? Behold, they which are gorgeously apparelled, and live delicately, are in king's courts.

in the RSV:

Matt. 11 8	Luke 7 25
Why then did you go out? To see a man[1] clothed in soft raiment? Behold, those who wear soft raiment are in king's houses.	What then did you go out to see? A man clothed in soft raiment? Behold, those who are gorgeously apparelled and live in luxury are in kings' courts.

and in the NEB:

Matt. 11 8	Luke 7 25
Then what did you go out to see? A man dressed in silks and satins? Surely you must look in palaces for that.	Then what did you go out to see? A man dressed in silks and satins? Surely you must look in palaces for grand clothes and luxury.

[1] A difference in the underlying Greek text is involved here. As an alternative the RSV offers in the margin 'Or *What then did you go out to see? A man . . .*'

It should not, of course, be inferred from these remarks that because in general the RV provides a more satisfactory basis for a Synopsis than either the NEB or the RSV it is therefore perfect in all particulars. The eagle-eyed will easily detect passages in the RV where identical words occur in parallel, but where the punctuation is different (*e.g.*, Matt. 12 45 ‖ Luke 11 26)—and for no apparent reason. They will also notice occasional instances where precisely the same kind of inconsistency in rendering occurs as has been remarked on in the RSV, and which is so noteworthy a feature of the NEB: thus, in the passage set out in full on the previous page, ἰδεῖν is rendered in the RV by 'to see' at Luke 7 25 and by 'for to see' at Matt. 11 8 (the probable explanation here is that the Revisers revised the AV's 'for to see' in Luke but overlooked the necessity for revising it also in Matthew! The American Standard Version of 1901, however, put this discrepancy right by reading 'to see' in both gospels). We have also to remember that since 1881 a number of hitherto unknown Greek manuscripts have been discovered and considerable advances made in the study of the text of the gospels. Full advantage of these discoveries and advances has been taken in the RSV and in the NEB, both of which are consequently very much more up to date in this respect than is the RV.

Nevertheless, the fundamental point remains that what is primarily required of a version which is to serve as the basis in an English Synopsis is that it shall as clearly and unambiguously as possible reflect in English the agreements and disagreements between the gospels as they exist in Greek; and, judged by this criterion, neither the RSV nor the NEB can compare with the RV. If we are looking for a version to serve as the basis for a Synopsis, the RV's mechanical exactness and word-for-word literalness, the characteristics for which it has been so often abused (but which the Revisers themselves understood as 'faithfulness'), so far from being a drawback, become an outstanding and decisive recommendation.

PART I

THE SYNOPTIC GOSPELS
WITH THE
JOHANNINE PARALLELS

PART I

TABLE OF CONTENTS

xvi

§ 1. **The Lucan Prologue**

Luke 1 1-4

cp. 13 19 *ff.*	*cp.* 2 2 ; 4 14 *ff.*, 33 ; 16 20.	**1** Forasmuch as many have taken in hand to draw up a narrative concerning those matters which have been [1] fulfilled among us, **2** even as they delivered them unto us, which from the beginning were eyewitnesses and ministers of the word [*cp.* 4 32 ; 8 12 *ff.*: *also* 5 1 ; 8 11, 21 ; 11 28], **3** it seemed good to me also, having traced the course of all things accurately from the first, to write unto thee in order, most excellent Theophilus ; **4** that thou mightest know the certainty concerning the [2] things [3] wherein thou wast instructed.	*cp.* 4 41 ; 5 24, 38 ; *etc.*

[1] Or, *fully established*   [2] Gr. *words.*
[3] Or, *which thou wast taught by word of mouth*

A. The Birth and Childhood (§§ 2-15)

(i) The Birth and Childhood according to Matthew (§§ 2-6)

§ 2. **The Genealogy of Jesus**

Matt. 1 1-17

1 [1] The book of the [2] generation of Jesus Christ, the son of David [*cp.* 9 27 ; 12 23 ; 15 22 ; 20 30, 31 ; 21 9, 15], the son of Abraham.
2 Abraham begat Isaac ; and Isaac begat Jacob ; and Jacob begat Judah and his brethren ; **3** and Judah begat Perez and Zerah of Tamar ; and Perez begat Hezron ; and Hezron begat [3] Ram ; **4** and [3] Ram begat Amminadab ; and Amminadab begat Nahshon ; and Nahshon begat Salmon ; **5** and Salmon begat Boaz of Rahab ; and Boaz begat Obed of Ruth ; and Obed begat Jesse ; **6** and Jesse begat David the king.

And David begat Solomon of her *that had been the wife* of Uriah ; **7** and Solomon begat Rehoboam ; and Rehoboam begat Abijah ; and Abijah begat [4] Asa ; **8** and [4] Asa begat Jehoshaphat ; and Jehoshaphat begat Joram ; and Joram begat Uzziah ; **9** and Uzziah begat Jotham ; and Jotham begat Ahaz ; and Ahaz begat Hezekiah ; **10** and Hezekiah begat Manasseh ; and Manasseh begat [5] Amon ; and [5] Amon begat Josiah ; **11** and Josiah begat Jechoniah and his brethren, at the time of the [6] carrying away to Babylon.
12 And after the [6] carrying away to Babylon, Jechoniah begat [7] Shealtiel ; and [7] Shealtiel begat Zerubbabel ; **13** and Zerubbabel begat Abiud ; and Abiud begat Eliakim ; and Eliakim begat Azor ; **14** and Azor begat Sadoc ; and Sadoc begat Achim ; and Achim begat Eliud ; **15** and Eliud begat Eleazar ; and Eleazar begat Matthan ; and Matthan

cp. 10 47, 48.

Luke 3 23-38

23 And Jesus himself, when he began *to teach,* was about thirty years of age, *cp.* 18 38, 39 ; *also* 1 32.

being the son (as was supposed) of Joseph, the *son* of Heli, **24** the *son* of Matthat, the *son* of Levi, the *son* of Melchi, the *son* of Jannai, the *son* of Joseph, **25** the *son* of Mattathias, the *son* of Amos, the *son* of Nahum, the *son* of Esli, the *son* of Naggai, **26** the *son* of Maath, the *son* of Mattathias, the *son* of Semein, the *son* of Josech, the *son* of Joda, **27** the *son* of Joanan, the *son* of Rhesa, the *son* of Zerubbabel, the *son* of [1] Shealtiel, the *son* of Neri, **28** the *son* of Melchi, the *son* of Addi, the *son* of Cosam, the *son* of Elmadam, the *son* of Er, **29** the *son* of Jesus, the *son* of Eliezer, the *son* of Jorim, the *son* of Matthat, the *son* of Levi, **30** the *son* of Symeon, the *son* of Judas, the *son* of Joseph, the *son* of Jonam, the *son* of Eliakim, **31** the *son* of Melea, the *son* of Menna, the *son* of Mattatha, the *son* of Nathan, the *son* of David, **32** the *son* of Jesse, the *son* of Obed, the *son* of Boaz, the *son* of [2] Salmon, the *son* of Nahshon, **33** the *son* of Amminadab, [3] the *son* of [4] Arni, the *son* of Hezron, the *son* of Perez, the *son* of Judah, **34** the *son* of Jacob, the *son* of Isaac, the *son* of Abraham, the *son* of Terah, the *son* of Nahor, **35** the *son* of Serug, the *son* of Reu, the *son* of Peleg, the *son* of

begat Jacob ; **16** and Jacob begat Joseph the husband of Mary, of whom was born Jesus, who is called Christ [*cp.* 27 17, 22].

17 So all the generations from Abraham unto David are fourteen generations ; and from David unto the ⁶ carrying away to Babylon fourteen generations ; and from the ⁶ carrying away to Babylon unto the Christ [*cp.* 11 2] fourteen generations.

¹ Or, *The genealogy of Jesus Christ*
² Or, *birth* : as in ver. 18.   ³ Gr. *Aram.*
⁴ Gr. *Asaph.*   ⁵ Gr. *Amos.*
⁶ Or, *removal to Babylon*   ⁷ Gr. *Salathiel.*

Eber, the *son* of Shelah, 36 the *son* of Cainan, the *son* of Arphaxad, the *son* of Shem, the *son* of Noah, the *son* of Lamech, 37 the *son* of Methuselah, the *son* of Enoch, the *son* of Jared, the *son* of Mahalaleel, the *son* of Cainan, 38 the *son* of Enos, the *son* of Seth, the *son* of Adam, the *son* of God.

cp. 4 25.

¹ Gr. *Salathiel.*
² Some ancient authorities write *Sala.*
³ Many ancient authorities insert *the son of Admin* : and one writes *Admin* for *Amminadab.*
⁴ Some ancient authorities write *Aram.*

§ 3. The Birth of Jesus

Matt. 1 18-25

18 Now the ¹ birth ² of Jesus Christ was on this wise : When his mother Mary had been betrothed to Joseph, before they came together she was found with child of the ³ Holy Ghost. **19** And Joseph her husband, being a righteous man, and not willing to make her a public example, was minded to put her away privily. **20** But when he thought on these things, behold, an angel of the Lord appeared unto him in a dream [*cp.* 2 12, 13, 19, 22 ; 27 19], saying, Joseph, thou son of David, fear not to take unto thee Mary thy wife : for that which is ⁴ conceived in her is of the Holy Ghost. **21** And she shall bring forth a son ; and thou shalt call his name JESUS ; for it is he that shall save his people from their sins. **22** Now all this is come to pass, that it might be fulfilled which was spoken by the Lord through the prophet, saying,

   23 Behold, the virgin shall be with child, and shall
      bring forth a son,
     And they shall call his name ⁵ Immanuel ;

which is, being interpreted, God with us [*cp.* 28 20]. **24** And Joseph arose from his sleep, and did as the angel of the Lord commanded him, and took unto him his wife ; **25** and knew her not till she had brought forth a son : and he called his name JESUS.

¹ Or, *generation* : as in ver. 1.   ³ Some ancient authorities read *of the Christ.*
² Or, *Holy Spirit* : and so throughout this book.
⁴ Gr. *begotten.*   ⁵ Gr. *Emmanuel.*

cp. 1 27 ; 2 5.
cp. 1 35.

cp. 1 26, 27.
cp. 1 27 ; 2 4.
cp. 1 35.
cp. 1 31.
cp. 2 11 ; 19 10.

cp. 3 17 ; 4 42 ; 5 34 ; 10 9 ; 12 47.

cp. 2 21.

Matt. 1 23. = Is. 7 14.

§ 4. The Visit of the Magi

Matt. 2 1-12

1 Now when Jesus was born in Bethlehem of Judæa in the days of Herod the king, behold, ¹ wise men from the east came to Jerusalem, **2** saying, ² Where is he that is born King of the Jews [*cp.* 27 11, 29, 37] ? for we saw his star in the east, and are come to worship him. **3** And when Herod the king heard it, he was troubled, and all Jerusalem with him. **4** And gathering together all the chief priests and scribes of the people, he inquired of them where the Christ should be born. **5** And they said unto him, In Bethlehem of Judæa : for thus it is written ³ by the prophet,

   6 And thou Bethlehem, land [*cp.* 2 20, 21 ; 4 15 ; 10 15 ; 11 24]
      of Judah,
     Art in no wise least among the princes of Judah :
     For out of thee shall come forth a governor,
     Which shall be shepherd of my people Israel.

7 Then Herod privily called the ¹ wise men, and learned of them carefully ⁴ what time the star appeared. **8** And he sent them to Bethlehem, and said, Go and search out carefully concerning the young child ; and when ye have found *him,*

cp. 15 2, 9, 12, 18, 26.

cp. 1 5 ; 2 4-7.
cp. 23 3, 37, 38.

cp. 18 33, 39 ; 19 3, 19, 21.

cp. 7 42.

cp. 3 22.

bring me word, that I also may come and worship him. **9** And they, having heard the king, went their way; and lo, the star, which they saw in the east, went before them, till it came and stood over where the young child was. **10** And when they saw the star, they rejoiced with exceeding great joy. **11** And they came into the house and saw the young child with Mary his mother; and they fell down [*cp.* 17 14] and worshipped him [*cp.* 8 2; 9 18; 14 33; 15 25; 20 20; 28 9, 17]; and opening their treasures they offered unto him gifts [*cp.* 5 23, 24; 8 4], gold and frankincense and myrrh. **12** And being warned *of God* in a dream [*cp.* 1 20; 2 13, 19, 22; 27 19] that they should not return to Herod, they departed into their own country another way.

> [1] Gr. *Magi.* Compare Esth. 1 13; Dan. 2 12.
> [2] Or, *Where is the King of the Jews that is born?*
> [3] Or, *through*
> [4] Or, *the time of the star that appeared*

cp. 1 40; 3 11; 5 22, 33; 7 25; 10 17: *also* 5 6.	*cp.* 5 8, 12; 8 28, 41, 47; 17 16: *also* 24 52.	*cp.* 11 32; 18 6: *also* 9 38.

Matt. 2 6=Mic. 5 2: *cp.* II Sam. 5 2; Mic. 5 4.

§ 5. The Flight to Egypt and the Slaughter of the Innocents

Matt. 2 13-18

13 Now when they were departed, behold, an angel of the Lord appeareth to Joseph in a dream [*cp.* 1 20; 2 12, 19, 22; 27 19], saying, Arise and take the young child and his mother, and flee into Egypt, and be thou there until I tell thee: for Herod will seek the young child to destroy him. **14** And he arose and took the young child and his mother by night, and departed into Egypt; **15** and was there until the death of Herod: that it might be fulfilled which was spoken by the Lord through the prophet, saying, Out of Egypt did I call my son. **16** Then Herod, when he saw that he was mocked of the [1] wise men, was exceeding wroth, and sent forth, and slew all the male children that were in Bethlehem, and in all the borders thereof, from two years old and under, according to the time which he had carefully learned of the [1] wise men. **17** Then was fulfilled that which was spoken [2] by Jeremiah the prophet, saying,

18 A voice was heard in Ramah,
Weeping and great mourning,
Rachel weeping for her children;
And she would not be comforted, because they are not.

> [1] Gr. *Magi.* Compare Esth. 1 13; Dan. 2 12.   [2] Or, *through*

Matt. 2 15=Hos. 11 1.   Matt. 2 18=Jer. 31 15.

§ 6. The Return from Egypt and the Settlement at Nazareth

Matt. 2 19-23

19 But when Herod was dead, behold, an angel of the Lord appeareth in a dream [*cp.* 1 20; 2 12, 13, 22; 27 19] to Joseph in Egypt, **20** saying, Arise and take the young child and his mother, and go into the land [*cp.* 2 6, 21; 4 15; 10 15; 11 24] of Israel: for they are dead that sought the young child's life. **21** And he arose and took the young child and his mother, and came into the land [*see above*] of Israel. **22** But when he heard that Archelaus was reigning over Judæa in the room of his father Herod, he was afraid to go thither; and being warned *of God* in a dream [*cp.* 1 20; 2 12, 13, 19; 27 19], he withdrew into the parts of Galilee, **23** and came and dwelt in a city called Nazareth: that it might be fulfilled which was spoken [1] by the prophets, that he should be called a Nazarene [*cp.* 21 11; 26 71].

> [1] Or, *through*

		cp. 3 22.
	cp. 2 39.	
cp. 1 24; 10 47; 14 67; 16 6.	*cp.* 4 34; 18 37; 24 19.	*cp.* 1 45; 18 5, 7; 19 19.

Matt. 2 23=?

(ii) The Birth and Childhood according to Luke (§§ 7-15)

§ 7. The Announcement of the Birth of John the Baptist

Luke 1 5-25

cp. 2 1.

5 There was in the days of Herod, king of Judæa, a certain priest named Zacharias, of the course of Abijah: and he had a wife of the daughters of Aaron, and her name was Elisabeth. 6 And they were both righteous before God, walking in all the commandments and ordinances of the Lord blameless. 7 And they had no child, because that Elisabeth was barren, and they both were *now* [1] well stricken in years.
8 Now it came to pass, while he executed the priest's office before God in the order of his course, 9 according to the custom of the priest's office, his lot was to enter into the [2] temple of the Lord and burn incense. 10 And the whole multitude of the people were praying without at the hour of incense. 11 And there appeared unto him an angel of the Lord standing on the right side of the altar of incense. 12 And Zacharias was troubled when he saw *him*, and fear fell upon him [*cp.* 1 65; 2 9; 5 26; 7 16; 8 25, 35, 37, 47; 9 34, 45; 24 5, 37].

cp. 9 8; 17 6; 27 54; 28 4, 8.

cp. 4 41; 5 15, 33; 9 6, 32; 10 32; 16 8.

13 But the angel said unto him, Fear not, Zacharias: because thy supplication is heard, and thy wife Elisabeth shall bear thee a son, and thou shalt call his name John. 14 And thou shalt have joy and gladness; and many shall rejoice at his birth. 15 For he shall be great in the sight of the Lord, and he shall drink no wine nor [3] strong drink [*cp.* 7 33]; and he shall be filled with the [4] Holy Ghost [*cp.* 1 41, 67; 4 1], even from his mother's womb. 16 And many of the children of Israel shall he turn unto the Lord their God. 17 And he shall [5] go before his face in the spirit and power [*cp.* 1 35; 4 14, 36; 5 17; 6 19; 8 46; 9 1; 24 49] of Elijah [*cp.* 1 76; 3 4; 7 27], to turn the hearts of the fathers to the children, and the disobedient *to walk* in the wisdom of the just; to make ready for the Lord a people prepared *for him.* 18 And Zacharias said unto the angel, Whereby shall I know this? for I am an old man, and my wife [6] well stricken in years. 19 And the angel answering said unto him, I am Gabriel, that stand in the presence of God; and I was sent to speak unto thee, and to bring thee these good tidings [*cp.* 2 10; 3 18; 4 18, 43; 7 22; 8 1; 9 6; 16 16; 20 1]. 20 And behold, thou shalt be silent and not able to speak, until the day that these things shall come to pass, because thou believedst not my words, which shall be fulfilled in their season. 21 And the people were waiting for Zacharias, and they marvelled [7] while he tarried in the [2] temple. 22 And when he came out, he could not speak unto them: and they perceived that he had seen a vision in the [2] temple: and he continued making signs unto them, and remained dumb. 23 And it came to pass, when the days of his ministration were fulfilled, he departed unto his house.

cp. 11 18.

cp. 5 30.

cp. 3 3, 4;
11 10, 14;
17 10-13.

cp. 1 2, 3, 6;
9 11-13.

cp. 1 21, 23;
3 28.

cp. 11 5.

24 And after these days Elisabeth his wife conceived; and she hid herself five months, saying, 25 Thus hath the Lord done unto me in the days wherein he looked upon *me*, to take away my reproach among men.

---

[1] Gr. *advanced in their days.*   [2] Or, *sanctuary*   [3] Gr. *sikera.*
[4] Or, *Holy Spirit*: and so throughout this book.
[5] Some ancient authorities read *come nigh before his face.*
[6] Gr. *advanced in her days.*   [7] Or, *at his tarrying*

Luke 1 17: *cp.* Mal. 4 5-6.

§ 8. The Announcement of the Birth of Jesus

Luke 1 26-38

cp. 1 20.

cp. 1 18.
cp. 1 20.

26 Now in the sixth month the angel Gabriel was sent from God unto a city of Galilee, named Nazareth, 27 to a virgin betrothed to a man whose name was Joseph [*cp.* 2 5], of the house of David [*cp.* 2 4]; and the virgin's name was Mary. 28 And he came in unto her, and said, Hail, thou that art

cp. 1 21.

cp.1 1; 9 27;
12 23; 15 22;
20 30, 31;
21 9, 15.
cp. 1 18, 20.

cp. 4 3, 6; 8
29; 14 33;
16 16; 26
63; 27 40,
43, 54: also
3 17; 17 5.

cp. 5 7.

cp. 10 47, 48.

cp. 5 30.
cp. 5 7.

cp. 1 1; 3 11;
5 7; 15 39:
also 1 11;
9 7.

[1] highly favoured, the Lord *is* with thee [2]. **29** But she was greatly troubled at the saying, and cast in her mind what manner of salutation this might be. **30** And the angel said unto her, Fear not, Mary: for thou hast found [3] favour with God. **31** And behold, thou shalt conceive in thy womb, and bring forth a son, and shalt call his name JESUS. **32** He shall be great, and shall be called the Son of the Most High [*cp.* 1 35, 76; 6 35; 8 28]: and the Lord God shall give unto him the throne of his father David [*cp.* 18 38, 39]: **33** and he shall reign over the house of Jacob [4] for ever; and of his kingdom there shall be no end. **34** And Mary said unto the angel, How shall this be, seeing I know not a man? **35** And the angel answered and said unto her, The Holy Ghost shall come upon thee, and the power [*cp.* 1 17; 4 14, 36; 5 17; 6 19; 8 46; 9 1; 24 49] of the Most High [*cp.* 1 32, 76; 6 35; 8 28] shall overshadow thee [*cp.* 24 49]: wherefore also [5] that which [6] is to be born [7] shall be called holy, the Son of God [*cp.* 4 3, 9, 41; 8 28; 22 70: *also* 3 22; 9 35]. **36** And behold, Elisabeth thy kinswoman, she also hath conceived a son in her old age: and this is the sixth month with her that [8] was called barren. **37** For no word from God shall be void of power [*cp.* Matt. 19 26: *also* 17 20; Mark 10 27; 14 36: *also* 9 23; Luke 18 27]. **38** And Mary said, Behold, the [9] handmaid of the Lord; be it unto me according to thy word. And the angel departed from her.

cp. 1 34; *etc.*

[1] Or, *endued with grace*
[2] Many ancient authorities add *blessed* art *thou among women.* See ver. 42.
[3] Or, *grace*   [4] Gr. *unto the ages.*
[5] Or, *the holy thing which is to be born shall be called the Son of God.*
[6] Or, *is begotten*   [7] Some ancient authorities insert *of thee.*
[8] Or, *is*   [9] Gr. *bondmaid.*

§ 9. Elizabeth visited by Mary

Luke 1 39-56

39 And Mary arose in these days and went into the hill country with haste, into a city of Judah; **40** and entered into the house of Zacharias and saluted Elisabeth. **41** And it came to pass, when Elisabeth heard the salutation of Mary, the babe leaped in her womb; and Elisabeth was filled with the Holy Ghost [*cp.* 1 15, 67; 4 1]; **42** and she lifted up her voice with a loud cry, and said, Blessed *art* thou among women, and blessed *is* the fruit of thy womb. **43** And whence is this to me, that the mother of my Lord should come unto me? **44** For behold, when the voice of thy salutation came into mine ears, the babe leaped in my womb for joy. **45** And blessed *is* she that [1] believed; for there shall be a fulfilment of the things which have been spoken to her from the Lord. **46** And Mary said,
My soul doth magnify the Lord,
47 And my spirit hath rejoiced in God my Saviour.
48 For he hath looked upon the low estate of his [2] handmaiden:
For behold, from henceforth [*cp.* 5 10; 12 52; 22 18, 69] all generations shall call me blessed [*cp.* 11 27].
49 For he that is mighty hath done to me great things;
And holy is his name [*cp.* 11 2].
50 And his mercy is unto generations and generations
On them that fear him.
51 He hath shewed strength with his arm;
He hath scattered the proud [3] in the imagination of their heart.
52 He hath put down princes from *their* thrones,
And hath exalted them of low degree.
53 The hungry he hath filled with good things;
And the rich he hath sent empty away.
54 He hath holpen Israel his servant,
That he might remember mercy
55 (As he spake unto our fathers)
Toward Abraham and his seed for ever.
56 And Mary abode with her about three months, and returned unto her house.

cp. § 18.

cp. 6 9.

cp. Luke 1 72-73.

[1] Or, *believed that there shall be*   [2] Gr. *bondmaiden.*   [3] Or, *by*

§ 10. The Birth and Childhood of John the Baptist

Luke 1 57-80

57 Now Elisabeth's time was fulfilled that she should be delivered; and she brought forth a son. **58** And her neighbours and her kinsfolk heard that the Lord had magnified his mercy towards her; and they rejoiced with her [*cp.* 15 6, 9]. **59** And it came to pass on the eighth day, that they came to circumcise the child; and they would have called him Zacharias, after the name of his father. **60** And his mother answered and said, Not so; but he shall be called John. **61** And they said unto her, There is none of thy kindred that is called by this name. **62** And they made signs to his father, what he would have him called. **63** And he asked for a writing tablet, and wrote, saying, His name is John. And they marvelled all. **64** And his mouth was opened immediately, and his tongue *loosed*, and he spake, blessing God [*cp.* 2 28; 24 53]. **65** And fear came on all that dwelt round about them [*cp.* 1 12; 2 9; 5 26; 7 16; 8 25, 35, 37, 47; 9 34, 45; 24 5, 37]: and all these sayings were noised abroad throughout all the hill country of Judæa. **66** And all that heard them laid them up in their heart [*cp.* 2 19, 51], saying, What then shall this child be? For the hand of the Lord was with him.

67 And his father Zacharias was filled with the Holy Ghost [*cp.* 1 15, 41; 4 1], and prophesied, saying,

68 Blessed *be* the Lord, the God of Israel;
For he hath visited [*cp.* 1 78; 7 16] and wrought redemption [*cp.* 2 38; 21 28; 24 21] for his people,

69 And hath raised up a horn of salvation [*cp.* 1 71, 77; 2 30; 3 6; 19 9] for us
In the house of his servant David

70 (As he spake by the mouth of his holy prophets which have been since the world began),

71 Salvation [*cp.* 1 69, 77; 2 30; 3 6; 19 9] from our enemies, and from the hand of all that hate us [*cp.* 6 22, 27; 21 17];

72 To shew mercy [*cp.* 10 37] towards our fathers,
And to remember his holy covenant;

73 The oath which he sware unto Abraham our father,

74 To grant unto us that we being delivered out of the hand of our enemies
Should serve him without fear,

75 In holiness and righteousness before him all our days.

76 Yea and thou, child, shalt be called the prophet [*cp.* 7 26; 20 6] of the Most High [*cp.* 1 32, 35; 6 35; 8 28]:
For thou shalt go before the face of the Lord to make ready his ways [*cp.* 1 17; 3 4; 7 27];

77 To give knowledge of salvation [*cp.* 1 69, 71; 2 30; 3 6; 19 9] unto his people
In the remission of their sins [*cp.* 3 3; 24 47],

78 Because of the [1] tender mercy of our God,
[2] Whereby the dayspring from on high [*cp.* 24 49] [3] shall visit [*cp.* 1 68; 7 16] us,

79 To shine upon them that sit in darkness and the shadow of death;
To guide our feet into the way of peace [*cp.* 2 14, 29; 10 5, 6; 19 38, 42].

80 And the child grew, and waxed strong [*cp.* 2 40] in spirit, and was in the deserts till the day of his shewing unto Israel.

[1] Or, *heart of mercy*   [2] Or, *Wherein*
[3] Many ancient authorities read *hath visited us.*

Left margin references:

cp. 9 8; 17 6; 27 54; 28 4, 8.

cp. 7 35.
cp. 4 41; 5 15, 33; 9 6, 32; 10 32; 16 8.

cp. 10 22; 24 9.
cp. 13 13.

cp. 11 9; 14 5; 21 26.
cp. 3 3; 11 10, 14; 17 10-13.
cp. 11 32.
cp. 5 7.
cp. 1 2, 3; 9 11-13.

cp. 26 28.
cp. 1 4.

cp. 5 9; 10 13.
cp. 9 50.

Right margin references:

cp. 4 22.

cp. 4 22.
cp. 15 18, 19; 17 14.

cp. Luke 54-55.

cp. 1 21, 23; 3 28.

cp. 4 22.

cp. 14 27; 16 33.

§ 11. The Birth of Jesus

Luke 2 1-7

1 Now it came to pass in those days, there went out a decree from Cæsar Augustus, that all [1] the world should be enrolled.

cp. 2 1.
cp. 1 20.
cp. 1 18.

2 This was the first enrolment made when Quirinius was governor of Syria. **3** And all went to enrol themselves, every one to his own city. **4** And Joseph also went up from Galilee, out of the city of Nazareth, into Judæa, to the city of David [cp. 2 11], which is called Bethlehem, because he was of the house and family of David [cp. 1 27]; **5** to enrol himself with Mary, who was betrothed to him [cp. 1 27], being great with child. **6** And it came to pass, while they were there, the days were fulfilled that she should be delivered. **7** And she brought forth her first-born son; and she wrapped him in swaddling clothes, and laid him in a manger, because there was no room for them in the inn.

cp. 7 42.

[1] Gr. *the inhabited earth.*

§ 12. **The Visit of the Shepherds**

Luke 2 8-20

cp. 9 8; 17 6; 27 54; 28 4, 8.
cp. 11 5.

cp. 1 21.

cp. 4 41; 5 15,33; 9 6, 32; 10 32; 16 8.

8 And there were shepherds in the same country abiding in the field, and keeping [1] watch by night over their flock. **9** And an angel of the Lord stood by them, and the glory of the Lord shone round about them: and they were sore afraid [cp. 1 12, 65; 5 26; 7 16; 8 25, 35, 37, 47; 9 34, 45; 24 5, 37]. **10** And the angel said unto them, Be not afraid; for behold, I bring you good tidings [cp. 1 19; 3 18; 4 18, 43; 7 22; 8 1; 9 6; 16 16; 20 1] of great joy which shall be to all the people: **11** for there is born to you this day in the city of David [cp. 2 4] a Saviour [cp. 19 10], which is [2] Christ the Lord. **12** And this *is* the sign unto you; Ye shall find a babe wrapped in swaddling clothes, and lying in a manger. **13** And suddenly there was with the angel a multitude of the heavenly host praising God [cp. 2 20; 18 43; 19 37], and saying,

cp. 3 17; 4 42; 5 34; 10 9; 12 47.

cp. 5 9; 10 13.
cp. 3 17; 11 26; 12 18; 17 5.

cp. 9 50.
cp. 1 11.

14 Glory to God in the highest [cp. 19 38],
And on earth [3] peace [cp. 1 79; 2 29; 10 5, 6; 19 38, 42] among [4] men in whom he is well pleased [cp. 3 22; 10 21; 12 32].

cp. 14 27; 16 33.

15 And it came to pass, when the angels went away from them into heaven, the shepherds said one to another, Let us now go even unto Bethlehem, and see this [5] thing that is come to pass, which the Lord hath made known unto us. **16** And they came with haste, and found both Mary and Joseph, and the babe lying in the manger. **17** And when they saw it, they made known concerning the saying which was spoken to them about this child. **18** And all that heard it wondered at the things which were spoken unto them by the shepherds. **19** But Mary kept all these [6] sayings, pondering them in her heart [cp. 1 66; 2 51]. **20** And the shepherds returned, glorifying [cp. 5 25, 26; 7 16; 13 13; 17 15, 18; 18 43; 23 47] and praising God [cp. 2 13; 18 43; 19 37] for all the things that they had heard and seen, even as it was spoken unto them.

cp. 5 16; 9 8; 15 31.

cp. 2 12.

cp. 9 24: also 15 8

[1] Or, *night-watches*   [2] Or, *Anointed Lord*
[3] Many ancient authorities read *peace, good pleasure among men.*
[4] Gr. *men of good pleasure.*   [5] Or, *saying*   [6] Or, *things*

§ 13. **The Circumcision**

Luke 2 21

cp. 1 25.

21 And when eight days were fulfilled for circumcising him, his name was called JESUS, which was so called by the angel before he was conceived in the womb.

§ 14. **The Presentation in the Temple and the Return to Nazareth**

Luke 2 22-40

22 And when the days of their purification according to the law of Moses were fulfilled, they brought him up to Jerusalem, to present him to the Lord **23** (as it is written in the law of the Lord, Every male that openeth the womb shall be called holy to the Lord), **24** and to offer a sacrifice according to that which is said in the law of the Lord, A pair of turtledoves, or two young pigeons. **25** And behold, there was a man in Jerusalem, whose name was Simeon; and this man was righteous and devout, looking for [*cp.* 2 38; 23 51] the consolation of Israel: and the Holy Spirit was upon him. **26** And it had been revealed unto him by the Holy Spirit, that he should not see death, before he had seen the Lord's Christ. **27** And he came in the Spirit into the temple: and when the parents brought in the child Jesus, that they might do concerning him after the custom of the law, **28** then he received him into his arms, and blessed God [*cp.* 1 64; 24 53], and said,

> **29** Now lettest thou thy [1] servant depart, O [2] Lord,
> According to thy word, in peace [*cp.* 1 79; 2 14; 10 5, 6; 19 38, 42];
> **30** For mine eyes have seen thy salvation [*cp.* 1 69, 71, 77; 3 6; 19 9],
> **31** Which thou hast prepared before the face of all peoples [*cp.* 3 6; 24 47: *also* 13 29; 14 21-24; 20 16];
> **32** A light for [3] revelation to the Gentiles,
> And the glory of thy people Israel.

33 And his father and his mother were marvelling at the things which were spoken concerning him; **34** and Simeon blessed them, and said unto Mary his mother, Behold, this *child* is set for the falling and rising up of many in Israel; and for a sign which is spoken against; **35** yea and a sword shall pierce through thine own soul; that thoughts out of many hearts may be revealed. **36** And there was one Anna, a prophetess, the daughter of Phanuel, of the tribe of Asher (she was [4] of a great age, having lived with a husband seven years from her virginity, **37** and she had been a widow [*cp.* 4 25, 26; 7 12; 18 3; 20 47; 21 2] even for fourscore and four years), which departed not from the temple, worshipping with fastings and supplications [*cp.* 5 33] night and day. **38** And coming up at that very hour she gave thanks unto God, and spake of him to all them that were looking for [*cp.* 2 25; 23 51] the redemption [*cp.* 1 68; 21 28; 24 21] of Jerusalem. **39** And when they had accomplished all things that were according to the law of the Lord, they returned into Galilee, to their own city Nazareth. **40** And the child grew, and waxed strong [*cp.* 1 80], [5] filled with wisdom: and the grace of God was upon him [*cp.* 2 52].

Left margin column 1: *cp.* 5 9; 10 13.

cp. 10 18; 24 14; 26 13; 28 19: *also* 8 11; 21 31, 41, 43; 22 7-10.

cp. 2 22, 23.

Left margin column 2: *cp.* 15 43.

cp. 9 50.

cp. 13 10; 14 9; 16 15: *also* 12 9.

cp. 12 40, 42.

cp. 15 43.

Right margin: *cp.* 14 27; 16 33. *cp.* 4 22.

cp. 10 16; 11 52.

[1] Gr. *bondservant.*   [2] Gr. *Master.*   [3] Or, *the unveiling of the Gentiles*
[4] Gr. *advanced in many days.*   [5] Gr. *becoming full of wisdom.*

Luke 2 22 : *cp.* Lev. 12 1-4.   Luke 2 23 = Exod. 13 2, 12.   Luke 2 24 = Lev. 12 8.

§ 15. **Jesus in the Temple at the Age of Twelve**

Luke 2 41-52

41 And his parents went every year to Jerusalem at the feast of the passover. **42** And when he was twelve years old, they went up after the custom of the feast; **43** and when they had fulfilled the days, as they were returning, the boy Jesus tarried behind in Jerusalem; and his parents knew it not; **44** but supposing him to be in the company, they went a day's journey; and they sought for him among their kinsfolk and acquaintance: **45** and when they found him not, they returned to Jerusalem, seeking for him. **46** And it came to pass, after three days they found him in the temple, sitting in the

cp. 7 28; 13 54; 19 25; 22 22, 33: also 8 27; 9 33; 12 23; 15 31; 21 20; 27 14.	cp. 1 22, 27; 6 2; 10 24, 26; 11 18; 12 17: also 2 12; 5 20, 42; 6 51; 7 37; 10 32; 15 5; 16 8.	midst of the ¹ doctors. both hearing them, and asking them questions: **47** and all that heard him were amazed at his understanding and his answers [cp. 4 22, 32, 36; 20 26: also 5 9, 26; 8 25, 56; 9 43; 11 14; 24 12, 41]. **48** And when they saw him, they were astonished [see verse 47 above]: and his mother said unto him, ² Son, why hast thou thus dealt with us? behold, thy father and I sought thee sorrowing. **49** And he said unto them, How is it that ye sought me? wist ye not that I must be ³ in my Father's house? **50** And	cp. 7 15, 21, 46.
cp. 15 16; 16 9, 11.	cp. 9 32; 4 13; 6 52; 7 18; 8 17, 21; 9 10; 16 14.	they understood not the saying which he spake unto them [cp. 9 45; 18 34]. **51** And he went down with them, and came to Nazareth; and he was subject unto them: and his mother kept all these ⁴ sayings in her heart [cp. 1 66; 2 19]. **52** And Jesus advanced in wisdom and ⁵ stature, and in ⁶ favour with God and men [cp. 2 40].	cp. 10 6; 12 16: 3 10; 4 33; 8 27, 43; 11 13; 13 7, 28, 36; 14 5-10, 22; 16 17, 18.

¹ Or, teachers   ² Gr. Child.
³ Or, about my Father's business   Gr. in the things of my Father.
⁴ Or, things   ⁵ Or, age   ⁶ Or, grace

B. The Preparation for the Ministry (§§ 16-22)

(i) The Mission and Message of John the Baptist (§§ 16-19)

§ 16. **The Appearance of John**

Matt. 3 1-6	**Mark 1** 1-6	**Luke 3** 1-6	John 1 6, 23
cp. 4 23; 9 35; 24 14; 26 13.	**1** The beginning of the gospel [cp. 1 14, 15; 8 35; 10 29; 13 10; 14 9; 16 15] of Jesus Christ, ¹ the Son of God [cp. 3 11; 5 7; 15 39: also 1 11; 9 7].		
cp. 4 3, 6; 8 29; 14 33; 16 16; 26 63; 27 40, 43, 54; also 3 17; 17 5.		cp. 1 35; 4 3, 9, 41; 8 28; 22 70: also 3 22; 9 35.	cp. 1 34; etc.
1 And in those days		**1** Now in the fifteenth year of the reign of Tiberius Cæsar, Pontius Pilate being governor of Judæa, and Herod being tetrarch of Galilee, and his brother Philip tetrarch of the region of Ituræa and Trachonitis, and Lysanias tetrarch of Abilene, **2** in the high-priesthood of Annas and Caiaphas, the word of God came unto	
cp. 26 3, 57.			cp. 18 13, 24. cp. 11 49; 18 13, 14, 24, 28.
cometh		John the son of Zacharias in the wilderness.	**1 6** There came a man, sent from God, whose name was John.
John the Baptist, preaching in the wilderness of Judæa [cp. vv. 5, 6],	verse 4	**3** And he came into all the region round about Jordan, preaching the baptism of repentance unto remission of sins [cp. 1 77; 24 47];	cp. 1 28; 3 23, 26; 10 40.
cp. 26 28. **2** saying, Repent ye; for the kingdom of heaven is at hand [cp. 4 17; 10 7; also 12 28]. **3** For this is he that was spoken of	cp. 1 15: also 6 12.	cp. 10 9, 11: also 9 2; 11 20; 17 20, 21; 19 11; 21 8.	
¹ by	**2** Even as it is written ² in [cp. 12 26]	**4** as it is written in the book [cp. 4 17; 20 42] of the words of	

Matt.

Isaiah the prophet, saying,

11 10

cp. 3 4; 11 14; 17 10-13.

The voice of one crying in the wilderness,
Make ye ready the way of the Lord,
Make his paths straight.

cp. 10 18; 24 14; 26 13; 28 19: *also* 8 11; 21 31, 41, 43; 22 7-10.

verse 1

cp. 26 28.

verses 5 *and* 6

cp. 14 5; 21 26, 32.
4 Now John himself had his raiment of camel's hair, and a leathern girdle about his loins [cp. 11 14; 17 10-13]; and his food was locusts and wild honey [cp. 11 18]. 5 Then went out unto him Jerusalem, and all Judæa, and all the region round about Jordan; 6 and they were baptized of him in the river Jordan, confessing their sins [cp. 14 5; 21 26, 32].

¹ Or, *through*

Mark.

Isaiah the prophet,
Behold, I send my messenger before thy face,
Who shall prepare thy way [*cp.* 1 6; 9 11-13];
3 The voice of one crying in the wilderness,
Make ye ready the way of the Lord,
Make his paths straight;

cp. 13 10; 14 9; 16 15: *also* 12 9.

4 John came, who baptized in the wilderness and preached the baptism of repentance unto remission of sins. 5 And there went out unto him all the country of Judæa, and all they of Jerusalem; and they were baptized of him in the river Jordan, confessing their sins [cp. 11 32]. 6 And John was clothed with camel's hair, and *had* a leathern girdle about his loins [cp. 1 2; 9 11-13], and did eat locusts and wild honey.

verse 5

cp. 11 32.

¹ Some ancient authorities omit *the Son of God.*
² Some ancient authorities read *in the prophets.*

Luke.

Isaiah the prophet,

7 27

cp. 1 17, 76.

The voice of one crying in the wilderness,
Make ye ready the way of the Lord,
Make his paths straight.
5 Every valley shall be filled,
And every mountain and hill shall be brought low;
And the crooked shall become straight,
And the rough ways smooth;
6 And all flesh [cp. 2 30-32; 24 47: *also* 13 29; 14 21-24; 20 16] shall see the salvation [cp. 1 69, 71, 77; 2 30; 19 9] of God.

verse 3

cp. 1 77; 24 47.

cp. *verse* 7.

cp. 7 29; 20 6.

cp. 1 17, 76.

cp. 7 33.

cp. *verse* 7.

cp. 7 29; 20 6.

John.

cp. 1 21; 3 28.
1 23 He said, I am the voice of one crying in the wilderness,

Make straight the way of the Lord, as said Isaiah the prophet.

cp. 10 16; 11 52.

cp. 4 22.

cp. 1 28; 3 23, 26; 10 40.

cp. 1 21.

Mark 1 2 = Exod. 23 20; Mal. 3 1.   Matt. 3 3 || Mark 1 3 || Luke 3 4 || John 1 23 = Is. 40 3.   Luke 3 5-6 = Is. 40 4-5.

§ 17. The Public Preaching of John

Matt. 3 7-10

    7 But when he saw many [cp. 5 1; 8 18; 9 36] of the Pharisees and Sadducees coming to his baptism [cp. 3 5, 6; 14 5; 21 26, 32], he said unto them, Ye offspring of vipers [cp. 12 34; 23 33], who warned you

cp. 1 5; 11 32.

Luke 3 7-14

7 He said therefore to the multitudes that went out to be baptized of him [cp. 7 29; 20 6], Ye offspring of vipers, who warned you

to flee from the wrath to come? **8** Bring forth therefore fruit worthy of [1] repentance: **9** and think not to say within yourselves, We have Abraham to our father:

for I say unto you, that God is able of these stones to raise up children unto Abraham. **10** And even now is the axe   laid unto the root of the trees: every tree therefore that bringeth not forth good fruit is hewn down, and cast into the fire [=7 19: cp. 3 12; 5 22, 29, 30; 10 28; 13 42, 50; 18 8, 9; 23 33; 25 41].

[1] Or, *your repentance*

cp. 19 16.

cp. 10 10.
cp. 21 32.

cp. 10 17.

cp. 6 9.

---

to flee from the wrath to come? **8** Bring forth therefore fruits worthy of [1] repentance, and begin not to say within yourselves, We have Abraham to our father [cp. 13 16; 16 24, 30; 19 9]: for I say unto you, that God is able of these stones to raise up children unto Abraham. **9** And even now is the axe also laid unto the root of the trees: every tree therefore that bringeth not forth good fruit is hewn down, and cast into the fire [cp. 13 7-9: also 3 17; 12 5]. **10** And the multitudes [cp. verse 7] asked him, saying, What then must we do [cp. 3 12, 14; 10 25; 18 18]? **11** And he answered and said unto them, He that hath two coats, let him impart to him that hath none [cp. 9 3]; and he that hath food, let him do likewise. **12** And there came also [2]publicans [cp. 7 29] to be baptized, and they said unto him, [3] Master, what must we do [cp. verse 10 etc., above]? **13** And he said unto them, Extort no more than that which is appointed you. **14** And [4] soldiers also asked him, saying, And we, what must we do [cp. verse 10, etc., above]? And he said unto them, Do violence to no man, neither [5] exact *anything* wrongfully [cp. 19 8]; and be content with your wages.

[1] Or, *your repentance*   [2] See footnote on Matt. 5 46.   [3] Or, *Teacher*
[4] Gr. *soldiers on service*.   [5] Or, *accuse* anyone

---

cp. 9 43, 45, 47.

cp. 8 33, 37, 39, 53.

cp. 15 2, 6.

cp. 6 28.

---

§ 18. The Testimony of John concerning his Relationship to the Christ

[*Cp.* Matt. 3 14; Luke 1 41-44; John 1 15, 29-34, 35-36; 3 26-30: *also* Matt. 11 2-19; 17 10-13; 21 24-32; Mark 9 11-13; 11 29-33; Luke 7 18-35; 16 16; 20 3-8; John 1 1-8; 5 33-36; 10 41; Acts 1 5; 11 16; 18 25; 19 1-7.]

Matt. 3 11-12	**Mark 1** 7-8	**Luke 3** 15-17	**John 1** 19-27	**Acts 13** 25
		15 And as the people were in expectation, and all men reasoned in their hearts concerning John, whether haply he were the Christ;	**19** And this is the witness of John, when the Jews sent unto him from Jerusalem priests and Levites to ask him, Who art thou? **20** And he confessed, and denied not; and he confessed, I am not the Christ. **21** And they asked him, What then? Art thou Elijah? And	**25** And as John was fulfilling his course, he said, What suppose ye that I am? I am not he.
cp. 3 4; 11 10, 14; 17 10-13.	cp. 1 2, 6; 9 11-13.	cp. 1 17, 76; 7 27.		
cp. 3 3. cp. 1 3.	cp. 3 4.	he saith, I am not. Art thou the prophet? And he answered, No. **22** They said therefore unto him, Who art thou? that we may give an answer to them that sent us. What sayest thou of thyself? **23** He said, I am the voice of one crying in the wilderness, Make straight the way of the Lord, as said Isaiah the prophet. **24** [1]And they had been sent from the Pharisees. **25** And they asked him, and said unto him, Why then baptizest thou, if thou art not the Christ, neither Elijah, neither the prophet?	**26** John answered them, saying, I baptize [2] with water: in the midst of you standeth one whom ye know not, **27** *even* he that cometh [cp. 1 15, 30; 3 31; 6 14; 11 27; 12 13]	
11 I indeed baptize you [1] with water unto repentance:	**7** And he preached, saying, *verse 8*	**16** John answered, saying unto them all, I indeed baptize you with water;		
but he that cometh [cp. 11 3; 21 9; 23 39]	There cometh [cp. 11 9]	but there cometh [cp. 7 19, 20; 13 35; 19 38]		But behold, there cometh

after me is mightier than I, whose shoes I am ²not worthy to bear:	after me he that is mightier than I, the latchet of whose shoes I am not ¹worthy to stoop down and unloose. **8** I baptized you ²with water;	he that is mightier than I, the latchet of whose shoes I am not ¹worthy to unloose:	after me, the latchet of whose shoe I am not worthy to unloose.	one after me, the shoes of whose feet I am not worthy to unloose.
he shall baptize you ¹with the Holy Ghost and *with* fire: **12** whose fan is in his hand, and he will throughly cleanse his threshing-floor; and he will gather his wheat into the garner [*cp.*13 30: *also* 24 31], but the chaff he will burn up with unquenchable fire [*cp.* 3 10; 5 22, 29, 30; 7 19; 10 28; 13 42, 50; 18 8, 9; 23 33; 25 41: *also* 13 49; 25 32].	but he shall baptize you ²with the ³Holy Ghost. *cp.* 13 27. *cp.* 9 43, 45, 47, 48.	he shall baptize you ²with the Holy Ghost and *with* fire [*cp.* 12 49, 50]: **17** whose fan is in his hand, throughly to cleanse his threshing-floor, and to gather the wheat into his garner; but the chaff he will burn up with unquenchable fire [*cp.* 3 9; 12 5].	*cp.* 1 33. *cp.* 15 2, 6.	*cp.* 11 16: *also* 1 5; 19 6.
¹ Or, *in* ² Gr. *sufficient*.	¹ Gr. *sufficient*. ² Or, *in* ³ Or, *Holy Spirit*: and so throughout this book.	¹ Gr. *sufficient*. ² Or, *in*	¹ Or, *And* certain *had been sent from among the Pharisees.* ² Or, *in*	

§ 19. The Imprisonment of John

Matt. 14 3-4	Mark 6 17-18	Luke 3 18-20	
cp. 11 5.		**18** With many other [*cp.* 22 65] exhortations therefore preached he ¹good tidings [*cp.* 1 19; 2 10; 4 18, 43; 7 22; 8 1; 9 6; 16 16; 20 1] unto the people; **19** but Herod the tetrarch,	
3 For Herod had laid hold on John, and bound him, and put him in prison for the sake of Herodias, his brother Philip's wife. **4** For John said unto him, It is not lawful for thee to have her.	**17** For Herod himself had sent forth and laid hold upon John, and bound him in prison for the sake of Herodias, his brother Philip's wife: for he had married her. **18** For John said unto Herod, It is not lawful for thee to have thy brother's wife.	being reproved by him for Herodias his brother's wife, and for all the evil things which Herod had done, **20** added yet this above all, that he shut up John in prison.	
cp. 4 12; 11 2.	*cp.* 1 14.		*cp.* 3 24.

¹ Or, *the gospel*

(ii) The Preparation of Jesus (§§ 20-22)

§ 20. The Baptism in the Jordan

Matt. 3 13-17	Mark 1 9-11	Luke 3 21-22	John 1 32-34
13 Then cometh Jesus from Galilee to the Jordan unto John, to be baptized	**9** And it came to pass in those days, that Jesus came from Nazareth of Galilee,	**21** Now it came to pass, when all the people were baptized,	

of him. **14** But John would have hindered him, saying, I have need to be baptized of thee, and comest thou to me? **15** But Jesus answering said unto him, Suffer [1] *it* now: for thus it becometh us to fulfil all righteousness [*cp.* 5 6, 10, 20; 6 1, 33; 21 32]. Then he suffereth him. **16** And Jesus, when he was baptized,

cp. 14 23; 19 13; 26 36, 39, 42, 44: *also* 11 25-26.

went up straightway from the water: and lo, the heavens were opened [2] unto him, and he saw the Spirit of God descending

as a dove, and coming upon him; **17** and lo, a voice out of the heavens [*cp.* 17 5], saying, [3] This is my beloved Son [*cp.* 12 18; 17 5: *also* 4 3; *etc.*], in whom I am well pleased [*cp.* 17 5: *also* 11 26; 12 18].

---

and was baptized of John [1] in the Jordan. **10** And

cp. 1 35; 6 46; 14 32, 35, 39.

straightway coming up out of the water, he saw the heavens rent asunder, and the Spirit as a dove descending

upon him: **11** and a voice came out of the heavens [*cp.* 9 7], Thou art my beloved Son [*cp.* 9 7; 12 6: *also* 1 1; *etc.*], in thee I am well pleased.

---

that, Jesus also having been baptized, and praying [*cp.* 5 16; 6 12; 9 18, 28, 29; 11 1; 22 41, 44: *also* 10 21],

the heaven was opened, **22** and the Holy Ghost descended in a bodily form, as a dove, upon him, and a voice came out of heaven [*cp.* 9 35], Thou art my beloved Son [*cp.* 9 35; 20 13: *also* 1 35; *etc.*], in thee I am well pleased [*cp.* 2 14; 10 21; 12 32].

---

32 And John bare witness, saying,

cp. 11 41-42; 12 27-28; 17 1-26.

I have beheld the Spirit descending as a dove out of heaven; and it abode upon him.

cp. 12 28.

verse 34

cp. 1 14, 18; 3 16, 18: *also* 1 34; *etc.*

33 And I knew him not: but he that sent me to baptize [1] with water, he said unto me, Upon whomsoever thou shalt see the Spirit descending, and abiding upon him, the same is he that baptizeth [1] with the Holy Spirit. **34** And I have seen, and have borne witness that this is the Son of God.

[1] Or, *in*

---

cp. 3 11.

verse 17

[1] Or, me
[2] Some ancient authorities omit *unto him.*
[3] Or, *This is my Son; my beloved in whom I am well pleased.* See ch. 12 18.

---

cp. 1 8.

verse 11

[1] Gr. *into.*

---

cp. 3 16.

verse 22

Matt. 3 17 ‖ Mark 1 11 ‖ Luke 3 22: *cp.* Ps. 2 7; Is. 42 1.

§ 21. The Genealogy of Jesus

Matt. 1 1-17

1 [1] The book of the [2] generation of Jesus Christ, the son of David, the son of Abraham.

cp. 4 17.

cp. 13 55.

2 Abraham begat Isaac; and Isaac begat Jacob; and Jacob begat Judah and his brethren; **3** and Judah begat Perez and Zerah of Tamar; and Perez begat Hezron; and Hezron begat [3] Ram; **4** and [3] Ram begat Amminadab; and Amminadab begat Nahshon; and Nahshon begat Salmon; **5** and Salmon begat Boaz of Rahab; and Boaz begat

---

Luke 3 23-38

23 And Jesus himself, when he began *to teach*, was about thirty years of age, being the son (as was supposed) of Joseph [*cp.* 4 22], the son of Heli, **24** the *son* of Matthat, the *son* of Levi, the *son* of Melchi, the *son* of Jannai, the *son* of Joseph, **25** the *son* of Mattathias, the *son* of Amos, the *son* of Nahum, the *son* of Esli, the *son* of Naggai, **26** the *son* of Maath, the *son* of Mattathias, the *son* of Semein, the *son* of Josech, the *son* of Joda, **27** the *son* of Joanan, the *son* of Rhesa,

cp. 1 45; 6 42.

Obed of Ruth ; and Obed begat Jesse ;
6 and Jesse begat David the king.

And David begat Solomon of her *that
had been the wife* of Uriah ; 7 and
Solomon begat Rehoboam ; and Rehoboam begat Abijah ; and Abijah begat
⁴ Asa ; 8 and ⁴ Asa begat Jehoshaphat ;
and Jehoshaphat begat Joram ; and
Joram begat Uzziah ; 9 and Uzziah
begat Jotham ; and Jotham begat
Ahaz ; and Ahaz begat Hezekiah ;
10 and Hezekiah begat Manasseh ; and
Manasseh begat ⁵ Amon ; and ⁵ Amon
begat Josiah ; 11 and Josiah begat
Jechoniah and his brethren, at the time
of the ⁶ carrying away to Babylon.

12 And after the ⁶ carrying away
to Babylon, Jechoniah begat ⁷ Shealtiel ; and ⁷ Shealtiel begat Zerubbabel ;
13 and Zerubbabel begat Abiud ; and
Abiud begat Eliakim ; and Eliakim
begat Azor ; 14 and Azor begat Sadoc ;
and Sadoc begat Achim ; and Achim
begat Eliud ; 15 and Eliud begat
Eleazar ; and Eleazar begat Matthan ;
and Matthan begat Jacob ; 16 and
Jacob begat Joseph the husband of
Mary, of whom was born Jesus, who is
called Christ.

17 So all the generations from Abraham
unto David are fourteen generations ;
and from David unto the ⁶ carrying
away to Babylon fourteen generations ;
and from the ⁶ carrying away to Babylon
unto the Christ fourteen generations.

¹ Or, *The genealogy of Jesus Christ*
² Or, *birth* : as in ver. 18.
³ Gr. *Aram.*   ⁴ Gr. *Asaph.*
⁵ Gr. *Amos.*   ⁶ Or, *removal to Babylon.*
⁷ Gr. *Salathiel.*

the *son* of Zerubbabel, the *son* of
¹ Shealtiel, the *son* of Neri, 28 the *son*
of Melchi, the *son* of Addi, the *son* of
Cosam, the *son* of Elmadam, the *son*
of Er, 29 the *son* of Jesus, the *son* of
Eliezer, the *son* of Jorim, the *son* of
Matthat, the *son* of Levi, 30 the *son*
of Symeon, the *son* of Judas, the *son*
of Joseph, the *son* of Jonam, the *son* of
Eliakim, 31 the *son* of Melea, the *son*
of Menna, the *son* of Mattatha, the
son of Nathan, the *son* of David, 32 the
son of Jesse, the *son* of Obed, the *son* of
Boaz, the *son* of ² Salmon, the *son* of
Nahshon, 33 the *son* of Amminadab,
³ the *son* of ⁴ Arni, the *son* of Hezron,
the *son* of Perez, the *son* of Judah,
34 the *son* of Jacob, the *son* of Isaac,
the *son* of Abraham, the *son* of Terah,
the *son* of Nahor, 35 the *son* of Serug,
the *son* of Reu, the *son* of Peleg, the
son of Eber, the *son* of Shelah, 36 the
son of Cainan, the *son* of Arphaxad,
the *son* of Shem, the *son* of Noah, the
son of Lamech, 37 the *son* of Methuselah, the *son* of Enoch, the *son* of
Jared, the *son* of Mahalaleel, the *son*
of Cainan, 38 the *son* of Enos, the *son*
of Seth, the *son* of Adam, the *son*
of God.

¹ Gr. *Salathiel.*
² Some ancient authorities write *Sala.*
³ Many ancient authorities insert *the son of
Admin* : and one writes *Admin* for *Amminadab.*
⁴ Some ancient authorities write *Aram.*

§ 22. The Temptation in the Wilderness

Matt. 4 1-11	Mark 1 12-13	Luke 4 1-13	
1 Then was Jesus led up of the Spirit into the wilderness	12 And straightway the Spirit driveth him forth into the wilderness. 13 And he was in the wilderness forty days tempted of Satan ;	1 And Jesus, full of the Holy Spirit [*cp.* 1 15, 41, 67], returned from the Jordan, and was led ¹ by the Spirit in the wilderness 2 during forty days, being tempted of the devil.	
to be tempted of the devil. 2 And when he had fasted forty days and forty nights, he afterward hungered.	and he was with the wild beasts ;	And he did eat nothing in those days : and when they were completed, he hungered.	
3 And the tempter came and said unto him, If thou art the Son of God [*cp.* 8 29 ; 14 33 ; 16 16 ; 26 63 ; 27 40, 43, 54 : *also* 3 17 ; 17 5], command that these stones become ¹ bread. 4 But he answered and said, It is written, Man shall not live by bread alone, but by every word that pro- ceedeth out of the mouth of God. 5 Then the devil taketh him into the	*cp.* 1 1 ; 3 11 ; 5 7 ; 15 39 : *also* 1 11 ; 9 7.	3 And the devil said unto him, If thou art the Son of God [*cp.* 1 35 ; 4 41 ; 8 28 ; 22 70 : *also* 3 22 ; 9 35], command this stone that it become ² bread. 4 And Jesus answered unto him, It is written, Man shall not live by bread alone. 9 And he led him to	*cp.* 1 34 ; *etc.* *cp.* 4 34.

[Matthew]

holy city [*cp.* 27 53]; and he set him on the [2] pinnacle of the temple, **6** and saith unto him, If thou art the Son of God [*see above*], cast thyself down: for it is written,
He shall give his angels charge concerning thee:
And on their hands they shall bear thee up,
Lest haply thou dash thy foot against a stone.
7 Jesus said unto him, Again it is written, Thou shalt not tempt the Lord thy God. **8** Again, the devil taketh him unto an exceeding high mountain, and sheweth him all the kingdoms of the world, and the glory of them;
9 and he said unto him, All these things will I give thee,

if thou wilt fall down and worship me.
10 Then saith Jesus unto him, Get thee hence, Satan [*cp.* 16 23]: for it is written, Thou shalt worship the Lord thy God, and him only shalt thou serve.

[Mark]
see above.

[Luke]

Jerusalem, and set him on the [3] pinnacle of the temple, and said unto him, If thou art the Son of God [*see above*], cast thyself down from hence: **10** for it is written,
He shall give his angels charge concerning thee, to guard thee:
11 and, On their hands they shall bear thee up,
Lest haply thou dash thy foot against a stone.
12 And Jesus answering said unto him, It is said, Thou shalt not tempt the Lord thy God. **5** And he led him up,
and shewed him all the kingdoms of [4] the world in a moment of time.
6 And the devil said unto him, To thee will I give all this authority, and the glory of them: for it hath been delivered unto me; and to whomsoever I will I give it. **7** If thou therefore wilt
worship before me, it shall all be thine.
8 And Jesus answered and said unto him,
It is written, Thou shalt worship the Lord thy God, and him only shalt thou serve. **9** And he led him to Jerusalem,

see above.

[Mark col] *cp.* 8 33.

[Luke col] *see above.*

[Matthew continued]

5 Then the devil taketh him into the holy city [*cp.* 27 53]; and he set him on the [1] pinnacle of the temple, **6** and saith unto him,
If thou art the Son of God [*see above*], cast thyself down:
for it is written,
He shall give his angels charge concerning thee:
And on their hands they shall bear thee up,
Lest haply thou dash thy foot against a stone.
7 Jesus said unto him, Again it is written, Thou shalt not tempt the Lord thy God.

11 Then the devil

[Luke continued]

and set him on the [3] pinnacle of the temple, and said unto him, If thou art the Son of God [*see above*], cast thyself down from hence: **10** for it is written,
He shall give his angels charge concerning thee, to guard thee:
11 and, On their hands they shall bear thee up,
Lest haply thou dash thy foot against a stone.
12 And Jesus answering said unto him, It is said, Thou shalt not tempt the Lord thy God.

13 And when the devil had completed every temptation [*cp.* 8 13; 22 28], he departed from him [5] for a season.

[Matthew bottom]
leaveth him; and behold, angels came and ministered unto him [*cp.* 26 53].

[Mark col bottom]
and the angels ministered unto him.

[Luke col bottom] *cp.* 22 43.

and

[far right col] *cp.* 1 51; 12 29.

[Matthew footnotes]
[1] Gr. *loaves.*   [2] Gr. *wing.*

[Luke footnotes]
[1] Or, *in*   [2] Or, *a loaf*
[3] Gr. *wing.*   [4] Gr. *the inhabited earth.*
[5] Or, *until*

Matt. 4 4 || Luke 4 4 = Deut. 8 3.   Matt. 4 6 || Luke 4 10-11 = Ps. 91 11-12.
Matt. 4 7 || Luke 4 12 = Deut. 6 16.   Matt. 4 10 || Luke 4 8 = Deut. 6 13.

C. The Ministry in Galilee and the North (§§ 23-133)

(i) The Beginning of the Ministry (§§ 23-31)

§ 23. **The Good News first proclaimed**

Matt. 4 12-17	Mark 1 14-15	Luke 4 14-15	John 4 1-3, 45
12 Now when he heard that John	**14** Now after that John	**14** And	**4 1** When therefore the Lord knew how that the Pharisees had heard that Jesus was making and baptizing more disciples than John **2** (although Jesus himself baptized not, but his disciples),
was delivered up [*cp.* 11 2; 14 3], he withdrew	was delivered up [*cp.* 6 17], Jesus came *cp.* 5 30.	*cp.* 3 19-20. Jesus returned in the power [*cp.* 4 36; 5 17; 6 19; 8 46: *also* 1 17, 35; 9 1; 24 49] of the Spirit into Galilee:	*cp.* 3 24. **3** he left Judæa, and departed again
into Galilee; **13** and leaving Nazareth, he came and dwelt in Capernaum [*cp.* 9 1: *also* 13 54], which is by the sea, in the borders of Zebulun and Naphtali: **14** that it might be fulfilled which was spoken [1] by Isaiah the prophet, saying,	into Galilee, *cp.* 1 21.	*cp.* 4 16, 23, 31.	into Galilee.
15 The land [*cp.* 2 6, 20, 21; 10 15; 11 24] of Zebulun and the land of Naphtali, [2] Toward the sea, beyond Jordan, Galilee of the [3] Gentiles,			*cp.* 3 22.
16 The people which sat in darkness Saw a great light, And to them which sat in the region and shadow of death, To them did light spring up.			
17 From that time began Jesus to preach, *cp.* 4 23; 9 35; 24 14; 26 13. and to say,	preaching the gospel [*cp.* 1 1; 8 35; 10 29; 13 10; 14 9; 16 15] of God, **15** and saying, The time is fulfilled, and the kingdom of God is at hand: repent ye [*cp.* 6 12], and believe in the gospel [*see above*].	*cp.* 3 23. *cp.* 4 21; 10 9, 11: *also* 9 2; 11 20; 17 20, 21; 19 11; 21 8.	
Repent ye [*cp.* 3 2]; for the kingdom of heaven is at hand [*cp.* 3 2; 10 7: *also* 12 28].			
cp. 4 24: *also* 9 26.	*cp.* 1 28.	*cp.* 10 9, 11; *etc., above.* and a fame went out concerning him through all the region round about [*cp.* 4 37; 5 15; 7 17]. **15** And he taught in their synagogues [*cp.* 4 44], being glorified of all.	**45** So when he came into Galilee, the Galilaeans received him, having seen all the things that he did in Jerusalem at the feast: for they also went unto the feast.
cp. 4 23; 9 35.	*cp.* 1 39.		*cp.* 18 20.

[1] Or, *through*
[2] Gr. *The way of the sea.*
[3] Gr. *nations:* and so elsewhere.

Matt. 4 15-16 = Is. 9 1-2.

§ 24. **The Rejection at Nazareth**

[*Cp*. Matt. 12 9-14 : Mark 1 21-28 ; 3 1-6 : Luke 4 31-37 ; 6 6-11 ; 13 10-17 : John 6 59]

Matt. 13 53-58	Mark 6 1-6	**Luke 4** 16-30	John 6 41-42 ; 4 43-44
53 And it came to pass, when Jesus had finished these parables, he departed thence. **54** And coming into his own country [*cp*. 9 1 : *also* 4 13]	1 And he went out from thence ; and he cometh into his own country ; and his disciples follow him. **2** And when the sabbath was come, he began to teach		
		16 And he came to Nazareth, where he had been brought up : and	*cp*. 1 11.
he taught them in their synagogue,	in the synagogue :	he entered, as his custom was [*cp*. 22 39], into the synagogue on the sabbath day, and stood up to read.	

17 And there was delivered unto him ¹ the book [*cp*. 3 4 ; 20 42] of the prophet Isaiah.   And he opened the ² book, and found the place where it was written, **18** The Spirit of the Lord is upon me,
    ³ Because he anointed me to preach ⁴ good tidings [*cp*. 1 19 ; 2 10 ; 3 18 ; 4 43 ; 7 22 ; 8 1 ; 9 6 ; 16 16 ; 20 1] to the poor [*cp*. 7 22] :
    He hath sent me to proclaim release to the captives,
    And recovering of sight to the blind [*cp*. 7 22 : *also* 7 21 ; 18 35-43],
    To set at liberty them that are bruised,
19 To proclaim the acceptable year of the Lord.
20 And he closed the ² book, and gave it back to the attendant, and sat down : and the eyes of all in the synagogue were fastened on him.   **21** And he began to say unto them, To-day hath this scripture been fulfilled

(margin Matt: cp. 12 26. ; cp. 11 5. ; cp. 9 27-31 ; 12 22 ; 15 30, 31 ; 20 29-34 ; 21 14.)
(margin Mark: cp. 8 22-26 ; 10 46-52.)
(margin Luke: cp. 4 17.)
(margin John: cp. 9 1-7.)

Matt.	Mark	Luke	John
insomuch that they were astonished [*cp*. 7 28 ; 19 25 ; 22 22, 33 : *also* 8 27 ; 9 33 ; 12 23 ; 15 31 ; 21 20 ; 27 14],	*cp*. 1 15. ¹ many hearing him were astonished [*cp*. 1 22, 27 ; 10 24, 26 ; 11 18 ; 12 17 : *also* 2 12 ; 5 20, 42 ; 6 51 ; 7 37 ; 10 32 ; 15 5 ; 16 5, 8],	in your ears. **22** And all bare him witness, and wondered [*cp*. 2 47, 48 ; 4 32, 36 ; 20 26 : *also* 5 9, 26 ; 8 25, 56 ; 9 43 ; 11 14 ; 24 12, 41] at the words of grace which proceeded out of his mouth : and they said,	6 **41** The Jews therefore murmured concerning him, *cp*. 7 15, 21, 46. because he said, I am the bread which came down out of heaven. **42** And they said,
and said, Whence hath this man *verse* 56. this wisdom, and these ¹ mighty works?	saying, Whence hath this man these things ? and, What is the wisdom that is given unto this man, and *what mean* such ² mighty works wrought by his hands ? **3** Is not this the carpenter,		
55 Is not this the carpenter's son ? is not his mother called Mary ? and his brethren, James, and Joseph, and Simon, and Judas ? **56** And his sisters, are they not all with us ? Whence then hath this man all these things ? **57** And they were ² offended in him.	the son of Mary, and brother of James, and Joses, and Judas, and Simon ? and are not his sisters here with us ? *verse* 2 And they were ³ offended in him.	Is not this Joseph's son [*cp*. 3 23] ?	Is not this Jesus, the son of Joseph [*cp*. 1 45], whose father and mother we know ? how doth he now say, I am come down out of heaven ?
cp. 27 40.	*cp*. 15 30.	**23** And he said unto them, Doubtless ye will say unto me this parable, Physician, heal thyself [*cp*. 23 37, 39] : whatsoever we have heard done at Capernaum [*cp*. 4 31], do also here in thine own country.	
cp. 4 13.	*cp*. 1 21.		4 **43** And after the two days he went forth from thence into Galilee.
But Jesus said unto them, A prophet [*cp*. 21 11, 46] is not without honour, save in his own	**4** And Jesus said unto them, A prophet [*cp*. 6 15] is not without honour, save in his own	**24** And he said, Verily I say unto you, No prophet [*cp*. 7 16, 39 ; 13 33 ; 24 19] is acceptable in his own	**44** For Jesus himself testified, that a prophet [*cp*. 4 19 ; 6 14 ; 7 40 ; 9 17] hath no honour in his own

Matt.	Mark	Luke	John
country, and in his own house.	country, and among his own kin, and in his own house.	country. **25** But of a truth	country.

cp. 12 40, 42.

I say unto you, There were many widows [*cp.* 2 37; 7 12; 18 3; 20 47; 21 2] in Israel in the days of Elijah, when the heaven was shut up three years and six months, when there came a great famine over all the land; **26** and unto none of them was Elijah sent, but only to ⁵ Zarephath, in the land of Sidon, unto a woman that was a widow. **27** And there were many lepers in Israel in the time of Elisha the prophet; and none of them was cleansed, but only Naaman the Syrian. **28** And they were all filled with wrath in the synagogue, as they heard these things; **29** and they rose up, and cast him forth out of the city [*cp.* 20 15], and led him unto the brow of the hill whereon their city was built, that they might throw him down headlong. **30** But he passing through the midst of them went his way.

Matt.	Mark	Luke	John
58 And he did not many ¹ mighty works there because of their unbelief.	**5** And he could there do no ⁴ mighty work, save that he laid his hands upon a few sick folk, and healed them. **6** And he marvelled because of their unbelief.		*cp.* 1 11. *cp.* 8 59; 10 39.

¹ Gr. *powers.*
² Gr. *caused to stumble.*

¹ Some ancient authorities insert *the.* ² Gr. *powers.*
³ Gr. *caused to stumble.*
⁴ Gr. *power.*

¹ Or, *a roll* ² Or, *roll*
³ Or, *Wherefore*
⁴ Or, *the gospel* ⁵ Gr. *Sarepta.*

Luke 4 18-19 = Is. 61 1-2; 58 6.

§ 25. The Call of the First Disciples (Matt. and Mark)

Matt. 4 18-22	**Mark 1** 16-20	Luke 5 1-11	John 1 35-42
		1 Now it came to pass, while the multitude pressed upon him and heard the word of God, that he was standing by the lake of Gennesaret [*cp.* 5 2; 8 22, 23, 33]; **2** and he saw two *cp.* 6 14. boats standing by the lake: but the fishermen had gone out of them, and were washing their nets.	**35** Again on the morrow John was standing, *cp.* 6 1; 21 1: *also* 6 16, *etc.* and two of his disciples; *verse* 42
18 And walking by the sea of Galilee [*cp.* 15 29: *also* 8 24; *etc.*], he saw two brethren, Simon who is called Peter [*cp.* 10 2; 16 16-18], and Andrew his brother,	**16** And passing along by the sea of Galilee [*cp.* 7 31: *also* 2 13; *etc.*], he saw [*cp.* 2 14] Simon *cp.* 3 16. and Andrew the brother of Simon		**36** and he looked upon Jesus as he walked, and saith, Behold, the Lamb of God!
casting a net into the sea; for they were fishers. **19** And he saith unto them, Come ye after me [*cp.* 8 22; 9 9; 16 24; 19 21], and I will make you fishers of men. **20** And they straightway left the nets, and followed him [*cp.* 4 22; 9 9; 19 27].	casting a net in the sea: for they were fishers. **17** And Jesus said unto them, Come ye after me [*cp.* 2 14; 8 34; 10 21], and I will make you to become fishers of men. **18** And straightway they left the nets, and followed him [*cp.* 1 20; 2 14; 10 28].	*cp.* 5 27; 9 23, 59; 18 22. *verse* 10	*cp.* 1 43; 12 26; 21 19, 22. **37** And the two disciples heard him speak, and they followed Jesus.

cp. 16 16.

he entered into one of the boats, which was Simon's, and asked him to put out a little from the land. And he sat down and taught the multitudes out of the boat. **4** And when he had left speaking, he said unto Simon, Put out into the deep, and let down your nets for a draught. **5** And Simon answered and said, Master, we toiled all night, and took nothing: but at thy word I will let down the nets. **6** And when they had this done, they inclosed a great multitude of fishes; and their nets were breaking; **7** and they beckoned unto their partners in the other boat, that they should come and help them. And they came, and filled both the boats, so that they began to sink. **8** But Simon Peter, when he saw it, fell down at Jesus' knees, saying, Depart from me; for I am a sinful man, O Lord. **9** For he was amazed, and all that were with him, at the draught of the fishes which they had taken; **10** and

Matt.	Mark	Luke	John
21 And going on from thence he saw other two	**19** And going on a little further, he saw	so were also	**38** And Jesus turned, and beheld them following, and saith unto them, What seek ye? And they said unto him, Rabbi (which is to say, being interpreted, ¹ Master), where abidest thou? **39** He saith unto them, Come, and ye shall see. They came therefore and saw where he abode; and they abode with him that day: it was about the tenth hour. **40** One of the two that heard John *speak*, and followed him, was Andrew, Simon Peter's [*cp.* 6 8, 68; *etc.*] brother. **41** He findeth first his own brother Simon, and

brethren, [1] James
the *son* of Zebedee, and
John his brother,
                in the boat
with Zebedee their father,
mending their nets; and
            he called
them.

verse 19
22 And

        they straightway left
the boat and their father
[*cp.* Luke 18 28],

            and fol-
lowed him [*cp.* 4 20; 9 9;
19 27].

[1] Or, *Jacob*: and so elsewhere.

        James
the *son* of Zebedee, and
John his brother, who
also were in the boat

mending the nets. **20** And
straightway he called
them:

verse 17
and

        their father
Zebedee in the boat with
the hired servants [*cp.*
Luke 18 28], and went
after him [*cp.* 1 18; 2 14;
10 28].

James and John,
sons of Zebedee,

which were partners
with Simon. And Jesus
said unto Simon, Fear
not; from henceforth
thou shalt [1] catch men.
11 And when they had
brought their boats to
land, they   left
all [*cp.* Matt. 19 27: Mark
10 28 : also Luke 5 28; 14
33],
            and fol-
lowed him [*cp.* 5 28;
18 28].

[1] Gr. *take alive*.

---

saith unto him, We have
found the Messiah (which is,
being interpreted, [2] Christ).
42 He brought him unto
Jesus. Jesus looked upon
him, and said, Thou art
Simon the son of [3] John:
thou shalt be called Cephas
(which is by interpretation,
[4] Peter).
[*cp.* 1 43-51: Philip and
    Nathanael]

[*cp. also* 21 1-23]

[1] Or, *Teacher*
[2] That is, *Anointed*.
[3] Gr. *Joanes*: called in Matt.
16. 17, *Jonah*.
[4] That is, *Rock* or *Stone*.

---

§ 26. In the Synagogue at Capernaum

[*Cp.* Matt. 12 9-14; 13 53-58 : Mark 3 1-6; 6 1-6 : Luke 4 16-30; 6 6-11; 13 10-17 : John 6 59]

Matt. 7 28-29	Mark 1 21-28	Luke 4 31-37	
cp. 4 13.	**21** And they go into Capernaum; and straightway on the sabbath day he entered into the synagogue and taught. **22** And they were astonished at his teaching	**31** And he came down to Capernaum, a city of Galilee. And he was teaching them on the sabbath day:	
28 And it came to pass, when Jesus ended these words, the multitudes were astonished at his teaching [*cp.* 22 33; 13 54; 19 25; 22 22: *also* 8 27; 9 33; 12 23; 15 31; 21 20; 27 14]:		**32** and they were astonished at his teaching [*cp.* 2 47, 48; 4 22, 36; 20 26: *also* 5 9, 26; 8 25, 56; 9 43; 11 14; 24 12, 41];	*cp.* 7 15, 21, 46.
29 for he taught them as *one* having authority [*cp.* 21 23 *ff.*; 9 6; 28 18], and not as their scribes.	[*cp.* 11 18; 1 27; 6 2; 10 24, 26; 12 17: *also* 2 12; 5 20, 42; 6 51; 7 37; 10 32; 15 5; 16 5, 8]: for he taught them as having authority [*cp.* 11 27 *ff.*; 1 27; 2 10], and not as the scribes. **23** And	for his word was with authority [*cp.* 20 1 *ff.*; 4 36; 5 24].	*cp.* 5 27; 17 2.
cp. 8 29.	straightway there was in their synagogue a man with an unclean spirit; and he cried out [*cp.* 3 11; 5 7],	**33** And in the synagogue there was a man, which had a spirit of an unclean [1] devil; and he cried out with a	
cp. 8 29.	**24** saying, What have we to do with thee [*cp.*	loud voice [*cp.* 8 28],	
cp. 2 23; 26 71: *also* 21 11.	5 7], thou Jesus of Nazareth [*cp.* 10	**34** [2] Ah! what have we to do with thee [*cp.* 8 28], thou Jesus of Nazareth [*cp.*	*cp.* 18 5, 7; 19 19: *also* 1 45.
cp. similarly 8 29.	47; 14 67; 16 6]? art thou come to destroy us? I know thee who thou art, the Holy One of God [*cp.*	18 37; 24 19]? art thou come to destroy us? I know thee who thou art, the Holy One of God [*cp.*	*cp.* 6 69.
cp. 8 26; 17 18.	*similarly* 3 11; 5 7]. **25** And Jesus rebuked [1] him [*cp.* 3 12; 4 39; 9 25], saying, Hold thy peace [*cp.* 4 39], and come out [*cp.* 5 8; 9 25] of him. **26** And the unclean spirit, [2] tearing	*similarly* 4 41; 8 28]. **35** And Jesus rebuked him [*cp.* 4 39, 41; 8 24; 9 42], saying, Hold thy peace, and come out of him. And when the [1] devil had thrown him down in the midst [*cp.* 9 39, 42],	
cp. 17 18.	him [*cp.* 9 18, 20, 26] and crying with a loud voice [*cp.* 5 7], came out of him [*cp.* 9 26].	he came out of him, having done him no hurt. **36** And amazement came	
cp. 7 28 *etc. above*.	**27** And they were all amazed [*cp.* 1 22 *etc. above*], insomuch that they questioned among themselves,	upon all [*cp.* 4 32 *etc. above*], and they spake together, one with another,	*cp.* 7 15, 21, 46.

cp. 8 27; 21 10. cp. 7 29 etc. above.	saying, What is this [cp. 2 7; 4 41]? a new teaching! with authority [cp. 1 22 etc. above]	saying, What is ³ this word [cp. 5 21; 7 49; 8 25; 9 9]? for with authority [cp. 4 32 etc. above] and power [cp. 4 14; 5 17; 6 19; 8 46: also 1	cp. 5 12: also 12 34. cp. 5 27; 17 2.

cp. 8 27.

cp. 4 24: also 9 26.

(Matthew column)

(Mark column) cp. 5 30.
he commandeth even the unclean spirits, and they obey him [cp. 4 41]. **28** And the report of him went out straightway everywhere into all the region of Galilee round about.

¹ Or, it   ² Or, convulsing

(Luke column) 17, 35; 9 1; 24 49] he commandeth the unclean spirits, and they come out [cp. 8 25]. **37** And there went forth a rumour concerning him into every place of the region round about [cp. 4 14; 5 15; 7 17].

¹ Gr. demon.   ² Or, Let alone
³ Or, this word, that with authority . . . come out?

§ 27. The Healing of Peter's Wife's Mother

Matt. 8 14-15	Mark 1 29-31	Luke 4 38-39	
14 And when Jesus was come into Peter's house,	**29** And straightway, ¹ when they were come out of the synagogue, they came into the house of Simon and Andrew, with James and John [cp. 5 37; 9 2; 13 3; 14 33].	**38** And he rose up from the synagogue, and entered into the house of Simon.	
cp. 17 1; 26 37. he saw his wife's mother lying sick of a fever.	**30** Now Simon's wife's mother lay sick of a fever; and straightway they tell him of her: **31** and he came and took her by the hand [cp. 5 41; 9 27; 1 41; 5 23; 6 2, 5; 7 33; 8 22, 23, 25; 10 13, 16: also 3 10; 5 27; 6 56], and raised her up;	cp. 8 51; 9 28. And Simon's wife's mother was holden with a great fever; and they besought him for her. **39** And he	cp. 9 6: also 20 17.
15 And he touched her hand [cp. 9 25; 8 3; 9 18, 29; 14 31; 17 7; 19 13, 15; 20 34: also 9 20; 14 36],		cp. 8 54; 4 40; 5 13; 7 14; 13 13; 14 4; 18 15; 22 51: also 6 19; 7 39; 8 44. stood over her, and rebuked	
cp. 8 26; 17 18: also 8 3, 8, 13, 16, 32; 9 6, 22, 29; 12 13; 15 28; 17 7.	cp. 1 25; 3 12; 4 39; 9 25: also 1 41; 2 11; 3 5; 5 8, 13, 34, 41; 7 29, 34; 10 52.	[cp. 4 35, 41; 8 24; 9 42: also 5 13, 24; 6 10; 7 7, 14; 8 29, 32, 48, 54; 13 12; 17 14; 18 42] the fever;	cp. 4 50; 5 8; 9 7; 11 43.
and the fever left her; and she arose, and ministered unto him.	and the fever left her, and she ministered unto them.	and it left her: and immediately she rose up and ministered unto them.	cp. 4 52.

¹ Some ancient authorities read *when he was come out of the synagogue, he came &c.*

§ 28. Healings in the Evening

Matt. 8 16-17	Mark 1 32-34	Luke 4 40-41	
16 And when even was come, they brought unto him many	**32** And at even, when the sun did set, they brought unto him all that were sick, and them that were	**40** And when the sun was setting, all they that had any sick with divers diseases brought them unto him;	
¹ possessed with devils:	¹ possessed with devils. **33** And all the city was gathered together at the door.		
cp. 9 18; 19 13, 15: 8 3, 15; 9 25, 29; 14 31; 17 7; 20 34: also 9 20; 14 36. and he cast out the spirits with a word [cp. 8 8: also 8 3, 13, 32; 9 6, 22, 29; 12 13; 15 28; 17 7, 18],	cp. 5 23; 6 5; 8 25; 10 16; 1 31, 41; 5 41; 6 2; 7 33; 9 27; 8 22, 23; 10 13: also 3 10; 5 27; 6 56.	and he laid his hands [cp. 13 13: 5 13; 7 14; 8 54; 14 4; 18 15; 22 51: also 6 19; 7 39; 8 44] on every one of them,	cp. 9 6: also 20 17.
and healed all [cp. 12 15] that were sick: cp. 4 24.	cp. 1 25, 41; 2 11; 3 5; 5 8, 13, 34, 41; 7 29, 34; 9 25; 10 52. **34** And he healed many that were sick with divers diseases, and cast out many ² devils;	[cp. 7 7: also 4 35, 39; 5 13, 24; 6 10; 7 14; 8 29, 32, 48, 54; 9 42; 13 12; 17 14; 18 42] and healed them. cp. 6 19. **41** And ¹ devils also	cp. 4 50; 5 8; 9 7; 11 43.

	3 10 for he had healed many; insomuch that as many as had [3] plagues [4] pressed upon him that they might touch him. **11** And the unclean spirits, whensoever they beheld him, fell down before him, and cried, saying, Thou art the Son of God [*cp.* 1 1; 5 7; 15 39: *also* 1 11; 9 7]. **12** And he charged them much [*cp.* 1 25; 4 39; 9 25] that they should not make him known. and he suffered not the [2] devils to speak [*cp.* 1 25; 3 12: 1 44; 5 43; 7 36; 8 26: *also* 8 30; 9 9], because they knew [*cp.* 1 24; 3 11; 5 7] him.[5]	came out from many, crying out, and saying, Thou art the Son of God [*cp.* 1 35; 4 3, 9; 8 28; 22 70: *also* 3 22; 9 35]. And rebuking them [*cp.* 4 35, 39; 8 24; 9 42], he suffered them not to speak [*cp.* 4 35: 5 14; 8 56: *also* 9 21, 36], because they knew [*cp.* 4 34; 8 28] that he was the Christ.	*cp.* 1 34; *etc.*
cp. 4 3, 6; 8 29; 14 33; 16 16; 26 63; 27 40, 43, 54: *also* 3 17; 17 5. *cp.* 8 26; 17 18.			
cp. 8 4; 9 30; 12 16: *also* 16 20; 17 9. *cp.* 8 29.			
17 that it might be fulfilled which was spoken [2] by Isaiah the prophet, saying, Himself took our infirmities, and bare our diseases.			

[1] Or, *demoniacs*   [2] Or, *through*

[1] Or, *demoniacs*   [2] Gr. *demons.*
[3] Gr. *scourges.*   [4] Gr. *fell.*
[5] Many ancient authorities add *to be Christ.* See Luke 4 41.

[1] Gr. *demons.*

Matt. 8 17 = Is. 53 4.

§ 29. Departure from Capernaum

Matt. 8 18	Mark 1 35-38	Luke 4 42-43	
18 Now when Jesus saw great multitudes about him, he gave commandment to depart unto the other side. *cp.* 14 13. *cp.* 14 23; 19 13; 26 36, 39, 42, 44: *also* 11 25-26.	**35** And in the morning, a great while before day, he rose up and went out, and departed into a desert place [*cp.* 1 45; 6 31, 32], and there prayed [*cp.* 6 46; 14 32, 35, 39]. **36** And Simon and they that were with him followed after him; **37** and they found him, and say unto him, All are seeking thee.	**42** And when it was day, he came out and went into a desert place [*cp.* 5 16; 9 10]: *cp.* 3 21; 5 16; 6 12; 9 18, 28, 29; 11 1; 22 41, 44: *also* 10 21.	*cp.* 11 41-42; 12 27-28; 17 1-26.
		and the multitudes sought after him, and came unto him [*cp.* 5 15], and would have stayed him, that he should not go from them. **43** But he said unto them,	
cp. 11 5.	**38** And he saith unto them, Let us go elsewhere into the next towns, that I may preach there also; for to this end came I forth.	I must preach the [1] good tidings [*cp.* 1 19; 2 10; 3 18; 4 18; 7 22; 8 1; 9 6; 16 16; 20 1] of the kingdom of God to the other cities also: for therefore was I sent.	*cp.* 8 42; 16 28.

[1] Or, *gospel*

§ 30. General Preaching and Healing in Galilee

Matt. 4 23-25	Mark 1 39	Luke 4 44	
23 And [1] Jesus went about in all Galilee, teaching in their synagogues, and preaching [*cp.* 9	**39** And he went into their synagogues throughout all Galilee, preaching	**44** And he was preaching in the synagogues [*cp.* 4 15] of [1] Galilee.	*cp.* 18 20.

35; 11 1] the [2] gospel of the kingdom [cp. 9 35; 24 14: also 26 13], and healing all manner of disease and all manner of sickness among the people.	cp. 1 1, 14, 15; 8 35; 10 29; 13 10; 14 9; 16 15. and casting out [1] devils.	
9 35 And Jesus went about all the cities and the villages, teaching in their synagogues, and preaching the gospel of the kingdom, and of healing all manner of disease and all manner of sickness.	6 6 And he went round about the villages teaching.	8 1 And it came to pass soon afterwards, that he went about through cities and villages, preaching and bringing the [2] good tidings of the kingdom of God, and with him the twelve.
24 And the report of him went forth [cp. 9 26] into all Syria: and they brought unto him all that were sick, holden with divers diseases and torments [cp. 8 6], [3] possessed with devils, and epileptic [cp. 17 15], and palsied [cp. 8 6; 9 2]; and he healed them. 25 And there followed him great multitudes from Galilee and Deca-polis and Jerusalem and Judæa and from beyond Jordan.	1 28 3 10 3 7 And a great multitude from Galilee followed: [cp. 5 20; 7 31] and from Judæa 8 and from Jerusalem, and from Idumæa, and beyond Jordan, and about Tyre and Sidon.	4 37: cp. 4 14; 5 15; 7 17. 6 18, 19. 6 17 and a great multitude of his disciples, and a great number of the people from all Judæa and Jerusalem, and the sea coast of Tyre and Sidon.
[1] Some ancient authorities read *he*. [2] Or, *good tidings*: and so elsewhere. [3] Or, *demoniacs*	[1] Gr. *demons*.	[1] Very many ancient authorities read *Judæa*. [2] Or, *gospel*

§ 31. The Call of the First Disciples (Luke)

Matt. 4 18-22	Mark 1 16-20	Luke 5 1-11	John 21 1-11
cp. 13 2. cp. 13 19 ff.	cp. 4 1; 3 9; 5 21. cp. 2 2; 4 14 ff., 33; 16 20.	1 Now it came to pass, while the multitude pressed upon him and heard the word of God [cp. 8 11, 21; 11 28: also 1 2; 4 32; 8 12 ff.], *himself* on this wise. 2 There were together Simon Peter, and Thomas called [1] Didymus, and Nathanael of Cana in Galilee, and the *sons* of Zebedee, and two other of his disciples. 3 Simon Peter saith unto them, I go a fishing. They say unto him, We also come with thee. They went forth, and entered	1 After these things Jesus manifested himself again to the disciples at the sea of Tiberias [cp. 6 1: also 6 16, *etc.*]; and he manifested himself on this wise.
		verse 5	4 But when day was now breaking, Jesus stood on the beach: howbeit the disciples knew not that it was Jesus.
18 And walking by the sea of Galilee [cp. 15 29: also 8 24; etc.], he saw two brethren, Simon who is called Peter [cp. 10 2: also 16 16-18], and Andrew his brother,	16 And passing along by the sea of Galilee [cp. 7 31: also 2 13; etc.], he saw Simon cp. 3 16. and Andrew the brother of Simon	that he was standing by the lake of Gennesaret [cp. 5 2; 8 22, 23, 33]; 2 and he saw two boats standing by the cp. 6 14. lake: but the fishermen had gone out of them, and were washing their nets.	cp. 1 42.
casting a net into the sea; for they were fishers. 19 And he saith unto them, Come ye after me, and I will make you fishers of men. 20 And they straightway left the nets, and followed him.	casting a net in the sea: for they were fishers. 17 And Jesus said unto them, Come ye after me, and I will make you to become fishers of men. 18 And straightway they left the nets, and followed him.	*verse 10* 3 And	5 Jesus therefore saith unto them, Children, have ye aught to eat? They answered him, No.

cp. 13 1-2.

cp. 4 1; 3 9.

he entered into one of the boats, which was Simon's, and asked him to put out a little [*cp.* Mark 1 19] from the land.   And he sat down and taught the multitudes out of the boat.   **4** And when he had left speaking, he said unto Simon, Put out into the deep, and let down your nets for a draught.   **5** And Simon answered and said, Master, we toiled all night, and took nothing: but at thy word I will let down the nets.   **6** And when they had this done,

they inclosed a great multitude of fishes;

and their nets were breaking;

6 And he said unto them, Cast the net on the right side of the boat, and ye shall find.

verse 3
They cast therefore, and now they were not able to draw it for the multitude of fishes.

cp. 16 16: *also* 4 18; 10 2.

cp. 2 11; 17 14; *etc.*

cp. 1 40; 3 11; *etc.*

7 and they beckoned unto their partners in the other boat, that they should come and help them.   And they came, and filled both the boats, so that they began to sink.   **8** But Simon Peter,   when he saw it,

verse 11
7 That disciple therefore whom Jesus loved saith unto Peter, It is the Lord.   So when Simon Peter [*cp.* 1 40; *etc.*] heard that it was the Lord, *cp.* 11 32; 18 6: *also* 9 38.

cp. 8 27; 9 33; 12 23; 15 31; 21 20; 27 14: *also* 7 28; *etc.*

cp. 2 12; 5 20, 42; 6 51; 7 37; 10 32; 15 5; 16 5, 8: *also* 1 22; *etc.*

fell down at Jesus' knees [*cp.* 5 12; 8 28, 41, 47; 17 16: *also* 24 52], saying, Depart from me; for I am a sinful man, O Lord.   **9** For he was amazed [*cp.* 5 26; 8 25, 56; 9 43; 11 14; 24 12, 41: *also* 2 47, 48; 4 22, 32, 36; 20 26], and all that were with him, at the draught of the fishes which they had taken;

cp. 7 15, 21, 46.

he girt his coat about him (for he was naked), and cast himself into the sea.   **8** But the other disciples came in the little boat (for they were not far from the land, but about two hundred cubits off), dragging the net *full* of fishes.   **9** So when they got out upon the land, they see [2] a fire of coals there, and [3] fish laid thereon, and [4] bread.   **10** Jesus saith unto them, Bring of the fish which ye have now taken.   **11** Simon Peter therefore went [5] up, and drew the net to land, full of great fishes, a hundred and fifty and three: and for all there were so many, the net was not rent.

verse 6
19 And going on a little [*cp.* Luke 5 3] further, he saw James the *son* of Zebedee, and John his brother, who also were in the boat

10 and so were also

21 And going on from thence

he saw other two brethren, [1] James the *son* of Zebedee, and John his brother,

in the boat with Zebedee their father, mending their nets; and   he called them.

James and John,

sons of Zebedee,

which were partners with Simon.   And Jesus said unto Simon, Fear not; from henceforth [*cp.* 1 48; 12 52; 22 18, 69] thou shalt [1] catch men.   **11** And when they had brought their boats to land, they   left all [*cp.* Matt. 19 27; Mark 10 28: *also* Luke 5 28; 14 33],

[*cp.* 21 15-23]

mending the nets.   **20** And straightway he called them:

verse 19
22 And

they straightway left the boat and their father [*cp.* Luke 18 28],

and fol-lowed him [*cp.* 4 20; 9 9; 19 27].

verse 17
and

they   left   their father Zebedee in the boat with the hired servants [*cp.* Luke 18 28], and went after him [*cp.* 1 18; 2 14; 10 28].

and fol-lowed him [*cp.* 5 28; 18 28].

[*cp. also* 1 35-51.]

[1] Or, *Jacob*: and so elsewhere.

[1] Gr. *take alive*.

[1] That is, *Twin*.
[2] Gr. *a fire of charcoal*.
[3] Or. *a fish*   [4] Or, *a loaf*
[5] Or, *aboard*

(ii) The Great Sermon (Matt.: §§ 32-51)

§ 32. **The Occasion of the Sermon**

Matt. 5 1-2			Luke 6 20		
1 And seeing the multitudes [*cp.* 3 7; 8 18; 9 36], he went up into the mountain [*cp.* 14 23; 15 29; 17 1; 28 16]: and when he had sat down [*cp.* 15 29; 24 3], his disciples came unto him [*cp.* 13 10, 36; 14 15; 15 12, 23; 17 19; 18 1; 24 1, 3; 26 17]: **2** and he opened his mouth and taught them, saying,	*cp.* 3 13; 6 46; 9 2. *cp.* 13 3. *cp.* 6 35.		*cp.* 6 12; 9 28. **20** And he lifted up his eyes on his disciples, *cp.* 9 12. and said,	*cp.* 6 5. *cp.* 6 3, 15. *cp.* 6 5.	

§ 33. **The Beatitudes**

Matt. 5 3-12			Luke 6 20-26		
3 Blessed are the poor in spirit: for theirs is the kingdom of heaven. **4** [1] Blessed are they that mourn: for they shall be comforted. **5** Blessed are the meek: for they shall inherit the earth. **6** Blessed are they that hunger and thirst after righteousness [*cp.* 6 33: *also* 3 15; 5 10, 20; 6 1; 21 32]: for they shall be filled.			Blessed *are* ye poor: for yours is the kingdom of God [*cp.* 16 25]. *verse 21: cp. also verse 25.*	*cp.* 16 20.	
verse 4			**21** Blessed *are* ye that hunger now:	*cp.* 7 37.	
7 Blessed are the merciful: for they shall obtain mercy. **8** Blessed are the pure in heart: for they shall see God. **9** Blessed are the peacemakers [*cp.* 10 13]: for they shall be called sons of God [*cp.* 5 45; 8 12; 13 38]. **10** Blessed are they that have been persecuted for righteousness' [*cp.* 3 15; 5 6, 20; 6 1, 33; 21 32] sake: for theirs is the kingdom of heaven. **11** Blessed are ye when *men* shall	*cp.* 9 50.		for ye shall be filled. Blessed *are* ye that weep now: for ye shall laugh. *cp.* 6 36. *cp.* 10 5, 6: *also* 1 79; 2 14, 29; 19 38, 42. *cp.* 20 36: *also* 6 35; 16 8.	*cp.* 16 20. *cp.* 14 27; 16 33. *cp.* 12 36: *also* 1 12; 11 52.	
	cp. 10 22; 24 9.	*cp.* 13 13.	**22** Blessed are ye, when men shall hate you [*cp.* 1 71; 6 27; 21 17], and when they shall separate you *from their company*, and reproach you,	*cp.* 15 18, 19; 17 14.	
reproach you, and persecute you, and say all manner of evil against you falsely, for my sake [*cp.* 10 18, 39; 16 25: *also* 10 22; 19 29; 24 9]. **12** Rejoice, and be exceeding glad: for great is your reward in heaven: for so persecuted they the prophets [*cp.* 21 35-36; 22 6; 23 29-34, 37] which were before you.	*cp.* 8 35; 10 29; 13 9: *also* 13 13. *cp.* 12 3-5.		and cast out your name as evil, for the Son of man's sake [*cp.* 9 24: *also* 21 12, 17: *and* 18 29]. **23** Rejoice in that day, and leap *for joy*: for behold, your reward is great in heaven: for in the same manner did their fathers unto the prophets [*cp.* 11 47-50; 13 33, 34; 20 10-12]. **24** But woe unto you that are rich! for ye have received your consolation [*cp.* 16 25]. **25** Woe unto	*cp.* 15 21.	

[1] Some ancient authorities transpose ver. 4 and 5.

you, ye that are full now! for ye shall hunger. Woe *unto you*, ye that laugh now! for ye shall mourn and weep. **26** Woe *unto you*, when all men shall speak well of you! for in the same manner did their fathers to the false prophets.

Matt. 5 5: *cp.* Ps. 37 11.

§ 34. **The Disciples as Salt and Light**

Matt. **5** 13-16	Mark 9 50; 4 21	Luke 14 34; 8 16; 11 33	
13 Ye are the salt of the earth: but if the salt have lost its savour, wherewith shall it be salted? it is thenceforth good for nothing, but to be cast out and trodden under foot of men. **14** Ye are the light of the world. A city set on a hill cannot be hid. **15** Neither do *men* light a lamp, and put it under the bushel, but on the stand; and it shineth unto all that are in the house. **16** Even so let your light shine before men, that they may see your good works, and glorify [*cp.* 9 8; 15 31] your Father which is in heaven [*cp.* 5 45; 6 1, 9; 7 11, 21; 10 32, 33; 12 50; 16 17; 18 10, 14, 19: *also* 5 48; 6 14, 26, 32; 15 13; 18 35; 23 9].	9 **50** Salt is good: but if the salt have lost its saltness, wherewith will ye season it? **4 21** Is the lamp brought to be put under the bushel, or under the bed, *and* not to be put on the stand? *cp.* 2 12. *cp.* 11 25, 26.	14 **34** Salt therefore is good: but if even the salt have lost its savour, wherewith shall it be seasoned? **35** It is fit neither for the land nor for the dunghill: *men* cast it out. 8 **16** And no man, when he hath lighted a lamp, covereth it with a vessel, or putteth it under a bed; but putteth it on a stand, that they which enter in may see the light.	11 **33** No man, when he hath lighted a lamp, putteth it in a cellar, neither under the bushel, but on the stand, that they which enter in may see the light. *cp.* 2 20; 5 25, 26; 7 16; 13 13; 17 15, 18; 18 43; 23 47. *cp.* 11 13.	*cp.* 8 12: *also* 1 4; 9 5; 12 46. *cp.* 15 8: *also* 9 24.

§ 35. **Jesus, the Disciples, and the Law**

Matt. **5** 17-20			
17 Think not that I came to destroy the law or the prophets [*cp.* 7 12; 11 13; 22 40]: I came not to destroy, but to fulfil. **18** For verily I say unto you, Till heaven and earth pass away [*cp.* 24 35], one jot or one tittle shall in no wise pass away from the law, till all things be accomplished. **19** Whosoever therefore shall break one of these least commandments, and shall teach men so, shall be called least in the kingdom of heaven [*cp.* 11 11]: but whosoever shall do and teach them, he shall be called great in the kingdom of heaven [*cp.* 11 11; 18 1, 4]. **20** For I say unto you, that except your righteousness [*cp.* 6 1: *also* 3 15; 5 6, 10; 6 33; 21 32] shall exceed *the righteousness* of the scribes and Pharisees ye shall in no wise enter into the kingdom of heaven [*cp.* 7 21; 18 3; 19 23, 24; 21 31; 23 13: *also* 7 13; 18 8, 9; 19 17; 25 21, 23].	*cp.* 13 31. *cp.* 9 47; 10 15, 23, 24, 25: *also* 9 43, 45.	*cp.* 16 16. Luke 16 **17** But it is easier for heaven and earth to pass away [*cp.* 21 33], than for one tittle of the law to fall. *cp.* 7 28. *cp.* 9 48. *cp.* 7 28. *cp.* 18 17, 24, 25: *also* 11 52; 13 24; 24 26.	*cp.* 3 5: *also* 10 1, 2, 9.

§ 36. **Murder, Anger, and the Need for Reconciliation in view of the Coming Judgement**

Matt. **5** 21-26		
21 Ye have heard that it was said to them of old time [*cp.* 5 27, 31, 33, 38, 43], Thou shalt not kill; and whosoever shall kill shall be in danger of the judgement: **22** but I say		

unto you, that every one who is angry with his brother [1] shall be in danger of the judgement; and whosoever shall say to his brother, [2] Raca, shall be in danger of the council; and whosoever shall say, [3] Thou fool [*cp.* 23 17], shall be in danger [4] of the [5] hell of fire [*cp.* 18 9: *also* 5 29, 30; 10 28; 23 15, 33: *and* 3 10, 12; 7 19; 13 42, 50; 18 8; 25 41]. **23** If therefore thou art offering thy gift [*cp.* 2 11; 8 4] at the altar, and there rememberest that thy brother hath aught against thee, **24** leave there thy gift before the altar, and go thy way, first [*cp.* 6 33; 7 5; 23 26] be reconciled to thy brother, and then come and offer thy gift. **25** Agree
with thine adversary quickly,
whiles thou art
with him in the way;
lest haply the adversary deliver thee to the judge, and the judge   [6] deliver thee to the officer, and   thou be cast   into prison. **26** Verily I say unto thee, Thou shalt by no means come out thence, till thou have paid the last farthing [*cp.* 18 34, 35].

cp. 9 43, 45, 47.

cp. 11 25.
cp. 7 27.

cp. 12 5: *also* 3 9, 17.

cp. 6 42.

cp. 15 6.

Luke 12 58 For as thou art going with thine adversary before the magistrate, on the way give diligence to be quit of him; lest haply he hale thee unto the judge, and the judge shall deliver thee to the [1] officer, and the [1] officer shall cast thee into prison. 59 I say unto thee, Thou shalt by no means come out thence, till thou have paid the very last mite.

[1] Many ancient authorities insert *without cause*.
[2] An expression of contempt.
[3] Or, *Moreh*, a Hebrew expression of condemnation.
[4] Gr. *unto* or *into*.   [5] Gr. *Gehenna of fire*.
[6] Some ancient authorities omit *deliver thee*.

[1] Gr. *exactor*.

Matt. 5 21 = Exod. 20 13; Deut. 5 17.

§ 37. Adultery, the Treatment of Offending Members, and Divorce

Matt. 5 27-32

27 Ye have heard that it was said [*cp.* 5 21, 31, 33, 38, 43], Thou shalt not commit adultery: **28** but I say unto you, that every one that looketh on a woman to lust after her hath committed adultery with her already in his heart. **29** And if thy right [*cp.* 5 30, 39; 27 29] eye causeth thee to stumble, pluck it out, and cast it from thee: for it is profitable for thee that one of thy members should perish, and not thy whole body be cast into [1] hell [*cp.* 5 30; 10 28; 23 15, 33: *also* 5 22; 18 9]. **30** And if thy right [*cp.* 5 29, 39; 27 29] hand causeth thee to stumble, cut it off, and cast it from thee: for it is profitable for thee that one of thy members should perish,

and not thy whole body

go into [1] hell [*see above*].
cp. 3 10, 12: 7 19.

verse 29

verse 9

Matt. 18 8 And if thy   hand or thy foot causeth thee to stumble, cut it off, and cast it from thee: it is good for thee
          to enter into life maimed or halt, rather than having two hands or two feet to be cast   into the eternal fire [*cp.* 25 41: *also* 13 42, 50].

9 And if thine eye causeth thee

verse 47

Mark 9 43 And if thy   hand cause thee to stumble, cut it off:
          it is good for thee
          to enter into life maimed, rather than having thy two hands   to go into [1] hell, into the unquenchable fire.[2] 45 And if thy foot cause thee to stumble, cut it off: it is good for thee to enter into life halt, rather than having thy two feet to be cast into [1] hell. 47 And if thine eye cause thee

cp. 6 6; 22 50.

cp. 12 5.

cp. 6 6; 22 50.

cp. 12 5.

cp. 12 5.

cp. 18 10.

cp. 18 10.

cp. 15 6.

to stumble, pluck it out, and cast it from thee: it is good for thee to enter into life with one eye, rather than having two eyes to be cast into the [1] hell of fire [cp. 5 22: also 5 29, 30 ; 10 28 ; 23 15, 33].

to stumble, cast it out: it is good for thee to enter into the kingdom of God with one eye, rather than having two eyes to be cast into [1] hell.

cp. 12 5.

31 It was said also [cp. 5 21, 27, 33, 38, 43], Whosoever shall put away his wife, let him give her a writing of divorcement:

32 but I say unto you, that every one that putteth away his wife, saving for the cause of fornication, maketh her an adulteress: and whosoever shall marry her when she is put away committeth adultery.

Matt. 19 7 They say unto him, Why then did Moses command to give a bill of divorcement, and to put her away? ... 9 And I say unto you, Whosoever shall put away his wife, [2] except for fornication, and shall marry another, committeth adultery: [3] and he that marrieth her when she is put away committeth adultery.

Mark 10 4 And they said, Moses suffered to write a bill of divorcement, and to put her away. ... 11 And he saith unto them, Whosoever shall put away his wife, and marry another, committeth adultery against her: 12 and if she herself shall put away her husband, and marry another, she committeth adultery.

Luke 16 18 Every one that putteth away his wife, and marrieth another, committeth adultery: and he that marrieth one that is put away from a husband committeth adultery.

[1] Gr. Gehenna.

[1] Gr. Gehenna of fire.
[2] Some ancient authorities read saving for the cause of fornication, maketh her an adulteress: as in ch. 5. 32.
[3] The following words, to the end of the verse, are omitted by some ancient authorities.

[1] Gr. Gehenna.
[2] Ver. 44 and 46 (which are identical with ver. 48) are omitted by the best ancient authorities.

Matt. 5 27 = Exod. 20 14 ; Deut. 5 18.   Matt. 5 31 (Matt. 19 7 ‖ Mark 10 4) = Deut. 24 1.

Matt. 5 32 ‖ Matt. 19 9 ‖ Mark 10 11 ‖ Luke 16 18 : cp. 1 Cor. 7 10-11, 'But unto the married I give charge, yea not I, but the Lord, That the wife depart not from her husband (but and if she depart, let her remain unmarried, or else be reconciled to her husband) ; and that the husband leave not his wife.'

§ 38. Oaths

[Cp. Matt. 23 16-22]

Matt. 5 33-37

33 Again, ye have heard that it was said to them of old time [cp. 5 21, 27, 31, 38, 43], Thou shalt not forswear thyself, but shalt perform unto the Lord thine oaths : **34** but I say unto you, Swear not at all; neither by the heaven, for it is the throne of God [cp. 23 22] ; **35** nor by the earth, for it is the footstool of his feet ; nor [1] by Jerusalem, for it is the city of the great King. **36** Neither shalt thou swear by thy head, for thou canst not make one hair white or black. **37** [2] But let your speech be, Yea, yea ; Nay, nay : and whatsoever is more than these is of [3] the evil one [cp. 5 39 ; 6 13 ; 13 19, 38].

cp. 17 15.

[1] Or, toward
[2] Some ancient authorities read But your speech shall be.
[3] Or, evil : as in ver. 39 ; 6 13.

Matt. 5 33 : cp. Lev. 19 12 ; Exod. 20 7 ; Deut. 5 11 ; Numb. 30 2 ; Deut. 23 21 ; Eccl. 5 4 ; Ecclus. 18 22.

§ 39. Non-resistance

Matt. 5 38-42

38 Ye have heard that it was said [*cp.* 5 21, 27, 31, 33, 43], An eye for an eye, and a tooth for a tooth: **39** but I say unto you, Resist not [1] him that is evil [*cp.* 5 37; 6 13; 13 19, 38]: but whosoever smiteth thee on thy right [*cp.* 5 29, 30; 27 29] cheek, turn to him the other also. **40** And if any man would go to law with thee, and take away thy coat, let him have thy cloke also. **41** And whosoever shall [2] compel thee to go one mile, go with him twain. **42** Give to him that asketh thee, and from him that would borrow of thee [*cp.* Luke 6 34, 35] turn not thou away.

[1] Or, *evil* [2] Gr. *impress.*

Matt. 5 38 = Exod. 21 24; Lev. 24 20; Deut. 19 21.

Luke 6 29-30

29 To him that smiteth thee on the *one* [*cp.* 6 6; 22 50] cheek offer also the other; and from him that taketh away thy cloke withhold not thy coat also.

30. Give to everyone that asketh thee; and of him that taketh away thy goods ask them not again.

cp. 17 15.

cp. 18 10.

cp. 19 23.

§ 40. The Love that is Perfect

Matt. 5 43-48

43 Ye have heard that it was said [*cp.* 5 21, 27, 31, 33, 38], Thou shalt love thy neighbour, and hate thine enemy: **44** but I say unto you, Love your enemies, and *cp.* 10 22; 24 9. pray for them that persecute you; **45** that ye may be sons [*cp.* 5 9; 8 12; 13 38] of your Father which is in heaven [*cp.* 5 16; 6 1, 9; 7 11, 21; 10 32, 33; 12 50; 16 17; 18 10, 14, 19: *also* 5 48; 6 14, 26, 32; 15 13; 18 35; 23 9: Mark 11 25, 26, *and* Luke 11 13]: for he maketh his sun to rise on the evil and the good, and sendeth rain on the just and the unjust [*cp.* 13 30]. **46** For if ye love them that love you, what reward [*cp.* Luke 6 35] have ye? do not even the [1] publicans [*cp.* 9 11; 11 19; 18 17; 21 31, 32] *cp.* 9 11, 13; 11 19; 26 45. the same? **47** And if ye salute your brethren only, what do ye more *than others*? do not even the Gentiles [*cp.* 6 7; 18 17: *also* 6 32 *and* Luke 12 30] the same?

verse 45

48 Ye therefore shall be

cp. 13 13.

cp. 2 16.

cp. 2 16, 17; 14 41.

cp. 5 7.

Luke 6 27-28, 32-36

27 But I say unto you which hear, Love your enemies, do good to them that hate you [*cp.* 1 71; 6 22; 21 17], **28** bless them that curse you, pray for them that despitefully use you [*cp.* 23 34]. *verse* 35

32 And if ye love them that love you, what thank have ye? for even [*cp.* 5 30; 7 29, 34; 15 1; 18 10] sinners [*cp.* 5 8, 30, 32; 7 34, 37; 15 1, 2; 18 13; 19 7; 24 7] love those that love them. **33** And if ye do good to them that do good to you, what thank have ye? for even sinners [*see above*] do the same. **34** And if ye lend [*cp.* Matt. 5 42] to them of whom ye hope to receive, what thank have ye? even sinners [*see above*] lend to sinners, to receive again as much. **35** But love your enemies, and do *them* good, and lend [*cp.* Matt. 5 42], [1] never despairing; and your reward [*cp.* Matt. 5 46] shall be great, and ye shall be sons [*cp.* 16 8; 20 36] of the Most High [*cp.* 1 32, 35, 76; 8 28]: for he is kind toward the unthankful and evil. **36** Be ye

cp. 15 18, 19; 17 14.

cp. 12 36: *also* 1 12; 11 52.

cp. 9 16, 24, 25, 31.

cp. 12 36: *also* 1 12; 11 52.

perfect [cp. 19 21],   as your
heavenly Father [cp. 6 14, 26, 32; 15
13; 18 35; 23 9: also 5 16, 45; 6 1, 9;
7 11, 21; 10 32, 33; 12 50; 16 17; 18
10, 14, 19: Mark 11 25, 26 and Luke
11 13] is perfect.

¹ That is, collectors or renters of Roman taxes: and so
elsewhere.

merciful [cp. Matt. 5 7], even as your
Father

is merciful.

¹ Some ancient authorities read despairing
of no man.

Matt. 5 43 = Lev. 19 18.

§ 41. Secrecy the Condition of the Heavenly Reward

Matt. 6 1

1 Take heed that ye do not your righteousness [cp. 5 20: also
3 15; 5 6, 10; 6 33; 21 32] before men, to be seen of them
[cp. 6 2, 5, 16; 23 5, 28]: else ye have no reward with your
Father which is in heaven [cp. 5 16, 45; 6 9; 7 11, 21; 10
32, 33; 12 50; 16 17; 18 10, 14, 19: also 5 48; 6 14, 26,
32; 15 13; 18 35; 23 9].   cp. 11 25, 26.   cp. 11 13.

§ 42. Almsgiving

Matt. 6 2-4

2 When therefore thou doest alms, sound not a trumpet before
thee, as the hypocrites [cp. 6 5, 16; 24 51] do in the synagogues
and in the streets, that they may have glory of men [cp. 6 1,
5, 16; 23 5, 28]. Verily I say unto you, They have received
their reward [cp. 6 5, 16]. **3** But when thou doest alms, let not
thy left hand know what thy right hand doeth: **4** that thine
alms may be in secret: and thy Father which seeth in secret
shall recompense thee [cp. 6 6, 18].

§ 43. Prayer and the Duty of Forgiveness

Matt. 6 5-15

5 And when ye pray [cp. Luke 11 2], ye shall not be as the
hypocrites [cp. 6 2, 16; 24 51]: for they love to stand and
pray in the synagogues and in the corners of the streets, that
they may be seen of men [cp. 6 1, 2, 16; 23 5, 28]. Verily
I say unto you, They have received their reward [cp. 6 2, 16].
6 But thou, when thou prayest, enter into thine inner
chamber, and having shut thy door, pray to thy Father which
is in secret, and thy Father which seeth in secret shall
recompense thee [cp. 6 4, 18]. **7** And in praying use not vain
repetitions, as the Gentiles [cp. 5 47; 18 17: also 6 32] do: for
they think that they shall be heard for their much speaking. **8** Be not therefore like unto them: for ¹ your Father
knoweth [cp. 6 32] what things ye have need of, before
ye ask him. **9** After this manner therefore pray ye:

cp. 12 40.   cp. 20 47.

cp. 12 30.

Luke 11 2 And he said unto them,
When ye pray [cp. Matt. 6 5], say,
    ¹ Father [cp. 10 21, 22; 22 42;
23 34, 46],

Our Father [cp. 11 25, 26; 26 39, 42]   cp. 14 36.
which art in heaven [cp. 5 16, 45;   cp. 11 25, 26.
6 1; 7 11, 21; 10 32, 33; 12 50;
16 17; 18 10, 14, 19: also 5 48; 6
14, 26, 32; 15 13; 18 35; 23 9],
Hallowed be thy name.
10 Thy kingdom come. Thy will be
done [cp. 26 39, 42: also 7 21; 12 50;
21 31], as in heaven, so on earth.
11 Give us this day ² our daily
bread. **12** And forgive us our debts,
as we   also have forgiven
our debtors.

    cp. 11 13.

Hallowed be thy name [cp. 1 49].
Thy kingdom come.²
    cp. 22 42.

3 Give us day by day ³ our daily
bread. **4** And forgive us our sins;
for we ourselves also   forgive
every one that is indebted to us.

cp. 11 41; 12
27, 28; 17
1, 5, 11, 21,
24, 25.

cp. 4 34; 5
30; 6 38;
7 17; 9 31.

13 And bring us not into temptation [*cp.* 26 41], but deliver us from ³ the evil *one* [*cp.* 5 37, 39; 13 19, 38].⁴

cp. 14 38.

And bring us not into temptation [*cp.* 22 40, 46].⁴

¹ Many ancient authorities read *Our Father, which art in heaven*. See Matt. 6 9.
² Many ancient authorities add *Thy will be done, as in heaven, so on earth*. See Matt. 6 10.
³ Gr. *our bread for the coming day*.
⁴ Many ancient authorities add *but deliver us from the evil one* (or, *from evil*). See Matt. 6 13.

cp. 17 15.

14 For if ye forgive men their trespasses, your heavenly Father [*cp.* 5 48; 6 26, 32; 15 13; 18 35; 23 9: *also* 5 16, 45; 6 1, 9; 7 11, 21; 10 32, 33; 12 50; 16 17; 18 10, 14, 19] will also forgive you. **15** But if ye forgive not men their trespasses, neither will your Father forgive your trespasses [*cp.* 18 21-35].

cp. 11 25.
cp. 11 25, 26.
cp. 11 26.

cp. 17 3-4.
cp. 11 13.

¹ Some ancient authorities read *God your Father*.
² Gr. *our bread for the coming day*.   ³ Or, *evil*
⁴ Many authorities, some ancient, but with variations, add *For thine is the kingdom, and the power, and the glory, for ever. Amen.*

Matt. 6 9 ‖ Luke 11 2 : *cp.* Rom. 8 15 ; Gal. 4 6.

§ 44. Fasting

[*Cp.* Matt. 9 14-15 ‖ Mark 2 18-20 ‖ Luke 5 33-35]

Matt. 6 16-18

16 Moreover when ye fast, be not, as the hypocrites [*cp.* 6 2, 5; 24 51], of a sad countenance: for they disfigure their faces, that they may be seen of men [*cp.* 6 1, 2, 5; 23 5, 28] to fast. Verily I say unto you, They have received their reward [*cp.* 6 2, 5]. **17** But thou, when thou fastest, anoint thy head, and wash thy face; **18** that thou be not seen of men to fast, but of thy Father which is in secret: and thy Father, which seeth in secret, shall recompense thee [*cp.* 6 4, 6].

§ 45. True Treasure and where it may be found

Matt. 6 19-34

19 Lay not up for yourselves treasures upon the earth, where moth and rust doth consume, and where thieves ¹ break through [*cp.* 24 43] and steal: **20** but lay up for yourselves treasures in heaven [*cp.* 19 21], where neither moth nor rust doth consume, and where thieves do not ¹ break through [*cp.* 24 43] nor steal: **21** for where thy treasure is, there will thy heart be also. **22** The lamp of the body is the eye: if therefore thine eye be single, thy whole body shall be full of light. **23** But if thine eye be evil [*cp.* 20 15], thy whole body shall be full of darkness. If therefore the light that is in thee be darkness, how great is the darkness !

cp. 10 21.

cp. 7 22.

Luke 11 34-36; 12 22-34; 16 13

cp. 12 39.
12 33 Sell that ye have, and give alms ; make for yourselves purses which wax not old, a treasure in the heavens [*cp.* 18 22] that faileth not, where no thief draweth near, neither moth destroyeth.
cp. 12 39.
34 For where your treasure is, there will your heart be also. 11 34 The lamp of thy body is thine eye : when thine eye is single, thy whole body also is full of light ; but when it is evil, thy body also is full of darkness. 35 Look therefore whether the light that is in thee be not darkness.
36 If therefore thy whole body be full of light, having no part dark, it shall be wholly full

24 No man can serve two masters: for either he will hate the one, and love the other; or else he will hold to one, and despise the other. Ye cannot serve God and mammon.

25 Therefore I say unto you, Be not anxious [*cp.* 6 31, 34; 10 19] for your life, what ye shall eat, or what ye shall drink; nor yet for your body, what ye shall put on. Is not   the life more than the food, and the body than the raiment? **26** Behold the birds of the heaven [*cp.* 8 20; 13 32: *also* Luke 8 5; 9 58; 13 19], that they sow not, neither do they reap, nor gather

into barns; and your heavenly Father [*cp.* 5 48; 6 14, 32; 15 13; 18 35; 23 9; *and* Luke 11 13: *also* 5 16, 45; 6 1, 9; 7 11, 21; 10 32, 33; 12 50; 16 17; 18 10, 14, 19] feedeth them. Are not ye of much more value   than they [*cp.* 10 31; 12 12]?   **27** And which of you by being anxious can add one cubit unto his ² stature? **28** And

why are ye anxious concerning raiment?

Consider the lilies of the field, how they grow; they toil not, neither do they spin: **29** yet I say unto you, that even Solomon in all his glory was not arrayed like one of these. **30** But if God doth so clothe the grass of the field, which to-day is, and to-morrow is cast into the oven, *shall he* not much more *clothe* you, O ye of little faith [*cp.* 8 26; 14 31; 16 8: *also* 17 20]? **31** Be not therefore anxious, saying, What shall we eat? or, What shall we drink? or, Wherewithal shall we be clothed?

32 For after all these things do the Gentiles [*cp.* 5 47; 6 7; 18 17] seek;   for your heavenly Father [*see references at verse* 26] knoweth [*cp.* 6 8] that ye have need of all these things. **33** But seek ye first [*cp.* 5 24; 7 5; 23 26] his kingdom, and his righteousness [*cp.* 5 6: *also* 3 15; 5 10, 20; 6 1; 21 32]; and all these things shall be added unto you [*cp.* 19 29]. **34** Be not therefore anxious for the morrow: for the morrow will be anxious for itself. Sufficient [*cp.* 10 25] unto the day is the evil thereof.

cp. 13 11.

cp. 4 32.

cp. 11 25, 26.

cp. 4 40; 11 22; 16 14.

cp. 7 27.

cp. 4 24; 10 29-30.

of light, as when the lamp with its bright shining doth give thee light. 16 **13** No ¹ servant can serve two masters: for either he will hate the one, and love the other; or else he will hold to one, and despise the other. Ye cannot serve God and mammon. 12 **22** And he said unto his disciples, Therefore I say unto you, Be not anxious [*cp.* 12 11] for *your* ² life, what ye shall eat; nor yet for your body, what ye shall put on. **23** For the ² life is more than the food, and the body than the raiment. **24** Consider the ravens,

that they sow not, neither do they reap;   which have no store-chamber nor barn; and God

feedeth them: of how much more value are ye than the birds [*cp.* 12 7]! **25** And which of you by being anxious can add a cubit unto his ³ stature? **26** If then ye are not able to do even that which is least, why are ye anxious concerning   the rest [*cp.* 8 10; 18 9, 11; 24 9, 10]? **27** Consider the lilies,   how they grow: they toil not, neither do they spin; yet I say unto you,

Even Solomon in all his glory was not arrayed like one of these. **28** But if God doth so clothe the grass in the field, which to-day is, and to-morrow is cast into the oven; how much more *shall he clothe* you, O ye of little faith [*cp.* 8 25; *etc.*]?   **29** And seek not ye   what ye shall eat, and what ye shall drink,

neither be ye of doubtful mind. **30** For   all these things do the nations of the world seek after: but your   Father knoweth   that ye have need of   these things. **31** Howbeit seek ye [*cp.* 6 42]   ⁴ his kingdom,

and   these things shall be added unto you [*cp.* 18 29-30].

32 Fear not, little flock; for it is your Father's good pleasure to give you the kingdom.

cp. 3 12; 6 64; 14 10; 20 27.

---

¹ Gr. *dig through.*   ² Or, *age*

¹ Gr. *household-servant.*   ² Or, *soul*
³ Or, *age*
⁴ Many ancient authorities read *the kingdom of God.*

§ 46. Judgement of Others

Matt. 7 1-5	Mark 4 24	Luke 6 37-38, 41-42
1 Judge not, that ye be not judged. **2** For with what judgement ye judge, ye shall be judged:		**37** And judge not, and ye shall not be judged:
		and condemn not, and ye shall not be condemned: release, and ye shall be released: **38** give, and it shall be given unto you; good measure, pressed down, shaken together, running over, shall they give into your bosom. For
and with what measure ye mete, it shall be measured unto you.	**24** And he said unto them, Take heed what ye hear: with what measure ye mete it shall be measured unto you: and more shall be given unto you [*cp.* 10 29-30].	with what measure ye mete it shall be measured to you again.
cp. 6 33; 19 29.		*cp.* 12 31; 18 29-30.
3 And why beholdest thou the mote that is in thy brother's eye, but considerest not the beam that is in thine own eye? **4** Or how wilt thou say to thy brother, Let me cast out the mote out of thine eye; and lo, the beam is in thine own eye? **5** Thou hypocrite, cast out first [*cp.* 5 24; 6 33; 23 26] the beam out of thine own eye; and then shalt thou see clearly to cast out the mote out of thy brother's eye.	*cp.* 7 27.	**41** And why beholdest thou the mote that is in thy brother's eye, but considerest not the beam that is in thine own eye? **42** Or how canst thou say to thy brother, Brother, let me cast out the mote that is in thine eye, when thou thyself beholdest not the beam that is in thine own eye? Thou hypocrite, cast out first the beam out of thine own eye, and then shalt thou see clearly to cast out the mote that is in thy brother's eye.

cp. 8 7-9.

§ 47. The Sanctity of Holy Things

Matt. 7 6	
6 Give not that which is holy unto the dogs [*cp.* 15 26], neither cast your pearls before the swine, lest haply they trample them under their feet, and turn and rend you.	*cp.* 7 27.

§ 48. Answer to Prayer and the Golden Rule

Matt. 7 7-12	Luke 11 9-13; 6 31	John 15 7	John 16 24
	9 And I say unto you, Ask,		Ask,
7 Ask, and it shall be given you [*cp.* 18 19; 21 22]; seek, and ye shall *cp.* 11 24.	and it shall be given you; seek, and ye shall	Ask whatsoever ye will, and it shall be done unto you.	and ye shall **receive** [*cp.* 14 13; 15 16; 16 23].
find; knock, and it shall be opened unto you: **8** for every one that asketh receiveth; and he that seeketh findeth; and to him that knocketh it shall be opened. **9** Or what man is there of you, who, if his son shall ask him for a loaf, will give him a stone; **10** or if he shall ask for a fish, will give him a serpent?		find; knock, and it shall be opened unto you. **10** For every one that asketh receiveth; and he that seeketh findeth; and to him that knocketh it shall be opened. **11** And of which of you that is a father shall his son ask ¹ a loaf, and he give him a stone? or a fish, and he for a fish give him a serpent? **12** Of if he shall ask an egg, will he give him a scorpion? **13** If ye then, being evil, know how to give good gifts	
11 If ye then, being evil [*cp.* 12 34], know how to give good gifts			

unto your children, how much more shall your Father which is in heaven [*cp.* 5 16, 45; 6 1, 9; 7 21; 10 32, 33; 12 50; 16 17; 18 10, 14, 19: *also* 5 48; 6 14, 26, 32; 15 13; 18 35; 23 9] give good things to them that ask him? **12** All things therefore whatsoever ye would that men should do unto you, even so do ye also unto them: for this is the law and the prophets [*cp.* 5 17; 11 13; 22 40: *also* Luke 16 16].	*cp.* 11 25, 26.	unto your children, how much more shall *your* heavenly Father give the Holy Spirit to them that ask him? **6 31** And as ye would that men should do to you, do ye also to them likewise. [1] Some ancient authorities omit *a loaf, and he give him a stone? or,*

§ 49. The Narrow Gate

Matt. 7 13-14		Luke 13 23-24	
13 Enter ye in [*cp.* 5 20; 7 21; 18 3, 8, 9; 19 17, 23, 24; 21 31; 23 13; 25 21, 23] by the narrow gate: for wide [1] is the gate, and broad is the way, that leadeth to destruction, and many be they that enter in thereby. **14** [2] For narrow is the gate, and straitened the way, that leadeth unto life, and few [*cp.* Luke 13 23] be they that find it. [1] Some ancient authorities omit *is the gate.* [2] Many ancient authorities read *How narrow is the gate, &c.*	*cp.* 9 43, 45, 47; 10 15, 23, 24, 25.	**23** And one said unto him, Lord, are they few [*cp.* Matt. 7 14] that be saved? And he said unto them, **24** Strive to enter in [*cp.* 11 52; 18 17, 24, 25; 24 26] by the narrow door: for many, I say unto you, shall seek to enter in, and shall not be able.	*cp.* 10 1, 2, 9; 3 5.

§ 50. The Criteria of the True Disciple

Matt. 7 15-27	Matt. 12 33-35		Luke 6 43-49; 13 26-27	
15 Beware of false prophets [*cp.* 24 11, 24], which come to you in sheep's clothing, but inwardly are ravening wolves. **16** By their fruits ye shall know them. Do *men* gather grapes of thorns, or figs of thistles? **17** Even so every good tree bringeth forth good fruit; but the corrupt tree bringeth forth evil fruit. **18** A good tree cannot bring forth evil fruit, neither can a corrupt tree bring forth good fruit. **19** Every tree that bringeth not forth good fruit is hewn down, and cast into the fire [= 3 10: *cp.* 3 12; 5 22, 29, 30; 10 28; 13 42, 50; 18 8, 9; 23 33; 25 41]. **20** Therefore by their fruits ye shall know them. *verse* 16		*cp.* 13 22. **33** Either make the tree good, and its fruit good; or make the tree corrupt, and its fruit corrupt: *cp.* 9 43, 45, 47. for the tree is known by its fruit.	6 44 **43** For there is no good tree that bringeth forth corrupt fruit; nor again a corrupt tree that bringeth forth good fruit. 3 9: *cp.* 13 7-9: *also* 3 17; 12 5. **44** For each tree is known by its own fruit. For of thorns men do not gather figs, nor of a bramble bush gather they grapes.	*cp.* 15 2, 6.

34 Ye offspring of vipers, how can ye, being evil, speak good things ?

verse 35

for out of the abundance of the heart the mouth speaketh. **35** The good man out of his good treasure bringeth forth good things : and the evil man out of his evil treasure bringeth forth evil things.

21 Not every one that saith unto me, Lord, Lord, shall enter into the kingdom of heaven [*cp.* 5 20; 18 3; 19 23, 24; 21 31; 23 13: *also* 7 13; 18 8, 9; 19 17; 25 21, 23]; but he that doeth   the will [*cp.* 12 50; 21 31: *also* 6 10; 26 39, 42] of my Father which is in heaven [*cp.* 5 16, 45; 6 1, 9; 7 11; 10 32, 33; 12 50; 16 17; 18 10, 14, 19: *also* 5 48; 6 14, 26, 32; 15 13; 18 35; 23 9]. **22** Many will say to me in that day [*cp.* 24 36: *also* 26 29], Lord, Lord, did we not prophesy by thy name, and by thy name cast out [1] devils, and by thy name do many [2] mighty works? **23** And then   will   I profess unto them [*cp.* 25 34, 41], I never knew   you [*cp.* 25 11, 12]: depart from me [*cp.* 25 41],   ye that work iniquity.   **24** Every one therefore   which heareth these words of mine, and doeth them,

shall be likened unto a wise [*cp.* 10 16; 24 45; 25 2 *ff.*] man, which built his house
            upon the rock [*cp.* 16 18] : **25** and the rain descended, and the floods came, and the winds blew, and   beat upon that house ; and it fell not : for it was founded upon the rock. **26** And every one that heareth these words of mine, and doeth them not, shall be likened unto a foolish [*cp.* 25 2 *ff.*] man, which built his house upon the sand : **27** and the rain descended, and the floods came, and the winds blew, and   smote upon that house ; and   it fell : and great was the fall thereof.

[1] Gr. *demons.*   [2] Gr. *powers.*

cp. 9 47; 10 15, 23, 24, 25 : *also* 9 43, 45. *cp.* 3 35 : *also* 14 36. *cp.* 11 25, 26.

cp. 13 32 : *also* 14 25.

cp. 9 38. *cp.* 9 39.

45 The good man out of the good treasure of his heart bringeth forth that which is good ; and the evil *man* out of the evil *treasure* bringeth forth that which is evil : for out of the abundance of the heart his mouth speaketh.

verse 45

46 And why call ye me, Lord, Lord, *cp.* 18 17, 24, 25 : *also* 11 52 ; 13 24 ; 24 26.   and do not the things which I say ? *cp.* 22 42. *cp.* 11 13.

13 26 Then shall ye begin to say, [*cp.* 10 12 ; 17 31 ; 21 34] We did eat and drink in thy presence, [*cp.* 9 49]   and thou didst teach in our streets ; **27** and he shall say, I tell you,   I   know not whence ye are ;   depart from me, all ye workers of iniquity. **6 47** Every one that cometh unto me, and heareth my words,   and doeth them, I will shew you to whom he is like : **48** he is like a   [*cp.* 12 42] man building a house, who digged and went deep, and laid a foundation upon the rock :   and when   a flood arose,   the stream brake against that house, and could not shake it : [1] because it had been well builded. **49** But he   that heareth,   and doeth not,   is like a   man that built a house upon the earth without a foundation ;   against which the stream brake,   and straightway it fell in ; and the ruin of that house was great.

[1] Many ancient authorities read *for it had been founded upon the rock* : as in Matt. 7 25.

cp. 13 13. *cp.* 3 5 : *also* 10 1, 2, 9.

cp. 4 34 ; 5 30 ; 6 38 ; 7 17 ; 9 31.

cp. 14 20 ; 16 23, 26.

cp. 7 27, 28 : 8 14 ; 9 29, 30.

Matt. **7** 23 || Luke 13 27 = Ps. **6** 8.

§ 51. The Effect of the Sermon

Matt. 7 28-29	Mark 1 21-22	Luke 7 1; 4 31-32	
28 And it came to pass, when Jesus ended these words [*cp.* 11 1; 13 53; 19 1; 26 1], the multitudes		**7 1** After he had ended all his sayings	
cp. 8 5.	**21** And they go into Capernaum; and straightway on the sabbath day he entered into the synagogue and taught. **22** And they were	in the ears of the people, he entered into Capernaum. **4 31** And he came down to Capernaum, a city of Galilee. And he was teaching them on the sabbath day: **32** and they were	
were astonished at his teaching [*cp.* 22 33; 13 54; 19 25; 22 22: *also* 8 27; 9 33; 12 23; 15 31; 21 20; 27 14]: **29** for he taught them as *one* having authority [*cp.* 21 23 *ff.*; 9 6; 28 18], and not as their scribes.	astonished at his teaching [*cp.* 11 18; 1 27; 6 2; 10 24, 26; 12 17: *also* 2 12; 5 20, 42; 6 51; 7 37; 10 32; 15 5; 16 5, 8]: for he taught them as having authority [*cp.* 11 27 *ff.*; 1 27; 2 10], and not as the scribes.	astonished at his teaching [*cp.* 2 47, 48; 4 22, 36; 20 26: *also* 5 9, 26; 8 25, 56; 9 43; 11 14; 24 12, 41]; for his word was with authority [*cp.* 20 1 *ff.*; 4 36; 5 24].	*cp.* 7 15, 21, 46. *cp.* 5 27; 17 2.

(iii) Events in Galilee I (§§ 52-64)

§ 52. The Healing of a Leper

[*Cp.* Luke 17 11-19]

Matt. 8 1-4	Mark 1 40-45	Luke 5 12-16	
1 And when he was come down from the mountain, great multitudes followed him. **2** And behold, there came to him a leper	**40** And there cometh to him a leper, beseeching him,	**12** And it came to pass, while he was in one of the cities; behold, a man full of leprosy: and when he saw Jesus, he fell on his face [*cp.* 5 8; 8 28, 41, 47; 17 16: *also* 24 52],	*cp.* 9 38; 11 32; 18 6.
and worshipped him [*cp.* 2 11; 9 18; 14 33; 15 25; 20 20; 28 9, 17: *also* 17 14], saying, Lord, if thou wilt, thou canst [*cp.* 9 28] make me clean. **3** And [*cp.* 20 34: *also* 9 36; 14 14; 15 32] he stretched forth his hand, and touched [*cp.* 8 15; 9 20, 29; 14 36; 17 7; 20 34: *also* 9 18, 25; 14 31; 19 13, 15] him, saying, I will; be thou made clean. And straightway his leprosy was cleansed.	¹ and kneeling down to him [*cp.* 10 17: *also* 3 11; 5 6, 22, 33; 7 25], and saying unto him, If thou wilt, thou canst [*cp.* 9 22, 23; 6 5] make me clean. **41** And being moved with compassion [*cp.* 6 34; 8 2], he stretched forth his hand, and touched [*cp.* 3 10; 5 27; 6 56; 7 33; 8 22; 10 13: *also* 1 31; 5 23, 41; 6 2, 5; 8 23, 25; 9 27; 10 16] him, and saith unto him, I will; be thou made clean. **42** And straightway the leprosy departed from him, and he was made clean.	and besought him, saying, Lord, if thou wilt, thou canst make me clean. **13** And [*cp.* 7 13: *also* 10 33; 15 20] he stretched forth his hand, and touched [*cp.* 6 19; 7 14, 39; 8 44; 18 15; 22 51: *also* 4 40; 8 54; 13 13; 14 4] him, saying, I will; be thou made clean. And straightway the leprosy departed from him.	*cp.* 9 6; 20 17.
4 And Jesus [*cp.* 9 30] saith unto him, See thou tell no man [*cp.* 9 30; 12 16: *also* 16 20; 17 9]; but go thy way, shew thyself to the priest,	**43** And he ² strictly charged him, and straightway sent him out, **44** and saith unto him, See thou say nothing to any man [*cp.* 5 43; 7 36; 8 26: *also* 1 25, 34; 3 12; 8 30; 9 9]: but go thy way, shew thyself to the priest,	**14** And he charged him to tell no man [*cp.* 8 56: *also* 4 35, 41; 9 21, 36]: but go thy way, and shew thyself to the priest [*cp.* 17	

and offer
the gift [*cp.* 2 11;
5 23, 24] that Moses commanded, for a testimony unto them [*cp.* 10 18; 24 14].

cp. 9 31.
cp. 4 24; 9 26.

cp. 14 13.

cp. 14 23; 19 13; 26 36, 39, 42, 44: *also* 11 25-26.

and offer for thy cleansing   the things
which Moses commanded, for a testimony unto them [*cp.* 6 11; 13 9]. **45** But he went out, and began to publish [*cp.* 7 36] it much, and to spread abroad the [3] matter, *cp.* 1 28.

insomuch that [4] Jesus could no more openly enter into [5] a city, but was without [*cp.* 1 35; 6 31, 32] in desert places: and they came to him from every quarter.
cp. 1 35; 5 46; 14 32, 35, 39.

14], and offer for thy cleansing, according as
Moses commanded, for a testimony unto them [*cp.* 9 5; 21 13]. **15** But

so much the more went abroad the report concerning him [*cp.* 4 14, 37; 7 17]: and great multitudes came together [*cp.* 4 42] to hear, and to be healed of their infirmities.

16 But he withdrew [*cp.* 4 42; 9 10] himself in the deserts,

and prayed [*cp.* 3 21; 6 12; 9 18, 28, 29; 11 1; 22 41, 44: *also* 10 21].

cp. 11 41-42; 12 27-28; 17 1-26.

[1] Some ancient authorities omit *and kneeling down to him.*
[2] Or, *sternly*   [3] Gr. *word.*
[4] Gr. *he.*   [5] Or, *the city*

Matt. 8 4 ‖ Mark 1 44 ‖ Luke 5 14: *cp.* Lev. 13 *and* 14.

§ 53. The Centurion at Capernaum

Matt. 8 5-13		Luke 7 1-10; 13 28-30	John 4 46-53
		7 **1** After he had ended all his sayings in the ears of the people,	

5 And when he was entered into Capernaum,

he entered into Capernaum.
2 And a certain centurion's [1] servant, who was [2] dear unto him, was sick and at the point of death [*cp.* 8 42].
3 And when he heard concerning Jesus,

46 And there was a certain [1] nobleman, whose son was sick
at Capernaum.

there came
unto him
a centurion, beseeching him,

he sent unto him elders of the Jews, asking him that he would come and save his [1] servant.

47 When he heard that Jesus was come out of Judæa into Galilee, he went unto him,
and besought *him* that he would come down, and heal his son; for he was at the point of death. **48** Jesus therefore said unto him, Except ye see signs and wonders, ye will in no wise believe.
49 The [1] nobleman saith unto him, [2] Sir, come down ere my child die.

6 and saying,
Lord,   my
[1] servant   lieth in the house sick of the palsy [*cp.* 4 24; 9 2 *ff.*], grievously tormented [*cp.* 4 24].

cp. 2 3 *ff.*

cp. 5 18 *ff.*

4 And they, when they came to Jesus, besought him earnestly, saying, He is worthy that thou shouldest do this for him: **5** for he loveth our nation, and himself built us our synagogue.

7 And he saith unto him, I will come and heal him.
8 And   the centurion answered and said,
Lord,
I am not [2] worthy that thou

cp. 5 35.

6 And Jesus went with them. And when he was now not far from the house, the centurion sent friends to him, saying unto him, Lord, trouble [*cp.* 8 49] not thyself: for I am not [3] worthy that thou

shouldest come under my roof:

but only say ³ the word [*cp.* 8 16: *also* 8 3, 13, 32; 9 6, 22, 29; 12 13; 15 28; 17 7, 18], and my ¹ servant shall be healed. **9** For I also am a man ⁴ under authority, having under myself soldiers: and I say to this one, Go, and he goeth; and to another, Come, and he cometh; and to my ⁵ servant, Do this, and he doeth it. **10** And when Jesus heard it, he marvelled, [*cp.* 9 22; 16 23]

and said to them that followed, Verily I say unto you, ⁶ I have not found so great faith, no, not in Israel. **11** And I say unto you, that many shall come from the east and the west, and shall ⁷ sit down [*cp.* 26 29]

with Abraham, and Isaac, and Jacob, in the kingdom of heaven [*cp.* 21 31, 41, 43; 22 7-10: *also* 10 18; 24 14; 26 13; 28 19]: **12** but the sons of the kingdom [*cp.* 13 38: *also* 5 9, 45] shall be cast forth into the outer darkness [*cp.* 22 13; 25 30]: there shall be the weeping and gnashing of teeth [*cp.* 13 42, 50; 22 13; 24 51; 25 30].

cp. 19 30; 20 16.

13 And Jesus said unto the centurion, Go thy way; as thou hast believed, *so* be it done unto thee [*cp.* 9 29; 15 28].

And the ¹ servant was healed in that hour [*cp.* 9 22; 15 28; 17 18].

cp. 8 15.

cp. 1 25, 41; 2 11; 3 5; 5 8, 34, 41; 7 29, 34; 9 25; 10 52.

cp. 5 30; 8 33.

cp. 14 25.

cp. 12 9; 13 10; 14 9; 16 15.

cp. 10 31.

cp. 7 29.

cp. 7 30.

cp. 1 31.

shouldest come under my roof: **7** wherefore neither thought I myself worthy to come unto thee: but ⁴ say the word [*cp.* 4 35, 39; 5 13, 24; 6 10; 7 14; 8 29, 32, 48, 54; 9 42; 13 12; 17 14; 18 42], and my ⁵ servant shall be healed. **8** For I also am a man set under authority, having under myself soldiers: and I say to this one, Go, and he goeth; and to another, Come, and he cometh; and to my ¹ servant, Do this, and he doeth it. **9** And when Jesus heard these things, he marvelled at him, and turned [*cp.* 7 44; 9 55; 10 23; 14 25; 22 61; 23 28] and said unto the multitude that followed him, I say unto you, I have not found so great faith, no, not in Israel.

cp. 14 15; 22 16, 18, 30.

13 28 There shall be the weeping and gnashing of teeth, when ye shall see Abraham, and Isaac, and Jacob, and all the prophets, in the kingdom of God [*cp.* 14 21-24; 20 16: *also* 2 30-32; 3 6; 24 47], and yourselves *cp.* 6 35　16 8; 20 36. cast forth without.

29 And they shall come from the east and west, and from the north and south, and shall ⁶ sit down in the kingdom of God. **30** And behold, there are last which shall be first, and there are first which shall be last.

7 10 And they that were sent, returning to the house, found the ¹ servant whole.

cp. 4 39.

cp. 4 50; 58; 9 7; 11 43.

cp. 1 38.

cp. 10 16; 11 52. *cp.* 12 36: *also* 1 12; 11 52.

50 Jesus saith unto him, Go thy way; thy son liveth. The man believed the word that Jesus spake unto him, and he went his way.

51 And as he was now going down, his ³ servants met him, saying, that his son lived.

52 So he inquired of them the hour when he began to amend. They said therefore unto him, Yesterday at the seventh hour the fever left him. **53** So the father knew that *it was* at that hour in which Jesus said unto him, Thy son liveth: and himself believed, and his whole house.

---

¹ Or, *boy*　　　　² Gr. *sufficient.*
³ Gr. *with a word.*
⁴ Some ancient authorities insert *set*: as in Luke 7 8.
⁵ Gr. *bondservant.*
⁶ Many ancient authorities read *With no man in Israel have I found so great faith.*
⁷ Gr. *recline.*

¹ Gr. *bondservant.*
² Or, *precious to him.* Or, *honourable with him.*
³ Gr. *sufficient.*
⁴ Gr. *say with a word.*
⁵ Or, *boy*　　　⁶ Gr. *recline.*

¹ Or, *king's officer*　　² Or, *Lord*
³ Gr. *bondservants.*

§ 54. The Healing of Peter's Wife's Mother

Matt. 8 14-15	Mark 1 29-31	Luke 4 38-39	
14 And when Jesus was come into Peter's house,	29 And straightway, [1] when they were come out of the synagogue, they came into the house of Simon and Andrew, with James and John [*cp.* 5 37; 9 2; 13 3; 14 33].	38 And he rose up from the synagogue, and entered into the house of Simon.	
cp. 17 1; 26 37.		*cp.* 8 51; 9 28.	
he saw his wife's mother lying sick of a fever.	30 Now Simon's wife's mother lay sick of a fever; and straightway they tell him of her: 31 and he came and took her by the hand [*cp.* 5 41; 9 27; 1 41; 5 23; 6 2, 5; 7 33; 8 22, 23, 25; 10 13, 16: *also* 3 10; 5 27; 6 56], and raised her up;	And Simon's wife's mother was holden with a great fever; and they besought him for her. 39 And he	
15 And he touched her hand [*cp.* 9 25; 8 3; 9 18, 29; 14 31; 17 7; 19 13, 15; 20 34: *also* 9 20; 14 36],		*cp.* 8 54; 4 40; 5 13; 7 14; 13 13; 14 4; 18 15; 22 51: *also* 6 19; 7 39; 8 44.	*cp.* 9 6: *also* 20 17.
		stood over her, and rebuked [*cp.* 4 35, 41; 8 24; 9 42: *also* 5 13, 24; 6 10; 7 7, 14; 8 29, 32, 48, 54; 13 12; 17 14; 18 42] the fever;	*cp.* 4 50; 5 8; 9 7; 11 43.
cp. 8 26; 17 18: *also* 8 3, 8, 13, 16, 32; 9 6, 22, 29; 12 13; 15 28; 17 7.	*cp.* 1 25; 3 12; 4 39; 9 25; *also* 1 41; 2 11; 3 5; 5 8, 13, 34, 41; 7 29, 34; 10 52.	and it left her: and immediately she rose up and ministered unto them.	*cp.* 4 52.
and the fever left her; and she arose, and ministered unto him.	and the fever left her, and she ministered unto them.		

§ 55. Healings in the Evening

Matt. 8 16-17	Mark 1 32-34	Luke 4 40-41	
16 And when even was come, they brought unto him many [1] possessed with devils:	32 And at even, when the sun did set, they brought unto him all that were sick, and them that were [1] possessed with devils. 33 And all the city was gathered together at the door.	40 And when the sun was setting, all they that had any sick with divers diseases brought them unto him;	
cp. 9 18; 19 13, 15: 8 3, 15; 9 25, 29; 14 31; 17 7; 20 34: *also* 9 20; 14 36.	*cp.* 5 23; 6 5; 8 25; 10 16: 1 31, 41; 5 41; 6 2; 7 33; 9 27; 8 22, 23; 10 13: *also* 3 10; 5 27; 6 56.	and he laid his hands [*cp.* 13 13: 5 13; 7 14; 8 54; 14 4; 18 15; 22 51: *also* 6 19; 7 39; 8 44] on every one of them,	*cp.* 9 6: *also* 20 17.
and he cast out the spirits with a word [*cp.* 8 8: *also* 8 3, 13, 32; 9 6, 22, 29; 12 13; 15 28; 17 7, 18], and healed all [*cp.* 12 15] that were sick: *cp.* 4 24.	*cp.* 1 25, 41; 2 11; 3 5; 5 8, 13, 34, 41; 7 29, 34; 9 25; 10 52. 34 And he healed many that were sick with divers diseases, and cast out many [2] devils; 3 10 for he had healed many; insomuch that as many as had [3] plagues [4] pressed upon him that they might touch him.	[*cp.* 7 7: *also* 4 35, 39; 5 13, 24; 6 10; 7 14; 8 29, 32, 48, 54; 9 42; 13 12; 17 14; 18 42] and healed them. *cp.* 6 19.	*cp.* 4 50; 5 8; 9 7; 11 43.
	11 And the unclean spirits, whensoever they beheld him, fell down before him, and cried, saying, Thou art the Son of God [*cp.* 1 1; 5 7; 15 39: *also* 1 11; 9 7]. 12 And he charged them much [*cp.* 1 25; 4 39; 9 25] that they should not make him known.	41 And [1] devils also came out from many, crying out, and saying, Thou art the Son of God [*cp.* 1 35; 4 3, 9; 8 28; 22 70: *also* 3 22; 9 35]. And rebuking them [*cp.* 4 35, 39; 8 24; 9 42],	
cp. 4 3, 6; 8 29; 14 33; 16 16; 26 63; 27 40, 43, 54: *also* 3 17; 17 5. *cp.* 8 26; 17 18.			*cp.* 1 34; *etc.*

cp. 8 4; 9 30; 12 16: *also* 16 20; 17 9.
cp. 8 29.

17 that it might be fulfilled which was spoken [2] by Isaiah the prophet, saying, Himself took our infirmities, and bare our diseases.

[1] Or, *demoniacs*   [2] Or, *through*

---

1 34 and he suffered not the [2] devils to speak [cp. 1 25; 3 12; 1 44; 5 43; 7 36; 8 26: *also* 8 30; 9 9], because they knew [cp. 1 24; 3 11; 5 7] him.[5]

[1] Or, *demoniacs*   [2] Gr. *demons.*
[3] Gr. *scourges.*   [4] Gr. *fell.*
[5] Many ancient authorities add *to be Christ.* See Luke 4 41.

---

he suffered them not to speak [cp. 4 35; 5 14; 8 56: *also* 9 21, 36], because they knew [cp. 4 34; 8 28] that he was the Christ.

[1] Gr. *demons.*

Matt. 8 17=Is. 53 4.

§ 56. Would-be Disciples

[*Cp.* Matt. 10 37: Luke 14 26]

Matt. 8 18-22

18 Now when Jesus saw great multitudes about him [cp. 3 7; 5 1; 9 36], he gave commandment to depart unto the other side [cp. 14 22]. **19** And there came [1] a scribe, and said unto him, [2] Master, I will follow thee whithersoever thou goest. **20** And Jesus saith unto him, The foxes have holes, and the birds of the heaven *have* [3] nests; but the Son of man hath not where to lay his head. **21** And another of the disciples
verse 22
said unto him, Lord, suffer me first to go and bury my father. **22** But Jesus saith unto him, Follow me [cp. 4 19; 9 9; 16 24; 19 21]; and leave the dead to bury their own dead.

[1] Gr. *one scribe.*   [2] Or, *Teacher*
[3] Gr. *lodging-places.*

verse 19

cp. 4 35; 6 45.

see below.

cp. 1 17; 2 14; 8 34; 10 21.

Luke 9 57-62

cp. 8 22.   57 And as they went in the way, a certain man said unto him, I will follow thee whithersoever thou goest. **58** And Jesus said unto him, The foxes have holes, and the birds of the heaven *have* [1] nests; but the Son of man hath not where to lay his head. **59** And he said unto another, Follow me [cp. 5 27; 9 23; 18 22]. But he said, Lord, suffer me first to go and bury my father. **60** But he said unto him,
verse 59
Leave the dead to bury their own dead; but go thou and publish abroad the kingdom of God. **61** And another also said, I will follow thee [cp. *verse* 57], Lord; but first suffer me [cp. *verse* 59] to bid farewell [cp. 14 33] to them that are at my house. **62** But Jesus said unto him, No man, having put his hand to the plough, and looking back, is fit for the kingdom of God.

[1] Gr. *lodging-places.*

cp. 6 5.

see below.

cp. 1 43; 12 26; 21 19, 22.

§ 57. The Stilling of a Storm

Matt. 8 23-27

23 And when he was entered into a boat, his disciples followed him.

cp. 8 18; 14 22.

24 And behold, there arose a great tempest in the sea [cp. 4 18; 8 32; *etc.*],

Mark 4 35-41

35 And on that day, when even was come, he saith unto them, Let us go over unto the other side [cp. 6 45]. **36** And leaving the multitude, they take him with them, even as he was, in the boat. And other boats were with him. **37** And there ariseth a great storm of wind,
cp. 1 16; 2 13; *etc.*
and the waves beat into the

Luke 8 22-25

22 Now it came to pass on one of those days, that he entered into a boat, himself and his disciples; and he said unto them, Let us go over unto the other side of the lake: and they launched forth.

23 But as they sailed he fell asleep: and there came down a storm of wind on the lake [cp. 5 1, 2; 8 33];

cp. 6 1, 16; *etc.*

insomuch that the boat was covered with the waves: but he

was

asleep. **25** And they came to him, and awoke him, saying, Save [*cp.* 14 30], Lord [*cp.* 17 4, 15; 20 30, 33: *and* 7 21; 8 2, 6, 8, 21; *etc.*];
    cp. 8 19; 12 38; 19 16; 22 16, 24, 36.

we perish.
26 And he saith unto them, Why are ye fearful, O ye of little faith [*cp.* 6 30; 14 31; 16 8: *also* 17 20]? Then he arose, and rebuked [*cp.* 17 18] the winds and the sea;

and there was a great calm.

cp. 17 20; 21 21.
27 And [*cp.* 9 8; 17 6; 27 54; 28 4, 8]

the men marvelled [*cp.* 9 33; 12 23; 15 31; 21 20; 27 14: *also* 7 28; 13 54; 19 25; 22 22, 33],
    saying,
What manner of man is this [*cp.* 21 10], that   even the winds and the sea obey him?

---

boat, insomuch that the boat was now filling.

38 And he himself was in the stern, asleep on the cushion: and they   awake him, and say unto him,
    cp. 7 28.

¹ Master [*cp.* 9 17, 38; 10 17, 20, 35; 12 14, 19, 32; 13 1],

    carest thou not that we perish?
39 And he awoke,

    and rebuked [*cp.* 1 25; 3 12; 9 25] the wind, and said unto the sea, Peace, be still [*cp.* 1 25]. And the wind ceased, and there was a great calm.
40 And he said unto them, Why are ye fearful? have ye not yet faith [*cp.* 11 22 16 14]?   **41** And they feared exceedingly [*cp.* 5 15, 33; 9 6, 32; 10 32; 16 8],
    [*cp.* 2 12; 5 20, 42; 6 51; 7 37; 10 32; 15 5; 16 5, 8: *also* 1 22, 27; 6 2; 10 24, 26; 11 18; 12 17] and said one to another, Who then   is this [*cp.* 1 27; 2 7], that   even the wind and the sea obey him [*cp.* 1 27]?

¹ Or, *Teacher*

---

    and they were filling *with water*, and were in jeopardy.

24 And they came to him, and awoke him, saying,
    [*cp.* 18 41: *and* 5 8, 12; 6 46; 7 6; *etc.*]
    [*cp.* 7 40; 9 38; 10 25; 11 45; 12 13; 18 18; 19 39; 20 21, 28, 39; 21 7] Master, master [*cp.* 9 33, 49: *and* 5 5; 8 45; 17 13],   we perish.
And he awoke,

    cp. 12 28.

    and rebuked [*cp.* 4 35, 39, 41; 9 42] the wind and the raging of the water: [*cp.* 4 35] and they   ceased, and there was a   calm.
25 And·he said unto them, Where is your faith [*cp.* 17 5, 6; 22 32; 24 25, 38]? And being afraid [*cp.* 1 12, 65; 2 9; 5 26; 7 16; 8 35, 37, 47; 9 34, 45; 24 5, 37] they marvelled [*cp.* 5 9, 26; 8 56; 9 43; 11 14; 24 12, 41: *also* 2 47, 48; 4 22, 32, 36; 20 26],
    saying one to another, Who then   is this [*cp.* 4 36; 5 21; 7 49; 9 9], that he commandeth even the winds and the water, and they obey him [*cp.* 4 36]?

---

cp. 4 11, 15, 19, 49; 5 7; *etc.*
cp. 1 38; 20 16.

cp. 3 12; 6 64; 14 10; 20 27.

cp. 7 15, 21, 46.

cp. 5 12: *also* 12 34.

---

§ 58. **The Gadarene Swine**

Matt. 8 28-34	Mark 5 1-20	Luke 8 26-39

28 And when he was come to the other side   into the country of the Gadarenes,

there met him two [*cp.* 9 27; 20 30] ¹ possessed with devils, coming forth out of the tombs,

exceeding fierce, so that no man could pass by that way.

---

1 And   they came to the other side of the sea, into the country of the Gerasenes.

2 And when he was come out of the boat, straightway there met him

    out of the tombs a man with an unclean spirit,

3 who had his dwelling in the tombs: and no man could any more bind him, no, not with a chain; **4** because that he had been often bound with fetters and chains, and the chains had been rent asunder by him, and the fetters broken in pieces: and no man had strength to tame him. **5** And always,

---

26 And   they arrived at

the country of the ¹ Gerasenes, which is over against Galilee. **27** And when he was come forth upon the land, there met him a certain man

    out of the city,   who had ² devils; and for a long time he had worn no clothes, and abode not in *any* house, but in the tombs.

verse 29

cp. 2 11 ; 8 2 ; 9 18 ; 14 33 ;
15 25 ; 17 14 ; 20 20 ; 28 9,
17.   **29** And behold,
they cried out,

saying,
What have we to do with thee,
[cp. 4 3, 6 ; 14 33 ; 16 16 ;
26 63 ; 27 40, 43, 54] of

God ?
cp. 26 63.
art thou come hither to
torment us before
the time ?

30 Now there
was afar off from them
a
herd of many swine feeding.
31 And the
[2] devils besought him, saying,
If thou cast us out, send us
away into the herd of swine.

32 And he said unto them,
Go. And they
came out,
and went into the swine :
and behold, the whole
herd rushed down the steep
into the sea [cp. 4 18 ;
8 24 ; etc.],
and
perished in the waters. **33** And
they that fed them

fled, and went away into
the city, and told everything,
and
what was befallen to them
that were [1] possessed with
devils. **34** And behold, all the
city came out to

meet Jesus :
and when they saw him,

night and day, in the tombs
and in the mountains, he was
crying out, and cutting himself with stones. **6** And when
he saw Jesus from afar, he ran
and worshipped him [cp. 1
40 ; 3 11 ; 5 22, 33 ; 7 25 ;
10 17] ; **7** and
crying out

with a
loud voice [cp. 1 26], he saith,
What have I to do with thee
[cp. 1 24], Jesus, thou Son
[cp. 1 1 ; 3 11 ; 15 39]
of
the Most High
God [cp. similarly
1 24 ; 3 11]? I adjure thee
cp. 1 24.
by God, torment me not.
8 For he said unto him,
Come forth [cp. 1 25 ; 9 25],
thou unclean spirit,
out of the man.

verses 4 *and* 5

9 And he   asked him,
What is thy name ? And he
saith unto him, My name is
Legion ; for we are many.

10 And he besought him
much that he would not
send them away out of
the country. **11** Now there
was   there
on the mountain side a
great herd of swine feeding.
12 And they
besought him, saying,
Send us
into the   swine,
that we may enter into
them. **13** And he gave them
leave. And the unclean spirits
came out,
and entered into the swine :
and   the
herd rushed down the steep
into the sea [cp. 1 16 ; 2 13 ;
etc.], *in number* about two
thousand ; and they were
choked in the sea. **14** And
they that fed them

fled,
and told it in the
city, and in the country.

verse 16
And
they came   to see what it
was that had come to pass.
15 And they come to Jesus,
and   behold [1] him

28 And when he
saw Jesus, he cried out,
and fell down [cp. 5 8,
12 ; 8 41, 47 ; 17 16 ; 24
52] before him, and with a
loud voice [cp. 4 33] said,
What have I to do with thee
[cp. 4 34], Jesus, thou Son
[cp. 1 35 ; 4 3, 9, 41 ; 22 70]
of
the Most High [cp. 1 32, 35,
76 ; 6 35] God [cp. similarly
4 34, 41]? I beseech thee,
cp. 4 34.
torment me not.
29 For he
cp. 4 35.
commanded the unclean spirit
to come out from the man.
For [3] oftentimes it had seized
him : and he was kept under
guard, and bound with chains
and fetters ; and breaking the
bands asunder, he was driven
of the [4] devil into the deserts.
30 And Jesus asked him,
What is thy name ? And he
said,
Legion ; for   many
[2] devils were entered into him.
31 And they intreated him
that he would not
command them to depart into
the abyss. **32** Now there
was   there
a
herd of many swine feeding
on the mountain : and they
intreated him

that he would give
them leave to enter into
them. And he gave them
leave. **33** And the [2] devils
came out from the man,
and entered into the swine :
and   the
herd rushed down the steep
into the lake [cp. 5 1, 2 ; 8
22, 23],
and   were
choked.   **34** And
when they that fed them saw
what had come to pass,
they fled,
and told it in the
city and in the country.

35 And
they went out to see what
had come to pass ;
and they came to Jesus,
and   found the

cp. 9 38 ; 11
32 ; 18 6.

cp. 1 34 ; etc.

cp. 6 1, 16 ;
etc.

	that was possessed with devils sitting, clothed and in his right mind,	man, from whom the 2 devils were gone out, sitting, clothed and in his right mind, at the feet of Jesus [*cp.* 7 38 ; 10 39]:

cp. 9 8; 17 6; 27 54; 28 4, 8.

verse 33

they

besought *him* that he would depart from their borders.

even him that had the legion : and they were afraid [*cp.* 4 41 ; 5 33 ; 9 6, 32 ; 10 32 ; 16 8].   **16** And they that saw it declared unto them how it befell 1 him that was possessed with devils,   and concerning the swine.   **17** And they

                 began to beseech him   to depart from their borders.

    18 And as he was entering into the boat,   he that had been possessed with 2 devils   besought him that he might be with him. **19** And he suffered him not, but saith unto him, Go to thy house unto thy friends, and tell them how great things the Lord hath done for thee, and *how* he had mercy on thee. **20** And he went his way, and began to publish in Decapolis [*cp.* 7 31] how great things Jesus had done for him : and all men did marvel [*cp.* 2 12 ; 5 42 ; 6 51 ; 7 37 ; 10 32 ; 15 5 ; 16 5, 8 : *also* 1 22, 27 ; 6 2 ; 10 24, 26 ; 11 18 ; 12 17].

    afraid [*cp.* 1 12, 65 ; 2 9 ; 5 26 ; 7 16 ; 8 25, 37, 47 ; 9 34, 45 ; 24 5, 37]. **36** And they that saw it told them how   he that was possessed with 2 devils was 5 made whole.

    37 And all the people of the country of the Gerasenes round about asked him   to depart from them ;   for they were holden with great fear [*cp. verse* 35 *above*] : and he   entered into a boat, and returned. **38** But the man from whom the 2 devils were gone out prayed him that he might be with him : but he sent him away,   saying,   **39** Return to thy house, and declare   how great things   God hath done for thee.

       And he went his way, publishing throughout the whole city how great things Jesus had done for him.

cp. 4 25.

cp. 8 27 ; 9 33 ; 12 23 ; 15 31 ; 21 20 ; 27 14 : *also* 7 28 ; 13 54 ; 19 25 ; 22 22, 33.

cp. 5 9, 26 ; 8 25, 56 ; 9 43 ; 11 14 ; 24 12, 41 : *also* 2 47, 48 ; 4 22, 32, 36 ; 20 26.

cp. 7 15, 21, 46.

1 Or, *demoniacs*   2 Gr. *demons.*

1 Or, *the demoniac*   2 Gr. *demons.*

1 Many ancient authorities read *Gergesenes*; others, *Gadarenes*: and so in ver. 37.
2 Gr. *demons.*   3 Or, *of a long time*
4 Gr. *demon.*   5 Or, *saved*

---

§ 59. The Healing of a Paralytic

Matt. 9 1-8	**Mark 2** 1-12	**Luke 5** 17-26	
1 And he entered into a boat, and crossed over, and came into his own city [*cp.* 4 13 : *also* 13 54].	**1** And when he entered again into Capernaum after some days, it was noised that he was 1 in the house. **2** And many were gathered together, so that there was no longer room *for them*, no, not even about the door : and he spake the word [*cp.* 4 33 : *also* 4 14 *ff.* ; 16 20] unto them.	**17** And it came to pass on one of those days,	
cp. 13 19 *ff.*		that he was teaching ; *cp.* 1 2 ; 8 12 *ff.* : *also* 4 32 : *and* 5 1 ; 8 11, 21 ; 11 28. and there were Pharisees and doctors of the law sitting by, which were come out of every village of Galilee and Judæa and Jerusalem : and the power [*cp.* 4 14, 36 ; 6 19 ; 8 46 : *also* 1 17, 35 ; 9 1 ; 24 49] of the Lord was with him 1 to heal. **18** And behold,	*cp.* 4 41 ; 5 24, 38 ; *etc.*
cp. 15 1.	*verse* 6		*cp.* 1 19.
	cp. 3 22 ; 7 1. *cp.* 5 30.		
2 And behold,	**3** And		

they brought to him a man sick of the palsy, lying on a bed: and Jesus seeing their faith said unto the sick of the palsy, [1] Son, be of good cheer [*cp.* 9 22; 14 27]; thy sins are forgiven. **3** And behold, certain of the scribes said within themselves, *cp.* 8 27; 21 10. This man blasphemeth [*cp.* 26 65]. **4** And Jesus [2] knowing their thoughts [*cp.* 12 25; 16 8] said, Wherefore think ye evil in your hearts? **5** For whether is easier, to say, Thy sins are forgiven; or to say, Arise, and walk? **6** But that ye may know that the Son of man hath [3] power [*cp.* 7 29; 21 23 *ff.*; 28 18] on earth to forgive sins (then saith he to the sick of the palsy), Arise, and take up thy bed, and go unto thy house. **7** And he arose, and departed to his house.

cp. Matt. 16 7-8; Mark 8 16-17.

8 But when the multitudes saw it, they were afraid [*cp.* 17 6; 27 54; 28 4, 8], *cp.* 8 27; 9 33; 12 23; 15 31; 21 20; 27 14: *also* 7 28; 13 54; 19 25; 22 22, 33. and glorified God [*cp.* 5 16; 15 31], which had given such [3] power unto men [*cp.* 11 27; 28 18: *also verse* 6 *above*]. *see above.*

they come, bringing unto him a man sick of the palsy, borne of four. **4** And when they could not [2] come nigh unto him for the crowd [*cp.* 3 9], they uncovered the roof where he was: and when they had broken it up, they let down the bed whereon the sick of the palsy lay. **5** And Jesus seeing their faith saith unto the sick of the palsy, [3] Son, *cp.* 6 50; 10 49. thy sins are forgiven. **6** But there were certain of the scribes sitting there, and reasoning in their hearts, *cp.* 4 41: *also* 1 27. **7** Why doth this man thus speak? he blasphemeth [*cp.* 14 64]: who can forgive sins but one, *even* God? **8** And straightway Jesus, perceiving in his spirit that they so reasoned within themselves [*cp.* 8 17], saith unto them, Why reason ye these things in your hearts? **9** Whether is easier, to say to the sick of the palsy, Thy sins are forgiven; or to say, Arise, and take up thy bed, and walk? **10** But that ye may know that the Son of man hath [4] power [*cp.* 1 22, 27; 11 28 *ff.*] on earth to forgive sins (he saith to the sick of the palsy), **11** I say unto thee, Arise [*cp.* 3 3; 5 41; 10 49], take up thy bed, and go unto thy house. **12** And he arose, and straightway took up the bed, and went forth, before them all; *cp.* 4 41; 5 15, 33; 9 6, 32; 10 32; 16 8. insomuch that they were all amazed [*cp.* 5 20, 42; 6 51; 7 37; 10 32; 15 5; 16 5, 8: *also* 1 22, 27; 6 2; 10 24, 26; 11 18; 12 17], and glorified God,

men bring on a bed a man that was palsied: and they sought to bring him in, and to lay him before him. **19** And not finding by what *way* they might bring him in because of the multitude [*cp.* 8 19; 19 3], they went up to the housetop, and let him down through the tiles with his couch into the midst before Jesus. **20** And seeing their faith, he said, Man, thy sins are forgiven thee [*cp.* 7 48]. **21** And the scribes and the Pharisees [*cp. verse* 17] began to reason, saying, Who is this [*cp.* 7 49; 8 25; 9 9: *also* 4 36] that speaketh blasphemies? Who can forgive sins, but God alone? **22** But Jesus perceiving their reasonings [*cp.* 6 8; 9 47; 11 17], answered and said unto them, [2] What reason ye in your hearts? **23** Whether is easier, to say, Thy sins are forgiven thee; or to say, Arise and walk? **24** But that ye may know that the Son of man hath [3] power [*cp.* 4 32, 36; 20 2 *ff.*] on earth to forgive sins (he said unto him that was palsied), I say unto thee, Arise [*cp.* 6 8; 7 14; 8 54], and take up thy couch, and go unto thy house. **25** And immediately he rose up before them, and took up that whereon he lay, and departed to his house, glorifying God [*cp. verse* 26]. *see below.* **26** And amazement took hold on all [*cp.* 5 9; 8 25, 56; 9 43; 11 14; 24 12, 41: *also* 2 47, 48; 4 22, 32, 36; 20 26], and they glorified God [*cp.* 2 20; 7 16; 13 13; 17 15, 18; 18 43; 23 47]; *cp.* 10 22. and they were filled with fear [*cp.* 1 12, 65; 2 9; 7 16; 8 25, 35, 37,

cp. 16 33.

cp. 5 12: *also* 12 34.

cp. 10 33, 36.

cp. 1 48; 2 24, 25; 4 19, 29; 5 6, 42; 6 61; 11 14; 13 18; 16 19, 30; 18 4; 21 17. *cp.* 5 8.

cp. 5 27; 17 2.

John 5 8 Jesus saith unto him, Arise, take up thy bed, and walk [*cp.* Matt. 9 5; Mark 2 9; Luke 5 23]. 9 And straightway the man was made whole, and took up his bed and walked.

cp. 7 15, 21, 46.

cp. 9 24.

cp. 3 35; 5 27; 13 3; 17 2.

| | saying, | 47; 9 34, 45; 24 5, 37], saying, |
| | We never saw it on this fashion. | We have seen strange things to-day. |

¹ Gr. *Child.*
² Many ancient authorities read *seeing.*
³ Or, *authority*

¹ Or, *at home*
² Many ancient authorities read *bring him unto him.*
³ Gr. *Child.*   ⁴ Or, *authority*

¹ Gr. *that he should heal.* Many ancient authorities read *that he should heal them.*   ² Or, *Why*
³ Or, *authority*

§ 60. The Call of Levi (Matthew)

Matt. 9 9-13	**Mark 2** 13-17	**Luke 5** 27-32	
	13 And he went forth again by the sea side [*cp.* 1 16]; and all the multitude resorted unto him, and he taught them. **14** And as he passed by,	**27** And after these things he went forth,	
9 And as Jesus passed by from thence [*cp.* 9 27], he saw a man, called Matthew [*cp.* 10 3: Mark 3 18: Luke 6 15], sitting at the place of toll: and he saith unto him, Follow me [*cp.* 4 19; 8 22; 16 24; 19 21]. And he [*cp.* 19 27] arose, and followed him [*cp.* 4 20, 22; 19 27]. **10** And it came to pass, as he ¹ sat at meat in the house, behold, many publicans and sinners came and sat down with Jesus and his disciples.	he saw [*cp.* 1 16] Levi the *son* of Alphæus sitting at the place of toll, and he saith unto him, Follow me [*cp.* 1 17; 8 34; 10 21]. And he [*cp.* 10 28] arose and followed him [*cp.* 1 18, 20; 10 28]. **15** And it came to pass, that he was sitting at meat in his house, and many ¹ publicans and sinners sat down with Jesus and his disciples: for there were many, and they followed him. **16** And the scribes ² of	and beheld a publican, named Levi, sitting at the place of toll, and said unto him, Follow me [*cp.* 9 23, 59; 18 22]. **28** And he forsook all [*cp.* 5 11; 14 33], and rose up and followed him [*cp.* 5 11; 18 28]. **29** And Levi made him a great feast in his house: and there was a great multitude of publicans and of others that were sitting at meat with them.	*cp.* 1 43; 12 26; 21 19, 22.
11 And when the Pharisees saw it, they said unto his disciples, Why eateth your ² Master with the publicans and sinners [*cp.* 11 19]? **12** But when he heard it, he said, They that are ³ whole have no need of a physician, but they that are sick. **13** But go ye and learn what *this* meaneth, I desire mercy, and not sacrifice [*cp.* 12 7: *also* 23 23]: for I came not to call the righteous, but sinners [*cp.* 21 31].	the Pharisees, when they saw that he was eating with the sinners and publicans, said unto his disciples, ³ He eateth ⁴ and drinketh with publicans and sinners. **17** And when Jesus heard it, he saith unto them, They that are ⁵ whole have no need of a physician, but they that are sick: *cp.* 12 33. I came not to call the righteous, but sinners.	**30** And ¹ the Pharisees and their scribes murmured against his disciples, saying, Why do ye eat and drink with the publicans and sinners [*cp.* 7 34, 39; 15 2; 19 7]? **31** And Jesus answering said unto them, They that are whole have no need of a physician; but they that are sick. **32** I am not come to call the righteous but sinners [*cp.* 19 10: *also* 7 29-30, 47; 18 14] to repentance [*cp.* 15 7, 10].	

§ 61. A Question about Fasting

[*Cp.* Matt. 12 1-8; 15 1-20: Mark 2 23-28; 7 1-23: Luke 6 1-5; 11 37-41]

Matt. 9 14-17	**Mark 2** 18-22	**Luke 5** 33-39	
14 Then come to him the disciples of John [*cp.* 11 2; 14 12], saying, Why do we and the Pharisees fast [1] oft,	**18** And John's disciples and the Pharisees were fasting: and they come and say unto him, Why do John's disciples [*cp.* 6 29] and the disciples of the Pharisees fast,	**33** And they said unto him, The disciples of John [*cp.* 7 18, 19; 11 1] fast often, and make supplications [*cp.* 2 37: *also* 11 1]; likewise also the *disciples* of the Pharisees; but thine eat and drink [*cp.* 6 2].	*cp.* 1 35, 37; 3 25; 4 1.
but thy disciples fast not [*cp.* 12 2; 15 2]? **15** And Jesus said unto them, Can the sons of the bride-chamber mourn, as long as the bridegroom is with them?	but thy disciples fast not [*cp.* 2 24; 7 5]? **19** And Jesus said unto them, Can the sons of the bride-chamber fast, while the bridegroom is with them? as long as they have the bridegroom with them, they cannot fast. **20** But the days will come,	**34** And Jesus said unto them, Can ye make the sons of the bride-chamber fast, while the bridegroom is with them?	*cp.* 3 29.
but the days will come,		**35** But the days will come [*cp.* 17 22; 21 6: *also* 19 43; 23 29]; and	
when the bridegroom shall be taken away from them, and then will they fast. **16** And	when the bridegroom shall be taken away from them, and then will they fast in that day.	when the bridegroom shall be taken away from them, then will they fast in those days. **36** And he spake also a parable unto them; No man rendeth a piece from a new garment and putteth it	*cp.* 16 19, 20.
no man	**21** No man		
putteth a piece of undressed cloth upon an old garment; for that which should fill it up taketh from the garment,	seweth a piece of undressed cloth on an old garment: else that which should fill it up taketh from it, the new from the old, and a worse rent is made.	upon an old garment; else he will rend the new, and also the piece from the new will not agree with the old.	
and a worse rent is made. **17** Neither do *men* put new wine into old [2] wine-skins: else the skins burst, and the wine is spilled, and the skins perish: but they put new wine into fresh wine-skins, and both are preserved.	**22** And no man putteth new wine into old [1] wine-skins: else the wine will burst the skins, and the wine perisheth, and the skins: but *they put* new wine into fresh wine-skins.	**37** And no man putteth new wine into old [1] wine-skins; else the new wine will burst the skins, and itself will be spilled, and the skins will perish. **38** But new wine must be put into fresh wine-skins.	
		39 And no man having drunk old *wine* desireth new: for he saith, The old is [2] good.	*cp.* 2 10.

---

[1] Some ancient authorities omit *oft*.
[2] That is, *skins used as bottles*.

[1] That is, *skins used as bottles*.

[1] That is, *skins used as bottles*.
[2] Many ancient authorities read *better*.

§ 62. A Ruler's Daughter and a Woman with an Issue of Blood

[*Cp.* Luke 7 11-17 ; John 11 1-46]

Matt. 9 18-26	Mark 5 21-43	Luke 8 40-56	
18 While he spake these things unto them,	**21** And when Jesus had crossed over again in the boat unto the other side, a great multitude was gathered unto him : and he was by the sea [*cp.* 3 7 ; 4 1].	**40** And as Jesus returned, the multitude welcomed him ;	
cp. 13 1.		[*cp.* 5 1] for they were all waiting for him. **41** And	
behold, there came [1] a	**22** And there cometh one of the	behold, there came a man	

Matthew

ruler,

and worshipped [cp. 2 11; 8 2; 14 33; 15 25; 20 20; 28 9, 17: *also* 17 14] him,

saying, My daughter is even now dead: but come and lay thy hand [cp. 19 13, 15: *also* 8 3, 15; 9 20, 25, 29; 14 31, 36; 17 7; 20 34] upon her, and she shall live. **19** And Jesus arose, and followed him, and *so did* his disciples.

20 And behold, a woman, who had an issue of blood twelve years,

came behind him, and touched [cp. 8 3, 15; 9 29; 14 36; 17 7; 20 34: *also* 9 18, 25; 14 31; 19 13, 15] the border [cp. 14 36] of his garment: **21** for she said within herself, If I do but touch his garment, I shall be [2] made whole.

cp. 9 22; 16 23.

cp. 9 8; 17 6; 27 54; 28 4, 8.

Mark

rulers of the synagogue, Jaïrus by name;

and seeing him, he falleth at his feet [cp. 3 11; 5 33; 7 25: *also* 1 40; 5 6; 10 17], **23** and beseecheth him much,

verse 42

saying, My little daughter is at the point of death: *I pray thee*, that thou come and lay thy hands [cp. 6 5; 8 25; 10 16: *also* 1 31, 41; 3 10; 5 27, 41; 6 2, 56; 7 33; 8 22, 23; 9 27; 10 13] on her, that she may be [1] made whole, and live. **24** And he went with him;

and a great multitude followed him, and they thronged him. **25** And a woman, which had an issue of blood twelve years, **26** and had suffered many things of many physicians, and had spent all that she had, and was nothing bettered, but rather grew worse, **27** having heard the things concerning Jesus, came in the crowd behind, and touched [cp. 1 41; 3 10; 6 56; 7 33; 8 22; 10 13: *also* 1 31; 5 23, 41; 6 2, 5; 8 23, 25; 9 27; 10 16] [cp. 6 56] his garment. **28** For she said, If I touch but his garments, I shall be [1] made whole. **29** And straightway the fountain of her blood was dried up; and she felt in her body that she was healed of her [1] plague. **30** And straightway Jesus, perceiving in himself that the power *proceeding* from him had gone forth, turned him about [cp. 8 33] in the crowd, and said, Who touched my garments? **31** And his disciples said unto him, Thou seest the multitude thronging thee, and sayest thou, Who touched me? **32** And he looked round about [cp. 3 5, 34; 9 8; 10 23; 11 11] to see her that had done this thing.

verse 30

33 But the woman fearing and trembling [cp. 4 41; 5 15; 9 6, 32; 10 32; 16 8], knowing what had been done to her, came and fell down [cp. *verse* 22 *above*] before him, and told him all the truth.

Luke

named Jaïrus, and he was a ruler of the synagogue [cp. 13 14]: and he fell down [cp. 5 8, 12; 8 28, 47; 17 16: *also* 24 52] at Jesus' feet, and besought him to come into his house; **42** for he had an only [cp. 7 12; 9 38] daughter, about twelve years of age, and she lay a dying [cp. 7 2].

cp. 4 40; 13 13: *also* 5 13; 6 19; 7 14, 39; 8 44, 54; 14 4; 18 15; 22 51.

But as he went the multitudes thronged him. **43** And a woman having an issue of blood twelve years [cp. 13 11], which [1] had spent all her living upon physicians, and could not be healed of any,

44 came behind him, and touched [cp. 5 13; 6 19; 7 14, 39; 18 15; 22 51: *also* 4 40; 8 54; 13 13; 14 4] the border of his garment:

and immediately the issue of her blood stanched.

45 And Jesus *verse* 46

cp. 7 9, 44; 9 55; 10 23; 14 25; 22 61; 23 28.

said, Who is it that touched me? And when all denied, Peter said, [1] and they that were with him, Master, the multitudes press thee and crush *thee*.

cp. 6 10.

46 But Jesus said, Some one did touch me: for I perceived that power [cp. 4 14, 36; 5 17; 6 19: *also* 1 17, 35; 9 1; 24 49] had gone forth from me. **47** And when the woman saw that she wa not hid, she came trembling [cp. 1 12, 65; 2 9; 5 26; 7 16; 8 25, 35, 37; 9 34, 45; 24 5, 37], and falling down [cp. *verse* 41 *above*] before him declared

(cross-references)

cp. 11 32; 18 6: *also* 9 38.

cp. 4 47.

cp. 9 6; 20 17.

cp. 20 17; 9 6.

cp. 1 38.

cp. 11 32; 18 6: *also* 9 38.

MATTHEW

22 But Jesus turning [cp. 16 23] and seeing her said, Daughter, be of good cheer [cp. 9 2; 14 27]; thy faith hath ³ made thee whole.

And the woman was ² made whole from that hour [cp. 8 13; 15 28; 17 18].

cp. 17 1; 26 37.

23 And when Jesus came into the ruler's house,

cp. 17 1; 26 37.

and saw the flute-players, and the crowd making a tumult, **24** he said, Give place:

for the damsel is not dead, but sleepeth. And they laughed him to scorn. **25** But when the crowd was put forth,

he entered in, and took her by the hand [cp. 8 15; 8 3; 9 18, 29; 14 31; 17 7; 19 13, 15; 20 34: also 9 20; 14 36];

cp. 9 6.

and the damsel arose.

cp. 8 27; 9 33; 12 23; 15 31; 21 20; 27 14: also 7 28; 13 54; 19 25; 22 22, 33.

MARK

34 And he [cp. 5 30; 8 33] said unto her, Daughter, [cp. 6 50; 10 49] thy faith hath ³ made thee whole [cp. 10 52]; go in peace, and be whole of thy ² plague.

35 While he yet spake, they come from the ruler of the synagogue's *house*, saying, Thy daughter is dead: why troublest thou the ⁴ Master any further? **36** But Jesus, ⁵ not heeding the word spoken, saith unto the ruler of the synagogue, Fear not, only believe.

37 And he suffered no man to follow with him, save Peter, and James, and John the brother of James [cp. 1 29; 9 2; 13 3; 14 33]. **38** And they come to the house of the ruler of the synagogue;

verse 37

verse 40

and he beholdeth a tumult, and *many* weeping and wailing greatly. **39** And when he was entered in, he saith unto them, Why make ye a tumult, and weep? the child is not dead, but sleepeth. **40** And they laughed him to scorn.

But he, having put them all forth, taketh the father of the child and her mother and them that were with him, and goeth in where the child was. **41** And taking the child by the hand [cp. 1 31; 9 27; 1 41; 5 23; 6 2, 5; 7 33; 8 22, 23, 25; 10 13, 16: also 3 10; 5 27; 6 56], he saith unto her, Talitha cumi; which is, being interpreted, Damsel, I say unto thee, Arise [cp. 2 11; 3 3; 10 49]. **42** And straightway the damsel rose up, and walked; for she was twelve years old.

verse 43

And they were amazed straightway with a great amazement [cp. 2 12; 5 20; 6 51; 7 37; 10 32; 15 5; 16 5, 8: also 1 22, 27; 6 2; 10 24, 26; 11 18; 12 17]. **43** And he charged them

LUKE

in the presence of all the people for what cause she touched him, and how she was healed immediately. **48** And he [cp. 7 9, 44; 9 55; 10 23; 14 25; 22 61; 23 28] said unto her, Daughter, thy faith hath ³ made thee whole [cp. 7 50; 17 19; 18 42]; go in peace [cp. 7 50].

49 While he yet spake, there cometh one from the ruler of the synagogue's *house*, saying, Thy daughter is dead; trouble [cp. 7 6] not the ⁴ Master. **50** But Jesus hearing it, answered him, Fear not: only believe, and she shall be ⁵ made whole.

verse 51

51 And when he came to the house, he suffered not any man to enter in with him, save Peter, and John, and James [cp. 9 28], and the father of the maiden and her mother. **52** And all were weeping, and bewailing her: but he said, Weep not [cp. 7 13; 23 28]; for she is not dead, but sleepeth. **53** And they laughed him to scorn, knowing that she was dead. **54** But he,

verse 51

taking her by the hand [cp. 4 40; 5 13; 7 14; 13 13; 14 4; 18 15; 22 51: also 6 19; 7 39; 8 44], called, saying, Maiden, arise [cp. 5 24; 6 8; 7 14]. **55** And her spirit returned, and she rose up immediately:

verse 42

and he commanded that *something* be given her to eat. **56** And her parents were amazed [cp. 5 9, 26; 8 25; 9 43; 11 14; 24 12, 41: also 2 47, 48; 4 22, 32, 36; 20 26]: but he charged them

Marginal references:

cp. 1 38.
cp. 16 33.
cp. 4 53.
cp. 20 13, 15.
cp. 11 11.
cp. 9 6: also 20 17.
cp. 5 8.
cp. 7 15, 21, 46.

cp. 8 4; 9 30; 12 16: *also* 16 20; 17 9.

much that no man should know this [*cp.* 1 44; 7 36; 8 26: *also* 1 25, 34; 3 12; 8 30; 9 9]: and he commanded that *something* should be given her to eat.

to tell no man what had been done [*cp.* 5 14: *also* 4 35, 41; 9 21, 36].

verse 55

26 And [4] the fame hereof went forth into all that land [*cp.* 4 24].

cp. 1 28.

cp. 4 14, 37; 5 15; 7 17.

[1] Gr. *one ruler.*   [2] Or, *saved*
[3] Or, *saved thee*   [4] Gr. *this fame.*

[1] Or, *saved*   [3] Gr. *scourge.*
[3] Or, *saved thee*   [4] Or, *Teacher*
[5] Or, *overhearing*

[1] Some ancient authorities omit *had spent all her living upon physicians, and.*
[2] Some ancient authorities omit *and they that were with him.*
[3] Or, *saved thee*   [4] Or, *Teacher*
[5] Or, *saved*

§ 63. **The Healing of Two Blind Men**

[*Cp.* Matt. 12 22; 15 30-31; 20 29-34; 21 14: Mark 8 22-26; 10 46-52: Luke 7 21; 18 35-43: John 9 1-7]

Matt. 9 27-31				
27 And as Jesus passed by from thence [*cp.* 9 9], two [*cp.* 8 28; 20 30] blind men followed him, crying out, and saying, Have mercy on us, thou son of David [*cp.* 15 22; 20 30, 31: *also* 17 15: *and* 1 1; 12 23; 21 9, 15]. **28** And when he was come into the house, the blind men came to him: and Jesus saith unto them, Believe ye that I am able [*cp.* 8 2] to do this? They say unto him, Yea, Lord. **29** Then touched [*cp.* 8 3, 15; 9 18, 25; 14 31; 17 7; 20 34: *also* 9 20; 14 36; 19 13, 15] he their eyes, saying, According to your faith be it done unto you [*cp.* 8 13; 15 28]. **30** And their eyes were opened. And Jesus [1] strictly charged them, saying, See that no man know it [*cp.* 8 4; 12 16: *also* 16 20; 17 9]. **31** But they went forth, and spread abroad his fame in all that land.	*cp.* 10 47, 48. *cp.* 1 40; 9 22, 23: *also* 6 5. *cp.* 1 41; *etc.* *cp.* 1 43. *cp.* 1 44; *etc.* *cp.* 1 45; 7 36.	*cp.* 18 38, 39: *also* 17 13: *and* 1 32. *cp.* 5 12. *cp.* 4 40; *etc.* *cp.* 5 14; *etc.* *cp.* 5 15.	*cp.* 9 6; 20 17.	

[1] Or, *sternly*

§ 64. **The Healing of a Dumb Demoniac**

[*Cp.* Matt. 15 29-31: Mark 7 31-37; 9 25]

Matt. 9 32-34	Matt. 12 22-24	Mark 3 22	Luke 11 14-15	
32 And as they went forth, behold, there was brought to him a dumb man possessed with a [1] devil. **33** And when the [1] devil was cast out, the dumb man spake: and the multitudes marvelled [*cp.* 8 27; 15 31; 21 20; 27 14: *also* 7 28; 13 54; 19 25; 22 22, 33], saying, It was never so seen in Israel. **34** But the Pharisees *cp.* 15 1.	**22** Then was brought unto him [1] one possessed with a devil, blind [*cp.* 9 27] and dumb: and he healed him, insomuch that the dumb man spake and saw. **23** And all the multitudes were amazed. and said, Is this the son of David [*cp.* 1 1; 9 27; 15 22; 20 30, 31; 21 9, 15]? **24** But when the Pharisees heard it, they	 *cp.* 2 12; 5 20, 42; 6 51; 7 37; 10 32; 15 5; 16 5, 8: *also* 1 22, 27; 6 2; 10 24, 26; 11 18; 12 17. *cp.* 10 47, 48. **22** And the scribes which came down from Jerusalem [*cp.* 7 1]	**14** And he was casting out a [1] devil *which was* dumb. And it came to pass, when the [1] devil was gone out, the dumb man spake; and the multitudes marvelled [*cp.* 5 9, 26; 8 25, 56; 9 43; 24 12, 41: *also* 2 47, 48; 4 22, 32, 36: 20 26]. *cp.* 1 32; 18 38, 39. **15** But some of them *cp.* 5 17.	*cp.* 7 15, 21, 46. *cp.* 1 19.

said, ² By the prince of the ³ devils casteth he out ³ devils.	said, This man doth not cast out ¹ devils, but ² by Beelzebub [cp. 10 25] the prince of the ² devils.	said, He hath Beelzebub, and, ¹ By the prince of the ² devils casteth he out the ² devils.	said, ² By Beelzebub the prince of the devils casteth he out ² devils.	cp. 7 20; 8 48, 52; 10 20.

¹ Gr. demon.   ² Or, In   ³ Gr. demons.

¹ Or, a demoniac   ² Gr. demons.   ³ Or, in

¹ Or, In   ² Gr. demons.

¹ Gr. demon.   ² Or, In   ³ Gr. demons.

Matt. 9 33 : cp. Judges 19 30.

(iv) The Mission of the Twelve (Matt. : §§ 65–72).

§ 65. The Occasion of the Mission

Matt. 9 35-**10** 1	Mark 6 6b, 34, 7	Luke 8 1; 10 2; 9 1	
35 And Jesus went about all the cities and the villages, teaching in their synagogues, and preaching [cp. 4 23; 11 1] the ¹ gospel cp. 11 5. of the kingdom [cp. 4 23; 24 14 : also 26 13], and healing all manner of disease and all manner of sickness.	6 6 And he went round about the villages teaching. cp. 1 1, 14, 15 ; 8 35 ; 10 29 ; 13 10 ; 14 9 ; 16 15.	8 1 And it came to pass soon afterwards, that he went about through cities and villages [cp. 13 22], preaching and bringing the ¹ good tidings [cp. 1 19 ; 2 10 ; 3 18 ; 4 18, 43 ; 7 22 ; 9 6 ; 16 16 ; 20 1] of the kingdom of God,	
4 23 And Jesus went about in all Galilee, teaching in their synagogues, and preaching the ¹ gospel of the kingdom, and healing all manner of disease and all manner of sickness among the people.	1 39 And he went into their synagogues throughout all Galilee, preaching and casting out ¹ devils.	and with him the twelve. 4 44 And he was preaching in the synagogues [cp. 4 15] of ² Galilee.	cp. 18 20.
36 But when he saw the multitudes [cp. 3 7; 5 1; 8 18], he was moved with compassion [cp. 14 14; 15 32 : also 20 34] for them, because they were distressed and scattered, as sheep not having a shepherd [cp. 10 6; 15 24 : also 26 31]. **37** Then saith he unto his disciples, The harvest truly is plenteous, but the labourers are few. **38** Pray ye therefore the Lord of the harvest, that he send forth labourers into his harvest. 10 1 And he called unto him his twelve disciples, and gave them authority over unclean spirits [cp. 10 8; 17 16], to cast them out, and to heal all manner of disease and all manner of sickness.	6 34 And he came forth and saw a great multitude, and he had compassion [cp. 8 2: also 1 41] on them, because they were as sheep not having a shepherd [cp. 14 27]. 6 7 And he called unto him the twelve [cp. 3 13-14], and began to send them forth by two and two; and he gave them authority over the unclean spirits [cp. 3 15 : also 6 12-13 ; 9 18].	cp. 7 13. 10 2 And he said unto them, The harvest is plenteous, but the labourers are few : pray ye therefore the Lord of the harvest, that he send forth labourers into his harvest. 9 1 And he called the twelve [cp. 6 13] together, [cp. 10 1] and gave them power and authority over all ³ devils [cp. 10 9 : also 9 6, 40 ; 10 17], and to cure diseases.	cp. 6 5. cp. 10 11-16. cp. 4 35-38.

¹ Or, good tidings

¹ Gr. demons.

¹ Or, gospel
² Very many ancient authorities read Judæa.
³ Gr. demons.

§ 66. **The Names of the Twelve**

Matt. 10 2-4	Mark 3 13-19a	Luke 6 12-16		Acts 1 13
	13 And he goeth up into the mountain,	12 And it came to pass in these days, that he went out into the mountain to pray; and he continued all night in prayer to God. 13 And when it was day, he called his disciples:		
1 And he called unto him	and calleth unto him whom he himself would: and they went unto him. 14 And he appointed twelve, 1 that they might be with him, and that he might send them forth to preach, 15 and to have authority	and he chose from them		
his twelve disciples,				
and gave them authority over unclean spirits, to cast them out [cp. 10 8; 17 16], and to heal all manner of disease and all manner of sickness.	to cast out 2 devils [cp. 6 7: also 6 12-13; 9 18]:	cp. 9 1, 2; 10 1, 9: also 9 6, 40; 10 17.		
2 Now the names of the twelve				
apostles	cp. 6 30.	twelve, whom also he named apostles [cp. 9 10; 17 5; 22 14; 24 10];		13 And when they were come in, they went up into the upper chamber, where they were abiding; both Peter
are these: The first, Simon, who is called Peter [cp. 4 18: also 16 16-18], and Andrew his brother;	16 3 and Simon he surnamed Peter;	14 Simon, whom he also named Peter [cp. 5 8], and Andrew his brother, and James	cp. 1 42: also 1 40; 6 8; etc.	
James the son of Zebedee, and John his brother;	17 and James the son of Zebedee, and John the brother of James; and them he surnamed Boanerges, which is, Sons of thunder: 18 And Andrew, and Philip,	and John,		and John and James
3 Philip, and Bartholomew; Thomas, and Matthew the publican [cp. 9 9]; James the son of Alphæus, and Thaddæus; 4 Simon the 1 Cananæan,	and Bartholomew, and Matthew, and Thomas, and James the son of Alphæus, and Thaddæus, and Simon the 4 Cananæan,	and Philip and Bartholomew, 15 and Matthew and Thomas, and James the son of Alphæus, and Simon which was called the Zealot, 16 and Judas the 1 son of James, and	cp. 14 22.	and Andrew, Philip and Thomas, Bartholomew and Matthew, James the son of Alphæus, and Simon the Zealot, and Judas the son of James.
and Judas Iscariot, who also 2 betrayed him.	19 and Judas Iscariot, which also betrayed him.	Judas Iscariot, which was the traitor.		
1 Or, Zealot. See Luke 6 15; Acts 1 13. 2 Or, delivered him up: and so always.	1 Some ancient authorities add whom also he named apostles. See Luke 6 13. 2 Gr. demons. 3 Some ancient authorities insert and he appointed twelve. 4 Or, Zealot. See Luke 6 15; Acts 1 13.	1 Or, brother. See Jude 1.		Or, brother. See Jude 1.

§ 67. **The Mission Charge** (i)

Matt. **10** 5-15	Mark 6 7-11	Luke 9 1-5	Luke 10 1-2, 4-12	
5 These twelve	7 And he called unto him the twelve,	1 And he called the twelve together, and gave them power and authority over all [1]devils, and to cure diseases. **2** And he sent them forth	1 Now after these things the Lord appointed seventy [1] others, and sent them	
Jesus sent forth,	and began to send them forth by two and two; and he gave them authority over the unclean spirits;		two and two before his face into every city and place, whither he himself was about to come. *cp. verse* 9.	
and charged them, saying, Go not into *any* way of the Gentiles, and enter not into any city of the Samaritans: **6** but go rather to the lost sheep of the house of Israel [*cp.* 15 24: *also* 9 36]. **7** And as ye go, preach, saying, The kingdom of heaven is at hand [*cp.* 3 2; 4 17: *also* 12 28]. **8** Heal the sick, raise the dead, cleanse the lepers, cast out [1] devils: freely ye received, freely give.	8 and he charged them	to preach the kingdom of God, and to heal [1] the sick. 3 And he said unto them,	2 And he said unto them. . . .	
	cp. 6 34.		*cp.* 9 52.	*cp.* 4 9.
				cp. 10 16.
	cp. 1 15: *also* 6 12.	*cp. verse* 2: *also* 9 6.	*verses* 9 *and* 11	
	cp. 6 13.	*cp.* 9 6.	*verse* 9	
9 Get you	that they should take nothing for *their* journey, save a staff only; no bread, no wallet,	Take nothing for your journey, neither staff, nor wallet, nor bread,	4 Carry	
no gold, nor silver, nor brass in your [2] purses; **10** no wallet for *your* journey, neither two coats, nor shoes, nor staff:	no [1] money in their [2] purse; 9 but *to go* shod with sandals: and, *said he,* put not on two coats.	nor money; neither have two coats [*cp.* 3 11].	no purse, no wallet, no shoes [*cp.* 22 35]:	
for the labourer is worthy of his food.			and salute no man on the way. *verse* 7	*cp.* 4 36.
11 And into whatsoever city or village ye shall enter, search out who in it is worthy; and there abide till ye go forth. **12** And as ye enter into the house, salute it.	10 And he said unto them, Wheresoever ye enter into a house, there abide till ye depart thence.	4 And into whatsoever house ye enter, there abide, and thence depart.	5 And into whatsoever house ye shall [1] enter, *verse* 7 first say, Peace *be* to this house. 6 And if a son of peace be there, your peace shall rest upon [2] him: but if not,	
13 And if the house be worthy, let your peace come upon it [*cp.* 5 9]: but if it be not worthy, let your peace return to you.	*cp.* 9 50.	*cp.* 1 79; 2 14, 29; 19 38.	it shall turn to you again. 7 And in that	*cp.* 14 27; 16 33.

verse 11

verse 10

verses 7 *and* 8

14 And whosoever

shall not receive you,
nor hear your words,
as ye go forth out of that house or that city,
          shake off the dust

of your feet.

cp. 8 4; 10 18; 24 14.

cp. 24 43.

15 Verily I say unto you, It shall be more tolerable [*cp.* 7 22; 24 36: *also* 26 29] for the land [*cp.* 2 6, 20, 21; 4 15; 11 24] of Sodom and Gomorrah in the day of judgement [*cp.* 11 22, 24; 12 36], than for that city [*cp.* 11 24].

¹ Gr. *demons.* ² Gr. *girdles.*

---

11 And whatsoever place

shall not recieve you,
and they hear you not,
as ye go forth thence,

          shake off the dust
          that is under your feet
for a testimony unto them [*cp.* 1 44; 13 9].

cp. 13 32 : *also* 14 25.

¹ Gr. *brass.* ² Gr. *girdle.*

---

cp. verse 2.

5 And as many as receive you not,

when ye depart from that city,
          shake off the dust

from your feet
for a testimony against them [*cp.* 5 14; 21 13].

¹ Gr. *demons.*
² Some ancient authorities omit *the sick.*

---

same house remain, eating and drinking such things as they give : for the labourer is worthy of his hire. Go not from house to house. **8** And into whatsoever city ye enter, and they receive you, eat such things as are set before you : **9** and heal the sick that are therein, and say unto them, The kingdom of God is come nigh unto you [*cp.* 11 20; 17 20, 21; 19 11; 21 8]. **10** But into whatsoever city ye shall enter, and they receive you not [*cp.* 9 53], go out into the streets thereof and say, **11** Even the dust from your city, that cleaveth to our feet, we do wipe off against you : howbeit know this, [*cp.* 12 39], that the kingdom of God is come nigh [*cp. verse* 9]. **12** I say unto you, It shall be more tolerable in that day [*cp.* 17 31; 21 34] for

Sodom,

          than
for that city.

¹ Many ancient authorities add *and two*: and so in ver. 17.
² Or, *enter first, say*
³ Or, *it*

---

cp. 14 20; 16 23, 26.
cp. 3 22.

---

§ 68. **The Mission Charge** (ii)

Matt. 10 16-23	Matt. 24 9, 13	Mark 13 9-13	Luke 21 12-19	Luke 10 3; 12 11-12
				10 3 Go your ways: behold, I send you forth as lambs in the midst of wolves.
16 Behold, I send you forth as sheep in the midst of wolves: be ye therefore wise [*cp.* 7 24; 24 45; 25 2 *ff.*] as serpents, and ¹ harmless as doves. **17** But beware of men: for they will			*cp.* 12 42.	
	9 Then shall they	**9** But take ye heed to yourselves : for they shall	**12** But before all these things, they shall lay their hands on you,	

Matthew

deliver you up to councils, and in their synagogues they will scourge you;

18 yea and before governors and kings shall ye be brought for my sake [*cp.* 5 11; 10 39; 16 25: *also* 10 22; 19 29; 24 9],

for a testimony to them [*cp.* 8 4; 24 14]

and to the Gentiles [*cp.* 24 14: *also* 8 11; 21 31, 41, 43; 22 7-10; 26 13; 28 19]. **19** But when they

deliver you up,

be not anxious [*cp.* 6 25, 31, 34] how or

what ye shall speak: for it shall be given you in that hour what ye shall speak. **20** For it is not ye that speak, but the Spirit of your Father that speaketh in you.

21 And brother shall deliver up brother to death, and the father his child: and children shall rise up against parents, and ² cause them to be put to death [*cp.* 10 35, 36]. **22** And ye shall be hated of all men for my name's sake [*cp.* 19 29: *also* 5 11; 10 18, 39; 16 25]:

---

deliver you up unto tribulation,

cp. 23 34.

and shall kill you:
and ye shall be hated of all the nations for my name's sake.

Mark

deliver you up to councils; and in synagogues shall ye be beaten;

and before governors and kings shall ye stand for my sake [*cp.* 8 35; 10 29: *also* 13 13],

for a testimony unto them [*cp.* 1 44; 6 11]. **10** And the gospel must first be preached unto all the nations [*cp.* 12 9; 14 9; 16 15].

11 And when they lead you *to judgement*, and

deliver you up,

be not anxious beforehand

what ye shall speak: but whatsoever shall be given you in that hour, that speak ye: For it is not ye that speak, but the Holy Ghost.

12 And brother shall deliver up brother to death, and the father his child; and children shall rise up against parents, and ¹ cause them to be put to death. **13** And ye shall be hated of all men for my name's sake [*cp.* 8 35; 10 29; 13 9]:

Luke

and shall persecute you, delivering you up to the synagogues and prisons,¹ bringing you before kings and governors for my name's sake [*cp.* 21 17: *also* 6 22; 9 24; 18 29].

13 It shall turn unto you for a testimony [*cp.* 5 14; 9 5].

cp. 2 30-32; 3 6; 13 29; 14 21-24; 20 16; 24 47.

verse 12

14 Settle it therefore in your hearts, not to meditate beforehand how to answer:

15 for I will give you a mouth and wisdom,

which all your adversaries shall not be able to withstand or to gainsay. **16** But ye shall be delivered up even by parents, and brethren, and kinsfolk, and friends; and *some* of you ² shall they cause to be put to death [*cp.* 12 53]. **17** And ye shall be hated of all men for my name's sake [*cp.* 21 12: *also* 6 22; 9 24; 18 29]. **18** And not

cp. 1 71; 6 22, 27.

---

cp. 12 11 *below.*

12 11 And when they bring you before the synagogues, and the rulers, and the authorities,

be not anxious [*cp.* 12 22] how or what ye shall answer, or what ye shall say: **12** for the Holy Spirit shall teach you in that very hour what ye ought to say.

---

cp. 15 21.

cp. 10 16; 11 52.

cp. 14 26.

cp. 16 2.

cp. 15 18-21; 17 14.

cp. 10 30.

but he that endureth to the end, the same shall be saved. **23** But when they persecute you in this city, flee into the next: for verily I say unto you, Ye shall not have gone through the cities of Israel, till the Son of man be come.

13 But he that endureth to the end, the same shall be saved.

cp. 23 34.

cp. 16 28: *also* 23 36; 24 34.

but he that endureth to the end, the same shall be saved.

cp. 9 1: *also* 13 30.

a hair of your head shall perish. **19** In your patience [*cp.* 8 15] ye shall win your 3 souls.

cp. 9 27: *also* 11 51; 21 32.

cp. 12 7.

1 Or, *simple*
2 Or, *put them to death*

1 Or, *put them to death*

1 Gr. *you being brought.*
2 Or, *shall they put to death*
3 Or, *lives*

§ 69. **The Mission Charge** (iii)

Matt. 10 24-33	Luke 6 40	John 13 16	John 15 20
24 A disciple is not above his 1 master, nor a 2 servant above his lord.	**40** The disciple is not above his 1 master:	**16** Verily, verily, I say unto you,	**20** Remember the word that I said unto you,
25 It is enough [*cp.* 6 34] for the disciple that he be as his 1 master, and the 2 servant as his lord. If they have called the master of the house 3 Beelzebub [*cp.* 9 34; 12 24], how much more *shall they call* them of his household [*cp.* 10 36]!	but every one when he is perfected shall be as his 1 master.	A 1 servant is not greater than his lord; neither 2 one that is sent greater than he that sent him.	A 1 servant is not greater than his lord.
	cp. 3 22.		If they persecuted me, they will also persecute you; if they kept my word, they will keep yours also.
	cp. 11 15, 18.	*cp.* 7 20; 8 48, 52; 10 20.	
1 Or, *teacher* 2 Gr. *bondservant.* 3 Gr. *Beelzebul.*	1 Or, *teacher*	1 Gr. *bondservant.* 2 Gr. *an apostle.*	1 Gr. *bondservant.*

26 Fear them not therefore: for there is nothing covered, that shall not be revealed; and hid, that shall not be known.

Mark **4 22** For there is nothing hid, save that it should be manifested; neither was *anything* made secret, but that it should come to light.

Luke **8 17** For nothing is hid, that shall not be made manifest; nor *anything* secret, that shall not be known and come to light.

Luke **12 2** But there is nothing covered up, that shall not be revealed: and hid, that shall not be known. **3** Wherefore whatsoever ye have said in the darkness shall be heard in the light; and what ye have spoken in the ear in the inner chambers shall be proclaimed upon the housetops. **4** And I say unto you my friends, Be not afraid of them which kill the body,

27 What I tell you in the darkness, speak ye in the light: and what ye hear in the ear, proclaim upon the housetops. **28** And be not afraid of them which kill the body, but are not able to kill the soul:

but rather

and after that have no more that they can do. **5** But I will warn you whom ye shall fear:

fear him which
is able to destroy
both soul and body in [1] hell [*cp.* 5 22, 29, 30; 18 9; 23 15, 33: *also* 3 10, 12; 7 19; 13 42, 50; 18 8; 25 41].
29 Are not two sparrows sold for a farthing? and not one of them shall fall on the ground without your Father: **30** but the very hairs of your head are all numbered. **31** Fear not therefore; ye are of more value than many sparrows [*cp.* 6 26: *also* 12 12]. **32** Every one therefore who shall confess [2] me before men, [3] him will I also confess before my Father which is in heaven [*cp.* 5 16, 45; 6 1, 9; 7 11, 21; 12 50; 16 17; 18 10, 14, 19: *also* 5 48; 6 14, 26, 32; 15 13; 18 35; 23 9].
33 But whosoever shall deny me before men, him will I also deny before my Father which is in heaven [*see above*].

Gr. *Gehenna*.   [2] Gr. *in me*.   [3] Gr. *in him*.

cp. 9 43, 45, 47.

cp. 11 25, 26.

Fear him, which after he hath killed hath [1] power to cast
into [2] hell [*cp.* 3 9, 17]; yea, I say unto you, Fear him.
6 Are not five sparrows sold for two farthings? and not one of them is forgotten in the sight of God. **7** But the very hairs of your head are all numbered [*cp.* 21 18]. Fear not: ye are of more value than many sparrows [*cp.* 12 24]. **8** And I say unto you, Every one who shall confess [3] me before men, [4] him shall the Son of man also confess before

cp. 11 13.

the angels of God [*cp.* 15 10]: **9** but he that denieth me in the presence of men shall be denied in the presence of

the angels of God [*see above*].

[1] Or, *authority*   [2] Gr. *Gehenna*.
[3] Gr. *in me*.   [4] Gr. *in him*.

cp. 15 6.

Matt. 16 **27** For the Son of man
shall come in the glory of his Father with his angels; and then shall he render unto every man according to his [1] deeds.

[1] Gr. *doing*.

Mark 8 **38** For whosoever shall be ashamed of me and of my words in this adulterous and sinful generation,
the Son of man also shall be ashamed of him,
when he cometh in the glory of his Father with the holy angels.

Luke 9 **26** For whosoever shall be ashamed of me and of my words,
of him shall the Son of man be ashamed,
when he cometh in his own glory, and *the glory* of the Father, and of the holy angels.

---

§ 70. **The Mission Charge** (iv)

Matt. 10 34-39

cp. 3 11.

34 Think not that I came to [1] send peace on the earth: I came not to [1] send peace, but a sword.

35 For I came to set a man at variance against his father,
and the daughter against her mother,
and the daughter in law against her mother in law: **36** and a man's foes *shall be* they of his own household [*cp.* 10 25: *also* 10 21].

37 He that loveth father or mother more

cp. 10 38, 39.

cp. 13 12.

Luke 12 49-53; 14 26-27; 17 33

12 49 I came to cast fire upon the earth [*cp.* 3 16]; and what will I, if it is already kindled? **50** But I have a baptism to be baptized with; and how am I straitened till it be accomplished! **51** Think ye that I am come to give peace in the earth? I tell you, Nay; but rather division: **52** for there shall be from henceforth five in one house divided, three against two, and two against three. **53** They shall be divided,
father against son, and son against father; mother against daughter, and daughter against her mother; mother in law against her daughter in law, and daughter in law against her mother in law.

cp. 21 16.

14 26 If any man cometh unto me, and hateth not his own father, and mother, and wife [*cp.* 18 29],

cp. 12 27.

than me is not worthy of me; and he that loveth son or daughter
cp. 19 27-29.

than me is not worthy of me.
cp. 8 18-22.

38 And he that doth not take his cross and follow after me, is not worthy of me.

39 He that
² findeth his ³ life shall lose it; and he that
⁴ loseth his ³ life for my sake [*see below*] shall find it.

Matt. 16 **24** If any man would come after me, let him deny himself, and take up his cross, and follow me [*cp.* 4 19; 8 22; 9 9; 19 21].

25 For whosoever would save his ³ life shall lose it: and whosoever shall lose his ³ life for my sake [*cp.* 5 11; 10 18: *also* 10 22; 19 29; 24 9] shall find it.

¹ Gr. *cast.* ² Or, *found* ³ Or, *soul* ⁴ Or, *lost*

---

cp. 10 28-30.

more

Mark 8 **34** If any man would come after me, let him deny himself, and take up his cross, and follow me [*cp.* 1 17; 2 14; 10 21].

35 For whosoever would save his ¹ life shall lose it; and whosoever shall lose his ¹ life for my sake [*cp.* 10 29; 13 9: *also* 13 13] and the gospel's [*cp.* 10 29] shall save it.

¹ Or, *soul*

---

and children, and brethren, and sisters [*cp.* 18 28-30], yea, and his own life also,
he cannot be my disciple [*cp.* 9 57-62].
27 Whosoever doth not bear his own cross, and come after me, cannot be my disciple.

Luke 17 **33** Whosoever shall seek to gain his ¹ life shall lose it: but whosoever shall lose *his* ¹ *life*
shall
² preserve it.

Luke 9 **23** If any man would come after me, let him deny himself, and take up his cross daily, and follow me [*cp.* 5 27; 9 59; 18 22].

24 For whosoever would save his ¹ life shall lose it; but whosoever shall lose his ¹ life for my sake [*cp.* 6 22; 18 29; 21 12, 17],

the same shall save it.

¹ Or, *soul* ² Gr. *save it alive.*

---

and

John 12 **25** He that loveth his ¹ life loseth it; and he that hateth his ¹ life in this world shall keep it unto life eternal.

26 If any man serve me, let him

follow me [*cp.* 1 43; 21 19, 22]; and where I am, there shall also my servant be: if any man . . .

cp. 15 21.

¹ Or, *soul*

Matt. 10 35-36 ∥ Luke 12 52-53 : Mic. 7 6 ; *cp.* Is. 19 2.

§ 71. **The Mission Charge** (v)

Matt. 10 40-42

40 He that receiveth you receiveth me, and he that receiveth me receiveth him that sent me.

Matt. 18 **5** And whoso shall receive one such little child in my name receiveth me.

41 He that receiveth a prophet in the name of a prophet shall receive a prophet's reward; and he that receiveth a righteous man in the name of a righteous man shall receive a righteous man's reward. **42** And whosoever shall give to drink unto one of these little ones [*cp.* 18 6, 10, 14] a cup of cold water only, in the name of a disciple,
verily I say unto you, he shall in no wise lose his reward [*cp.* 25 34-40].

Luke 10 16

16 He that heareth you heareth me; and he that rejecteth you rejecteth me; and he that rejecteth me rejecteth him that sent me.

Mark 9 **37** Whosoever shall receive one of such little children in my name, receiveth me: and whosoever receiveth me, receiveth not me, but him that sent me.

Mark 9 **41** For whosoever shall give you a cup of water to drink,
cp. 9 42.

¹ because ye are Christ's, verily I say unto you, he shall in no wise lose his reward.

¹ Gr. *in name that ye are.*

John 13 20

20 Verily, verily, I say unto you, He that receiveth whomsoever I send receiveth me; and he that receiveth me receiveth him that sent me [*cp.* 12 44-48].

Luke 9 **48** Whosoever shall receive this little child in my name receiveth me: and whosoever shall receive me receiveth him that sent me.

cp. 17 2.

§ 72. **The Conclusion of the Charge**

Matt. **11** 1

1 And it came to pass, when Jesus had made an end [*cp.* 7 28; 13 53; 19 1; 26 1] of commanding his twelve disciples, he departed thence to teach and preach [*cp.* 4 23; 9 35] in their cities.

cp. 7 1.

(v) Events in Galilee II (§§ 73–80)

§ 73. **The Question of John the Baptist and the Testimony of Jesus concerning him**

Matt. **11** 2-19		Luke 7 18-35; 16 16	
2 Now when John heard in the prison [*cp.* 4 12; 14 3] the works of the Christ [*cp.* 1 17], he sent by his disciples [*cp.* 9 14; 14 12],	*cp.* 1 14; 6 17. *cp.* 2 18; 6 29. *cp.* 16 19, 20.	**7 18** And the disciples of John told him of all these things. **19** And John *cp.* 3 20. calling unto him [1] two of his disciples [*cp.* 5 33; 11 1] sent them to the Lord [*cp.* 7 13; 10 1, 39, 41; 11 39; 12 42; 13 15; 17 5, 6; 18 6; 19 8; 22 61; 24 34: *also* 24 3], saying, Art thou he that cometh, or look we for another ? **20** And when the men were come unto him, they said, John the Baptist hath sent us	*cp.* 3 24. *cp.* 1 35, 37; 3 25; 4 1. *cp.* 4 1; 6 23; 11 2; 20 2, 18, 20, 25; 21 7, 12.
3 and said unto him, Art thou he that cometh [*cp.* 3 11; 21 9; 23 39], or look we for another ? *cp.* 18 1; 26 55.	*cp.* 11 9.	unto thee, saying, Art thou he that cometh [*cp.* 13 35; 19 38], or look we for another ? **21** In that hour [*cp.* 10 21; 13 31] he cured many of diseases and [2] plagues and evil spirits ; and on many that were blind he bestowed sight. **22** And	*cp.* 1 15, 27; 3 31; 6 14; 11 27; 12 13.
4 And Jesus answered and said unto them, Go your way and tell John the things which ye do hear and see : **5** the blind receive their sight, and the lame walk, the lepers are cleansed, and the deaf hear [*cp.* 15 31], and the dead are raised up, and the poor have [1] good tidings preached to them.		he answered and said unto them, Go your way, and tell John what things ye have seen and heard ; the blind receive their sight, the lame walk, the lepers are cleansed, and the deaf hear, the dead are raised up, the poor have [3] good tidings preached [*cp.* 1 19; 2 10; 3 18; 4 18, 43; 8 1; 9 6; 16 16; 20 1] to them [*cp.* 4 18]. **23** And blessed is he, whoso-	
6 And blessed is he, whoso- ever shall find none occasion of stumbling [*cp.* 13 57; 15 12; 26 31, 33: *also* 13 21; 24 10] in me. **7** And as these	*cp.* 6 3; 14 27, 29 : *also* 4 17.	ever shall find none occasion of stumbling in me. **24** And	*cp.* 6 61 : *also* 16 1.
went their way, Jesus began to say unto the multitudes concerning John, What went ye out into the wilderness to behold ? a reed shaken with the wind ? **8** But what went ye out for to see ? a man clothed in soft *raiment* ? Behold, they that wear soft *raiment*		when the messengers of John were departed, he began to say unto the multitudes concerning John, What went ye out into the wilderness to behold ? a reed shaken with the wind ? **25** But what went ye out to see ? a man clothed in soft raiment ? Behold, they which are gorgeously apparelled, and live deli-	
are in kings' houses. **9** [2] But wherefore went ye out ? to see a pro- phet [*cp.* 14 5; 21 26] ? Yea, I say unto you, and much more than a prophet. **10** This is he, of whom it is written,	*cp.* 11 32.	cately, are in kings' courts. **26** But what went ye out to see ? a pro- phet [*cp.* 1 76; 20 6] ? Yea, I say unto you, and much more than a prophet. **27** This is he of whom it is written,	
Behold, I send my messenger before thy face,		Behold, I send my messenger before thy face,	
Who shall prepare thy way be- fore thee.	1 2	Who shall prepare thy way be- fore thee [*cp.* 1 17, 76].	*cp.* 1 21, 23; 3 28.
11 Verily I say unto you, Among them		**28** I say unto you, Among them	

that are born of women there hath not arisen a greater than John the Baptist: yet he that is [3] but little   in the kingdom of heaven is greater [*cp.* 5 19; 18 1, 4] than he.

cp. 21 32.

cp. 21 25, 32 : *also* 3 7.

cp. 9 13; 21 31.
12 And from the days of John the Baptist until now the kingdom of heaven suffereth violence, and men of violence take it by force. **13** For all the prophets and the law [*cp.* 5 17; 7 12; 22 40]   prophesied until John.

14 And if ye are willing to receive [4] *it*, this is Elijah, which is to come [*cp.* 17 12, 13: *also* 3 3, 4]. **15** He that hath ears [5] to hear, let him hear [*cp.* 13 9, 43: *also* 19 12]. **16** But whereunto   shall I liken this generation?
    It is like unto children sitting in the market-places, which call unto their fellows, **17** and say, We piped unto you, and ye did not dance; we wailed, and ye did not [6] mourn. **18** For John   came neither eating [*cp.* 3 4]   nor drinking, and they say, He hath a [7] devil. **19** The Son of man   came eating and drinking, and they say, Behold, a gluttonous man, and a wine-bibber, a friend of publicans and sinners [*cp.* 9 11] !
    And wisdom [8] is justified by   her   [9] works.

[1] Or, *the gospel*
[2] Many ancient authorities read *But what went ye out to see ? a prophet ?*
[3] Gr. *lesser.*   [4] Or, *him*
[5] Some ancient authorities omit *to hear.*
[6] Gr. *beat the breast.*   [7] Gr. *demon.*
[8] Or, *was*
[9] Many ancient authorities read *children*: as in Luke 7 35.

---

that are born of women there is none greater than John:
yet he that is [4] but little [*cp.* 9 48] in the kingdom of God is greater
    than he. **29** And all the people [*cp.* 3 10] when they heard, and the publicans [*cp.* 3 12], justified God, [5] being baptized with the baptism of John. **30** But the Pharisees and the lawyers rejected for themselves [*cp.* 20 5] the counsel of God, [6] being not baptized of him [*cp.* 5 32 ; 7 47; 15 7, 10 ; 18 14 ; 19 10].

16 **16** The law and the prophets

were until John : from that time the gospel of the kingdom of God is preached [*cp.* 1 19; 2 10; 3 18; 4 18, 43; 7 22; 8 1; 9 6; 20 1], and every man entereth violently into it.

7 31 Whereunto then shall I liken the men of this generation, and to what are they like ? **32** They are like unto children that sit in the market-place, and call one to another ; which say, We piped unto you, and ye did not dance ; we wailed, and ye did not weep. **33** For John the Baptist is come   eating no bread nor drinking wine [*cp.* 1 15] ; and ye say, He hath a [7] devil. **34** The Son of man is come eating [*cp.* 7 36] and drinking ; and ye say, Behold, a gluttonous man, and a wine-bibber, a friend of publicans and sinners [*cp.* 5 30 : *also* 7 37, 39 ; 15 2 ; 19 7] ! **35** And wisdom [*cp.* 11 49] [8] is justified of all her children.

[1] Gr. *certain two.*   [2] Gr. *scourges.*
[3] Or, *the gospel*   [4] Gr. *lesser.*
[5] Or, *having been*   [6] Or, *not having been*
[7] Gr. *demon.*   [8] Or, *was*

Marginal references:
cp. 11 31. — *cp.* 2 17.
cp. 9 13: *also* 1 2-3, 6. — *cp.* 4 9, 23; 7 16.
cp. 1 6.
cp. 2 16.
cp. 1 17. — *cp.* 1 21.
cp. 8 8 ; 14 35. — *cp.* 6 60.

Matt. 11 5 ‖ Luke 7 22 : *cp.* Is. 29 18-19 ; 35 5-6 ; 61 1.
Matt. 11 10 ‖ Luke 7 27 = Exod. 23 20 ; Mal. 3 1.   Matt. 11 14 : *cp.* Mal. 4 5.

§ 74. The Upbraiding of the Cities

Matt. 11 20-24   Luke 10 12-15

20 Then began he to upbraid the cities wherein most of his [1] mighty works were done, because they repented not.
    cp. 7 22; 24 36: *also* 26 29.
      verse 24
    21 Woe unto thee, Chorazin ! woe unto thee, Bethsaida ! for if the [1] mighty works had been done in Tyre and Sidon

12 I say unto you, It shall be more tolerable in that day [*cp.* 17 31 ; 21 34] for Sodom, than for that city. **13** Woe unto thee, Chorazin ! woe unto thee, Bethsaida ! for if the [1] mighty works had been done in Tyre and Sidon,

Marginal references:
cp. 13 32: *also* 14 25. — *cp.* 14 20; 16 23, 26.

which were done in you, they would have repented long ago   in sackcloth and ashes. **22** Howbeit I say unto you, it shall be more tolerable for Tyre and Sidon in the day of judgement [*cp.* 10 15; 11 24; 12 36], than for you. **23** And thou, Capernaum, shalt thou be exalted unto heaven? thou shalt ² go   down unto Hades: for if the ¹ mighty works had been done in Sodom which were done in thee, it would have remained until this day [*cp.* 27 8; 28 15]. **24** Howbeit I say unto you, that it shall be more tolerable for the land [*cp.* 2 6, 20, 21; 4 15; 10 15] of Sodom in the day of judgement [*cp. above*], than for thee [*cp.* 10 15].

¹ Gr. *powers.*
² Many ancient authorities read *be brought down.*

which were done in you, they would have repented long ago, sitting in sackcloth and ashes. **14** Howbeit   it shall be more tolerable for Tyre and Sidon in the   judgement,   than for you. **15** And thou, Capernaum, shalt thou be exalted unto heaven? thou shalt be brought down unto Hades.

verse 12

cp. 3 22.

¹ Gr. *powers.*

Matt. 11 23 ‖ Luke 10 15 : *cp.* Is. 14 13-15.

§ 75. **The Thanksgiving of Jesus and His Invitation to the Weary**

Matt. 11 25-30		Luke 10 21-24	

25 At that season [*cp.* 12 1; 14 1: *also* 18 1; 26 55] Jesus answered and said, I ¹ thank thee, O Father [*cp.* 26 39, 42: *also* 6 9], Lord of heaven and earth, that thou didst hide these things from the wise and understanding, and didst reveal them unto babes [*cp.* 16 17]: **26** yea, Father [*see above*], ² for so it was well-pleasing [*cp.* 3 17; 12 18; 17 5] in thy sight. **27** All things have been delivered unto me of my Father [*cp.* 9 8; 28 18]: and no one knoweth   the Son,   save the Father; neither doth any know the Father,   save the Son, and he to whomsoever the Son willeth to reveal *him*. **28** Come unto me, all ye that labour and are heavy laden, and I will give you rest. **29** Take my yoke upon you, and learn of me; for I am meek and lowly in heart: and ye shall find rest unto your souls. **30** For my yoke is easy, and my burden is light.

cp. 9 22; 16 23.

cp. 17 1, 19; 20 17; 24 3.   **13 16** But blessed are your eyes, for they see; and your ears, for they hear. **17** For verily I say unto you, that many prophets and righteous men desired to see the things which ye see, and saw them not; and to hear the things which ye hear, and heard them not.

¹ Or, *praise*   ² Or, *that*

cp. 14 36.

cp. 1 11.

cp. 5 30; 8 33.
cp. 4 10, 34; 6 31, 32; 9 2, 28; 13 3.

21 In that same hour [*cp.* 7 21; 13 31] he rejoiced ¹ in the Holy Spirit, and said, I ² thank thee, O Father [*cp.* 2 42; 23 34, 46: *also* 11 2], Lord of heaven and earth, that thou didst hide these things from the wise and understanding, and didst reveal them unto babes: yea, Father [*see above*]; ³ for so it was well-pleasing [*cp.* 2 14; 3 22; 12 32] in thy sight. **22** All things have been delivered unto me of my Father: and no one knoweth who the Son is, save the Father; and   who the Father is, save the Son, and he to whomsoever the Son willeth to reveal *him*.

23 And turning [*cp.* 7 9, 44; 9 55; 14 25; 22 61; 23 28] to the disciples, he said privately [*cp.* 9 10], Blessed *are* the eyes which see the things that ye see: **24** for   I say unto you, that many prophets and kings   desired to see the things which ye see, and saw them not; and to hear the things which ye hear, and heard them not.

¹ Or, *by*   ² Or, *praise*   ³ Or, *that*

cp. 11 41; 12 27, 28; 17 1, 5, 11, 21, 24, 25.

see above.

cp. 3 35; 5 27; 13 3; 17 2.
cp. 1 18; 6 46; 7 29; 8 19; 10 15; 17 25-26.
cp. 6 37; 7 37.

cp. 1 38.

Matt. 11 28–30 : *cp.* Ecclus. 51 23-27; Jer. 6 16; Zech. 9 9.

§ 76. A Controversy in the Cornfields on the Sabbath

[*Cp.* Matt. 12 9-14; Mark 3 1-6; Luke 6 6-11; 13 10-17; 14 1-6; John 5 2-18; 7 21-24; 9 1-34]

Matt. 12 1-8	**Mark 2** 23-28	**Luke 6** 1-5
1 At that season [*cp.* 11 25; 14 1] Jesus went on the sabbath day through the cornfields; and his disciples were an hungred, and began to pluck ears of corn, and to eat. **2** But the Pharisees, when they saw it, said unto him, Behold, thy disciples do that which it is not lawful to do upon the sabbath [*cp.* 9 14; 15 2]. **3** But he said unto them, Have ye not read [*cp.* 12 5; 19 4; 21 16, 42; 22 31] what David did, when he was an hungred, and they that were with him; **4** how he entered into the house of God, and [1] did eat the shewbread, which it was not lawful for him to eat, neither for them that were with him, but only for the priests? **5** Or have ye not read [*see verse* 3 *above*] in the law, how that on the sabbath day the priests in the temple profane the sabbath, and are guiltless? **6** But I say unto you, that [2] one greater than the temple is here [*cp.* 12 41, 42]. **7** But if ye had known what this meaneth, I desire mercy, and not sacrifice [*cp.* 9 13: *also* 23 23], ye would not have condemned the guiltless. **8** For the Son of man is lord of the sabbath.	**23** And it came to pass, that he was going on the sabbath day through the cornfields; and his disciples [1] began, as they went, to pluck the ears of corn. **24** And the Pharisees said unto him, Behold, why do they on the sabbath day that which is not lawful [*cp.* 2 18; 7 5]? **25** And he said unto them, Did ye never read [12 10, 26] what David did, when he had need, and was an hungred, he, and they that were with him? **26** How he entered into the house of God [2] when Abiathar was high priest, and did eat the shewbread, which it was not lawful to eat save for the priests, and gave also to them that were with him? *cp.* 12 33. **27** And he said unto them, The sabbath was made for man, and not man for the sabbath: **28** so that the Son of man is lord even of the sabbath.	**1** Now it came to pass on a [1] sabbath, that he was going through the cornfields; and his disciples plucked the ears of corn, and did eat, rubbing them in their hands. **2** But certain of the Pharisees said, Why do ye that which it is not lawful to do on the sabbath day [*cp.* 5 33]? **3** And Jesus answering them said, Have ye not read [*cp.* 10 26] even this, what David did, when he was an hungred, he, and they that were with him; **4** how he entered into the house of God, and did take and eat the shewbread, and gave also to them that were with him; which it is not lawful to eat save for the priests alone? *cp.* 7 22-23. *cp.* 11 31, 32. **5** And he said unto them, The Son of man is lord of the sabbath.
[1] Some ancient authorities read *they did eat.* [2] Gr. *a greater thing.*	[1] Gr. *began to make their way plucking.* [2] Some ancient authorities read *in the days of Abiathar the high priest.*	[1] Many ancient authorities insert *second-first.*

Matt. 12 3-4 ‖ Mark 2 25-26 ‖ Luke 6 3-4 : *cp.* I Sam. 21 1-6.   Matt. 12 4b ‖ Mark 2 26b ‖ Luke 6 4b : *cp.* Lev. 24 5-9.
Matt. 12 5 : *cp.* Num. 28 9-10.   Matt. 12 7 = Hos. 6 6.

§ 77. The Healing of a Man with a Withered Hand

[*Cp*. Matt. 12 1-8; Mark 2 23-28; Luke 6 1-5; 13 10-17; John 5 2-18; 7 21-24; 9 1-34]

Matt. 12 9-14	**Mark 3** 1-6	**Luke 6** 6-11	Luke 14 1-6	
9 And he departed thence, and went into their synagogue [*cp.* 13 54: *also* 4 23; 9 35]: **10** and behold, a man having [*cp.* 5 29, 30, 39; 27 29] a withered hand.	**1** And he entered again into the synagogue [*cp.* 1 21; 6 2: *also* 1 39]; and there was a man there which had his hand withered.	**6** And it came to pass on another sabbath, that he entered into the synagogue [*cp.* 4 16, 33; 13 10: *also* 4 15, 44] and taught: and there was a man there, and his right [*cp.* 22 50] hand was withered. **7** And the scribes and the Pharisees	**1** And it came to pass, when he went into the house of one of the rulers of the Pharisees on a sabbath to eat bread [*cp.* 7 36; 11 37], that they were watching him [*cp.* 20 20].	*cp.* 6 59; 18 20.
				cp. 18 10.
verse 14	*verse 6* **2** And they watched him, whether he would heal him on the sabbath day; that they might	watched him, whether he would heal on the sabbath; that they might find		
see below.	accuse him [*cp.* 12 13].	how to accuse him [*cp.* 11 53-54; 20 20].		*cp.* 8 6.
			2 And behold, there was before him a certain man which had the dropsy.	
cp. 9 4; 12 25; 16 8.	*cp.* 2 8; 8 17. **3** And he saith unto the man that had his hand withered, ¹ Stand	**8** But he knew their thoughts [*cp.* 5 22; 9 47; 11 17]; and he said to the man that had his hand withered, Rise up, and stand		*cp.* 1 48: 2 24, 25; 4 19, 29; 5 6, 42; *etc.*
cp. 9 6.	forth [*cp.* 2 11; 5 41; 10 49].	forth [*cp.* 5 24; 7 14; 8 54] in the midst. And he arose and stood forth. **9** And Jesus said		*cp.* 5 8.
And they asked him, saying, Is it lawful [*cp.* 19 3; 22 17] to heal on the sabbath day? that they might accuse him [*cp.* 22 15].	**4** And he saith unto them, Is it lawful [*cp.* 10 2; 12 14] on the sabbath day *verse 2* to do good, or to do harm? to save a life, or to kill? But they held their peace.	unto them, I ask you, Is it lawful [*cp.* 20 22] on the sabbath *verse 7* to do good, or to do harm? to save a life, or to destroy it?	**3** And Jesus answering spake unto the lawyers and Pharisees, saying, Is it lawful to heal on the sabbath, or not?	
11 And he said unto them, What man shall there be of you, that shall have one sheep, and if this fall into a pit on the sabbath day, will he not lay hold on it, and lift it out?			**4** But they held their peace. And he took him, and healed [*cp.* 6 19; 9 2, 11, 42; 22 51] him, and let him go. **5** And he said unto them, Which of you shall have ¹ an ass or an ox fallen into a well, and will not straightway draw him up on a sabbath day?	
12 How much then is a man of more value		*cp.* 13 15-16.		

_cp. 12 7, 24._

_cp. 7 23._

than a sheep [_cp._ 6 26; 10 31]! Wherefore it is lawful to do good on the sabbath day. **13** Then

5 And when he had looked round about [_cp._ 3 34; 5 32; 9 8; 10 23; 11 11] on them with anger, being grieved at the hardening of their heart [_cp._ 10 5: _also_ 6 52; 8 17; 16 14],

10 And he looked round about on them all,

_cp._ 12 40.

_cp._ 19 8.

saith he to the man, Stretch forth thy hand. And he stretched it forth; and it was restored whole, as the other. **14** But the Pharisees went out, and

he saith unto the man, Stretch forth thy hand. And he stretched it forth: and his hand was restored. **6** And the Pharisees went out, and straightway with the Herodians [_cp._ 12 13]

and said unto him, Stretch forth thy hand. And he did _so_: and his hand was restored.

verse 7

_cp._ 22 16.

11 But they were filled with [1] madness; and communed one with another what they might do to Jesus [_cp._ 19 47; 20 19, 20; 22 2].

took counsel [_cp._ 22 15; 27 1, 7; 28 12] against him, how they might destroy him [_cp._ 21 46; 26 4].
_cp._ 22 46.

took counsel [_cp._ 15 1] against him, how they might destroy him [_cp._ 11 18; 12 12; 14 1].

6 And they could not answer again unto these things.

_cp._ 5 16, 18; 7 30, 32; 11 53.

[1] Gr. _Arise into the midst._

[1] Or, _foolishness_

[1] Many ancient authorities read _a son._ See ch. 13 15.

§ 78. **The Choice of the Twelve** (Luke)

Matt. 10 1-4	Mark 3 13-19a	Luke 6 12-16		Acts 1 13

_cp._ 5 1; 14 23; 15 29; 17 1; 28 16.
_cp._ 14 23; 19 13; 26 36, 39, 42, 44: _also_ 11 25-26.

13 And he goeth up into the mountain [_cp._ 6 46; 9 2],
_cp._ 1 35; 6 46; 14 32, 35, 39.

12 And it came to pass in these days, that he went out into the mountain [_cp._ 9 28] to pray [_cp._ 3 21; 5 16; 9 18, 28, 29; 11 1; 22 41, 44: _also_ 10 21]; and he continued all night in prayer to God. **13** And when it was day, he called his disciples:

_cp._ 6 3, 15.

_cp._ 11 41-42; 12 27-28; 17 1-26.

1 And he called unto him

and calleth unto him whom he himself would: and they went unto him. **14** And he appointed twelve, [1] that they might be with him, and that he might send them forth to preach, **15** and to have authority

his twelve disciples,

and he chose from them twelve,

_cp._ 6 70; 13 18; 15 16, 19.

and gave them authority over unclean spirits, to cast them out [_cp._ 10 8; 17 16], and to heal all manner of disease and all manner of sickness.
2 Now the names of the twelve

to cast out [2] devils [_cp._ 6 7: _also_ 6 12-13; 9 18]:

_cp._ 9 1, 2; 10 1, 9: _also_ 9 6, 40; 10 17.

whom also

13 And when

[Matt.]

apostles

are these:
The first, Simon, who is
called Peter [cp. 4 18:
also 16 16-18], and
Andrew his brother;
James the son
of Zebedee, and John
his brother;

3 Philip,
and Bartholomew;
Thomas, and Matthew
the publican [cp. 9 9];
James the son of
Alphæus, and Thad-
dæus; 4 Simon the
1 Cananæan,

and
Judas Iscariot, who
also 2 betrayed him.

1 Or, Zealot. See Luke
6 15; Acts 1 13.
2 Or, delivered him up: and
so always.

[Mark]

cp. 6 30.

16 3 and Simon he
surnamed Peter;

17 and James the son
of Zebedee, and John
the brother of James;
and them he sur-
named Boanerges,
which is, Sons of thun-
der: 18 and Andrew,
and Philip,
and Bartholomew,
and Matthew,
and Thomas,
and James the son of
Alphæus, and Thad-
dæus, and Simon the
4 Cananæan,

19 and
Judas Iscariot, which
also betrayed him.

1 Some ancient authori-
ties add whom also he
named apostles. See
Luke 6 13.
2 Gr. demons.
3 Some ancient authori-
ties insert and he
appointed twelve.
4 Or, Zealot. See Luke
6 15; Acts 1 13.

[Luke]

he named apostles
[cp. 9 10; 17 5; 22
14; 24 10];
14 Simon, whom he
also named Peter [cp.
5 8], and
Andrew his brother,
and James
and John,

and Philip
and Bartholomew,
15 and Matthew
and Thomas,
and James the son of
Alphæus,
and Simon which
was called the Zealot,
16 and Judas the
1 son of James, and
Judas Iscariot, which
was the traitor;

1 Or, brother. See Jude 1.

cp. 1 42: also
1 40; 6 8;
etc.

cp. 14 22.

[Acts]

they were come in,
they went up into the
upper chamber, where
they were abiding;
both Peter

and John
and James

and Andrew,
Philip and Thomas,
Bartholomew
and Matthew,

James the son of
Alphæus,
and Simon
the Zealot,
and Judas the
1 son of James.

1 Or, brother. See Jude 1.

§ 79. Healings of the Multitude

Matt. 12 15-21	**Mark 3** 7-12	**Luke 6** 17-19	
15 And Jesus perceiving it [cp. 16 8; 22 18; 26 10]	7 And Jesus cp. 8 17.	17 and he	cp. 5 6; 6 15.

Matt. 12 15-21

15 And Jesus perceiving it
[cp. 16 8; 22 18; 26 10]

withdrew
from thence [cp. 13 1]: and
many
followed him;
4 24 And the report of him went
forth into all Syria: and they
brought unto him all that were
sick, holden with divers diseases
and torments, 1 possessed with
devils, and epileptic, and palsied;
and he healed them. 25 And there
followed him great multitudes from
Galilee and Decapolis
and
Jerusalem and Judæa
and from
beyond Jordan.

Mark 3 7-12

7 And Jesus
cp. 8 17.

with his disciples withdrew
to the sea [cp. 4 1; 5 21]: and
a great multitude

from
Galilee followed:
and from Judæa, 8 and
from Jerusalem, and
from Idumæa, and
beyond Jordan, and about
Tyre and Sidon,
a great multitude, hearing
1 what great things he did,
came unto him.

9 And he
spake to his disciples, that

Luke 6 17-19

17 and he

came down with them,
and stood on a level place,
and a great multitude
of his disciples,
[cp. 5 1] and
a great number of the people

from all Judæa and
Jerusalem,

and the
sea coast of Tyre and Sidon,

which
came to hear him, and to
be healed of their diseases;
18 and they that were
troubled with unclean spirits
were healed.

cp. 5 6; 6 15.

cp. 13 2.

a little boat [*cp.* 4 1] should wait on him because of the crowd [*cp.* 2 4], lest they should throng him: **10** for he had healed many; insomuch that as many as had [2] plagues [3] pressed upon him that they might touch him [*cp.* 5 27; 6 56: *also* 1 31, 41; *etc.*].

cp. 5 3.

19 And all the multitude [*cp.* 5 19; 8 19; 19 3]

cp. 9 20; 14 36: *also* 8 3, 15; *etc.*

cp. 5 30.

sought to touch him [*cp.* 7 39; 8 44: *also* 5 13; *etc.*]: for power came forth from him [*cp.* 4 14, 36; 5 17; 8 46: *also* 1 17, 35; 9 1; 24 49], and   healed [*cp.* 9 2, 11, 42; 14 4; 22 51] *them* all [*cp.* 4 40]. **4 41** And [1] devils also came out from many,

and he healed

them all [*cp.* 8 16],

11 And the unclean spirits, whensoever they beheld him, fell down before him [*cp.* 5 6: *also* 1 40; 5 22, 33; 7 25; 10 17], and cried, saying [*cp.* 1 24; 5 7],

[*cp.* 2 11; 8 2; 9 18; 14 33; 15 25; 17 14; 20 20; 28 9, 17] *cp.* 8 29.

[*cp.* 4 3, 6; 8 29; 14 33; 16 16; 26 63; 27 40, 43, 54: *also* 3 17; 17 5] **16** and charged them   that they should not make him known [*cp.* 8 4; 9 30: *also* 16 20; 17 9]:

Thou art the Son of God [*cp.* 1 1; 5 7; 15 39: *also* 1 11; 9 7]. **12** And he charged them much that they should not make him known [*cp.* 1 25, 34, 44; 5 43; 7 36; 8 26: *also* 8 30; 9 9: *and* 7 24; 9 30].

crying out, and saying [*cp.* 4 33; 8 28], Thou art the Son of God [*cp.* 1 35; 4 3, 9; 8 28; 22 70: *also* 3 22; 9 35]. And rebuking them,   he suffered them not to speak [*cp.* 4 35; 5 14; 8 56: *also* 9 21, 36], because they knew that he was the Christ.

cp. 9 38; 11 32; 18 6.

cp. 1 34; *etc.*

17 that it might be fulfilled which was spoken [2] by Isaiah the prophet, saying, **18** Behold, my servant whom I have chosen; My beloved in whom my soul is well pleased [*cp.* 3 17; 11 26; 17 5]: I will put my Spirit upon him, And he shall declare judgement to the Gentiles. **19** He shall not strive, nor cry aloud; Neither shall any one hear his voice in the streets. **20** A bruised reed shall he not break, And smoking flax shall he not quench, Till he send forth judgement unto victory. **21** And in his name shall the Gentiles hope.

[1] Or, *all the things that he did*   [2] Gr. *scourges.*   [3] Gr. *fell.*

[1] Gr. *demons.*

cp. 1 11.

cp. 2 14; 3 22; 10 21; 12 32.

[1] Or, *demoniacs*   [2] Or, *through*

Matt. 12 18-21 = Is. 42 1-4.

§ 80. The Appointment of the Twelve (Mark)

Matt. 10 1-4	Mark 3 13-19a	Luke 6 12-16	Acts 1 13
cp. 5 1; 14 23; 15 29; 17 1; 28 16. *cp.* 14 23; 19 13; 26 36, 39, 42, 44: *also* 11 25-26.	**13** And he goeth up into the mountain [*cp.* 6 46; 9 2], *cp.* 1 35; 6 46; 14 32, 35, 39.	**12** And it came to pass in these days, that he went out into the mountain [*cp.* 9 28] to pray [*cp.* 3 21; 5 16; 9 18, 28, 29; 11 1; 22 41, 44: *also* 10 21]; and he continued all night in prayer to God. **13** And when it was day, he called his disciples:	
		cp. 6 3, 15. *cp.* 11 41-42; 12 27-28; 17 1-26.	
1 And he called unto him	and calleth unto him whom he himself would: and they went unto him. **14** And he appointed twelve, [1] that they might be with him, and that he might send them forth to		
his twelve disciples,		and he chose from them twelve,	*cp.* 6 70; 13 18; 15 16, 19.

Matt.	Mark	(Mark cp.)		Luke
and gave them authority over unclean spirits, to cast them out [*cp.* 10 8 ; 17 16], and to heal all manner of disease and all manner of sickness. **2** Now the names of the twelve apostles	preach, **15** and to have authority to cast out ² devils [*cp.* 6 7 : *also* 6 12-13 ; 9 18] :	*cp.* 6 30.	*cp.* 9 1, 2 ; 10 1, 9 : *also* 9 6, 40 ; 10 17.	
are these : The first, Simon, who is called Peter [*cp.* 4 18 : *also* 16 16 - 18], and Andrew his brother ; James the *son* of Zebedee, and John his brother	**16** ³ and Simon he surnamed Peter ; **17** and James the *son* of Zebedee, and John the brother of James ; and them he surnamed Boanerges, which is, Sons of thunder : **18** and Andrew,		whom also he named apostles [*cp.* 9 10 ; 17 5 ; 22 14 ; 24 10] ; **14** Simon, whom he also named Peter [*cp.* 5 8], and Andrew his brother, and James and John,	**13** And when they were come in, they went up into the upper chamber, where they were abiding ; both Peter and John and James
		cp. 1 42 : *also* 1 40 ; 6 8 ; *etc.*		
3 Philip, and Bartholomew ; Thomas, and Matthew the publican [*cp.* 9 9] ; James the *son* of Alphæus, and Thaddæus ; **4** Simon the ¹ Cananæan,	and Philip, and Bartholomew, and Matthew and Thomas, and James the *son* of Alphæus, and Thaddæus, and Simon the ⁴ Cananæan,		and Philip and Bartholomew, **15** and Matthew and Thomas, and James *the son* of Alphæus, and Simon which was called the Zealot, **16** and Judas *the* ¹ *son* of James, and	and Andrew, Philip and Thomas, Bartholomew and Matthew, James *the son* of Alphæus, and Simon the Zealot, and Judas *the* ¹ *son* of James.
		cp. 14 22.		
and Judas Iscariot, who also ² betrayed him.	**19** and Judas Iscariot, which also betrayed him.		Judas Iscariot, which was the traitor.	
¹ Or, *Zealot*. See Luke 6 15; Acts 1 13. ² Or, *delivered him up* : and so always.	¹ Some ancient authorities add *whom also he named apostles*. See Luke 6 13. ² Gr. *demons*. ³ Some ancient authorities insert *and he appointed twelve*. ⁴ Or, *Zealot*. See Luke 6 15 ; Acts 1 13.		¹ Or, *brother*. See Jude 1.	¹ Or, *brother*. See Jude 1.

(vi) The Great Sermon (Luke : §§ 81–84)

§ 81. **The Beatitudes and the Woes**

Matt. 5 1-12	(Matt. cp.)	Luke 6 20-26	(Luke cp.)
			cp. 6 5.
1 And seeing the multitudes [*cp.* 3 7 ; 8 18 ; 9 36], he went up into the mountain [*cp.* 14 23 ; 15 29 ; 17 1 ; 28 16] : and when he had sat down [*cp.* 15 29 ; 24 3],	*cp.* 3 13 ; 6 46 ; 9 2. *cp.* 13 3.	*cp.* 6 12 ; 9 28.	*cp.* 6 3 : *also* 6 15.
his disciples came unto him [*cp.* 13 10, 36 ; 14 15 ; 15 12, 23 ; 17 19 ; 18 1 ; 24 1, 3 ; 26 17] : **2** and he opened his mouth and taught them, saying, **3** Blessed are the poor in spirit : for theirs is the kingdom of heaven.	*cp.* 6 35.	**20** And he lifted up his eyes on his disciples, *cp.* 9 12. and said, Blessed *are* ye poor : for yours is the kingdom of God [*cp.* 16 25].	*cp.* 6 5.
4 ¹ Blessed are they that mourn : for they shall be comforted. **5** Blessed are the meek : for they shall inherit the earth. **6** Blessed are they that hunger and thirst after righteousness [*cp.* 6 33 : *also* 3 15 ; 5 10, 20 ; 6 1 ; 21 32] : for they shall be filled.		*verse 21 : cp. also verse 25.*	*cp.* 16 20.
		21 Blessed *are* ye that hunger now :	*cp.* 7 37.
verse 4		for ye shall be filled. Blessed *are* ye that weep now : for ye shall laugh.	*cp.* 16 20.

Matthew

7 Blessed are the merciful: for they shall obtain mercy. 8 Blessed are the pure in heart: for they shall see God. 9 Blessed are the peacemakers [cp. 10 13]: for they shall be called sons of God [cp. 5 45; 8 12; 13 38]. 10 Blessed are they that have been persecuted for righteousness' [cp. 3 15; 5 6, 20; 6 1, 33; 21 32] sake: for theirs is the kingdom of heaven. 11 Blessed are ye when men shall [cp. 10 22; 24 9]

reproach you, and persecute you, and say all manner of evil against you falsely, for my sake [cp. 10 18, 39; 16 25: also 10 22; 19 29; 24 9]. 12 Rejoice, and be exceeding glad: for great is your reward in heaven: for so persecuted they the prophets [cp. 21 35-36; 22 6; 23 29-34, 37] which were before you.

¹ Some ancient authorities transpose ver. 4 and 5.

(cross-references, Mark column): cp. 9 50. — cp. 13 13. — cp. 8 35; 10 29; 13 9: also 13 13. — cp. 12 3-5.

(cross-references): cp. 6 36. — cp. 10 5, 6: also 1 79; 2 14, 29; 19 38. cp. 20 36: also 6 35; 16 8.

Luke

22 Blessed are ye, when men shall hate you [cp. 1 71; 6 27; 21 17], and when they shall separate you *from their company*, and reproach you, and cast out your name as evil, for the Son of man's sake [cp. 9 24: also 21 12, 17: and 18 29]. 23 Rejoice in that day, and leap *for joy*: for behold, your reward is great in heaven: for in the same manner did their fathers unto the prophets [cp. 11 47-50; 13 33, 34; 20 10-12]. 24 But woe unto you that are rich! for ye have received your consolation [cp. 16 25]. 25 Woe unto you, ye that are full now! for ye shall hunger. Woe *unto you*, ye that laugh now! for ye shall mourn and weep. 26 Woe *unto you*, when all men shall speak well of you! for in the same manner did their fathers to the false prophets.

(cross-references, right column): cp. 14 27; 16 33. cp. 12 36: also 1 12; 11 52. — cp. 15 18, 19; 17 14. — cp. 15 21.

Matt, 5 5: *cp.* Ps. 37 11.

§ 82. Love of Enemies and Judgement of Others

Matt. 5 44, 39-42; 7 12; 5 46-47, 45, 48; 7 1-2

5 44 But I say unto you, Love your enemies, cp. 10 22; 24 9. and pray for them that persecute you; 39 but I say unto you, Resist not ¹ him that is evil: but whosoever smiteth thee on thy right [cp. 5 29, 30; 27 29] cheek, turn to him the other also. 40 And if any man would go to law with thee, and take away thy coat, let him have thy cloke also. 41 And whosoever shall ² compel thee to go one mile, go with him twain. 42 Give to him that asketh thee, and from him that would borrow [cp. Luke 6 35] of thee turn not thou away. 7 12 All things therefore whatsoever ye would that men should do unto you, even so do ye also unto them: for this is the law and the prophets [cp. 5 17; 11 13; 22 40]. 5 46 For if ye love them that love you, what reward [cp. Luke 6 35] have ye? do not even the cp. 9 11, 13; 11 19; 26 45.

³ publicans [cp. 9 11; 11 19; 18 17; 21 31, 32]

the same?

(cross-references): cp. 13 13. — cp. 2 16, 17; 14 41. — cp. 2 16.

Luke 6 27-38

27 But I say unto you which hear, Love your enemies, do good to them that hate you [cp. 1 71; 6 22; 21 17], 28 bless them that curse you, pray for them that despitefully use you [cp. 23 34]. 29 To him that smiteth thee on the [cp. 6 6; 22 50] *one* cheek offer the other; also and from him that taketh away thy cloke withhold not thy coat also.

30 Give to every one that asketh thee; and of him that taketh away thy goods ask them not again. 31 And as ye would that men should do to you, do ye also to them likewise. cp. 16 16. 32 And if ye love them that love you, what thank have ye? for even sinners [cp. 5 8, 30, 32; 7 34, 37, 39; 15 1, 2; 18 13; 19 7; 24 7] cp. 5 30; 7 29, 34; 15 1; 18 13. love those that love them. 33 And if ye do good to them that do good to you, what thank have ye? for even sinners do the same.

(cross-references, right column): cp. 15 18, 19; 17 14. — cp. 18 10. — cp. 19 23. — cp. 9 16, 24, 25, 31.

47 And if ye salute your brethren only, what do ye more *than others* ? do not even the Gentiles [*cp.* 6 7 ; 18 17 : *also* 6 32 *and* Luke 12 30] the same ?

cp. 5 42.

45 that ye may be sons [*cp.* 5 9 ; 8 12 ; 13 38] of your Father which is in heaven [*cp.* 5 16 ; 6 1, 9 ; 7 11, 21 ; 10 32, 33 ; 12 50 ; 16 17 ; 18 10, 14, 19 : *also* 5 48 ; 6 14, 26, 32 ; 15 13 ; 18 35 ; 23 9] : for he maketh his sun to rise on the evil and the good, and sendeth rain on the just and the unjust [*cp.* 13 30]. **48** Ye therefore shall be perfect [*cp.* 19 21], as your heavenly Father [*cp.* 6 14, 26, 32 ; 15 13 ; 18 35 ; 23 9 : *also* 5 16, 45 ; 6 1, 9 ; 7 11, 21 ; 10 32, 33 ; 12 50 ; 16 17 ; 18 10, 14, 19] is perfect. **7 1** Judge not, that ye be not judged. **2** For with what judgement ye judge, ye shall be judged :

and with what measure ye mete, it shall be measured unto you.

cp. 6 33.

[1] Or, *evil*   [2] Gr. *impress.*
[2] That is, *collectors or renters of Roman taxes* : and so elsewhere.

cp. 5 7.
cp. 11 25, 26.

cp. 11 25, 26.

Mark **4 24** And he said unto them, Take heed what ye hear : with what measure ye mete it shall be measured unto you : and more shall be given unto you.

34 And if ye lend to them of whom ye hope to receive, what thank have ye ? even sinners lend to sinners, to receive again as much.

35 But love your enemies, and do *them* good, and lend, [1] never despairing ; and your reward [*cp.* Matt. 5 46] shall be great, and ye shall be sons [*cp.* 16 8 ; 20 36] of the Most High [*cp.* 1 32, 35, 76 ; 8 28] :

cp. 11 13.

for he is kind toward the unthankful and evil.

36 Be ye merciful [*cp.* Matt. 5 7], even as your Father *cp.* 11 13. is merciful.

37 And judge not, and ye shall not be judged :

and condemn not, and ye shall not be condemned : release, and ye shall be released : **38** give, and it shall be given unto you ; good measure, pressed down, shaken together, running over, shall they give into your bosom.

For with what measure ye mete it shall be measured to you again.

cp. 12 31.

[1] Some ancient authorities read *despairing of no man.*

cp. 12 36: *also* 1 12 ; 11 52.

§ 83. **The Criteria of the True Disciple** (i)

Matt. 15 14 ; 10 24-25 ; 7 3-5, 16-18 ; 12 33-35

15 14 And if the blind guide the blind [*cp.* 23 16, 17, 19, 24, 26], both shall fall into a pit. **10 24** A disciple is not above his [1]master, nor a [2]servant above his lord. **25** It is enough for the disciple that he be as his [1]master, and the [2]servant as his lord. **7 3** And why beholdest thou the mote that is in thy brother's eye, but considerest not the beam that is in thine own eye ? **4** Or how wilt thou say to thy brother, Let me cast out the mote out of thine eye ; and lo, the beam is in thine own eye ? **5** Thou hypocrite, cast out first [*cp.* 5 24 ; 6 33 ; 23 26] the beam out of thine own eye ; and then shalt thou see clearly to cast out the mote out of thy brother's eye.

cp. 7 27.

Luke 6 39-45

39 And he spake also a parable unto them, Can the blind guide the blind ? shall they not both fall into a pit ? **40** The disciple is not above his [1] master : but every one when he is perfected shall be as his [1] master. **41** And why beholdest thou the mote that is in thy brother's eye, but considerest not the beam that is in thine own eye ? **42** Or how canst thou say to thy brother, Brother, let me cast out the mote that is in thine eye, when thou thyself beholdest not the beam that is in thine own eye ? Thou hypocrite, cast out first the beam out of thine own eye, and then shalt thou see clearly to cast out the mote that is in thy brother's eye.

cp. 9 39-41.

cp. 13 16 ; 15 20.

cp. 8 7-9.

7 16 By their fruits ye shall know them. Do *men* gather grapes of thorns, or figs of thistles ? 17 Even so every good tree bringeth forth good fruit ; but the corrupt tree bringeth forth evil fruit. 18 A good tree cannot bring forth evil fruit, neither can a corrupt tree bring forth good fruit.

cp. verse 16 above.

cp. verse 33 below.

12 33 Either make the tree good, and its fruit good ; or make the tree corrupt, and its fruit corrupt :

the tree is known by its fruit.

34 Ye offspring of vipers [*cp.* 3 7 ; 23 33], how can ye, being evil [*cp.* 7 11], speak good things ? for out of the abundance of the heart the mouth speaketh [*cp.* 15 18, 19]. 35 The good man out of his good treasure [*cp.* 13 52] bringeth forth good things : and the evil man out of his evil treasure bringeth forth evil things.

verse 34

cp. verse 44.

verse 44

43 For there is no good tree that bringeth forth corrupt fruit ; nor again a corrupt tree that bringeth forth good fruit. 44 For each tree is known by its own fruit. For of thorns men do not gather figs, nor of a bramble bush gather they grapes.

cp. 3 7.
cp. 11 13.

verse 45

45 The good man out of the good treasure of his heart bringeth forth that which is good ; and the evil *man* out of the evil *treasure* bringeth forth that which is evil : for out of the abundance of the heart his mouth speaketh.

Or, *teacher*   ² Gr. *bondservant*.

¹ Or, *teacher*

§ 84. **The Criteria of the True Disciple** (ii)

Matt. 7 21-27

21 Not every one that saith unto me, Lord, Lord, shall enter into the kingdom of heaven [*cp.* 5 20 ; 18 3 ; 19 23, 24 ; 21 31 ; 23 13 : *also* 7 13 ; 18 8, 9 ; 19 17 ; 25 21, 23]; but he that doeth the will [*cp.* 12 50 ; 21 31 : *also* 6 10 ; 26 39, 42] of my Father which is in heaven [*cp.* 5 16, 45 ; 6 1, 9 ; 7 11 ; 10 32, 33 ; 12 50 ; 16 17 ; 18 10, 14, 19 : *also* 5 48 ; 6 14, 26, 32 ; 15 13 ; 18 35 ; 23 9]. 22 Many will say to me in that day, Lord, Lord, did we not prophesy by thy name, and by thy name cast out ¹ devils, and by thy name do many ² mighty works ? 23 And then will I profess unto them [*cp.* 25 34, 41], I never knew you [*cp.* 25 11, 12]: depart from me [*cp.* 25 41], ye that work iniquity. 24 Every one therefore which heareth these words of mine, and doeth them, shall be likened unto a wise [*cp.* 10 16 ; 24 45 ; 25 2 *ff.*] man, which built his house

cp. 9 47; 10 15, 23, 24, 25: *also* 9 43, 45.
cp. 3 35: *also* 14 36.
cp. 11 25, 26.

cp. 9 38.
cp. 9 39.

Luke 6 46-49

46 And why call ye me, Lord, Lord,
cp. 18 17, 24, 25: *also* 11 52 ; 13 24 ; 24 26.
and do not the things which I say ?
cp. 22 42.
cp. 11 13.

13 26 then shall ye begin to say,
We did eat and drink in thy presence,
cp. 9 49.
and thou didst teach in our streets ;
27 and he shall say,
I tell you, I know not whence ye are ; depart from me, all ye workers of iniquity.

47 Every one that cometh unto me, and heareth my words, and doeth them, I will shew you to whom he is like : 48 he is like a [*cp.* 12 42] man building a house, who digged and went deep, and laid a foundation

cp. 13 13.
cp. 3 5: *also* 10 1, 2, 9.

cp. 4 34 ; 5 30 ; 6 38 ; 7 17 ; 9 31.

upon the rock [cp. 16 18]: 25 and the rain descended, and the floods came, and the winds blew, and   beat upon that house ; and it fell not :
for it was founded upon the rock. 26 And every one that heareth these words of mine, and doeth them not, shall be likened unto a foolish [cp. 25 2 ff.] man, which built his house upon the sand :
    27 and the rain descended, and the floods came, and the winds blew, and   smote upon that house ; and   it fell : and
great was the fall thereof.

    ¹ Gr. demons.   ² Gr. powers.

Matt. 7 23 ‖ Luke 13 27 = Ps. 6 8.

upon the rock :   and when a flood arose, the stream brake against that house, and could not shake it : ¹ because it had been well builded. 49 But he   that heareth, and doeth not,   is like a man that built a house upon the earth without a foundation ;

against which the stream brake,   and straightway it fell in ; and the ruin of that house was great.

    ¹ Many ancient authorities read *for it had been founded upon the rock*: as in Matt. 7 25.

(vii) Events in Galilee III (§§ 85-92)

§ 85. The Centurion at Capernaum

Matt. 7 28; 8 5-13	Luke 7 1-10	John 4 46-53
7 28 And it came to pass, when Jesus ended these words [cp. 11 1; 13 53; 19 1; 26 1], the multitudes were astonished at his teaching.	1 After he had ended all his sayings in the ears of the people,	
8 5 And when he was entered into Capernaum,	he entered into Capernaum. 2 And a certain centurion's ¹servant, who was ²dear unto him, was sick and at the point of death [cp. 8 42]. 3 And when he heard concerning Jesus,	46 And there was a certain ¹nobleman, whose son was sick at Capernaum.
there came unto him a centurion, beseeching him,	he sent unto him elders of the Jews, asking him that he would come and save his ¹servant.	47 When he heard that Jesus was come out of Judæa into Galilee, he went unto him, and besought *him* that he would come down, and heal his son ; for he was at the point of death. 48 Jesus therefore said unto him, Except ye see signs and wonders, ye will in no wise believe. 49 The ¹nobleman saith unto him, ²Sir, come down ere my child die.
6 and saying, Lord. my ¹servant lieth in the house sick of the palsy [cp. 4 24; 9 2 ff.], grievously tormented [cp. 4 24].	cp. 2 3 ff.	cp. 5 18 ff.
7 And he saith unto him, I will come and heal him. 8 And the centurion answered and said, Lord, I am not ²worthy that thou	4 And they, when they came to Jesus, besought him earnestly, saying, He is worthy that thou shouldest do this for him : 5 for he loveth our nation, and himself built us our synagogue. 6 And Jesus went with them. And when he was now not far from the house, the centurion sent friends to him, saying unto him, Lord, trouble [cp. 8 49] not thyself : for I am not ³ worthy that thou	
	cp. 5 35.	

[Matthew]

shouldest come under my roof:

but only say 3 the word [cp. 8 16: also 8 3, 13, 32; 9 6, 22, 29; 12 13; 15 28; 17 7, 18], and my 1 servant shall be healed. 9 For I also am a man 4 under authority, having under myself soldiers: and I say to this one, Go, and he goeth; and to another, Come, and he cometh; and to my 5 servant, Do this, and he doeth it. 10 And when Jesus heard it, he marvelled, [cp. 9 22; 16 23]

and said to them that followed, Verily I say unto you, 6 I have not found so great faith, no, not in Israel. 11 And I say unto you that many shall come from the east and the west, and shall 7 sit down [cp. 26 29]

with Abraham, and Isaac, and Jacob, in the kingdom of heaven [cp. 21 31, 41, 43; 22 7-10: also 10 18; 24 14; 26 13; 28 19]: 12 but the sons of the kingdom [cp. 13 38: also 5 9, 45] shall be cast forth into the outer darkness [cp. 22 13; 25 30]: there shall be the weeping and gnashing of teeth [cp. 13 42, 50; 22 13; 24 51; 25 30].

13 And Jesus said unto the centurion, Go thy way; as thou hast believed, so be it done unto thee [cp. 9 29; 15 28].

And the 1 servant was healed in that hour [cp. 9 22 15 28; 17 18].

[cross-references, Mark]

cp. 1 25, 41; 2 11; 3 5; 5 8, 34 41; 7 29, 34; 9 25; 10 52.

cp. 5 30; 8 33.

cp. 14 25.

cp. 12 9; 13 10; 14 9; 16 15.

cp. 19 30; 20 16.

cp. 7 29.

cp. 7 30.

cp. 1 31.

cp. 10 31.

[Luke]

shouldest come under my roof: 7 wherefore neither thought I myself worthy to come unto thee: but 4 say the word [cp. 4 35, 39; 5 13, 24; 6 10; 7 14; 8 29, 32, 48, 54; 9 42; 13 12; 17 14; 18 42], and my 5 servant shall be healed. 8 For I also am a man set under authority, having under myself soldiers: and I say to this one, Go, and he goeth; and to another, Come, and he cometh; and to my 1 servant, Do this, and he doeth it. 9 And when Jesus heard these things, he marvelled at him, and turned [cp. 7 44; 9 55; 10 23; 14 25; 22 61; 23 28] and said unto the multitude that followed him, I say unto you, I have not found so great faith, no, not in Israel.

cp. 14 15; 22 16, 18, 30.

13 28 There shall be the weeping and gnashing of teeth, when ye shall see Abraham, and Isaac, and Jacob, and all the prophets, in the kingdom of God [cp. 14 21-24; 20 16: also 2 30-32; 3 6; 24 47], and yourselves cp. 6 35; 16 8; 20 36. cast forth without.

29 And they shall come from the east and west, and from the north and south, and shall 6 sit down in the kingdom of God. 30 And behold, there are last which shall be first, and there are first which shall be last.

10 And they that were sent, returning to the house, found the 1 servant whole.

cp. 4 39.

[John]

cp. 4 50; 5 8; 9 7; 11 43.

cp. 1 38.

cp. 10 16; 11 52.

cp. 12 36: also 1 12; 11 52.

50 Jesus saith unto him, Go thy way; thy son liveth. The man believed the word that Jesus spake unto him, and he went his way.

51 And as he was now going down, his 3 servants met him, saying, that his son lived.

52 So he inquired of them the hour when he began to amend. They said therefore unto him, Yesterday at the seventh hour the fever left him. 53 So the father knew that it was at that hour in which Jesus said unto him, Thy son liveth: and himself believed, and his whole house.

---

cp. 8 15.

---

1 Or, boy   2 Gr. sufficient.
3 Gr. with a word.
4 Some ancient authorities insert set: as in Luke 7 8.
5 Gr. bondservant.
6 Many ancient authorities read With no man in Israel have I found so great faith.   7 Gr. recline.

1 Gr. bondservant.
2 Or, precious to him Or, honourable with him.
3 Gr. sufficient.
4 Gr. say with a word.   5 Or, boy
6 Gr. recline.

1 Or, king's officer   2 Or, Lord
3 Gr. bondservants.

§ 86. The Widow's Son at Nain

[*Cp.* Matt. 9 18-26 ‖ Mark 5 21-43 ‖ Luke 8 40-56: John 11 1-46]

Luke 7 11-17

	cp. 5 35; 9 26.		
	cp. 12 40, 42.		
	cp. 16 19, 20.		
cp. 9 36; *etc.*	*cp.* 1 41; *etc.*		*cp.* 4 1; 6 23; 11 2; 20 2, 18; *etc.*
	cp. 5 39.		
cp. 8 3, 15; *etc.*	*cp.* 1 41; 3 10; *etc.*		*cp.* 20 13, 15.
cp. 9 6.	*cp.* 2 11; 3 3; 5 41.		*cp.* 5 8.
cp. 9 8; 17 6; *etc.*	*cp.* 4 41; 5 15, 33; *etc.*		
cp. 9 8; *etc.*	*cp.* 2 12.		*cp.* 9 24.
cp. 13 57; 21 11, 46.	*cp.* 6 4, 15.		*cp.* 4 19, 44; 6 14; 7 40; 9 17.
cp. 4 24; 9 26.	*cp.* 1 28.		

11 And it came to pass [1] soon afterwards, that he went to a city called Nain; and his disciples went with him, and a great multitude. **12** Now when he drew near to the gate of the city, behold, there was carried out one that was dead [*cp.* 8 49], the only [*cp.* 8 42; 9 38] son of his mother, and she was a widow [*cp.* 2 37; 4 25, 26; 18 3; 20 47; 21 2]: and much people of the city was with her. **13** And when the Lord [*cp.* 7 19; 10 1, 39, 41; 11 39; 12 42; 13 15; 17 5, 6; 18 6; 19 8; 22 61; 24 3, 34] saw her, he had compassion [*cp.* 10 33; 15 20] on her, and said unto her, Weep not [*cp.* 8 52; 23 28]. **14** And he came nigh and touched [*cp.* 5 13; 6 19; 7 39; 8 44; 18 15; 22 51: *also* 4 40; 8 54; 13 13; 14 4] the bier: and the bearers stood still. And he said, Young man, I say unto thee, Arise [*cp.* 5 24; 6 8; 8 54]. **15** And he that was dead sat up, and began to speak. And he gave him to his mother [*cp.* 9 42]. **16** And fear [*cp.* 1 12, 65; 2 9; 5 26; 8 25, 35, 37, 47; 9 34, 45; 24 5, 37] took hold on all: and they glorified God [*cp.* 2 20; 5 25, 26; 13 13; 17 15, 18; 18 43; 23 47], saying, A great prophet [*cp.* 4 24; 7 39; 13 33; 24 19] is arisen among us: and, God hath visited [*cp.* 1 68, 78] his people. **17** And this report went forth concerning him in the whole of Judæa, and all the region round about [*cp.* 4 14, 37; 5 15].

[1] Many ancient authorities read *on the next day*.

Luke 7 15: *cp.* I Kings 17 23.

§ 87. The Question of John the Baptist and the Testimony of Jesus concerning him

Matt. 11 2-19

	cp. 1 14; 6 17.	
	cp. 2 18; 6 29.	
	cp. 16 19, 20.	
	cp. 11 9.	
	cp. 6 3; 14 27, 29: *also* 4 17.	

2 Now when John heard in the prison [*cp.* 4 12; 14 3] the works of the Christ [*cp.* 1 17], he sent   by his disciples [*cp.* 9 14; 14 12],

3 and said unto him, Art thou he that cometh [*cp.* 3 11; 21 9; 23 39], or look we for another?
          cp. 18 1; 26 55.

4 And Jesus answered and said unto them, Go your way and tell John the things which ye do hear and see: **5** the blind receive their sight, and the lame walk, and the lepers are cleansed, and the deaf hear [*cp.* 15 31], and the dead are raised up, and the poor have [1] good tidings preached
          to them.
6 And blessed is he, whosoever shall find none occasion of stumbling [*cp.* 13 57; 15 12; 26 31, 33: *also* 13 21; 24 10] in me. **7** And as these

went their way, Jesus began to

Luke 7 18-35

		cp. 3 24.
		cp. 1 35, 37; 3 25; 4 1.
		cp. 4 1; 6 23; 11 2; 20 2, 18, 20, 25; 21 7, 12.
		cp. 1 15, 27; 3 31; 6 14; 11 27; 12 13.
		cp. 6 61: *also* 16 1.

18 And the disciples of John told him of all these things. **19** And John
          cp. 3 20.

calling unto him [1] two of his disciples [*cp.* 5 33; 11 1] sent them to the Lord [*cp.* 7 13; 10 1, 39, 41; 11 39; 12 42; 13 15; 17 5, 6; 18 6; 19 8; 22 61; 24 34; *also* 24 3], saying, Art thou he that cometh, or look we for another? **20** And when the men were come unto him, they said, John the Baptist hath sent us unto thee, saying, Art thou he that cometh [*cp.* 13 35; 19 38], or look we for another? **21** In that hour [*cp.* 10 21; 13 31] he cured many of diseases and [2] plagues and evil spirits; and on many that were blind he bestowed sight. **22** And he answered and said unto them, Go your way, and tell John what things ye have seen and heard; the blind receive their sight,   the lame walk, the lepers are cleansed, and the deaf hear,   the dead are raised up,   the poor have [3] good tidings preached [*cp.* 1 19; 2 10; 3 18; 4 18, 43; 8 1; 9 6; 16 16; 20 1] to them [*cp.* 4 18]. **23** And blessed is he, whosoever shall find none occasion of stumbling
          in me. **24** And when the messengers of John were departed, he began to

say unto the multitudes concerning John, What went ye out into the wilderness to behold? a reed shaken with the wind? **8** But what went ye out for to see? a man clothed in soft *raiment*? Behold, they that wear soft *raiment*

are in kings' houses. **9** [2] But wherefore went ye out? to see a prophet [*cp.* 14 5; 21 26]? Yea, I say unto you, and much more than a prophet. **10** This is he, of whom it is written,

Behold, I send my messenger before thy face,
Who shall prepare thy way before thee.

11 Verily I say unto you, Among them that are born of women there hath not arisen a greater than John the Baptist: yet he that is [3] but little   in the kingdom of heaven is greater [*cp.* 5 19; 18 1, 4] than he.

cp. 21 32.

cp. 21 25, 32: *also* 3 7.

cp. 9 13; 21 31.
12 And from the days of John the Baptist until now the kingdom of heaven suffereth violence, and men of violence take it by force. **13** For all the prophets and the law [*cp.* 5 17; 7 12   22 40] prophesied until John.

14 And if ye are willing to receive [4] *it*, this is Elijah, which is to come [*cp.* 17 12, 13: *also* 3 3, 4]. **15** He that hath ears [5] to hear, let him hear [*cp.* 13 9, 43: *also* 19 12]. **16** But whereunto   shall I liken this generation?

It is like unto children sitting in the market-places, which call unto their fellows, **17** and say, We piped unto you, and ye did not dance; we wailed, and ye did not [6] mourn. **18** For John   came neither eating [*cp.* 3 4]   nor drinking, and they say, He hath a [7] devil. **19** The Son of man   came eating and drinking, and they say, Behold, a gluttonous man, and a wine-bibber, a friend of publicans and sinners [*cp.* 9 11]!

And wisdom [8] is justified by   her   [9] works.

¹ Or, *the gospel*
² Many ancient authorities read *But what went ye out to see? a prophet?*
³ Gr. *lesser.*   ⁴ Or, *him*
⁵ Some ancient authorities omit *to hear.*
⁶ Gr. *beat the breast.*   ⁷ Gr. *demon.*
⁸ Or, *was*
⁹ Many ancient authorities read *children*: as in Luke 7 35.

---

cp. 11 32.

1 2

cp. 11 31.
cp. 2 17.

cp. 9 13: *also* 1 2-3, 6.
cp. 4 9, 23; 7 16.

cp. 1 6.

cp. 2 16.

---

say unto the multitudes concerning John, What went ye out into the wilderness to behold? a reed shaken with the wind? **25** But what went ye out   to see? a man clothed in soft raiment? Behold, they which are gorgeously apparelled, and live delicately, are in king's courts. **26** But what went ye out to see? a prophet [*cp.* 1 76; 20 6]? Yea, I say unto you, and much more than a prophet. **27** This is he of whom it is written,

Behold, I send my messenger before thy face,
Who shall prepare thy way before thee [*cp.* 1 17, 76].

28 I say unto you, Among them that are born of women there is none greater than John: yet he that is [4] but little [*cp.* 9 48] in the kingdom of God is greater   than he. **29** And all the people [*cp.* 3 10] when they heard, and the publicans [*cp.* 3 12], justified God, [5] being baptized with the baptism of John. **30** But the Pharisees and the lawyers rejected for themselves [*cp.* 20 5] the counsel of God, [6] being not baptized of him [*cp.* 5 32; 7 47; 15 7, 10; 18 14; 19 10].

16 16 The law and the prophets

were until John: from that time the gospel of the kingdom of God is preached [*cp.* 1 19; 2 10; 3 18; 4 18, 43; 7 22; 8 1; 9 6; 20 1], and every man entereth violently into it.

cp. 1 17.

cp. 8 8; 14 35.
31 Whereunto then shall I liken the men of this generation, and to what are they like? **32** They are like unto children that sit in the market-place, and call one to another; which say, We piped unto you, and ye did not dance; we wailed, and ye did not weep. **33** For John the Baptist is come   eating no bread nor drinking wine [*cp.* 1 15]; and ye say, He hath a [7] devil. **34** The Son of man is come eating [*cp.* 7 36] and drinking; and ye say, Behold, a gluttonous man, and a wine-bibber, a friend of publicans and sinners [*cp.* 5 30: *also* 7 37, 39; 15 2; 19 7]! **35** And wisdom [*cp.* 11 49] [8] is justified of all her children.

¹ Gr. *certain two.*   ² Gr. *scourges.*
³ Or, *the gospel*   ⁴ Gr. *lesser.*
⁵ Or, *having been*   ⁶ Or, *not having been*
⁷ Gr. *demon.*   ⁸ Or, *was*

---

cp. 1 21, 23; 3 28.

cp. 1 21.

cp. 6 60.

Matt. 11 5 ‖ Luke 7 22 : *cp.* Is. 29 18-19; 35 5-6; 61 1.
Matt. 11 10 ‖ Luke 7 27 = Exod. 23 20; Mal. 3 1.   Matt. 11 14 : *cp.* Mal. 4 5.

§ 88. The Anointing in Galilee

Matt. 26 6-13	Mark 14 3-9	Luke 7 36-50	John 12 1-8
		36 And one of the Pharisees desired him that he would eat [*cp.* 7 34] with him. And he entered into the Pharisee's house,	
6 Now when Jesus was in Bethany, in the house of Simon the leper,	**3** And while he was in Bethany in the house of Simon the leper,	*cp.* 7 40, 43, 44.	**1** Jesus therefore six days before the passover came to Bethany, where Lazarus was, whom Jesus raised from the dead. **2** So they made him a supper there: and Martha served; but Lazarus was one of them that sat at meat with him.
		cp. 10 40.	
7 there came unto him a woman	as he sat at meat, there came a woman	and sat down to meat [*cp* 11 37; 14 1]. **37** And behold, a woman which was in the city, a sinner [*cp.* 7 34]; and when she knew that he was sitting at meat in the Pharisee's house, she brought **1** an alabaster cruse of ointment,	**3** Mary therefore
having **1** an alabaster cruse of exceeding precious ointment, and she poured it upon his head, as he sat at meat.	having **1** an alabaster cruse of ointment of **2** spikenard very costly *and* she brake the cruse, and poured it over his head.	**38** and standing behind at his feet [*cp.* 8 35; 10 39], weeping, she began to wet his feet with her tears, and wiped them with the hair of her head, and **2** kissed his feet, and anointed them with the ointment.	took a pound of ointment of **1** spikenard, very precious, and anointed the feet of Jesus, and wiped his feet with her hair: and the house was filled with the odour of the ointment.
8 But when the disciples saw it, they had indignation, saying, To what purpose is this waste? **9** For this *ointment* might have been sold for much, and given to the poor.	**4** But there were some that had indignation among themselves, *saying,* To what purpose hath this waste of the ointment been made? **5** For this ointment might have been sold for above three hundred **3** pence, and given to the poor. And they murmured against her [*cp.* 10 13].	**39** Now when the Pharisee which had bidden him saw it, he spake within himself [*cp.* 11 38], saying,	**4** But Judas Iscariot, one of his disciples, which should betray him, saith, **5** Why was not this ointment sold for three hundred **2** pence, and given to the poor? **6** Now this he said, not because he cared for the poor; but because he was a thief, and having the **3** bag [*cp.* 13 29] **4** took away what was put therein. **7** Jesus therefore
cp. 15 23; 19 13.		*cp.* 18 15.	*cp.* 5 6; 6 15. said,
10 But Jesus perceiving it [*cp.* 12 15; 16 8; 22 18] said unto them, Why trouble ye the woman? for she hath wrought a good work upon me. *cp.* 19 14.	**6** But Jesus *cp.* 8 17. said, Let her alone; why trouble ye her? she hath wrought a good work on me. *cp.* 10 14.	*cp.* 18 16.	**5** Suffer her to keep it against

[Matt.]

11 For
ye have the poor
always with you ;

but me ye have not
always.
12 For in that she ² poured
this ointment upon my body,
she did it to prepare
me for burial.
13 Verily I say unto you,
Wheresoever ³ this gospel [cp.
4 23; 9 35; 24 14]
shall
be preached in the
whole world [cp. 24 14: also 8 11;
10 18; 21 31, 41, 43; 22 7-10; 28
19], that also which this woman
hath done shall be spoken
of for a memorial of her.

¹ Or, a flask   ² Gr. cast.
³ Or, these good tidings

[Mark]

7 For
ye have the poor
always with you, and whensoever ye will ye can do them
good : but me ye have not
always. 8 She hath done what
she could :   she hath
anointed   my body
aforehand
for the burying. 9 And
verily I say unto you,
Wheresoever the gospel [cp.
1 1, 14, 15; 8 35; 10 29;
13 10;   16 15] shall
be preached throughout the
whole world [cp. 13 10: also
12 9; 16 15],
that also which this woman
hath done shall be spoken
of for a memorial of her.

¹ Or, a flask
² Gr. pistic nard, pistic being
perhaps a local name. Others
take it to mean genuine; others,
liquid.
³ See marginal note on Matt. 18 28.

cp. 2 30-32;
3 6; etc.

[Luke]

the day of my burying. 8 For
the poor ye have
always with you ;

but me ye have not
always.

cp. 10 16; 11 52.

¹ See marginal note on Mark 14 3.
² See marginal note on Matt. 18 28.
³ Or, box
⁴ Or, carried what was put therein
⁵ Or, Let her alone: it was that she
might keep it

---

cp. 13 57;   cp. 6 4, 15.
21 11, 46.

cp. 9 11;   cp. 2 16.
11 19.
cp. 26 6.   cp. 14 3.
cp. 18 23-34.

cp. 18 25.

cp. 9 22;   cp. 5 30;
16 23.   8 33.

cp. 9 13;   cp. 2 17.
21 31.
cp. 9 2.   cp. 2 5.
cp. 8 27;   cp. 1 27; 2 7;
21 10.   4 41.
cp. 9 22.   cp. 5 34;
10 52.

This man, if he were ³ a prophet [cp. 4 24; 7 16; 13 33; 24 19],
would have perceived who and what manner of woman this
is which toucheth [cp. 6 19; 8 44: Matt. 9 20; 14 36: Mark
3 10; 5 27; 6 56: John 20 17] him, that she is a sinner
[cp. 5 30; 15 2; 19 7]. 40 And Jesus answering said unto him,
Simon, I have somewhat to say unto thee. And he saith,
⁴ Master, say on. 41 A certain lender had two debtors : the one
owed five hundred ⁵ pence, and the other fifty. 42 When they
had not wherewith to pay, he forgave them both. Which of
them therefore will love him most? 43 Simon answered and
said, He, I suppose, to whom he forgave the most. And he
said unto him, Thou hast rightly judged [cp. 10 28]. 44 And
turning [cp. 7 9; 9 55; 10 23; 14 25; 22 61; 23 28] to the
woman, he said unto Simon, Seest thou this woman? I entered
into thine house, thou gavest me no water for my feet : but she
hath wetted my feet with her tears, and wiped them with her
hair. 45 Thou gavest me no kiss : but she, since the time I
came in, hath not ceased to ⁶ kiss my feet. 46 My head with
oil thou didst not anoint : but she hath anointed my feet with
ointment. 47 Wherefore I say unto thee, Her sins, which are
many, are forgiven; for she loved much : but to whom little
is forgiven, the same loveth little [cp. 5 32; 7 29, 30; 15 7, 10;
18 14; 19 10]. 48 And he said unto her, Thy sins are
forgiven [cp. 5 20]. 49 And they that sat at meat with him
began to say ⁷ within themselves, Who is this [cp. 5 21: also 4 36;
8 25; 9 9] that even forgiveth sins? 50 And he said unto the
woman, Thy faith hath saved thee [cp. 8 48; 17 19; 18 42];
go in peace [cp. 8 48].

¹ Or, a flask   ² Gr. kissed much.
³ Some ancient authorities read the prophet. See John 1 21, 25.
⁴ Or, Teacher   ⁵ See footnote on Matt. 18 28.
⁶ Gr. kiss much.   ⁷ Or, among

cp. 4 19, 44;
6 14; 7 40;
9 17.

cp. 1 38.

cp. 5 12:
also 12 34.

---

§ 89. A Controversy about Casting out Devils

Matt. 12 22-37	Matt. 9 32-34; 7 16-18	Mark 3 19b-30	Luke 11 14-23; 12 10; 6 43-45
		And he cometh ¹ into a house. 20 And the multitude cometh together again, so that they could not so much as eat bread [cp. 6 31]. 21 And when his friends	

22 Then was brought unto him [1] one possessed with a devil, blind [*cp.* 9 27] and dumb: and he healed him, insomuch that the dumb man spake and saw. **23** And all the multitudes were amazed,

and said, Is this the son of David [*cp.* 1 1; 9 27; 15 22; 20 30, 31; 21 9, 15]? **24** But when the Pharisees

heard it, they said, This man doth not cast out [2] devils, but [3] by Beelzebub [*cp.* 10 25] the prince of the [2] devils.

---

cp. 13 57-58.
9 **32** And as they went forth, behold, there was brought to him a dumb man possessed with a [1] devil.

33 And when the [1] devil was cast out, the dumb man spake: and the multitudes marvelled [*cp.* 8 27; 15 31; 21 20; 27 14: *also* 7 28; 13 54; 19 25; 22 22, 33], saying, It was never so seen in Israel.

34 But the Pharisees

cp. 15 1.
said,

[2] By the prince of the [3] devils casteth he out [3] devils.

[1] Gr. *demon.* [2] Or, *In* [3] Gr. *demons.*

---

heard it, they went out to lay hold on him [*cp.* 3 31]: for they said, He is beside himself [*cp.* 6 3-6].

cp. 2 12; 5 20, 42; 6 51; 7 37; 10 32; 15 5; 16 5, 8: *also* 1 22, 27; 6 2; 10 24, 26; 11 18; 12 17.

cp. 10 47, 48.

22 And the scribes which came down from Jerusalem [*cp.* 7 1] said, He hath Beelzebub, and,

[2] By the prince of the [3] devils casteth he out the [3] devils.

---

11 **14** And he was casting out a [1] devil *which was* dumb. And it came to pass, when the [1] devil was gone out, the dumb man spake; and the multitudes marvelled [*cp.* 5 9, 26; 8 25, 56; 9 43; 24 12, 41: *also* 2 47, 48; 4 22, 32, 36 20 26].

cp. 1 32; 18 38, 39.

15 But some of them

cp. 5 17.
said,

[2] By Beelzebub the prince of the [3] devils casteth he out [3] devils.

---

cp. 7 5.

cp. 7 15, 21, 46.

cp. 1 19.

cp. 7 20; 8 48, 52; 10 20.

---

cp. 16 1: *also* 19 3; 22 18, 35: *and* 12 38.

25 And knowing their thoughts [*cp.* 9 4; 16 8] he said unto them,

Every kingdom divided against itself is brought to desolation; and every city or house divided against itself shall not stand: **26** And if Satan casteth out Satan, he is divided against himself; how then shall his kingdom stand?

27 And if I [3] by Beelzebub cast out [2] devils, [3] by whom do your sons cast them out? therefore shall they be your judges. **28** But if I [3] by the Spirit of God cast out [2] devils, then is the kingdom of God come upon you [*cp.* 3 2; 4 17; 10 7].
29 Or how can one enter

---

cp. 8 11: *also* 10 2; 12 15.

23 And he
cp. 2 8; 8 17.
called them unto him, and said unto them in parables, How can Satan cast out Satan? **24** And if a kingdom be divided against itself, that kingdom cannot stand. **25** And if a house be divided against itself, that house will not be able to stand. **26** And if Satan hath risen up against himself, and is divided, he cannot stand, but hath an end.

cp. 1 15; 6 12.

27 But no one can enter

---

16 And others, tempting *him* [*cp.* 10 25], sought of him a sign from heaven. **17** But he, knowing their thoughts [*cp.* 5 22; 6 8; 9 47], said unto them,

Every kingdom divided against itself is brought to desolation; [4] and a house *divided* against a house falleth. **18** And if Satan also is divided against himself, how shall his kingdom stand? because ye say that I cast out [3] devils [2] by Beelzebub. **19** And if I [2] by Beelzebub cast out [3] devils, by whom do your sons cast them out? therefore shall they be your judges. **20** But if I by the finger of God cast out [3] devils, then is the kingdom of God come upon you [*cp.* 9 2; 10 9, 11; 17 20, 21; 19 11; 21 8].

---

cp. 8 6.
cp. 2 18; 6 30.

cp. 1 48; 2 24, 25; 4 19, 29; 5 6, 42; 6 61; 11 14; 13 18; 16 19, 30; 18 4; 21 17.

into the house of the strong *man,*

and spoil his goods, except he first bind the strong *man* ? and then

he will spoil his house. **30** He that is not with me is against me ; and he that gathereth not with me scattereth.
31 Therefore I say unto you, Every sin and blasphemy shall be forgiven [4] unto men ;

but the blasphemy against the Spirit shall not be forgiven. **32** And whosoever shall speak a word against the Son of man, it shall be forgiven him ; but whosoever shall speak against the Holy Spirit, it shall not be forgiven him, neither in this [5] world, nor in that which is to come.
cp. 18 8 ; 25 41, 46.

cp. verse 33 below.

33 Either make the tree good, and its fruit good ; or make the tree corrupt, and its fruit corrupt :

for the tree is known by its fruit.

34 Ye offspring of vipers [*cp.* 3 7 ; 23 33], how can ye, being evil [*cp.* 7 11], speak good things ? for out of the abundance of the heart the mouth speaketh [*cp.* 15 18, 19]. **35** The good man out of his good treasure [*cp.* 13 52] bringeth forth good things : and the evil man out of his evil treasure bringeth forth evil things.
verse 34
36 And I say unto you, that every idle word that men shall speak, they shall give account thereof in the day of judgement [*cp.* 10 15 ; 11 22, 24]. **37** For by thy words thou shalt be justified, and by thy words thou shalt be condemned.

[1] Or, *a demoniac*   [2] Gr. *demons.*   [3] Or, *in*
[4] Some ancient authorities read *unto you men.*
[5] Or, *age*

---

into the house of the strong *man,*

and spoil his goods, except he first bind the strong *man* ; and then

he will spoil his house.

cp. 9 40.
28 Verily I say unto you, All their sins shall be forgiven unto the sons of men, and their blasphemies wherewith soever they shall blaspheme :

29 but whosoever shall blaspheme against the Holy Spirit hath never forgiveness,

cp. 10 30.
but is guilty of an eternal sin : **30** because they said, He hath an unclean spirit.

[1] Or, *home*   [2] Or, *In*   [3] Gr. *demons.*

7 16 By their fruits ye shall know them. Do *men* gather grapes of thorns, or figs of thistles ? **17** Even so every good tree bringeth forth good fruit ; but the corrupt tree bringeth forth evil fruit. **18** A good tree cannot bring forth evil fruit, neither can a corrupt tree bring forth good fruit.
cp. verse 16 above.

verse 16 above

---

21 When the strong *man* fully armed guardeth his own court, his goods are in peace :
22 but when a stronger than he shall come upon him, and overcome him, he taketh from him his whole armour wherein he trusted, and divideth his spoils.
23 He that is not with me is against me ; and he that gathereth not with me scattereth [*cp.* 9 50].

12 10 And everyone who shall speak a word against the Son of man, it shall be forgiven him : but unto him that blasphemeth against the Holy Spirit it shall not be forgiven.

cp. 18 30.

6 44

6 43 For there is no good tree that bringeth forth corrupt fruit ; nor again a corrupt tree that bringeth forth good fruit. **44** For each tree is known by its own fruit. For of thorns men do not gather figs, nor of a bramble bush gather they grapes.
cp. 3 7.
cp. 11 13.

verse 45
45 The good man out of the good treasure of his heart bringeth forth that which is good ; and the evil *man* out of the evil *treasure* bringeth forth that which is evil : for out of the abundance of the heart his mouth speaketh.

[1] Gr. *demon.*   [2] Or, *In*   [3] Gr. *demons.*
[4] Or, *and house falleth upon house*

§ 90. **A Request for a Sign refused**

Matt. 12 38-45	Matt. 16 1-2, 4	Mark 8 11-13	Luke 11 29-32, 24-26	

38 Then certain of the scribes and   Pharisees

                    1 And the Pharisees and Sadducees came, and tempting him [*cp.* 19 3; 22 35: *also* 22 18]

                        11 And the Pharisees   came forth, and

                                                29 And when the multitudes   were gathering together unto him,
                                cp. 10 25; 11 16.   *cp.* 8 6.

                        began to question with him [*cp* 9 14, 16; 12 28],

answered him, saying, 1 Master,   we would see a sign from thee.

            asked him to shew them a sign from heaven.

            seeking of him a sign from heaven, tempting him [*cp.* 10 2: *also* 12 15].

                    11 16   *cp.* 2 18; 6 30.
            cp. 10 25; 11 16.   *cp.* 8 6.

39 But he

    2 But he

12 And he sighed deeply [*cp.* 7 34] in his spirit, and saith, Why doth this generation

            answered and said unto them,

                    answered and said unto them, . . .

            he began to say,   This generation is an evil   generation

            An evil and adulterous generation [*cp.* 12 45] seeketh after a sign;

        4 An evil and adulterous generation [*cp.* 17 17] seeketh after a sign;

cp. 8 38; 9 19. seek   a sign? verily I say unto you,

[*cp.* 9 41]: it seeketh after a sign;

and there shall no sign be given to it

and there shall no sign be given unto it,

        There shall no sign be given unto this generation.

and there shall no sign be given to it

        but the sign of Jonah the prophet:

        but the sign of Jonah. And he left them, and   departed.

                                                but the sign of Jonah.

13 And he left them, and again entering into *the boat* departed to the other side.

40 for
    as Jonah
was three days and three nights in the belly of the 2 whale; so shall the Son of man
    be three days and three nights in the heart of the earth [*cp.* 16 21; 17 23; 20 19; 26 61; 27 40, 63, 64].
41 The men of Nineveh shall stand up in the judgement with this generation, and shall condemn it: for they repented at the preaching of Jonah; and behold, 3 a greater than Jonah is here [*cp.* 12 6]. **42** The queen of the south shall rise up in the judgement with   this generation, and shall condemn it: for she came from the ends of the earth to hear the wisdom of Solomon; and behold, 3 a greater than Solomon is here [*cp.* 12 6].

cp. 8 31; 9 31; 10 34; 14 58; 15 29.

                30 For
even as Jonah became a sign unto the Ninevites,
            so shall also the Son of man be to this generation.
    cp. 9 22; 13 32; 18 33; 24 7, 21, 46.

cp. 2 19-22.

                verse 32

                31 The queen of the south shall rise up in the judgement with the men of this generation, and shall condemn them: for she came from the ends of the earth to hear the wisdom of Solomon; and behold, 1 a greater than Solomon is here. **32** The men of Nineveh shall stand up in the judgement with this generation, and shall condemn it: for they repented at the preaching of Jonah; and behold, 1 a greater than Jonah is here. **24** The unclean spirit when 2 he is gone out of the man, passeth through waterless places, seeking rest; and finding none, 2 he saith, I will turn back unto my house whence I came out. **25** And when 2 he is come, 2 he findeth it   swept and garnished. **26** Then goeth 2 he, and taketh *to him* seven other spirits more evil than 3 himself; and they enter in and dwell there: and the last state of that

            verse 41

43 But the unclean spirit, when 4 he is gone out of the man, passeth through waterless places, seeking rest, and findeth it not. **44** Then 4 he saith, I will return into my house whence I came out; and when 4 he is come, 4 he findeth it empty,   swept,   and garnished. **45** Then goeth 4 he, and taketh with 5 himself seven other spirits more evil than 5 himself, and they enter in and dwell there: and the last state of that

man becometh worse than the first. Even so shall it be also unto this evil generation [*cp. verse* 39].	man becometh worse than the first.
[1] Or, *Teacher* [2] Gr. *sea-monster*. [3] Gr. *more than*. [4] Or, *it* [5] Or, *itself*	[1] Gr. *more than*. [2] Or, *it* [3] Or, *itself*

Matt. 12 39 ; 16 4 ‖ Luke 11 29 : *cp.* Jonah 3 4.   Matt. 12 40 : *cp.* Jonah 1 17.   Matt. 12 41 ‖ Luke 11 32 : *cp.* Jonah 3 5.
Matt. 12 42 ‖ Luke 11 31 : *cp.* I Kings 10 1 *ff.*

§ 91. The True Brethren of Jesus
[*Cp.* Luke 11 27-28]

Matt. 12 46-50	**Mark 3** 31-35	Luke 8 19-21	
46 While he was yet speaking [*cp.* 17 5; 26 47] to the multitudes, behold, his mother and his brethren	*cp.* 5 35; 14 43. **31** And there come his mother and his brethren [*cp.* 3 21] ;	*cp.* 8 49; 22 47, 60. **19** And there came to him his mother and brethren, and they could not come at him for the crowd [*cp.* 5 19; 19 3].	
stood without, seeking to speak to him.	*cp.* 2 4; 3 9. and, standing without, they sent unto him, calling him. **32** And a multitude was sitting about him; and they say unto him, Behold, thy mother and thy brethren without seek for thee.		
47 [1] And one said unto him, Behold, thy mother and thy brethren stand without, seeking to speak to thee. **48** But he answered and said unto him that told him, Who is my mother? and who are my brethren? **49** And	**33** And **he** answereth them, and saith, Who is my mother and my brethren? **34** And looking round [*cp.* 3 5; 5 32; 9 8; 10 23; 11 11] on them which sat round about him,	**20** And it was told him, Thy mother and thy brethren stand without, desiring to see thee. **21** But he answered and said unto them,	
he stretched forth his hand towards his disciples, and said, Behold, my mother and my brethren! **50** For whosoever *cp.* 13 19-23.	he saith, Behold, my mother and my brethren! **35** For whosoever *cp.* 2 2; 4 14-20, 33; 16 20.	*cp.* 6 10.	
shall do the will [*cp.* 7 21; 21 31: *also* 6 10; 26 39, 42] of my Father which is in heaven [*cp.* 5 16, 45; 6 1, 9; 7 11, 21; 10 32, 33; 16 17; 18 10, 14, 19: *also* 5 48; 6 14, 26, 32; 15 13; 18 35; 23 9], he is my brother, and sister, and mother.	shall do the will [*cp.* 14 36] of God, *cp.* 11 25, 26.	My mother and my brethren are these which hear the word of God [*cp.* 5 1; 8 11; 11 28: *also* 1 2; 8 12-15; *and* 4 32], and do it. *cp.* 22 42. *cp.* 11 13.	*cp.* 4 41; 5 24, 38; *etc.* *cp.* 4 34; 5 30; 6 38; 7 17; 9 31.
	the same is my brother, and sister, and mother.		
[1] Some ancient authorities omit ver. 47.			

§ 92. General Preaching with the Twelve and the Ministering Women

Matt. 9 35	Mark 6 6b	Luke 8 1-3	
35 And Jesus went about all the cities and the villages, teaching in their synagogues, and preaching [*cp.* 4 23 ; 11 1] the [1] gospel *cp.* 11 5. of the kingdom [*cp.* 4 23 ; 24 14: *also* 26 13], and healing all manner	**6** And he went round about the villages teaching. *cp.* 1 1, 14, 15; 8 35; 10 29; 13 10; 14 9; 16 15.	**1** And it came to pass soon afterwards, that he went about through cities and villages [*cp.* 13 22], preaching and bringing the [1] good tidings [*cp.* 1 19; 2 10; 3 18; 4 18, 43; 7 22; 9 6; 16 16; 20 1] of the kingdom of God,	

Matt.	Mark	Luke	
of disease and all manner of sickness.		and with him the twelve,	
cp. 10 1.	*cp.* 6 7.	4 44 And he was	
4 23 And Jesus went about in all Galilee, teaching in their synagogues,	1 39 And he went into their synagogues throughout all Galilee, preaching	preaching in the synagogues [*cp.* 4 15] of 4 Galilee.	*cp.* 18 20.
and preaching the ¹ gospel of the kingdom, and healing all manner of disease and all manner of sickness among the people.	and casting out ¹ devils.		
cp. 27 55.	*cp.* 15 40.	2 and certain women [*cp.* 23 49, 55; 24 1, 10, 22, 24] which had been healed of evil spirits and infirmities, Mary that was	
cp. 27 56, 61 ; 28 1.	*cp.* 15 40, 47; 16 1, 9.	called Magdalene [*cp.* 24 10], from whom seven ² devils had gone out, 3 and Joanna [*cp.* 24 10] the wife of Chuza Herod's steward, and	*cp.* 19 25; 20 1, 18.
cp. 27 55.	*cp.* 15 41.	Susanna, and many others, which ministered unto ³them of their substance.	
¹ Or, *good tidings*	¹ Gr. *demons.*	¹ Or, *gospel* ² Gr. *demons.* ³ Many ancient authorities read *him.* ⁴ Very many ancient authorities read *Judæa.*	

(viii) Teaching by Parables (§§ 93-104)

§ 93. The Sower

Matt. 13 1-9	Mark 4 1-9	Luke 8 4-8	
1 On that day went Jesus out of the house, and sat by the sea side.	1 And again he began to teach by the sea side [*cp.* 3 7; 5 21]. And there is gathered unto him a very great multitude,	*cp.* 5 1. 4 And when a great multitude came together, and they of every city resorted unto him,	
2 And there were gathered unto him great multitudes, so that he entered into a boat, and sat; and all the multitude stood on the beach. 3 And he spake to them many things in parables, saying,	so that he entered into a boat, and sat in the sea [*cp.* 3 9]; and all the multitude were by the sea on the land. 2 And he taught them many things in parables, and said unto them in his teaching [*cp.* 12 38], 3 Hearken: Behold, the sower went forth to sow:	*cp.* 5 3. he spake by a parable:	*cp.* 16 25.
Behold, the sower went forth to sow; 4 and as he sowed, some *seeds* fell by the way side, and the birds *cp.* 6 26; 8 20; 13 32. came and devoured them:	4 and it came to pass, as he sowed, some *seed* fell by the way side, and the birds *cp.* 4 32. came and devoured it.	5 The sower went forth to sow his seed: and as he sowed, some fell by the way side; and it was trodden under foot, and the birds of the heaven [*cp.* 9 58; 13 19] devoured it.	
5 and others fell upon the rocky places, where they had not much earth: and straightway they sprang up, because they had no deepness of earth: 6 and when the sun was risen, they were scorched; and because they had no root, they withered away.	5 And other fell on the rocky *ground*, where it had not much earth; and straightway it sprang up, because it had no deepness of earth: 6 and when the sun was risen, it was scorched; and because it had no root, it withered away.	6 And other fell on the rock; and as soon as it grew, it withered away, because it had no moisture.	
7 And others fell upon the thorns; and the thorns grew up, and choked them:	7 And other fell among the thorns, and the thorns grew up, and choked it, and it yielded no	7 And other fell amidst the thorns; and the thorns grew with it, and choked it.	

Matt.	Mark	Luke	
8 and others fell upon the good ground, and yielded fruit,	fruit. **8** And others fell into the good ground, and yielded fruit, growing up and increasing; and brought forth, thirtyfold, and sixtyfold, and a hundredfold.	**8** And other fell into the good ground, and grew, and brought forth fruit a hundredfold.	
some a hundredfold, some sixty, some thirty. **9** He that hath ears[1], let him hear [*cp.* 11 15; 13 43: *also* 19 12].	**9** And he said, Who hath ears to hear, let him hear [*cp.* 4 23; 7 16].	As he said these things, he cried, He that hath ears to hear, let him hear [*cp.* 14 35].	*cp.* 6 60.

[1] Some ancient authorities add here, and in ver. 43, *to hear*: as in Mark 4 9: Luke 8 8.

§ 94. The Interpretation of the Sower

Matt. 13 10-23	**Mark 4** 10-20	**Luke 8** 9-15	
10 And *cp.* 17 1, 19; 20 17; 24 3. the disciples came [*cp.* 5 1; 13 36; 14 15; 15 12, 23; 17 19; 18 1; 24 1, 3; 26 17], and said unto him, Why speakest thou unto them in parables [*cp.* 13 36; 15 15]? **11** And he answered and said unto them, Unto you it is given to know the mysteries of the kingdom of heaven [*cp.* 13 51], but to them it is not given [*cp.* 19 11].	**10** And when he was alone [*cp.* 4 34; 6 31, 32; 9 2, 28; 13 3], they that were about him with the twelve *cp.* 6 35. asked of him the parables [*cp.* 7 17]. **11** And he said unto them, Unto you is given the mystery of the kingdom of God: but unto them that are without, all things are done	**9** And *cp.* 9 10; 10 23. his disciples *cp.* 9 12. asked him what this parable might be. **10** And he said, Unto you it is given to know the mysteries of the kingdom of God: but to the rest [*cp.* 12 26; 18 9, 11; 24 9, 10]	
12 For whosoever hath, to him shall be given, and he shall have abundance: but whosoever hath not, from him shall be taken away even that which he hath. 25 **29** For unto every one that hath shall be given, and he shall have abundance: but from him that hath not, even that which he hath shall be taken away.	4 **25** For he that hath, to him shall be given: and he that hath not, from him shall be taken away even that which he hath.	8 **18** For whosoever hath, to him shall be given; and whosoever hath not, from him shall be taken away even that which he [1] thinketh he hath. 19 **26** I say unto you, that unto every one that hath shall be given; but from him that hath not, even that which he hath shall be taken away from him.	
13 Therefore speak I to them in parables; because seeing they see not, and hearing they hear not, neither do they understand.	in parables: **12** that seeing they may see, and not perceive; and hearing they may hear, and not understand [*cp.* 8 18]; lest haply they should turn again, and it should be forgiven them.	in parables; that seeing they may not see, and hearing they may not understand.	*cp.* 9 39.
14 And unto them is fulfilled the prophecy of Isaiah, which saith, By hearing ye shall hear, and shall in no wise understand; And seeing ye shall see, and shall in no wise perceive: **15** For this people's heart is waxed gross, And their ears are dull of hearing, And their eyes they have closed; Lest haply they should perceive with their eyes, And hear with their ears, And understand with their heart, And should turn again, And I should heal them. *cp.* 9 22; 16 23.			*cp.* 12 39-40.
cp. 17 1, 19; 20 17; 24 3. **16** But blessed are your eyes, for they see; and your ears, for they hear. **17** For verily I say unto you,	*cp.* 5 30; 8 33. *cp.* 4 10, 34; 6 31, 32; 9 2, 28; 13 3.	10 **23** And turning [*cp.* 7 9, 44; 9 55; 14 25; 22 61; 23 28] to the disciples, he said privately [*cp.* 9 10], Blessed *are* the eyes which see the things that ye see: **24** for I say unto you,	*cp.* 1 38.

[1] thinketh he hath.

Matthew

that many prophets and righteous men desired to see the things which ye see, and saw them not; and to hear the things which ye hear, and heard them not.

cp. 15 16; 16 8-12.

18 Hear then ye the parable of the sower [cp. 13 37].

19 When any one heareth the word of the kingdom, and understandeth it not, *then* cometh the evil *one* [cp. 5 37, 39; 6 13; 13 38], and snatcheth away that which hath been sown in his heart. This is he that was sown by the way side. 20 And he that was sown upon the rocky places, this is he that heareth the word, and straightway with joy receiveth it; 21 yet hath he not root in himself, but endureth for a while; and when tribulation or persecution ariseth because of the word, straightway he stumbleth [cp. 24 10: also 11 6; 13 57; 15 12; 26 31, 33]. 22 And he that was sown among the thorns, this is he that heareth the word; and the care of the ¹ world, and the deceitfulness of riches, choke the word, and he becometh unfruitful. 23 And he that was sown upon the good ground, this is he that heareth the word, and understandeth it; who verily beareth fruit, and bringeth forth, some a hundredfold, some sixty, some thirty.

¹ Or, age

Mark

13 And he saith unto them, Know ye not this parable [cp. 6 52; 7 18; 8 17-21; 9 10, 32; 16 14]? and how shall ye know all the parables? 14 The sower soweth the word [cp. 2 2; 4 33; 16 20]. 15 And these are they by the way side, where the word is sown; and when they have heard, straightway cometh Satan, and taketh away the word which hath been sown in them. 16 And these in like manner are they that are sown upon the rocky *places*, who, when they have heard the word, straightway receive it with joy; 17 and they have no root in themselves, but endure for a while; then, when tribulation or persecution ariseth because of the word, straightway they stumble [cp. 6 3; 14 27, 29]. 18 And others are they that are sown among the thorns; these are they that have heard the word, 19 and the cares of the ¹ world, and the deceitfulness of riches, and the lusts of other things entering in, choke the word, and it becometh unfruitful. 20 And those are they that were sown upon the good ground; such as hear the word, and accept it, and bear fruit, thirtyfold, and sixtyfold, and a hundredfold.

¹ Or, age

Luke

that many prophets and kings desired to see the things which ye see, and saw them not; and to hear the things which ye hear, and heard them not.

cp. 2 50; 9 45; 18 34.

11 Now the parable is this: The seed is the word of God [cp. 5 1; 8 21; 11 28: also 1 2 *and* 4 32]. 12 And those by the way side are they that have heard; then cometh the devil, and taketh away the word from their heart, that they may not believe and be saved. 13 And those on the rock *are* they which, when they have heard, receive the word with joy; and these have no root, which for a while believe, and in time of temptation [cp. 4 13; 22 28]

cp. 7 23.

fall away. 14 And that which fell among the thorns, these are they that have heard, and as they go on their way they are choked with cares [cp. 21 34] and riches and pleasures of *this* life [cp. 21 34], and bring no fruit to perfection. 15 And that in the good ground, these are such as in an honest and good heart, having heard the word, hold it fast, and bring forth fruit with patience [cp. 21 19].

¹ Or, *seemeth to have*

(marginal references) cp. 3 10; 4 33; 8 27, 43; *etc.* — cp. 17 15. — cp. 6 61; 16 1. — cp. 15 4, 8, 16.

Matt. 13 13 ‖ Mark 4 12 ‖ Luke 8 10 : cp. Is. 6 9-10.   Matt. 13 14-15 = Is. 6 9-10.

§ 95. Miscellaneous Sayings

Matt. 5 15; 10 26-27; 7 2; 13 12; 25 29	Mark 4 21-25	Luke 8 16-18	Luke 11 33; 12 2-3; 6 38; 19 26
5 15 Neither do *men* light	21 And he said unto them, Is	16 And no man, when he hath lighted	11 33 No man, when he hath lighted

Matthew

a lamp,

and put it, under the bushel, but on the stand ; and it shineth unto all that are in the house.

10 26 For there is nothing covered, that shall not be revealed ; and hid,

that shall not be known. 27 What I tell you in the darkness, speak ye in the light : and what ye hear in the ear, proclaim upon the house-tops.

cp. 11 15 ; 13 9, 43 : also 19 12.

7 2 And with what measure ye mete, it shall be measured unto you.

cp. 6 33 : also 19 28-29. 13 12 For whosoever hath, to him shall be given, and he shall have abundance : but whosoever hath not, from him shall be taken away even that which he hath.

25 29 For unto every one that hath shall be given, and he shall have abundance : but from him that hath not, even that which he hath shall be taken away.

Mark

the lamp brought to be put under the bushel, or under the bed, *and* not to be put on the stand ?

22 For there is nothing hid, save that it should be manifested ; neither was *anything* made secret, but that it should come to light.

23 If any man hath ears to hear, let him hear [*cp.* 4 9 ; 7 16]. 24 And he said unto them, Take heed what ye hear : with what measure ye mete it shall be measured unto you : and more shall be given unto you [*cp.* 10 29-30]. 25 For he that hath, to him shall be given : and he that hath not, from him shall be taken away even that which he hath.

Luke 8

a lamp, covereth it with a vessel, or putteth it under a bed ; but putteth it on a stand,

that they which enter in may see the light. 17 For nothing is hid, that shall not be made manifest ; nor *anything* secret, that shall not be known and come to light.

cp. 8 8 ; 14 35.

18 Take heed therefore how ye hear :

cp. 12 31 : also 18 29-30. for whosoever hath, to him shall be given ;

and whosoever hath not, from him shall be taken away even that which he ¹ thinketh he hath.

¹ Or, *seemeth to have*

Luke

a lamp, putteth it in a cellar, neither under the bushel, but on the stand,

that they which enter in may see the light. 12 2 But there is nothing covered up, that shall not be revealed : and hid,

that shall not be known. 3 Wherefore whatsoever ye have said in the darkness shall be heard in the light ; and what ye have spoken in the ear in the inner chambers shall be proclaimed upon the house-tops.

cp. 6 60.

6 38 For with what measure ye mete it shall be measured to you again.

19 26 I say unto you, that unto every one that hath shall be given ;

but from him that hath not, even that which he hath shall be taken away from him.

§ 96. The Tares (Matt.) : The Seed Growing Secretly (Mark)

Matt. 13 24-30

24 Another parable set he before them, saying, The kingdom of heaven is likened unto a man that sowed good seed in his field : 25 but while men slept, his enemy came and sowed

Mark 4 26-29

26 And he said, So is the kingdom of God, as if a man should cast seed upon the earth ; 27 and should sleep and rise night and day,

[1] tares also among the wheat, and went away. **26** But when the blade sprang up, and

brought forth fruit,

then appeared the tares also. **27** And the [2] servants of the householder [*cp*. 13 52; 20 1; 21 33] came and said unto him, Sir, didst thou not sow good seed in thy field? whence then hath it tares? **28** And he said unto them, [3] An enemy hath done this. And the [2] servants say unto him, Wilt thou then that we go and gather them up? **29** But he saith, Nay; lest haply while ye gather up the tares, ye root up [*cp*. 15 13] the wheat with them. **30** Let both grow together until the harvest [*cp*. 5 45: *also* 13 47 *ff*.; 22 10; 25 32]:

and in the time of the harvest I will say to the reapers, Gather up first the tares, and bind them in bundles to burn them: but gather the wheat into my barn [*cp*. 3 12: *also* 24 31].

[1] Or, *darnel*   [2] Gr. *bondservants.*
[3] Gr. *A man* that is *an enemy.*

and the seed should spring up and grow, he knoweth not how. **28** The earth [1] beareth fruit of herself; first the blade, then the ear, then the full corn in the ear.

29 But when the fruit [2] is ripe, straightway he [3] putteth forth the sickle, because the harvest is come.

cp. 13 27.

[1] Or, *yieldeth*   [2] Or, *alloweth*
[3] Or, *sendeth forth*

cp. 14 21.

cp. 6 35.

cp. 3 17.

§ 97. The Mustard Seed

Matt. 13 31-32	Mark 4 30-32	Luke 13 18-19
31 Another parable set he before them, saying, The kingdom of heaven is like unto a grain of mustard seed [*cp*. 17 20], which a man took, and sowed in his field: **32** which indeed is less than all seeds; but when it is grown, it is greater than the herbs, and becometh a tree, so that the birds of the heaven come and lodge in the branches thereof.	**30** And he said, How shall we liken the kingdom of God? or in what parable shall we set it forth? **31** [1] It is like a grain of mustard seed, which, when it is sown upon the earth, though it be less than all the seeds that are upon the earth, **32** yet when it is sown, groweth up, and becometh greater than all the herbs, and putteth out great branches; so that the birds of the heaven can lodge under the shadow thereof. [1] Gr. *As unto.*	**18** He said therefore, Unto what is the kingdom of God like? and whereunto shall I liken it? **19** It is like unto a grain of mustard seed [*cp*. 17 6], which a man took, and cast into his own garden; and it grew, and became a tree; and the birds of the heaven lodged in the branches thereof.

§ 98. The Leaven

Matt. 13 33	Luke 13 20-21
33 Another parable spake he unto them; The kingdom of heaven is like unto leaven, which a woman took, and hid in three [1] measures of meal, till it was all leavened. [1] The word in the Greek denotes the Hebrew seah, a measure containing nearly a peck and a half.	**20** And again he said, Whereunto shall I liken the kingdom of God? **21** It is like unto leaven, which a woman took and hid in three [1] measures of meal, till it was all leavened. [1] See footnote on Matt. 13 33.

§ 99. The Parabolic Method

Matt. 13 34-35	**Mark 4** 33-34		
34 All these things spake Jesus [*cp.* 13 19 *ff.*] in parables unto the multitudes; and without a parable spake he nothing unto them: *cp.* 17 1, 19; 20 17; 24 3. **35** that it might be fulfilled which was spoken [1] by the prophet, saying, I will open my mouth in parables; I will utter things hidden from the foundation [2] of the world [*cp.* 25 34].	**33** And with many such parables spake he the word [*cp.* 2 2; 4 14 *ff.*; 16 20] unto them, as they were able to hear it: **34** and without a parable spake he not unto them: but privately [*cp.* 4 10; 6 31,32; 9 2,28; 13 3] to his own disciples he expounded all things.	*cp.* 5 1; 8 11 *ff.*, 21; 11 28: *also* 1 2 *and* 4 32. *cp.* 9 10; 10 23. *cp.* 11 50.	*cp.* 6 60; 16 12, 25. *cp.* 17 24.

[1] Or, *through*
[2] Many ancient authorities omit *of the world*.

Matt. 13 35 = Ps. 78 2.

§ 100. The Interpretation of the Tares

Matt. 13 36-43			
36 Then he left the multitudes, and went into the house [*cp.* 17 25]: and his disciples came unto him [*cp.* 5 1; 13 10; 14 15; 15 12, 23; 17 19; 18 1; 24 1, 3; 26 17: *also* Mark 6 35; *and* Luke 9 12], saying, Explain unto us the parable [*cp.* 15 15] of the field. **37** And he answered and said, He that soweth [*cp.* 13 18, 24: *also* Mark 4 14] the good seed is the Son of man; **38** and the field is the world; and the good seed, these are the sons of the kingdom [*cp.* 8 12: *also* 5 9, 45]; and the tares are the sons of the evil *one* [*cp.* 5 37, 39; 6 13; 13 19: *also* John 17 15]; **39** and the enemy that sowed them is the devil: and the harvest is [1] the end of the world [*cp.* 13 40, 49; 24 3; 28 20]; and the reapers are angels. **40** As therefore the tares are gathered up and burned with fire; so shall it be in [1] the end of the world [*cp. verse* 39 *above*]. **41** The Son of man shall send forth his angels [*cp.* 24 31: *also* 13 49; 16 27; 25 31], and they shall gather out of his kingdom all things that cause stumbling, and them that do iniquity, **42** and shall cast them into the furnace of fire [*cp.* 13 50: *also* 3 10, 12; 5 22, 29, 30; 7 19; 10 28; 18 8, 9; 23 33; 25 41]: there shall be the weeping and gnashing of teeth [*cp.* 8 12; 13 50; 22 13; 24 51; 25 30]. **43** Then shall the righteous shine forth as the sun in the kingdom of their Father [*cp.* 26 29]. He that hath ears, let him hear [*cp.* 11 15; 13 9: *also* 19 12].	*cp.* 7 17; 9 28, 33; 10 10. *cp.* 4 10, 13; 7 17. *cp.* 13 27: *also* 8 38. *cp.* 9 43, 45, 47. *cp.* 4 9, 23; 7 16.	*cp.* 8 9. *cp.* 6 35; 16 8; 20 36. *cp.* 10 19. *cp.* 9 26; 12 8, 9. *cp.* 3 9, 17; 12 5. *cp.* 13 28. *cp.* 8 8; 14 35.	*cp.* 12 36: *also* 1 12; 11 52. *cp.* 15 6. *cp.* 6 60.

[1] Or, *the consummation of the age*

Matt. 13 43: *cp.* Dan. 12 3.

§ 101. The Hidden Treasure

Matt. 13 44		
44 The kingdom of heaven is like unto a treasure hidden in the field; which a man found, and hid; and [1] in his joy he goeth and selleth all that he hath, and buyeth that field.		

[1] Or, *for joy thereof*

§ 102. The Pearl of Great Price

Matt. 13 45-46		
45 Again, the kingdom of heaven is like unto a man that is a merchant seeking goodly pearls: **46** and having found one pearl of great price, he went and sold all that he had, and bought it.		

§ 103. The Drag-Net

Matt. 13 47-50

47 Again, the kingdom of heaven is like unto a [1] net, that was cast into the sea, and gathered of every kind [cp. 13 30; 22 10; 25 32] : 48 which, when it was filled, they drew up on the beach; and they sat down, and gathered the good into vessels, but the bad they cast away. 49 So shall it be in [2] the end of the world [cp. 13 39, 40; 24 3; 28 20] : the angels shall come forth [cp. 13 41; 16 27; 24 31; 25 31], and sever the wicked from among the righteous [cp. 25 32 : also 3 12], 50 and shall cast them into the furnace of fire [cp. 13 42 : also 3 10, 12; 5 22, 29, 30; 7 19; 10 28; 18 8, 9; 23 33; 25 41] : there shall be the weeping and gnashing of teeth [cp. 8 12; 13 42; 22 13; 24 51; 25 30].

cp. 8 38; 13 27.	cp. 9 26; 12 8, 9.	
	cp. 3 17.	
cp. 9 43, 45, 47.	cp. 3 9, 17; 12 5.	cp. 15 6.
	cp. 13 28.	

[1] Gr. drag-net.   [2] Or, the consummation of the age

§ 104. The Householder and his Treasure

Matt. 13 51-52

51 Have ye understood all these things? They say unto him, Yea [cp. 13 11]. 52 And he said unto them, Therefore every scribe who hath been made a disciple [cp. 27 57; 28 19] to the kingdom of heaven is like unto a man that is a householder [cp. 20 1; 21 33 : also 13 27], which bringeth forth out of his treasure [cp. 12 35] things new and old.

cp. 4 11.	cp. 8 10.
	cp. 14 21.
	cp. 6 45.

(ix) Events in Galilee IV (§§ 105-113).

§ 105. The True Brethren of Jesus

[Cp. Luke 11 27-28]

Matt. 12 46-50	Mark 3 31-35	Luke 8 19-21	
46 While he was yet speaking [cp. 17 5; 26 47] to the multitudes,	cp. 5 35; 14 43.	cp. 8 49; 22 47, 60.	
behold, his mother and his brethren	31 And there come his mother and his brethren [cp. 3 21];	19 And there came to him his mother and brethren, and they could not come at him for the crowd [cp. 5 19; 19 3].	
stood without,	cp. 2 4; 3 9. and, standing without, they sent unto him, calling him. 32 And a multitude was sitting about		
seeking to speak to him.	him; and they say unto him, Behold, thy mother and thy		
47 [1] And one said unto him, Behold, thy mother and thy brethren stand without, seeking to speak to thee. 48 But he answered and said unto him that told him, Who is my mother? and who are my brethren? 49 And	brethren without seek for thee. 33 And he answereth them, and saith, Who is my mother and my brethren? 34 And looking round [cp. 3 5; 5 32; 9 8; 10 32; 11 11] on them which sat round about him,	20 And it was told him, Thy mother and thy brethren stand without, desiring to see thee. 21 But he answered and said unto them, cp. 6 10.	
he stretched forth his hand towards his disciples, and said, Behold, my mother and my brethren! 50 For whosoever cp. 13 19-23.	he saith, Behold, my mother and my brethren! 35 For whosoever cp. 2 2; 4 14-20, 33; 16 20.	My mother and my brethren are these which hear the word of God [cp. 5 1; 8 11; 11 28: also 1 2; 8 12-15; and 4 32], and do it cp. 22 42.	cp. 4 41; 5 24, 38; etc.
shall do the will [cp. 7 21; 21 31 : also 6 10; 26 39, 42] of my Father which is in heaven	shall do the will [cp. 14 36] of God,		cp. 4 34; 5 30; 6 38; 7 17; 9 31.

[*cp.* 5 16, 45; 6 1, 9; 7 11, 21; 10 32, 33; 16 17; 18 10, 14, 19: *also* 5 48; 6 14, 26, 32; 15 13; 18 35; 23 9],	*cp.* 11 25, 26.	*cp.* 11 13.

<table>
<tr><td>he is my brother, and sister, and mother.</td><td>the same is my brother, and sister, and mother.</td><td></td></tr>
</table>

¹ Some ancient authorities omit ver. 47.

§ 106. The Stilling of a Storm

<table>
<tr><th>Matt. 8 23-27</th><th>Mark 4 35-41</th><th>Luke 8 22-25</th><th></th></tr>
<tr>
<td>

3 And
when
he was entered into a boat, his disciples followed him.

cp. 8 18; 14 22.

</td>
<td>

35 And   on that day, when even was come,

he saith unto them, Let us go over unto the other side [*cp.* 6 45]. 36 And leaving the multitude, they take him with them, even as he was, in the boat. And other boats were with him.

</td>
<td>

22 Now it came to pass on one of those days, that he entered into a boat, himself and his disciples; and he said unto them, Let us go over unto the other side of the lake: and they launched forth.

</td>
<td></td>
</tr>
<tr>
<td>

24 And behold, there arose a great tempest in the sea [*cp.* 4 18; 8 32; *etc.*],

insomuch that the boat was covered with the waves: but he
was
asleep. 25 And they came to him, and awoke him, saying,   Save [*cp.* 14 30], Lord [*cp.* 17 4, 15; 20 30, 33: *and* 7 21; 8 2, 6, 8, 21; *etc.*];

[*cp.* 8 19; 12 38; 19 16; 22 16, 24, 36.

</td>
<td>

37 And   there ariseth a great storm of wind,
cp. 1 16; 2 13; *etc.*
and the waves beat into the boat, insomuch that the boat was now filling.

38 And he himself was in the stern, asleep on the cushion: and they   awake him, and say unto him,
cp. 7 28.

¹ Master [*cp.* 9 17, 38; 10 17, 20, 35; 12 14, 19, 32; 13 1],

</td>
<td>

23 But as they sailed he fell asleep: and   there came down a   storm of wind on the lake [*cp.* 5 1, 2; 8 33];

and they were filling *with water*, and were in jeopardy.

24 And they came to him, and awoke him, saying,
[*cp.* 18 41: *and* 5 8, 12; 6 46; 7 6; *etc.*]
[*cp.* 7 40; 9 38; 10 25; 11 45; 12 13; 18 18; 19 39; 20 21, 28, 39; 21 7] Master, master [*cp.* 9 33, 49: *and* 5 5; 8 45; 17 13],

</td>
<td>

cp. 6 1, 16; *etc.*

cp. 4 11, 15, 19, 49; 5 7; *etc.*
cp. 1 38; 20 16.

</td>
</tr>
<tr>
<td>

we perish.
26 And he saith unto them, Why are ye fearful, O ye of little faith [*cp.* 6 30; 14 31; 16 8: *also* 17 20]? Then he arose, and rebuked [*cp.* 17 18]
the winds and   the sea;

and there was a great calm.

cp. 17 20; 21 21.
27 And
[*cp.* 9 8; 17 6; 27 54; 28 4, 8]

the men marvelled [*cp.* 9 33; 12 23; 15 31; 21 20; 27 14: *also* 7 28; 13 54; 19 25; 22 22, 33],
saying,
What manner of man is this [*cp.* 21 10],
that   even the winds and the sea obey him?

</td>
<td>

carest thou not that we perish? 39 And he awoke,

and rebuked [*cp.* 1 25; 3 12; 9 25] the wind, and said unto the sea, Peace, be still [*cp.* 1 25]. And the wind ceased, and there was a great calm. 40 And he said unto them, Why are ye fearful? have ye not yet faith [*cp.* 11 22; 16 14]?   41 And they feared exceedingly [*cp.* 5 15, 33; 9 6, 32; 10 32; 16 8],
[*cp.* 2 12; 5 20, 42; 6 51; 7 37; 10 32; 15 5; 16 5, 8: *also* 1 22, 27; 6 2; 10 24, 26; 11 18; 12 17] and said one to another, Who then   is this [*cp.* 1 27; 2 7],
that   even the wind and the sea obey him [*cp.* 1 27]?

¹ Or, *Teacher*

</td>
<td>

we perish.
And he awoke,

cp. 12 28.

and rebuked [*cp.* 4 35, 39, 41; 9 42] the wind and the raging of the water: [*cp.* 4 35] and they   ceased, and there was a   calm. 25 And he said unto them, Where is your faith [*cp.* 17 5, 6; 22 32; 24 25, 38]? And being afraid [*cp.* 1 12, 65; 2 9; 5 26; 7 16; 8 35, 37, 47; 9 34, 45; 24 5, 37] they marvelled [*cp.* 5 9, 26; 8 56; 9 43; 11 14; 24 12, 41: *also* 2 47, 48; 4 22, 32, 36; 20 26], saying one to another, Who then   is this [*cp.* 4 36; 5 21; 7 49; 9 9], that he commandeth even the winds and the water, and they obey him [*cp.* 4 36]?

</td>
<td>

cp. 3 12; 6 64; 14 10; 20 27.

cp. 7 15, 21, 46.

cp. 5 12: *also* 12 34.

</td>
</tr>
</table>

§ 107. The Gerasene Demoniac

Matt. 8 28-34	Mark 5 1-20	Luke 8 26-39
28 And when he was come to the other side into the country of the Gadarenes,	**1** And they came to the other side of the sea, into the country of the Gerasenes.	**26** And they arrived at the country of the [1] Gerasenes, which is over against Galilee.
there met him two [cp. 9 27; 20 30] [1] possessed with devils, coming forth out of the tombs,	**2** And when he was come out of the boat, straightway there met him out of the tombs a man with an unclean spirit,	**27** And when he was come forth upon the land, there met him a certain man out of the city, who had [2] devils; and for a long time he had worn no clothes, and abode not in *any* house, but in the tombs.
	3 who had his dwelling in the tombs: and no man could any more bind him, no, not with a chain; **4** because that he had been often bound with fetters and chains, and the chains had been rent asunder by him, and the fetters broken in pieces: and no man had strength to tame him. **5** And always, night and day, in the tombs and in the mountains, he was crying out, and cutting himself with stones. **6** And when he saw Jesus from afar, he ran and worshipped him [cp. 1 40; 3 11; 5 22, 33; 7 25; 10 17]; **7** and crying out	*verse 29*
exceeding fierce, so that no man could pass by that way.		
cp. 2 11; 8 2; 9 18; 14 33; 15 25; 17 14; 20 20; 28 9, 17. **29** And behold, they cried out,	with a loud voice [cp. 1 26], he saith,	**28** And when he saw Jesus, he cried out, and fell down [cp. 5 8, 12; 8 41, 47; 17 16; 24 52] before him, and with a loud voice [cp. 4 33] said, cp. 9 38; 11 32; 18 6.
saying, What have we to do with thee, thou Son [cp. 4 3, 6; 14 33; 16 16; 26 63; 27 40, 43, 54] of	What have I to do with thee [cp. 1 24], Jesus, thou Son [cp. 1 1; 3 11; 15 39] of the Most High	What have I to do with thee [cp. 4 34], Jesus, thou Son [cp. 1 35; 4 3, 9, 41; 22 70] of the Most High [cp. 1 32, 35, 76; 6 35] God [cp. similarly
God? cp. 26 63. art thou come hither to torment us before the time?	God [cp. similarly 1 24; 3 11]? I adjure thee cp. 1 24. by God, torment me not. **8** For he said unto him, Come forth [cp. 1 25; 9 25], thou unclean spirit, out of the man.	4 34, 41]? I beseech thee, cp. 4 34. torment me not. **29** For he cp. 4 35. commanded the unclean spirit to come out from the man. For [3] oftentimes it had seized him: and he was kept under guard, and bound with chains and fetters; and breaking the bands asunder, he was driven of the [4] devil into the deserts. cp. 1 34; etc.
	verses 4 and 5	**30** And Jesus asked him, What is thy name? And he said, Legion; for many [2] devils were entered into him.
	9 And he asked him, What is thy name? And he saith unto him, My name is Legion; for we are many.	**31** And they intreated him that he would not command them to depart into the abyss. **32** Now there was there a
30 Now there was afar off from them a herd of many swine feeding.	**10** And he besought him much that he would not send them away out of the country. **11** Now there was there on the mountain side a great herd of swine feeding.	herd of many swine feeding

31 And the
² devils besought him, saying,
If thou cast us out, send us
away into the herd of swine.

32 And he said unto them,
Go.   And they
came out,
and went into the swine:
and behold, the whole
herd rushed down the steep
into the sea [*cp. 4 18;
8 24; etc.*],
                        and
perished in the waters. 33 And
they that fed them

        fled, and went away into
the city, and told everything,
                            and
what was befallen to them
that were ¹ possessed with
devils. 34 And behold, all the
city came out to

                meet Jesus:
and when they saw him,

cp. 9 8; 17 6; 27 54;
        28 4, 8.

verse 33

        they

besought *him* that he would
depart from their borders.

cp. 4 25.

cp. 8 27; 9 33; 12 23; 15 31;
21 20; 27 14: *also* 7 28; 13 54;
        19 25; 22 22, 33.

¹ Or, *demoniacs*   ² Gr. *demons.*

---

12 And they
besought him, saying,
                Send us
into the   swine,
that we may enter into
them. 13 And he gave them
leave. And the unclean spirits
came out,
and entered into the swine:
and   the
herd rushed down the steep
into the sea [*cp.* 1 16; 2 13;
etc.], *in number* about two
thousand; and they were
choked in the sea.   14 And
they that fed them

fled,
        and told it in the
city, and in the country.

verse 16
    And
they came   to see what it
was that had come to pass.
15 And they come to Jesus,
and   behold ¹ him
that   was   possessed   with
devils   sitting,
clothed and in his right mind,

        even him that had
the legion: and they were
afraid [*cp.* 4 41; 5 33; 9 6,
32; 10 32; 16 8].
                16 And they
that saw it declared unto
them how it befell ¹ him that
was possessed with devils,
            and concerning the
swine. 17 And they

                began to
beseech him   to
depart from their borders.

                18 And
as he was entering into the
boat,   he that
had   been   possessed   with
² devils   besought
him that he might be with
him. 19 And he suffered him
not, but saith unto him, Go
to thy house unto thy friends,
and tell them how great
things the Lord hath done
for thee, and *how* he had
mercy on thee. 20 And he
went his way, and began to
publish in Decapolis [*cp.* 7
31] how   great   things
Jesus had done for him: and
all men did marvel [*cp.* 2 12;
5 42; 6 51; 7 37; 10 32;
15 5; 16 5, 8: *also* 1 22, 27;
6 2; 10 24, 26; 11 18; 12 17].

¹ Or, *the demoniac*   ² Gr. *demons.*

---

on the mountain: and they
        intreated him

        that he would give
them leave to enter into
them.   And he gave them
leave. 33 And the ² devils
came out from the man,
and entered into the swine:
and   the
herd rushed down the steep
into the lake [*cp.* 5 1, 2; 8
22, 23],
        and   were
choked.   34 And
when they that fed them saw
what had come to pass,
they fled,
        and told it in the
city and in the country.

        35 And
they went out to see what
        had come to pass;
and they came to Jesus,
and   found the
man, from whom the
² devils were gone out, sitting,
clothed and in his right mind,
at the feet of Jesus [*cp.* 7 38;
10 39]:
        and they were
afraid [*cp.* 1 12, 65; 2 9; 5
26; 7 16; 8 25, 37, 47; 9 34,
45; 24 5, 37]. 36 And they
that saw it told
them how   he that
was possessed with ² devils
was ⁵ made whole.
37 And all the people of the
country of the Gerasenes
round about
asked him   to
depart from them; for
they were holden with great
fear [*cp. verse* 35 *above*]: and
he   entered into a
boat, and returned. 38 But
the man from whom the
² devils were gone out prayed
him that he might be with
him: but he sent him away,
        saying,   39 Return
to thy house,
and declare   how great
things   God hath done
for thee.

                And he
went his way,
publishing throughout the
whole city how great things
Jesus had done for him.

cp. 5 9, 26; 8 25, 56; 9 43;
11 14; 24 12, 41: *also* 2 47,
    48; 4 22, 32, 36; 20 26.

¹ Many ancient authorities read
Gergesenes: others,   *Gadarenes*:
and so in ver. 37.
² Gr. *demons.*   ³ Or, *of a long time*
⁴ Gr. *demon.*   ⁵ Or, *saved*

---

cp. 6 1, 16;
etc.

cp. 7 15, 21,
46.

§ 108. **Jaïrus's Daughter and a Woman with an Issue of Blood**

[*Cp.* Luke 7 11-17; John 11 1-46]

Matt. 9 18-26	**Mark 5** 21-43	**Luke 8** 40-56	
18 While he spake these things unto them,	21 And when Jesus had crossed over again in the boat unto the other side, a great multitude was gathered unto him: and he was by the sea [*cp.* 3 7; 4 1].	40 And as Jesus returned, the multitude welcomed him; [*cp.* 5 1] for they were all waiting for him. 41 And behold, there came a man	
cp. 13 1.	22 And there cometh one of the rulers of the synagogue, Jaïrus by name;	named Jaïrus, and he was a ruler of the synagogue [*cp.* 13 14]: and	
behold, there came ¹a ruler,	and seeing him, he falleth at his feet [*cp.* 3 11; 5 33; 7 25: *also* 1 40; 5 6; 10 17], 23 and beseecheth him much,	he fell down [*cp.* 5 8, 12; 8 28, 47; 17 16: *also* 24 52] at Jesus' feet, and besought him to come into his house; 42 for he had an only [*cp.* 7 12; 9 38] daughter, about twelve years of age, and she lay a dying [*cp.* 7 2].	*cp.* 11 32; 18 6: *also* 9 38.
and worshipped [*cp.* 2 11; 8 2; 14 33; 15 25; 20 20; 28 9, 17: *also* 17 14] him,	*verse* 42		
saying, My daughter is even now dead: but come and lay thy hand [*cp.* 19 13, 15: *also* 8 3, 15; 9 20, 25, 29; 14 31, 36; 17 7; 20 34] upon her, and she shall live. 19 And Jesus arose, and followed him, and *so did* his disciples.	saying, My little daughter is at the point of death: *I pray thee*, that thou come and lay thy hands [*cp.* 6 5; 8 25; 10 16: *also* 1 31, 41; 3 10; 5 27, 41; 6 2, 56; 7 33; 8 22, 23; 9 27; 10 13] on her, that she may be ¹made whole, and live. 24 And he went with him;	*cp.* 4 40; 13 13: *also* 5 13; 6 19; 7 14, 39; 8 44, 54; 14 4; 18 15; 22 51.	*cp.* 9 6; 20 17.
	and a great multitude followed him, and they thronged him. 25 And a woman, which had an issue of blood twelve years,	But as he went the multitudes thronged him. 43 And a woman having an issue of blood twelve years [*cp.* 13 11],	
20 And behold, a woman, who had an issue of blood twelve years,	26 and had suffered many things of many physicians, and had spent all that she had, and was nothing bettered, but rather grew worse, 27 having heard the things concerning Jesus, came in the crowd behind,	which ¹ had spent all her living upon physicians, and could not be healed of any,	
came behind him, and touched [*cp.* 8 3, 15; 9 29; 14 36; 17 7; 20 34: *also* 9 18, 25; 14 31; 19 13, 15] the border [*cp.* 14 36] of his garment: 21 for she said within herself, If I do but touch his garment, I shall be ²made whole.	and touched [*cp.* 1 41; 3 10; 6 56; 7 33; 8 22; 10 13: *also* 1 31; 5 23, 41; 6 2, 5; 8 23, 25; 9 27; 10 16] [*cp.* 6 56] his garment. 28 For she said, If I touch but his garments, I shall be ¹made whole. 29 And	44 came behind him, and touched [*cp.* 5 13; 6 19; 7 14, 39; 18 15; 22 51: *also* 4 40; 8 54; 13 13; 14 4] the border of his garment:	*cp.* 20 17; 9 6.
	straightway the fountain of her blood was dried up; and she felt in her body that she was healed of her ² plague. 30 And straightway Jesus, perceiving in himself that the power *proceeding* from him had gone forth, turned him about [*cp.* 8 33] in the crowd, and said, Who touched my garments? 31 And his disciples	and immediately the issue of her blood stanched. 45 And Jesus *verse* 46 said, Who is it that touched me? And when all denied, Peter	
cp. 9 22; 16 23.		*cp.* 7 9, 44; 9 55; 10 23; 14 25; 22 61; 23 28.	*cp.* 1 38.

cp. 14 28; 15 15; 16 22; 17 4; 18 21; 19 27; 26 33: also 16 16; 17 24.

[cp. 8 32; 9 5; 10 28; 11 21; 14 29: also 8 29] said unto him,

Thou seest the multitude thronging thee, and sayest thou, Who touched me? **32** And he looked round about [cp. 3 5, 34; 9 8; 10 23; 11 11] to see her that had done this thing.

[cp. 9 33; 12 41; 18 28: also 5 8; 9 20] said,
2 and they that were with him, Master, the multitudes press thee and crush *thee*.

cp. 13 36, 37; 21 21: also 6 68.

verse 30

cp. 6 10.

46 But Jesus said, Some one did touch me: for I perceived that power [cp. 4 14, 36; 5 17; 6 19: *also* 1 17, 35; 9 1; 24 49] had gone forth from me. **47** And when the woman saw that she was not hid, she came trembling [cp. 1 12, 65; 2 9; 5 26; 7 16; 8 25, 35, 37; 9 34, 45; 24 5, 37], and falling down [cp. *verse* 41 *above*] before him declared in the presence of all the people for what cause she touched him, and how she was healed immediately.

cp. 9 8; 17 6; 27 54; 28 4, 8.

33 But the woman fearing and trembling [cp. 4 41; 5 15; 9 6, 32; 10 32; 16 8], knowing what had been done to her, came and fell down [cp. *verse* 22 *above*] before him, and told him all the truth.

cp. 11 32; 18 6: *also* 9 38.

22 But Jesus turning [cp. 16 23] and seeing her said, Daughter, be of good cheer [cp. 9 2; 14 27]; thy faith hath 3 made thee whole.

34 And he [cp. 5 30; 8 33] said unto her, Daughter, [cp. 6 50; 10 49] thy faith hath 3 made thee whole [cp. 10 52]; go in peace, and be whole of thy 2 plague.

48 And he [cp. 7 9, 44; 9 55: 10 23; 14 25; 22 61; 23 28] said unto her, Daughter, thy faith hath 3 made thee whole [cp. 7 50; 17 19; 18 42]; go in peace [cp. 7 50].

cp. 1 38.

cp. 16 33.

And the woman was 2 made whole from that hour [cp. 8 13; 15 28; 17 18].

cp. 4 53.

35 While he yet spake, they come from the ruler of the synagogue's *house*, saying, Thy daughter is dead [cp. 9 26]: why troublest thou the 4 Master any further? **36** But Jesus, 5 not heeding the word spoken, saith unto the ruler of the synagogue, Fear not, only believe. **37** And he suffered no man to follow with him, save Peter, and James, and John the brother of James [cp. 1 29; 9 2; 13 3; 14 33].

49 While he yet spake, there cometh one from the ruler of the synagogue's *house*, saying, Thy daughter is dead [cp. 7 12]; trouble [cp. 7 6] not the 4 Master. **50** But Jesus hearing it, answered him, Fear not: only believe, and she shall be 5 made whole.

verse 51

cp. 17 1; 26 37.
23 And when Jesus came into the ruler's house,

38 And they come to the house of the ruler of the synagogue;

51 And when he came to the house, he suffered not any man to enter in with him, save Peter, and John, and James [cp. 9 28], and the father of the maiden and her mother. **52** And all were weeping, and bewailing her: but he said,

cp 17 1; 26 37.

verse 37

verse 40
and he beholdeth a tumult, and *many* weeping and wailing greatly. **39** And when he was entered in, he saith unto them, Why make ye a tumult, and weep?

and saw the flute-players, and the crowd making a tumult,

Weep not [cp. 7 13; 23 28]; for she is not dead, but sleepeth. **53** And they laughed him to scorn, knowing that she was dead. **54** But he,

cp. 20 13, 15.

cp. 11 11.

24 he said, Give place: for the damsel is not dead, but sleepeth. And they laughed him to scorn. **25** But when the crowd was put forth,

the child is not dead, but sleepeth. **40** And they laughed him to scorn. But he, having put them all forth, taketh the father of the child and her mother and them that were with him, and goeth in where the child was. **41** And taking the child by the hand [cp. 1 31; 9 27; 1 41; 5 23; 6 2, 5; 7 33; 8 22, 23, 25; 10

he entered in, and took her by the hand [cp. 8 15; 8 3; 9 18, 29; 14 31; 17 7; 19 13, 15; 20 34: *also* 9 20;

verse 51

taking her by the hand [cp. 4 40; 5 13; 7 14; 13 13; 14 4; 18 15; 22 51: *also* 6

cp. 9 6: *also* 20 17.

14 36];	13, 16: *also* 3 10; 5 27; 6 56], he saith unto her, Talitha cumi; which is, being interpreted, Damsel, I say unto thee, Arise [*cp.* 2 11; 3 3; 10 49]. **42** And straight-way　　　the damsel rose up,　　and walked; for she was twelve years old.	19; 7 39; 8 44], called, saying,	

Top section (three parallel columns):

Matthew

14 36];

cp. 9 6.
and
the damsel
arose.

cp. 8 27; 9 33; 12 23; 15 31;
21 20; 27 14: *also* 7 28;
13 54; 19 25 22 22, 33.

cp. 8 4; 9 30; 12 16: *also*
16 20; 17 9.

26 And
4 the fame hereof went forth
into all that land [*cp.* 4 24].

1 Gr. *one ruler.*　　2 Or, *saved*
3 Or, *saved thee*　　4 Gr. *this fame.*

Mark

13, 16: *also* 3 10; 5 27; 6 56], he saith unto her, Talitha cumi; which is, being interpreted, Damsel, I say unto thee, Arise [*cp.* 2 11; 3 3; 10 49]. **42** And straight-way　　　the damsel rose up,　　and walked; for she was twelve years old.

verse 43
And they　　　were amazed straightway with a great amazement [*cp.* 2 12; 5 20; 6 51; 7 37; 10 32; 15 5; 16 5, 8: *also* 1 22, 27; 6 2; 10 24, 26; 11 18; 12 17]. **43** And he charged them much that no man should know this [*cp.* 1 44; 7 36; 8 26: *also* 1 25, 34; 3 12; 8 30; 9 9]: and he com-manded that *something* should be given her to eat.

cp. 1 28.

1 Or, *saved*　　2 Gr. *scourge.*
3 Or, *saved thee*　　4 Or, *Teacher*
5 Or, *overhearing*

Luke

19; 7 39; 8 44], called, saying,

Maiden,
arise [*cp.* 5 24; 6 8; 7 14]. **55** And her spirit returned, and she rose up immediately:
verse 42
and he commanded that *something* be given her to eat. **56** And her parents were amazed [*cp.* 5 9, 26; 8 25; 9 43; 11 14; 24 12, 41: *also* 2 47, 48; 4 22, 32, 36; 20 26]:

but he charged them to tell no man what had been done [*cp.* 5 14: *also* 4 35, 41; 9 21, 36].

verse 55
cp. 4 14, 37; 5 15; 7 17.

1 Some ancient authorities omit *had spent all her living upon physicians, and.*
2 Some ancient authorities omit *and they that were with him.*
3 Or, *saved thee*　　4 Or, *Teacher*
5 Or, *saved*

cp. 5 8.

cp. 7 15, 21, 46.

---

§ 109. The Rejection in the Synagogue

[*Cp.* Matt. 12 9-14: Mark 1 21-28; 3 1-6: Luke 4 31-37; 6 6-11; 13 10-17: John 6 59]

Matt. 13 53-58

53 And it came to pass, when Jesus had finished [*cp.* 7 28; 11 1; 19 1; 26 1] these parables, he depar-ted thence. **54** And coming into his own country [*cp.* 9 1: *also* 4 13]

he
taught
them in their synagogue,

cp. 4 17.

insomuch that they were astonished [*cp.* 7 28; 19 25; 22 22, 33: *also* 8 27; 9 33; 12 23; 15 31; 21 20; 27 14],

and said, Whence hath this man [*cp. verse* 56] this wisdom,

and　　these
1 mighty works?

Mark 6 1-6a

1 And

he went out from thence; and he cometh into his own country; and his disciples follow him. **2** And when the sabbath was come, he began to teach in the synagogue:

cp. 1 15.
and
1 many hearing him were astonished [*cp.* 1 22, 27; 10 24, 26; 11 18; 12 17: *also* 2 12; 5 20, 42; 6 51; 7 37; 10 32; 15 5; 16 8],

saying, Whence hath this man these things? and, What is the wisdom that is given unto this man, and *what mean* such 2 mighty works wrought

Luke 4 16-30

cp. 7 1.

16 And he came to Nazareth, where he had been brought up:

and

he entered, as his custom was, into the synagogue on the sabbath day, and stood up to read. ...
21 And he began to say unto them, To-day hath this scripture been fulfilled in your ears. 22 And all bare him witness, and wondered [*cp.* 2 47, 48; 4 32, 36; 20 26: *also* 5 9, 26; 8 25, 56; 9 43; 11 14; 24 12, 41] at the words of grace which pro-ceeded out of his mouth: and they said,

John 6 41-42; **4** 43-44

cp. 1 11.

6 41 The Jews therefore murmured concerning him,
cp. 7 15, 21, 46.

because he said. I am the bread which came down out of heaven. 42 And they said,

cp. 8 3, 15; 9 18, 25, 29; 20 34: *also* 14 31; 17 7; 19 13, 15.

55 Is not this   the carpenter's son ?
        is not his mother called
Mary ? and his brethren, James, and Joseph, and Simon, and Judas? **56** And his sisters, are they not all with us ? Whence then hath this man all these things ? **57** And they were ² offended [*cp.* 11 6; 15 12; 26 31, 33: *also* 13 21; 24 10] in him.

cp. 27 40.

cp. 4 13.

But Jesus
said unto them, A prophet [*cp.* 21 11, 46]
    is not without honour, save in his own country,

and in his own house. **58** And he
cp. 9 28: *also* 8 2.
did not many ¹ mighty works there
cp. 8 3, 15; *etc.*

    because of their unbelief.

---

by his hands [*cp.* 1 31, 41; 5 23, 41; 6 5; 7 33; 8 22, 23, 25; 9 27: *also* 10 13, 16]?
3 Is not this   the carpenter,

        the son of Mary, and brother of James, and Joses, and Judas, and Simon ? and are not his sisters here with us ?
    verse 2
      And they were ³ offended [*cp.* 14 27, 29: *also* 4 17]
     in him.

cp. 15 30.

cp. 1 21.

4 And Jesus
said unto them, A prophet [*cp.* 6 15]
    is not without honour, save in his own country, and among his own kin, and in his own house. **5** And he could [*cp.* 9 22, 23: *also* 1 40] there do no   ⁴ mighty work,   save that he laid his hands [*cp.* 1 31, 41; *etc.*] upon a few sick folk, and healed them. **6** And he marvelled because of their unbelief [*cp.* 16 14].

---

cp. 4 40; 5 13; 7 14; 8 54; 13 13; 14 4; 22 51: *also* 18 15.
Is not this
    Joseph's son [*cp.* 3 23] ?

cp. 7 23.

23 And he said unto them, Doubtless ye will say unto me this parable, Physician, heal thyself [*cp.* 23 37, 39]: whatsoever we have heard done at Capernaum [*cp.* 4 31], do also here in thine own country. **24** And he said, Verily I say unto you, No prophet [*cp.* 7 16, 39; 13 33; 24 19] is acceptable
    in his own country . . . .

cp. 5 12.

cp. 4 40; 5 13; *etc.*

28 And they were all filled with wrath in the synagogue, as they heard these things ; **29** and they rose up, and cast him forth out of the city [*cp.* 20 15], and led him unto the brow of the hill whereon their city was built, that they might throw him down headlong. **30** But he passing through the midst of them went his way.

---

cp. 9 6.

Is not this Jesus, the son of Joseph [*cp.* 1 45], whose father and mother we know ?

how doth he now say, I am come down out of heaven ?
    cp. 6 61: *also* 16 1.

4 43 And after the two days he went forth from thence into Galilee. **44** For Jesus himself testified, that a prophet [*cp.* 4 19; 6 14; 7 40; 9 17]   hath no honour   in his own country.

cp. 7 5.

cp. 1 11.

cp. 8 59; 10 39.

---

² Gr. *powers.*
² Gr. *caused to stumble.*

¹ Some ancient authorities insert *the.* ² Gr. *powers.*
³ Gr. *caused to stumble.*
⁴ Gr. *power.*

Luke 4 18-19 = Is. 61 1-2 ; 58 6.

---

§ 110. General Teaching

Matt. 9 35	Mark 6 6b	Luke 8 1

35 And Jesus went about all the cities and the villages, teaching in their synagogues, and preaching [*cp.* 4 23 ; 11 1] the ¹ gospel
cp. 11 5.
      of the kingdom [*cp.* 4 23 ; 24 14: *also* 26 13], and healing all manner

       6 And he went round about   the villages teaching.

cp. 1 1, 14, 15; 8 35; 10 29; 13 10; 14 9; 16 15.

1 And it came to pass soon afterwards, that he went about through cities and   villages [*cp.* 13 22],

    preaching and bringing the ¹ good tidings [*cp.* 1 19 ; 2 10 ; 3 18 ; 4 18, 43 ; 7 22 ; 9 6 ; 16 16 ; 20 1] of the kingdom of God,

of disease and all manner of sickness. *cp.* 10 1. **4 23** And Jesus went about in all Galilee, teaching in their synagogues, and preaching the ¹ gospel of the kingdom, and healing all manner of disease and all manner of sickness among the people.	*cp.* 6 7. **1 39** And he went into their synagogues throughout all Galilee, preaching and casting out ¹ devils.	and with him the twelve. **4 44** And he was preaching in the synagogues [*cp.* 4 15] of ² Galilee.
¹ Or, *good tidings*	¹ Gr. *demons.*	¹ Or, *gospel* ² Very many ancient authorities read *Judæa.*

cp. 18 20.

§ 111. The Mission of the Twelve

Matt. 10 1, 5-8; 9 37-38; 10 16, 9-15	**Mark 6** 7-13	**Luke 9** 1-6	Luke 10 1-12	
1 And he	**7** And he *cp.* 16 19, 20.	**1** And he	**1** Now after these things the Lord [*cp.* 7 13, 19; 10 39, 41; 11 39; 12 42; 13 15; 17 5, 6; 18 6; 19 8; 22 61; 24 3, 34]	*cp.* 4 1; 6 23; 11 2; 20 2, 18, 20, 25; 21 7, 12.

called unto him his twelve   disciples,
          and
gave them
 	
          authority over   unclean spirits [*cp.* 10 8; 17 16], to cast them out, and to heal all manner of disease and all manner of sickness. **5** These twelve
	called unto him the twelve [*cp.* 3 13, 14],
	
	          cp. 5 30.
		called the twelve [*cp.* 6 13] together,
		          and gave them power [*cp.* 1 17, 35; 4 14, 36; 5 17; 6 19; 8 46; 24 49] and authority over all ¹ devils [*cp.* 9 6, 40; 10 9, 17], and to cure diseases.
			appointed seventy ¹ others,	

Jesus sent forth, *cp.* 21 1.	and began to send them forth by two and two [*cp.* 11 1; 14 13]; and he gave them authority over the unclean spirits [*cp.* 3 15: *also* 6 12, 13; 9 18];	**2** And he sent them forth *cp.* 19 29; 22 8.	and sent them two and two	
verses 7 and 8		to preach the kingdom of God, and to heal [*cp.* 6 19; 9 11, 42; 14 4; 22 51] ² the sick.	*verses 9 and 11*	
			before his face into every city and place, whither he himself was about to come [*cp.* 9 52]. **2** And he said unto them,	

and charged them, saying, Go not into *any* way of the Gentiles, and enter not into any city of the Samaritans : **6** but go rather to the lost sheep of the house of Israel [*cp.* 15 24 : *also* 9 36]. **7** And as ye go, preach, saying, The kingdom of heaven is at hand [*cp.* 3 2; 4 17: *also* 12 28]. **8** Heal the sick, raise the dead, cleanse the lepers, cast out	**8** and he charged them
	
	          cp. 6 34.
	
	cp. 1 15: *also* 6 12.
		3 And he said unto them,
		
		          cp. 9 52.
		
		cp. verse 2: also 9 6.
			cp. 4 9.
			cp. 10 16.
			
			verses 9 and 11	

Column 1 (Matthew)

[1] devils : freely ye received, freely give. 9 37 The harvest truly is plenteous, but the labourers are few. 38 Pray ye therefore the Lord of the harvest, that he send forth labourers into his harvest.
10 16 Behold, I send you forth as sheep in the midst of wolves :
9 Get you

no gold, nor silver, nor brass in your [2] purses ; 10 no wallet for *your* journey, neither two coats, nor shoes, nor staff :

for the labourer is worthy of his food. 11 And into whatsoever city or village ye shall enter, search out who in it is worthy ; and there abide till ye go forth. 12 And as ye enter into the house, salute it.

13 And if the house be worthy, let your peace come upon it [*cp.* 5 9] : but if it be not worthy, let your peace return to you.

verse 11

verse 10

verses 7 *and* 8

14 And whosoever

shall not receive you, nor hear your words, as ye go forth out of that house or that city, shake off

Column 2 (Mark)

cp. verse 13.

that they should take nothing for *their* journey, save a staff only ; no bread, no wallet, no [1] money in their [2] purse ;

9 but *to go* shod with sandals : and, *said he*, put not on two coats.

10 And he said unto them, Wheresoever ye enter into a house, there abide till ye depart thence.

cp. 9 50.

11 And whatsoever place

shall not receive you, and they hear you not, as ye go forth thence, shake off

Column 3 (Luke 9)

Take nothing for your journey, neither staff, nor wallet, nor bread, nor money ;

neither have two coats [*cp.* 3 11].

4 And into whatsoever house ye enter, there abide, and thence depart.

cp. 1 79; 2 14, 29; 19 38.

verse 2

5 And as many as receive you not, when ye depart from that city, shake off

Column 4 (Luke 10)

The harvest is plenteous, but the labourers are few : pray ye therefore the Lord of the harvest, that he send forth labourers into his harvest. 3 Go your ways : behold, I send you forth as lambs in the midst of wolves.
4 Carry

no purse, no wallet, no shoes [*cp.* 22 35] :

and salute no man on the way.
verse 7

5 And into whatsoever house ye shall [2] enter,

verse 7

first say, Peace *be* to this house. 6 And if a son of peace be there, your peace shall rest upon [3] him : but if not, it shall turn to you again. 7 And in that same house remain, eating and drinking such things as they give : for the labourer is worthy of his hire. Go not from house to house. 8 And into whatsoever city ye enter, and they receive you, eat such things as are set before you : 9 and heal the sick that are therein, and say unto them, The kingdom of God is come nigh unto you [*cp.* 11 20 ; 17 20, 21 ; 19 11 ; 21 8]. 10 But into whatsoever city ye shall enter, and they receive you not [*cp.* 9 53], go out into the streets thereof and say, 11 Even

Right margin cross-references

cp. 4 35-38.

cp. 4 36.

cp. 14 27; 16 33.

cp. 4 36.

[Matt.]

the dust

of your feet.

cp. 8 4; 10 18; 24 14.

cp. 24 43.

15 Verily I say unto you, It shall be more tolerable [cp. 7 22; 24 36: *also* 26 29] for the land [cp. 2 6, 20, 21; 4 15; 11 24] of Sodom and Gomorrah in the day of judgement [cp. 11 22, 24; 12 36], than for that city [cp. 11 24].

cp. 11 5.

cp. 3 2; 4 17.

cp. *verse* 8.

¹ Gr. *demons*. ² Gr. *girdles*.

[Mark]

the dust

that is under your feet for a testimony unto them [cp. 1 44; 13 9].

cp. 13 32: *also* 14 25.

12 And they went out, and preached

that *men* should repent [cp. 1 15]. **13** And they cast out many ³ devils, and anointed with oil many that were sick, and healed them.

¹ Gr. *brass*. ² Gr. *girdle*. ³ Gr. *demons*.

[Luke 9]

the dust

from your feet for a testimony against them [cp. 5 14; 21 13].

6 And they departed, and went throughout the villages, preaching the gospel [cp. 1 19; 2 10; 3 18; 4 18, 43; 7 22; 8 1; 16 16; 20 1],

and healing everywhere.

¹ Gr. *demons*. ² Some ancient authorities omit *the sick*.

[Luke 10]

the dust from your city, that cleaveth to our feet, we do wipe off against you: howbeit know this [cp. 12 39], that the kingdom of God is come nigh [cp. *verse* 9]. **12** I say unto you, It shall be more tolerable in that day [cp. 17 31; 21 34] for

Sodom,

than

for that city.

cp. 13 3, 5.

¹ Many ancient authorities add *and two*: and so in ver. 17. ² Or, *enter first, say* ³ Or, *it*

[references]

cp. 14 20; 16 23, 26. cp. 3 22.

---

§ 112. Herod's Opinion on Jesus and the Death of John the Baptist

Matt. 14 1-12

1 At that season [cp. 11 25; 12 1] Herod the tetrarch heard the report concerning Jesus, **2** and said [cp. 16 14] unto his servants, This is John the Baptist; he is risen from the dead; and therefore do these powers work in him.

cp. 13 57; 21 11, 46.

cp. 8 27; 21 10.

3 For Herod had laid hold on John, and bound him, and put him in prison [cp. 4 12; 11 2] for the sake of

Mark 6 14-29

14 And king Herod heard *thereof*; for his name had become known: and

verse 20

¹ he said [8 28], John ² the Baptist is risen from the dead, and therefore do these powers work in him. **15** But others said, It is Elijah. And others said, *It is* a prophet [cp. 6 4], *even* as one of the prophets. **16** But Herod, when he heard *thereof*, said, John, whom I beheaded, he is risen.

cp. 1 27; 2 7; 4 41.

17 For Herod himself had sent forth and laid hold upon John, and bound him in prison [cp. 1 14] for the sake of

Luke 9 7-9

7 Now Herod the tetrarch heard of all that was done [cp. 23 8]: and he was much perplexed, because that it was said by some [cp. 9 19], that John was risen from the dead; **8** and by some, that Elijah had appeared; and by others, [cp. 4 24; 7 16, 39; 13 33; 24 19] that one of the old prophets was risen again. **9** And Herod said, John I beheaded: but who is this [cp. 4 36; 5 21; 7 49; 8 25], about whom I hear such things? And he sought to see him [cp. 23 8: *also* 19 3].

3 19 But Herod the tetrarch, being reproved by him for

[references]

cp. 4 19, 44; 6 14; 7 40; 9 17.

cp. 5 12: *also* 12 34.

cp. 3 24.

Herodias, his brother Philip's wife.

4 For John said unto him, It is not lawful for thee to have her.

5 And when he would have put him to death,

he feared   the multitude [*cp.* 21 26: *also* 21 46; 26 5], because they counted him as a prophet [*cp.* 21 26 *and* 46: *also* 11 9].

6 But when   Herod's   birthday came,

the daughter of Herodias danced in the midst, and   pleased Herod.

7 Whereupon he promised with an oath to give her whatsoever she should ask.

8 And she, being put forward by her mother,

saith, Give me here in a charger the head of John the Baptist. **9** And the king was grieved; but for the sake of his oaths, and of them which sat at meat with him, he commanded it to be given; **10** and he sent,

and beheaded John in the prison. **11** And his head was brought in a charger, and given to the damsel: and she brought it to her mother. **12** And his disciples [*cp.* 9 14; 11 2] came, and took up the corpse, and buried him; and they went and told Jesus.

Herodias, his brother Philip's wife: for he had married her. **18** For John said unto Herod, It is not lawful for thee to have thy brother's wife. **19** And Herodias set herself against him, and desired to kill him; and she could not; **20** for Herod feared John,

cp. 11 32: *also* 11 18; 12 12; 14 2.

cp. 11 32.

knowing that he was a righteous man and a holy, and kept him safe. And when he heard him, he [3] was much perplexed; and he heard him gladly [*cp.* 12 37].

21 And when a convenient day was come, that Herod on his birthday made a supper to his lords, and the [4] high captains, and the chief men of Galilee; **22** and when [5] the daughter of Herodias herself came in and danced, [6] she pleased Herod and them that sat at meat with him; and the king said unto the damsel, Ask of me whatsoever thou wilt, and I will give it thee. **23** And he sware unto her, Whatsoever thou shalt ask of me, I will give it thee, unto the half of my kingdom. **24** And she went out, and said unto her mother, What shall I ask? And she said, The head of John [2] the Baptist. **25** And she came in straightway with haste unto the king, and asked, saying, I will that thou forthwith give me in a charger the head of John the Baptist. **26** And the king was exceeding sorry; but for the sake of his oaths, and of them that sat at meat, he would not reject her. **27** And straightway the king sent forth a soldier of his guard, and commanded to bring his head: and he went and beheaded him in the prison, **28** and brought his head in a charger, and gave it to the damsel; and the damsel gave it to her mother. **29** And when his disciples [*cp.* 2 18] heard *thereof*, they came and took up his corpse, and laid it in a tomb.

cp. 6 30.

[1] Some ancient authorities read *they*.
[2] Gr. *the Baptizer*.
[3] Many ancient authorities read *did many things*.
[4] Or, *military tribunes* Gr. *chiliarchs*.
[5] Some ancient authorities read *his daughter Herodias*.   [6] Or, *it*

Herodias his brother's wife, and for all the evil things which Herod had done, **20** added yet this above all, that he shut up John in prison.

cp. 20 6: *also* 20 19; 22 2.

cp. 20 6: *also* 1 76; 7 26.

verse 7

cp. 5 33; 7 18; 11 1.

cp. 1 35, 37; 3 25; 4 1.

Matt. 14 4 ‖ Mark 6 18: *cp.* Lev. 18 16; 20 21.

§ 113. The Return of the Twelve and the Feeding of the Five Thousand

[*Cp*. Matt. 15 32-39: Mark 8 1-10]

Matt. 14 13-21	Mark 6 30-44	Luke 9 10-17	John 6 1-14
cp. 10 2.	30 And the apostles	10 And the apostles [*cp*. 6 13; 17 5; 22 14; 24 10], when they were returned [*cp*. 10 17],	
13 Now when Jesus *cp*. 14 12.	gather themselves together unto Jesus; and they told him all things, whatsoever they had done, and whatsoever they had taught.	declared unto him what things they had done.	1 After these things Jesus
heard *it*,	31 And he saith unto them, Come ye yourselves apart [*cp*. 4 10, 34; 9 2, 28; 13 3] into a desert place, and rest a while. For there were many coming and going, and they had no leisure so much as to eat [*cp*. 3 20].	And he took them, *cp*. 10 23.	
cp. 17 1, 19; 20 17; 24 3.			
[*cp*. 8 18] he withdrew from thence in a boat, to a desert place apart [*see above*]:	32 And they went away [*cp*. 1 35, 45] in the boat to a desert place apart [*see above*]. *cp*. 6 45; 8 22.	and withdrew [*cp*. 4 42; 5 16] apart [*see above*] to a city called Bethsaida.	went away to the other side of the sea of Galilee, which is *the sea of Tiberias*. 2 And a great multitude
and when the multitudes heard thereof, they followed him [1] on foot from the cities.	33 And *the people* saw them going, and many knew *them*, and they ran there together [1] on foot from all the cities, and outwent them.	11 But the multitudes perceiving it followed him:	followed him,
14 And he came forth, and saw a great multitude, and he had compassion on them [*cp*. 9 36; 15 32: also 20 34],	34 And he came forth and saw a great multitude, and he had compassion on them [*cp*. 8 2: also 1 41], because they were as sheep not having a shepherd [*cp*. 14 27]: and he began to teach them many things.	and he welcomed them [*cp*. 7 13: *and* 10 33; 15 20],	*cp*. 10 11-16.
cp. 9 36: *also* 10 6; 15 24; 26 31.		and spake to them of the kingdom of God, and them that had need of healing he healed [*cp*. 6 19; 9 2, 42; 14 4; 22 51].	
and healed			because they beheld the signs which he did on them that were sick. 3 And Jesus went up into the mountain [*cp*. 6 15], and there he sat with his disciples. 4 Now the passover, the feast of the Jews, was at hand. 5 Jesus therefore lifting up his eyes, and seeing that a great multitude cometh unto him, saith unto Philip,
their sick. *cp*. 5 1; 14 23; 15 29; 17 1; 28 16. *cp*. 15 29: *also* 5 1; 24 3.	*cp*. 3 13; 6 46; 9 2. *cp*. 13 3.	*cp*. 6 12; 9 28.	
		cp. 6 20.	
cp. 3 7; 5 1; 8 18; 9 36.			
15 And when even was come, the disciples came to him, saying, The place is desert, and the time is already past; send the multitudes away [*cp*. 15 23], that they may go into the villages,	35 And when the day was now far spent, his disciples came unto him, and said, The place is desert, and the day is now far spent: 36 send them away, that they may go into the country and villages round about,	12 And the day began to wear away; and the twelve came, and said unto him, Send the multitude away, that they may go into the villages and country round about, and lodge,	
and buy themselves food.	and buy themselves some-	and get victuals:	Whence are we to buy [1] bread, that these

[Matthew]

16 But Jesus said unto them, They have no need to go away; give ye them to eat. 17 And they say unto him,

cp. 15 34.

We have here but five loaves, and two fishes.

verse 21
18 And he said, Bring them hither to me [*cp.* 17 17]. 19 And he commanded the multitudes to ² sit down on the grass;

verse 21
and he took the five loaves, and the two fishes, and looking up to heaven, he blessed [*cp.* 26 26: *also* 15 36; 26 27], and brake and gave the loaves to the disciples, and the disciples to the multitudes.

20 And they did all eat, and were filled:

and they took up

that which remained over of the broken pieces, twelve baskets full.
21 And they that did eat were about five thousand men, beside women and children [*cp.*

[Mark]

what to eat.

37 But he answered and said unto them,

Give ye them to eat. And they say unto him, Shall we go and buy two hundred ² pennyworth of bread, and give them to eat ?
38 And he saith unto them, How many loaves have ye [*cp.* 8 5] ? go *and* see. And when they knew,

they say,

Five, and two fishes.

verse 44
39 And he commanded them that all should ³ sit down by companies upon the green grass. 40 And they

sat down in ranks, by hundreds, and by fifties.

verse 44
41 And he took the five loaves and the two fishes, and looking up to heaven [*cp.* 7 34], he blessed [*cp.* 8 7; 14 22: *also* 8 6; 14 23], and brake the loaves; and he gave to the disciples to set before them; and the two fishes divided he among them all. 42 And they did all eat, and were filled.

43 And they took up

broken pieces, twelve basketfuls, and also of the fishes. 44 And they that ate the loaves were five thousand men.

[Luke]

for we are here in a desert place. 13 But he said unto them,

Give ye them to eat. And they said,

We have no more than five loaves and two fishes; except we should go and buy food for all this people. 14 For they were about five thousand men. And he said unto his disciples,

Make them ¹ sit down in companies, about fifty each. 15 And they did so, and made them all ¹ sit down.

verse 14
16 And he took the five loaves and the two fishes, and looking up to heaven, he blessed [*cp.* 24 30; *also* 22 17, 19] them, and brake; and gave to the disciples to set before the multitude.

17 And they did eat, and were all filled:

and there was taken up

that which remained over to them of broken pieces, twelve baskets.

verse 14

[John]

may eat ? 6 And this he said to prove him : for he himself knew what he would do.

7 Philip answered him, Two hundred ² pennyworth of ¹ bread is not sufficient for them, that every one may take a little.

8 One of his disciples, Andrew, Simon Peter's brother, saith unto him, 9 There is a lad here, which hath five barley loaves, and two fishes : but what are these among so many ?

verse 10
10 Jesus said,

Make the people sit down. Now there was much grass in the place. So the men sat down, in number about five thousand. 11 Jesus therefore took the loaves; and
cp. 11 41; 17 1.

having given thanks,

he distributed to them that were set down; likewise also of the fishes as much as they would. 12 And when they were filled, he saith unto his disciples, Gather up the broken pieces which remain over, that nothing be lost. 13 So they gathered them up, and filled twelve baskets with broken pieces from the five barley loaves, which remained over unto them

that had eaten.
verse 10

15 38].

cp. 12 23; 14 2; 21 11; 27 54: *also* 8 27; 21 10. *cp.* 13 57; 21 11, 46.	*cp.* 6 15; 15 39: *also* 2 7; 4 41, *and* 1 27. *cp.* 6 4, 15.	*cp.* 23 47: *also* 5 21; 7 49; 8 25; 9 9, *and* 4 36. *cp.* 4 24; 7 16, 39; 13 33; 24 19.	14 When therefore the people saw the [3] sign which he did, they said, This is [*cp.* 1 34; 4 29, 42; 7 41] of a truth the prophet [*cp.* 4 19, 44; 7 40; 9 17] that cometh [*cp.* 1 15, 27; 3 31; 11 27; 12 13] into the world.
cp. 3 11; 11 3: 21 9; 23 39.	*cp.* 11 9.	*cp.* 7 19, 20; 13 35; 19 38.	

[1] Or, *by land* [2] Gr. *recline.*	[1] Or, *by land* [2] See marginal note on Matt. 18 28. [3] Gr. *recline.*	[1] Gr. *recline.*	[1] Gr. *oaves.* [2] See marginal note on Matt. 18 28. [3] Some ancient authorities read *signs.*

(x) Journeying in the North (Matt. and Mark: in Galilee, Luke: §§ 114-128).

§ 114. **Jesus walks on the Water**

[*Cp.* Matt. 8 23-27: Mark 4 35-41: Luke 8 22-25]

Matt. 14 22-33	**Mark 6** 45-52		John 6 15-21
cp. 12 15; 16 8; 22 18; 26 10.	*cp.* 8 17.		15 Jesus therefore perceiving [*cp.* 5 6] that they were about to come and take him by force, to make him king,
22 And straightway he constrained the disciples to enter into the boat, and to go before him unto the other side [*cp.* 8 18], till he should send the multitudes away. **23** And after he had sent the multitudes away, he went up into the mountain [*cp.* 5 1; 15 29; 17 1; 28 16] apart to pray [*cp.* 19 13; 26 36, 39, 42, 44; *and* 11 25]: and when even was come,	**45** And straightway he constrained his disciples to enter into the boat, and to go before *him* unto the other side [*cp.* 4 35] to Bethsaida [*cp.* 8 22], while he himself sendeth the multitude away. **46** And after he had taken leave of them, he departed into the mountain [*cp.* 3 13; 9 2] to pray [*cp.* 1 35; 14 32, 35, 39].	*cp.* 8 22. *cp.* 9 10.	with-drew again into the mountain [*cp.* 6 3] himself alone. *cp.* 11 41; 12 27-28; 17 1 *ff*.
	47 And when even was come,	*cp.* 6 12; 9 28: *also* 3 21; 5 16; 9 18, 29; 11 1; 22 41, 44; *and* 10 21.	16 And when evening came, his disciples went down unto the sea; **17** and they entered into a boat, and were going over the sea unto Capernaum.
he was there alone. **24** But the boat [1] was now in the midst of the sea,	the boat was in the midst of the sea, and he alone on the land.		And it was now dark, and Jesus had not yet come to them. **18** And the sea was rising by reason of a great wind that blew. **19** When therefore they had rowed about
distressed by the waves; for the wind was contrary. **25** And	**48** And seeing them distressed in rowing, for the wind was contrary unto them,		five and twenty or thirty furlongs,
in the fourth watch of the night he came unto them, walking upon the sea.	about the fourth watch of the night he cometh unto them, walking on the sea; and he would have passed by them:		
26 And when the disciples saw him walking on the sea, they were troubled, saying, It is an apparition; and they cried out	**49** but they, when they saw him walking on the sea, supposed that it was an apparition, and cried out: **50** for they all saw him, and were troubled.		they behold Jesus walking on the sea, and drawing nigh unto the boat:
for fear. **27** But straightway Jesus spake unto them, saying, Be of good cheer [*cp.* 9 2, 22]; it is I; be not afraid [*cp.* 17 7; 28 10]. **28** And Peter [*cp.* 15 15; 16 22; 17 4; 18 21;	But he straightway spake with them, and saith unto them, Be of good cheer [*cp.* 10 49]: it is I; be not afraid. *cp.* 8 32; 9 5; 10 28; 11 21; 14 29: *also* 8 29.	*cp.* 24 37. *cp.* 8 45; 9 33; 12 41;	and they were afraid. **20** But he saith unto them, *cp.* 16 33. It is I; be not afraid. *cp.* 13 36, 37; 21 21: *also* 6 68.

19 27; 26 33: *also* 16 16; 17 24] answered him and said, Lord, if it be thou, bid me come unto thee upon the waters. **29** And he said, Come. And Peter went down from the boat, and walked upon the waters, ² to come to Jesus. **30** But when he saw the ³ wind, he was afraid; and beginning to sink, he cried out, saying, Lord, save me [*cp.* 8 25]. **31** And immediately Jesus stretched forth his hand, and took hold of him [*cp.* 8 3; 9 25: *also* 8 15; 9 18, 29; 17 7; 19 13, 15; 20 34], and saith unto him, O thou of little faith [*cp.* 6 30; 8 26; 16 8: *also* 17 20], wherefore didst thou doubt [*cp.* 21 21; 28 17]? **32** And when they were gone up into the boat, the wind ceased.

      cp. 14 34.

    33 And they that were in the boat worshipped him [*cp.* 28 9, 17: *also* 2 11; *and* 8 2; 9 18; 15 25; 17 14; 20 20], saying, Of a truth thou art the Son of God [*cp.* 4 3, 6; 8 29; 16 16; 26 63; 27 40, 43, 54: *also* 3 17; 17 5].

cp. 8 27; 21 20: *also* 9 33; 12 23; 15 31; 27 14: *and* 7 28; 13 54; 19 25; 22 22, 33.

    cp. 16 8-12: *also* 15 16.

      cp. 19 8.

¹ Some ancient authorities read *was many furlongs distant from the land.*
² Some ancient authorities read *and came.*
³ Many ancient authorities add *strong.*

---

cp. 1 31, 41; 5 41; 8 23; 9 27: *also* 5 23; 6 2, 5; 7 33; 8 22, 25; 10 13, 16.

    cp. 4 40; 11 22; 16 14.

cp. 11 23; 16 14.   **51** And he went up unto them into the boat; and the wind ceased [*cp.* 4 39]:
      cp. 6 53.
    and they were

cp. 3 11; 5 33; *and* 1 40; 5 6, 22; 7 25; 10 17.

cp. 1 1; 3 11; 5 7; 15 39: *also* 1 11; 9 7.

sore amazed in themselves [*cp.* 10 32; 16 5, 8: *also* 2 12; 5 20, 42; 7 37; 15 5: *and* 1 22, 27; 6 2; 10 24, 26; 11 18; 12 17]; **52** for they understood not concerning the loaves [*cp.* 8 17-21: *also* 4 13; 7 18; 9 10, 32], but their heart was hardened [*cp.* 8 17; 16 14: *also* 3 5; 10 5].

---

18 28: *also* 5 8; 9 20.

cp. 5 13; 8 54: *also* 4 40; *etc.*

cp. 12 28: *also* 8 25; 17 5, 6; 22 32; 24 25, 38.

cp. 5 8; 24 52: *also* 8 47; 17 16; *etc.*

cp. 1 35; 4 3, 9, 41; 8 28; *etc.*

cp. 5 9; 8 25; 24 12, 41: *also* 5 26; *etc.*

cp. 2 50; 9 45; 18 34.

---

    cp. 21 7.

cp. 3 12; 6 64; 14 10; 20 27.

    21 They were willing therefore to receive him into the boat: and straightway the boat was at the land whither they were going.

cp. 9 38; 18 6; *and* 11 32.

    cp. 1 34; *etc.*

    cp. 7 15, 21, 46.

cp. 4 33: *also* 3 10; 8 27, 43 10 6; *etc.*
    cp. 12 40.

---

§ 115. Healings in Gennesaret

Matt. 14 34-36	Mark 6 53-56		
34 And when they had crossed over, they came to the land, unto Gennesaret. **35** And when the men of that place knew him, they sent into all that region round about, and brought unto him [*cp.* 9 2] all that were sick;	**53** And when they had ¹ crossed over, they came to the land unto Gennesaret, and moored to the shore. **54** And when they were come out of the boat, straightway *the people* knew him, **55** and ran round about that whole region, and began to carry about on their beds [*cp.* 2 4] those that were sick, where they heard he was. **56** And wheresoever he entered, into villages, or into cities, or into the country, they laid the sick in the marketplaces, and	*cp.* 6 21.	
36 and they besought him that they might only touch [*cp.* 9 20: *also* 8 3, *etc.*] the	besought him that they might touch [*cp.* 3 10; 5 27: *also* 1 31, 41; *etc.*] if it were but the	*cp.* 5 18	*cp.* 5 3-6.
		cp. 6 19; 7 39; 8 44; *etc.*	

border [*cp*. 9 20] of his garment: and as many as touched were made whole.	border of his garment: and as many as touched ² him were made whole.	*cp.* 8 44.

¹ Or, *crossed over to the land, they came unto Gennesaret*
² Or, *it*

§ 116. A Question about the Tradition of the Elders

[*Cp*. Luke 11 38-41: *also* Matt. 9 14-17; Mark 2 18-22; Luke 5 33-39]

Matt. 15 1-20	Mark 7 1-23		
1 Then there come to Jesus from Jerusalem Pharisees and scribes,	**1** And there are gathered together unto him the Pharisees, and certain of the scribes, which had come from Jerusalem [*cp*. 3 22], **2** and had seen that some of his disciples ate their bread with ¹ defiled, that is, unwashen, hands.	*cp.* 5 17.	*cp.* 1 19.
cp. verse 20.	**3** For the Pharisees, and all the Jews, except they wash their hands ² diligently, eat not, holding the tradition of the elders: **4** and *when they come* from the marketplace, except they ³ wash themselves, they eat not: and many other things there be, which they have received to hold, ⁴ washings		
cp. 23 25.	of cups, and pots, and brasen vessels.⁵	*cp.* 11 39.	
saying, **2** Why do thy disciples transgress [*cp*. 9 14; 12 2] the tradition of the elders ? for they wash not their hands when they eat bread.	**5** And the Pharisees and the scribes ask him, Why walk not thy disciples [*cp*. 2 18, 24] according to the tradition of the elders, but eat their bread with ¹ defiled hands ? **6** And he said unto them, Well did Isaiah prophesy of you hypocrites [*cp*. 12 15], as it is written,	*cp.* 5 33; 6 2. *cp.* 11 38. *cp.* 12 56; 13 15: *also* 12 1.	
verses 7-9	This people honoureth me with their lips, But their heart is far from me. **7** But in vain do they worship me, Teaching *as their* doctrines the precepts of men. **8** Ye leave the commandment of God, and hold fast the tradition of		
3 And he answered and said unto them, Why do ye also transgress the commandment of God because of your tradition ? **4** For God said, Honour thy father and thy mother: and, He that speaketh evil of father or mother, let him ¹ die the death. **5** But ye say, Whosoever shall say to his father or his mother, That wherewith thou mightest have been profited by me is given *to God*; **6** he shall not honour his father.² And ye have made void the ³ word of God because of your tradition.	men. **9** And he said unto them, Full well do ye reject the commandment of God, that ye may keep your tradition. **10** For Moses said, Honour thy father and thy mother; and, He that speaketh evil of father or mother, let him ⁶ die the death: **11** but ye say, If a man shall say to his father or his mother, That wherewith thou mightest have been profited by me is Corban, that is to say, Given *to God*; **12** ye no longer suffer him to do aught for his father or his mother; **13** making void the word of God by your tradition, which ye have delivered: and many such like things ye do.		
7 Ye hypocrites [*cp*. 22 18; 23 13, 15, 23, 25, 27 29: *also* 6 2, 5, 16; 24 51: *and* 23 28], well did Isaiah prophesy of you, saying, **8** This people honoureth me with their lips; But their heart is far from me. **9** But in vain do they worship me,	*verses* 6-7	*cp.* 12 56; 13 15: *also* 12 1.	

Teaching *as their* doctrines the precepts of men.
10 And he called to him the multitude, and said unto them, Hear, and understand: **11** Not that which entereth into the mouth defileth the man; but that which proceedeth out of the mouth, this defileth the man.

cp. 11 15; 13 9, 43: *also* 19 12.
cp. 13 36; 17 25.

12 Then came the disciples [cp. 5 1; 13 10, 36; 14 15; 15 23; 17 19; 18 1; 24 1, 3; 26 17], and said unto him, Knowest thou that the Pharisees were 4 offended [cp. 11 6; 13 57; 26 31, 33; *also* 13 21; 24 10], when they heard this saying? **13** But he answered and said, Every 5 plant which my heavenly Father [cp. 5 48; 6 14, 26, 32; 18 35; 23 9: *also* 5 16, 45; 6 1; *etc.*] planted not, shall be rooted up [cp. 13 29]. **14** Let them alone: they are blind guides [cp. 23 16, 17, 19, 24, 26]. And if the blind guide the blind, both shall fall into a pit. **15** And Peter [cp. 14 28; 16 22; 17 4; 18 21; 19 27; 26 33: *also* 16 16; 17 24] answered and said unto him, Declare unto us the parable [cp. 13 36]. **16** And he said, Are ye also even yet without understanding [cp. 16 8-12]? **17** Perceive ye not, that whatsoever goeth into the mouth passeth into the belly, and is cast out into the draught?

cp. 23 26.

18 But the things which proceed out of the mouth come forth out of the heart [cp. 12 34]; and they defile the man. **19** For [cp. 23 25, 26, 28] out of the heart come forth evil thoughts, murders, adulteries, fornications, thefts,

[cp. 6 23; 20 15] false witness, railings:
20 these are the things which defile the man: but to eat with unwashen hands defileth not the man.

1 Or, *surely die*
2 Some ancient authorities add *or his mother*.
3 Some ancient authorities read *law*.
4 Gr. *caused to stumble*.   5 Gr. *planting*.

14 And he called to him the multitude again, and said unto them, Hear me all of you, and understand: **15** there is nothing from without the man, that going into him can defile him: but the things which proceed out of the man are those that defile the man. 7[cp. 4 9, 23]. **17** And when he was entered into the house [cp. 9 28, 33; 10 10] from the multitude, his disciples [cp. 6 35]

Luke 6 **39** And he spake also a parable unto them. Can the blind guide the blind? shall they not both fall into a pit?
cp. 8 45; 9 33; 12 41; 18 28: *also* 5 8; 9 20.

asked of him the parable [cp. 4 10]. **18** And he saith unto them, Are ye so without understanding also [cp. 4 13; 8 17-21: *also* 6 52; 9 10, 32; 16 14]? Perceive ye not, that whatsoever from without goeth into the man, *it* cannot defile him; **19** because it goeth not into his heart, but into his belly, and goeth out into the draught? *This he said*, making all meats clean. **20** And he said, That which proceedeth out of the man, that defileth the man. **21** For from within, out of the heart of men, 8 evil thoughts proceed, fornications, **22** thefts, murders, adulteries, covetings, wickednesses, deceit, lasciviousness, an evil eye, railing, pride, foolishness: **23** all these evil things proceed from within, and defile the man.

cp. verse 2.

1 Or, *common*
2 Or, *up to the elbow* Gr. *with the fist*.
3 Gr. *baptize*. Some ancient authorities read *sprinkle themselves*.
4 Gr. *baptizings*.
5 Many ancient authorities add *and couches*.
6 Or, *surely die*
7 Many ancient authorities insert ver. 16, *If any man hath ears to hear, let him hear*.
8 Gr. *thoughts that are evil*.

Cross-references (right-hand columns):

cp. 8 8; 14 35.   cp. 6 60.
cp. 9 12.
cp. 6 3; 14 27, 29: *also* 4 17.   cp. 7 23.   cp. 6 61: *also* 16 1.
cp. 11 25, 26.   cp. 11 13.
cp. 9 39-41.
cp. 8 32; 9 5; 10 28; 11 21; 14 29: *also* 8 29.   cp. 13 36, 37; 21 21: *also* 6 68.
cp. 8 9.
cp. 2 50; 9 45; 18 34.   cp. 3 10; 4 33; 8 27, 43; *etc.*
cp. 11 41.
cp. 6 45.
cp. 11 39, 41.
cp. 11 34.

Matt. 15 4 || Mark 7 10: Exod. 20 12; 21 17; Lev. 20 9; Deut. 5 16.   Matt. 15 8-9 || Mark 7 6-7: Is. 29 13.

§ 117. The Syrophœnician Woman

Matt. 15 21-28

21 And Jesus went out thence, and withdrew into the parts of Tyre and Sidon.

cp. 8 4; etc.

22 And behold, a Canaanitish woman came out from those borders, and cried, saying,

cp. 2 11: also 17 14.

Have mercy on me [cp. 9 27; 17 15; 20 30, 31], O Lord, thou son of David [cp. 9 27; 20 30, 31: also 1 1; 12 23; 21 9, 15]; my daughter is grievously vexed with a ¹ devil. **23** But he answered her not a word [cp. 26 63; 27 12, 14]. And his disciples came [cp. 5 1; 13 10, 36; 14 15; 15 12; 17 19; 18 1; 24 1, 3; 26 17] and besought him, saying, Send her away [cp. 14 15: also 19 13; 26 8-9]; for she crieth after us. **24** But he answered and said, I was not sent but unto the lost sheep of the house of Israel [cp. 10 6: also 9 36; 26 31]. **25** But she came and worshipped [cp. 2 11; 8 2; 9 18; 14 33; 20 20; 28 9, 17] him, saying, Lord, help me. **26** And he answered and said, [cp. 5 24; 6 33; 7 5; 23 26] It is not meet to take the children's ² bread and cast it to the dogs [cp. 7 6]. **27** But she said, Yea, Lord: for even the dogs eat of the crumbs which fall from their masters' table. **28** Then Jesus answered and said unto her, O woman, great is thy faith: be it done unto thee even as thou wilt [cp. 8 13; 9 29].
cp. 8 13. And her daughter was healed from that hour [cp. 8 13; 9 22; 17 18].

¹ Gr. demon.　　² Or, loaf

Mark 7 24-30

24 And from thence he arose, and went away into the borders of Tyre ¹ and Sidon. And he entered into a house, and would have no man know it [cp. 9 30: also 1 25; etc.]: and he could not be hid. **25** But straightway a woman, whose little daughter had an unclean spirit, having heard of him, came and fell down at his feet [cp. 3 11; 5 22, 33: also 1 40; 10 17]. **26** Now the woman was a ² Greek, a Syrophœnician by race. And she besought him that he would cast forth the ³ devil out of her daughter.

cp. 10 47, 48.

cp. 10 47, 48.

cp. 14 61; 15 5.

cp. 6 35.

cp. 6 36: also 10 13; 14 4-5.

cp. 6 34; 14 27.

cp. 5 6.

cp. 9 22. **27** And he said unto her, Let the children first be filled: for it is not meet to take the children's ⁴ bread and cast it to the dogs. **28** But she answered and saith unto him, Yea, Lord: even the dogs under the table eat of the children's crumbs.

29 And he said unto her, For this saying go thy way; the ³ devil is gone out of thy daughter. **30** And she went away unto her house, and found the child laid upon the bed, and the ³ devil gone out.

¹ Some ancient authorities omit and Sidon.
² Or, Gentile　³ Gr. demon.　⁴ Or, loaf

cp. 4 35; etc.		
cp. 5 8, 12; 8 28, 41, 47; 17 16.	cp. 11 32; 18 6.	
cp. 17 13; 18 38, 39.		
cp. 18 38, 39: also 1 32.		
cp. 23 9.	cp. 19 9.	
cp. 9 12.		
cp. 9 12: also 18 15.	cp. 12 5.	
	cp. 10 11-16.	
cp. 24 52.	cp. 9 38.	
cp. 6 42.		
cp. 16 21.		
	cp. 4 50.	
cp. 7 10.	cp. 4 53.	

§ 118. Healings by the Sea of Galilee (Matt.): The Healing of a Deaf-Mute (Mark)

[Cp. Matt. 9 32-34; 12 22: Mark 9 17, 25: Luke 11 14: also Matt. 11 5 and Luke 7 22]

Matt. 15 29-31

29 And Jesus departed thence, and came nigh unto the sea of Galilee;
cp. 4 25. and he

Mark 7 31-37

31 And again he went out from the borders of Tyre, and came through Sidon unto the sea of Galilee, through the midst of the borders of Decapolis [cp. 5 20].

cp. 6 1.

Matt.

went up into the mountain [*cp.* 5 1; 14 23; 17 1; 28 16], and sat there [*cp.* 5 1; 24 3]. **30** And there came unto him great multitudes, having with them the lame, blind,

dumb,

maimed, and many others, and they cast them down at his feet;

cp. 8 3, 15; 9 29; 17 7; 20 34: *also* 9 25; 14 31; 19 13, 15: *and* 9 18.

cp. 14 19.

and he healed them:

cp. 8 4; 9 30; 12 16: *also* 16 20; 17 9.

cp. 9 31.

31 insomuch that the multitude wondered [*cp.* 9 33; 12 23; 27 14: *also* 8 27; 21 20: *and* 7 28; 13 54; 19 25; 22 22, 33], when they saw

the dumb speaking, the maimed whole, and the lame walking, and the blind seeing [*cp.* 11 5]: and they glorified the God [*cp.* 9 8: *also* 5 16] of Israel.

Mark

cp. 3 13; 6 46; 9 2.

cp. 13 3.   **32** And they bring unto him

one that was deaf, and had an impediment in his speech;

and they beseech him to lay his hand upon him [*cp.* 8 22]. **33** And he took him aside from the multitude privately [*cp.* 8 23], and put his fingers into his ears, and he spat [*cp.* 8 23], and touched [*cp.* 1 41; 8 22; 10 13: *also* 1 31; 5 41; 8 23, 25; 9 27; 10 16: *and* 5 23; 6 2, 5] his tongue; **34** and looking up to heaven [*cp.* 6 41], he sighed [*cp.* 8 12], and saith unto him, Ephphatha, that is, Be opened. **35** And his ears were opened, and the bond of his tongue was loosed, and he spake plain [*cp.* 8 25].

36 And he charged them that they should tell no man [*cp.* 1 44; 5 43; 8 26: *also* 1 25, 34; 3 12: *and* 8 30; 9 9]: but the more he charged them, so much the more a great deal they published it [*cp.* 1 45]. **37** And they were beyond measure astonished [*cp.* 2 12; 5 20, 42; 15 5: *also* 6 51; 10 32; 16 5, 8: *and* 1 22, 27; 6 2; 10 24, 26; 11 18; 12 17], saying, He hath done all things well: he maketh even the deaf to hear, and the dumb to speak.

cp. 2 12.

Luke

cp. 6 12; 9 28.

cp. 5 13; 7 14; 18 15; 22 51; *etc.*

cp. 9 16.

cp. 1 64.

cp. 5 14; 8 56: *also* 4 35; *etc.*

cp. 5 15.

cp. 5 26; 8 56; 9 43; 11 14; *etc.*

cp. 7 22.

cp. 5 25, 26: *also* 2 20; 7 16; 13 13; 17 15, 18; 18 43; 23 47.

John

cp. 6 3, 15.

cp. 9 6.

cp. 11 41; 17 1.

cp. 9 24.

§ 119. The Feeding of the Four Thousand

[*Cp.* Matt. 14 13-21: Mark 6 30-44: Luke 9 10-17: John 6 1-14]

Matt. 15 32-39

32 And Jesus called unto him his disciples, and said, I have compassion [*cp.* 9 36; 14 14: *also* 20 34] on the multitude, because they continue with me now three days and have nothing to eat: and I would not send them away fasting, lest haply they faint in the way. **33** And the disciples say unto him, Whence should we have so many loaves in a desert place, as to fill so great a multitude?

34 And Jesus saith unto them, How many loaves have ye? And they said, Seven, and a few small fishes. **35** And he commanded the multitude to sit down on the ground; **36** and

Mark 8 1-10

1 In those days, when there was again a great multitude, and they had nothing to eat, he called unto him his disciples, and saith unto them, **2** I have compassion [*cp.* 6 34: *also* 1 41] on the multitude, because they continue with me now three days, and have nothing to eat: **3** and if I send them away fasting to their home, they will faint in the way; and some of them are come from far. **4** And his disciples answered him, Whence shall one be able to fill these men with ¹ bread here in a desert place? **5** And he asked them, How many loaves have ye [*cp.* 6 38]? And they said, Seven. **6** And he commandeth the multitude to sit down on the ground: and

cp. 7 13: *and* 10 33; 15 20.

he took the seven loaves and the fishes; and he gave thanks [*cp.* 26 27] and brake, and gave to the disciples. and the disciples to the multitudes. *cp.* 14 19; 26 26.	he took the seven loaves, and having given thanks [*cp.* 14 23], he brake, and gave to his disciples, to set before them; and they set them before the multitude. **7** And they had a few small fishes: and having blessed [*cp.* 6 41; 14 22] them, he commanded to set these also before them. **8** And they did eat, and were filled: and they took up, of broken pieces that remained over, seven baskets. **9** And they were about four thousand:	*cp.* 22 17, 19. *cp.* 9 16; 24 30.	*cp.* 6 11.
37 And they did all eat, and were filled: and they took up that which remained over of the broken pieces, seven baskets full. **38** And they that did eat were four thousand men, beside women and children [*cp.* 14 21]. **39** And he sent away the multitudes, and entered into the boat, and came into the borders of Magadan.	and he sent them away. **10** And straightway he entered into the boat with his disciples, and came into the parts of Dalmanutha.		

¹ Gr. *loaves.*

§ 120. A Request for a Sign refused

Matt. 12 38-39	**Matt. 16** 1-4	**Mark 8** 11-13	Luke 12 54-56; 11 29		
38 Then certain of the scribes and Pharisees	**1** And the Pharisees and Sadducees came, and tempting him [*cp.* 19 3; 22 35: *also* 22 18]	**11** And the Pharisees came forth, and began to question with him [*cp.* 9 14, 16; 12 28],			
answered him, saying, ¹ Master, we would see a sign from thee.	asked him to shew them a sign from heaven.	seeking of him a sign from heaven, tempting him [*cp.* 10 2: *also* 12 15].	11 16 *cp.* 10 25; 11 16.	*cp.* 2 18; 6 30. *cp.* 8 6.	
39 But he answered and said unto them,	**2** But he answered and said unto them, ¹ When it is evening, ye say, *It will be* fair weather: for the heaven is red. **3** And in the morning, *It will be* foul weather to-day: for the heaven is red and lowring.	**12** And he sighed deeply [*cp.* 7 34] in his spirit, and saith,	**54** And he said to the multitudes also, When ye see a cloud rising in the west, straightway ye say, There cometh a shower; and so it cometh to pass. **55** And when *ye see* a south wind blowing, ye say, There will be a ¹ scorching heat; and it cometh to pass. **56** Ye hypocrites [*cp.* 13 15: *also* 12 1], ye		
cp. 15 7; 22 18; 23 13, *etc.: also* 6 2, 5, 16; 24 51: *and* 23 28.	Ye know how to discern the face of the heaven; but ye cannot *discern* the signs of the times [*cp.* 24 32-33].	*cp.* 7 6: *also* 12 15. *cp.* 13 28-29.	know how to ² interpret the face of the earth and the heaven; but how is it that ye know not how to ² interpret this time [*cp.* 21 29-31]? **11 29** And when the multitudes were gathering together unto him, he began to say,		
An	**4** An	Why doth this generation	This generation is an		

evil and adulterous generation [*cp.* 12 45] seeketh after a sign ;

and there shall no sign be given to it
       but the sign of Jonah the prophet. *cp.* 21 17.

¹ Or, *Teacher.*

evil and adulterous generation [*cp.* 17 17] seeketh after **a** sign;

and there shall no sign be given unto it,
       but the sign of Jonah.
       And he left them, and
       departed.

¹ The following words, to the end of ver. 3, are omitted by some of the most ancient and other important authorities.

cp. 8 38; 9 19. seek a sign ? verily I say unto you, There shall no sign be given unto this generation.

13 And he left them, and again entering into *the boat* departed to the other side [*cp.* Matt. 16 5].

evil generation [*cp.* 9 41] : it seeketh after a sign ;

and there shall no sign be given to it
       but the sign of Jonah.

¹ Or, *hot wind*
² Gr. *prove.*

§ 121. The Leaven of the Pharisees and Sadducees (Matt.: **Herod,** Mark)

Matt. 16 5-12	**Mark 8** 14-21	Luke 12 1
5 And the disciples came to the other side [*cp.* Mark 8 13] and forgot to take ¹ bread. **6** And Jesus said unto them, Take heed and beware of the leaven of the Pharisees and Sadducees. *cp.* 23 28: *also* 6 2, 5, 16; 15 7; 22 18; 23 13, *etc*; 24 51.	**14** And they forgot to take bread; and they had not in the boat with them more than one loaf. **15** And he charged them, saying, Take heed, beware [*cp.* 12 38] of the leaven of the Pharisees and the leaven of Herod. *cp.* 12 15: *also* 7 6.	**1** In the mean time, when ¹ the many thousands of the multitude were gathered together, insomuch that they trode one upon another, he began to ² say unto his disciples first of all, Beware [*cp.* 20 46: *also* 17 3; 21 34] ye of the leaven of the Pharisees, which is hypocrisy [*cp.* 12 56; 13 15]. ¹ Gr. *the myriads of.* ² Or, *say unto his disciples, First of all beware ye*

cp. Matt. 9 3-4; Mark 2 6-8; Luke 5 21-22.

7 And they reasoned among themselves, saying, ² We took no ¹ bread. **8** And Jesus perceiving it [*cp.* 12 15; 22 18; 26 10] said, O ye of little faith [*cp.* 6 30; 8 26; 14 31: *also* 17 20: 21 21; 28 17], why reason ye among yourselves, because ye have no ¹ bread ? **9** Do ye not yet perceive, neither

cp. 19 8.

cp. 13 13: *also* 15 16; 16 11.

remember the five loaves of the five thousand, and how many ³ baskets ye took up ? **10** Neither the seven loaves of the four thousand, and how many ³ baskets ye took up ?

   11 How is it that ye do not [*see verse 9 above*] perceive that I spake not to you concerning ¹ bread ? But beware of the leaven of the Pharisees and Sadducees. **12** Then understood they [*cp.* 17 13] how that he bade them not

16 And they reasoned one with another, ¹ saying, ² We have no bread. **17** And Jesus perceiving it saith unto them, *cp.* 4 40; 11 22; 16 14. Why reason ye, because ye have no bread ? do ye not yet perceive, neither understand ? have ye your heart hardened [*cp.* 6 52; 16 14: *also* 3 5; 10 5] ? **18** Having eyes, see ye not ? and having ears, hear ye not [*cp.* 4 12: *also* 4 13; 6 52; 7 18; 8 21; 9 10, 32; 16 14] ? and do ye not remember ? **19** When I brake the five loaves among the five thousand, how many ³ baskets full of broken pieces took ye up ? They say unto him, Twelve. **20** And when the seven among the four thousand, how many ³ basketfuls of broken pieces took ye up ? And they say unto him, Seven. **21** And he said unto them, Do ye not yet understand [*see verse 18 above*] ?

cp. 12 28: *also* 8 25; 17 5, 6; 22 32; 24 25, 38.

cp. 8 10: *also* 2 50; 9 45; 18 34.

see above.

cp. 5 6; 6 15; *etc.*
cp. 3 12; 6 64; 14 10; 20 27.

cp. 12 40.

cp. 3 10; 4 33; 8 27, 43; *etc.*

see above.

beware of the leaven of [1] bread, but of
the teaching of the Pharisees and
Sadducees.

[1] Gr. *loaves.*
[2] Or, It is *because we took no bread.*
[3] *Basket* in ver. 9 and 10 represents different Greek words.

[1] Some ancient authorities read *because they had no bread.*
[2] Or, It is *because we have no bread.*
[3] *Basket* in ver. 19 and 20 represents different Greek words.

Mark **8** 17-18 : *cp.* Ps. 115 5-6 ; 135 16-17 ; Is. 6 9-10 ; 43 8 ; Jer. 5 21 ; Ezek. 12 2.

§ 122. **The Healing of a Blind Man at Bethsaida**

[*Cp.* Matt. 9 27-31 ; 12 22 ; 15 30-31 ; 20 29-34 ; 21 14: Mark 10 46-52 : Luke 7 21 ;
18 35-43 : John 9 1-7]

Mark 8 22-26

cp. 19 13, 15:
also 8 3, 15;
9 25, 29; 14
31; 17 7; 20
34; *and* 9 18.

cp. 8 4; 9 30;
12 16: *also*
16 20; 17 9.

22 And they come unto Bethsaida [*cp.* 6 45]. And they bring to him a blind man, and beseech him to touch him [*cp.* 7 32]. **23** And he took hold of the blind man by the hand, and brought him out of the village [*cp.* 7 33] ; and when he had spit [*cp.* 7 33] on his eyes, and laid his hands [*cp.* 8 25; 10 16: *also* 1 31, 41; 5 41; 7 33; 8 22; 9 27; 10 13; *and* 5 23; 6 2, 5] upon him, he asked him, Seest thou aught ? **24** And he looked up, and said, I see men; for I behold *them* as trees, walking. **25** Then again he laid his hands [*see above*] upon his eyes ; and he looked stedfastly, and was restored, and saw all things clearly [*cp.* 7 35]. **26** And he sent him away to his home, saying, Do not even enter into the village [*cp.* 1 44; 5 43; 7 36: *also* 1 25, 34; 3 12; *and* 7 24; 8 30; 9 9, 30].

cp. 9 10.

cp. 4 40; 13
13: *also* 5
13; 7 14;
8 54; 14
4; 18 15;
22 51.

cp. 5 14; 8
56: *also* 4
35, 41 ; *and*
9 21, 36.

cp. 9 6.
cp. 9 6.

§ 123. **Peter's Confession**

Matt. 16 13-20	**Mark 8** 27-30	**Luke 9** 18-21	John 6 66-69 ; 1 41-42 ; 20 22-23
13 Now when Jesus came into the parts of Cæsarea Philippi, *cp.* 14 23; 19 13; 26 36, 39, 42, 44: *also* 11 25.	**27** And Jesus went forth, and his disciples, into the villages of Cæsarea Philippi : and in the way *cp.* 1 35; 6 46, 47; 14 32, 35, 39.	**18** And it came to pass, as he was praying [*cp.* 3 21; 5 16; 6 12; 9 28, 29; 11 1; 22 41, 44: *also* 10 21] alone, the disciples were with him : and he asked them, saying,	6 **66** Upon this many of his disciples went back, and walked no more with him. *cp.* 11 41 ; 12 27-28 ; 17 1-26.
he asked his disciples, saying, Who do men say [1] that the Son of man is ? **14** And they said [*cp.* 14 2], Some *say* John the Baptist ; some, Elijah : and others, Jeremiah, or one of the prophets. **15** He saith unto them, But who say ye that I am ? **16** And Simon [*cp.* 4 18; 10 2] Peter answered and said,	he asked his disciples, saying unto them, Who do men say that I am ? **28** And they told him, saying [*cp.* 6 14, 15], John the Baptist : and others, Elijah ; but others, One of the prophets. **29** And he asked them, But who say ye that I am ? Peter answereth and saith unto him,	Who do the multitudes say that I am ? **19** And they answering said [*cp.* 9 7, 8], John the Baptist ; but others *say*, Elijah ; and others, that one of the old prophets is risen again. **20** And he said unto them, But who say ye that I am ? And *cp.* 5 8. Peter answering said,	**67** Jesus said therefore unto the twelve, Would ye also go away ? **68** Simon [*cp.* 1 40; 6 8; 13 6; *etc.*] Peter answered him, Lord, to whom shall we go ? thou [1] hast the words of eternal life. **69** And we have believed and know that thou art
Thou art	**Thou art**		

[Matthew]

the Christ [*cp.* 26 63: *also* 26 68; 27 17, 22],

the Son [*cp.* 4 3, 6; 8 29; 14 33; 26 63; 27 40, 43, 54: *also* 3 17; 17 5] of the living [*cp.* 26 63] God.

17 And Jesus answered and said unto him, Blessed art thou, Simon [*cp.* 17 25] Bar-Jonah: for flesh and blood hath not revealed it unto thee [*cp.* 11 25], but my Father which is in heaven [*cp.* 5 16, 45; 6 1, 9; 7 11, 21; 10 32, 33; 12 50; 18 10, 14, 19: *also* 5 48; 6 14, 26, 32; 15 13; 18 35; 23 9]. **18** And I also say unto thee, that thou art

² Peter, and upon this ³ rock [*cp.* 7 24] I will build my church; and the gates of Hades shall not prevail against it. **19** I will give unto thee the keys of the kingdom of heaven [*cp.* 23 13]: and whatsoever thou shalt bind on earth shall be bound in heaven: and whatsoever thou shalt loose on earth shall be loosed in heaven. **20** Then charged he the disciples that they should tell no man [*cp.* 17 9: *also* 8 4; 9 30; 12 16] that he was the Christ.

¹ Many ancient authorities read *that I the Son of man am.* See Mark 8 27; Luke 9 18.
² Gr. *Petros.*   ³ Gr. *petra.*

[Mark]

the Christ [*cp.* 14 61; *also* 15 32].

cp. 1 24.

cp. 1 1; 3 11; 5 7; 15 39: *also* 1 11; 9 7.

cp. 14 37.

cp. 11 25, 26.

cp. 3 16.

cp. 18 17.

Matt. 18 18 Verily I say unto you, What things soever ye shall bind on earth shall be bound in heaven: and what things soever ye shall loose on earth shall be loosed in heaven.

30 And he charged them that they should tell no man [*cp.* 9 9: *also* 1 25, 34, 44; 3 12; 5 43; 7 36; 8 26] of him.

[Luke]

The Christ [*cp.* 22 67: *also* 23 2, 35, 39]

cp. 4 34.

cp. 1 35; 4 3, 9, 41; 8 28; 22 70: *also* 3 22; 9 35.

of God [*cp.* 23 35].

cp. 22 31.

cp. 10 21.

cp. 11 13.

cp. 6 14.

cp. 6 48.
cp. 22 32.

21 But he charged them, and commanded *them* to tell this to no man [*cp.* 9 36: *also* 4 35, 41; 5 41; 8 56];

[John]

[*cp.* 1 41; 4 25, 26, 29; 7 26, 41; 9 22; 10 24; 11 27] the Holy One *cp.* 1 34; *etc.*

of God.   **1 41** He findeth first his own brother Simon, and saith unto him, We have found the Messiah (which is, being interpreted, ² Christ). **42** He brought him unto Jesus. Jesus looked upon him, and said, Thou art Simon [*cp.* 21 15, 16, 17] the son of ³ John [*cp.* 21 15, 16, 17]:

thou shalt be called Cephas (which is by interpretation, ⁴ Peter).

cp. 21 15-17.

20 22 And when he had said this, he breathed on them, and saith unto them, Receive ye the ⁵ Holy Ghost: **23** whose soever sins ye forgive, they are forgiven unto them; whose soever *sins* ye retain, they are retained.

¹ Or, *hast words*
² That is, *Anointed.*
³ Gr. *Joanes:* called in Matt. 16 17, *Jonah.*
⁴ That is, *Rock* or *Stone.*
⁵ Or, *Holy Spirit*

Matt. 16 19: *cp.* Is. 22 22.

§ 124. The First Prediction of the Passion and Resurrection

[*Cp.* Matt. 17 22-23 ‖ Mark 9 30-32 ‖ Luke 9 43b-45; Matt. 20 17-19 ‖ Mark 10 32-34 ‖ Luke 18 31-34: *also* Matt. 17 9, 12; 20 28; 26 2, 12, 18, 24, 32, 45: Mark 9 9, 12; 10 45; 14 8, 21, 28, 41: Luke 13 32-33; 17 25; 22 22; 24 7, *and* 26, 44, 46: John 2 19-22; 3 14; 12 32-33]

Matt. 16 21-23	**Mark 8** 31-33	**Luke 9** 22
21 From that time began ¹ Jesus to shew unto his disciples, how that he must go unto Jerusalem [*cp.* 20 18], and suffer many things	**31** And he began to teach them, *cp.* 10 33. that the Son of man must suffer many things, and be	**22** saying, *cp.* 9 31, 51; 13 33; 18 31. The Son of man must suffer many things, and be

of the elders and chief priests and scribes, and be killed, *cp.* 27 63.

and the third day [*cp.* 17 23; 20 19; *also* 12 40; 26 61; 27 40, 64] *cp.* 17 9. be raised up [*cp.* 17 23; 20 19; 26 32; 27 63, 64; 28 6, 7].

22 And Peter [*cp.* 14 28; 15 15; 17 4; 18 21; 19 27; 26 33: *also* 16 16; 17 24] took him, and began to rebuke him, saying, ² Be it far from thee, Lord: this shall never be unto thee. **23** But he turned [*cp.* 9 22], and said unto Peter, Get thee behind me, Satan [*cp.* 4 10]: thou art a stumbling block unto me: for thou mindest not the things of God, but the things of men.

¹ Some ancient authorities read *Jesus Christ.*
² Or, God *have mercy on thee*

rejected by the elders, and the chief priests, and the scribes, and be killed, and after three days [*cp.* 9 31; 10 34: *also* 14 58; 15 29]

rise again [*cp.* 9 9, 31; 10 34; 16 9]. *cp.* 14 28; 16 6, 14.

32 And he spake the saying openly. And Peter [*cp.* 9 5; 10 28; 11 21; 14 29: *also* 8 29] took him, and began to rebuke him.

33 But he turning about [*cp.* 5 30], and seeing his disciples, rebuked Peter, and saith, Get thee behind me, Satan:

for thou mindest not the things of God, but the things of men.

rejected [*cp.* 17 25] of the elders and chief priests and scribes, and be killed,

cp. 2 19.

and the third day [*cp.* 13 32; 18 33; 24 7, 46: *also* 24 21] *cp.* 18 33; 24 7, 46. be raised up [*cp.* 24 6, 34]. *cp.* 20 9. *cp.* 2 19-22; 21 14. *cp.* 7 4, 13, 26; 10 24. *cp.* 8 45; 9 33; 12 41; 18 28: *also* 5 8; 9 20. *cp.* 13 36, 37; 21 21: *also* 6 68.

cp. 7 9, 44; 9 55; 10 23; 14 25; 22 61; 23 28. *cp.* 1 38.

---

§ 125. The Cost and Rewards of Discipleship

[*Cp.* Matt. 10 16-42; 19 27-30; 24 9: Mark 10 28-31; 13 9-13: Luke 12 8-12; 14 25-35; 18 28-30; 21 12-19; 22 28-30: John 14 2-3; 15 18-21; 16 2-3, 33]

Matt. **16** 24-28	Mark 8 34-9 1	Luke **9** 23-27	John 12 26, 25
24 Then said Jesus unto his disciples, If any man would come after me, let him deny himself, and take up his cross, and follow me [*cp.* 4 19; 8 22; 9 9; 19 21].	**34** And he called unto him the multitude with his disciples, and said unto them, If any man would come after me, let him deny himself, and take up his cross, and follow me [*cp.* 1 17; 2 14; 10 21].	**23** And he said unto all, If any man would come after me, let him deny himself, and take up his cross daily, and follow me [*cp.* 5 27; 9 59; 18 22].	**26** If any man serve me, let him follow me [*cp.* 1 43; 21 19, 22]; and where I am, there shall also my servant be: if any man serve me, him will the Father honour. **25** He that loveth his ¹ life loseth it; and he that hateth his ¹ life *cp.* 15 21.
25 For whosoever would save his ¹ life shall lose it: and whosoever shall lose his ¹ life for my sake [*cp.* 5 11; 10 18, 39: *also* 10 22; 19 29; 24 9] *cp.* 4 23; 9 35; 24 14; 26 13. shall find it.	**35** For whosoever would save his ¹ life shall lose it; and whosoever shall lose his ¹ life for my sake [*cp.* 10 29; 13 9: *also* 13 13] and the gospel's [*cp.* 10 29: *also* 1 1, 14, 15; 13 10; 14 9; 16 15] shall save it.	**24** For whosoever would save his ¹ life shall lose it; but whosoever shall lose his ¹ life for my sake [*cp.* 6 22; 18 29; 21 12, 17], the same shall save it.	in this world shall keep it unto life eternal.

Matt. 10 **37** He that loveth father or mother more than me is not worthy of me; and he that loveth son or daughter more

Luke 14 **26** If any man cometh unto me, and hateth not his own father, and mother, and wife, and children, and brethren, and sisters, yea, and his own life also,

Matt.	Mark	Luke	
than me is not worthy of me [*cp.* 19 27-29]. 38 And he that doth not take his cross and follow after me, is not worthy of me. 39 He that [2] findeth his [1] life shall lose it; and he that [3] loseth his [1] life for my sake [*see above*] shall find it.	*cp.* 10 28-30.	he cannot be my disciple [*cp.* 18 28-30]. 27 Whosoever doth not bear his own cross, and come after me, cannot be my disciple. 17 33 Whosoever shall seek to gain his [1] life shall lose it: but whosoever shall lose *his* [1] *life* shall [2] preserve it.	
26 For what shall a man be profited, if he shall gain the whole world, and forfeit his [1] life? or what shall a man give in exchange for his [1] life? **27** For *cp.* 12 39, 45; 16 4; 17 17. the Son of man shall come in *cp.* 19 28; 25 31. the glory of his Father with his angels [*cp.* 24 30, 31; 25 31; 26 64: *also* 13 41, 49]; and then shall he render unto every man according to his [4] deeds [25 31-46].	**36** For what doth it profit a man, to gain the whole world, and forfeit his [1] life? **37** For what should a man give in exchange for his [1] life? **38** For whosoever shall be ashamed of me and of my words in this adulterous and sinful generation [*cp.* 9 19], the Son of man also shall be ashamed of him, when he cometh in *cp.* 10 37. the glory of his Father with the holy angels [*cp.* 13 26, 27; 14 62].	**25** For what is a man profited, if he gain the whole world, and lose or forfeit his own self? **26** For whosoever shall be ashamed of me and of my words, *cp.* 9 41; 11 29. of him shall the Son of man be ashamed, when he cometh in his own glory [*cp.* 9 32; 24 26], and *the glory* of the Father, and of the holy angels [*cp.* 21 27].	*cp.* 1 14; 2 11; 12 41; 17 5, 22, 24.
Matt. 10 32 Every one therefore who shall confess [5] me before men, [6] him will I also confess before my Father which is in heaven [*cp.* 5 16, 45; 6 1, 9; 7 11, 21; 12 50; 16 17; 18 10, 14, 19: *also* 5 48; 6 14, 26, 32; 15 13; 18 35; 23 9]. 33 But whosoever shall deny me before men, him will I also deny before my Father which is in heaven [*see above*].	*cp.* 11 25, 26.	Luke 12 8 Every one who shall confess [3] me before men, [4] him shall the Son of man also confess before *cp.* 11 13. the angels of God [*cp.* 15 10]: 9 but he that denieth me in the presence of men shall be denied in the presence of the angels of God [*see above*].	
28 Verily I say unto you, There be some of them that stand here [*cp.* 27 47; *also* 26 73], which shall in no wise taste of death, till they see [*cp.* 26 64: *also* 10 23; 23 36; 24 34] the Son of man coming in his [*cp.* 20 21] kingdom [*see verse* 27].	9 **1** And he said unto them, Verily I say unto you, There be some here of them that stand *by* [*cp.* 11 5; 14 47; 15 35: *also* 14 69, 70; 15 39], which shall in no wise taste of death, till they see [*cp.* 14 62: *also* 13 30] the kingdom of God come with power.	**27** But I tell you of a truth [*cp.* 12 44; 21 3], There be some of them that stand here [*cp.* 19 24], which shall in no wise taste of death, till they see *cp.* 11 51; 21 32. the kingdom of God. *cp.* 22 29-30; 23 42.	*cp.* 12 29. *cp.* 8 51, 52. *cp.* 1 51. *cp.* 18 36.
[1] Or, *soul* [2] Or, *found* [3] Or, *lost* [4] Gr. *doing.* [5] Gr. *in me.* [6] Gr. *in him.*	[1] Or, *soul*	[1] Or, *soul* [2] Gr. *save it alive.* [3] Gr. *in me.* [4] Gr. *in him.*	[1] Or, *soul*

§ 126. The Transfiguration

Matt. 17 1-8	Mark 9 2-8	Luke 9 28-36		
1 And after six days Jesus taketh with him Peter, and James, and John his brother, and bringeth them up into a high mountain [*cp.* 5 1; 14 23; 15 29; 28 16] apart [*cp.* 17 19; 20 17; 24 3]:	**2** And after six days Jesus taketh with him Peter, and James, and John, and bringeth them up into a high mountain [*cp.* 3 13; 6 46] apart [*cp.* 4 10, 34; 6 31, 32; 9 28; 13 3] by themselves:	**28** And it came to pass about eight [*cp.* 1 59; 2 21] days after these sayings, he took with him Peter and John and James, and went up into the mountain [*cp.* 6 12] *cp.* 9 10; 10 23.	*cp.* 20 26. *cp.* 6 3, 15.	*cp.* Ma 37: M 29; 5 3; 14 Luke

Matthew

cp. 14 23; 19 13; 26 36, 39, 42, 44: *also* 11 25-26.

2 and he was transfigured before them: and his face did shine as the sun, and his garments became white [*cp.* 28 3] as the light.

3 And behold, there appeared unto them Moses and Elijah talking with him.

cp. 16 21; 20 18.

cp. 26 40, 43.

cp. 19 28; 25 31

4 And Peter [*cp.* 14 28; 15 15; 16 22; 18 21; 19 27; 26 33: *also* 16 16; 17 24] answered, and said unto Jesus, Lord [*cp.* 8 25; 17 15; 20 30, 33: *and* 7 21; 8 2, 6, 8, 21; *etc.*], *cp.* 26 25, 49: *also* 23 7, 8.

it is good for us to be here: if thou wilt, I will make here three 1 tabernacles; one for thee, and one for Moses, and one for Elijah.

verse 6

5 While he was yet speaking [*cp.* 12 46; 26 47], behold, a bright cloud over-shadowed them:
verse 6

and behold, a voice out of the cloud [*cp.* 3 17], saying, This is my beloved Son [*cp.* 3 17; 12 18: *also* 4 3; *etc.*], in whom I am well pleased [*cp.* 3 17: *also* 11 26; 12 18]; hear ye him.
6 And when the disciples heard it, they fell on their face, and were sore afraid [*cp.* 9 8; 27 54; 28 4, 8].
7 And Jesus came and touched them [*cp.* 8 3, 15; 9 18, 25, 29; 14 31; 19 13, 15; 20 34: *also* 9 20; 14 36] and said, Arise [*cp.* 9 5, 6; 26 46], and

Mark

cp. 1 35; 6 46; 14 32, 35, 39.

and he was transfigured before them:

3 and his garments became glistering, exceeding white [*cp.* 16 5]; so as no fuller on earth can whiten them.
4 And there appeared unto them Elijah with Moses: and they were talking with Jesus.

cp. 10 33.

cp. 14 37, 40.

cp. 10 37.

5 And Peter [*cp.* 8 32; 10 28; 11 21; 14 29: *also* 8 29] answereth and saith to Jesus, *cp.* 7 28.

Rabbi [*cp.* 11 21; 14 45: *and* 10 51],

it is good for us to be here: and let us make three 1 tabernacles; one for thee, and one for Moses, and one for Elijah.
6 For he wist not what to answer [*cp.* 14 40]; for they became sore afraid [*cp.* 4 41; 9 32; 10 32: *also* 5 15, 33; 16 8]. **7** And *cp.* 5 35; 14 43.
there came a cloud over-shadowing them:
verse 6

and there came a voice out of the cloud [*cp.* 1 11], This is my beloved Son [*cp.* 1 11; 12 6: *also* 1 1; *etc.*]:
cp. 1 11.
hear ye him.

verse 6
cp. 1 31, 41; 5 23, 41; 6 2, 5; 7 33; 8 22, 23, 25; 9 27; 10 13, 16: *also* 3 10; 5 27; 6 56.
cp. 2 9, 11; 3 3; 5 41; 14 42.

Luke

to pray [*cp.* 5 16; 6 12; 22 41, 44: *also* 10 21]. **29** And as he was praying [*cp.* 3 21; 9 18; 11 1],
the fashion of his countenance was altered, and his raiment *became* white *and* dazzling [*cp.* 24 4].

30 And behold, there talked with him two men, which were Moses and Elijah; **31** who appeared in glory, and spake of his 1 decease which he was about to accomplish at Jerusalem [*cp.* 9 51; 13 33; 18 31]. **32** Now Peter and they that were with him were heavy with sleep [*cp.* 22 45]: but 2 when they were fully awake, they saw his glory [*cp.* 9 26; 24 26], and the two men that stood with him. **33** And it came to pass, as they were parting from him, Peter [*cp.* 8 45; 12 41; 18 28: *also* 5 8; 9 20]
said unto Jesus, *cp.* 18 41: *and* 5 8, 12; 6 46; 7 6; 9 54, 59, 61; *etc.*

Master [*cp.* 8 24; 9 49: *and* 5 5; 8 45; 17 13], it is good for us to be here: and let us make three 3 tabernacles; one for thee, and one for Moses, and one for Elijah: not knowing what he said.

verse 34

34 And while he said these things [*cp.* 8 49; 22 47, 60], there came a cloud and over-shadowed them: and they feared [*cp.* 8 25; 9 45; 24 5, 37: *also* 1 12, 65; 2 9; 5 26; 7 16; 8 35, 37, 47] as they entered into the cloud. **35** And a voice came out of the cloud [*cp.* 3 22], saying, This is 4 my Son [*cp.* 3 22; 20 13: *also* 1 35; *etc.*], my chosen [*cp.* 23 35]: *cp.* 3 22: *also* 2 14; 10 21; 12 32. hear ye him.

verse 34
cp. 4 40; 5 13; 7 14; 8 54; 13 13; 14 4; 18 15; 22 51: *also* 6 19; 7 39; 8 44.
cp. 5 23, 24; 6 8; 7 14; 8 54.

John

cp. 11 41; 12 27-28; 17 1-26.

cp. 20 12.

cp. 1 14; 2 11; 12 41; 17 5, 22, 24.
cp. 13 36, 37; 21 21: *also* 6 68.
cp. 4 11, 15, 19, 49; 5 7; *etc.*
cp. 1 38, 49; 3 2; *etc.*: *and* 20 16.

cp. 12 28.
cp. 1 14, 18, 34; *etc.*

cp. 9 6; 20 17.

cp. 5 8; 14 31.

be not afraid [*cp.* 14 27; 28 10]. **8** And   lifting up their eyes,

cp. 6 50.

they saw no one, save Jesus only.

8 And suddenly looking round about [*cp.* 3 5, 34; 5 32; 10 23; 11 11],   they saw no one any more, save Jesus only with themselves.

36 And

cp. 6 10.
        when the voice
5 came,
        Jesus was found alone. And they held their peace, and told no man in those days any of the things which they had seen.

cp. 6 20.

cp. 17 9.

cp. 9 9.

1 Or, *booths*

Or, *booths*

1 Or, *departure*
2 Or, *having remained awake*
3 Or, *booths*
4 Many ancient authorities read *my beloved Son.* See Matt. 17 5; Mark 9 7.   5 Or, *was past*

Matt. 17 5 ‖ Mark 9 7 ‖ Luke 9 35 : *cp.* Ps. 2 7 ; Is. 42 1 ; Deut. 18 15.

§ 127. A Question about Elijah

Matt. 17 9-13

9 And as they were coming down from the mountain, Jesus commanded them, saying, Tell the vision to no man [*cp.* 16 20: *also* 8 4; 9 30; 12 16],   until the Son of man be risen from the dead [*cp.* 16 21; 17 23; 20 19; 26 32; 27 63, 64; 28 6].

cp. 15 16; 16 8-12.

10 And his disciples asked him, saying, Why then say the scribes that Elijah must first come? **11** And he answered and said, Elijah indeed cometh, and shall restore all things :
cp. 21 42; 26 24, 31, 54, 56.

verse 12

12 but I say unto you, that Elijah is come already, and they knew him not, but   did unto him whatsoever they listed.   Even so shall the Son of man also suffer of them [*cp.* 16 21-23; *etc.*].   **13** Then understood the disciples [*cp.* 16 12] that he spake unto them of John the Baptist [*cp.* 11 10, 14: *also* 3 3, 4].

Mark 9 9-13

9 And as they were coming down from the mountain, he charged them that they should tell no man [*cp.* 8 30: *also* 1 25, 34, 44; 3 12; 5 43; 7 36; 8 26] what things they had seen, save when the Son of man should have risen again from the dead [*cp.* 8 31; 9 31; 10 34; 14 28].   **10** And they kept the saying, questioning among themselves [*cp.* 4 13; 6 52; 7 18; 8 17-21; 9 32: *also* 16 14] what the rising again from the dead should mean. **11** And they   asked him, saying,   1 The scribes [*cp.* 12 35] say that Elijah must first [*cp.* 13 10] come. **12** And he   said unto them, Elijah indeed cometh first, and   restoreth all things : and how is it written [*cp.* 12 10; 14 21, 27, 49] of the Son of man, that he should suffer many things and be set at nought [*cp.* 8 31-33; *etc.*] ? **13** But I say unto you, that Elijah is come, and they have also done unto him whatsoever they listed, even as it is written of him.

verse 12

cp. 1 2-3, 6.

1 Or, How is it *that the scribes say . . . come ?*

9 37

cp. 9 36 *and* 9 21: *also* 4 35, 41; 5 14; 8 56.
cp. 9 22; 13 32; 18 33; 24 7, 26, 46.
cp. 2 50; 9 45; 18 34.

cp. 17 25; 21 9.

cp. 18 31; 20 17; 22 37; 24 25-27, 44-46.

cp. 9 22; *etc.*: *also* 23 11.

cp. 1 17, 76; 7 27.

cp. 2 19-22.

cp. 3 10; 4 33; 8 27, 43; 10 6; 11 13; 12 16; *etc.*

cp. 5 39; 13 18; 15 25; 17 12.

cp. 2 19-22; 3 14; 12 32-33.

cp. 1 21, 23; 3 28.

Matt. 17 10, 11 ‖ Mark 9 11 12 : *cp.* Mal. 4 5.

§ 128. The Healing of an Epileptic Boy

Matt. 17 14-20 (21)

17 9
14 And when they were come to the   multitude,

Mark 9 14-29

9 9
14 And when they   came to the disciples, they saw a great multitude about them,

Luke 9 37-43a

37 And it came to pass, on the next day, when they were come down from the mountain,

great multitude

a

Matthew

there came to him a man,
kneeling
to him [cp. 8 2; 9 18; 14 33; 15 25; 20 20], and saying, **15** Lord [cp. 8 25; 17 4; 20 30, 33: and 7 21; 8 2, 6, 8, 21; 9 28; etc.], cp. 8 19; 12 38; 19 16; 22 16, 24, 36.

have mercy [cp. 9 27; 15 22; 20 30, 31] on my son: for he is

epileptic [cp. 4 24], and suffereth grievously: cp. 9 32-34; 12 22; 15 30-31: also 11 5.

for oft-times he falleth into the fire, and oft-times into the water.

16 And I brought him to thy disciples, cp. 10 1, 8. and they could not cure him. **17** And Jesus answered and said, O faithless and perverse generation [cp. 12 39, 45; 16 4], how long shall I be with you? how long shall I bear with you? bring him hither to me [cp. 14 18].

verse 15

cp. 15 25.

cp. 8 2; 9 28. verse 20

Mark

and scribes questioning with them [cp. 8 11; 9 16; 12 28]. **15** And straightway all the multitude, when they saw him, were greatly amazed, and running to him saluted him. **16** And he asked them, What question ye with them [see above]? **17** And one of the multitude [cp. 1 40; 3 11; 5 6, 22, 33; 7 25; 10 17] answered him,

cp. 7 28.

1 Master [cp. 4 38; 9 38; 10 17, 20, 35; 12 14, 19, 32; 13 1], I brought unto thee cp. 10 47, 48. my son,

which hath a dumb [cp. 7 32-37] spirit; **18** and wheresoever it taketh him, it 2 dasheth him down: verse 22

and he foameth, and grindeth his teeth, and pineth away:

and I spake to thy disciples that they should cast it out [cp. 3 15; 6 7, 13]; and they were not able. **19** And he answereth them and saith, O faithless generation [cp. 8 38], how long shall I be with you? how long shall I bear with you? bring him unto me. **20** And they brought him unto him: and when he saw him, straightway the spirit 3 tare him grievously [cp. 1 26]; and he fell on the ground, and wallowed foaming. **21** And he asked his father, How long time is it since this hath come unto him? And he said, From a child. **22** And oft-times it hath cast him both into the fire and into the waters, to destroy him: but if thou canst do anything, have compassion on us, and help us. **23** And Jesus said unto him, If thou canst [cp. 1 40; 6 5-6]! All things are possible [cp. 10 27; 14 36] to him that believeth. **24** Straightway the father of the child cried out, and said 4, I believe; help thou mine unbelief.

Luke

met him.

38 And behold, a man from the multitude [cp. 5 8, 12; 8 28, 41, 47; 17 16] cried, saying, [cp. 18 41: and 5 8, 12; 6 46; 7 6; 9 54, 59, 61; etc.] 1 Master [cp. 7 40; 10 25; 11 45; 12 13; 18 18; 19 39; 20 21, 28, 39; 21 7], I beseech thee to look cp. 17 13; 18 38, 39. upon my son; for he is mine only [cp. 7 12; 8 42] child:

39 and behold, a [cp. 11 14: also 7 22] spirit taketh him, and he suddenly crieth out; and it 2 teareth him

that he foameth,

and it hardly departeth from him, bruising him sorely. **40** And I besought thy disciples to cast it out [cp. 9 1, 6; 10 9, 17]; and they could not. **41** And Jesus answered and said, O faithless and perverse generation [cp. 11 29], how long shall I be with you, and bear with you? bring hither thy son. **42** And as he was yet a coming,

the 3 devil 4 dashed him down, and 5 tare him grievously [cp. 4 35].

cp. 5 12. cp. 1 37; 18 27.

Cross-references

cp. 4 11, 15, 19, 49; 5 7; etc.
cp. 1 38; 20 16.

cp. 14 9.

Matthew

18 And Jesus rebuked [cp. 8 26] him; and out the ¹ devil went from him:
cp. 28 4.

cp. 9 25; 14 31: also 8 3, 15; 9 18, 29; 17 7; 19 13, 15; 20 34.
and the boy was cured from that hour [cp. 8 13; 9 22; 15 28].

cp. 8 27; 9 33; 12 23; 15 31; 21 20; 27 14: and 7 28; etc.

cp. 13 36; 17 25.
19 Then came the disciples to Jesus [cp. 5 1; 13 10, 36; 14 15; 15 12, 23; 18 1; 24 1, 3; 26 17] apart [cp. 17 1; 20 17; 24 3], and said, Why could not we cast it out? **20** And he saith unto them, Because of your little faith [cp. 6 30; 8 26; 14 31; 16 8]: for verily I say unto you, If ye have faith as a grain of mustard seed [cp. 13 31], ye shall say unto this mountain, Remove hence to yonder place; and it shall remove; and nothing shall be impossible unto you [cp. 19 26].²

21 **21** And Jesus answered and said unto them, Verily I say unto you, If ye have faith, and doubt not, ye shall not only do what is done to the fig tree, but even if ye shall say unto this mountain, Be thou taken up and cast into the sea,

it shall be done.

22 And all things, whatsoever

Mark

25 And when Jesus saw that a multitude came running together, he rebuked [cp. 1 25; 3 12; 4 39] the unclean spirit, saying unto him, Thou dumb and deaf spirit [see verse 17], I command thee, come out of him [cp. 1 25; 5 8], and enter no more into him. **26** And having cried out, and ³ torn him much, he came out [cp. 1 26]: and the child became as one dead; insomuch that the more part said, He is dead [cp. 5 35]. **27** But Jesus took him by the hand, and raised him up [cp. 1 31; 5 41: also 1 41; 5 23; 6 2, 5; 7 33; 8 22, 23, 25; 10 13, 16]; and he arose.

cp. 2 12; 5 20, 42; 6 51; 7 37; 10 32; 15 5; 16 5, 8: and 1 22; etc.

28 And when he was come into the house [cp. 7 17; 9 33; 10 10], his disciples
cp. 6 35.

asked him privately [cp. 4 10, 34; 6 31, 32; 9 2; 13 3], ⁵ saying, We could not cast it out. **29** And he said unto them,

cp. 4 40.

cp. 4 31.

verse 23
This kind can come out by nothing, save by prayer ⁶.

11 **22** And Jesus answering saith unto them, Have faith in God. **23** Verily I say unto you,

Whosoever shall say unto this mountain, Be thou taken up and cast into the sea; and shall not doubt in his heart, but shall believe that what he saith cometh to pass; he shall have it. **24** Therefore I say unto you, All things whatsoever

Luke

But Jesus rebuked [cp. 4 35, 39, 41; 8 24] the unclean spirit,

cp. 4 35.

cp. 4 35.

cp. 7 12; 8 49.

cp. 8 54: also 4 40; 5 13; 7 14; 13 13; 14 4; 18 15; 22 51.
and healed [cp. 6 19; 9 2, 11; 14 4; 22 51] the boy,

and gave him back to his father [cp. 7 15]. **43** And they were all astonished [cp. 5 9, 26; 8 25, 56; 11 14; 24 12, 41: and 2 47, 48; 4 22; etc.] at the majesty of God.

cp. 9 12.

cp. 9 10; 10 23.

17 6 And the Lord said,

cp. 12 28: and 8 25; 17 5; 22 32.
If ye have faith as a grain of mustard seed [cp. 13 19], ye would say unto this sycamine tree,

cp. 1 37; 18 27.

Be thou rooted up, and be thou planted in the sea; and

it would have obeyed you.

Right margin references

cp. 9 6.

cp. 4 53.

cp. 7 15, 21, 46.

cp. 3 12; 6 64; 14 10.

ye shall ask [*cp.* 7 7; 18 19] in prayer, believing, ye shall receive.	ye pray and ask for, believe that ye have received them, and ye shall have them.	*cp.* 11 9.	*cp.* 14 13, 14; 15 7, 16; 16 23, 24.

[1] Gr. *demon.*
[2] Many authorities, some ancient, insert verse 21 *But this kind goeth not out save by prayer and fasting.* See Mark 9 29.

[1] Or, *Teacher*
[2] Or, *rendeth him*   [3] Or, *convulsed*
[4] Many ancient authorities add *with tears.*
[5] Or, How is it *that we could not cast it out?*
[6] Many ancient authorities add *and fasting.*

[1] Or, *Teacher*
[3] Gr. *demon.*
[5] Or, *convulsed*

[2] Or, *convulseth*
[4] Or, *rent him*

Matt. 17 17 ‖ Mark 9 19 ‖ Luke 9 41 : *cp.* Deut. 32 5.

(xi) Events in Galilee V (§§ 129-133)

§ 129. The Second Prediction of the Passion and Resurrection

[*Cp.* Matt. 16 21-23 ‖ Mark 8 31-33 ‖ Luke 9 22; Matt. 20 17-19 ‖ Mark 10 32-34 ‖ Luke 18 31-34: *also* Matt. 17 9, 12; 20 28; 26 2, 12, 18, 24, 32, 45: Mark 9 9, 12; 10 45; 14 8, 21, 28, 41: Luke 13 32-33; 17 25; 22 22; 24 7, *and* 26, 44, 46: John 2 19-22; 3 14; 12 32-33]

Matt. 17 22-23	**Mark 9** 30-32	**Luke 9** 43b-45	
22 And while they [1] abode in Galilee, *cp.* 8 4; *etc.* *cp.* 8 27; 9 33; 12 23; 15 31; 21 20; 27 14: *also* 7 28; 13 54; 19 25; 22 22, 33. Jesus said unto them, The Son of man shall be delivered up into the hands of men; **23** and they shall kill him, and *cp.* 27 63. the third day [*cp.* 16 21; 20 19: *also* 12 40; 26 61; 27 40, 64] he shall *cp.* 17 9. be raised up [*cp.* 16 21; 20 19; 26 32; 27 63, 64; 28 6, 7]. And they *cp.* 15 16; 16 8-12. *cp.* 17 6: *also* 9 8; 27 54; 28 4, 8. were exceeding sorry [*cp.* 18 31: *also* 26 22 *and* 37].	**30** And they went forth from thence, and passed through Galilee; and he would not that any man should know it [*cp.* 7 24: *also* 1 25; *etc.*]. **31** For *cp.* 2 12; 5 20, 42; 6 51; 7 37; 10 32; 15 5; 16 5, 8: *also* 1 22, 27; 6 2; 10 24, 26; 11 18; 12 17. he taught his disciples, and said unto them, The Son of man is delivered up into the hands of men, and they shall kill him; and when he is killed, after three days [*cp.* 8 31; 10 34: *also* 14 58; 15 29] he shall rise again [*cp.* 8 31; 9 9; 10 34; 16 9]. *cp.* 14 28; 16 6, 14. **32** But they understood not the saying [*cp.* 4 13; 6 52; 7 18; 8 17-21; 9 10], and were afraid [*cp.* 4 41; 9 6; 10 32: *also* 5 15, 33; 16 8] to ask him. *cp.* 14 19.	*cp.* 24 6-7. *cp.* 4 35; *etc.* But while all were marvelling [*cp.* 5 9, 26; 8 25, 56; 11 14; 24 12, 41: *also* 2 47, 48; 4 22, 32, 36; 20 26] at all the things which he did, he said unto his disciples, **44** Let these words sink into your ears: for the Son of man shall be delivered up into the hands of men. *cp.* 9 22; 13 32; 18 33; 24 7, 46: *also* 24 21. *cp.* 18 33; 24 7, 46. *cp.* 9 22; 24 6, 34. **45** But they understood not this saying [*cp.* 2 50; 18 34], and it was concealed from them, that they should not perceive it: and they were afraid [*cp.* 8 25; 9 34; 24 5, 37: *also* 1 12, 65; 2 9; 5 26; 7 16; 8 35, 37, 47] to ask him about this saying. *cp.* 22 45.	*cp.* 7 15, 21, 46. *cp.* 2 19. *cp.* 20 9. *cp.* 2 19-22; 21 14. *cp.* 10 6; 12 16: *also* 3 10; 4 33; 8 27, 43; 11 13; 13 7, 28, 36; 14 5-10, 22; 16 17-18. *cp.* 16 6, 20, 22.

[1] Some ancient authorities read *were gathering themselves together.*

§ 130. A Question about Payment of the Temple-Tax

Matt. 17 24-27			
24 And when they were come to Capernaum, they that received the [1] half-shekel came to Peter, and said, Doth not your [2] master pay the [1] half-shekel? **25** He saith, Yea. And	9 33		

when he came into the house [*cp.* 13 36], Jesus spake first to him, saying, What thinkest thou [*cp.* 18 12; 21 28; 22 17, 42; 26 66], Simon [*cp.* 16 17] ? the kings of the earth, from whom do they receive toll or tribute ? from their sons, or from strangers ? **26** And when he said, From strangers, Jesus said unto him, Therefore the sons are free. **27** But, lest we cause them to stumble, go thou to the sea, and cast a hook, and take up the fish that first cometh up ; and when thou hast opened his mouth, thou shalt find a ³ shekel : that take, and give unto them for me and thee.	9 33: *cp.* 7 17; 9 28; 10 10. *cp.* 14 37.	*cp.* 22 31.	*cp.* 11 56. *cp.* 1 42; 21 15, 16, 17.

¹ Gr. *didrachma*.   ² Or, *teacher*   ³ Gr *stater*.

Matt. 17 24 : *cp.* Exod. 30 13 ; 38 26.

§ 131. **Rivalry among the Disciples and Sayings of Rebuke** (Mark and Luke)
A Question about Who is the Greatest and Sayings about Little Ones (Matt.)

[*Cp.* Matt. 20 20-28; Mark 10 35-45; Luke 22 24-27]

Matt. 18 1-14	**Mark 9** 33-50	**Luke 9** 46-50	
17 24	**33** And they came to Capernaum : and when he was in the house [*cp.* 7 17; 9 28; 10 10] he asked them, What were ye reasoning in the way ? **34** But they held their peace : for they had disputed one with another in the way,	**46** And there arose a reasoning among them,	
17 25: *cp.* 13 36.		*cp.* 7 21; 10 21; 13 31. *cp.* 9 12.	
1 In that hour [*cp.* 26 55] came the disciples unto Jesus [*cp.* 5 1; 13 10, 36; 14 15; 15 12, 23; 17 19; 24 1,3; 26 17], saying, Who then is ¹ greatest in the kingdom of heaven [*cp.* 5 19; 18 4: *also* 11 11] ? **2** And he called	*cp.* 6 35. who *was* the ¹ greatest.	which of them should be ¹ greatest [*cp.* 22 24].	
	35 And he sat down, and called the twelve ; and he saith unto them, If any man would be first, he shall be last of all, and minister of all.	*cp.* 7 28.	
		verse 48	
20 26 But whosoever would become great among you shall be your ² minister ; **27** and whosoever would be first among you shall be your ³ servant. **23 11** But he that is ¹ greatest among you shall be your ⁴ servant.	**10 43** But whosoever would become great among you, shall be your ² minister : **44** and whosoever would be first among you, shall be ³ servant of all.	**22 26** But he that is the greater among you, let him become as the younger ; and he that is chief, as he that doth serve.	*cp.* 13 2 *ff.*
cp. 9 4; 12 25; 16 8. to him a little child, and set him in the midst of them, **3** and said,	**36** And *cp.* 2 8; 8 17. he took a little child, and set him in the midst of them : and taking him in his arms [*cp.* 10 16], he said unto them,	**47** But when Jesus saw the reasoning of their heart [*cp.* 5 22; 6 8; 11 17], he took a little child, and set him by his side, **48** and said unto them,	*cp.* 1 48; 2 24, 25; 4 19, 29; 5 6, 42; *etc.*
Verily I say unto you, Except ye turn, and become as little children,	**10 15** Verily I say unto you, Whosoever shall not receive the kingdom of God as a little child,	**18 17** Verily I say unto you, Whosoever shall not receive the kingdom of God as a little child,	**3 3** Verily, verily, I say unto thee, Except a man be born ¹ anew, he cannot see the kingdom of God. . . . **5** Verily, verily, I say unto thee, Except a man be born of water and the Spirit, he cannot
ye shall in no wise enter [*cp.* 5 20; 7 21; 19 23, 24; 21 31; 23 13:	he shall in no wise enter [*cp.* 9 47; 10 23, 24, 25 : *also* 9 43,	he shall in no wise enter [*cp.* 18 24, 25: *also* 11 52 ; 13 24 ; 24 26]	enter [*cp.* 10 1, 2, 9]

[Matthew]

also 7 13; 18 8, 9; 19 17; 25 21, 23] into the kingdom of heaven. **4** Whosoever therefore shall humble himself [cp. 23 12] as this little child, the same is the ¹ greatest in the kingdom of heaven [cp. 5 19; 18 1: also 11 11]. **5** And whoso shall receive one such little child in my name [cp. 18 20; 24 5: also 7 22] receiveth me:

10 40 He that receiveth you receiveth me, and he that receiveth me receiveth him that sent me.

cp. 11 11.

cp. 8 19; 12 38; 19 16; 22 16, 24, 36.

cp. 7 22.

cp. 19 14.

cp. 7 22.

cp. 12 30.   10 42 And whosoever shall give to drink unto one of these little ones a cup of cold water only, in the name of a disciple, verily I say unto you, he shall in no wise lose his reward [cp. 25 34-40].

verse 7

6 but whoso shall cause one of these little ones which believe on me to stumble, it is profitable for him that ⁵ a great millstone should be hanged about his neck, and that he should be sunk in the depth of the sea.

7 Woe unto the world because of occasions of stumbling! for it must needs

[Mark]

45] therein.

37 Whosoever shall receive one of such little children in my name [cp. 9 38, 39; 13 6; 16 17], receiveth me: and whosoever receiveth me, receiveth not me, but him that sent me.

verse 35

38 John said unto him, ⁴ Master [cp. 4 38; 9 17: also 10 17, 20, 35; 12 14, 19, 32; 13 1],

we saw one casting out ⁵ devils in thy name [see above]: and we forbade him, because he followed not us. **39** But Jesus said, Forbid him not [cp. 10 14]: for there is no man which shall do a ⁶ mighty work in my name [see above], and be able quickly to speak evil of me. **40** For he that is not against us is for us. **41** For whosoever shall give you a cup of water to drink,

⁷ because ye are Christ's, verily I say unto you, he shall in no wise lose his reward.

cp. 14 21.

42 And whosoever shall cause one of these little ones that believe ⁸ on me to stumble, it were better for him if ⁹ a great millstone were hanged about his neck, and he were cast into the sea.

[Luke]

therein.

cp. 14 11; 18 14.

cp. 7 28.   Whosoever shall receive this little child in my name [cp. 9 49; 10 17; 21 8; 24 47] receiveth me: and whosoever shall receive me receiveth him that sent me:

10 16 He that heareth you heareth me; and he that rejecteth you rejecteth me; and he that rejecteth me rejecteth him that sent me.

for he that is ² least [cp. 7 28] among you all, the same is great.

49 And John answered and said, [cp. 7 40; 9 38; 10 25; 11 45; 12 13; 18 18; 19 39; 20 21, 28, 39; 21 7] Master [cp. 8 24; 9 33: also 5 5; 8 45; 17 13], we saw one casting out ³ devils in thy name [see above]; and we forbade him, because he followeth not with us. **50** But Jesus said unto him, Forbid him not [cp. 18 16]:

for he that is not against you is for you [cp. 11 23].

17 1 And he said unto his disciples, It is impossible but that occasions of stumbling should come: but woe unto him [cp. 22 22: also 11 42 ff.], through whom they come!

2 It were well for him if a millstone were hanged about his neck, and he were thrown into the sea, rather than that he should cause one of these little ones to stumble.

[John]

into the kingdom of God.

cp. 14 13, 14, 26; 15 16; 16 23, 24, 26.
12 44 He that believeth on me, believeth not on me, but on him that sent me.

13 20 He that receiveth whomsoever I send receiveth me; and he that receiveth me receiveth him that sent me.

¹ Or, from above

cp. 1 38; 20 16.

cp. 14 13, 14, 26; 15 16; 16 23, 24, 26.

cp. 14 13, 14, 26; 15 16; 16 23, 24, 26.

be that the occasions come; but woe to that man [*cp.* 26 24: *also* 23 13 *ff.*] through whom the occasion cometh !

cp. 14 21.

17 1

8 And if thy hand or thy foot causeth thee to stumble, cut it off, and cast it from thee : it is good for thee to enter [*see verse 3 above*] into life maimed or halt,

rather than having two hands or two feet to be cast into the eternal [*cp.* 25 41: *also* 13 42, 50] fire.

Matt. **5 30** And if thy right [*cp.* 5 29, 39 ; 27 29] hand causeth thee to stumble, cut it off, and cast it from thee : for it is profitable for thee that one of thy members should perish, and not thy whole body go into [6] hell [*cp.* 5 29; 10 28; 23 15, 33 : *also* 5 22 ; 18 9].

cp. 3 12.

43 And if thy hand cause thee to stumble, cut it off : it is good for thee to enter [*cp.* 9 45, 47; 10 15, 23, 24, 25] into life maimed, rather than having thy two hands to go into [10] hell, into the unquenchable fire.[11] **45** And if thy foot cause thee to stumble, cut it off: it is good for thee to enter [*see verse 43 above*] into life halt, rather than having thy two feet to be cast into [10] hell. **47** And if thine eye cause thee to stumble, cast it out : it is good for thee to enter [*see verse 43 above*] into the kingdom of God with one eye, rather than having two eyes to be cast into [10] hell; **48** where their worm dieth not, and the fire is not quenched.

cp. 6 6; 22 50.

cp. 18 17, 24, 25 : *also* 11 52; 13 24; 24 26.

cp. 12 5.

cp. 3 17.

cp. 18 17, etc., above.

cp. 12 5.

cp. 6 6; 22 50.

cp. 18 17, etc., above.

cp. 12 5.

cp. 18 10.

cp. 3 5: *also* 10 1, 2, 9.

cp. 3 5: *also* 10 1, 2, 9.

cp. 18 10.

cp. 3 5: *also* 10 1, 2, 9.

9 And if thine eye causeth thee to stumble, pluck it out, and cast it from thee : it is good for thee to enter [*see verse 3 above*] into life with one eye, rather than having two eyes to be cast into the [6] hell of fire [*cp.* 5 22 : *also* 5 29, 30; 10 28; 23 15, 33].

29 And if thy right [*see above*] eye causeth thee to stumble, pluck it out, and cast it from thee : for it is profitable for thee that one of thy members should perish, and not thy whole body be cast into [6] hell [*see above*].

10 See that ye despise not one of these little ones; for I say unto you, that in heaven their angels do always behold the face of my Father which is in heaven [*cp.* 5 16, 45 ; 6 1, 9; *etc.*].[7]

cp. 11 25, 26.

cp. 11 13.

Luke **15 3** And he spake unto them this parable, saying,

12 How think ye [*cp.* 17 25; 21 28; 22 17, 42; 26 66] ? if any man have a hundred sheep, and one of them be gone astray, doth he not leave the ninety and nine, and go unto the mountains, and seek that which goeth astray ? **13** And if so be that he find it, verily I say unto you, he rejoiceth over it

4 What man of you, having a hundred sheep, and having lost one of them, doth not leave the ninety and nine in the wilderness, and go after that which is lost, until he find it [*cp.* 15 8 : *also* 19 10] ? **5** And when he hath found it, he layeth it on his shoulders, rejoicing.

6 And when he cometh home, he calleth together his friends and his neighbours, saying unto them, Rejoice with me [*cp.* 15 9: *also* 1 58], for I have found my sheep which was lost [*cp.* 15 9, 24, 32]. **7** I say unto you, that even so there shall be joy in heaven over one sinner that repenteth [*cp.* 15 10], *more* than over ninety and nine righteous persons, which need no repentance [*cp.* 5 32].

cp. 11 56.
cp. 10 1 *ff.*

cp. 6 39.

more than over the ninety and nine which have not gone astray.

14 Even so it is not [8] the will of [9] your Father which is in heaven [*cp.* 5 16, 45; 6 1, 9; *etc.*], that one of these little ones should perish.

cp. 11 25, 26.

cp. 11 13.

Matt. 5 **13** Ye are the salt of the earth : but if the salt have lost its savour, wherewith shall it be salted ? it is thenceforth good for nothing,

but to be cast out and trodden under foot of men.

cp. 5 9; 10 13.

49 For every one shall be salted with fire [12].   **50** Salt is good : but if the salt have lost its saltness, wherewith will ye season it ?

Have salt in yourselves, and be at peace one with another.

Luke 14 **34** Salt therefore is good : but if even the salt have lost its savour, wherewith shall it be seasoned ? **35** It is fit neither for the land nor for the dunghill : *men* cast it out.

cp. 10 5, 6 : *also* 1 79; 2 14, 29 ; 19 38.

cp. 14 27; 16 33.

[1] Gr. *greater*.   [2] Or, *servant*
[3] Gr. *bondservant*.   [4] Or, *minister*
[5] Gr. *a millstone turned by an ass*.
[6] Gr. *Gehenna*.
[7] Many authorities, some ancient, insert ver. 11 *For the Son of man came to save that which was lost.* See Luke 19 10.
[8] Gr. *a thing willed before your Father*.
[9] Some ancient authorities read *my*.

[1] Gr. *greater*.   [2] Or, *servant*
[3] Gr. *bondservant*.   [4] Or, *Teacher*
[5] Gr. *demons*.   [6] Gr. *power*.
[7] Gr. *in name that ye are*.
[8] Many ancient authorities omit *on me*.
[9] Gr. *a millstone turned by an ass*.
[10] Gr. *Gehenna*.
[11] Ver. 44 and 46 (which are identical with ver. 48) are omitted by the best ancient authorities.
[12] Many ancient authorities add *and every sacrifice shall be salted with salt.* See Lev. 2 13.

[1] Gr. *greater*.   [2] Gr. *lesser*.
[3] Gr. *demons*.

Mark 9 48 : Is. 66 24.   Mark 9 49 : *cp.* Lev. 2 13.

§ 132. **The Treatment of a Brother's Fault and the Authority of the Church**

Matt. 18 15-20

Luke 17 3-4

15 And if thy brother sin [1] against thee, go, shew him his fault between thee and him alone : if he hear thee, thou hast gained thy brother.

18 21

3 Take heed to yourselves : if thy brother sin, rebuke him ;

and if he repent, forgive him [*cp.* 11 4]. **4** And if he sin against thee seven times in the day, and seven times turn again to thee, saying, I repent; thou shalt forgive him.

cp. 11 25.

16 But if he hear *thee* not, take with thee one or two more, that at the mouth of two witnesses or three every word may be established. **17** And if he refuse to hear them, tell it unto the [2] church [*cp.* 16 18] : and if he refuse to hear the [2] church also, let him be unto thee as the Gentile [*cp.* 5 47; 6 7, 32] and the publican [*cp.* 5 46; 9 11; 11 19; 21 31, 32].

cp. 8 17.

cp. 2 16.

cp. 12 30: *and* 5 30; 7 34; 15 1; 18 10.

18 Verily I say unto you,

What things soever ye shall bind on earth shall be bound in heaven : and what things soever ye shall loose on earth shall be loosed in heaven.

Matt. 16 **19** I will give unto thee the keys of the kingdom of heaven : and whatsoever thou shalt bind on earth shall be bound in heaven : and whatsoever thou shalt loose on earth shall be loosed in heaven.

John 20 **22** And when he had said this, he breathed on them, and saith unto them, Receive ye the [1] Holy Ghost :
23 whose soever sins ye forgive, they are forgiven unto them ;
whose soever *sins* ye retain, they are retained.

[1] Or, *Holy Spirit*

19 Again I say unto you, that if two of you shall agree on earth as touching anything that they shall ask, it shall be done for them [*cp.* 7 7; 21 22] of my Father which is in heaven [*cp.* 5 16, 45; 6 1, 9; 7 11, 21; 10 32, 33; 12 50; 16 17; 18 10, 14: *also* 5 48; 6 14, 26, 32; 15 13; 18 35; 23 9]. **20** For where two or three are gathered together in my name [*cp.* 18 5; 24 5: *also* 7 22], there am I in the midst of them [*cp.* 28 20].

cp. 11 24.
cp. 11 25, 26.

cp. 9 37, 39; 13 6; 16 17: *also* 9 38.

cp. 11 9.
cp. 11 13.

cp. 9 48; 21 8: *also* 9 49; 10 17; 24 47.

cp. 14 13, 14; 15 7, 16; 16 23, 24.

cp. 14 13, 14, 26; 15 16; 16 23, 24, 26.

[1] Some ancient authorities omit *against thee*.

[2] Or, *congregation*

Matt. 18 16 : *cp.* Deut. 19 15 ; *also* Num. 35 30.

§ 133. The Obligation to Forgive a Brother and the Parable of the Two Debtors

[*Cp.* Luke 7 40-48]

Matt. 18 21-35			**Luke 17** 3-4	
18 15			3 Take heed to yourselves: if thy brother sin, rebuke him; and if he repent, forgive him [*cp.* 11 4].	*cp.* 13 36, 37; 21 21: *also* 6 68.
21 Then came Peter [*cp.* 14 28; 15 15; 16 22; 17 4; 19 27; 26 33: *also* 16 16; 17 24], and said to him, Lord, how oft shall my brother sin against me, and I forgive him [*cp.* 6 12, 14, 15]? until seven times?	*cp.* 8 32; 9 5; 10 28; 11 21; 14 29: *also* 8 29. *cp.* 11 25.		*cp.* 8 45; 9 33; 12 41; 18 28: *also* 5 8; 9 20. **4** And if he sin against thee	
			seven times in the day, and seven times turn again to thee, saying, I repent; thou shalt forgive him.	
22 Jesus saith unto him, I say not unto thee, Until seven times; but, Until ¹ seventy times seven. **23** Therefore is the kingdom of heaven likened unto a certain king [*cp.* 22 2 *ff.*: *also* 25 34, 40], which would make a reckoning [*cp.* 25 19] with his ² servants [*cp.* 25 14]. **24** And when he had begun to reckon, one was brought unto him, which owed him ten thousand ³ talents [*cp.* 25 15, *etc.*]. **25** But forasmuch as he had not *wherewith* to pay, his lord [*cp.* 25 18, *etc.*] commanded him to be sold, and his wife, and children, and all that he had, and payment to be made. **26** The ⁴ servant therefore fell down and worshipped him, saying, Lord, have patience with me, and I will pay thee all. **27** And the lord of that ⁴ servant [*cp.* 24 50; 25 19], being moved with compassion, released him, and forgave him the ⁵ debt. **28** But that ⁴ servant went out, and found one of his fellow-servants [*cp.* 24 49], which owed him a hundred ⁶ pence: and he laid hold on him, and took *him* by the throat, saying, Pay what thou owest. **29** So his fellow-servant fell down and besought him, saying, Have patience with me, and I will pay thee. **30** And he would not: but went and cast him into prison, till he should pay that which was due. **31** So when his fellow-servants saw what was done, they were exceeding sorry [*cp.* 17 23; 26 22], and came and told unto their lord all that was done. **32** Then his lord called him unto him, and saith to him, Thou wicked ⁴ servant [*cp.* 25 26: *also* 24 48], I forgave thee all that debt, because thou besoughtest me: **33** shouldest not thou also have had mercy on thy fellow-servant, even as I had mercy on thee? **34** And his lord was wroth [*cp.* 22 7], and delivered him to the tormentors, till he should pay all that was due [*cp.* 5 25, 26]. **35** So shall also my heavenly Father [*cp.* 5 48; 6 14, 26, 32; 15 13; 23 9: *also* 5 16, 45; *etc.*] do unto you, if ye forgive not every one his brother from your hearts [*cp.* 6 15].	*cp.* 11 25, 26. *cp.* 11 26.		*cp.* 19 12, 15, 27. *cp.* 7 42. *cp.* 12 46. *cp.* 19 22. *cp.* 14 21. *cp.* 12 58, 59. *cp.* 11 13.	

¹ Or, *seventy times and seven*   ² Gr. *bondservants*.
³ This talent was probably worth about £240.   ⁴ Gr. *bondservant*.
⁵ Gr. *loan*.
⁶ The word in the Greek denotes a coin worth about eight pence halfpenny.

D. The Journey to Jerusalem (§§ 134-193)

(i) Events on the Journey I (§§ 134-146)

§ 134. The Start of the Journey and Rejection in a Samaritan Village

[*Cp.* § 183]

Matt. 19 1	**Mark 10** 1	**Luke 9** 51-56
1 And it came to pass when Jesus had finished these words [*cp.* 7 28; 11 1; 13 53; 26 1],	**1** And	**51** And it came to pass, when
		cp. 7 1. the days ¹ were well - nigh come that he should be received up, he stedfastly set his face to go to Jerusalem

cp. 16 21; 20 17, 18.	*cp*. 10 32, 33.	[*cp*. 9 53; 13 22; 17 11; 19 11, 41: *also* 9 31; 13 33; 18 31],	
he departed from Galilee, and came into the borders of Judæa beyond Jordan;	he arose from thence, and cometh into the borders of Judæa and beyond Jordan:		*cp*. 10 40.

he departed from Galilee, and came into the borders of Judæa beyond Jordan;

cp. 10 5.

cp. 10 14.   *cp*. 6 11.

cp. 20 20.   *cp*. 10 35.

cp. 9 22;
16 23.   *cp*. 5 30;
      8 33.

he arose from thence, and cometh into the borders of Judæa and beyond Jordan:

52 and sent messengers before his face [*cp*. 10 1]: and they went, and entered into a village [*cp*. 9 56; 10 38; 17 12] of the Samaritans [*cp*. 17 11: *also* 10 33; 17 16], to make ready for him. **53** And they did not receive him [*cp*. 10 10: *also* 9 5], because his face was *as though he were* going to Jerusalem [*see above*]. **54** And when his disciples James and John saw *this*, they said, Lord, wilt thou that we bid fire to come down from heaven, and consume them [2] ? **55** But he turned [*cp*. 7 9, 44; 10 23; 14 25; 22 61; 23 28], and rebuked them [3]. **56** And they went to another village [*see verse* 52].

cp. 10 40.

cp. 4 4, 5, 39, 40.

cp. 4 9.

cp. 1 38.

[1] Gr. *were being fulfilled.*   [2] Many ancient authorities add *even as Elijah did.*
[3] Some ancient authorities add *and said, Ye know not what manner of spirit ye are of.*
Some, but fewer, add also *For the Son of man came not to destroy men's lives, but to save them.*

Luke 9 54 : *cp*. II Kings 1 10, 12.

§ 135. **Would-be Disciples**

[*Cp*. Matt. 10 37; Luke 14 26]

Matt. 8 18-22

18 Now when Jesus saw great multitudes about him [*cp*. 3 7; 5 1; 9 36], he gave commandment to depart unto the other side. **19** And there came [1] a scribe, and said unto him, [2] Master, I will follow thee whithersoever thou goest. **20** And Jesus saith unto him, The foxes have holes, and the birds of the heaven *have* [3] nests ; but the Son of man hath not where to lay his head. **21** And another of the disciples *verse* 22
said unto him, Lord, suffer me first to go and bury my father. **22** But Jesus saith unto him, Follow me [*cp*. 4 19 ; 9 9 ; 16 24 ; 19 21] ; and leave the dead to bury their own dead.

[1] Gr. *one scribe.*   [2] Or, *Teacher*
[3] Gr. *lodging-places.*

verse 19

Luke 9 57-62

57 And as they went in the way,

     a certain man said unto him,   I will follow thee [*cp. verse* 61] whithersoever thou goest. **58** And Jesus said unto him, The foxes have holes, and the birds of the heaven *have* [1] nests ; but the Son of man hath not where to lay his head. **59** And he said unto another, Follow me [*cp*. 5 27 ; 9 23 ; 18 22]. But he said,   Lord, suffer me first [*cp. verse* 61] to go and bury my father. **60** But he said unto him, *verse* 59
Leave the dead to bury their own dead ; but go thou and publish abroad the kingdom of God. **61** And another also said, I will follow thee [*cp. verse* 57], Lord ; but first suffer me [*cp. verse* 59] to bid farewell [*cp*. 14 33] to them that are at my house. **62** But Jesus said unto him, No man, having put his hand to the plough, and looking back, is fit for the kingdom of God.

[1] Gr. *lodging-places.*

cp. 6 5.

cp. 1 17; 2 14; 8 34; 10 21.

see above.

cp. 1 43; 12 26; 21 19, 22.

see above.

§ 136. **The Mission of the Seventy**

Matt. 10 1, 5-8; 9 37-38; 10 16, 9-15; 11 21-24	Mark 6 7-11	Luke 9 1-5	**Luke 10** 1-16	
1 And he	**7** And he *cp*. 16 19, 20.	**1** And he	**1** Now after these things the Lord [*cp*. 7 13, 19; 10 39, 41; 11 39; 12 42; 13 15; 17 5, 6; 18 6; 19 8; 22 61; 24 3, 34]	*cp*. 4 1; 6 23; 11 2; 20 2, 18, 20, 25; 21 7, 12.
called unto him his twelve disciples, and gave them	called unto him the twelve [*cp*. 3 13, 14], *cp*. 5 30.	called the twelve [*cp*. 6 13] together, and gave them power [*cp*.	appointed seventy [1] others,	

authority over unclean spirits [*cp.* 10 8 ; 17 16], to cast them out, and to heal all manner of disease and all manner of sickness.		1 17, 35 ; 4 14, 36 ; 5 17 ; 6 19 ; 8 46 ; 24 49] and authority over all [1] devils [*cp.* 9 6, 40 ; 10 9, 17], and to cure diseases.		
5 These twelve Jesus sent forth, *cp.* 21 1.	and began to send them forth by two and two [*cp.* 11 1 ; 14 13] ; and he gave them authority over the unclean spirits [*cp.* 3 15 : *also* 6 12, 13 ; 9 18] ;	2 And he sent them forth *cp.* 19 29 ; 22 8.	and sent them two and two	
verses 7 *and* 8		to preach the kingdom of God, and to heal [*cp.* 6 19 ; 9 11, 42 ; 14 4 ; 22 51] [2] the sick.	*verses* 9 *and* 11 before his face into every city and place, whither he himself was about to come [*cp.* 9 52].	
and charged them, saying,	8 and he charged them	3 And he said unto them,	2 And he said unto them,	
Go not into *any* way of the Gentiles, and enter not into any city of the Samaritans : 6 but go rather to the lost sheep of the house of Israel [*cp.* 15 24 : *also* 9 36].	*cp.* 6 34.	*cp.* 9 52.		*cp.* 4 9. *cp.* 10 16.
7 And as ye go, preach, saying, The kingdom of heaven is at hand [*cp.* 3 2; 4 17: *also* 12 28].	*cp.* 1 15 : *also* 6 12.	*cp. verse* 2 : *also* 9 6.	*verses* 9 *and* 11	
8 Heal the sick, raise the dead, cleanse the lepers, cast out [1] devils : freely ye received, freely give.	*cp. verse* 13.			
9 37 The harvest truly is plenteous, but the labourers are few. 38 Pray ye therefore the Lord of the harvest, that he send forth labourers into his harvest.			The harvest is plenteous, but the labourers are few : pray ye therefore the Lord of the harvest, that he send forth labourers into his harvest.	*cp.* 4 35-38.
10 16 Behold, I send you forth as sheep in the midst of wolves :			3 Go your ways : behold, I send you forth as lambs in the midst of wolves.	
9 Get you	that they should take nothing for *their* journey, save a staff only ; no bread, no wallet,	Take nothing for your journey, neither staff, nor wallet, nor bread,	4 Carry	
no gold, nor silver, nor brass in your [2] purses ; 10 no wallet for *your* journey, neither two coats, nor shoes, nor staff :	no [1] money in their [2] purse ; 9 but *to go* shod with sandals : and, *said he*, put not on two coats.	nor money ; neither have two coats [*cp.* 3 11].	no purse, no wallet, no shoes [*cp.* 22 35]: and salute no men on the way.	
for the labourer is worthy of his food.			*verse* 7	*cp.* 4 36.
11 And into whatsoever city or village ye shall	10 And he said unto them, Wheresoever ye	4 And into whatsoever house ye	5 And into whatsoever house ye shall	

[Matthew]

enter,
search out who in it is worthy; and there abide till ye go forth. 12 And as ye enter into the house, salute it.

13 And if the house be worthy, let your peace come upon it [cp. 5 9]: but if it be not worthy, let your peace return to you.

verse 11

verse 10

verses 7 and 8

14 And whosoever shall not receive you, nor hear your words, as ye go forth out of that house or that city, shake off the dust of your feet.

cp. 8 4; 10 18; 24 14.

cp. 24 43.

15 Verily I say unto you, It shall be more tolerable [cp. 7 22; 24 36: *also* 26 29] for the land [cp. 2 6, 20, 21; 4 15; 11 2A] of Sodom and Gomorrah in the day of judgement [cp. 11 22, 24; 12 36], than for that city [cp. 11 24]. 11 21 Woe unto thee, Chorazin! woe unto thee, Bethsaida! for if the 3 mighty works had been done in Tyre and Sidon which were done in you, they would have repented long ago in sackcloth and ashes. 22 Howbeit I say unto you, it shall be more tolerable for Tyre and Sidon in the day of judgement [cp. 10 15; 11 24; 12 36], than for you. 23 And thou, Capernaum, shalt thou be exalted unto heaven? thou shalt 4 go down unto

[Mark]

enter into a house,

there abide till ye depart thence.

cp. 9 50.

11 And whatsoever place shall not receive you, and they hear you not, as ye go forth thence, shake off the dust that is under your feet for a testimony unto them [cp. 1 44; 13 9].

cp. 13 32: *also* 14 25.

1 Gr. *brass.* 2 Gr. *girdle.*

[Luke]

enter,

there abide, and thence depart.

cp. 1 79; 2 14, 29; 19 38.

verse 2

5 And as many as receive you not, when ye depart from that city, shake off the dust from your feet for a testimony against them [cp. 5 14; 21 13].

1 Gr. *demons.*
2 Some ancient authorities omit *the sick.*

2 enter,

verse 7

first say, Peace *be* to this house. 6 And if a son of peace be there, your peace shall rest upon 3 him: but if not, it shall turn to you again. 7 And in that same house remain, eating and drinking such things as they give: for the labourer is worthy of his hire. Go not from house to house. 8 And into whatsoever city ye enter, and they receive you, eat such things as are set before you: 9 and heal the sick that are therein, and say unto them, The kingdom of God is come nigh unto you [cp. 11 20; 17 20, 21; 19 11; 21 8]. 10 But into whatsoever city ye shall enter, and they receive you not [cp. 9 53], go out into the streets thereof and say, 11 Even the dust from your city, that cleaveth to our feet, we do wipe off against you: howbeit know this [cp. 12 39], that the kingdom of God is come nigh [cp. v. 9]. 12 I say unto you, It shall be more tolerable in that day [cp. 17 31; 21 34] for

Sodom,

than

for that city. 13 Woe unto thee, Chorazin! woe unto thee, Bethsaida! for if the 4 mighty works had been done in Tyre and Sidon, which were done in you, they would have repented long ago, sitting in sackcloth and ashes. 14 Howbeit it shall be more tolerable for Tyre and Sidon in the judgement, than for you. 15 And thou, Capernaum, shalt thou be exalted unto heaven? thou shalt be brought down unto

[marginal references]

cp. 14 27; 16 33.

cp. 4 36.

cp. 14 20; 16 23, 26.
cp. 3 22.

Hades: for if the [3] mighty works had been done in Sodom which were done in thee, it would have remained until this day [*cp.* 27 8; 28 15]. **24** Howbeit I say unto you, that it shall be more tolerable for the land [*cp.* 2 6, 20, 21; 4 15; 10 15] of Sodom in the day of judgement, than for thee [*cp.* 10 15].

Hades.

verse 12

16 He that heareth you heareth me; and he that rejecteth you rejecteth me;

and he that rejecteth me rejecteth him that sent me.

cp. 3 22.

John 12 **48** He that rejecteth me, and receiveth not my sayings . . .

Matt. 10 **40** He that receiveth you receiveth me, and he that receiveth me receiveth him that sent me. 18 **5** And whoso shall receive one such little child in my name receiveth me.

Mark 9 **37** Whosoever shall receive one of such little children in my name, receiveth me: and whosoever receiveth me, receiveth not me, but him that sent me.

Luke 9 **48** Whosoever shall receive this little child in my name receiveth me: and whosoever shall receive me receiveth him that sent me.

13 **20** He that receiveth whomsoever I send receiveth me; and he that receiveth me receiveth him that sent me [*cp.* 12 44, 45].

[1] Gr. *demons.*   [2] Gr. *girdles.*
[3] Gr. *powers.*
[4] Many ancient authorities read *be brought down.*

[1] Many ancient authorities add *and two*: and so in ver. 17.
[2] Or, *enter first, say*
[3] Or, *it*   [4] Gr. *powers.*

Matt. 11 23 ‖ Luke 10 15: *cp.* Is. 14 13-15.

§ 137. **The Return of the Seventy**

[*Cp.* Mark 6 30: Luke 9 10]

	Mark 16 17-18	Luke 10 17-20	
	17 And these signs shall follow them that believe: in my name [*cp.* 9 38, 39: *also* 9 37; 13 6] shall they cast out [1] devils; they shall speak with [2] new tongues; 18 they shall	**17** And the seventy returned with joy, saying, Lord, even the [1] devils are subject unto us in thy name [*cp.* 9 49: *also* 9 48; 21 8; 24 47].	

cp. 7 22: *also* 18 5, 20; 24 5.

cp. 10 1, 8: *also* 17 16. *cp.* 13 39.

[*cp.* 3 15; 6 7: *also* 6 13; 9 18] take up serpents,

and if they drink any deadly thing, it shall in no wise hurt them; they shall lay hands on the sick, and they shall recover.

18 And he said unto them, I beheld Satan fallen as lightning from heaven. **19** Behold, I have given you authority [*cp.* 10 9; 9 1: *also* 9 6, 40] to tread upon serpents and scorpions, and over all the power of the enemy: and nothing shall in any wise hurt you.

20 Howbeit in this rejoice not, that the spirits are subject unto you; but rejoice that your names are written in heaven.

cp. 14 13, 14, 26; 15 16; 16 23, 24, 26. *cp.* 12 31; 16 11.

[1] Gr. *demons.*
[2] Some ancient authorities omit *new.*

[1] Gr. *demons.*

Luke 10 20: *cp.* Dan. 12 1.

§ 138. **The Thanksgiving of Jesus and the Blessedness of His Disciples**

Matt. 11 25-30; 13 16-17		Luke 10 21-24	
25 At that season [*cp.* 12 1; 14 1: *also* 18 1; 26 55] Jesus answered and said, I [1] thank thee, O Father [*cp.* 26 39, 42: *also* 6 9], Lord of heaven and	*cp.* 14 36.	**21** In that same hour [*cp.* 7 21; 13 31] he rejoiced [1] in the Holy Spirit, and said, I [2] thank thee, O Father [*cp.* 22 42; 23 34, 46: *also* 11 2], Lord of heaven and	*cp.* 11 41; 12 27, 28;

earth, that thou didst hide these things from the wise and understanding, and didst reveal them unto babes [*cp.* 16 17]: **26** yea, Father [*see above*], ² for so it was well-pleasing [*cp.* 3 17; 12 18; 17 5] in thy sight. **27** All things have been delivered unto me of my Father [*cp.* 9 8; 28 18]: and no one knoweth the Son, save the Father; neither doth any know the Father, save the Son, and he to whomsoever the Son willeth to reveal *him*. **28** Come unto me, all ye that labour and are heavy laden, and I will give you rest. **29** Take my yoke upon you, and learn of me; for I am meek and lowly in heart: and ye shall find rest unto your souls. **30** For my yoke is easy, and my burden is light.	*cp.* 1 11.	earth, that thou didst hide these things from the wise and understanding, and didst reveal them unto babes: yea, Father [*see above*]; ³ for so it was well-pleasing [*cp.* 2 14; 3 22; 12 32] in thy sight. **22** All things have been delivered unto me of my Father: and no one knoweth who the Son is, save the Father; and who the Father is, save the Son, and he to whomsoever the Son willeth to reveal *him*.	17 1, 5, 11, 21, 24, 25. *see above.* *cp.* 3 35; 5 27; 13 3; 17 2. *cp.* 1 18; 6 46; 7 29; 8 19; 10 15; 17 25-26. *cp.* 6 37; 7 37.
cp. 9 22; 16 23.	*cp.* 5 30; 8 33.	**23** And turning [*cp.* 7 9, 44; 9 55; 14 25; 22 61; 23 28] to the disciples, he said privately [*cp.* 9 10],	*cp.* 1 38.
cp. 17 1, 19; 20 17; 24 3. **13 16** But blessed are your eyes, for they see; and your ears, for they hear. **17** For verily I say unto you, that many prophets and righteous men desired to see the things which ye see, and saw them not; and to hear the things which ye hear, and heard them not.	*cp.* 4 10, 34; 6 31, 32; 9 2, 28; 13 3.	Blessed *are* the eyes which see the things that ye see: **24** for I say unto you, that many prophets and kings desired to see the things which ye see, and saw them not; and to hear the things which ye hear, and heard them not.	

¹ Or, *praise*   ² Or, *that*   ¹ Or, *by*   ² Or, *praise*   ³ Or, *that*

Matt. 11 28-30 : *cp.* Ecclus. 51 23-27 ; Jer. 6 16 ; Zech. 9 9.

§ 139. **A Lawyer's Question and the Parable of the Good Samaritan**

[*Cp.* Matt. 19 16-22 ‖ Mark 10 17-22 ‖ Luke 18 18-23]

Matt. 22 34-40	Mark 12 28-31	Luke 10 25-37	
34 But the Pharisees, when they heard that he had put the Sadducees to silence, gathered themselves together. **35** And one of them, a lawyer,			
	28 And one of the scribes came, and heard them questioning together [*cp.* 8 11 ; 9 14, 16], and knowing that he had answered them well,	**25** And behold, a certain lawyer	
asked him a question, tempting [*cp.* 16 1 ; 19 3 : *also* 22 18] him, **36** ¹ Master,	asked him, *cp.* 8 11 ; 10 2 : *also* 12 15.	stood up and tempted [*cp.* 11 16] him, saying, ¹ Master, what shall I do [*cp.* 3 10, 12, 14] to inherit eternal life [*cp.* 18 18, 30] ?	*cp.* 8 6. *cp.* 6 28. *cp.* 3 15 ; *etc.*
cp. 19 16, 29 ; 25 46. which is the great commandment in the law ? **37** And he said unto him,	*cp.* 10 17, 30. What commandment is the first of all? **29** Jesus	**26** And he said unto him, What is written in the law ? how readest thou [*cp.* 6 3] ? **27** And he answering said,	
cp. 12 3, 5 ; 19 4 ; 21 16, 42 ; 22 31.	*cp.* 2 25 ; 12 10, 26. answered, The first is, Hear, O Israel ; ¹ The Lord our God, the Lord is one :		
Thou shalt love the Lord thy God with all thy heart, and with all thy soul, and with all thy mind.	**30** and thou shalt love the Lord thy God ² with all thy heart, and ² with all thy soul, and ² with all thy mind, and ² with all thy strength.	Thou shalt love the Lord thy God ² with all thy heart, and with all thy soul, and with all thy strength, and with all thy mind ;	
38 This is the great and first com-			

Matthew	Mark	Luke
mandment. 39 [2] And a second like *unto it* is this, Thou shalt love thy neighbour as thyself [*cp.* 19 19]. 40 On these two commandments hangeth the whole law, and the prophets [*cp.* 5 17; 7 12; 11 13].	31 The second is this, Thou shalt love thy neighbour as thyself. There is none other commandment greater than these.	and thy neighbour as thyself. *cp.* 16 16. 28 And he said unto him, Thou hast answered right [*cp.* 7 43]: this do, and thou shalt live.
[1] Or, *Teacher* [2] Or, *And a second is like unto it, Thou shalt love &c.*	[1] Or, *The Lord is our God; the Lord is one* [2] Gr. *from.*	

29 But he, desiring to justify himself [*cp.* 16 15], said unto Jesus, And who is my neighbour? 30 Jesus made answer and said, A certain man was going down from Jerusalem to Jericho; and he fell among robbers, which both stripped him and beat him, and departed, leaving him half dead. 31 And by chance a certain priest was going down that way: and when he saw him, he passed by on the other side. 32 And in like manner a Levite also, when he came to the place, and saw him, passed by on the other side. 33 But a certain Samaritan [*cp.* 17 16: *also* 9 52; 17 11], as he journeyed, came where he was: and when he saw him, he was moved with compassion [*cp.* 15 20: *also* 7 13], 34 and came to him, and bound up his wounds, pouring on *them* oil and wine; and he set him on his own beast, and brought him to an inn, and took care of him. 35 And on the morrow he took out two [3] pence, and gave them to the host, and said, Take care of him; and whatsoever thou spendest more, I, when I come back again, will repay thee. 36 Which of these three, thinkest thou, proved neighbour unto him that fell among the robbers? 37 And he said, He that shewed mercy [*cp.* 1 72] on him. And Jesus said unto him, Go, and do thou likewise.

cp. 4 9: *also* 4 39, 40.

[1] Or, *Teacher*   [2] Gr. *from.*   [3] See footnote on Matt. 18 28.

Mark 12 29=Deut. 6 4.   Matt. 22 37 ‖ Mark 12 30 ‖ Luke 10 27=Deut. 6 5.
Matt. 22 39 ‖ Mark 12 31 ‖ Luke 10 27=Lev. 19 18.   Luke 10 28 : *cp.* Lev. 18 5.

§ 140. **In the House of Martha and Mary**

Luke 10 38-42

38 Now as they went on their way, he entered into a certain village [*cp.* 9 52, 56; 17 12]: and a certain woman named Martha received him into her house. 39 And she had a sister called Mary, which also sat at the Lord's [*see below*] feet [*cp.* 7 38; 8 35], and heard his word. 40 But Martha was [1] cumbered about much serving; and she came up to him, and said, Lord, dost thou not care that my sister did leave me to serve alone? bid her therefore that she help me. 41 But the Lord [*cp.* 7 13, 19; 10 1, 39; 11 39; 12 42; 13 15; 17 5, 6; 18 6; 19 8; 22 61; 24 3, 34] answered and said unto her, [2] Martha, Martha, thou art anxious and troubled about many things: 42 [3] but one thing is needful: for Mary hath chosen the good part, which shall not be taken away from her.

cp. 16 19, 20.

cp. 11 1.

cp. 12 2.

cp. 4 1; 6 23; 11 2; 20 2, 18, 20, 25; 21 7, 12.

[1] Gr. *distracted.*
[2] A few ancient authorities read *Martha, Martha, thou art troubled: Mary hath chosen &c.*
[3] Many ancient authorities read *but few things are needful, or one.*

§ 141. **The Lord's Prayer**

Matt. 6 9-13		Luke 11 1-4	
cp. 14 23 ; 19 13 ; 26 36, 39, 42, 44 : *also* 11 25.	*cp.* 1 35; 6 46; 14 32, 35, 39.	1 And it came to pass, as he was praying [*cp.* 3 21 ; 5 16; 6 12; 9 18, 28, 29; 22 41, 44: *also* 10 21] in a certain place, that when he ceased, one of his disciples said unto him,	*cp.* 11 41-42; 12 27-28; 17 1-26.

cp. 9 14 ; 11 2 ; 14 12.

9 After this manner therefore pray ye:
          Our Father
[cp. 11 25, 26 ; 26 39, 42] which art
in heaven [cp. 5 16, 45 ; 6 1 ; 7 11, 21 ;
10 32, 33 ; 12 50 ; 16 17 ; 18 10, 14, 19 ;
also 5 48 ; 6 14, 26, 32 ; 15 13 ; 18 35 ;
23 9], Hallowed be thy name.
10 Thy kingdom come. Thy will be done
[cp. 26 39, 42 : also 7 21 ; 12 50 ; 21 31],
as in heaven, so on earth. **11** Give us
this day   1 our daily bread.
12 And forgive us our debts, as we
          also have forgiven
          our debtors [cp. 6 14, 15 ; 18 21-35].
13 And bring us not into temptation
[cp. 26 41], but deliver us from 2 the evil
one [cp. 5 37, 39 ; 13 19, 38].3

1 Gr. our bread for the coming day.
2 Or, evil
3 Many authorities, some ancient, but with variations, add For thine is the kingdom, and the
power, and the glory, for ever. Amen.

cp. 2 18 ;
6 29.

cp. 14 36.
cp. 11 25, 26.

cp. 14 36 :
also 3 35.

cp. 11 25.

cp. 14 38.

Lord, teach us to pray, even as John
also taught his disciples [cp. 5 33 : also
7 18]. **2** And he said unto them,
          When ye pray
[cp. Matt. 6 5], say,   1 Father
[cp. 10 21, 22 ; 22 42 ; 23 34, 46],
          cp. 11 13.

Hallowed be thy name [cp. 1 49].
Thy kingdom come.2
          cp. 22 42.
          3 Give us
          day by day 3 our daily bread.
4 And forgive us our sins ; for we ourselves also   forgive every one that
is indebted to us [cp. 17 3-4].
And bring us not into temptation
[cp. 22 40, 46].4

1 Many ancient authorities read Our Father, which
art in heaven. See Matt. 6 9.
2 Many ancient authorities add Thy will be done,
as in heaven, so on earth. See Matt. 6 10.
3 Gr. our bread for the coming day.
4 Many ancient authorities add but deliver us from
the evil one (or, from evil). See Matt. 6 13.

cp. 1 35, 37 ;
3 25 ; 4 1.

cp. 11 41 ;
12 27, 28 ;
17 1, 5, 11,
21, 24, 25.

cp. 4 34 ; 5
30 ; 6 38 ;
7 17 ; 9 31.

cp. 17 15.

§ 142. **Teaching about Prayer**

Luke 11 5-13

5 And he said unto them, Which of you shall have a friend,
and shall go unto him at midnight, and say to him, Friend
[cp. 14 10], lend me three loaves ; **6** for a friend of mine is come
to me from a journey, and I have nothing to set before him ;
7 and he from within shall answer and say, Trouble me [cp. 18 5]
not : the door is now shut, and my children are with me in
bed ; I cannot rise and give thee ? **8** I say unto you, Though
he will not rise and give him, because he is his friend, yet because
of his importunity [cp. 18 4, 5] he will arise and give him 1 as
many as he needeth.   **9** And I say unto you,

cp. 26 10.   cp. 14 6.

Matt. 7 7-11

Ask,
and it shall be given
you [cp. 18 19 ; 21
22] ; seek, and ye shall
find ; knock, and it shall be opened
unto you : **8** for every one that
asketh receiveth ; and he that seeketh
findeth ; and to him that knocketh
it shall be opened. **9** Or what man
is there of you, who,   if
his son shall ask him for a loaf,
will   give him a stone ; **10** or if he
shall ask for a fish, will
give him a serpent ?

          11 If ye then, being evil
[cp. 12 34], know how to give good gifts
unto   your   children,   how   much
more shall your   Father
which is in heaven [cp. 5 16, 45 ; 6 1,
9 ; 7 21 ; 10 32, 33 ; 12 50 ; 16 17 ;
18 10, 14, 19 : also 5 48 ; 6 14, 26, 32 ;
15 13 ; 18 35 ; 23 9] give good things
to them that ask him ?

cp. 11 24.

Ask,
and it shall be given
you ;
     seek, and ye shall

John 15 7

Ask whatsoever ye will,
and it shall be done
unto you.

John 16 24

Ask,
and ye shall receive
[cp. 14 13 ; 15 16 ;
16 23].

find ; knock, and it shall be opened
unto you. **10** For every one that
asketh receiveth ; and he that seeketh
findeth ; and to him that knocketh
it shall be opened. **11** And of
which of you that is a father shall
his son   ask   2 a loaf,
and he give him a stone ? or
          a fish, and he for a fish
give him a serpent ? **12** Of if he
shall ask an egg, will he give him a
scorpion ? **13** If ye then, being evil,
          know how to give good gifts
unto   your   children,   how   much
more   shall   your heavenly Father

cp. 11 25, 26.

          give the Holy Spirit
to them that ask him ?

1 Or, whatsoever things
2 Some ancient authorities omit a loaf, and he give
him a stone ? or,

§ 143. **A Controversy about Casting out Devils**

Matt. 12 22-30, 43-45	Matt. 9 32-34	Mark 3 22-27	Luke 11 14-26	
22 Then was brought unto him ¹ one possessed with a devil, blind [*cp.* 9 27] and dumb : and he healed him, insomuch that the dumb man spake and saw. **23** And all the multitudes were amazed,	**32** And as they went forth, behold, there was brought to him a dumb man possessed with a ¹ devil. **33** And when the ¹ devil was cast out, the dumb man spake : and the multitudes marvelled [*cp.* 8 27; 15 31; 21 20; 27 14: *also* 7 28; 13 54; 19 25; 22 22, 33], saying, It was never so seen in Israel.	*cp.* 2 12 ; 5 20, 42 ; 6 51 ; 7 37; 10 32; 15 5 ; 16 5, 8 : *also* 1 22, 27 ; 6 2 ; 10 24, 26 ; 11 18 ; 12 17.	**14** And he was casting out a ¹ devil *which was* dumb. And it came to pass, when the ¹ devil was gone out, the dumb man spake; and the multitudes marvelled [*cp.* 5 9, 26; 8 25, 56; 9 43; 24 12, 41: *also* 2 47, 48; 4 22, 32, 36; 20 26].	*cp.* 7 15, 21, 46.
and said, Is this the son of David [*cp.* 1 1 ; 9 27; 15 22; 20 30, 31 ; 21 9, 15]? **24** But when the Pharisees	**34** But the Pharisees *cp.* 15 1. said,	*cp.* 10 47, 48. **22** And the scribes which came down from Jerusalem [*cp.* 7 1] said, He hath Beelzebub, and,	*cp.* 1 32; 18 38, 39. **15** But some of them *cp.* 5 17. said,	*cp.* 1 19. *cp.* 7 20; 8 48, 52; 10 20.
heard it, they said, This man doth not cast out ² devils, but ³ by Beelzebub [*cp.* 10 25] the prince of the ² devils.	² By the prince of the ³ devils casteth he out ³ devils. ¹ Gr. *demon.* ³ Gr. *demons.*	¹ By the prince of the ² devils casteth he out the ² devils. ¹ Or, *In*	² By Beelzebub the prince of the ³ devils casteth he out ³ devils.	
cp. 16 1: *also* 19 3; 22 18, 35: *and* 12 38. **25** And knowing their thoughts [*cp.* 9 4; 16 8] he said unto them, Every kingdom divided against itself is brought to desolation ; and every city or house divided against itself shall not stand : **26** and if Satan casteth out Satan, he is divided against himself; how then shall his kingdom stand ?	*cp.* 8 11 : *also* 10 2 ; 12 15. **23** And he *cp.* 2 8 ; 8 17. called them unto him, and said unto them in parables, How can Satan cast out Satan ? **24** And if a kingdom be divided against itself, that kingdom cannot stand. **25** And if a house be divided against itself, that house will not be able to stand. **26** And if Satan hath risen up against himself, and is divided, he cannot stand, but hath an end.	**16** And others, tempting *him* [*cp.* 10 25], sought of him a sign from heaven. **17** But he, knowing their thoughts [*cp.* 5 22 ; 6 8; 9 47], said unto them, Every kingdom divided against itself is brought to desolation ; ⁴ and a house *divided* against a house falleth. **18** And if Satan also is divided against himself, how shall his kingdom stand ? because ye say that I cast out ³ devils ² by Beelzebub.	*cp.* 8 6. *cp.* 2 18; 6 30. *cp.* 1 48; 2 24, 25; 4 19, 29; 5 6, 42; 6 61; 11 14; 13 18; 16 19, 30; 18 4; 21 17.
27 And if I ³ by Beelzebub cast out ² devils, ³ by whom do your sons cast them out ? therefore shall they be your judges. **28** But if I ³ by the Spirit of God cast out ² devils, then is the kingdom of God come upon you [*cp.* 3 2 ; 4 17; 10 7]. **29** Or how can one enter into the house of the strong *man,*	*cp.* 1 15 ; 6 12. **27** But no one can enter into the house of the strong *man,*	**19** And if I ² by Beelzebub cast out ³ devils, by whom do your sons cast them out ? therefore shall they be your judges. **20** But if I by the finger of God cast out ³ devils, then is the kingdom of God come upon you [*cp.* 9 2; 10 9, 11; 17 20, 21; 19 11; 21 8]. **21** When the strong *man* fully armed guardeth his	

Matt.

and spoil his goods,
except he first
bind the strong *man* ? and then

he will
spoil his house. **30** He that is
not with me is against me ; and
he that gathereth not with me
scattereth. . . . . **43** But the
unclean spirit, when [4] he is
gone out of the man, passeth
through waterless places, seeking rest, and findeth it not.
44 Then [4] he saith, I will return
into my house whence I came
out ; and when [4] he is come,
[4] he findeth it empty, swept,
and garnished. **45** Then goeth
[4] he, and taketh with [5] himself
seven other spirits more evil
than [5] himself, and they enter
in and dwell there : and the
last state of that man becometh
worse than the first. Even so
shall it be also unto this evil
generation [cp. 12 39 ; 16 4 ;
17 17].

[1] Or, *a demoniac*   [2] Gr. *demons.*
[3] Or, *in*   [4] Or, *it*   [5] Or, *itself*

Mark

and spoil his goods,
except he first
bind the strong *man*; and then

he will
spoil his house.

cp. 9 40.

cp. 8 38 ; 9 19.

[1] Or, *In*   [2] Gr. *demons.*

Luke

own court,   his goods
are in peace :

22 but when a stronger than
he shall come upon him, and
overcome him, he taketh from
him his whole armour wherein
he trusted, and divideth his
spoils.   **23** He that is
not with me is against me ; and
he that gathereth not with me
scattereth [cp. 9 50]. **24** The
unclean spirit when [5] he is
gone out of the man, passeth
through waterless places, seeking rest ; and finding none,
[5] he saith, I will turn back
unto my house whence I came
out. **25** And when [5]he is come,
[5] he findeth it   swept
and garnished. **26** Then goeth
[5] he, and taketh *to him*
seven other spirits more evil
than [6] himself; and they enter
in and dwell there : and the
last state of that man becometh
worse than the first.

cp. 9 41 ; 11 29.

[1] Gr. *demon.*   [2] Or, *In*
[3] Gr. *demons.*
[4] Or, *and house falleth upon house.*
[5] Or, *it*   [6] Or, *itself*

§ 144. The Truly Blessed

[Cp. Matt. 12 46-50; Mark 3 31-35; Luke 8 19-21]

Luke 11 27-28

cp. 13 19-23.   cp. 2 2 ; 4 14-20, 33 ; 16 20.

27 And it came to pass, as he said these things, a certain woman out of the multitude lifted up her voice [cp. 17 13], and said unto him, Blessed is the womb that bare thee, and the breasts which thou didst suck [cp. 1 48]. **28** But he said, Yea rather, blessed are they that hear the word of God [cp. 5 1 ; 8 11, 21 : also 1 2 ; 8 12-15 : *and* 4 32], and keep it.

cp. 4 41 ; 5 24, 38 ; etc.

§ 145. A Sign refused

Matt. 12 38-42

38 Then certain of the
scribes and   Pharisees

answered him, saying,
[1] Master,   we
would see a sign from
thee.

39 But he

answered
and said unto them,

An evil and

Matt. 16 1-2, 4

1 And the Pharisees
and Sadducees came,
and tempting him
[cp. 19 3 ; 22 35 :
also 22 18]

asked him to
shew them a sign from
heaven.

2 But he

answered
and said unto them,
. . .

4 An evil and

Mark 8 11-13

11 And the Pharisees
came
forth, and

began to
question with him
[cp. 9 14, 16 ; 12 28],

seeking of him
a sign from
heaven, tempting him
[cp. 10 2 : *also* 12 15].
12 And he sighed
deeply [cp. 7 34] in
his spirit,
and saith,
Why doth this genera-
tion

Luke 11 29-32

29 And when the
multitudes   were
gathering   together
unto him,
cp. 10 25 ; 11 16.

11 16

cp. 10 25 ; 11 16.

he began
to say,
This genera-
tion is an evil

cp. 8 6.

cp. 2 18 ; 6 30.

cp. 8 6.

adulterous generation [*cp.* 12 45] seeketh after a sign;

and there shall no sign be given to it
    but the sign of Jonah the prophet :

    40 for
as Jonah
    was three days and three nights in the belly of the [2] whale ; so shall
    the Son of man
    be three days and three nights in the heart of the earth [*cp.* 16 21 ; 17 23 ; 20 19 ; 26 61 ; 27 40, 63, 64]. 41 The men of Nineveh shall stand up in the judgement with this generation, and shall condemn it : for they repented at the preaching of Jonah; and behold, [3] a greater than Jonah is here [*cp.* 12 6]. 42 The queen of the south shall rise up in the judgement with   this generation, and shall condemn it : for she came from the ends of the earth to hear the wisdom of Solomon ; and behold, [3] a greater than Solomon is here [*cp.* 12 6].

    verse 41

[1] Or, *Teacher*   [2] Gr. *sea-monster.*
[3] Gr. *more than.*

---

adulterous generation [*cp.* 17 17] seeketh after a sign;

and there shall no sign be given unto it,
    but the sign of Jonah.
And he left them, and
    departed.

---

cp. 8 38 ; 9 19.
seek   a sign ? verily I say unto you, There shall no sign be given unto this generation.

13 And he left them, and again entering into *the boat* departed to the other side.

cp. 8 31; 9 31; 10 34; 14 58; 15 29.

---

    generation [*cp.* 9 41]: it seeketh after a sign;

and there shall no sign be given to it
    but the sign of Jonah.

30 For even as Jonah became a sign unto the Ninevites,
    so shall also the Son of man be to this generation.
cp. 9 22; 13 32; 18 33; 24 7, 21, 46.

    verse 32

31 The queen of the south shall rise up in the judgement with the men of this generation, and shall condemn them : for she came from the ends of the earth to hear the wisdom of Solomon; and behold, [1] a greater than Solomon is here.
32 The men of Nineveh shall stand up in the judgement with this generation, and shall condemn it: for they repented at the preaching of Jonah; and behold, [1] a greater than Jonah is here.

[1] Gr. *more than.*

---

cp. 2 19-22.

Luke 11 29 ‖ Matt. 12 39 ; 16 4 : *cp.* Jonah 3 4.
Luke 11 31 ‖ Matt. 12 42 : *cp.* I Kings 10 1 *ff.*

Matt. 12 40 : *cp.* Jonah 1 17.
Luke 11 32 ‖ Matt. 12 41 : *cp.* Jonah 3 5.

§ 146. Sayings about Light

Matt. 5 15; 6 22-23

5 15 Neither do   *men*

light   a lamp,

    and put it

under the bushel,

    but   on the stand ; and it shineth unto all that are in the house.

6 22 The lamp of the body is the eye : if therefore thine eye be single, thy whole body shall be full of light. 23 But if thine eye be evil [*cp.* 20 15], thy whole body shall be full of darkness. If therefore the light that is in thee be   darkness, how great is the darkness !

Mark 4 21

21 Is the lamp brought   to be put

under the bushel, or under the bed, *and* not to be   put on the stand ?

cp. 7 22.

Luke 8 16

16 And no man, when   he hath lighted   a lamp, covereth it with a vessel, or putteth it

under a bed ;
    but putteth it on a stand,

that they which enter in may see the light.

Luke 11 33-36

33 No man, when   he hath lighted   a lamp,

    putteth it in a cellar, neither under the bushel,

    but   on the stand,

that they which enter in may see the light. 34 The lamp of thy body is thine eye: when thine eye is single, thy whole body also is full of light; but when   it is evil, thy   body also is full of darkness. 35 Look therefore whether the light that is in thee be not darkness. 36 If therefore thy whole body be full of light, having no part dark, it shall be wholly full of light, as when the lamp with its bright shining doth give thee light.

(ii) Jesus a Guest in the House of a Pharisee (§§ 147-150)

§ 147. Ritual Washing and Moral Cleanliness

[*Cp.* Matt. 15 1-20; Mark 7 1-23: *also* Matt. 9 14-17; Mark 2 18-22; Luke 5 33-39]

Matt. 23 25-26		Luke 11 37-41	
		37 Now as he spake, a Pharisee asketh him to ¹ dine with him: and he went in, and sat down to meat [*cp.* 7 36; 14 1]. **38** And when the Pharisee saw it, he marvelled [*cp.* 7 39] that he had not first washed before ¹dinner. **39** And the Lord [*cp.* 7 13, 19; 10 1, 39, 41; 12 42; 13 15; 17 5, 6; 18 6; 19 8; 22 61; 24 3, 34] said unto him,	
cp. 15 2.	*cp.* 7 5. *cp.* 16 19, 20.		*cp.* 4 1; 6 23; 11 2; 20 2, 18, 20, 25; 21 7, 12.
25 Woe unto you [*cp.* 23 13, *etc.*: *also* 18 7; 26 24], scribes and Pharisees, hypocrites [*cp.* 15 7; 22 18; 23 13, *etc.*: *also* 6 2, 5, 16; 23 28; 24 51]! for ye cleanse the outside of the cup and of the platter, but within [*cp.* 15 19; 23 28] they are full from extortion and excess. *cp.* 22 18. *cp.* 23 17. 26 Thou blind [*cp.* 15 14; 23 16, 17, 19, 24] Pharisee,	*cp.* 14 21. *cp.* 7 6: *also* 12 15. *cp.* 7 4. *cp.* 7 21-23. *cp.* 12 40.	*cp.* 11 42, *etc.*: *also* 17 1; 22 22. *cp.* 12 56; 13 15: *also* 12 1. Now do ye Pharisees cleanse the outside of the cup and of the platter; but your inward part is full of extortion [*cp.* 16 14; 20 47] and wickedness. **40** Ye foolish ones [*cp.* 12 20], *cp.* 6 39. did not he that made the outside make the inside also? **41** Howbeit give for alms	 *cp.* 9 39, 40, 41.
cleanse first [*cp.* 5 24; 6 33; 7 5] the inside of the cup and of the platter, that the outside thereof may become clean also.	*cp.* 7 27. *cp.* 7 19.	[*cp.* 12 33] *cp.* 6 42. those things which ² are within; and behold, all things are clean unto you.	

¹ Gr. *breakfast.*   ² Or, *ye can*

§ 148. Woes against Pharisees

Matt. 23 23-24, 6-7, 27-28			Luke 11 42-44	
23 Woe unto you [*cp.* 23 13, *etc.*: *also* 18 7; 26 24], scribes and Pharisees, hypocrites [*cp.* 15 7; 22 18; 23 13, *etc.*: *also* 6 2, 5, 16; 23 28; 24 51]! for ye tithe mint and ¹ anise and cummin,	*cp.* 14 21. *cp.* 7 6: *also* 12 15.		**42** But woe unto you [*cp.* 11 43, 44, 46, 47, 52: *also* 17 1; 22 22] Pharisees ! *cp.* 12 56; 13 15: *also* 12 1. for ye tithe mint and rue and every herb, and pass over judgement and the love of God [*cp.* 10 27]:	
cp. 22 37. and have left undone the weightier matters of the law, judgement, and mercy [*cp.* 9 13; 12 7], and faith: but these ye ought to have done, and not to have left the other undone. **24** Ye blind guides [*cp.* 15 14; 23 16, 17, 19, 26], which strain out the gnat, and swallow the camel.	*cp.* 12 30, 33.		 but these ought ye to have done, and not to leave the other undone. *cp.* 6 39. **43** Woe unto you [*see above*] Pharisees ! for ye	*cp.* 5 42. *cp.* 9 39, 40, 41.
cp. 16 6.	Mark 12 38 Beware of [*cp.* 8 15] the scribes, which desire to walk in long robes, and *to have*	Luke 20 46 Beware of the scribes, which desire to walk in long robes, and love	*cp.* 12 1.	
6 and love the chief place at feasts, and the chief seats in the synagogues, 7 and the salutations in the marketplaces,	salutations in the marketplaces, 39 and chief seats in the synagogues, and chief places at feasts.	salutations in the marketplaces, and chief seats in the synagogues, and chief places at feasts.	love the chief seats in the synagogues, and the salutations in the marketplaces.	

27 Woe unto you [*see above*], scribes and Pharisees, hypocrites [*see above*]! for ye are like unto whited sepulchres, which outwardly appear   beautiful, but inwardly are full of dead men's bones, and of all uncleanness.

28 Even so ye also outwardly appear [*cp.* 6 1, 2, 5, 16 ; 23 5] righteous unto men, but inwardly [*cp.* 15 19 ; 23 25, 26] ye are full of hypocrisy [*see verse 23 above*] and iniquity.

¹ Or, *dill*

44 Woe unto you [*see above*] !
                              for ye
are as   the tombs which
     appear not,

                    and the men
that walk over *them* know it not.

cp. 7 21-23.
cp. 12 15:
also 7 6.

cp. 11 39-41.
cp. 12 1: *also* 12 56; 13 15.

§ 149. Woes against Lawyers

Matt. 23 4, 29-36, 13

Luke 11 45-52

cp. 23 13, *etc.*: *also* 18 7 ; 26 24.

cp. 14 21.

45 And one of the lawyers answering saith unto him, ¹ Master, in saying this thou reproachest us also. **46** And he said, Woe unto you [*cp.* 11 42, 43, 44, 47, 52: *also* 17 1 ; 22 22] lawyers also ! for ye lade men with
burdens   grievous to be borne,
                         and ye
yourselves   touch not
the burdens with one of your fingers.
47 Woe unto you [*see above*] !
     cp. 12 56; 13 15: *also* 12 1.

4 Yea, they bind   heavy burdens ¹ and grievous to be borne, and lay them on men's shoulders ; but they themselves will not move
them   with   their finger.
29 Woe unto you [*see above*], scribes and Pharisees, hypocrites [*cp.* 15 7 ; 22 18 ; 23 13, *etc.*: *also* 6 2, 5, 16 ; 23 28 ; 24 51]! for ye build the sepulchres of the prophets, and garnish the tombs of the righteous, 30 and say, If we had been in the days of our fathers, we should not have been partakers with them in the blood of the prophets. 31 Wherefore ye   witness to yourselves,
               that ye are sons of
them that slew the prophets [*cp.* 5 12 ; 21 35-36 ; 22 6 ; 23 37].
          32 Fill ye up then the measure of your fathers. 33 Ye serpents, ye offspring of vipers [*cp.* 3 7 ; 12 34], how shall ye escape the judgement of ² hell [*cp.* 5 29, 30 ; 10 28 ; 23 15 : *also* 5 22 ; 18 9] ? 34 Therefore,
cp. 11 19.   behold, I
          send unto you prophets, and wise men, and scribes :
               cp. 10 2.
          some of them   shall ye kill and crucify [*cp.* 20 19 ; 27 26] ; and some of them shall ye scourge in your synagogues [*cp.* 10 17], and persecute from city to city [*cp.* 10 23] : 35 that upon you may come all the righteous blood
               shed on the earth,
          cp. 13 35 ; 25 34.

          from the blood of Abel the righteous unto the blood of Zachariah son of Barachiah, whom ye slew between the sanctuary and the altar.
          36 Verily I say unto you, All these things shall come upon
          this generation [*cp.* 24 34 : *also* 10 23 ; 16 28]. 13 But woe unto you [*see above*], scribes and Pharisees, hypocrites [*see above*]! because ye shut the kingdom of heaven ³ against men :

cp. 7 6:
also 12 15.

cp. 12 3-5.

cp. 9 43, 45, 47.

cp. 6 30.

cp. 15 15.
cp. 13 9.

cp. 13 30:
also 9 1.

for ye build the tombs of the prophets, and

your fathers
     killed them.
          48 So ye are witnesses
          and consent unto the works of your fathers: for
they   killed them [*cp.* 6 23; 13 33, 34; 20 10-12], and ye build *their tombs*.

          cp. 3 7.

     cp. 12 5.
          49 Therefore also said the wisdom [*cp.* 7 35] of God,   I will send unto them prophets
                         and apostles
[*cp.* 6 13; 9 10; 17 5; 22 14; 24 10]; and *some* of them they shall   kill

          and persecute ;
          50 that
          the   blood of all the prophets, which was shed
from the foundation of the world, may be required of this generation [*see below*]; **51** from the blood of Abel
          unto the blood of Zachariah,
               who perished between
                    the altar and the
² sanctuary: yea, I say unto you, it   shall   be required of this generation [*cp.* 21 32 : *also* 9 27].   **52** Woe unto you [*see above*] lawyers !
          for ye
               took away the

cp. 13 16.

cp. 17 24.

cp. 16 19.   for ye enter
[cp. 5 20; 7 13, 21; 18 3, 8, 9; 19 17, 23, 24; 25 21, 23] not in yourselves [cp. 21 31], neither suffer ye them that are entering in to enter.

1 Many ancient authorities omit *and grievous to be borne.*   2 Gr. *Gehenna.*   3 Gr. *before.*

cp. 9 43, 45, 47; 10 15, 23, 24, 25.

key of knowledge: ye entered [cp. 13 24; 18 17, 24, 25: *also* 24 26] not in yourselves, and   them that were entering in   ye hindered.

1 Or, *Teacher*   2 Gr. *house.*

cp. 3 5; 10 1, 2, 9.

Luke 11 50-51 || Matt. 23 35: cp. Gen. 4 8; II Chron. 24 20-22.

§ 150. The Increasing Hostility of the Scribes and Pharisees

Luke 11 53-54

cp. 12 10; 22 15.

cp. 3 2; 12 13.

53 And when he was come out from thence, the scribes and the Pharisees began to 1 press upon *him* vehemently, and to provoke him to speak of 2 many things; **54** laying wait for him, to catch something out of his mouth [cp. 6 7; 20 20].

1 Or, *set themselves vehemently against* him   2 Or, *more*

cp. 8 6.

(iii) A Sermon to the Disciples in the Presence of the Multitude (§§ 151-159).

§ 151. Miscellaneous Teaching

Luke 12 1-12

Matt. 16 **5** And the disciples came to the other side and forgot to take 1 bread.

6 And Jesus said unto them, Take heed and beware of the leaven of the Pharisees and Sadducees.

cp. 23 28: *also* 6 2, 5, 16; 15 7; 22 18; 23 13, *etc.*; 24 51.

Mark 8 **14** And they forgot to take bread; and they had not in the boat with them more than one loaf. **15** And he charged them, saying, Take heed, beware [cp. 12 38] of the leaven of the Pharisees and the leaven of Herod.

cp. 12 15: *also* 7 6.

1 In the mean time, when 1 the many thousands of the multitude were gathered together, insomuch that they trode one upon another, he began to 2 say unto his disciples first of all, Beware [cp. 20 46] ye [cp. 17 3; 21 34] of the leaven of the Pharisees, which is hypocrisy [cp. 12 56; 13 15].

Matt. 10 **26** For there is nothing covered, that shall not be revealed; and hid, that shall not be known.

Mark 4 **22** For there is nothing hid, save that it should be manifested; neither was *anything* made secret, but that it should come to light.

Luke 8 **17** For nothing is hid, that shall not be made manifest; nor *anything* secret, that shall not be known and come to light.

2 But there is nothing covered up, that shall not be revealed: and hid, that shall not be known.

27 What I tell you in the darkness, speak ye in the light: and what ye hear in the ear, proclaim upon the housetops. **28** And be not afraid of them which kill the body, but are not able to kill the soul: but rather fear him which is able to destroy both soul and body in 2 hell [cp. 5 22, 29, 30; 18 9; 23 15, 33: *also* 3 10, 12; 7 19; 13 42, 50; 18 8; 25 41]. **29** Are not two sparrows sold for a farthing? and not one of them shall fall on the ground without your Father: **30** but the very hairs of your head are all numbered. **31** Fear not therefore; ye are of more value than many

cp. 9 43, 45, 47.

3 Wherefore whatsoever ye have said in the darkness shall be heard in the light; and what ye have spoken in the ear in the inner chambers shall be proclaimed upon the housetops. **4** And I say unto you my friends, Be not afraid of them which kill the body, and after that have no more that they can do. **5** But I will warn you whom ye shall fear: Fear him, which after he hath killed hath 3 power to cast into 4 hell [cp. 3 9, 17]; yea, I say unto you, Fear him. **6** Are not five sparrows sold for two farthings? and not one of them is forgotten in the sight of God. **7** But the very hairs of your head are all numbered [cp. 21 18]. Fear not: ye are of more value than many

cp. 15 14, 15.

cp. 15 6.

sparrows [cp. 6 26: also 12 12].
32 Every one therefore who shall confess 3 me before men, 4 him will I also confess before my Father which is in heaven [cp. 5 16, 45; 6 1, 9; 7 11, 21; 12 50; 16 17; 18 10, 14, 19: also 5 48; 6 14, 26, 32; 15 13; 18 35; 23 9]. 33 But whosoever shall deny me before men, him will I also deny before my Father which is in heaven [see above].

cp. 11 25, 26.

sparrows [cp. 12 24]. 8 And I say unto you, Every one who shall confess 5 me before men, 6 him shall the Son of man also confess before cp. 11 13.

the angels of God [cp. 15 10]: 9 but he that denieth me in the presence of men shall be denied in the presence of the angels of God [see above].

Matt. 16 27 For the Son of man shall come in the glory of his Father with his angels; and then shall he render unto every man according to his 5 deeds. 12 31 Therefore I say unto you, Every . sin and blasphemy shall be forgiven 6 unto men;

but the blasphemy against the Spirit shall not be forgiven. 32 And whosoever shall speak a word against the Son of man, it shall be forgiven him; but whosoever shall speak against the Holy Spirit, it shall not be forgiven him, neither in this 7 world, nor in that which is to come.
cp. 18 8; 25 41, 46.

Mark 8 38 For whosoever shall be ashamed of me and of my words in this adulterous and sinful generation, the Son of man also shall be ashamed of him, when he cometh in the glory of his Father with the holy angels.

Mark 3 28 Verily I say unto you, All their sins shall be forgiven unto the sons of men, and their blasphemies wherewith soever they shall blaspheme:

29 but whosoever shall blaspheme against the Holy Spirit hath never forgiveness, but is guilty of an eternal sin.

Luke 9 26 For whosoever shall be ashamed of me and of my words, of him shall the Son of man be ashamed, when he cometh in his own glory, and the glory of the Father, and of the holy angels.

10 And every one who shall speak a word against the Son of man, it shall be forgiven him: but unto him that blasphemeth against the Holy Spirit it shall not be forgiven.

Matt. 10 17 For they will deliver you up to councils, and in their synagogues [cp. 23 34] they will scourge you; 18 yea and before governors and kings shall ye be brought for my sake [cp. 5 11; 10 39; 16 25: also 10 22; 19 29; 24 9], for a testimony to them [cp. 8 4; 24 14] and to the Gentiles [cp. 24 14: also 8 11; 21 31, 41, 43; 22 7-10; 26 13; 28 19]. 19 But when they deliver you up,

be not anxious [cp. 6 25, 31, 34] how or

Mark 13 9 For they shall deliver you up to councils; and in synagogues shall ye be beaten; and before governors and kings shall ye stand for my sake [cp. 8 35; 10 29: also 13 13], for a testimony unto them [cp. 1 44; 6 11]. 10 And the gospel must first be preached unto all the nations [cp. 12 9; 14 9; 16 15].

11 And when they lead you to judgement, and deliver you up,

be not anxious beforehand

Luke 21 12 But before all these things, they shall lay their hands on you, and shall persecute you, delivering you up to the synagogues and prisons, 7 bringing you before kings and governors for my name's sake. 13 It shall turn unto you for a testimony.

cp. 2 30-32; 3 6; 13 29; 14 21-24; 20 16; 24 47.

14 Settle it therefore in your hearts, not to meditate beforehand how to answer:

11 And when they bring you before the synagogues, and the rulers, and the authorities [cp. 20 20],

cp. 21 17: also 6 22; 9 24; 18 29.

cp. 5 14; 9 5.

be not anxious [cp. 12 22] how or what ye shall answer,

cp. 15 21.

cp. 10 16; 11 52.

what ye shall speak : for it shall be given you in that hour what ye shall speak. **20** For it is not ye that speak, but the Spirit of your Father that speaketh in you.	what ye shall speak : but whatsoever shall be given you in that hour, that speak ye : for it is not ye that speak, but the Holy Ghost.	**15** for I will give you a mouth and wisdom, which all your adversaries shall not be able to withstand or to gainsay.	or what ye shall say : **12** for the Holy Spirit shall teach you in that very hour what ye ought to say.	*cp.* 14 26.

¹ Gr. *loaves.* ² Gr. *Gehenna.*
³ Gr. *in me.* ⁴ Gr. *in him.*
⁵ Gr. *doing.*
⁶ Some ancient authorities read *unto you men.*
⁷ Or, *age*

¹ Gr. *the myriads of.*
² Or, *say unto his disciples. First of all beware ye*
³ Or, *authority* ⁴ Gr. *Gehenna.* ⁵ Gr. *in me.*
⁶ Gr. *in him.* ⁷ Gr. *you being brought.*

§ 152. A Request to Divide an Inheritance and the Parable of the Rich Fool

Luke 12 13-21

13 And one out of the multitude said unto him, ¹ Master, bid my brother divide the inheritance with me. **14** But he said unto him, Man, who made me a judge or a divider over you ? **15** And he said unto them, Take heed, and keep yourselves from all covetousness : ² for a man's life consisteth not in the abundance of the things which he possesseth. **16** And he spake a parable unto them, saying, The ground of a certain rich man [*cp.* 16 1, 19] brought forth plentifully : **17** and he reasoned within himself, saying, What shall I do [*cp.* 16 3; 20 13], because I have not where to bestow my fruits ? **18** And he said, This will I do : I will pull down my barns [*cp.* 12 24], and build greater ; and there will I bestow all my corn and my goods. **19** And I will say to my ³ soul [*cp.* 12 22], ³ Soul, thou hast much goods laid up for many years ; take thine ease, eat [*cp.* 12 22], drink [*cp.* 12 22], be merry [*cp.* 15 23]. **20** But God said unto him, Thou foolish one [*cp.* 11 40], this night ⁴ is thy ³ soul required of thee ; and the things which thou hast prepared, whose shall they be ? **21** So is he that layeth up treasure for himself, and is not rich toward God [*cp.* 12 33-34; 18 22].

cp. 6 19-21; 19 21.

cp. 10 21.

¹ Or, *Teacher* ⁵ Gr. *for not in a man's abundance consisteth his*
² Or, *life* ⁴ Gr. *they require thy soul.* *life, from the things which he possesseth.*

Luke 12 19 : *cp.* Eccl. 2 24; Is. 22 13.

§ 153. True Treasure and where it may be found

Matt. 6 25-34, 19-21		Luke 12 22-34
25 Therefore I say unto you, Be not anxious [*cp.* 6 31, 34 ; 10 19] for your life, what ye shall eat, or what ye shall drink ; nor yet for your body, what ye shall put on. Is not the life more than the food, and the body than the raiment ? **26** Behold the birds of the heaven [*cp.* 8 20 ; 13 32], that they sow not, neither do they reap, nor gather into barns ; and your heavenly Father [*cp.* 5 48 ; 6 14, 32 ; 15 13 ; 18 35 ; 23 9 : *also* 5 16, 45, *etc.*] feedeth them. Are not ye of much more value than they [*cp.* 10 31 ; 12 12] ? **27** And which of you by being anxious can add one cubit unto his ¹ stature ? **28** And why are ye anxious concerning raiment ? Consider the	*cp.* 13 11. *cp.* 4 32. *cp.* 11 25, 26. *cp.* 4 19.	**22** And he said unto his disciples, Therefore I say unto you, Be not anxious [*cp.* 12 11] for *your* ¹ life [*cp.* 12 19], what ye shall eat [*cp.* 12 19] ; [*cp.* 12 19] nor yet for your body, what ye shall put on. **23** For the ¹ life is more than the food, and the body than the raiment. **24** Consider the ravens [*cp.* 8 5 ; 9 58 ; 13 19], that they sow not, neither reap ; which have no store chamber nor barn [*cp.* 12 18] ; and God *cp.* 11 13. feedeth them : of how much more value are ye than the birds [*cp.* 12 7] ! **25** And which of you by being anxious can add a cubit unto his ² stature ? **26** If then ye are not able to do even that which is least [*cp.* 16 10 ; 19 17], why are ye anxious concerning the rest [*cp.* 8 10 ; 18 9, 11 ; 24 9, 10] ? **27** Consider the

lilies of the field, how they grow ; they toil not, neither do they spin : **29** yet I say unto you, that even Solomon in all his glory was not arrayed like one of these. **30** But if God doth so clothe the grass of the field, which to-day is, and to-morrow is cast into the oven, *shall he* not much more *clothe* you, O ye of little faith [*cp.* 8 26 ; 14 31 ; 16 8 : *also* 17 20] ? **31** Be not therefore anxious, saying, What shall we eat ? or, What shall we drink ? or, Wherewithal shall we be clothed ?

32 For after all these things do the Gentiles [*cp.* 5 47 ; 6 7 ; 18 17] seek ; for your heavenly Father [*see verse* 26] knoweth [*cp.* 6 8] that ye have need of all these things. **33** But seek ye first [*cp.* 5 24 ; 7 5 ; 23 26] his kingdom, and his righteousness [*cp.* 5 6 : *also* 3 15 ; 5 10, 20 ; 6 1 ; 21 32] ; and all these things shall be added unto you. **34** Be not therefore anxious for the morrow : for the morrow will be anxious for itself. Sufficient [*cp.* 10 25] unto the day is the evil thereof.

cp. 26 31.

cp. 3 17 ; 11 26 ; 12 18 ; 17 5.

19 Lay not up for yourselves treasures upon the earth, where moth and rust doth consume, and where thieves [2] break through [*cp.* 24 43] and steal : **20** but lay up [*cp.* 19 21] for yourselves

treasures in heaven [*cp.* 19 21], where neither moth nor rust doth consume, and where thieves do not [2] break through [*cp.* 24 43] nor steal : **21** for where thy treasure is, there will thy heart be also.

[1] Or, *age*   [2] Gr. *dig through.*

---

cp. 4 40 ; 11 22 ; 16 14.

cp. 7 27.

cp. 4 24 ; *also* 10 29-30.

cp. 14 27.
cp. 1 11.

cp. 10 21.

cp. 10 21.

---

lilies, how they grow : they toil not, neither do they spin ; yet I say unto you, Even Solomon in all his glory was not arrayed like one of these. **28** But if God doth so clothe the grass in the field, which to-day is, and to-morrow is cast into the oven ; how much more *shall he clothe* you, O ye of little faith [*cp.* 8 25 ; 17 5, 6 ; 22 32 ; 24 25, 38] ? **29** And seek not ye what ye shall eat, and what ye shall drink, neither be ye of doubtful mind. **30** For all these things do the nations of the world seek after : but your Father knoweth that ye have need of these things. **31** Howbeit seek ye [*cp.* 6 42] [3] his kingdom, and these things shall be added unto you.

32 Fear not, little flock ; for it is your Father's good pleasure [*cp.* 2 14 ; 3 22 ; 10 21] to give you the kingdom.

cp. 12 39.

33 Sell [*cp.* 18 22 : *also* 22 36] that ye have, and give alms [*cp.* 11 41] ; make for yourselves [*cp.* 16 9] purses which wax not old, a treasure in the heavens [*cp.* 18 22 : *also* 12 21] that faileth not, where no thief draweth near, neither moth destroyeth.

cp. 12 39.

34 For where your treasure is, there will your heart be also.

[1] Or, *soul*   [2] Or, *age*   [3] Many ancient authorities read *the kingdom of God.*

---

cp. 3 12 ; 6 64 ; 14 10 ; 20 27.

cp. 10 1 *ff.*

---

§ 154. **Injunctions to be Ready for the End**

Matt. 25 13 ; 24 42-44	Mark 13 33-36	Luke 12 35-40
		35 Let your loins be girded about [*cp.* 12 37 ; 17 8], and your lamps burning ; **36** and be ye yourselves like unto men looking for their lord, when he shall return from the marriage feast ; that, when he cometh and knocketh, they may straightway open unto him.
cp. 25 1-13.		
25 13 Watch [*cp.* 24 42 ; 26 38, 41] therefore, [*cp.* 26 41] for ye know not the day nor the hour.	13 33 Take ye heed, watch [*cp.* 13 35, 37 : 14 34, 38] [1] and pray [*cp.* 14 38] : for ye know not when the time is.	21 36 But watch [*cp.* 12 37] ye at every season, making supplication [*cp.* 22 40, 46], that ye may prevail to escape all these things that shall come to pass, and to stand before the Son of man.
cp. 25 14-15.	34 *It is* as *when* a man, sojourning in another country, having left his house, and given	*cp.* 19 12-13.

Matthew

cp. 24 46.

24 **42** Watch [cp. 25 13 : 26 38, 41] therefore : for ye know not on what day your Lord cometh.

cp. 25 5 ; 26 40, 43.

43 ¹ But know this, that if the master of the house had known in what watch the thief was coming, he would have watched, and would not have suffered his house to be ² broken through [cp. 6 19, 20]. **44** Therefore be ye also ready [cp. 25 10] : for in an hour that ye think not [cp. 24 36, 42, 50 ; 25 13] the Son of man cometh.

¹ Or, *But this ye know.*
² Gr. *digged through.*

Mark

authority to his ² servants,

to each one his work, commanded also the porter to watch. **35** Watch [*see verse* 33] therefore : for ye know not when the lord of the house cometh,

whether at even, or at midnight, or at cockcrowing, or in the morning ; **36** lest coming suddenly he find you sleeping [cp. 14 37, 40].

cp. 13 32, 33, 35.

¹ Some ancient authorities omit *and pray.*   ² Gr. *bondservants.*

Luke

37 Blessed are those ¹ servants, whom the lord when he cometh shall find [cp. 12 38, 43]

watching [cp. 21 36]:

verily I say unto you, that he shall gird himself [cp. 12 35; 17 8], and make them sit down to meat, and shall come and serve them [cp. 22 27: *also* 17 8]. **38** And if he shall come in the second watch, and if in the third,

and find [cp. 22 45] *them* so, blessed are those *servants* [cp. 12 37, 43]. **39** ² But know this [cp. 10 11], that if the master of the house had known in what hour the thief was coming, he would have watched, and not have left his house to be ³ broken through. **40** Be ye also ready [cp. 12 47: *also* 17 8]: for in an hour that ye think not [cp. 12 46] the Son of man cometh.

¹ Gr. *bondservants.*
² Or, *But this ye know*
³ Gr. *digged through.*

(right margin references) cp. 13 17. — cp. 13 4. — cp. 13 5. — cp. 13 17.

§ 155. The Obligations of Stewards in the Interim

[*Cp.* Matt. 25 14-30; Luke 19 11-27]

Matt. 24 45-51	Mark 13 37	Luke 12 41-48	

Matthew 24 45-51

cp. 14 28; 15 15; 16 22; 17 4; 18 21 ; 19 27; 26 33: *also* 16 16 ; 17 24.

45 Who then is the faithful [cp. 25 21, 23] and wise [cp. 7 24 ; 10 16 ; 25 2 ff.] ¹ servant, whom his lord hath set over [cp. 24 47 ; 25 21, 23] his household, to give them their food in due season ? **46** Blessed is that ¹ servant, whom his lord when he cometh shall find so doing. **47** Verily I say unto you, that he will set him over [cp. 25 21, 23 : *also* 24 45] all that he hath. **48** But if that evil [cp. 18 32 ; 25 26] ¹ servant shall say in his heart, My lord tarrieth [cp. 25 5]; **49** and shall begin to beat his fellow-servants [cp. 18 28, 29, 31, 33], and shall eat and drink with the drunken ; **50** the lord of that ¹ servant [cp. 18 27 ; 25 19] shall come in a day when he expecteth not,

Mark 13 37

37 And [cp. 8 32 ; 9 5; 10 28 ; 11 21 ; 14 29 : *also* 8 29] what I say unto you I say unto all, Watch [*see* 13 33].
cp. 16 19, 20.

Luke 12 41-48

41 And Peter [cp. 8 45 ; 9 33; 18 28 : *also* 5 8 ; 9 20] said, Lord, speakest thou this parable unto us, or even unto all ? **42** And the Lord [cp. 7 13, 19 ; 10 1, 39, 41; 11 39; 13 15; 17 5, 6; 18 6; 19 8; 22 61; 24 3, 34] said, Who then is ¹ the faithful [cp. 16 10, 11, 12 ; 19 17] and wise [cp. 16 8] steward [cp. 16 1 ff.], whom his lord shall set over [cp. *verse* 44] his household, to give them their portion of food in due season ? **43** Blessed is that ² servant, whom his lord when he cometh shall find [cp. 12 37, 38] so doing. **44** Of a truth [cp. 9 27 ; 21 3] I say unto you, that he will set him over [cp. *verse* 42 : *also* 19 17,19] all that he hath. **45** But if that [cp. 19 22] ² servant shall say in his heart, My lord delayeth his coming ; and shall begin to beat the menservants and the maidservants, and to eat and drink, and to be drunken [cp. 21 34]; **46** the lord of that ² servant shall come in a day when he expecteth not,

(right margin references) cp. 13 36, 37; 21 21: *also* 6 68. — cp. 4 1 ; 6 23; 11 2; 20 2, 18, 20, 25; 21 7, 12. — cp. 13 17.

and in an hour when he knoweth not [*cp.* 24 36, 42, 44 ; 25 13], **51** and shall ² cut him asunder, and appoint his portion with the hypocrites [*cp.* 6 2, 5, 16 : *also* 15 7 ; 22 18 ; 23 13 *ff.*] : there shall be the weeping and gnashing of teeth [*cp.* 8 12 ; 13 42, 50 ; 22 13 ; 25 30].

¹ Gr. *bondservant*.   ² Or, *severely scourge him*

cp. 25 14-30.

cp. 13 32, 33, 35.

cp. 7 6 ; 12 15.

and in an hour when he knoweth not [*cp.* 12 40],   and shall ³ cut him asunder, and appoint his portion with the   [*cp.* 12 1, 56 ; 13 15]   unfaithful.

cp. 13 28.

47 And that ² servant, which knew his lord's will, and made not ready [*cp.* 12 40 : *also* 17 8], nor did according to his will, shall be beaten with many *stripes* ; **48** but he that knew not, and did things worthy of stripes, shall be beaten with few *stripes*. And to whomsoever much is given, of him shall much be required : and to whom they commit much, of him will they ask the more [*cp.* 19 11-27].

¹ Or, *the faithful steward, the wise* man *whom &c.*   ² Gr. *bondservant*.
² Or, *severely scourge him*

§ 156. **Divisions within Families**

Matt. 10 34-36		Luke 12 49-53	
cp. 3 11.		**49** I came to cast fire upon the earth [*cp.* 3 16] ; and what will I, if it is already kindled ? **50** But I have a baptism to be baptized with ; and how am I straitened till it be accomplished [*cp.* 18 31 ; 22 37 : *also* 13 32] ! **51** Think ye that I am come to give peace in the earth ? I tell you, Nay ; but rather division : **52** for there shall be from henceforth [*cp.* 1 48 ; 5 10 ; 22 18, 69] five in one house divided, three against two, and two against three. **53** They shall be divided,	*cp.* 12 27. *cp.* 19 28, 30 : *also* 4 34 ; 5 36 ; 17 4.
	cp. 10 38, 39.		
34 Think not that I came to ¹ send peace on the earth : I came not to ¹ send peace, but a sword.			
35 For I came to set a man at variance against his father,			
and the daughter against her mother,		father against son, and son against father ; mother against daughter, and daughter against her mother ; mother in law against her daughter in law, and daughter in law against her mother in law.	
and the daughter in law against her mother in law : **36** and a man's foes *shall be* they of his own household [*cp.* 10 25 : *also* 10 21].			
¹ Gr. *cast*.	*cp.* 13 12.	*cp.* 21 16.	

Luke 12 52-53 ‖ Matt. 10 35-36 : Mic. 7 6 ; *cp.* Is. 19 2.

§ 157. **The Signs of the Times and the Need for Reconciliation in view of the Coming Judgement**

Matt. 16 2-3 ; 5 25-26		Luke 12 54-59	
16 2 But he answered and said unto them, ¹ When it is [*cp.* 24 15, 33] evening,	*cp.* 13 14, 29.	**54** And he said to the multitudes also, When ye see [*cp.* 12 55 ; 21 20, 31] a cloud rising in the west, straightway ye say, There cometh a shower ; and so it cometh to pass. **55** And when *ye see* [*cp.* 12 54 ; 21 20, 31] a south wind blowing, ye say, There will be a ¹ scorching heat ;	
ye say, *It will be* fair weather : for the heaven is red. **3** And in the morning, [*cp.* 24 15, 33]			
It will be foul weather to-day : for the heaven is red and lowring.	*cp.* 13 14, 29.		
cp. 15 7 ; 22 18 ; 23 13, *etc.* : *also* 6 2, 5, 16 ; 24 51 : *and* 23 28.		and it cometh to pass. **56** Ye hypocrites [*cp.* 13 15 : *also* 12 1],	
Ye know how to discern the face of the heaven ; but	*cp.* 7 6 : *also* 12 15.	ye know how to ² interpret the face of the earth and the heaven ; but how is it that ye know not how to ² interpret	
ye cannot *discern* the signs of the times [*cp.* 24 32-33].	*cp.* 13 28-29.	this time [*cp.* 21 29-31] ?	

5 **25** Agree with thine adversary quickly, whiles thou art with him in the way; lest haply the adversary deliver thee to the judge, and the judge ² deliver thee to the officer, and thou be cast into prison. **26** Verily I say unto thee, Thou shalt by no means come out thence, till thou have paid the last farthing [*cp.* 18 34, 35].	**57** And why even of yourselves [*cp.* 21 30] judge ye not what is right? **58** For as thou art going with thine adversary before the magistrate, on the way give diligence to be quit of him; lest haply he hale thee unto the judge, and the judge shall deliver thee to the ³ officer, and the ³ officer shall cast thee into prison. **59** I say unto thee, Thou shalt by no means come out thence, till thou have paid the very last mite.	*cp.* 7 24.

¹ The following words, to the end of ver. 3, are omitted by some of the most ancient and other important authorities.
² Some ancient authorities omit *deliver thee*.

¹ Or, *hot wind*   ² Gr. *prove*.   ³ Gr. *exactor*.

§ 158. An Exhortation to Repentance

[*Cp.* John 9 1-12]

Luke 13 1-5

cp. 3 2; 4 17: *also* 11 20.	*cp.* 1 15; 6 12.	**1** Now there were some present at that very season which told him of the Galilæans, whose blood Pilate had mingled with their sacrifices. **2** And he answered and said unto them, Think ye that these Galilæans were sinners above all the Galilæans, because they have suffered these things? **3** I tell you, Nay: but, except ye repent, ye shall all in like manner perish. **4** Or those eighteen [*cp.* 13 11, 16], upon whom the tower in Siloam fell, and killed them, think ye that they were ¹ offenders above all the men that dwell in Jerusalem? **5** I tell you, Nay: but, except ye repent, ye shall all likewise perish.	*cp.* 9 7, 11.

¹ Gr. *debtors*.

§ 159. The Parable of the Fig Tree

[*Cp.* Matt. 24 32-33 ‖ Mark 13 28-29 ‖ Luke 21 29-31: *also* Matt 21 18-20 ‖ Mark 11 12-14, 20-21]

Luke 13 6-9

cp. 20 1; 21 28, 33. *cp.* 21 19. *cp.* 3 10; 7 19.	*cp.* 12 1. *cp.* 11 13.	**6** And he spake this parable; A certain man had a fig tree planted in his vineyard [*cp.* 20 9]; and he came seeking fruit thereon, and found none. **7** And he said unto the vinedresser, Behold, these three years I come seeking fruit on this fig tree, and find none: cut it down [*cp.* 3 9]; why doth it also cumber the ground? **8** And he answering saith unto him, Lord, let it alone this year also, till I shall dig about it, and dung it: **9** and if it bear fruit thenceforth, *well*; but if not, thou shalt cut it down.	*cp.* 15 2, 6.

(iv) Events on the Journey II (§§ 160-163)

§ 160. The Healing of a Woman with a Spirit of Infirmity

[*Cp.* Matt. 12 9-14 ‖ Mark 3 1-6 ‖ Luke 6 6-11; Luke 14 1-6; John 5 2-18, 7 21-24, 9 1-34: *also* Matt. 12 1-8 ‖ Mark 2 23-28 ‖ Luke 6 1-5]

Luke 13 10-17

cp. 12 9; 13 54: *also* 4 23; 9 35. *cp.* 9 20.	*cp.* 1 21; 3 1; 6 2: *also* 1 39. *cp.* 5 25-26.	**10** And he was teaching in one of the synagogues [*cp.* 4 16, 31-33; 6 6: *also* 4 15, 44] on the sabbath day. **11** And behold, a woman which had a spirit of infirmity eighteen [*cp.* 13 4] years; and was bowed together, and could in no wise lift herself up [*cp.* 8 43]. **12** And when Jesus saw her, he called her, and said to her, Woman, thou art loosed from thine	*cp.* 6 59: *also* 18 20.

Matt.	Mark	Luke (center)		Luke refs
cp. 9 18; 19 13, 15; etc. cp. 9 8; 15 31: also 5 16.	cp. 5 23; 6 5; 8 23, 25; etc. cp. 2 12. cp. 5 22.	infirmity. **13** And he laid his hands [cp. 4 40: also 5 13; 7 14; 8 54; 14 4; 18 15; 22 51] upon her: and immediately she was made straight, and glorified God [cp. 2 20; 5 25, 26; 7 16; 17 15, 18; 18 43; 23 47]. **14** And the ruler of the synagogue [cp. 8 41], being moved with indignation because Jesus had healed on the sabbath, answered and said to the multitude, There are six days in which men ought to work: in them therefore come and be healed, and not on the day of the sabbath.		cp. 9 6; 20 17. cp. 9 24.
12 11 And he	cp. 16 19, 20.	**15** But the Lord [cp. 7 13, 19; 10 1, 39, 41; 11 39; 12 42; 17 5, 6; 18 6; 19 8; 22 61; 24 3, 34] answered him, and said, Ye hypocrites [cp. 12 56: also 12 1], doth not each one of you on the sabbath loose his ox or his ass from the ¹ stall,	Luke 14 5 And he	cp. 4 1; 6 23; 11 2; 20 2, 18, 20, 25; 21 7, 12.
said unto them, cp. 15 7; 22 18; 23 13 ff.: also 6 2, 5, 16; 24 51. What man shall there be of you, that shall have one sheep, and if this fall into a pit on the sabbath day, will he not lay hold on it, and lift it out? **12** How much then is a man of more value [cp. 6 26; 10 31] than a sheep! cp. 3 9.	cp. 7 6: also 12 15.	and lead him away to watering? **16** And ought not this woman, cp. 12 7, 24. being a daughter of Abraham [cp. 19 9: also 3 8; 16 24, 30], whom Satan had bound, lo, *these* eighteen years [*see above*], to have been	said unto them, Which of you shall have ¹ an ass or an ox fallen into a well, and will not straightway draw him up on a sabbath day? ¹ Many ancient authorities read *a son*. See ch. 13 15.	cp. 8 33, 37, 39, 53.
Wherefore it is lawful to do good on the sabbath day.	cp. 3 4.	loosed from this bond on the day of the sabbath? **17** And as he said these things, all his adversaries were put to shame: and all the multitude rejoiced for all the glorious things that were done by him.	cp. 6 9.	cp. 7 23.

¹ Gr. *manger*.

Luke 13 14: cp. Exod. 20 9-10; Deut. 5 13-14.

§ 161. The Parables of the Mustard Seed and the Leaven

Matt. 13 31-33	Mark 4 30-32	**Luke 13** 18-21
31 Another parable set he before them, saying, The kingdom of heaven is like unto a grain of mustard seed [cp. 17 20], which a man took, and sowed in his field: **32** which indeed is less than all seeds; but when it is grown, it is greater than the herbs, and becometh a tree, so that the birds of the heaven come and lodge in the branches thereof.	**30** And he said, How shall we liken the kingdom of God? or in what parable shall we set it forth? **31** ¹ It is like a grain of mustard seed, which, when it is sown upon the earth, though it be less than all the seeds that are upon the earth, **32** yet when it is sown, groweth up, and becometh greater than all the herbs, and putteth out great branches; so that the birds of the heaven can lodge under the shadow thereof.	**18** He said therefore, Unto what is the kingdom of God like? and whereunto shall I liken it? **19** It is like unto a grain of mustard seed [cp. 17 6], which a man took, and cast into his own garden; and it grew, and became a tree; and the birds of the heaven lodged in the branches thereof.

33 Another parable spake he unto them ;
The kingdom
of heaven   is like unto leaven,
which a woman took, and hid in three
¹ measures of meal, till it was all
leavened.

¹ The word in the Greek denotes the Hebrew
seah, a measure containing nearly a peck and
a half.

20 And again he said,
Whereunto shall I liken the kingdom
of God ? **21** It is like unto leaven,
which a woman took and hid in three
¹ measures of meal, till it was all
leavened.

¹ Gr. *As unto.*   ¹ See footnote on Matt. 13 33.

§ 162. A Question about Salvation

Matt. 7 13-14 ; 25 10-12 ; 7 22-23 ;
8 11-12.

cp. 9 35.

cp. 16 21 ; 20 17, 18.

          7 13 Enter
ye in [*cp.* 5 20 ; 7 21 ; 18 3, 8, 9 ; 19
17, 23, 24 ; 21 31 ; 23 13 ; 25 21, 23] by
the narrow gate : for wide ¹ is the gate,
and broad is the way, that leadeth to
destruction, and many
be they that enter in thereby. **14** ² For
narrow is the gate, and straitened the way,
that leadeth unto life, and few [*cp.* Luke
13 23] be they that find it.
25 10 And while they went away to buy,
the bridegroom came ; and they that
were ready went in with him to the
marriage feast :
                    and
the door was shut. **11** Afterward come
also the other virgins,

          saying, Lord, Lord, open to us.
12 But he answered and said,
Verily I say unto you, I know you not.
                    7 22 Many
will say to me in that day [*cp.* 24 36 : *also*
26 29], Lord, Lord, did we not prophesy
by thy name, and by thy name cast out
³ devils, and by thy name do many
⁴ mighty works ?

          23 And then will I profess
unto them [*cp.* 25 34, 41],   I
never knew   you : depart from
me [*cp.* 25 41], ye that work
iniquity. **8 11** And I say unto you, that
many shall come from the east and the
west, and shall ⁵ sit down with

          Abraham, and
Isaac, and Jacob,
in the kingdom of heaven :
12 but the sons of the kingdom [*cp.* 13 38 :
also 5 9, 45] shall be cast forth into the
outer darkness [*cp.* 22 13 ; 25 30] : there
shall be the weeping and gnashing of
teeth [*cp.* 13 42, 50 ; 22 13 ; 24 51 ; 25 30].

cp. 26 29.

cp. 6 6.

cp. 10 32, 33.

cp. 9 43, 45,
47 ; 10 15,
23, 24, 25.

cp. 13   32 :
also 14 25.

cp. 9 38, 39.

cp. 14 25.

Luke 13 22-30

22 And he went on his way through
cities and villages [*cp.* 8 1], teaching,
and journeying on unto Jerusalem
[*cp.* 9 51, 53 ; 17 11 ; 19 11, 41 : *also*
9 31 ; 13 33 ; 18 31]. **23** And one
said unto him, Lord, are they few
[*cp.* Matt. 7 14] that be saved ? And
he said unto them, **24** Strive to enter
in [*cp.* 11 52 ; 18 17, 24, 25 ; 24 26]
                    by
the narrow door :

          for many, I say unto you,
shall seek to enter in,

          and shall not be ¹ able.

          25 When once the master
of the house is risen up, and hath shut
to the door,
                    and ye begin to
stand without, and to knock at the
door, saying, Lord,   open to us ;
and he shall answer and say to you,
          I know you not
whence ye are ; **26** then shall ye begin
to say,   [*cp.* 10 12 ; 17
31 ; 21 34] We did

          cp. 9 49.

          eat and drink in
thy presence, and thou didst teach in
our streets ; **27** and   he shall say,
          I tell you, I
know not whence ye are ; depart from
me,   all ye workers of
iniquity.

          28 There
shall be the weeping and gnashing of
teeth, when ye shall see Abraham, and
Isaac, and Jacob, and all the prophets,
in the kingdom of God, and yourselves   [*cp.* 6 35 ;
16 8 ; 20 36]   cast forth
without.

29 And they shall come from the east
and west, and from the north and
south, and shall ² sit down [*cp.* 14 15 ;
22 16, 18, 30] in the kingdom of God

cp. 10 1, 2,
9 ; 3 5.

cp. 7 27, 28 ;
etc. below.
cp. 14 20 ;
16 23, 26.

cp. 7 27, 28 ;
8 14 ; 9
29, 30.

cp. 12 36.

cp. 21 31, 41, 43 ; 22 7-10 : *also* 10 18 ; 24 14 ; 26 13 ; 28 19.	cp. 12 9 : *also* 13 10 ; 14 9 ; 16 15.	[cp. 14 21-24 ; 20 16 : *also* 2 30-32 ; 3 6 ; 24 47]. **30** And behold, there are last which shall be first, and there are first which shall be last.	cp. 10 16 ; 11 52.
cp. 19 30 ; 20 16.	cp. 10 31.		

¹ Some ancient authorities omit *is the gate.*
² Many ancient authorities read *How narrow is the gate, &c.*
³ Gr. *demons.*   ⁴ Gr. *powers.*   ⁵ Gr. *recline.*

¹ Or, *able, when once*   ² Gr. *recline.*

Luke 13 27 ‖ Matt. 7 23 = Ps. 6 8.   Luke 13 29 ‖ Matt. 8 11 : *cp.* Ps. 107 3 *and* Is. 49 12.

§ 163. Advice from the Pharisees and a Lament over Jerusalem

[Cp. Luke 19 41-44 : *also* 23 27-31 *and* 21 20]

Luke 13 31-35

cp. 18 1 ; 26 55.		**31** In that very hour [cp. 7 21 ; 10 21] there came certain Pharisees, saying to him, Get thee out, and go hence : for Herod would fain kill thee. **32** And he said unto them, Go and	
cp. 12 40 ; 16 21 ; *etc.*	cp. 8 31 ; *etc.*	say to that fox, Behold, I cast out ¹ devils and perform cures to-day and to-morrow, and the third *day* [cp. 9 22 ; 18 33 ; 24 7, 21, 46] I am perfected [cp. 12 50 ; 18 31 ; 22 37 : John 19 28, 30 : *also* John 4 34 ; 5 36 ; 17 4]. **33** Howbeit I must go on my way to-day and to-morrow and the *day* following : for it cannot be that a	cp. 2 19.
cp. 13 57 ; 21 11, 46. cp. 16 21 ; 20 17, 18. Matt. 23 **37** O Jerusalem, Jerusalem, which killeth the prophets [cp. 5 12 ; 21 35-36 ; 22 6 ; 23 29-34], and stoneth [cp. 21 35] them that are sent unto her ! how often would I have gathered thy children together, even as a hen gathereth her chickens under her wings, and ye would not ! **38** Behold, your house is left unto you ¹ desolate.	cp. 6 4, 15. cp. 10 32, 33. cp. 12 3-5.	prophet [cp. 4 24 ; 7 16, 39 ; 24 19] perish out of Jerusalem [cp. 9 31, 51 ; 18 31]. **34** O Jerusalem, Jerusalem, which killeth the prophets [cp. 6 23 ; 11 47-50 ; 20 10-12], and stoneth them that are sent unto her ! how often would I have gathered thy children [cp. 19 44] together, even as a hen *gathereth* her own brood under her wings, and ye would not ! **35** Behold, your house is left unto you *desolate* [cp. 21 20 : *also* 19 43-44 ; 23 29-31] :	cp. 4 19, 44 ; 6 14 ; 7 40 ; 9 17.
39 For I say unto you, Ye shall not see me henceforth [cp. 26 29, 64], till ye shall say, Blessed *is* he that cometh [cp. 3 11 ; 11 3] in the name of the Lord [= 21 9 *and* John 12 13].	cp. 1 7. 11 9.	and I say unto you, Ye shall not see me, until ye shall say, Blessed *is* he that cometh [cp. 7 19, 20 : *also* 3 16] in the name of the Lord [= 19 38 *and* John 12 13].	cp. 13 19 ; 14 7. cp. 1 15, 27 ; 3 31 ; 6 14 ; 11 27 : *also* 1 30.

¹ Some ancient authorities omit *desolate.*

¹ Gr. *demons.*

Luke 13 35 ‖ Matt. 23 39 = Ps. 118 26.

(v) Jesus a Guest in the House of a Ruler of the Pharisees on the Sabbath (§§ 164-167)

§ 164. The Healing of a Man with the Dropsy

[Cp. Matt. 12 1-8 ; Mark 2 23-28 ; Luke 6 1-5 ; 13 10-17 ; John 5 2-18 ; 7 21-24 ; 9 1-34]

Matt. 12 9-14	Mark 3 1-6	Luke 6 6-11	Luke 14 1-6	
9 And he departed thence, and went into their synagogue [cp. 13 54 : *also* 4 23 ; 9 35] :	**1** And he entered again into the synagogue [cp. 1 21 ; 6 2 : *also* 1 39] ;	**6** And it came to pass on another sabbath, that he entered into the synagogue [cp. 4 16, 33 ; 13 10 : *also* 4 15, 44] and taught : and there was	**1** And it came to pass, when he went into the house	cp. 6 59 ; 18 20.
10 and behold, a man having [cp. 5 29, 30, 39 ; 27 29] a withered hand.	and there was a man there which had his hand withered.	a man there, and his right [cp. 22 50] hand was withered. **7** And the scribes and the Pharisees	of one of the rulers of the Pharisees on a sabbath to eat bread [cp. 7 36 ; 11 37], that	cp 18 10.
verse 14	*verse* 6			
	2 And they watched	watched	they were watching	

Matthew	Mark	(Mark p. 156)	Luke 14	
see below.	him, whether he would heal him on the sabbath day; that they might accuse him [cp. 12 13].	him, whether he would heal on the sabbath; that they might find how to accuse him [cp. 11 53-54; 20 20].	him [cp. 20 20]. 2 And behold, there was before him a certain man which had the dropsy.	cp. 8 6.
cp. 9 4 ; 12 25 ; 16 8.	cp. 2 8; 8 17. 3 And he saith unto the man that had his hand withered, 1 Stand forth [cp. 2 11 ; 5 41 ; 10 49].	8 But he knew their thoughts [cp. 5 22 ; 9 47 ; 11 17] ; and he said to the man that had his hand withered, Rise up, and stand forth [cp. 5 24 ; 7 14 ; 8 54] in the midst. And he arose and stood forth. 9 And Jesus said unto them,	3 And Jesus answering spake unto the lawyers and Pharisees, saying, Is it lawful [cp. 20 22] to heal on the sabbath, or not?	cp. 1 48; 2 24, 25; 4 19, 29; 5 6, 42; etc.
cp. 9 6.	4 And he saith unto them,			cp. 5 8.
And they asked him, saying, Is it lawful [cp. 19 3; 22 17] to heal on the sabbath day? that they might accuse him [cp. 22 15].	Is it lawful [cp. 10 2; 12 14] on the sabbath day *verse 2* to do good, or to do harm? to save a life, or to kill? But they held their peace.	I ask you, Is it lawful on the sabbath *verse 7* to do good, or to do harm? to save a life, or to destroy it?	4 But they held their peace. And he took him, and healed [cp. 6 19; 9 2, 11, 42; 22 51] him, and let him go. 5 And he said unto them, Which of you shall have 1 an ass or an ox fallen into a well,	
11 And he said unto them, What man shall there be of you, that shall have one sheep, and if this fall into a pit on the sabbath day, will he not lay hold on it, and lift it out? 12 How much then is a man of more value than a sheep [cp. 6 26; 10 31]! Wherefore it is lawful to do good on the sabbath day. 13 Then		cp. 13 15-16.	and will not straightway draw him up on a sabbath day? cp. 12 7, 24.	
				cp. 7 23.
cp. 19 8.	5 And when he had looked round about [cp. 3 34; 5 32; 9 8; 10 23; 11 11] on them with anger, being grieved at the hardening of their heart [cp. 10 5: *also* 6 52; 8 17; 16 14],	10 And he looked round about on them all,		cp. 12 40.
saith he to the man, Stretch forth thy hand. And he stretched it forth; and it was restored whole, as the other. 14 But the Pharisees went out, and	he saith unto the man, Stretch forth thy hand. And he stretched it forth: and his hand was restored. 6 And the Pharisees went out, and straightway with	and said unto him, Stretch forth thy hand. And he did *so*: and his hand was restored. *verse 7*		

cp. 22 16.	the Herodians [cp. 12 13]	11 But they were filled with ¹ madness; and communed one with another
took counsel [cp. 22 15; 27 1, 7; 28 12] against him, how they might destroy him [cp. 21 46; 26 4].	took counsel [cp. 15 1] against him, how they might destroy him [cp. 11 18; 12 12; 14 1].	what they 19 47; 20 19, 20; 22 might do to Jesus [cp. 2].
cp. 22 46.		

6 And they could not answer again unto these things.

cp. 5 16, 18; 7 30, 32; 11 53.

¹ Gr. *Arise into the midst.*   Or, *foolishness*   ¹ Many ancient authorities read *a son.* See ch. 13 15.

§ 165. **Advice to Guests**

Luke 14 7-11

cp. 23 6.

cp. 22 2 *ff.*

cp. 12 39.

7 And he spake a parable unto those which were bidden, when he marked how they chose out the chief seats [cp. 20 46: *also* 11 43]; saying unto them, 8 When thou art bidden of any man to a marriage feast, ¹ sit not down in the chief seat; lest haply a more honourable man than thou be bidden of him, 9 and he that bade thee and him shall come and say to thee, Give this man place; and then thou shalt begin with shame to take the lowest place. 10 But when thou art bidden, go and sit down in the lowest place; that when he that hath bidden thee cometh, he may say to thee, Friend [cp. 11 5], go up higher: then shalt thou have glory in the presence of all that sit at meat with thee.

Matt. 23 12 And whosoever shall exalt himself shall be humbled; and whosoever shall humble himself [cp. 18 4] shall be exalted.

11 For every one that exalteth himself shall be humbled; and he that humbleth himself shall be exalted.

Luke 18 14 For every one that exalteth himself shall be humbled; but he that humbleth himself shall be exalted.

¹ Gr. *recline not.*

§ 166. **Advice to Hosts**

Luke 14 12-14

12 And he said to him also that had bidden him, When thou makest a dinner or a supper, call not thy friends, nor thy brethren, nor thy kinsmen, nor rich neighbours; lest haply they also bid thee again, and a recompense be made thee. 13 But when thou makest a feast, bid the poor, the maimed, the lame, the blind [cp. 14 21]: 14 and thou shalt be blessed; because they have not *wherewith* to recompense thee: for thou shalt be recompensed in the resurrection of the just.

§ 167. **The Parable of the Great Supper**

[*Cp.* Matt. 8 11; 21 31, 41-43: *also* 10 18; 24 14; 26 13; 28 19: Mark 12 9-11: *also* 13 10; 14 9; 16 15: Luke 13 29; 20 16-17: *also* 2 30-32; 3 6; 24 47: John 10 16; 11 52]

Matt. 22 1-14   Luke 14 15-24

15 And when one of them that sat at meat with him heard these things, he said unto him, Blessed is he that shall eat bread in the kingdom of God [cp. 13 29; 22 16, 18, 30].
16 But he

cp. 8 11; 26 29.   cp. 14 25.
1 And Jesus answered and spake again in parables unto them, saying,
2 The kingdom of heaven is likened unto a certain king [cp. 18 23: *also* 25 34, 40], which made a marriage feast for his son,

said unto him,

A certain   [cp. 19 12, 15, 27] man made   [cp. 14 8]
a great supper; and he bade many:

3 and   sent forth his ¹ servants [cp. 21   cp. 12 2.   17 and he sent forth his ¹ servant [cp. 20
34]   to call them that   10] at supper time to say to them that

were bidden to the marriage feast : and they would not come.   **4** Again he sent forth other [1] servants [*cp.* 21 36], saying, Tell them that are bidden, Behold, I have made ready my dinner : my oxen and my fatlings are killed, and all things are ready : come

to the marriage feast.   **5** But they made
light of it, and went their ways, one

to his own
farm,

another   to his mer-
chandise :

6 and the rest laid hold on his [1] servants, and entreated them shamefully, and killed them [*cp.* 21 35, 36 : *also* 5 12 ; 23 29-34, 37].

cp. 13 27, 52 ; 20 1 ; 21 33.
          7 But the king was wroth [*cp.* 18 34] ; and he sent his armies, and destroyed those murderers [*cp.* 21 41], and burned their city.   **8** Then saith he to his [1] servants, The wedding is ready, but they that were bidden were not worthy.   **9** Go ye therefore unto

the partings of the highways,
          and as many as ye shall
find, bid to the marriage feast.

          10 And those [1] servants went out into the highways, and gathered together all as many as they found, both bad and good [*cp.* 13 30, 47 ; 25 32] : and the wedding was filled with guests.   **11** But when the king came in to behold the guests, he saw there a man which had not on a wedding-garment : **12** and he saith unto him, Friend [*cp.* 20 13 ; 26 50], how camest thou in hither not having a wedding-garment ?   And he was speechless.   **13** Then the king said to the [2] servants, Bind him hand and foot, and cast him out into the outer darkness [*cp.* 8 12 ; 25 30] ; there shall be the weeping and gnashing of teeth [*cp.* 8 12 ; 13 42, 50 ; 24 51 ; 25 30].   **14** For many are called, but few chosen.

          [1] Gr. *bondservants.*   [2] Or, *ministers*

cp. 12 4-5.

cp. 12 3, 4, 5.

cp. 12 9.

were bidden,

cp. 20 11-12.

          Come ; for *all* things are now ready.   **18** And they all with one *consent* began to make excuse.   The first said unto him, I have bought a field, and I must needs go out and see it : I pray thee have me excused. **19** And another said, I have bought five yoke of oxen, and I go to prove them : I pray thee have me excused. **20** And another said, I have married a wife, and therefore I cannot come.

cp. 20 10, 11, 12 ; *also* 6 23 ; 11 47-50 ;
          13 33, 34.
          21 And the [1] servant came, and told his lord these things. Then the master of the house being angry

cp. 20 16.
          said   to his
[1] servant,
          Go
out quickly into the streets and lanes of the city, and bring in hither the poor and maimed and blind and lame [*cp.* 14 13].   **22** And the [1] servant said, Lord, what thou didst command is done, and yet there is room.   **23** And the lord said unto the [1] servant, Go out into the   highways and hedges,
and constrain *them* to come in, that my house may be filled.   **24** For I say unto you, that none of those men which were bidden shall taste of my supper.

          [1] Gr. *bondservant.*

cp. 13 28.

(vi) An Address to the Multitudes (§ 168)

§ 168. **The Cost of Discipleship**

cp. 9 22 ; 16 23.

Matt. 10 **37** He
          that loveth

cp. 5 30 ; 8
33.

Luke 14 25-35

25 Now there went with him great multitudes : and he turned [*cp.* 7 9, 44 ; 9 55 ; 10 23 ; 22 61 ; 23 28], and said unto them, **26** If any man cometh unto me, and hateth not his own

cp. 1 38.

cp. 12 25.

father or mother
        more than me is not worthy of me;
and he that loveth son or daughter
                cp. 19 29.
        cp. 10 39; 16 25-26.
more than me is not worthy of me.
                cp. 8 18-22.

                38 And he that
doth not take his   cross and follow
after me, is not worthy of me.

cp. 10 29.
cp. 8 35-37.

father, and mother, and wife [*cp.* 18 29],
and   children,   and
brethren, and sisters [*cp.* 18 29], yea,
and his own life [*cp.* 9 24; 17 33] also,
                he
cannot be my disciple [*cp. verses* 27 *and* 33: *also* 9 57-62].   27 Whosoever
doth not bear his own cross, and come
after me,   cannot
be my disciple [*cp. verses* 26 *and* 33].

cp. 12 25.

Matt. 16 24 If any man
would come after
me, let him deny him-
self, and take up his
cross,   and follow
me [*cp.* 4 19; 8 22; 9 9; 19 21].

Mark 8 34 If any man
would come after
me, let him deny him-
self, and take up his
cross,   and follow
me [*cp.* 1 17; 2 14; 10 21].

Luke 9 23 If any man
would come after
me, let him deny him-
self, and take up his
cross daily, and follow
me [*cp.* 5 27; 9 59; 18 22].

John 12 26 If any man
serve
me, let him

        follow
me [*cp.* 1 43; 21 19, 22]; and where I am,
there shall also my ser-
vant be.

28 For which of you, desiring to build a tower, doth not first sit down and count the cost, whether he have *wherewith* to complete it? 29 Lest haply, when he hath laid a foundation, and is not able to finish, all that behold begin to mock him, 30 saying, This man began to build, and was not able to finish. 31 Or what king, as he goeth to encounter another king in war, will not sit down first and take counsel whether he is able with ten thousand to meet him that cometh against him with twenty thousand? 32 Or else, while the other is yet a great way off, he sendeth an ambassage [*cp.* 19 14], and asketh conditions of peace. 33 So therefore whosoever he be of you that renounceth [*cp.* 9 61] not all that he hath [*cp.* 5 11, 28], he cannot be my disciple [*cp. verses* 26 *and* 27].

cp. 19 27.

cp. 10 28.

Matt. 5 13 Ye are the salt of the earth: but if   the salt have lost its savour, wherewith shall it be salted?   it is thenceforth good for nothing,   but to be cast out and trodden under foot of men.

Mark 9 50 Salt   is good: but if   the salt have lost its saltness, wherewith will ye season it?

        34 Salt therefore is good: but if even the salt have lost its savour, wherewith shall it be seasoned?   35 It is   fit neither for the land nor for the dunghill: *men* cast it out.
        He that hath ears to hear, let him hear [*cp.* 8 8].

cp. 11 15; 13 9, 43: *also* 19 12.

cp. 4 9, 23; 7 16.

cp. 6 60.

(vii) Three Parables on Things Lost and Found (§§ 169-172)

§ 169. **The Occasion of the Parables**

Luke 15 1-2

1 Now all the publicans and sinners were drawing near unto him for to hear him. 2 And both the Pharisees and the scribes murmured, saying, This man receiveth sinners, and eateth with them [*cp.* 5 30; 7 34, 39; 19 7].

cp. 9 11; 11 19.

cp. 2 16.

§ 170. **The Lost Sheep**

Matt. 18 12-13

12 How think ye [*cp.* 17 25; 21 28; 22 17, 42; 26 66]? if any man   have a hundred sheep, and   one of them be gone astray, doth he not leave the ninety and nine,   and go unto the mountains, and seek that which goeth astray?

Luke 15 3-7

3 And he spake unto them this parable, saying,

4 What man of you, having a hundred sheep, and having lost one of them,   doth   not leave the ninety and nine in the wilderness, and go   after that which is lost, until he find it [*cp.* 15 8:

cp. 11 56.
cp. 10 1 *ff.*

	13 And if so be that he	*also* 19 10]? **5** And when he hath found it, he layeth it on his shoulders, rejoicing.

find it,
verily I say unto you, he rejoiceth
over it

6 And when he cometh home, he calleth together his friends and his neighbours, saying unto them, Rejoice with me [*cp.* 15 9: *also* 1 58], for I have found my sheep which was lost [*cp.* 15 9, 24, 32]. **7** I say unto you, that even so there shall be joy in heaven over one sinner that repenteth [*cp.* 15 10, 32], *more* than over

cp. 6 39.

more than over the

ninety and nine
which have not gone astray.

ninety and nine righteous persons, which need no repentance [*cp.* 5 32].

§ 171. The Lost Coin

Luke 15 8-10

8 Or what woman having ten [1] pieces of silver, if she lose one piece, doth not light a lamp, and sweep the house, and seek diligently until she find it [*cp.* 15 4: *also* 19 10] ? **9** And when she hath found it, she calleth together her friends and neighbours, saying, Rejoice with me [*cp.* 15 6: *also* 1 58], for I have found the piece which I had lost [*cp.* 15 6, 24, 32]. **10** Even so, I say unto you, there is joy in the presence of the angels of God [*cp.* 12 8, 9] over one sinner that repenteth [*cp.* 15 7, 32: *also* 5 32].

[1] Gr. *drachma*, a coin worth about eight pence.

§ 172. The Lost Son

[*Cp.* Matt. 21 28-32]

Luke 15 11-32

cp. 21 28.

11 And he said, A certain man had two sons: **12** and the younger of them said to his father, Father, give me the portion of [1] *thy* substance that falleth to me. And he divided unto them his living. **13** And not many days after the younger son gathered all together, and took his journey into a far country [*cp.* 19 12]; and there he wasted his substance with riotous living. **14** And when he had spent all, there arose a mighty famine in that country; and he began to be in want. **15** And he went and joined himself to one of the citizens of that country; and he sent him into his fields to feed swine. **16** And he would fain have been filled with [2] the husks that the swine did eat: and no man gave unto him. **17** But when he came to himself he said, How many hired servants of my father's have bread enough and to spare, and I perish here with hunger ! **18** I will arise and go to my father, and will say unto him, Father, I have sinned against heaven, and in thy sight: **19** I am no more worthy to be called thy son: make me as one of thy hired servants. **20** And he arose, and came to his father. But while he was yet afar off, his father saw him, and was moved with compassion [*cp.* 10 33: *also* 7 13], and ran, and fell on his neck, and [3] kissed him. **21** And the son said unto him, Father, I have sinned against heaven, and in thy sight: I am no more worthy to be called thy son.[4] **22** But the father said to his [5] servants, Bring forth quickly the best robe, and put it on him; and put a ring on his hand, and shoes on his feet: **23** and bring the fatted calf, *and* kill it, and let us eat, and make merry: **24** for this my son was dead, and is alive again; he was lost, and is found [*cp. verse* 32: *also* 15 6, 9]. And they began to be merry. **25** Now his elder son was in the field: and as he came and drew nigh to the house, he heard music and dancing. **26** And he called to him one of the servants, and inquired what these things might be. **27** And he said unto him, Thy brother is come; and thy father hath killed the fatted calf, because he

hath received him safe and sound.   **28** But he was angry, and
would not go in: and his father came out, and intreated him.
29 But he answered and said to his father, Lo, these many years
do I serve thee, and I never transgressed a commandment of
thine: and *yet* thou never gavest me a kid, that I might make
merry with my friends: **30** but when this thy son came, which
hath devoured thy living with harlots, thou killedst for him the
fatted calf.   **31** And he said unto him, [6] Son, thou art ever with
me, and all that is mine is thine.   **32** But it was meet to make
merry, and be glad: for this thy brother was dead, and is alive
again; and *was* lost, and is found [*cp. verse* 24: *also* 15 6, 9].

[1] Gr. *the*.   [2] Gr. *the pods of the carob tree*.   [3] Gr. *kissed him much*.
[4] Some ancient authorities add *make me as one of thy hired servants*. See ver. 19.
[5] Gr. *bondservants*.   [6] Gr. *Child*.

(viii) A Discourse mainly on Money, its Uses, and its Effects (§§ 173-175)

[*Cp*. Matt. 19 16-24 ‖ Mark 10 17-25 ‖ Luke 18 18-25]

§ 173. **The Parable of the Unrighteous Steward**

Luke 16 1-13

1 And he said also unto the disciples, There was a certain
rich man [*cp*. 12 16; 16 19], which had a steward [*cp*. 12 42];
and the same was accused unto him that he was wasting his
goods.   **2** And he called him, and said unto him, What is this
that I hear of thee? render the account of thy stewardship;
for thou canst be no longer steward.   **3** And the steward said
within himself, What shall I do [*cp*. 12 17; 20 13], seeing that
my lord taketh away the stewardship from me? I have not
strength to dig; to beg I am ashamed.   **4** I am resolved what to
do, that, when I am put out of the stewardship, they may receive
me into their houses.   **5** And calling to him each one of his
lord's debtors, he said to the first, How much owest thou unto
my lord?   **6** And he said, A hundred [1] measures of oil.   And
he said unto him, Take thy [2] bond, and sit down quickly and
write fifty.   **7** Then said he to another, And how much owest
thou? And he said, A hundred [3] measures of wheat.   He saith
unto him, Take thy [2] bond, and write fourscore.   **8** And his lord
commended [4] the unrighteous steward [*cp*. 18 6; *also* 13 27]
because he had done wisely: for the sons of this [5] world [*cp*.
20 34] are, for their own generation wiser [*cp*. 12 42] than the
sons of the light [*cp*. 6 35; 20 36: Matt. 5 9, 45; 8 12; 13 38].
9 And I say unto you, Make to yourselves [*cp*. 12 33] friends
[6] by means of the mammon of unrighteousness [*cp*. 18 6; *also*
13 27]; that, when it shall fail, they may receive you into the
eternal tabernacles.   **10** He that is faithful [*cp*. 12 42; 19 17]
in a very little [*cp*. 19 17: *also* 12 26] is faithful also in much:
and he that is unrighteous in a very little is unrighteous also in
much.   **11** If therefore ye have not been faithful in the unrighteousness mammon, who will commit to your trust the true
riches [*cp*. 19 15-26]?   **12** And if ye have not been faithful in
that which is another's, who will give you that which is [7] your
own?   **13** No [8] servant can serve two
masters: for either he will hate the
one, and love the other; or else he will
hold to one, and despise the other.   Ye
cannot serve God and mammon.

cp. 7 24; 10
16; 24 45;
25 2 *ff*.

cp. 24 45;
25 21, 23.

cp. 25 19-30.

cp. 12 36:
also 1 12;
11 52.

Matt. 6 **24** No man can serve two
masters: for either he will hate the
one, and love the other; or else he will
hold to one, and despise the other.   Ye
cannot serve God and mammon.

[1] Gr. *baths*, the bath being a Hebrew measure.
See Ezek. 45 10, 11, 14.   [2] Gr. *writings*.
[3] Gr. *cors*, the cor being a Hebrew measure.
See Ezek. 45 14.
[4] Gr. *the steward of unrighteousness*.
[5] Or, *age*   [6] Gr. *out of*.
[7] Some ancient authorities read *our own*.
[8] Gr. *household-servant*.

§ 174. **The Pharisees rebuked and Three Detached Sayings**

Luke 16 14-18

cp. 23 25.

14 And the Pharisees, who were lovers of money [cp. 11 39; 20 47], heard all these things; and they scoffed [cp. 23 35] at him. **15** And he said unto them, Ye are they that justify yourselves [cp. 10 29] in the sight of men; but God knoweth your hearts: for that which is exalted among men is an abomination in the sight of God.

Matt. 11 **12** And from the days of John the Baptist until now the kingdom of heaven

cp. 11 5.

suffereth violence, and men of violence take it by force. **13** For all the prophets and the law [cp. 5 17; 7 12; 22 40] prophesied until John.

Matt. 5 **18** For verily I say unto you, Till heaven and earth pass away [cp. 24 35], one jot or one tittle shall in no wise pass away from the law, till all things be accomplished.

16 The law and the prophets *were* until John: from that time the gospel of the kingdom of God is preached [cp. 1 19; 2 10; 3 18; 4 18, 43; 7 22; 8 1; 9 6; 20 1], and every man entereth violently into it.

cp. 13 31.

17 But it is easier for heaven and earth to pass away [cp. 21 33], than for one tittle of the law to fall.

Matt. 5 **32** But I say unto you, that every one that putteth away his wife, saving for the cause of fornication,

Matt. 19 **9** And I say unto you, Whosoever shall put away his wife, [1] except for fornication, and shall marry another, committeth adultery:

Mark 10 **11** And he saith unto them, Whosoever shall put away his wife,

18 Every one that putteth away his wife,

maketh her an adulteress: and whosoever shall marry her when she is put away committeth adultery.

[2] and he that marrieth her when she is put away committeth adultery.

and marry another, committeth adultery against her:

and marrieth another, committeth adultery:

12 and if she herself shall put away her husband, and marry another, she committeth adultery.

and he that marrieth one that is put away from a husband committeth adultery.

[1] Some ancient authorities read *saving for the cause of fornication, maketh her an adulteress*: as in ch. 5 32.
[2] The following words, to the end of the verse, are omitted by some ancient authorities.

§ 175. **The Parable of the Rich Man and Lazarus**

Luke 16 19-31

cp. 15 27.   cp. 7 28.

cp. 3 9.

19 Now there was a certain rich man [cp. 12 16; 16 1], and he was clothed in purple and fine linen, [1] faring sumptuously every day: **20** and a certain beggar named Lazarus was laid at his gate, full of sores, **21** and desiring to be fed with the *crumbs* that fell from the rich man's table; yea, even the dogs came and licked his sores. **22** And it came to pass, that the beggar died, and that he was carried away by the angels into Abraham's bosom: and the rich man also died, and was buried. **23** And in Hades he lifted up his eyes, being in torments, and seeth Abraham afar off, and Lazarus in his bosom. **24** And he cried and said, Father Abraham [cp. *verse* 30: *also* 3 8; 13 16; 19 9], have mercy on me, and send Lazarus, that he may dip the tip of his finger in water, and cool my tongue; for I am in anguish in this flame. **25** But Abraham said, [2] Son, remember that thou in thy lifetime receivedst thy good things, and Lazarus in like manner evil things: but now here he is comforted, and thou art in anguish [cp. 6 20, 24]. **26** And [3] beside all this, between

cp. 8 33, 37, 39, 53.

		us and you there is a great gulf fixed, that they which would pass from hence to you may not be able, and that none may cross over from thence to us. **27** And he said, I pray thee therefore, father, that thou wouldest send him to my father's house; **28** for I have five brethren; that he may testify unto them, lest they also come into this place of torment. **29** But Abraham saith, They have Moses and the prophets [*cp. verse* 31 *and* 24 27]; let them hear them. **30** And he said, Nay, father Abraham [*cp. verse* 24: *also* 3 8; 13 16; 19 9]: but if one go to them from the dead, they will repent. **31** And he said unto him, If they hear not Moses and the prophets [*see above*], neither will they be persuaded, if one rise from the dead.	
	cp. 3 9.		*cp.* 1 45. *cp.* 8 33, 37, 39, 53. *cp.* 1 45. *cp.* 12 9.

¹ Or, *living in mirth and splendour every day*
² Gr. *Child.*   ³ Or, *in all these things*

(ix) Events on the Journey III (§§ 176-182)

§ 176. **Sayings about Occasions of Stumbling, the Treatment of a Brother's Fault, and the Obligation to Forgive him**

Matt. 18 7, 6, 15, 21-22	Mark 9 42	Luke 17 1-4	
7 Woe unto the world [*cp.* 26 24: *also* 23 13 *ff.*] because of occasions of stumbling! for it must needs be that the occasions come; but woe to that man [*cp.* 26 24: *also* 23 13 *ff.*] through whom the occasion cometh! **6** But whoso shall cause one of these little ones [*cp.* 10 42; 18 10, 14] which believe on me to stumble, it is profitable for him that ¹ a great millstone should be hanged about his neck, and *that* he should be sunk in the depth of the sea.	*cp.* 14 21. *cp.* 14 21. **42** And whosoever shall cause one of these little ones that believe ¹ on me to stumble, it were better for him if ² a great millstone were hanged about his neck, and he were cast into the sea. ¹ Many ancient authorities omit *on me.* ² Gr. *a millstone turned by an ass.*	**1** And he said unto his disciples, It is impossible but that occasions of stumbling should come: but woe unto him [*cp.* 22 22: *also* 11 42 *ff.*], through whom they come! **2** It were well for him if a millstone were hanged about his neck, and he were thrown into the sea, rather than that he should cause one of these little ones to stumble. **3** Take heed to yourselves [*cp.* 12 1; 21 34]:	
15 And if thy brother sin ²against thee, go, shew him his fault between thee and him alone: if he hear thee, thou hast gained thy brother. . . . **21** Then came Peter, and said to him, Lord, how oft shall my brother sin against me, and I forgive him [*cp.* 6 12, 14, 15]? until seven times? **22** Jesus saith unto him, I say not unto thee, Until seven times; but, Until ³ seventy times seven.	*cp.* 11 25.	if thy brother sin, rebuke him; and if he repent, forgive him [*cp.* 11 4]. **4** And if he sin against thee seven times in the day, and seven times turn again to thee, saying, I repent; thou shalt forgive him.	

¹ Gr. *a millstone turned by an ass.*
² Some ancient authorities omit *against thee.*
³ Or, *seventy times and seven*

§ 177. **Sayings about Faith and the Obligations of Servants**

Matt. 17 19-20; 21 21-22	Mark 9 28-29; 11 22-24	Luke 17 5-10	
cp. 10 2.	*cp.* 6 30. *cp.* 16 19, 20.	**5** And the apostles [*cp.* 6 13; 9 10; 22 14; 24 10] said unto the Lord [*cp.* 7 13, 19; 10 1, 39, 41; 11 39; 12 42; 13 15; 18 6; 19 8; 22 61; 24 3, 34], Increase our faith.	*cp.* 4 1; 6 23; 11 2; 20 2, 18, 20, 25; 21 7, 12.
17 19 Then	**9** 28 And when he was	

came   the disciples to Jesus
apart, and said, Why could
not we cast it out ? **20** And he
saith unto
them, Because of your little
faith [*cp.* 6 30; 8 26; 14 31;
16 8] :

for verily I say unto you, If ye
have faith as a grain of mustard seed [*cp.* 13 31], ye shall
say unto this
mountain, Remove hence to
yonder place ; and it shall remove ; and nothing shall be
impossible unto you [*cp.* 19 26].[1]
21 21 And Jesus answered and
said unto them,
            Verily I say unto
you, If ye have faith, and doubt
not, ye shall not only do what
is done to the fig tree, but
even if ye shall say unto this
mountain, Be thou taken up
and   cast into the
sea,

            it shall be
done.
            22 And all things,
whatsoever ye   shall
ask [*cp.* 7 7; 18 19] in prayer,
believing,
            ye shall receive.

[1] Many authorities, some ancient,
insert ver. 21 *But this kind goeth not
out save by prayer and fasting.*
See Mark 9 29.

cp. 25 30.

---

come into the house, his disciples   asked him
privately, [1] *saying,* We could
not cast it out. **29** And he
            said unto
them,
            cp. 4 40; 16 14.
            This kind can come out
by nothing, save by prayer.[2]

            cp. 4 31.

cp. 9 23; 10 27; 14 36.
11 22 And Jesus answering
saith unto them, Have faith
in God. **23** Verily I say unto
you,

Whosoever shall say unto this
mountain, Be thou taken up
and   cast into the
sea ; and shall not doubt in
his heart, but shall believe
that what he saith cometh to
pass ;   he shall have
it.   **24** Therefore I
say unto you,   All things
whatsoever ye pray and
ask for,
believe that ye have received
them, and ye shall have them.

[1] Or, How is it *that we could not cast
it out ?*
[2] Many ancient authorities add
and fasting.

---

            6 And the
Lord [*see above*] said,

cp. 12 28: *also* 8 25; 22 32;
            24 25, 38.

            If ye
have faith as a grain of mustard seed [*cp.* 13 19], ye would
say unto this sycamine tree,

            cp. 1 37; 18 27.

            Be thou rooted up,
and be thou planted   in the
sea ;

            and it would have
obeyed you.

            cp. 11 9.

7 But who is there of you,
having a [1] servant plowing or
keeping sheep, that will say
unto him, when he is come in

---

cp. 3 12; 6
64; 14 10;
    20 27.

cp. 14 13,
14; 15 7,
16; 16 23,
    24.

---

from the field, Come straightway and sit down to meat ; **8** and
will not rather say unto him, Make ready [*cp.* 12 47] wherewith
I may sup, and gird thyself [*cp.* 12 35, 37], and serve me
[*cp.* 12 37; 22 27], till I have eaten and drunken ; and afterward thou shalt eat and drink ? **9** Doth he thank the [1] servant
because he did the things that were commanded ? **10** Even so
ye also, when ye shall have done all the things that are commanded you, say, We are unprofitable [2] servants ; we have done
that which it was our duty to do.

[1] Gr. *bondservant.*   [2] Gr. *bondservants.*

cp. 13 4-5.

---

§ 178. The Healing of Ten Lepers

[*Cp.* Matt. 8 1-4 ‖ Mark 1 40-45 ‖ Luke 5 12-16]

Luke 17 11-19

cp. 16 21;   *cp.* 10 32, 33.
20 17, 18.

cp. 9 27; 15   *cp.* 10 47, 48.
22 ; *etc.*
cp. 8 4.   *cp.* 1 44.

cp. 9 8; 15 31.   *cp.* 2 12.

11 And it came to pass, [1] as they were on the way to Jerusalem [*cp.* 9 51, 53; 13 22; 19 11, 41: *also* 9 31; 13 33; 18 31],
that he was passing [2] through the midst of Samaria [*cp.* 9 52]
and Galilee. **12** And as he entered into a certain village [*cp.* 9
52, 56; 10 38], there met him ten men that were lepers, which
stood afar off: **13** and they lifted up their voices [*cp.* 11 27],
saying, Jesus, Master, have mercy on us [*cp.* 18 38, 39]. **14** And
when he saw them, he said unto them, Go and shew yourselves
unto the priests [*cp.* 5 14]. And it came to pass, as they went,
they were cleansed. **15** And one of them, when he saw that he
was healed, turned back, with a loud voice glorifying God
[*cp.* 2 20; 5 25, 26; 7 16; 13 13; 18 43; 23 47]; **16** and he

cp. 4 4.
cp. 4 5.

cp. 9 24.

cp. 2 11: also 8 2; 9 18; etc.	cp. 3 11; 5 22, 33; 7 25: also 1 40; 5 6; 10 17.	fell upon his face [cp. 5 8, 12; 8 28, 41, 47: also 24 52] at his feet, giving him thanks: and he was a Samaritan [cp. 10 33]. **17** And Jesus answering said, Were not the ten cleansed? but where are the nine? **18** [3] Were there none found that returned to give glory to God [see verse 15], save this [4] stranger? **19** And he said unto him, Arise, and go thy way: thy faith hath [5] made thee whole [cp. 7 50; 8 48; 18 42].	cp. 11 32; etc. cp. 4 39-42.
cp. 9 22.	cp. 5 34; 10 52.		

[1] Or, *as he was*   [2] Or, *between*   [3] Or, *There were none found . . . save this stranger.*   [4] Or, *alien*   [5] Or, *saved thee*

Luke 7 12: cp. Lev. 13 45-46.   Luke 17 14: cp. Lev. 13 49; 14 2.

§ 179. A Question and Answer about the Coming of the Kingdom

Luke 17 20-21

cp. 24 23, 26. cp. 3 2; 4 17; 10 7; 12 28.	cp. 13 21. cp. 1 15; 6 12.	**20** And being asked by the Pharisees, when the kingdom of God cometh [cp. 19 11], he answered them and said, The kingdom of God cometh not with observation: **21** neither shall they say, Lo, here! or, There [cp. 17 23]! for lo, the kingdom of God is [1] within you [cp. 9 2; 10 9, 11; 11 20: also 19 11; 21 8].

[1] Or, *in the midst of you*

§ 180. A Description of the Day of the Son of Man

Matt. 24 23, 26-27, 37-39, 17-18; 10 39; 24 40-41, 28.	Mark 13 21, 15-16	Luke 17 22-37	
cp. 9 15.	cp. 2 20.	**22** And he said unto the disciples, The days will come [cp. 5 35; 19 43; 21 6; 23 29], when ye shall desire to see one of the days of the Son of man, and ye shall not see it. **23** And they shall say to you, Lo, there! Lo, here [cp. 17 21]!	
24 23 Then if any man shall say unto you, Lo, here is the Christ [cp. 24 5], or, Here; believe [1] *it* not. **26** If therefore they shall say unto you, Behold, he is in the wilderness; go not forth: Behold, he is in the inner chambers; believe [2] *it* not. **27** For as the lightning cometh forth from the east, and is seen even unto the west; so shall be the [3] coming [cp. 24 3, 37, 39] of the Son of man.	**21** And then if any man shall say unto you, Lo, here is the Christ [cp. 13 6]; or, Lo, there; believe [1] *it* not. [1] Or, *him*	go not away, nor follow after *them* [cp. 21 8]: **24** for as the lightning, when it lighteneth out of the one part under the heaven, shineth unto the other part under heaven; so shall the Son of man be [1] in his day.	
cp. 17 10. cp. 16 21-23; 17 12, 22-23; 20 17-19, 28; 26 2, 12, 18, 24, 45.	cp. 9 11, 12; 13 10. cp. 8 31-33; 9 12, 30-32; 10 32-34, 45; 14 8, 21, 41. cp. 8 31.	**25** But first [cp. 21 9] must he suffer [cp. 9 22, 43-45; 13 32, 33; 18 31-34; 22 22; 24 7, 26, 44, 46] many things and be rejected [cp. 9 22] of this generation. **26** And as it came to pass in the days of Noah, even so shall it be also in the days of the Son of man.	cp. 2 19, 22; 3 14; 12 32-33.
24 37 And as *were* the days of Noah, so shall be the [3] coming cp. 24 3, 27, 39] of the Son of man. **38** For as in those days which were before the flood they were eating and drinking, marrying and giving in marriage, until the day that Noah entered into the ark, **39** and they knew not until the flood came, and took them all away;		**27** They ate, they drank, they married, they were given in marriage, until the day that Noah entered into the ark, and the flood came, and destroyed them all. **28** Likewise even as it came to	

pass in the days of Lot; they ate, they drank, they bought, they sold, they planted, they builded; **29** but in the day that Lot went out from Sodom it rained fire and brimstone from heaven, and destroyed them all: **30** after the same manner shall it be in the day that the Son of man is revealed.

so shall be the [3] coming [cp. 24 3, 27, 37] of the Son of man.

cp. 7 22; 24 36: also 26 29.

24 17 Let him that is on the housetop

not go down to take out the things that are in his house: **18** and let him that is in the field not return back to take his cloke.

cp. 13 32: also 14 25.

15 And let him that is on the housetop

not go down, nor enter in, to take anything out of his house: **16** and let him that is in the field not return back to take his cloke.

31 In that day [cp. 10 12; 21 34], he which shall be on the housetop, and his goods in the house, let him not go down to take them away: and let him that is in the field likewise not return back [cp. 21 21]. **32** Remember Lot's wife. **33** Whosoever shall seek to gain his [2] life shall lose it: but whosoever shall lose *his* [2] *life* shall [3] preserve it.

cp. 14 20; 16 23, 26.

10 39 He that [4] findeth his [5] life shall lose it; and he that [6] loseth his [5] life for my sake [see below] shall find it.

Matt. 16 **25** For whosoever would save his [5] life shall lose it: and whosoever shall lose his [5] life for my sake [cp. 5 11; 10 18, 39: also 10 22; 19 29; 24 9] cp. 4 23; 9 35; 24 14; 26 13.

shall find it.

Mark 8 **35** For whosoever would save his [1] life shall lose it; and whosoever shall lose his [1] life for my sake [cp. 10 29; 13 9: also 13 13] and the gospel's [cp. 10 29: also 1 1, 14, 15; 13 10; 14 9; 16 15] shall save it.

[1] Or, *soul*

Luke 9 **24** For whosoever would save his [2] life shall lose it; but whosoever shall lose his [2] life for my sake [cp. 6 22; 18 29; 21 12, 17], the same shall save it.

John 12 **25** He that loveth his [1] life loseth it; and he that hateth his [1] life cp. 15 21. in this world shall keep it unto life eternal.

[1] Or. *soul*

34 I say unto you, In that night there shall be two men on one bed; the one shall be taken, and the other shall be left. **35** There shall be two women grinding together; the one shall be taken, and the other shall be left.[4] **37** And they answering say unto him, Where, Lord? And he said unto them, Where the body *is*, thither will the [5] eagles also be gathered together.

24 40 Then shall two men be in the field; one is taken, and one is left: **41** two women *shall* be grinding at the mill; one is taken, and one is left.

28 Wheresoever the carcase is, there will the [7] eagles be gathered together.

[1] Or, *him*   [2] Or, *them*
[3] Gr. *presence.*   [4] Or, *found*
[5] Or, *soul*   [6] Or, *lost*
[7] Or, *vultures*

[1] Some ancient authorities omit *in his day.*
[2] Or, *soul*   [3] Gr. *save it alive.*
[4] Some ancient authorities add ver. 36, *There shall be two men in the field; the one shall be taken, and the other shall be left.*
[5] Or, *vultures*

Luke 17 26-27 ‖ Matt. 24 37-39: Gen. 6 11-13; 7 7, 21-23. Luke 17 28-29: Gen. 18 20 *ff.*; 19 16, 24-25. Luke 17 32: Gen. 19 26.

§ 181. The Parable of the Unrighteous Judge

Luke 18 1-8

cp. 12 40, 42.

1 And he spake a parable unto them to the end that they ought always to pray, and not to faint; **2** saying, There was in a city a judge, which feared not God, and regarded not man: **3** and there was a widow [cp. 2 37; 4 25, 26; 7 12; 20 47; 21 2] in that city; and she came oft unto him, saying, [1] Avenge

cp. 26 10.	*cp.* 14 6.	me of mine adversary. **4** And he would not for a while: but afterward he said within himself, Though I fear not God, nor regard man; **5** yet because this widow troubleth me [*cp.* 11 7], I will avenge her, lest she ² wear me out by her continual coming [*cp.* 11 8]. **6** And the Lord [*cp.* 7 13, 19; 10 1, 39, 41; 11 39; 12 42; 13 15; 17 5, 6; 19 8; 22 61; 24 3, 34] said, Hear what ³ the unrighteous judge [*cp.* 16 8, 9: *also* 13 27] saith. **7** And shall not God avenge [*cp.* 21 22] his elect, which cry to him day and night, and he is longsuffering over them? **8** I say unto you, that he will avenge them speedily. Howbeit when the Son of man cometh, shall he find ⁴ faith on the earth?	*cp.* 4 1; 6 23; 11 2; 20 2, 18, 20, 25; 21 7, 12.
	cp. 16 19, 20.		
cp. 24 22, 24, 31.	*cp.* 13 20, 22, 27.		

¹ Or, *Do me justice of*: and so in ver. 5, 7, 8.
² Gr. *bruise*.   ³ Gr. *the judge of unrighteousness*.   ⁴ Or, *the faith*

§ 182. The Parable of the Pharisee and the Publican

[*Cp.* Matt. 9 13; 21 31: Mark 2 17: Luke 5 32; 7 29-30, 47; 15 7, 10; 19 10]

Luke 18 9-14

9 And he spake also this parable unto certain which trusted in themselves that they were righteous, and set ¹ all others at nought: **10** Two men went up into the temple to pray; the one a Pharisee, and the other a publican. **11** The Pharisee stood and prayed thus with himself, God, I thank thee, that I am not as the rest of men, extortioners, unjust, adulterers, or even as this publican. **12** I fast twice in the week; I give tithes of all that I get. **13** But the publican, standing afar off, would not lift up so much as his eyes unto heaven, but smote his breast [*cp.* 23 48], saying, God, ² be merciful to me ³ a sinner. **14** I say unto you, This man went down to his house justified rather than the other:

Matt. 23 12 And whosoever shall exalt himself shall be humbled; and whosoever shall humble himself [*cp.* 18 4] shall be exalted.		Luke 14 11 For every one that exalteth himself shall be humbled; and he that humbleth himself shall be exalted.	for every one that exalteth himself shall be humbled; but he that humbleth himself shall be exalted.

¹ Gr. *the rest*.
² Or, *be propitiated*
³ Or, *the sinner*

(x) In 'the Borders of Judæa and beyond Jordan' (§§ 183-189)

§ 183. General Teaching (Mark) and Healing (Matt.)

[*Cp.* § 134]

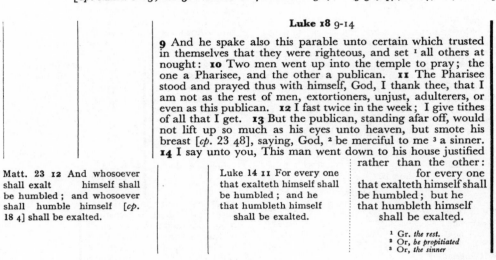

Matt. 19 1-2	Mark 10 1	Luke 9 51
1 And it came to pass when Jesus had finished these words [*cp.* 7 28; 11 1; 13 53; 26 1],	**1** And	**51** And it came to pass, when
		cp. 7 1.
		the days ¹ were well-nigh come that he should be received up, he stedfastly set his face to go to Jerusalem [*cp.* 9 53; 13 22; 17 11; 19 11, 41: *also* 9 31; 13 33; 18 31],
cp. 16 21; 20 17, 18.	*cp.* 10 32, 33.	
he departed from Galilee, and came into the borders of Judæa beyond Jordan; **2** and great multitudes followed him; and he healed them there.	he arose from thence, and cometh into the borders of Judæa and beyond Jordan: and multitudes come together unto him again; and, as he was wont, he taught them again.	*cp.* 10 40.

¹ Gr. *were being fulfilled*.

§ 184. **A Question about Divorce**

Matt. 19 3-12

3 And there came unto him [1] Pharisees, tempting [*cp.* 16 1; 22 35: *also* 22 18] him, and saying, Is it lawful [*cp.* 12 10; 22 17] *for a man* to put away his wife for every cause?   **4** And he answered and said,

verses 7 and 8

Have ye not read [*cp.* 12 3, 5; 21 16, 42; 22 31], that he which [2] made *them* from the beginning   made them male and female, **5** and said, For this cause shall a man leave his father and mother, and shall cleave to his wife; and the twain shall become one flesh? **6** So that they are no more twain, but one flesh. What therefore God hath joined together, let not man put asunder. **7** They say unto him, Why then did Moses command to give a bill of divorcement, and to put *her* away [*cp.* 5 31]? **8** He saith unto them, Moses for your hardness of heart suffered you to put away your wives: but from the beginning it hath not been so.

cp. 13 36; 17 25.

9 And I say unto you, Whosoever shall put away his wife, [3] except for fornication, and shall marry another, committeth adultery:

[4] and he that marrieth her when she is put away committeth adultery.

10 The disciples say unto him, If the case of the man is so with his wife, it is not expedient to marry. **11** But he said unto them, All men cannot receive this saying [*cp.* verse 12], but they to whom it is given [*cp.* 13 11]. **12** For there are eunuchs, which were so born from their mother's womb: and there are eunuchs, which were made eunuchs by men: and there are eunuchs, which made themselves eunuchs for the kingdom of heaven's

Matt. 5 32 But I say unto you, that every one that putteth away his wife, saving for the cause of fornication   maketh her an adulteress: and whosoever shall marry her when she is put away   committeth adultery.

Mark 10 2-12

2 And there came unto him Pharisees,   and asked him, Is it lawful [*cp.* 3 4; 12 14] for a man to put away *his* wife? tempting [*cp.* 8 11: *also* 12 15] him. **3** And he answered and said unto them, What did Moses command you? **4** And they said, Moses suffered to write a bill of divorcement, and to put her away. **5** But Jesus said unto them, For your hardness of heart [*cp.* 3 5: *also* 6 52; 8 17; 16 14] he wrote you this commandment. **6** But   *cp.* 2 25; 12 10, 26.   from the beginning of the creation [*cp.* 13 19; 16 15],   Male and female made he them. **7** For this cause shall a man leave his father and mother, [1] and shall cleave to his wife; **8** and the twain shall become one flesh: so that they are no more twain, but one flesh. **9** What therefore God hath joined together, let not man put asunder.

verses 3-5

10 And in the house [*cp.* 7 17; 9 28, 33] the disciples asked him again of this matter. **11** And he saith unto them, Whosoever shall put away his wife,   and marry another, committeth adultery against her:

12 and if she herself shall put away her husband, and marry another, she committeth adultery.

[1] Some ancient authorities omit *and shall cleave to his wife.*

Luke 16 18

Every one that putteth away his wife,   and marrieth another, committeth adultery:

and he that marrieth one that is put away from a husband committeth adultery.

cp. 10 25; 11 16.   cp. 8 6.

cp. 6 9; 14 3; 20 22.

cp. 10 25; 11 16.   cp. 8 6.

cp. 12 40.

cp. 6 3; 10 26.

cp. 4 11.   cp. 8 10.   cp. 8 37.

sake. He that is able to receive it, let him receive it [cp. verse 11: also 11 15; 13 9, 43].	cp. **4** 9, 23; **7** 16.	cp. **8** 8; **14** 35.	cp. **8** 37: also **6** 60.

1 Many authorities, some ancient, insert *the*.
2 Some ancient authorities read *created*.
3 Some ancient authorities read *saving for the cause of fornication, maketh her an adulteress*: as in ch. **5** 32.
4 The following words, to the end of the verse, are omitted by some ancient authorities.

Matt. 19 4 ‖ Mark 10 6 = Gen. 1 27; 5 2.   Matt. 19 5 ‖ Mark 10 7-8 = Gen. 2 24.
Matt. 19 7 ‖ Mark 10 4 : Deut. 24 1.

§ 185. The Blessing of Little Children

Matt. 19 13-15	**Mark 10** 13-16	**Luke 18** 15-17	John 3 3, 5
13 Then were there brought unto him little children, that he should lay his hands on them [cp. **8** 3, 15; **9** 18, 25, 29; **14** 31; **17** 7; **20** 34: also **9** 20; **14** 36], and pray: and the disciples rebuked them [cp. **15** 23; **26** 8-9]. **14** But Jesus	**13** And they brought unto him little children, that he should touch them [cp. **1** 31, 41; **5** 23, 41; **6** 2, 5; **7** 33; **8** 22, 23, 25; **9** 27: also **3** 10; **5** 27; **6** 56]: and the disciples rebuked them [cp. **14** 4-5]. **14** But when Jesus saw it, he was moved with indignation, and	**15** And they brought unto him also their babes, that he should touch them [cp. **4** 40; **5** 13; **7** 14; **8** 54; **13** 13; **14** 4; **22** 51: also **6** 19; **7** 39; **8** 44]: but when the disciples saw it, they rebuked them. **16** But Jesus	cp. **9** 6: also **20** 17.

cp. **12** 5. |
| said, Suffer [cp. **26** 10] the little children,   and forbid them not,   to come unto me: for of such is the kingdom of heaven. **18** 3 Verily I say unto you, Except ye turn, and become   as little children, | said unto them, Suffer [cp. **14** 6] the little children to come unto me; forbid them not [cp. **9** 39]:   for of such is the kingdom of God. **15** Verily I say unto you,   Whosoever shall not receive the kingdom of God as a little child, | called them unto him, saying, Suffer   the little children to come unto me, and forbid them not [cp. **9** 50]:   for of such is the kingdom of God. **17** Verily I say unto you,   Whosoever shall not receive the kingdom of God as a little child, | cp. **12** 7.

3 3 Verily, verily, I say unto thee, Except a man be born 1 anew, he cannot see the kingdom of God. . . .5 Verily, verily, I say unto thee, Except a man be born of water and the Spirit, he |
| ye shall in no wise enter [cp. **5** 20; **7** 21; **19** 23, 24; **21** 31; **23** 13: also **7** 13; **18** 8, 9; **19** 17; **25** 21, 23] into the kingdom of heaven. **15** And he   laid his hands on them [cp. verse 13], and departed thence. | he shall in no wise enter [cp. **9** 47; **10** 23, 24, 25: also **9** 43, 45]   therein. **16** And he took them in his arms [cp. **9** 36], and blessed them, laying his hands upon them [cp. verse 13]. | he shall in no wise enter [cp. **18** 24, 25: also **11** 52; **13** 24; **24** 26]   therein.

cp. verse 15. | cannot   enter [cp. **10** 1, 2, 9]   into the kingdom of God.

1 Or, *from above* |

§ 186. A Question about Inheriting Eternal Life

Matt. 19 16-22	**Mark 10** 17-22	**Luke 18** 18-23	
16 And behold, one came to him and cp. **17** 14: and **2** 11; **8** 2; etc. said, 1, 2 Master, what good thing shall I do,	**17** And as he was going forth 1 into the way, there ran one to him, and kneeled to him [cp. **1** 40: and **3** 11; etc.], and asked him, Good 2 Master, what shall I do	**18** And a certain ruler cp. **5** 8, 12; etc. asked him, saying, Good 1 Master, what shall I do [cp. **3** 10, 12, 14;	cp. **9** 38; **11** 32; **18** 6.

cp. **6** 28. |

that I may have eternal life [*cp.* 19 29: *also* 25 46]? **17** And he said unto him, ³ Why askest thou me concerning that which is good?

One there is who is good: but if thou wouldest enter into life [*cp.* 18 8, 9: *also* 5 20; 7 21; 18 3; 19 23, 24; 21 31; 23 13: *and* 7 13; 25 21, 23], keep the commandments. **18** He saith unto him, Which? And Jesus said, Thou shalt not kill, Thou shalt not commit adultery, Thou shalt not steal, Thou shalt not bear false witness, **19** Honour thy father and thy mother: and, Thou shalt love thy neighbour as thyself [*cp.* 22 39]. **20** The young man saith unto him, All these things have I observed:

what lack I yet?

21 Jesus said unto him, If thou wouldest be perfect [*cp.* 5 48], go, sell that thou hast, and give to the poor, and thou shalt have treasure in heaven [*cp.* 6 19-21]: and come, follow me [*cp.* 4 19; 8 22; 9 9; 16 24]. **22** But when the young man heard the saying, he went away sorrowful: for he was one that had great possessions.

¹ Or, *Teacher*
² Some ancient authorities read *Good Master*. See Mark 10 17; Luke 18 18.
³ Some ancient authorities read *Why callest thou me good? None is good save one*, even *God*. See Mark 10 18; Luke 18 19.

---

that I may inherit eternal life [*cp.* 10 30]? **18** And Jesus said unto him, Why callest thou me good? none is good save one, *even* God. **19** Thou knowest [*cp.* 9 43, 45: *also* 9 47; 10 15, 23, 24, 25] the commandments,

Do not kill, Do not commit adultery, Do not steal, Do not bear false witness, Do not defraud, Honour thy father and mother.

cp. 12 31.

20 And he said unto him, ² Master, all these things have I observed from my youth.

21 And Jesus looking upon him loved him [*cp.* 12 34], and said unto him, One thing thou lackest:

go, sell whatsoever thou hast, and give to the poor, and thou shalt have treasure in heaven: and come, follow me [*cp.* 1 17; 2 14; 8 34]. **22** But his countenance fell at the saying, and he went away sorrowful: for he was one that had great possessions.

¹ Or, *on his way*　² Or, *Teacher*

---

10 25] to inherit eternal life [*cp.* 18 30: *also* 10 25]? **19** And Jesus said unto him, Why callest thou me good? none is good, save one, *even* God. **20** Thou knowest [*cp.* 18 17, 24, 25: *also* 11 52; 13 24: *and* 24 26] the commandments,

Do not commit adultery, Do not kill, Do not steal, Do not bear false witness, Honour thy father and mother.

cp. 10 27.

21 And he said, All these things have I observed from my youth up. **22** And when Jesus heard it, he said unto him, One thing thou lackest yet:

sell all that thou hast [*cp.* 12 33: *also* 22 36], and distribute unto the poor, and thou shalt have treasure in heaven [*cp.* 12 33, 34: *also* 12 21]: and come, follow me [*cp.* 5 27; 9 23, 59]. **23** But when he heard these things, he became exceeding sorrowful; for he was very rich.

¹ Or, *Teacher*

---

cp. 3 15; *etc.*

cp. 3 5: *also* 10 1, 2, 9.

cp. 1 43; 12 26; 21 19, 22.

Matt. 19 18, 19a ‖ Mark 10 19 ‖ Luke 18 20: Exod. 20 12-16; Deut. 5 16-20.　　　Matt. 19 19b: Lev. 19 18.

§ 187. Sayings on the Danger of Riches and the Rewards of Discipleship. The Parable of the Labourers in the Vineyard

[*Cp.* Luke 16 1-31]

[*Cp.* Matt. 10 16-42; 16 24-28: Mark 8 34-9 1; 13 9-13: Luke 9 23-27; 21 12-19; 22 28-30: John 14 2-3]

Matt. 19 23-20 16	**Mark 10** 23-31	**Luke 18** 24-30	
23 And Jesus said unto his disciples, Verily I say unto you, It is hard for a rich man to enter into the kingdom of heaven [*cp.* 5 20; 7 21; 18 3; 19 24; 21 31; 23 13: *also* 18 8, 9; 19 17: *and*	**23** And Jesus looked round about [*cp.* 3 5, 34; 5 32; 9 8; 11 11], and saith unto his disciples, How hardly shall they that have riches enter into the kingdom of God [*cp.* 9 47; 10 15, 24, 25: *also* 9 43, 45]!	**24** And Jesus seeing him *cp.* 6 10. said, How hardly shall they that have riches enter into the kingdom of God [*cp.* 18 17, 25: *also* 11 52; 13 24: *and* 24 26]!	*cp.* 3 5: *also* 10 1, 2, 9.

Matthew

1 73; 25 21, 23]. **24** And

cp. 7 28; 13 54; 19 25; 22 22, 33: *also* 8 27; *etc.*

again ...... I say unto you,

...... It is easier for a camel to go through a needle's eye, than for a rich man to enter into the kingdom of God [*see verse* 23]. **25** And when the disciples heard it, they were astonished exceedingly [*see verse* 24], saying, ... Who then can be saved? **26** And Jesus looking upon *them* said to them,

...... With men this is impossible; but ...... with God all things are possible [*cp.* 17 20]. **27** Then answered Peter [*cp.* 14 28; 15 15; 16 22; 17 4; 18 21; 26 33: *also* 16 16; 17 24] ...... and said unto him, Lo, we have left all, ... and followed thee [*cp.* 4 20, 22; 9 9]; what then shall we have? **28** And Jesus said unto them, Verily I say unto you, that ye ...... which have followed ...... me,

in the regeneration when the Son of man shall sit on the throne of his glory [*cp.* 25 31: *also* 16 27],

cp. 8 11; 26 29.

[*cp.* 16 28; 20 21] ...... ye also shall sit upon twelve thrones, judging the twelve tribes of Israel. **29** And every one ...... that hath left houses, ... or brethren, or sisters, ... or father, or mother, [1] or children [*cp.* 10 37], or lands, for my name's sake [*cp.* 10 22; 24 9: *also* 5 11; 10 18, 39; 16 25], *cp.* 4 23; 9 35; 24 14; 26 13.

...... shall receive[2] a hundredfold [*cp.* 13 8, 23: *and* 6 33],

cp. 13 21.

...... and [*cp.* 12 32] shall inherit eternal life [*cp.* 19 16: *also* 25 46]. **30** But many shall be last *that are* first; and

Mark

24 And the disciples were amazed at his words [*cp.* 1 22, 27; 6 2; 10 26; 11 18; 12 17: *also* 2 12; *etc.*]. But Jesus answereth again, and saith unto them, Children, how hard is it [1] for them that trust in riches to enter into the kingdom of God [*see verse* 23]! **25** It is easier for a camel to go through a needle's eye, than for a rich man to enter into the kingdom of God [*see verse* 23]. **26** And ...... they were astonished exceedingly [*see verse* 24], saying [2] unto him, Then who can be saved? **27** Jesus looking upon them saith,

...... With men it is impossible, but not with God: for all things are possible with God [*cp.* 14 36: *also* 9 23]. **28** Peter [*cp.* 8 32; 9 5; 11 21; 14 29: *also* 8 29] ...... began to say unto him, Lo, we have left all, ... and have followed thee [*cp.* 1 18, 20; 2 14].

29 Jesus said, Verily I say unto you,

cp. 10 37: *also* 8 38.

cp. 14 25.

...... There is no man that hath left house, ... or brethren, or sisters, or mother, or father, or children, ... or lands, for my sake [*cp.* 8 35; 13 9: *also* 13 13], ... and for the gospel's sake [*cp.* 8 35: *also* 1 1, 14, 15; 13 10; 14 9; 16 15],

30 but he shall receive a hundredfold [*cp.* 4 8, 20, *and* 24] now in this time, houses, and brethren, and sisters, and mothers, and children, and lands, with persecutions [*cp.* 4 17]; and in the [3] world to come eternal life [*cp.* 10 17]. **31** But many *that are* first shall be last; ...... and

Luke

cp. 2 47, 48; 4 22, 32, 36; 20 26: *also* 5 9; *etc.*

25 For it is easier for a camel to enter in through a needle's eye, than for a rich man to enter into the kingdom of God [*see verse* 24]. **26** And ...... they that heard it ...... said, ... Then who can be saved? **27** But he ...... said, The things which are impossible with men ...... are possible with God [*cp.* 1 37]. **28** And ...... Peter [*cp.* 8 45; 9 33; 12 41: *also* 5 8; 9 20] ...... said, Lo, we have left [*cp.* 5 11, 28; 14 33] [1] our own, and followed thee [*cp.* 5 11, 28].

29 And he said unto them, Verily I say unto you, 22 **28** But ye are they which have continued with me in my temptations [*cp.* 4 13; 8 13];

[*cp.* 9 26, 32; 24 26] **29** and [2] I appoint unto you a kingdom, even as my Father appointed unto me, **30** that ye may eat and drink at my table [*cp.* 13 29; 14 15; 22 16, 18] in my kingdom [*cp.* 23 42]; and ye shall sit on thrones judging the twelve tribes of Israel.

...... There is no man that hath left house, or wife [*cp.* 14 26], or brethren, ... or parents, or children [*cp.* 14 26],

cp. 6 22; 9 24; 21 12, 17.

for the kingdom of God's sake, **30** who shall not receive [*cp.* 8 8] manifold more [*cp.* 12 31] in this time,

...... and in the [3] world to come eternal life [*cp.* 18 18: *also* 10 25].

13 **30** And

John (marginal references)

cp. 7 15, 21, 46.

see above.

see above.

cp. 13 36, 37; 21 21: *also* 6 68.

cp. Joh 13 36-14...

cp. 1 14; 2 11; 12 41; 17 5, 22, 24.

cp. 18 36.

cp. 15 21.

cp. 3 15; *etc.*

the last
first.

behold, there are last which shall be first, and there are first which shall be last.

first *that are* last [*cp.* 20 8, 16].
20 **1** For the kingdom of heaven is like unto a man that is a householder [*cp.* 13 52; 21 33: *also* 13 27 *and* Luke 14 21], which went out early in the morning to hire labourers into his vineyard [*cp.* 21 28, 33]. **2** And when he had agreed with the labourers for a ³ penny a day, he sent them into his vineyard. **3** And he went out about the third hour, and saw others standing in the marketplace idle; **4** and to them he said, Go ye also into the vineyard [*cp.* 21 28], and whatsoever is right I will give you. And they went their way. **5** Again he went out about the sixth and the ninth hour, and did likewise. **6** And about the eleventh *hour* he went out, and found others standing; and he saith unto them, Why stand ye here all the day idle? **7** They say unto him, Because no man hath hired us. He saith unto them, Go ye also into the vineyard [*cp.* 21 28]. **8** And when even was come, the lord of the vineyard [*cp.* 21 40] saith unto his steward, Call the labourers, and pay them their hire, beginning from the last unto the first [*cp.* 19 30; 20 16]. **9** And when they came that *were hired* about the eleventh hour, they received every man a ³ penny. **10** And when the first came, they supposed that they would receive more; and they likewise received every man a ³ penny. **11** And when they received it, they murmured against the householder, **12** saying, These last have spent *but* one hour, and thou hast made them equal unto us, which have borne the burden of the day and the ⁴ scorching heat. **13** But he answered and said to one of them, Friend [*cp.* 22 12; 26 50], I do thee no wrong: didst not thou agree with me for a ³ penny? **14** Take up that which is thine, and go thy way; it is my will to give unto this last, even as unto thee. **15** Is it not lawful for me to do what I will with mine own? or is thine eye evil [*cp.* 6 23], because I am good? **16** So the last shall be first, and the first last [*cp.* 19 30; 20 8].

¹ Some ancient authorities omit *for them that trust in riches.*
² Many ancient authorities read *among themselves.*
³ Or, *age*

¹ Or, *our own* homes
² Or, *I appoint unto you, even as my Father appointed unto me a kingdom, that ye may eat and drink &c.*
³ Or, *age*

cp. 12 1.

cp. 13 6; 20 9.

cp. 12 9.

cp. 20 13, 15.

cp. 7 22.

cp. 11 34.

¹ Many ancient authorities add *or wife*: as in Luke 18 29.
² Some ancient authorities read *manifold*.   ³ See marginal note on ch. 18 28.
⁴ Or, *hot wind*

§ 188. The Third Prediction of the Passion and Resurrection

[*Cp.* Matt. 16 21-23 ‖ Mark 8 31-33 ‖ Luke 9 22; Matt. 17 22-23 ‖ Mark 9 30-32 ‖ Luke 9 43b-45: *also* Matt. 17 9, 12; 20 28; 26 2, 12, 18, 24, 32, 45; Mark 9 9, 12; 10 45; 14 8, 21, 28, 41: Luke 13 32-33; 17 25; 22 22; 24 7, *and* 26, 44, 46: John 2 19-22; 3 14; 12 32-33]

Matt. 20 17-19	Mark 10 32-34	Luke 18 31-34	
17 And as Jesus was going up to Jerusalem,	**32** And they were in the way, going up to Jerusalem; and Jesus was going before them: and they	*cp.* 19 28: *also* 9 51, 53; 13 22; 17 11.	
cp. 8 27; 9 33; 12 23; 15 31; 21 20; 27 14: *also* 7 28; 13 54; 19 25; 22 22, 33.	were amazed [*cp.* 2 12; 5 20, 42; 6 51; 7 37; 15 5; 16 5, 8: *also* 1 22, 27; 6 2; 10 24, 26; 11 18; 12 17]; ¹ and they	*cp.* 5 9, 26; 8 25, 56; 9 43; 11 14; 24 12, 41: *also* 2 47, 48; 4 22, 32, 36; 20 26.	*cp.* 7 15, 21, 46.
cp. 17 6: *also* 9 8; 27 54; 28 4, 8.	that followed were afraid [*cp.* 4 41; 9 6, 32: *also* 5 15, 33; 16 8]. And he	*cp.* 8 25; 9 34, 45; 24 5, 37: *also* 1 12, 65; 2 9; 5 26; 7 16; 8 35, 37, 47. **31** And he	
he took the twelve disciples apart [*cp.* 17 1, 19; 24 3], and in the way he	took again the twelve, [*cp.* 4 10, 34; 6 31, 32; 9 2, 28; 13 3] and began to tell them the things that were to happen unto him, **33** *saying*, Behold, we go up to Jerusalem; and	took unto him the twelve, [*cp.* 9 10; 10 23] and	
said unto them, **18** Behold, we go up to Jerusalem [*cp.* 16 21]; and		said unto them, Behold, we go up to Jerusalem [*cp.* 9 31, 51; 13 33], and all	

Matt.	Mark	Luke	
		the things that are written [1] by the prophets [*cp.* 20 17; 22 37; 24 25-27, 44-46] shall be accomplished [*cp.* 12 50; 22 37: *also* 13 32] unto the Son of man. **32** For he shall be delivered up	*cp.* 5 39; 13 18; 15 25; 17 12. *cp.* 4 34; 5 36; 17 4; 19 28, 30.
cp. 21 42; 26 24, 31, 54, 56.	*cp.* 9 12; 12 10; 14 21, 27, 49.		
the Son shall be of man delivered unto the chief priests and scribes; and they shall condemn him to death, **19** and shall deliver him unto the Gentiles to mock [*cp.* 27 27-31: *also* 27 41],	the Son shall of man delivered unto the chief priests and the scribes; and they shall condemn him to death, and shall deliver him unto the Gentiles: **34** and they shall mock [*cp.* 15 16-20: *also* 15 31] him, and shall spit upon [*cp.* 15 19: *also* 14 65] him, and shall scourge [*cp.* 15 15] him, and shall kill him;	unto the Gentiles, and shall be mocked [*cp.* 23 36: *also* 22 63; 23 11, 35], and shamefully entreated, and spit upon: **33** and they shall scourge and kill him:	*cp.* 19 2-3. *cp.* 19 1.
cp. 27 30: *also* 26 67. and to scourge [*cp.* 27 26], and to crucify [*cp.* Luke 24 7: *also* Matt. 23 34]: *cp.* 27 63. and the third day [*cp.* 16 21; 17 23: *also* 12 40; 26 61; 27 40, 64] he shall [*cp.* 17 9] be raised up [*cp.* 16 21; 17 23; 26 32; 27 63, 64; 28 6, 7].	and after three days [*cp.* 8 31; 9 31: *also* 14 58; 15 29] he shall rise again [*cp.* 8 31; 9 9, 31; 16 9]. *cp.* 14 28; 16 6, 14.	and the third day [*cp.* 9 22; 13 32; 24 7, 46: *also* 24 21] he shall rise again [*cp.* 24 7, 46]. *cp.* 9 22; 24 6, 34.	*cp.* 2 19. *cp.* 20 9. *cp.* 2 19-22; 21 14.
cp. 15 16; 16 8-12.	*cp.* 4 13; 6 52; 7 18; 8 17-21; 9 10, 32.	**34** And they understood none of these things [*cp.* 2 50; 9 45]; and this saying was hid from them, and they perceived not the things that were said.	*cp.* 10 6; 12 16: *also* 3 10; 4 33; 8 27, 43; 11 13; 13 7, 28, 36; 14 5-10; 16 17, 18.

[1] Or, *but some as they followed were afraid* (Mark)

[1] Or, *through* (Luke)

§ 189. Rivalry among the Disciples and Sayings of Rebuke

[*Cp.* Matt. 18 1–14; Mark 9 33-50; Luke 9 46-50]

Matt. 20 20-28	Mark 10 35-45		
20 Then came to him the mother [*cp.* 27 56] of the sons of Zebedee with her sons, worshipping *him* [*cp.* 2 11; 8 2; 9 18; 14 33; 15 25; 28 9, 17: *also* 17 14], and	**35** And there come near unto him James and John, the sons of Zebedee, *cp.* 5 6: *also* 1 40; 3 11; 5 22, 33; 7 25; 10 17. saying unto him, [1] Master, we would that thou shouldest do for us whatsoever we shall ask	*cp.* 9 54. *cp.* 24 52: *also* 5 8, 12; *etc.*	*cp.* 9 38; 11 32; 18 6.
asking a certain thing of him. **21** And he said unto her, What wouldest thou [*cp.* 20 32]? She saith unto him, Command that these my two sons may sit, one on thy right hand, and one on thy left hand, in thy [*cp.* 19 28; 25 31: *also* 16 27] kingdom [*cp.* 16 28]. **22** But Jesus answered and said, Ye know not what ye ask. Are ye able to drink the cup [*cp.* 26 39] that I am about to drink?	of thee. **36** And he said unto them, What would ye that I should do for you [*cp.* 10 51]? **37** And they said unto him, Grant unto us that we may sit, one on thy right hand, and one on *thy* left hand, in thy glory [*cp.* 8 38]. **38** But Jesus said unto them, Ye know not what ye ask. Are ye able to drink the cup [*cp.* 14 36] that I	*cp.* 18 41. *cp.* 9 26, 32; 24 26: *and* 22 29, 30; 23 42. *cp.* 22 42.	*cp.* 1 14; 2 11; 12 41; 17 5, 22, 24; *and* 18 36. *cp.* 18 11.
They say unto him, We are able. **23** He saith unto them, My cup indeed ye shall drink:	drink? or to be baptized with the baptism that I am baptized with? **39** And they said unto him, We are able. And Jesus said unto them, The cup that I drink ye shall drink; and with the baptism that I am baptized withal shall ye be baptized:	*cp.* 12 50.	
but to sit on my right hand, and on	**40** but to sit on my right hand or on		

my left hand, is not mine to give, but *it is for them* for whom it hath been prepared [*cp.* 25 34] of my Father. **24** And when the ten heard it, they were moved with indignation concerning the two brethren.

cp. 18 1.

25 But Jesus called them unto him, and said, Ye know that the rulers of the Gentiles lord it over them, and their great ones exercise authority over them. **26** Not so shall it be among you: but whosoever would become great among you shall be your ¹ minister; **27** and whosoever would be first among you shall be your ² servant:

23 11 But he that is ³ greatest among you shall be your ⁴ servant.

28 even as the Son of man came [*cp.* 18 11] not to be ministered unto, but to minister, and to give his life a ransom for many [*cp.* 26 28].

¹ Or, *servant*   ² Gr. *bondservant.*
³ Gr. *greater.*   ⁴ Or, *minister*

---

my left hand is not mine to give: but *it is for them* for whom it hath been prepared. **41** And when the ten heard it, they began to be moved with indignation concerning James and John.

cp. 9 33-34.

42 And Jesus called them to him, and saith unto them, Ye know that they which are accounted to rule over the Gentiles lord it over them; and their great ones exercise authority over them. **43** But it is not so among you: but whosoever would become great among you, shall be your ² minister: **44** and whosoever would be first among you, shall be ³ servant of all.

9 35 If any man would be first, he shall be last of all, and minister of all.

45 For verily the Son of man came not to be ministered unto, but to minister, and to give his life a ransom for many [*cp.* 14 24].

¹ Or, *Teacher*   ² Or, *servant*
³ Gr. *bondservant.*

Luke 22 **24** And there arose also a contention among them [*cp.* 9 46], which of them is accounted to be ¹ greatest. **25** And he said unto them, The kings of the Gentiles have lordship over them; and they that have authority over them are called Benefactors. **26** But ye *shall* not *be* so: but he that is the greater among you, let him become as the younger; and he that is chief, as he that doth serve. **9 48** For he that is ² least among you all, the same is great. **22 27** For whether is greater, he that ³ sitteth at meat, or he that serveth? is not he that ³ sitteth at meat [*cp.* 17 7-8]? but I am in the midst [*cp.* 9 55; 19 10] of you as he that serveth [*cp.* 12 37].

¹ Gr. *greater.*   ² Gr. *lesser.*
³ Gr. *reclineth.*

---

cp. John 13 2-17.

cp. 10 11, 15, 17; 11 51, 52.

Matt. 20 28 ‖ Mark 10 45: *cp.* Is. 52 15; 53 4-6, 8, 11, 12.

(xi) At Jericho (§§ 190-193)

§ 190. **The Healing of a Blind Man** (Mark and Luke: **of Two Blind Men,** Matt.)

[*Cp.* Matt. 9 27-31; 12 22; 15 30-31; 21 14: Mark 8 22-26: Luke 7 21: John 9 1-7]

Matt. 20 29-34	**Mark 10** 46-52	**Luke 18** 35-43	
29 And as they went out from Jericho, a great multitude followed him. **30** And behold, two [*cp.* 8 28; 9 27] blind men sitting by the way side,	**46** And they come to Jericho: and as he went out from Jericho, with his disciples and a great multitude, the son of Timæus, Bartimæus, a blind beggar, was sitting by the way side.	**35** And it came to pass, as he drew nigh unto Jericho, a certain blind man sat by the way side begging: **36** and hearing a multitude going by, he inquired what this meant. **37** And they told him, that Jesus of Nazareth [*cp.* 4 34; 24 19] passeth by. **38** And he cried, saying, Jesus, [*cp.* 18 41: *and* 5 8, 12; *etc.*]	*cp.* 9 8.
when they heard that Jesus [*cp.* 2 23; 21 11; 26 71] was passing by, cried out, saying, Lord [*cp.* 8 25; 17 4, 15; 20 33: *and* 7 21; 8 2; *etc.*], have mercy on us	**47** And when he heard that it was Jesus of Nazareth [*cp.* 1 24; 14 67; 16 6], he began to cry out, and say, Jesus, [*cp.* 7 28]		*cp.* 1 45; 18 5, 7; 19 19. *cp.* 4 11, 15; *etc.*

[cp. 9 27; 15 22; 17 15; 20 31], thou son of David [cp. 1 1; 9 27; 12 23; 15 22; 20 31; 21 9, 15].
31 And the multitude [cp. 21 9] rebuked them, that they should hold their peace: but they cried out the more, saying, Lord, have mercy on us thou son of David.
32 And Jesus stood still, and called them,

cp. 9 2, 22; 14 27.

and said, What will ye [cp. 20 21] that I should do unto you?
33 They say unto him, Lord [cp. 8 25; 17 4, 15; 20 30: and 7 21; 8 2; etc.], cp. 26 25, 49: also 23 7, 8. that our eyes may be opened. 34 And Jesus, being moved with compassion [cp. 9 36; 14 14; 15 32], touched [cp. 8 3, 15; 9 18, 25, 29; 14 31; 17 7; 19 13, 15: also 9 20; 14 36] their eyes: cp. 8 3, 8, 13, 16, 32; 9 6, 22, 29; 12 13; 15 28; 17 7, 18.

cp. 9 22.
and straightway they received their sight, and followed him.
cp. 9 8; 15 31: also 5 16.

---

thou son of David,
have mercy on me.
48 And many [cp. 11 9] rebuked him, that he should hold his peace: but he cried out the more a great deal, Thou son of David, have mercy on me.
49 And Jesus stood still, and said, Call ye him.
And they call the blind man, saying unto him, Be of good cheer [cp. 6 50]: rise, he calleth thee. 50 And he, casting away his garment, sprang up, and came to Jesus. 51 And Jesus answered him, and said, What wilt thou [cp. 10 36] that I should do unto thee? And the blind man said unto him, [cp. 7 28]

Rabboni [cp. 9 5; 11 21; 14 45], that I may receive my sight. 52 And Jesus
cp. 1 41; 6 34; 8 2.
cp. 1 31, 41; 5 23, 41; 6 2, 5; 7 33; 8 22, 23, 25; 9 27; 10 13, 16: also 3 10; 5 27; 6 56.
said [cp. 1 25, 41; 2 11; 3 5; 5 8, 13, 34, 41; 7 29, 34; 9 25] unto him, Go thy way; thy faith hath ¹ made thee whole [cp. 5 34]. And straightway he received his sight, and followed him in the way. cp. 2 12.

¹ Or, *saved thee*

---

thou son of David [cp. 1 32],
have mercy on me [cp. 17 13]. 39 And they that went before rebuked [cp. 19 39] him, that he should hold his peace [cp. 19 40]: but he cried out [cp. 19 40] the more a great deal, Thou son of David, have mercy on me.
40 And Jesus stood, and commanded him to be brought unto him:

and when he was come near, he asked him, 41 What wilt thou that I should do unto thee? And he said, Lord [cp. 5 8, 12; etc.], that I may receive my sight. 42 And Jesus
cp. 7 13: also 10 33; 15 20.
cp. 4 40; 5 13; 7 14; 8 54; 13 13; 14 4; 18 15; 22 51: also 6 19; 7 39; 8 44.
said [cp. 4 35, 39; 5 13, 24; 6 10; 7 7, 14; 8 29, 32, 48, 54; 9 42; 13 12; 17 14] unto him, Receive thy sight: thy faith hath ¹ made thee whole [cp. 7 50; 8 48; 17 19]. 43 And immediately he received his sight, and followed him, glorifying God [cp. 2 20; 5 25, 26; 7 16; 13 13; 17 15; 23 47]: and all the people, when they saw it, gave praise [cp. 2 13, 20; 19 37] unto God.

¹ Or, *saved thee*

---

cp. 16 33.

cp. 4 11, 15; etc.
cp. 20 16: also 1 38; etc.

cp. 9 6; 20 17.

cp. 4 50; 5 8; 9 7; 11 43.

cp. 9 24.

---

§ 191. Zacchæus

[*Cp.* Matt. 9 13; 21 31: Mark 2 17: Luke 5 32; 7 29-30, 47; 15 7, 10; 18 14]

Luke 19 1-10

1 And he entered and was passing through Jericho. 2 And behold, a man called by name Zacchæus; and he was a chief publican, and he was rich. 3 And he sought to see Jesus who he was; and could not for the crowd [cp. 5 19; 8 19], because he was little of stature. 4 And he ran on before, and climbed up into a sycomore tree to see him: for he was to pass that way. 5 And when Jesus came to the place, he looked up, and said unto him, Zacchæus, make haste, and come down; for to-day I must abide at thy house. 6 And he made haste, and came down, and received him joyfully. 7 And when they saw it, they all murmured, saying, He is gone in to lodge with a man that is a sinner [cp. 5 30; 7 34, 39; 15 2]. 8 And Zacchæus

cp. 2 4; 3 9.

cp. 9 11; 11   cp. 2 16.

19: *also* 21 31.	*cp.* 16 19, 20.	stood, and said unto the Lord [*cp.* 7 13, 19; 10 1, 39, 41; 11 39; 12 42; 13 15; 17 5, 6; 18 6; 22 61; 23, 3, 34], Behold, Lord, the half of my goods I give to the poor; and if I have wrongfully exacted aught [*cp.* 3 14] of any man, I restore fourfold. **9** And Jesus said unto him, To-day is salvation [*cp.* 1 69, 71, 77; 2 30; 3 6] come to this house, forasmuch as he also is a son of Abraham [*cp.* 3 8; 13 16; 16 24, 30]. **10** For the Son of man came [*cp.* 9 55] to seek and to save [*cp.* 2 11] that which was lost [*cp.* 15 4, 8].	*cp* 4 1; 6 23; 11 2; 20 2, 18, 20, 25; 21 7, 12.
cp. 3 9. *cp.* 18 11: *also* 20 28: *and* 1 21.	*cp.* 10 45.		*cp.* 4 22. *cp.* 8 33 *ff.* *cp.* 3 17; 4 42; 5 34; 10 9; 12 47.

§ 192. The Parable of the Pounds

[*Cp.* Matt. 24 45-51 : Luke 12 41-48; 16 10-12]

Matt. 25 14-30		Luke 19 11-27	
cp. 16 21; 20 17, 18.	*cp.* 10 32, 33.	**11** And as they heard these things, he added and spake a parable, because he was nigh to Jerusalem [*cp.* 19 41: *also* 9 51, 53; 13 22; 17 11: *and* 9 31; 13 33; 18 31], and *because* they supposed that the kingdom of God was immediately to appear [*cp.* 9 2; 10 9, 11; 11 20; 17 20, 21; 21 8]. **12** He said therefore, A certain nobleman went into a far [*cp.* 15 13] country [*cp.* 20 9], to receive for himself a kingdom, and to return.	
cp. 3 2; 4 17; 10 7; 12 28.	*cp.* 1 15; 6 12.		
14 For *it is* as *when* a man, going into another country [*cp.* 21 33], *cp.* 18 23; 22 2 *ff.*; 25 34, 40.	Mark 13 **34** *It is* as *when* a man, sojourning in another country [*cp.* 12 1],	**13** And he called ten [1] servants of his,	
called his own [1] servants,	having left his house, and given authority to his [1] servants, to each one his work, commanded also the porter to watch.		
and delivered unto them his goods. **15** And unto one he gave five talents [*cp.* 18 24], to another two, to another one; to each according to his several ability;	[1] Gr. *bondservants*.	and gave them ten [2] pounds,	
and he went on his journey [*cp.* 21 33].	*cp.* 12 1.	and said unto them, trade ye *herewith* till I come. *cp.* 20 9. **14** But his citizens hated him, and sent an ambassage [*cp.* 14 32] after him, saying, We will not that this man reign over us.	*cp.* 21 22, 23.
16 Straightway he that received the five talents went and traded with them, and made other five talents. **17** In like manner he also that *received* the two gained other two. **18** But he that received the one went away and digged in the earth, and hid his lord's [*cp.* 18 25, *etc.*] money. **19** Now after a long time the lord of those [1] servants [*cp.* 18 27; 24 50] cometh,			
and maketh a reckoning with them [*cp.* 18 23]. **20** And he that received the five talents came and brought other five talents, saying, Lord, thou deliveredst unto me five talents: lo, I have gained other five talents. **21** His lord said unto him, Well done, good and faith-		**15** And it came to pass, when he [*cp.* 12 46] was come back again, having received the kingdom, that he commanded these [1] servants, unto whom he had given the money, to be called to him, that he might know what they had gained by trading. **16** And the first came before him, saying, Lord, thy pound hath made ten pounds more. **17** And he said unto him, Well done, thou good	

ful [*cp.* 24 45] ² servant :   thou hast been faithful over a few things,   I will set thee over [*cp.* 24 47 *and* 45] many things : enter [*cp.* 7 13 ; *etc.*] thou into the joy of thy lord. **22** And he also that *received* the two talents came and said, Lord, thou deliveredst unto me two talents : lo, I have gained other two talents. **23** His lord said unto him,   Well done, good and faithful [*cp.* 24 45] ² servant ; thou hast been faithful over a few things, I will set thee over [*cp.* 24 47 *and* 45] many things : enter [*cp.* 7 13 ; *etc.*] thou into the joy of thy lord. **24** And he also that had received the one talent came and said, Lord,

            I knew thee   that thou art a hard man,

            reaping where thou didst not sow, and gathering where thou didst not scatter : **25** and I was afraid, and went away and hid thy talent in the earth : lo, thou hast thine own. **26** But his lord answered and said unto him,

        Thou wicked [*cp.* 18 32 : *also* 24 48] and slothful ² servant, thou knewest that I

       reap where I sowed not, and gather where I did not scatter ; **27** thou oughtest therefore to have put   my money to the bankers, and   at my coming I should have received back mine own with interest.

cp. 16 28 ; 26 73 ; 27 47.

28 Take ye away therefore the talent from him,   and give it unto him that hath the ten talents [*cp.* 21 43].

29 For unto every one that hath shall be given, and he shall have abundance : but from him that hath not, even that which he hath shall be taken away.

Matt. 13 12 For whosoever hath, to him shall be given, and he shall have abundance : but whosoever hath not, from him shall be taken away even that which he   hath. **30** And cast ye out the unprofitable ² servant into the outer darkness [*cp.* 8 12 ; 22 13] :

        there shall be the weeping and gnashing of teeth [*cp.* 8 12 ; 13 42, 50 ; 22 13 ; 24 51].

¹ Gr. *bondservants.*   ² Gr. *bondservant.*

---

cp. 9 43 ; *etc.*

cp. 9 43 ; *etc.*

cp. 9 1 ; 11 5 ; 14 47, 69, 70 ; 15 35, 39.

Mark 4 **25** For he that hath, to him shall be given :   and he that hath not, from him shall be taken away even that which he   hath.

[*cp.* 12 42] ³ servant : because thou wast found faithful in a very little [*cp.* 16 10 : *also* 12 26], have thou authority over [*cp.* 12 44 *and* 42] ten cities.   *cp.* 13 24 ; *etc.*

18 And the second   came, saying, Thy pound, Lord,   hath made   five pounds. **19** And he said unto him also,

          cp. 12 42.

       cp. 16 10 : *also* 12 26.

Be thou also over [*cp.* 12 44 *and* 42] five cities.

         cp. 13 24 ; *etc.*

20 And ⁴ another   came, saying, Lord, behold, *here is* thy pound, which I kept laid up in a napkin : **21** for I feared thee, because thou art an austere man : thou takest up that thou layedst not down, and reapest that thou didst not sow.

        22 He   saith unto him, Out of thine own mouth will I judge thee, thou wicked ³ servant. Thou knewest that I am an austere man, taking up that I laid not down, and reaping that I did not sow ;

           23 then wherefore gavest thou not my money into the bank, and ⁵ I at my coming   should have required it   with interest ? **24** And he said unto them that stood by [*cp.* 9 27], Take   away from him the pound, and give it unto him that hath the ten pounds. **25** And they said unto him, Lord, he hath ten pounds. **26** I say unto you, that unto every one that hath shall be given ;   but from him that hath not, even that which he hath shall be taken away from him.

Luke 8 18 For whosoever hath, to him shall be given ;   and whosoever hath not, from him shall be taken away even that which he ⁶ thinketh he hath.

       cp. 17 10.

       27 Howbeit these mine enemies, which would not that I should reign over them, bring hither, and slay them before me.

      cp. 13 28.

¹ Gr. *bondservants.*
² *Mina,* here translated a pound, is equal to one hundred drachmas. See ch. 15 8.
³ Gr. *bondservant.*   ⁴ Gr. *the other.*
⁵ Or, *I should have gone and required*
⁶ Or, *seemeth to have*

---

cp. 3 5 ; 10 1, 2, 9 : *and* 15 11 ; 17 13.

cp. 3 5 ; 10 1, 2, 9 : *and* 15 11 ; 17 13.

cp. 12 29.

§ 193. **Departure from Jericho**

Luke 19 28

cp. 20 17: also 16 21; 20 18.	cp. 10 32: also 10 33.	**28** And when he had thus spoken, he went on before, going up to Jerusalem [cp. 9 51, 53; 13 22; 17 11: also 9 31; 13 33; 18 31; 19 11, 41].

E. The Ministry in Jerusalem (§§ 194-224)

(i) Arrival and Initial Activity (§§ 194-200)

§ 194. **The Triumphal Entry**

Matt. 21 1-11	**Mark 11** 1-10	**Luke 19** 29-40	John 12 12-19
1 And when they drew nigh unto Jerusalem, and came unto Bethphage, unto the mount of Olives, then Jesus sent two disciples, **2** saying unto them, Go into the village that is over against you, and straightway ye shall find an ass tied, and a colt with her: loose *them*, and bring *them* unto me. **3** And if any one say aught unto you, ye shall say, The Lord hath need of them; and straightway he will send them. **4** Now this is come to pass, that it might be fulfilled which was spoken ¹ by the prophet, saying, **5** Tell ye the daughter of Zion, Behold, thy King cometh unto thee, Meek, and riding upon an ass, And upon a colt the foal of an ass. **6** And the disciples went, and did cp. 16 28: 27 47: also 26 73. even as Jesus appointed them [cp. 26 19],	**1** And when they draw nigh unto Jerusalem, unto Bethphage and Bethany, at the mount of Olives, he sendeth two [cp. 14 13: also 6 7] of his disciples, **2** and saith unto them, Go your way into the village that is over against you: and straightway as ye enter into it, ye shall find a colt tied, whereon no man ever yet sat; loose him, and bring him. **3** And if any one say unto you, Why do ye this? say ye, The Lord hath need of him; and straightway he ¹ will send him ² back hither. **4** And they went away, and found a colt tied at the door without in the open street; and they loose him. **5** And certain of them that stood there [cp. 9 1; 14 47; 15 35: also 14 69, 70; 15 39] said unto them, What do ye, loosing the colt? **6** And they said unto them even as Jesus had said: and they let them go.	**29** And it came to pass, when he drew nigh unto Bethphage and Bethany, at the mount that is called *the mount* of Olives, he sent two [cp. 22 8: also 10 1] of the disciples, **30** saying, Go your way into the village over against *you*; in the which as ye enter ye shall find a colt tied, whereon no man ever yet sat [cp. 23 53]: loose him, and bring him. **31** And if any one ask you, Why do ye loose him? thus shall ye say, The Lord hath need of him. **32** And they that were sent went away, and found even as he had said unto them [cp. 22 13]. **33** And as they were loosing the colt, cp. 9 27: also 19 24. the owners thereof said unto them, Why loose ye the colt? **34** And they said, The Lord hath need of him.	cp. 12 1. cp. 19 41. verse 15 cp. 12 29.

7 and brought the ass, and the colt, and put on them their garments; and he sat thereon. **8** And the most part of the multitude

spread their garments in the way; and others cut branches from the trees, and spread them in the way. **9** And

the multitudes that went before him, and that followed, cried,

saying, Hosanna [*cp.* 21 15] to the son of David [*cp.* 1 1; 9 27; 12 23; 15 22; 20 30, 31; 21 15]: Blessed *is* he [*cp.* 2 2; 21 5; 25 34, 40; 27 11, 29, 37, 42] that cometh [*cp.* 3 11; 11 3] in the name of the Lord [=23 39];

cp. 5 9; 10 13.
Hosanna in the highest.

verse 7

verses 4 and 5

cp. 15 16; 16 8-12.

cp. 26 75.

---

7 And they bring the colt unto Jesus, and cast on him their garments; and he sat upon him. **8** And

many

spread their garments upon the way; and others 3 branches, which they had cut from the fields. **9** And

they that went before, and they that followed, cried,

Hosanna; *cp.* 10 47, 48.

Blessed *is* he [*cp.* 15 2, 9, 12, 18, 26, 32] that cometh [*cp.* 1 7] in the name of the Lord: **10** Blessed *is* the kingdom that cometh, *the kingdom* of our father David: *cp.* 9 50.
Hosanna in the highest.

verse 7

cp. 4 13; 6 52; 7 18; 8 17-21; 9 10, 32: *also* 16 14.

---

35 And they brought him to Jesus: and they threw their garments upon the colt, and set Jesus thereon. **36** And

as he went, they spread their garments in the way.

37 And as he was now drawing nigh, *even* at the descent of the mount of Olives, the whole multitude of the disciples *cp.* 18 39. began to rejoice and praise God [*cp.* 2 13, 20; 18 43] with a loud voice for all the 1 mighty works which they had seen; **38** saying, *cp.* 18 38, 39: *also* 1 32.

Blessed *is* the King [*cp.* 23 2, 3, 37, 38: *also* 1 33] that cometh [*cp.* 7 19, 20: *also* 3 16] in the name of the Lord [=13 35]:

peace [*cp.* 2 14: *also* 1 79; 2 29; 19 42] in heaven, and glory in the highest [*cp.* 2 14].

verse 35

cp. 9 45; 18 34: *also* 2 50.

cp. 24 6, 8.

verse 37

---

verse 14
12 On the morrow 1 a great multitude that had come to the feast, when they heard that Jesus was coming to Jerusalem,

13 took the branches of the palm trees,

and

went forth to meet him, and cried out,

verses 17 and 18

Hosanna:

Blessed *is* he [*cp.* 1 49; 12 15; 18 33, 37, 39; 19 3, 12, 14, 15, 19, 21: *also* 6 15] that cometh [*cp.* 1 15, 27; 3 31; 6 14; 11 27: *also* 1 30] in the name of the Lord, even the King of Israel.

cp. 14 27; 16 33.

14 And Jesus, having found a young ass, sat thereon; as it is written, **15** Fear not, daughter of Zion: behold, thy King cometh, sitting on an ass's colt. **16** These things understood not his disciples [*cp.* 4 33; 11 13; 13 7, 28, 36; 14 5-10; 16 17-18: *also* 3 10; 8 27, 43; 10 6] at the first: but when Jesus was glorified, then [*cp.* 13 7] remembered they that these things were written of him, and that they had done these things unto him [*cp.* 2 22]. **17** The multitude therefore that was with him when he called Lazarus out of the tomb, and raised him from the dead, bare witness. **18** For this cause also the multitude went

			and met him, for that they heard that he had done this sign.
		39 And some of the Pharisees from the multitude said unto him, ² Master, rebuke [cp. 18 39] thy disciples. **40** And he answered and said, I tell you that, if these shall hold their peace [cp. 18 39], the stones will cry out [cp. 18 39].	19 The Pharisees therefore said
			among themselves, ² Behold how ye prevail nothing : lo, the world is gone after him.
cp. 21 15-16.			
10 And when he was come into Jerusalem, all the city was stirred, saying, Who is this [cp. 8 27]? **11** And the multitudes said, This is the prophet [cp. 13 57; 21 46], Jesus, from Nazareth [cp. 2 23; 26 71] of Galilee.	**11** And he entered into Jerusalem ...		
	cp. 4 41: also 1 27.	cp. 5 21; 7 49; 8 25; 9 9: also 4 36.	cp. 5 12: also 12 34.
	cp. 6 4, 15.	cp. 4 24; 7 16, 39; 13 33; 24 19.	cp. 4 19, 44; 6 14; 7 40; 9 17.
	cp. 1 24; 10 47; 14 67; 16 6.	cp. 4 34; 18 37; 24 19.	cp. 1 45; 18 5, 7; 19 19.
¹ Or, through	¹ Gr. sendeth. ² Or, again ³ Gr. layers of leaves.	¹ Gr. powers. ² Or, Teacher	¹ Some ancient authorities read the common people. ² Or, Ye behold

Matt. 21 5=Is. 62 11.   Matt. 21 5 ‖ John 12 15=Zech. 9 9.   Matt. 21 9 ‖ Mark 11 9 ‖ Luke 19 38 ‖ John 12 13 : cp. Ps. 118 25-26.

§ 195. **A Lament over Jerusalem**

[Cp. Matt. 23 37-39 ‖ Luke 13 34-35 : also Luke 23 27-31 and 21 20]

Luke 19 41-44

cp. 16 21; 20 17, 18.	cp. 10 32, 33.	**41** And when he drew nigh, he saw the city [cp. 9 51, 53; 13 22; 17 11; 19 11: also 9 31; 13 33; 18 31] and wept over it [cp. 23 28], **42** saying, ¹ If thou hadst known in this day, even thou, the things which belong unto peace [cp. 1 79; 2 14, 29; 19 38] ! but now they are hid from thine eyes. **43** For the days shall come [cp. 5 35; 17 22; 21 6; 23 29] upon thee, when thine enemies shall cast up a ² bank about thee, and compass thee round [cp. 21 20], and keep thee in on every side, **44** and shall dash thee to the ground, and thy children [cp. 13 34] within thee; and they shall not leave in thee one stone upon another [cp. 21 6]; because thou knewest not the time of thy visitation.	cp. 14 27; 16 33.
cp. 5 9; 10 13.	cp. 9 50.		
cp. 9 15.	cp. 2 20.		
cp. 23 37.			
cp. 24 2.	cp. 13 2.		

¹ Or, O that thou hadst known   ² Gr. palisade.

Luke 19 44 : cp. Ps. 137 9.

§ 196. **A Visit to the Temple** (Mark); **The Cleansing of the Temple** (Matt.)
Retirement to Bethany

[Cp. Mal. 3 1: Zech. 14 21]

Matt. 21 (10-11) 12-17	**Mark 11** 11 (15-17)	Luke 19 45-46	John 2 13-17
			13 And the passover of the Jews was at hand, and Jesus went up to Jerusalem.
10 And when he was come into Jerusalem, all the city was stirred, saying, Who is this [cp. 8 27]? **11** And the multitudes said, This is the prophet [cp. 13 57; 21 46], Jesus, from Nazareth	**11** And he entered into Jerusalem, into the temple;		
	cp. 4 41: also 1 27.	cp. 5 21; 7 49; 8 25; 9 9: also 4 36.	cp. 5 12: also 12 34.
	cp. 6 4, 15.	cp. 4 24; 7 16, 39; 13 33; 24 19.	cp. 4 19, 44; 6 14; 7 40; 9 17.

[*cp.* 2 23; 26 71] of Galilee.	*cp.* 1 24; 10 47; 14 67; 16 6.	*cp.* 4 34; 18 37; 24 19.	*cp.* 1 45; 18 5, 7; 19 19.
12 And Jesus entered into the temple [1] of God,	**15** And they come to Jerusalem: and he entered into the temple,	**45** And he entered into the temple,	**14** And he found in the temple those that sold oxen and sheep and doves, and the changers of money sitting: **15** and he made a scourge of cords, and
and cast out all them that sold and bought in the temple,	and began to cast out them that sold and them that bought in the temple,	and began to cast out them that sold,	cast all out of the temple, both the sheep and the oxen; and he poured out the changers' money, and
and overthrew the tables of the money-changers, and the seats of them that sold the doves;	and overthrew the tables of the money-changers, and the seats of them that sold the doves; **16** and he would not suffer that any man should carry a vessel through the temple.		overthrew their tables; **16** and to them that sold the doves
13 and he saith unto them, It is written, My house shall be called a house of prayer: but ye make it a den of robbers.	**17** And he taught, and said unto them, Is it not written, My house shall be called a house of prayer for all the nations? but ye have made it a den of robbers.	**46** saying unto them, It is written, And my house shall be a house of prayer: but ye have made it a den of robbers.	he said, Take these things hence; make not my Father's house a house of merchandise. **17** His disciples remembered that it was written, The zeal of thine house shall eat me up.
14 And the blind and the lame came to him in the temple: and he healed them. **15** But when the chief priests and the scribes saw the wonderful things that he did,	*cp.* 11 18.	*cp.* 19 47.	*cp.* 2 18.
and the children that were crying in the temple and saying, Hosanna [*cp.* 21 9] to the son of David [*cp.* 1 1; 9 27; 12 23; 15 22; 20 30, 31; 21 9];	*cp.* 11 9, 10. *cp.* 10 47, 48.	*cp.* 18 38, 39: *also* 1 32.	*cp.* 12 13.
they were moved with indignation, **16** and said unto him, Hearest thou what these are saying?		*cp.* 19 39-40.	*cp.* 12 19.
And Jesus saith unto them, Yea: did ye never read [*cp.* 12 3, 5; 19 4; 21 42; 22 31], Out of the mouth of babes and sucklings thou hast perfected praise?	*cp.* 2 25; 12 10, 26.	*cp.* 6 3: *also* 10 26.	
17 And	and when he had looked round about [*cp.* 3 5, 34; 5 32; 9 8; 10 23] upon all things, it being now eventide, he	*cp.* 6 10.	
he left them [*cp.* 16 4], and went forth out [*cp.* 26 30] of the city to Bethany, and lodged there.	[*cp.* 8 13] went out [*cp.* 11 19; 14 26] unto Bethany with the twelve.	*cp.* 21 37; 22 39.	*cp.* 18 1-2: *also* 8 1.

[1] Many ancient authorities omit *of God*.

Mark 11 16: *cp.* Zech. 14 21. Matt. 21 13 ‖ Mark 11 17 ‖ Luke 19 46 = Is. 56 7: *cp.* Jer. 7 11. Matt. 21 16 = Ps. 8 2. John 2 17 = Ps. 69 9.

§ 197. **The Cursing of a Fig Tree**

[*Cp.* Matt. 24 32-33 ‖ Mark 13 28-29 ‖ Luke 21 29-31 ; Luke 13 6-9]

Matt. 21 18-19	Mark 11 12-14	
18 Now in the morning as he returned to the city, he hungered. **19** And seeing ¹ a fig tree by the way side, he came to it, and found nothing thereon, but leaves only; and he saith unto it, Let there be no fruit from thee henceforward for ever. And immediately the fig tree withered away. ¹ Or, *a single*	**12** And on the morrow, when they were come out from Bethany, he hungered. **13** And seeing a fig tree afar off having leaves, he came, if haply he might find anything thereon : and when he came to it, he found nothing but leaves ; for it was not the season of figs. **14** And he answered and said unto it, No man eat fruit from thee henceforward for ever. And his disciples heard it.	*cp.* 13 6.

§ 198. **The Cleansing of the Temple**

[*Cp.* Mal. 3 1 : Zech. 14 21]

Matt 21 12-13	Mark 11 15-18	Luke 19 45-48	John 2 13-17
12 And Jesus entered into the temple ¹ of God, and cast out all them that sold and bought in the temple, and overthrew the tables of the money-changers, and the seats of them that sold the doves ;	**15** And they come to Jerusalem : and he entered into the temple, and began to cast out them that sold and them that bought in the temple, and overthrew the tables of the money-changers, and the seats of them that sold the doves ; **16** and he would not suffer that any man should carry a vessel through the temple.	**45** And he entered into the temple, and began to cast out them that sold,	**13** And the passover of the Jews was at hand, and Jesus went up to Jerusalem. **14** And he found in the temple those that sold oxen and sheep and doves, and the changers of money sitting : **15** and he made a scourge of cords, and cast all out of the temple, both the sheep and the oxen ; and he poured out the changers' money, and overthrew their tables ; **16** and to them that sold the doves
13 and he saith unto them, It is written, My house shall be called a house of prayer : but ye make it a den of robbers.	**17** And he taught, and said unto them, Is it not written, My house shall be called a house of prayer for all the nations ? but ye have made it a den of robbers.	**46** saying unto them, It is written, And my house shall be a house of prayer : but ye have made it a den of robbers.	he said, Take these things hence ; make not my Father's house a house of merchandise. **17** His disciples remembered that it was written, The zeal of thine house shall eat me up.
cp. 26 55 : *also* 21 23. *cp.* 21 15.	*cp.* 14 49 : *also* 12 35. **18** And the chief priests and the scribes	**47** And he was teaching daily in the temple [*cp.* 21 37 ; 22 53 : *also* 20 1]. But the chief priests and the scribes and the principal men of the	*cp.* 18 20 : *also* 7 28 ; 8 20. *cp.* 2 18.

cp. 12 14 ; 21 46 ; 26 4. cp. 21 46 ; 26 5 : also 14 5 ; 21 26. cp. 7 28 ; 13 54 ; 19 25 ; 22 22, 33 : also 8 27 ; 9 33 ; etc.	heard it, and sought how they might destroy him [cp. 3 6 ; 12 12 ; 14 1] : for they feared [cp. 12 12 ; 14 2 : also 11 32] him, for all the multitude was astonished [cp. 1 22, 27 ; 6 2 ; 10 24, 26 ; 12 17 : also 2 12 ; 5 20 ; etc.] at his teaching. cp. 12 37.	people sought to destroy him [cp. 6 11 ; 20 19 ; 22 2] : **48** and they [cp. 20 19 ; 22 2 : also 20 6] could not find what they might do ; for the people all cp. 2 47, 48 ; 4 22, 32, 36 ; 20 26 : also 5 9, 26 ; etc. hung upon him, listening [cp. 21 38].	cp. 5 16, 18 ; 7 30, 32 ; 11 53, 57. cp. 7 15, 21, 46.
[1] Many ancient authorities omit of God.			

Mark 11 16 : cp. Zech. 14 21.   Matt. 21 13 ‖ Mark 11 17 ‖ Luke 19 46 = Is. 56 7 : cp. Jer. 7 11.   John 2 17 = Ps. 69 9.

§ 199. Retirement in the Evenings

	Mark 11 19	Luke 21 37-38	
cp. 26 55 : also 21 23. cp. 21 17 ; 26 30. cp. 24 3 ; 26 30.	cp. 14 49 : also 12 35. **19** And [1] every evening [2] he went forth out [cp. 11 11 ; 14 26] of the city. cp. 13 3 ; 14 26. cp. 12 37.	**37** And every day he was teaching in the temple [cp. 19 47 ; 22 53 : also 20 1] ; and every night he went out [cp. 22 39], and lodged in the mount that is called the mount of Olives [cp. 22 39]. **38** And all the people came early in the morning to him in the temple, to hear him [cp. 19 48].	cp. 18 20 : also 7 28 ; 8 20. cp. 18 1-2. cp. 8 1. cp. 8 2.
	[1] Gr. whenever evening came. [2] Some ancient authorities read they.		

§ 200. The Fig Tree withered and Sayings about Faith

Matt. 21 20-22	**Mark 11** 20-25 (26)	Luke 17 6	

20 And when
  the disciples saw it,
 	
cp. 14 28 ; 15 15 ; 16 22 ; 17 4 ;
18 21 ; 19 27 ; 26 33 : also
  16 16 ; 17 24.
they marvelled [cp. 8 27 ; etc. :
also 19 25 ; etc.],
  saying,
  cp. 26 25, 49.
  How did the fig tree
 	
immediately wither away ?
 	
17 19 Then   came
  the disciples
to Jesus   apart,
and said, Why   could not
we cast it out ? **20** And he
saith unto them, Because of your
little faith [cp. 6 30 ; 8 26 ;
14 31 ; 16 8] :
 	
for verily I say unto you, If
ye have faith as a grain of
mustard seed [cp. 13 31], ye
shall say unto this mountain,
  Remove hence
to yonder place ; and it shall
remove ; and nothing shall be
impossible unto you [cp. 19 26].[1]
	20 And as they passed by in
	the morning, they saw the fig
	tree withered away from the
	roots. **21** And Peter [cp. 8 32 ;
	9 5 ; 10 28 ; 14 29 : also 8
	29] calling to remembrance
	  [cp. 6 51 ; 10 32 ;
	16 8 ; etc. : also 10 24, 26 ;
	etc.] saith unto him, Rabbi
	[cp. 9 5 ; 14 45 : also 10 51],
	behold, the fig tree
	which thou cursedst is
	  withered away.
	
	9 28 And when he was come
	into the house, his disciples
	  asked him privately,
	[1] saying, We could not
	  cast it out. **29** And he
	said unto them,
	  cp. 4 40 ; 16 14.
	  This kind can
	come out by nothing, save by
	prayer.[2]
	
	  cp. 4 31.
		cp. 8 45 ; 9 33 ; 12 41 ; 18 28 :
		  also 5 8 ; 9 20.
		
		cp. 5 9 ; 8 25 ; 24 12, 41 ; etc.
		
		  6 And the Lord
		said,
		cp. 12 28 : also 8 25 ; 17 5 ;
		  22 32 ; 24 25, 38.
		
		  If
		ye have faith as a grain of
		mustard seed [cp. 13 19], ye
		would say unto this
		sycamine tree,
		
		  cp. 1 37 ; 18 27.
			cp. 13 36, 37 ;
			21 21 : also
			  6 68.
			
			cp. 1 38, 49 ;
			etc. : also
			  20 16.
			
			cp. 3 12 ; 6
			64 ; 14 10 ;
			  20 27.

21 And Jesus answered and said unto them,
          Verily I say unto you, If ye have faith, and doubt not, ye shall not only do what is done to the fig tree, but even if ye shall say unto this mountain, Be thou taken up and   cast   into the sea,

          it shall be done.

22 And all things, whatsoever ye shall ask   in prayer,
          believ-
ing,

ye shall receive.

cp. 18 19.

Matt. 7 **7** Ask,

and it shall be given you ; seek, and ye shall find; knock, and it shall be opened unto   you.

cp. 5 23.

cp. 6 14-15: *also* 6 12; 18 21-35.

Many authorities, some ancient, insert ver. 21 *But this kind goeth not out save by prayer and fasting.* See Mark 9 29.

---

22 And Jesus answering saith unto them, Have faith in God. **23** Verily I say unto you,

Whosoever shall say unto this mountain, Be thou taken up and   cast   into the sea ; and shall not doubt in his heart, but shall believe that what he saith cometh to pass ; he shall have it.

24 Therefore I say unto you, All things whatsoever ye

pray and ask for,
          believe
          that ye have received them, and ye shall have them.

Luke 11 **9** Ask,

and it shall be given you ; seek, and ye shall find; knock, and it shall be opened unto   you.

25 And whensoever ye stand praying, forgive, if ye have aught against any one ; that your Father also which is in heaven may forgive you your trespasses.[3]

[1] Or, How is it *that we could not cast it out?*
[2] Many ancient authorities add *and fasting.*
[3] Many ancient authorities add ver. 26 *But if ye do not forgive, neither will your Father which is in heaven forgive your trespasses.*

                    Be thou rooted up, and be thou   planted in the sea ; and

          it would have obeyed you.

John 14 **13**
And whatsoever ye shall ask

in my name,

that will I do. . . .
          14 If ye shall ask [1] me anything

          in my name, that will I do.

John 15 **7** Ask whatsoever ye will, and it shall be done unto you.

[1] Many ancient authorities omit *me.*

cp. 11 4; 17 3-4.

John 15 **16**
. . . that whatsoever ye shall ask of the Father

in my name,

he may give it you. **16 23** If ye shall ask anything of the Father, he will give it you in my name.
          24 Hitherto have ye asked nothing in my name : ask,

and ye shall receive.

(ii) Debate and Teaching in the Temple (§§ 201-212)

§ 201. **A Question about Authority**

Matt. 21 23-32	**Mark 11** 27-33	**Luke 20** 1-8	
23 And when he was come	**27** And they come again to Jerusalem : and as he was walking [*cp.* 12 35; 14 49]	**1** And it came to pass, on one of the days, as he was teaching [*cp.* 19 47; 21 37; 22 53] the people in the temple, and preaching the gospel [*cp.* 1 19; 2 10; 3 18; 4 18, 43; 7 22; 8 1; 9 6; 16 16], there came upon	*cp.* 18 20; *also* 7 28; 8 20.
into the temple, *cp.* 11 5.	in the temple,		
the chief priests and the elders of the people came unto him as he was teaching [*cp.* 26 55], and said,	there come to him the chief priests, and the scribes, and the elders; *cp.* 12 35; 14 49.	him the chief priests and the scribes with the elders;	
	28 and they said unto	**2** and they spake, saying unto	*cp.* 18 20: *also* 7 28; 8 20.

Matthew

By what authority [cp. 7 29; 9 6; 28 18] doest thou these things? and who gave thee this authority? **24** And Jesus answered and said unto them, I also will ask you one [1] question, which if ye tell me, I likewise will tell you by what authority I do these things. **25** The baptism of John, whence was it? from heaven or from men?

And they reasoned with themselves, saying, If we shall say, From heaven; he will say unto us, Why then did ye not believe him [cp. verse 32]? **26** But if we shall say, From men; we fear the multitude [cp. 14 5: also 21 46; 26 5]; for all hold John as a prophet [cp. 14 5: also 11 9: and 21 46]. **27** And they answered Jesus, and said, We know not.

He also said unto them, Neither tell I you by what authority I do these things. **28** But what think ye [cp. 17 25; 18 12; 22 17, 42; 26 66]? A man had two sons; and he came to the first, and said, [2] Son, go work to-day in the vineyard [cp. 20 1, 2, 4, 7: also 21 33; Mark 12 1; Luke 20 9 and 13 6].

1 Gr. word.

Mark

him, By what authority [cp. 1 22, 27; 2 10] doest thou these things? or who gave thee this authority to do these things? **29** And Jesus said unto them, I will ask of you one [1] question, and answer me, and I will tell you by what authority I do these things. **30** The baptism of John, was it from heaven, or from men? answer me. **31** And they reasoned with themselves, saying, If we shall say, From heaven; he will say, Why then did ye not believe him? **32** [2] But should we say, From men—they feared the people [cp. 11 18; 12 12; 14 2]: [3] for all verily held John to be a prophet.

33 And they answered Jesus and say, We know not.

And Jesus saith unto them, Neither tell I you by what authority I do these things.

cp. 15 11-32.

1 Gr. word.
2 Or, But shall we say, From men?
3 Or, for all held John to be a prophet indeed.

Luke

him, Tell us: By what authority [cp. 4 32, 36; 5 24] doest thou these things? or who is he that gave thee this authority? **3** And he answered and said unto them, I also will ask you a [1] question; and tell me: **4** The baptism of John, was it from heaven, or from men? **5** And they reasoned with themselves, saying, If we shall say, From heaven; he will say, Why did ye not believe him [cp. 7 30]? **6** But if we shall say, From men; all the people [cp. 20 19; 22 2] will stone us: for they be persuaded that John was a prophet [cp. 1 76; 7 26]. **7** And they answered, that they knew not whence it was. **8** And Jesus said unto them, Neither tell I you by what authority I do these things.

1 Gr. word.

(right-hand cross references): cp. 2 18: also 5 27; 17 2. — cp. 3 27. — cp. 11 56.

---

29 And he answered and said, I will not: but afterward he repented himself, and went. **30** And he came to the second, and said likewise. And he answered and said, I go, sir: and went not. **31** Whether of the twain did the will [cp. 7 21; 12 50: also 6 10; 26 39, 42] of his father? They say, The first. Jesus saith unto them, Verily I say unto you, that the publicans and the harlots go into the kingdom of God [cp. 5 20; 7 21; 18 3; 19 23, 24; 23 13: also 7 13; 18 8, 9; 19 17; 25 21, 23] before you [cp. 9 13: Mark 2 17: Luke 5 32; 7 29, 30, 47; 15 7, 10; 18 14; 19 10]. **32** For John came unto you in the way of righteousness [cp. 3 15; 5 6, 10, 20; 6 1, 33], and ye believed him not [cp. verse 25: Mark 11 31: Luke 20 5]: but the publicans and the harlots believed him: and ye, when ye saw it, did not even repent yourselves afterward, that ye might believe him.

1 Gr. word.   2 Gr. Child.

(cross references, Mark column): cp. 3 35: also 14 36. cp. 9 47; 10 15, 23-25: also 9 43, 45.

(cross references, Luke column): cp. 22 42. cp. 18 17, 24, 25: also 11 52; 13 24; 24 26. cp. 7 30. cp. 3 12; 7 29.

(far right): cp. 4 34; 5 30; 6 38; 7 17; 9 31. cp. 3 5: also 10 1, 2, 9.

---

§ 202. The Parable of the Wicked Husbandmen

Matt. 21 33-46

33 Hear another parable: There was a man that was a householder [cp. 13 52; 20 1: also 13 27], which planted a vineyard [cp. 20 1; 21 28], and set a hedge about it, and digged a winepress in it, and built a tower, and let it out to husbandmen, and went into another country

Mark 12 1-12

1 And he began to speak unto them in parables. A man planted a vineyard, and set a hedge about it, and digged a pit for the winepress, and built a tower, and let it out to husbandmen, and went into another country

Luke 20 9-19

9 And he began to speak unto the people this parable: A man

cp. 14 21.

planted a vineyard [cp. 13 6], and let it out to husbandmen, and went into another country

[*cp.* 25 14, 15].
34 And when the season of the fruits drew near, he sent his [1] servants [*cp.* 22 3] to the husbandmen, to receive [2] his fruits.
35 And the husbandmen took his [1] servants, and beat one, and killed another, and stoned [*cp.* 23 37] another.
36 Again, he sent other [1] servants [*cp.* 22 4] more than the first: and they [*cp.* 22 6: *also* 5 12; 23 29-34, 37] did unto them in like manner.
37 But *cp.* 3 17; 12 18; 17 5. afterward he sent unto them his son, saying, *cp.* 3 17; 12 18; 17 5. They will reverence my son.
38 But the husbandmen, when they saw the son, said among themselves, This is the heir; come, let us kill him, and take his inheritance.
39 And they took him, and cast him forth out of the vineyard, and killed him.
40 When therefore the lord of the vineyard [*cp.* 20 8] shall come, what will he do unto those husbandmen?
41 They say unto him, He will miserably destroy those miserable men [*cp.* 22 7], and will let out the vineyard unto other husbandmen [*cp.* 8 11; 21 31; 22 7-10: *also* 10 18; 24 14; 26 13; 28 19], which shall render him the fruits in their seasons [*cp. verse* 43].
42 Jesus saith unto them, Did ye never read [*cp.* 12 3, 5; 19 4; 21 16; 22 31] in the scriptures,

The stone which the builders rejected,
The same was made the head of the corner [*cp.* 26 24, 31, 54, 56]:

[*cp.* 13 34].
2 And at the season he sent to the husbandmen a [1] servant, that he might receive from the husbandmen of the fruits of the vineyard.
3 And they took him, and beat him, and sent him away empty.
4 And again he sent unto them another [1] servant; and him they wounded in the head, and handled shamefully.
5 And he sent another; and him they killed: and many others; beating some, and killing some.
6 He had yet one, a beloved son [*cp.* 1 11; 9 7]: he sent him last unto them, saying, They will reverence my son.
7 But those husbandmen said among themselves, This is the heir; come, let us kill him, and the inheritance shall be ours.
8 And they took him, and killed him, and cast him forth out of the vineyard.
9 What therefore will the lord of the vineyard do? he will come and destroy the husbandmen, and will give the vineyard unto others [*cp.* 13 10; 14 9; 16 15].
10 Have ye not read [*cp.* 2 25; 12 26] even this scripture;

The stone which the builders rejected,
The same was made the head of the corner [*cp.* 9 12; 14 21, 27, 49]:

[*cp.* 19 12] for a long time.
10 And at the season he sent unto the husbandmen a [1] servant [*cp.* 14 17], that they should give him of the fruit of the vineyard: but the husbandmen beat him, *cp.* 13 34. and sent him away empty.
11 And he sent yet another [1] servant: and him also they beat, and handled him shamefully, and sent him away empty.
12 And he sent yet a third: and him also they wounded, and cast him forth. *cp.* 6 23; 11 47-50; 13 33, 34.
13 And the lord of the vineyard said, What shall I do [*cp.* 12 17; 16 3]? I will send my beloved son [*cp.* 3 22; 9 35]: it may be they will reverence him.
14 But when the husbandmen saw him, they reasoned one with another, saying, This is the heir: let us kill him, that the inheritance may be ours.
15 And they cast him forth out of the vineyard [*cp.* 4 29], and killed him. What therefore will the lord of the vineyard do unto them?
16 He will come and destroy these husbandmen, and will give the vineyard unto others [*cp.* 13 29; 14 21-24: *also* 2 30-32; 3 6; 24 47]. And when they heard it, they said, [2] God forbid.
17 But he looked upon them, and said, *cp.* 6 3; 10 26. What then is this that is written,

The stone which the builders rejected,
The same was made the head of the corner [*cp.* 18 31; 22 37; 24 25-27,

---

cp. 1 11.

cp. 10 16; 11 52.

cp. 5 39; 13 18; 15 25; 17 12.

This was from the Lord, And it is marvellous in our eyes ?

43 Therefore say I unto you, The kingdom of God shall be taken away from you, and shall be given to a nation bringing forth the fruits thereof [cp. 25 28: *also verse* 41 *above*]. **44** ³ And he that falleth on this stone shall be broken to pieces: but on whomsoever it shall fall, it will scatter him as dust. **45** And when the chief priests and the Pharisees heard his parables, they perceived that he spake of them. **46** And when they sought to lay hold on him [cp. 12 14; 26 4], cp. 18 1; 26 55.

feared the multitudes [cp. 26 5: *also* 14 5; 21 26],

because they took him for a prophet [cp. 14 5; 21 26: *also* 13 57; 21 11]. cp. 22 22.

¹ Gr. bondservants.
² Or, *the fruits of it*
³ Some ancient authorities omit ver. 44.

---

11 This was from the Lord, And it is marvellous in our eyes ?

cp. verse 9 above.

12 And they sought to lay hold on him [cp. 3 6; 11 18; 14 1]; and they feared the multitude [cp. 11 18; 14 2: *also* 11 32]; for they perceived that he spake the parable against them:

cp. 11 32: *also* 6 4, 15. and they left him, and went away.

¹ Gr. bondservant.

44-46] ?

cp. 19 24: *also verse* 16 *above*. **18** Every one that falleth on that stone shall be broken to pieces; but on whomsoever it shall fall, it will scatter him as dust. **19** And the scribes and the chief priests

sought to lay hands on him [cp. 6 11; 19 47; 22 2] in that very hour [cp. 7 21; 10 21; 13 31]; and they feared the people [cp. 22 2: *also* 20 6]: for they perceived that he spake this parable against them.

cp. 20 6: *also* 4 24; 7 16, 39; 13 33; 24 19.

¹ Gr. bondservant.
² Gr. Be it not so.

---

cp. 5 16, 18; 7 30, 32; 11 53, 57.

cp. 4 19, 44; 6 14; 7 40; 9 17.

Matt. 21 33-34 ‖ Mark 12 1-2 ‖ Luke 20 9-10 : cp. Is. 5 1-2.   Matt. 21 42 ‖ Mark 12 10-11 ‖ Luke 20 17 = Ps. 118 22-23.
Matt. 21 44 ‖ Luke 20 18 : cp. Is. 8 14-15.

---

§ 203. The Parable of the Marriage Feast

[*Cp.* Matt. 8 11; 21 31, 41-43: *also* 10 18; 24 14; 26 13; 28 19: Mark 12 9-11: *also* 13 10; 14 9; 16 15: Luke 13 29; 20 16-17: *also* 2 30-32; 3 6; 24 47: John 10 16; 11 52]

Matt. 22 1-14   **Luke 14** 15-24

15 And when one of them that sat at meat with him heard these things, he said unto him, Blessed is he that shall eat bread in the kingdom of God [cp. 13 29; 22 16, 18, 30]. 16 But he

cp. 8 11; 26 29.   cp. 14 25.

1 And Jesus answered and spake again in parables unto them, saying, **2** The kingdom of heaven is likened unto a certain king [cp. 18 23: *also* 25 34, 40], which made a marriage feast for his son,

said unto him,

A certain [cp. 19 12, 15, 27] man made [cp. 14 8] a great supper; and he bade many : 17 and he sent forth his ¹ servant [cp. 20 10] at supper time to say to them that were bidden,

3 and sent forth his ¹ servants [cp. 21 34] to   cp. 12 2.
call them that were bidden to the marriage feast: and they would not come. **4** Again he sent forth other ¹ servants [cp. 21 36], saying, Tell them   cp. 12 4-5.
that are bidden, Behold, I have made ready my dinner: my oxen and my fatlings are killed, and all things are ready: come to the marriage feast.   **5** But they made
light of it, and went their ways, one to his own

cp. 20 11-12.

Come; for *all* things are now ready. 18 And they all with one *consent* began to make excuse. The first said unto him, I have bought a

Matt.	Mark	Luke
farm,		field, and I must needs go out and see it : I pray thee have me excused. **19** And another said, I have bought five yoke of oxen, and I go to prove them : I pray thee have me excused. **20** And another said, I have married a wife, and therefore I cannot come.
another to his mer-chandise :	*cp.* 12 3, 4, 5.	*cp.* 20 10, 11, 12 : *also* 6 23 ; 11 47-50 ; 13 33, 34.
6 and the rest laid hold on his ¹ servants, and entreated them shamefully, and killed them [*cp.* 21 35, 36 : *also* 5 12 ; 23 29-34, 37].		**21** And the ¹ servant came, and told his lord these things. Then the master of the house being angry
cp. 13 27, 52 ; 20 1 ; 21 33. **7** But the king was wroth [*cp.* 18 34] ; and he sent his armies, and destroyed those murderers [*cp.* 21 41], and burned their city. **8** Then saith he to his ¹ servants, The wedding is ready, but they that were bidden were not worthy. **9** Go ye therefore unto	*cp.* 12 9.	*cp.* 20 16. said to his ¹ servant,
		Go out quickly into the streets and lanes of the city, and bring in hither the poor and maimed and blind and lame [*cp.* 14 13]. **22** And the ¹ servant said, Lord, what thou didst command is done, and yet there is room. **23** And the lord said unto the ¹ servant, Go out into the
the partings of the highways, and as many as ye shall find, bid to the marriage feast.		highways and hedges, and constrain *them* to come in, that my house may be filled. **24** For I say unto you, that none of those men which were bidden shall taste of my supper.
		¹ Gr. *bondservant.*
10 And those ¹ servants went out into the highways, and gathered together all as many as they found, both bad and good [*cp.* 13 30, 47 ; 25 32] : and the wedding was filled with guests. **11** But when the king came in to behold the guests, he saw there a man which had not on a wedding-garment : **12** and he saith unto him, Friend [*cp.* 20 13 ; 26 50], how camest thou in hither not having a wedding-garment ? And he was speechless. **13** Then the king said to the ² servants, Bind him hand and foot, and cast him out into the outer darkness [*cp.* 8 12 ; 25 30] ; there shall be the weeping and gnashing of teeth [*cp.* 8 12 ; 13 42, 50 ; 24 51 ; 25 30]. **14** For many are called, but few chosen.		*cp.* 13 28.
¹ Gr. *bondservants.* ² Or, *ministers*		

§ 204. A Question about Tribute

Matt. 22 15-22	**Mark 12** 13-17	**Luke 20** 20-26	
	13 And they [*cp.* 3 2] send	**20** And they watched him [*cp.* 6 7 ; 14 1], and sent forth spies, which feigned themselves to be righteous,	
15 Then went the Pharisees, and took counsel [*cp.* 12 14 ; 27 1, 7 ; 28 12] how they might ensnare him in *his* talk [*cp.* 12 10].	unto him certain of the Pharisees and of the Herodians [*cp.* 3 6], *cp.* 3 6 ; 15 1. that they might catch him in talk [*cp.* 3 2].	that they might take hold of his speech [*cp.* 6 7 ; 11 53, 54], so as to deliver him up [*cp.* 23 2] to the rule and to the authority [*cp.* 12 11] of the governor. **21** And	*cp.* 8 6.
cp. 27 2, *etc.* ; 28 14. **16** And they send to him their disciples, with the Herodians,	**14** And when they were come, they	they	

saying,
[1] Master, we know that thou art true,

and teachest the way of God in truth, and carest not for any one: for thou regardest not the person of men.

17 Tell us therefore, What thinkest thou [*cp.* 17 25; 18 12; 21 28; 22 42; 26 66]? Is it lawful [*cp.* 12 10; 19 3]   to give tribute unto Cæsar, or not?

18 But Jesus perceived [*cp.* 12 15; 16 8; 26 10] their wickedness [*cp.* Luke 11 39],   and said, Why tempt ye me [*cp.* 16 1; 19 3; 22 35], ye hypocrites [*cp.* 15 7; 23 13, (14,) 15, *etc.*: *also* 6 2, 5, 16; 24 51]? **19** Shew me the tribute money. And they brought unto him a [2] penny.

20 And he saith unto them, Whose is this image and superscription?
21 They say unto him, Cæsar's. Then saith he unto them, Render therefore unto Cæsar the things that are Cæsar's; and unto God the things that are God's.

22 And when they heard it, they marvelled [*cp.* 7 28; 13 54; 19 25; 22 33: *also* 8 27; 9 33; 12 23; 15 31; 21 20; 27 14],

and left him, and went their way.

[1] Or, *Teacher*
[2] See marginal note on ch. 18 28.

say unto him,
[1] Master, we know that thou art true,

and carest not for any one: for thou regardest not the person of men, but of a truth teachest the way of God:

Is it lawful [*cp.* 3 4; 10 2]   to give tribute unto Cæsar, or not? **15** Shall we give, or shall we not give? But he, knowing [*cp.* 8 17] their hypocrisy [*cp.* Matt. 23 28; Luke 12 1],   said unto them, Why tempt ye me [*cp.* 8 11; 10 2]?
cp. 7 6.

bring   me a [2] penny, that I may see it. **16** And they brought it. And he saith unto them, Whose is this image and superscription? And they said unto him, Cæsar's. **17** And Jesus said   unto them, Render   unto Cæsar the things that are Cæsar's, and unto God the things that are God's.

And they marvelled [*cp.* 1 22, 27; 6 2; 10 24, 26; 11 18: *also* 2 12; 5 20, 42; 6 51; 7 37; 10 32; 15 5; 16 5, 8] greatly at him.

cp. 12 12.

[1] Or, *Teacher*
[2] See marginal note on Matt. 18 28.

asked him, saying,
[1] Master, we know that thou sayest and teachest rightly,   and

acceptest not the person *of any*, but of a truth teachest the way of God:

22 Is it lawful [*cp.* 6 9; 14 3] for us to give tribute unto Cæsar, or not?

23 But he perceived their craftiness,   and said unto them,
cp. 10 25; 11 16.
cp. 12 56; 13 15.

24 Shew me   a [2] penny.

Whose image and superscription hath it? And they said, Cæsar's. **25** And he said   unto them, Then render   unto Cæsar the things that are Cæsar's, and unto God the things that are God's. **26** And they were not able to take hold of the saying before the people: and they marvelled [*cp.* 2 47, 48; 4 22, 32, 36: *also* 5 9, 26; 8 25, 56; 9 43; 11 14; 24 12, 41] at his answer, and held their peace.

[1] Or, *Teacher*
[2] See marginal note on Matt. 18 28.

cp. 3 2.

cp. 11 56.

cp. 5 6; 6 15.

cp. 8 6.

cp. 7 15, 21, 46.

§ 205. **A Question about Resurrection**

Matt. 22 23-33	**Mark 12** 18-27	**Luke 20** 27-40

23 On that day there came to him   Sadducees,   [1] which say that there is no resurrection: and they asked him, **24** saying, [2] Master, Moses said,
If a man   die,

having no children,   his brother [3] shall marry his wife, and raise up seed unto his brother. **25** Now there were   with us seven brethren: and the first married   and deceased, and having no seed left his wife unto his brother; **26** in like

18 And   there come unto him   Sadducees,   which say that there is no resurrection; and they asked him, saying, **19** [1] Master, Moses wrote unto us,   If a man's brother die, and leave a wife behind him, and leave no child, that his brother should take his wife, and raise up seed unto his brother. **20** There were   seven brethren: and the first took a wife, and dying left no seed;

27 And   there came to him certain of the Sadducees, they which say that there is no resurrection; and they asked him, **28** saying, [1] Master, Moses wrote unto us, that if a man's brother die, having a wife, and he be childless,   his brother should take the wife, and raise up seed unto his brother. **29** There were   seven brethren: and the first took a wife, and died childless;

Matt.	Mark	Luke		
manner the second also,	**21** and the second took her, and died, leaving no seed behind him; and the third likewise: **22** and the seven left no seed.	**30** and the second;		
and the third, unto the [4] seventh.		**31** and the third took her; and likewise the seven also left no children, and died. **32** Afterward the woman also died.		
27 And after them all the woman died.	Last of all the woman also died.			
28 In the resurrection therefore whose wife shall she be of the seven? for they all had her. **29** But Jesus answered and said unto them,	**23** In the resurrection whose wife shall she be of them? for the seven had her to wife. **24** Jesus said unto them, Is it not for this cause that ye err, that ye know not the scriptures, nor the power of God?	**33** In the resurrection therefore whose wife of them shall she be? for the seven had her to wife. **34** And Jesus said unto them,		
Ye do err, not knowing the scriptures, nor the power of God.		The sons of this [2] world [cp. 16 8] marry, and are given in marriage: **35** but they that are accounted worthy to attain to that [2] world, and the resurrection from the dead,		
30 For in the resurrection they neither marry, nor are given in marriage,	**25** For when they shall rise from the dead, they neither marry, nor are given in marriage;	neither marry, nor are given in marriage: **36** for neither can they die any more: for they are equal unto the angels; and are sons of God [cp. 6 35; 16 8], being sons of the resurrection. **37** But that	cp. 1 12; 11 52; 12 36.	
but are as angels [5] in heaven. cp. 5 9: also 5 45; 8 12; 13 38.	but are as angels in heaven.			
31 But as touching the resurrection of the dead, have ye not read [cp. 12 3, 5; 19 4; 21 16, 42]	**26** But as touching the dead, that they are raised; have ye not read [2 25; 12 10] in the book of Moses, in *the place concerning* the Bush, how God spake unto him,	the dead are raised, cp. 6 3; 10 26. [cp. 3 4; 4 17; 20 42] even Moses shewed in *the place concerning* the Bush, when he calleth the Lord		
that which was spoken unto you by God, saying, **32** I am the God of Abraham, and the God of Isaac, and the God of Jacob?	saying, I *am* the God of Abraham, and the God of Isaac, and the God of Jacob?	the God of Abraham, and the God of Isaac, and the God of Jacob.		
God is not *the God* of the dead, but of the living.	**27** He is not the God of the dead, but of the living: ye do greatly err.	**38** Now he is not the God of the dead, but of the living: for all live unto him.		
33 And when the multitudes heard it, they were astonished at his teaching [cp. 7 28; 13 54; 19 25; 22 22: also 8 27; etc.].	cp. 1 22, 27; 6 2; 10 24, 26; 11 18; 12 17: also 2 12; etc.	cp. 2 47, 48; 4 22, 32, 36; 20 26: also 5 9; etc.	cp. 7 15, 21, 46.	
	12 28, 32.	**39** And certain of the scribes answering said, [1] Master, thou hast well said. **40** For they durst not any more ask him any question.		
22 46	12 34			

[1] Gr. *saying.*   [2] Or, *Teacher*
[3] Gr. *shall perform the duty of a husband's brother to his wife.*   Compare Deut. 25 5.   [4] Gr. *seven.*
[5] Many ancient authorities add *of God.*

[1] Or, *Teacher*

[1] Or, *Teacher*   [2] Or, *age*

Matt. 22 24 ‖ Mark 12 19 ‖ Luke 20 28 : cp. Deut. 25 5.   Matt. 22 32 ‖ Mark 12 26 ‖ Luke 20 37 = Exod. 3 6, 15.

§ 206. A Question about the 'First' Commandment

Matt. 22 34-40	**Mark 12** 28-34	Luke 10 25-28; 20 39-40	
34 But the Pharisees, when they heard that he had put the Sadducees to silence, gathered themselves together. **35** And one of them, a lawyer,	**28** And one of the scribes came, and heard them questioning together [cp. 8	**25** And behold, a certain lawyer	

asked him a question, tempting [cp. 16 1; 19 3: also 22 18] him, 36 ¹ Master,

cp. 19 16, 29; 25 46.
which is the great commandment in the law? 37 And he said unto him,

cp. 12 3, 5; 19 4; 21 16, 42; 22 31.

Thou shalt love the Lord thy God with all thy heart, and with all thy soul, and with all thy mind.

38 This is the great and first commandment. 39 ² And a second like unto it is this, Thou shalt love thy neighbour as thyself [cp. 19 19].

40 On these two commandments hangeth the whole law, and the prophets [cp. 5 17; 7 12; 11 13].

cp. 9 13; 12 7; 23 23.

22 46 And no one was able to answer him a word, neither durst any man from that day forth ask him any more questions.

¹ Or, Teacher
² Or, And a second is like unto it, Thou shalt love &c.

11; 9 14, 16], and knowing that he had answered them well [cp. verse 32], asked him, cp. 8 11; 10 2: also 12 15.

cp. 10 17, 30.
What commandment is the first of all? 29 Jesus

cp. 2 25; 12 10, 26.
answered, The first is, Hear, O Israel; ¹ The Lord our God, the Lord is one: 30 and thou shalt love the Lord thy God ² with all thy heart, and ² with all thy soul, and ² with all thy mind, and ² with all thy strength.

31 The second is this, Thou shalt love thy neighbour as thyself. There is none other commandment greater than these.

32 And the scribe said unto him, Of a truth, ³ Master, thou hast well said [cp. verse 28] that he is one; and there is none other but he: 33 and to love him with all the heart, and with all the understanding, and with all the strength, and to love his neighbour as himself, is much more than all whole burnt offerings and sacrifices. 34 And when Jesus saw that he answered discreetly, he said unto him, Thou art not far from the kingdom of God [cp. 10 21]. And no man after that durst ask him any question.

¹ Or, The Lord is our God; the Lord is one
² Gr. from. ³ Or, Teacher

[cp. 20 39] stood up and tempted [cp. 11 16] him, saying, ¹ Master, what shall I do [cp. 3 10, 12, 14] to inherit eternal life [cp. 18 18, 30]?

26 And he said unto him, What is written in the law? how readest thou [cp. 6 3]? 27 And he answering said,

Thou shalt love the Lord thy God ² with all thy heart, and with all thy soul, and with all thy strength, and with all thy mind;

and thy neighbour as thyself.

cp. 16 16.
28 And he said unto him, Thou hast answered right [cp. 7 43]: this do, and thou shalt live. 20 39 And certain of the scribes answering said, ¹ Master, thou hast well said.

40 For they
cp. 14 6.
durst not any more ask him any question.

¹ Or, Teacher ² Gr. from.

---

cp. 8 6.

cp. 6 28.
cp. 3 15; etc.

Mark 12 29=Deut. 6 4. Matt. 22 37 || Mark 12 30 || Luke 10 27=Deut. 6 5.
Matt. 22 39 || Mark 12 31 || Luke 10 27=Lev. 19 18. Luke 10 28: cp. Lev. 18 5.
Mark 12 33: cp. I Sam. 15 22.

§ 207. A Question about the Christ as Son of David

Matt. 22 41-46	**Mark 12** 35-37	**Luke 20** 41-44	
41 Now while the Pharisees were gathered together, Jesus asked them a question, **42** saying, *cp.* 21 23; 26 55. *cp.* 17 10. What think ye [*cp.* 17 25; 18 12; 21 28; 22 17; 26 66] of the Christ? whose son is he? They say unto him, *The son of David.* **43** He saith unto them, How then doth David in the Spirit call him Lord, saying, **44** The Lord said unto my Lord, Sit thou on my right hand, Till I put thine enemies underneath thy feet? **45** If David then calleth him Lord, how is he his son? **46** And no one was able to answer him a word, neither durst any man from that day forth ask him any more questions.	**35** And Jesus answered and said, as he taught in the temple [*cp.* 14 49], How say the scribes [*cp.* 9 11] that the Christ is the son of David? **36** David himself said in the Holy Spirit, [*cp.* 12 26] The Lord said unto my Lord, Sit thou on my right hand, Till I make thine enemies ¹ the footstool of thy feet. **37** David himself calleth him Lord; and whence is he his son? And ² the common people heard him gladly [*cp.* 6 20]. 12 34	**41** And he said unto them, *cp.* 19 47; 20 1; 21 37; 22 53. How say they that the Christ is David's son? **42** For David himself saith in the book [*cp.* 3 4; 4 17] of Psalms [*cp.* 24 44], The Lord said unto my Lord, Sit thou on my right hand, **43** Till I make thine enemies the footstool of thy feet. **44** David therefore calleth him Lord, and how is he his son? *cp.* 19 48; 21 38. *cp.* 14 6. 20 40	*cp.* 18 20: *also* 7 28; 8 20. *cp.* 11 56.

¹ Some ancient authorities read *underneath thy feet.*
² Or, *the great multitude*

Matt. 22 44 ‖ Mark 12 36 ‖ Luke 20 42-43 = Ps. 110 1.

§ 208. A Warning against Scribes (Mark and Luke) and Pharisees (Matt.)

Matt. 23 1-12	**Mark 12** 38-40	**Luke 20** 45-47	
1 Then spake Jesus to the multitudes and to his disciples, **2** saying, The scribes and the Pharisees sit on Moses' seat: **3** all things therefore whatsoever they bid you, *these* do and observe: but do not ye after their works; for they say, and do not [*cp.* 7 21]. **4** Yea, they bind heavy burdens ¹ and grievous to be borne, and lay them on men's shoulders; but they themselves will not move them with their finger. **5** But all their works they do for to be seen of men [*cp.* 6 1, 2, 5, 16; 23 28]: for they make broad their phylacteries, and enlarge the borders *of their garments,* *cp.* 16 6.	**38** And in his teaching [*cp.* 4 2] he said,	**45** And in the hearing of all the people he said unto his disciples, 11 46 And he said, Woe unto you lawyers also! for ye lade men with burdens grievous to be borne, and ye yourselves touch not the burdens with one of your fingers.	
	Beware of [*cp.* 8 15] the scribes, which desire to walk	Luke 11 43 Woe unto you Pharisees!	**46** Beware of [*cp.* 12 1] the scribes, which desire to walk

Matt.	Mark	Luke	
6 and love the chief place at feasts, and the chief seats in the synagogues, **7** and the salutations in the market places,	in long robes, and *to have* salutations in the market places, **39** and chief seats in the synagogues, and chief places at feasts:	in long robes, and love for ye love the chief seats in the synagogues, and the salutations in the market places.	
cp. 23 25.			
	40 they which devour widows' [cp. 12 42]	*cp.* 14 7-11. **47** which devour [cp. 11 39; 16 14] widows' [cp. 21 2: *also* 2 37; 4 25-26; 7 12; 18 3] houses, and for a pretence make long prayers: these shall receive greater condemnation.	
cp. 6 5.	houses, ¹ and for a pretence make long prayers; these shall receive greater condemnation.		
and to be called of men, Rabbi. **8** But be not ye called Rabbi: for one is your teacher [cp. 26 18, 25, 49: *also* 10 24, 25], and all ye are brethren. **9** And call no man your father on the earth: for one is your Father, ² which is in heaven [cp. 5 48; 6 14, 26, 32; 15 13; 18 35: *also* 5 16, 45; 6 1, 9; 7 11, 21; 10 32, 33; 12 50; 16 17; 18 10, 14, 19]. **10** Neither be ye called masters: for one is your master, *even* the Christ.	cp. 4 38; 9 5, 38; 10 35; 11 21; 13 1; 14 14, 45. cp. 11 25, 26.	cp. 5 5; 8 24, 45; 9 33, 49; 21 7; 22 11: *also* 6 40. cp. 11 13.	cp. 1 38, 49; 4 31; 9 2; 11 8, 28; 13 13, 14; 20 16.
11 But he that is ³ greatest among you shall be ⁴ servant.	**9 35** If any man would be first, he shall be last of all, and minister of all.	**9 48** For he that is ¹ least among you all, the same is great.	
20 26 But whosoever would become great among you shall be ⁵ minister; **27** and whosoever would be first among you shall be your ⁶ servant.	**10 43** But whosoever would become great among you, shall be ² minister: **44** and whosoever would be first among you, shall be ³ servant of all.	**22 26** But he that is the greater among you, let him become as the younger; and he that is chief, as he that doth serve.	cp. 13 2-17.
12 And whosoever shall exalt himself shall be humbled; and whosoever shall humble himself [cp. 18 4] shall be exalted.		**14 11** *and* **18 14** For every one that exalteth himself shall be humbled; and [but] he that humbleth himself shall be exalted.	

¹ Many ancient authorities omit *and grievous to be borne.*
⁴ Gr. *the heavenly.* ³ Gr. *greater.*
Or, *minister.* ⁵ Or, *servant*
⁶ Gr. *bondservant.*

¹ Or, *even while for a pretence they make*
² Or, *servant* ³ Gr. *bondservant.*

¹ Gr. *lesser.*

§ 209. Woes against Scribes and Pharisees

Matt. 23 13-36		Luke 11 52, 42, 39-41, 44, 47-51	
13 But woe unto you [cp. *verses* 15, 16, 23, 25, 27, 29: *also* 18 7; 26 24], scribes and Pharisees, hypocrites [cp. 15 7; 22 18; 23 15, 23, 25, 27, 29: *also* 6 2, 5, 16; 23 28; 24 51]! because ye shut the kingdom of heaven ¹ against men:	cp. 14 21. cp. 7 6: *also* 12 15.	**52** Woe unto you [cp. 11 42, 43, 44, 46, 47: *also* 17 1; 22 22] lawyers! cp. 12 56; 13 15: *also* 12 1. for ye	
cp. 16 19. for ye enter [cp. 5 20; 7 13, 21; 18 3, 8, 9; 19 17, 23, 24; 25 21, 23] not in yourselves [cp. 21 31], neither suffer ye them that are entering in to enter.² **15** Woe unto you,	cp. 9 43, 45, 47; 10 15, 23, 24, 25.	key of knowledge: ye entered [cp. 13 24; 18 17, 24, 25: *also* 24 26] not in yourselves, and them that were entering in ye hindered.	cp. 3 5; 10 1, 2, 9.

scribes and Pharisees, hypocrites [see above] ! for ye compass sea and land to make one proselyte; and when he is become so, ye make him twofold more a son of [3] hell [cp. 5 29, 30; 10 28; 23 33: also 5 22; 18 9] than yourselves. **16** Woe unto you [see above], ye blind guides [cp. 15 14; 23 17, 19, 24, 26], which say, Whosoever shall swear by the [4] temple, it is nothing; but whosoever shall swear by the gold of the [4] temple, he is [5] a debtor. **17** Ye fools [cp. 5 22] and blind [cp. verse 16]: for whether is greater, the gold, or the [4] temple that hath sanctified the gold ? **18** And, Whosoever shall swear by the altar, it is nothing; but whosoever shall swear by the gift that is upon it, he is [5] a debtor. **19** Ye blind [cp. verse 16]: for whether is greater, the gift, or the altar that sanctifieth the gift ? **20** He therefore that sweareth by the altar, sweareth by it, and by all things thereon. **21** And he that sweareth by the [4] temple, sweareth by it, and by him that dwelleth therein. **22** And he that sweareth by the heaven, sweareth by the throne of God [cp. 5 34], and by him that sitteth thereon.

(Mark): cp. 9 43, 45, 47.   *(Luke 20 47):* cp. 12 5.   cp. 6 39.   *(Luke 21 1):* cp. 9 39, 40, 41.   cp. 11 40.

Matt. 5 33-37.

23 Woe unto you, scribes and Pharisees, hypocrites [see above]! for ye tithe mint and [6] anise and cummin, and

cp. 22 37.

have left undone the weightier matters of the law, judgement, and mercy [cp. 9 13; 12 7], and faith: but these ye ought to have done, and not to have left the other undone. **24** Ye blind guides [cp. 15 14; 23 16, etc.], which strain out the gnat, and swallow the camel. **25** Woe unto you, scribes and Pharisees, hypocrites [see above] ! for ye cleanse the outside of the cup and of the platter, but within [cp. 15 19; 23 28] they are full from extortion and excess. cp. 22 18. **26** Thou blind [cp. verse 16] Pharisee, cp. verse 17.

cleanse first [cp. 5 24; 6 33; 7 5]

the inside of the cup and of the platter, that the outside thereof may become clean also. **27** Woe unto you, scribes and Pharisees, hypocrites [see above] ! for ye are like unto whited sepulchres, which outwardly appear beautiful, but inwardly are full of dead men's bones, and of all uncleanness.

28 Even so ye also outwardly appear [cp. 6 1, 2, 5, 16; 23 5] righteous unto men, but inwardly [cp. 15 19; 23 25, 26] ye are full of hypocrisy [cp. verse 13] and iniquity. **29** Woe unto you, scribes and Pharisees, hypocrites [see above] ! for ye build the sepulchres of the prophets, and garnish the tombs of the righteous, **30** and say, If we had been in the days of our fathers, we should not have been partakers with them in the blood of the prophets. **31** Wherefore ye witness to yourselves, that ye are sons of them that slew the prophets [cp. 5 12; 21 35-36; 22 6; 23 37]. **32** Fill ye up then the measure of your fathers. **33** Ye ser-

(Mark): cp. 12 30, 33.   cp. 7 4.   cp. 7 21-23.   cp. 12 40.   cp. 7 27.   cp. 7 19.   cp. 7 21-23.   cp. 12 15: also 7 6.   cp. 12 3-5.

(Luke):

42 But woe unto you [see above] Pharisees ! for ye tithe mint and rue and every herb, and pass over judgement and the love of God [cp. 10 27]: but these ought ye to have done, and not to leave the other undone.

cp. 6 39.

39 Now do ye Pharisees cleanse the outside of the cup and of the platter; but your inward part is full of extortion [cp. 16 14; 20 47] and wickedness. cp. 6 39. **40** Ye foolish ones [cp. 12 20], did not he that made the outside make the inside also ? **41** Howbeit [cp. 6 42] give for alms [cp. 12 33] those things which [1] are within; and behold, all things are clean unto you. **44** Woe unto you [see above] ! for ye are as the tombs which appear not, and the men that walk over *them* know it not.

cp. 11 39-41.
cp. 12 1: also 12 56; 13 15.
47 Woe unto you [see above]!

for ye build the tombs of the prophets, and your fathers killed them. **48** So ye are witnesses and consent unto the works of your fathers: for they killed them [cp. 6 23; 13 33, 34; 20 10-12], and ye build *their tombs.*

(far right): cp. 9 39, 40, 41.   cp. 5 42.   cp. 9 39, 40, 41.   cp. 9 39, 40, 41.

Matt.

pents, ye offspring of vipers [*cp.* 3 7; 12 34], how shall ye escape the judgement of ³ hell [*cp.* 5 29, 30; 10 28; 23 15: *also* 5 22; 18 9] ? **34** Therefore, behold, I send unto you prophets, and wise men, and scribes:
some of them shall ye kill and crucify [*cp.* 20 19; 27 26]; and some of them shall ye scourge in your synagogues [*cp.* 10 17], and persecute from city to city [*cp.* 10 23]: **35** that upon you may come all the righteous blood shed on the earth,

from the blood of Abel the righteous unto the blood of Zachariah son of Barachiah, whom ye slew between the sanctuary and the altar. **36** Verily I say unto you, All these things shall come upon this generation [*cp.* 24 34: *also* 10 23; 16 28].

¹ Gr. *before.*
² Some ancient authorities insert here, or after ver. 12, ver. 14 *Woe unto you, scribes and Pharisees, hypocrites! for ye devour widows' houses, even while for a pretence ye make long prayers: therefore ye shall receive greater condemnation.* See Mark 12 40; Luke 20 47. ³ Gr. *Gehenna.*
Or, *sanctuary*: as in ver. 35.
⁵ Or, *bound by his oath*   ⁶ Or, *dill*

Mark

cp. 9 43, 45, 47.

cp. 6 30.

cp. 15 15.

cp. 13 9.

cp. 13 30: *also* 9 1.

Luke

cp. 3 7.

cp. 12 5.
49 Therefore also said the wisdom [*cp.* 7 35] of God, I will send unto them prophets and apostles [*cp.* 6 13; 9 10; 17 5; 22 14; 24 10]; and *some* of them they shall kill

and persecute; **50** that the blood of all the prophets, which was shed from the foundation of the world, may be required of this generation [*see below*]; **51** from the blood of Abel unto the blood of Zachariah, who perished between the altar and the ² sanctuary: yea, I say unto you, it shall be required of this generation [*cp.* 21 32: *also* 9 27].

¹ Or, *ye can*   ² Gr. *house.*

cp. 13 16.

cp. 17 24.

Matt. 23 35 ‖ Luke 11 50-51 : *cp.* Gen. 4 8 ; II Chron. 24 20-22.

§ 210. **A Lament over Jerusalem**

[*Cp.* Luke 19 41-44: *also* 23 27-31 *and* 21 20]

Matt. 23 37-39

37 O Jerusalem, Jerusalem, which killeth the prophets [*cp.* 5 12; 21 35, 36; 22 6; 23 29-34], and stoneth [*cp.* 21 35] them that are sent unto her ! how often would I have gathered thy children together, even as a hen gathereth her chickens under her wings, and ye would not ! **38** Behold, your house is left unto you ¹ desolate. **39** For I say unto you, Ye shall not see me henceforth [*cp.* 26 29, 64], till ye shall say, Blessed *is* he that cometh [*cp.* 3 11; 11 3] in the name of the Lord [= 21 9 *and* John 12 13].

¹ Some ancient authorities omit *desolate.*

cp. 12 3-5.

cp. 1 7. 11 9.

Luke 13 34- 5

34 O Jerusalem, Jerusalem, which killeth the prophets [*cp.* 6 23; 11 47-50; 20 10-12], and stoneth them that are sent unto her ! how often would I have gathered thy children [*cp.* 19 44] together, even as a hen *gathereth* her own brood under her wings, and ye would not ! **35** Behold, your house is left unto you *desolate* [*cp.* 21 20: *also* 19 43-44; 23 29-31]: and I say unto you, Ye shall not see me, until ye shall say, Blessed *is* he that cometh [*cp.* 7 19, 20: *also* 3 16] in the name of the Lord [= 19 38 *and* John 12 13].

cp. 13 19; 14 7.

cp. 1 15, 27; 3 31; 6 14; 11 27: *also* 1 30.

Matt. 23 39 ‖ Luke 13 35 = Ps. 118 26.

§ 211. **A Widow's Mites**

Mark 12 41-44

41 And he sat down over against the treasury, and beheld how the multitude cast ¹ money into the treasury: and many that were

Luke 21 1-4

1 And he looked up, ¹ and saw the

rich cast in much. **42** And there came **2** a poor widow [*cp.* 12 40],	rich men that were casting their gifts into the treasury. **2** And he saw a certain poor widow [*cp.* 20 47: *also* 2 37; 4 25, 26; 7 12; 18 3] casting in	

and she cast in two mites, which make a farthing. **43** And he called unto him his disciples, and said unto them, Verily I say unto you, This poor widow cast in more than all they which are casting into the treasury: **44** for they all did cast in of their superfluity; but she of her want did cast in all that she had, *even* all her living.	thither two mites. **3** And he said, Of a truth [*cp.* 9 27; 12 44] I say unto you, This poor widow cast in more than they all: **4** for all these did of their superfluity cast in unto the gifts: but she of her want did cast in all the living that she had.	

¹ Gr. *brass.*   ² Gr. *one.*   ¹ Or, *and saw them that . . . treasury, and they were rich.*

§ 212. A Prophecy of the Destruction of the Temple

Matt. 24 1-2	Mark 13 1-2	Luke 21 5-6
1 And Jesus went out from the temple, and was going on his way; and his disciples came to him [*cp.* 5 1; 13 10, 36; 14 15; 15 12, 23; 17 19; 18 1; 24 3; 26 17] to shew him the buildings of the temple. **2** But he answered and said unto them, See ye not all these things? verily I say unto you, *cp.* 9 15. There shall not be left here one stone upon another, that shall not be thrown down.	**1** And as he went forth out of the temple, one of his disciples *cp.* 6 35. saith unto him, ¹ Master, behold, what manner of stones and what manner of buildings! **2** And Jesus said unto him, Seest thou these great buildings? *cp.* 2 20. there shall not be left here one stone upon another, which shall not be thrown down.	**5** And as some spake of the temple, *cp.* 9 12. how it was adorned with goodly stones and offerings, he said, **6** As for these things which ye behold, the days will come [*cp.* 5 35; 17 22: *also* 19 43; 23 29], in which there shall not be left here one stone upon another [*cp.* 19 44], that shall not be thrown down.

¹ Or, *Teacher*

(iii) The Great Apocalyptic Discourse (§§ 213-223)

§ 213. The Occasion of the Discourse

False Christs; Wars among Nations; Disturbances in Nature

Matt. 24 3-8	Mark 13 3-8	Luke 21 7-11	
3 And as he sat on the mount of Olives [*cp.* 26 30], the disciples *cp.* 17 1; 26 37. came unto him [*cp.* 5 1; 13 10, 36; 14 15; 15 12, 23; 17 19; 18 1; 24 1; 26 17] privately [*cp.* 17 1, 19; 20 17], saying, Tell us, when shall these things be? and what *shall be* the sign [*cp.* 24 30] of thy ¹ coming [*cp.*	**3** And as he sat on the mount of Olives [*cp.* 14 26] over against the temple, Peter and James and John [*cp.* 1 29; 5 37; 9 2; 14 33] and Andrew *cp.* 6 35. asked him privately [*cp.* 4 10, 34; 6 31, 32; 9 2, 28], **4** Tell us, when shall these things be? and what *shall be* the sign when these things are all about to be accomplished?	**7** And *cp.* 21 37; 22 39. they *cp.* 8 51; 9 28. *cp.* 9 12. asked him, [*cp.* 9 10; 10 23] saying, ¹ Master, when therefore shall these things be? and what *shall be* the sign [*cp.* 21 25] when these things are about to come to pass?	*cp.* 8 1.

24 27, 37, 39], and of [2] the end of the world [*cp.* 13 39, 40, 49; 28 20]? **4** And Jesus answered and said unto them, Take heed
that no man lead you astray.
5 For many shall come in my name [*cp.* 7 22; 18 5, 20], saying, I am the Christ;

cp. 3 2; 4 17; 10 7.
cp. 24 26.
and shall lead many astray [*cp.* 24 11, 24]. **6** And ye shall hear of wars and rumours of wars: see that ye be not troubled: for *these things* must needs come to pass;   [*cp.* 17 10]   but the end is not yet.

7 For nation shall rise against nation, and kingdom against kingdom: and there shall be famines and   earthquakes   in divers places.

cp. 16 1: *also* 24 29.
8 But all these things are the beginning of travail.

[1] Gr. *presence.*
[2] Or, *the consummation of the age*

---

5 And Jesus began to say unto them, Take heed [*cp.* 13 9, 23, 33] that no man lead you astray.
6 Many shall come in my name [*cp.* 9 37, 38, 39; 16 17], saying, I am *he* [*cp.* 14 62];
cp. 1 15.
and shall lead many astray [*cp.* 13 22]. **7** And when ye shall hear of wars and rumours of wars, be not troubled: *these things* must needs come to pass; [*cp.* 9 11, 12; 13 10] but the end is not yet.

8 For nation shall rise against nation, and kingdom against kingdom: there shall be   earthquakes   in divers places; there shall be famines:

cp. 8 11: *also* 13 24, 25.
       these things are the beginning of travail.

---

8 And he   said,
Take heed
that   ye be not led astray: for many shall come in my name [*cp.* 9 48, 49: *also* 10 17; 24 47], saying, I am *he* [*cp.* 22 70]: and, The time is at hand [*cp.* 10 9, 11]: go ye not after them [*cp.* 17 23].
cp. 17 21, 23.
       9 And when ye shall hear of wars and tumults, be not terrified: for these things must needs come to pass first [*cp.* 17 25]; but the end is not immediately.
10 Then said he unto them, Nation shall rise against nation, and kingdom against kingdom: **11** and there shall be   great earthquakes, and in divers places   famines and pestilences; and there shall be terrors and great signs from heaven [*cp.* 11 16: *also* 21 25, 26].

[1] Or, *Teacher*

cp. 14 13, 14, 26; 15 16; 16 23, 24, 26;   *also* 8 24, 28; 13 19.

---

§ 214. **Persecution of Disciples**

Matt. 24 9-14	Matt. 10 17-22	**Mark 13** 9-13	**Luke 21** 12-19	
	17 But beware of men: [*cp.* 13 5, 23, 33] for they will	**9** But take ye heed to yourselves: for they shall	**12** But before all these things, they shall lay their hands on you, and shall persecute you, delivering you up to	
9 Then shall they deliver you up unto tribulation, *cp.* 23 34.	deliver you up to councils, and in their synagogues they will scourge you; **18** yea and before governors and kings shall ye be brought for my sake [*cp.* 5 11; 10 39; 16 25: *also* 10 22; 19 29; 24 9], for a testimony to them [*cp.* 8 4; 24 14]	deliver you up to councils; and in synagogues shall ye be beaten; and before governors and kings shall ye stand for my sake [*cp.* 8 35; 10 29: *also* 13 13], for a testimony unto them [*cp.* 1 44; 6 11]. **10** And the gospel [*cp.* 1 1, 14, 15; 8 35; 10 29; 14 9; 16 15]	the synagogues and prisons, [1] bringing you before kings and governors for my name's sake [*cp.* 21 17: *also* 6 22; 9 24; 18 29]. **13** It shall turn unto you for a testimony. *cp.* 5 14; 9 5.	*cp.* 15 21.
verse 14	*cp.* 17 10. and to the Gentiles [*cp.* 8 11; 21 31, 41, 43; 22 7-10; 26 13; 28 19].	must first [*cp.* 9 11, 12] be preached unto all the nations [*cp.* 12 9; 14 9; 16 15].	*cp.* 2 30-32; 3 6; 13 29; 14 21-24; 20 16; 24 47.	*cp.* 10 16; 11 52.
	19 But when they	**11** And when they lead you to *judgement,*	Luke 12 11 And when they bring you before the	

Matthew	Mark	Luke (12)	Luke (21)	
	and	synagogues, and the rulers, and the authorities,		
deliver you up,	deliver you up,		**14** Settle it therefore in your hearts, not to meditate beforehand how to answer:	
be not anxious [*cp.* 6 25, 31, 34] how or what ye shall	be not anxious beforehand what ye shall	be not anxious [*cp.* 12 22] how or what ye shall answer, or what ye shall say: **12** for the Holy Spirit shall teach you in that very hour what ye ought to say.	**15** for I will give you	
speak: for it shall be given you in that hour what ye shall speak. **20** For it is not ye that speak, but the Spirit of your Father that speaketh in you.	speak: but whatsoever shall be given you in that hour, that speak ye: for it is not ye that speak, but the Holy Ghost.		a mouth and wisdom,	*cp.* 14 26; 15 26.

Matthew	Mark	Luke (12)	Luke (21)	
			which all your adversaries shall not be able to withstand or to gainsay. **16** But ye shall be delivered up even by parents, and brethren, and kinsfolk, and friends;	
verse 10	**21** And brother shall deliver up brother to death, and the father his child: and children shall rise up against parents, and ¹ cause them to be put to death [*cp.* 10 35, 36]. **22** And ye shall be hated	**12** And brother shall deliver up brother to death, and the father his child; and children shall rise up against parents, and ¹ cause them to be put to death. **13** And ye shall be hated	and *some* of you ² shall they cause to be put to death [*cp.* 12 53]. **17** And ye shall be hated [*cp.* 1 71; 6 22, 27]	*cp.* 16 2.
and shall kill you: and ye shall be hated of all the nations for my name's sake [*cp.* 19 29: *also* 5 11; 10 18, 39; 16 25].	of all men for my name's sake:	of all men for my name's sake [*cp.* 8 35; 10 29; 13 9]:	of all men for my name's sake [*cp.* 21 12: *also* 6 22; 9 24; 18 29]. **18** And not a hair of your head [*cp.* 12 7] shall perish.	*cp.* 15 18-21; 17 14.

Matthew	Mark	Luke (12)	Luke (21)	
10 And then shall many stumble [*cp.* 13 21: *also* 11 6; 13 57; 15 12; 26 31, 33], and shall deliver up one another, and shall hate one another. **11** And many false prophets [*cp.* 24 24: *also* 7 15] shall arise, and shall lead many astray [*cp.* 24 5, 24]. **12** And because iniquity shall be multiplied, the love of the many shall wax cold. **13** But he that endureth to the end, the same shall be saved. **14** And ¹ this gospel of the kingdom [*cp.* 4 23; 9 35: *also* 26 13] shall be preached in the whole ² world [*cp.* 26 13] for a testimony [*cp.* 8 4; 10 18] unto	*cp.* 10 30. *verse* 21 but he that endureth to the end, the same shall be saved.	*cp.* 4 17: *also* 6 3; 14 27, 29. *verse* 12 *cp.* 13 22. *cp.* 13 6, 22. but he that endureth to the end, the same shall be saved. *verse* 10 *cp.* 14 9.	*cp.* 7 23. *verse* 16 **19** In your patience [*cp.* 8 15] ye shall win your ³ souls.	*cp.* 16 1: *also* 6 61.
	cp. 1 44; 6 11; 13 9.	*cp.* 5 14; 9 5; 21 13.		

all the nations [*cp.* 8 11; 10 18; 21 31,41, 43; 22 7-10; 26 13; 28 19]; and then shall the end come.	*cp.* 12 9; 13 10; 14 9; 16 15.	*cp.* 2 30-32; 3 6; 13 29; 14 21-24; 20 16; 24 47.	*cp.* 10 16; 11 52.

¹ Or, *put them to death*

¹ Or, *put them to death*

¹ Gr. *you being brought.*
² Or, *shall they put to death*
³ Or, *lives*

§ 215. Desolation and Tribulation in Judæa: The Lure of False Teachers

Matt. 24 15-28	**Mark 13** 14-23	**Luke 21** 20-24
15 When therefore ye see [*cp.* 24 33] the abomination of desolation [*cp.* 23 38], which was spoken of ¹ by Daniel the prophet, standing in ² the holy place (let him that readeth understand), **16** then let them that are in Judæa flee unto the mountains:	**14** But when ye see [*cp.* 13 29] the abomination of desolation standing where he ought not (let him that readeth understand), then let them that are in Judæa flee unto the mountains:	**20** But when ye see [*cp.* 12 54, 55; 21 31] Jerusalem compassed with armies [*cp.* 19 43], then know that her desolation [*cp.* 13 35: *also* 19 43-44; 23 29-31] is at hand.
17 let him that is on the housetop not go down to take out the things that are in his house: **18** and let him that is in the field not return back to take his cloke.	**15** and let him that is on the housetop not go down, nor enter in, to take anything out of his house: **16** and let him that is in the field not return back to take his cloke.	**21** Then let them that are in Judæa flee unto the mountains; and let them that are in the midst of her depart out; 17 31 In that day, he which shall be on the housetop, and his goods in the house, let him not go down to take them away: and let him that is in the field likewise not return back. and let not them that are in the country enter therein. **22** For these are days of vengeance [*cp.* 18 7, 8], that all things which are written may be fulfilled.
19 But woe unto them that are with child and to them that give suck in those days! **20** And pray ye that your flight be not in the winter, neither on a sabbath: **21** for then shall be great tribulation,	**17** But woe unto them that are with child and to them that give suck in those days! **18** And pray ye that it be not in the winter. **19** For those days shall be tribulation,	**23** Woe unto them that are with child and to them that give suck in those days! for there shall be great distress upon the ¹ land, and wrath unto this people. **24** And they shall fall by the edge of the sword, and shall be led captive into all the nations: and Jerusalem shall be trodden down of the Gentiles, until the times of the Gentiles be fulfilled.
such as hath not been from the beginning of the world until now, nor ever shall be. **22** And except those days had been shortened, no flesh would have been saved: but for the elect's [*cp.* 24 24, 31] sake those days shall be shortened. **23** Then if any man shall say unto you, Lo,	such as there hath not been the like from the beginning of the creation [*cp.* 10 6; 16 15] which God created until now, and never shall be. **20** And except the Lord had shortened the days, no flesh would have been saved: but for the elect's [*cp.* 13 22, 27] sake, whom he chose, he shortened the days. **21** And then if any man shall say unto you, Lo,	*cp.* 18 7. 17 23 And they shall say to you, Lo,

here is the Christ [*cp.* 24 5], or,   Here; believe [3] *it* not. **24** For there shall arise false Christs, and false prophets [*cp.* 24 11: *also* 7 15], and shall shew great signs and wonders;   so as to lead astray [*cp.* 24 5, 11], if possible, even the elect [*cp.* 24 22, 31].

25 Behold, I have told you   beforehand. **26** If therefore they shall say unto you, Behold, he is in the wilderness; go not forth:

Behold, he is in the inner chambers; believe [4] *it* not. **27** For as the lightning   cometh forth from the

east, and is seen even unto the   west; so shall be the [5] coming [*cp.* 24 3, 37, 39] of the Son of man.

28 Wheresoever the carcase is, there will the [6] eagles be gathered together.

[1] Or, *through* [2] Or, *a holy place*
[3] Or, *him* [4] Or, *them*
[5] Gr. *presence.* [6] Or, *vultures*

---

here is the Christ [*cp.* 13 6]; or, Lo, there; believe [1] *it* not: **22** for there shall arise false Christs and false prophets, and shall shew signs and wonders, that they may lead astray [*cp.* 13 6], if possible,   the elect [*cp.* 13 20, 27]. **23** But take ye heed [*cp.* 13 5, 9, 33]: behold, I have told you all things beforehand.

[1] Or, *him*

---

there !   *cp.* 21 8. Lo, here [*cp.* 17 21] !

cp. 18 7.

go not *away*, nor follow after *them* [*cp.* 21 8]:

24 for as the lightning, when it lighteneth out of the one part under the heaven,   shineth   unto the other part under heaven ; so shall   the Son of man be [2] in his day . . . . . **37** And they answering say unto him, Where, Lord ? And he said unto them, Where   the body *is*, thither will the [3] eagles also be gathered together.

[1] Or, *earth*
[2] Some ancient authorities omit *in his day.*   [3] Or, *vultures*

---

cp. 13 19; 14 29; 16 4.

Matt. 24 15 ‖ Mark 13 14: *cp.* Dan. 9 27 ; 11 31 ; 12 11.

§ 216. **Signs in Heaven and the Coming of the Son of Man**

Matt. 24 29-31	**Mark 13** 24-27	**Luke 21** 25-28
29 But immediately, after the tribulation of those days, *cp.* 24 3, 30. the sun shall be darkened, and the moon shall not give her light, and the stars shall fall from heaven,	**24** But in those days, after that tribulation, *cp.* 13 4. the sun shall be darkened, and the moon shall not give her light, **25** and the stars shall be falling from heaven,	**25** And there shall be signs [*cp.* 21 7, 11] in sun and moon and stars; and upon the earth distress of nations, in perplexity for the roaring of the sea and the billows; **26** men [1] fainting for fear, and for expectation of the things which are coming on [2] the world : for the powers of
and the powers of the heavens shall be shaken : **30** and then shall appear the sign [*cp.* 24 3] of the Son of man in heaven : and then shall all the tribes of the earth mourn, and they shall see the Son of man coming on the clouds of heaven with power and great glory [*cp.* 16 27; 25 31; 26 64]. **31** And he shall send forth his angels [*cp.* 13 41: *also* 13 49; 16 27; 25 31]	and the powers that are in the heavens shall be shaken. *cp.* 13 4. **26** And then shall they see the Son of man coming in clouds with great power and glory [*cp.* 8 38; 14 62]. **27** And then shall he send forth the angels [*cp.* 8 38],	the heavens shall be shaken. *cp.* 21 7, 11, 25. **27** And then shall they see the Son of man coming in a cloud with power and great glory [*cp.* 9 26]. *cp.* 9 26; 12 8, 9.

[1] with [2] a great sound of a trumpet, and they shall gather together his elect [*cp.* 24 22, 24: *also* 3 12; 13 30] from the four winds, from one end of heaven to the other.	and shall gather together his elect [*cp.* 13 20, 22] from the four winds, from the uttermost part of the earth to the uttermost part of heaven.	*cp.* 18 7: *also* 3 17. **28** But when these things begin to come to pass, look up, and lift up your heads; because your redemption [*cp.* 1 68; 2 38; 24 21] draweth nigh.

[1] Many ancient authorities read *with a great trumpet, and they shall gather &c.*
[2] Or, *a trumpet of great sound*

[1] Or, *expiring*
[2] Gr. *the inhabited earth.*

Matt. 24 30 ‖ Mark 13 26 ‖ Luke 21 27: *cp.* Dan. 7 13-14.

§ 217. The Parable of the Fig Tree and the Date of the Coming

[*Cp.* Luke 13 6-9: *also* Matt. 21 18-20 ‖ Mark 11 12-14, 20-21; *and* Matt. 16 2-3 ‖ Luke 12 54-56]

Matt. 24 32-36	Mark 13 28-32	Luke 21 29-33	
32 Now from the fig tree learn her parable: when her branch is now become tender, and putteth forth its leaves, ye know that the summer is nigh; **33** even so ye also, when ye see [*cp.* 24 15] all these things, know ye that [1] he is nigh, *even* at the doors. **34** Verily I say unto you, This generation shall not pass away, till all these things be accomplished [*cp.* 23 36: *also* 10 23; 16 28]. **35** Heaven and earth shall pass away [*cp.* 5 18], but my words shall not pass away. **36** But of that day [*cp.* 7 22: *also* 26 29] and hour knoweth no one [*cp.* 24 42, 44, 50; 25 13], not even the angels of heaven, [2] neither the Son, but the Father only.	**28** Now from the fig tree learn her parable: when her branch is now become tender, and putteth forth its leaves, ye know that the summer is nigh; **29** even so ye also, when ye see [*cp.* 13 14] these things coming to pass, know ye that [1] he is nigh, *even* at the doors. **30** Verily I say unto you, This generation shall not pass away, until all these things be accomplished [*cp.* 9 1]. **31** Heaven and earth shall pass away: but my words shall not pass away. **32** But of that day [*cp.* 14 25] or that hour knoweth no one [*cp.* 13 33, 35], not even the angels in heaven, neither the Son, but the Father.	**29** And he spake to them a parable: Behold the fig tree, and all the trees: **30** when they now shoot forth, ye see it and know of your own selves [*cp.* 12 57] that the summer is now nigh. **31** Even so ye also, when ye see [*cp.* 12 54, 55; 21 20] these things coming to pass, know ye that the kingdom of God is nigh. **32** Verily I say unto you, This generation shall not pass away, till all things be accomplished [*cp.* 11 51: *also* 9 27]. **33** Heaven and earth shall pass away [*cp.* 16 17]: but my words shall not pass away. *cp.* 10 12; 17 31; 21 34. *cp.* 12 40, 46.	*cp.* 14 20; 16 23, 26.

[1] Or, *it*   [2] Many authorities, some ancient, omit *neither the Son.*

[1] Or, *it*

§ 218. A Description of the Coming

Matt. 24 37-41	Luke 17 26-30, 34-35
37 And as *were* the days of Noah, so shall be the [1] coming [*cp.* 24 3, 27, 39] of the Son of man. **38** For as in those days which were before the flood they were eating and drinking, marrying and giving in marriage, until the day that Noah entered into the ark, **39** and they knew not until the flood came, and took them all away;	**26** And as it came to pass in the days of Noah, even so shall it be also in the days of the Son of man. **27** They ate, they drank, they married, they were given in marriage, until the day that Noah entered into the ark, and the flood came, and destroyed them all. **28** Likewise

		even as it came to pass in the days of Lot; they ate, they drank, they bought, they sold, they planted, they builded ; **29** but in the day that Lot went out from Sodom it rained fire and brimstone from heaven, and destroyed them all : **30** after the same manner shall it be in the day that
so shall be the [1] coming [cp. 24 3, 27, 37] of the Son of man.		the Son of man is revealed. . . . **34** I say unto you, In that night there shall be two men on one bed ;
40 Then shall two men be in the field ; one is taken, and one is left : **41** two women *shall* be grinding at the mill; one is taken, and one is left.		the one shall be taken, and the other shall be left. **35** There shall be two women grinding together ; the one shall be taken, and the other shall be left.[1]
[1] Gr. *presence.*		[1] Some ancient authorities add ver. 36 *There shall be two men in the field; the one shall be taken, and the other shall be left.*

Matt. 24 37-39 ‖ Luke 17 26-27 : Gen. 6 11-13 ; 7 7, 21-23.   Luke 17 28-29 : Gen. 18 20 *ff.*; 19 16, 24-25.

§ 219. Injunctions to Watch

Matt. 24 42-44	Mark 13 33-37	Luke 21 34-36	
	33 Take ye heed [cp. 13 5, 9, 23],	**34** But take heed to yourselves [cp. 12 1; 17 3], lest haply your hearts be overcharged with surfeiting, and drunkenness [cp. 12 45], and cares of this life [cp. 8 14], and that day [cp. 10 12; 17 31] come on you suddenly as a snare: **35** for *so* shall it come upon all them that dwell on the face of all the earth. **36** But	
cp. 13 22.	*cp.* 4 19.		
cp. 7 22 ; 24 36: *also* 26 29.	*cp.* 13 32: *also* 14 25.	watch [cp. 12 37] ye at every season, making supplication [cp. 22 40, 46], that ye may prevail to escape all these things that shall come to pass, and to stand before the Son of man.	*cp.* 14 20; 16 23, 26.
25 13 Watch [cp. 24 42; 26 38, 41] therefore, *cp.* 26 41.	watch [cp. 13 35, 37; 14 34, 38] [1] and pray [cp. 14 38] :		
for ye know not [cp. 24 36, 42, 44, 50] the day nor the hour. **14** For *it is* as *when* a man, going into another country [cp. 21 33],	for ye know not [cp. 13 32, 35] when the time is. **34** *It is* as *when* a man, sojourning in another country [cp. 12 1],	*cp.* 12 40, 46. 19 12 A certain nobleman went into a far [cp. 15 13] country [cp. 20 9], to receive for himself a kingdom, and to return. **13** And he	
called his own [1] servants, and delivered unto them his goods.	having left his house, and given authority to his [2] servants,	called ten [1] servants of his, and gave them ten [2] pounds. 12 37 Blessed are those [1] servants, whom the lord when he cometh shall find [cp. 12 38, 43]	*cp.* 13 17.
	to each one his work, commanded also the porter to watch. **35** Watch [*see verse* 33] therefore:	watching [cp. 21 36] :	
42 Watch [cp. 25 13 ; 26 38, 41] therefore: for ye know not [cp. 24 36, 44, 50; 25 13] on what day your Lord cometh.	for ye know not [cp. 13 32, 33] when the lord of the house cometh,	*cp.* 12 40, 46.	
		verily I say unto you, that he shall gird himself [cp. 12 35 ; 17 8], and make them sit down to meat, and shall come and serve them [cp. 22 27 :	*cp.* 13 4. *cp.* 13 5.

Matt.	Mark	Luke	
		also 17 8]. **38** And if he shall come in the second watch, and if in the third,	
cp. 25 6.	whether at even, or at midnight, or at cockcrowing, or in the morning; **36** lest coming suddenly he find you sleeping [*cp.* 14 37, 40].		
cp. 25 5; 26 40, 43.		and find [*cp.* 22 45] *them* so, blessed are those *servants* [*cp.* 12 37, 43]. **39** [3] But	*cp.* 13 17.
43 [2] But that if know this, the master of the house had known in what watch the thief was coming, he would have watched, and would not have suffered his house to be [3] broken through [*cp.* 6 19, 20]. **44** Therefore be ye also ready [*cp.* 25 10]: for in an hour that ye think not [*cp.* 24 36, 42, 50; 25 13] the Son of man cometh. *cp.* 14 28; 15 15; 16 22; 17 4; 18 21; 19 27; 26 33: *also* 16 16; 17 24.	*cp.* 13 32, 33, 35. **37** And [*cp.* 8 32; 9 5; 10 28; 11 21; 14 29: *also* 8 29] what I say unto you I say unto all, Watch [*see verse* 33].	know this [*cp.* 10 11], that if the master of the house had known in what hour the thief was coming, he would have watched, and not have left his house to be [4] broken through. **40** Be ye also ready [*cp.* 12 47: *also* 17 8]: for in an hour that ye think not [*cp.* 12 46] the Son of man cometh. **41** And Peter [*cp.* 8 45; 9 33; 18 28: *also* 5 8; 9 20] said, Lord, speakest thou this parable unto us, or even unto all?	*cp.* 13 36, 37; 21 21: *also* 6 68.

[1] Gr. *bondservants.*
[2] Or, *But this ye know*
[3] Gr. *digged through.*

[1] Some ancient authorities omit *and pray.*   [2] Gr. *bondservants.*

[1] Gr. *bondservants.*
[2] *Mina,* here translated a pound, is equal to one hundred drachmas. See ch. 15 8.   [3] Or, *But this ye know*
[4] Gr. *digged through.*

§ 220. The Obligations of Servants in the Interim

[*Cp.* Matt. 25 14-30; Luke 19 11-27]

Matt. 24 45-51		Luke 12 42-46	
45 Who then is the faithful [*cp.* 25 21, 23] and wise [*cp.* 7 24; 10 16; 25 2 *ff.*] [1] servant, whom his lord hath set over [*cp.* 24 47; 25 21, 23] his household, to give them their food in due season? **46** Blessed is that [1] servant, whom his lord when he cometh shall find so doing. **47** Verily I say unto you, that he will set him over [*cp.* 25 21, 23: *also* 24 45] all that he hath. **48** But if that evil [*cp.* 18 32; 25 26] [1] servant shall say in his heart, My lord tarrieth [*cp.* 25 5]; **49** and shall begin to beat his fellow-servants [*cp.* 18 28, 29, 31, 33], and shall eat and drink with the drunken; **50** the lord of that [1] servant [*cp.* 18 27; 25 19] shall come in a day when he expecteth not, and in an hour when he knoweth not [*cp.* 24 36, 42, 44; 25 13], **51** and shall [2] cut him asunder, and appoint his portion with the hypocrites [*cp.* 6 2, 5, 16: *also* 15 7; 22 18; 23 13 *ff.*]: there shall be the weeping and gnashing of teeth [*cp.* 8 12; 13 42, 50; 22 13; 25 30].	*cp.* 13 32, 33, 35. *cp.* 7 6; 12 15.	**42** And the Lord said, Who then is [1] the faithful [*cp.* 16 10, 11, 12; 19 17] and wise [*cp.* 16 8] steward [*cp.* 16 1 *ff.*], whom his lord shall set over [*cp. verse* 44] his household, to give them their portion of food in due season? **43** Blessed is that [2] servant, whom his lord when he cometh shall find [*cp.* 12 37, 38] so doing. **44** Of a truth [*cp.* 9 27; 21 3] I say unto you, that he will set him over [*cp. verse* 42: *also* 19 17, 19] all that he hath. **45** But if that [*cp.* 19 22] [2] servant shall say in his heart, My lord delayeth his coming; and shall begin to beat the menservants and the maidservants, and to eat and drink, and to be drunken [*cp.* 21 34]; **46** the lord of that [2] servant shall come in a day when he expecteth not, and in an hour when he knoweth not [*cp.* 12 40], and shall [3] cut him asunder, and appoint his portion with the [*cp.* 12 1, 56; 13 15] unfaithful. *cp.* 13 28.	*cp.* 13 17.

[1] Gr. *bondservant.*   [2] Or, *severely scourge him*

[1] Or, *the faithful steward, the wise* man *whom &c.*
[2] Gr. *bondservant.*
[3] Or, *severely scourge him*

§ 221. **The Parable of the Ten Virgins**

[*Cp*. Luke 12 35-36]

Matt. 25 1-13

1 Then shall the kingdom of heaven be likened unto ten virgins, which took their [1] lamps, and went forth to meet the bridegroom. **2** And five of them were foolish [*cp*. 7 26], and five were wise [*cp*. 7 24; 10 16; 24 45]. **3** For the foolish, when they took their [1] lamps, took no oil with them: **4** but the wise took oil in their vessels with their [1] lamps. **5** Now while the bridegroom tarried [*cp*. 24 48], they all slumbered and slept [*cp*. 26 40, 43]. **6** But at midnight [*cp*. Mark 13 35] there is a cry, Behold, the bridegroom! Come ye forth to meet him. **7** Then all those virgins arose, and trimmed their [1] lamps. **8** And the foolish said unto the wise, Give us of your oil; for our [1] lamps are going out. **9** But the wise answered, saying, Peradventure there will not be enough for us and you: go ye rather to them that sell, and buy for yourselves. **10** And while they went away to buy, the bridegroom came; and they that were ready [*cp*. 24 44] went in with him to the marriage feast:

and the door was shut.

11 Afterward come also the other virgins, saying, Lord, Lord, open to us. **12** But he answered and said, Verily I say unto you, I know you not [*cp*. 7 23].

13 Watch [*cp*. 26 38, 41] therefore,

cp. 26 41.

for ye know not [*cp*. 24 36, 44, 50] the day nor the hour.

24 **42** Watch therefore: for ye know not on what day your Lord   cometh.

[1] Or, *torches*

---

cp. 13 36; 14 37, 40.

Mark 13 **33** Take ye heed, watch [*cp*. 13 37; 14 34, 38]

[1] and pray [*cp*. 14 38]:
            for ye know not [*cp*. 13 32]
            when the time is.
    35 Watch therefore: for ye know not when   the lord of the house cometh.

[1] Some ancient authorities omit *and pray*.

---

cp. 12 42.

cp. 22 45.

cp. 12 40, 47.

Luke 13 **25** When once the master of the house is risen up, and hath shut to the door, and ye begin to stand without, and to knock at the door,

        saying, Lord, open to us; and he shall answer and say to you, I know you not [*cp*. 13 27] whence ye are.   21 36 But watch [*cp*. 12 37]   ye at every season, making supplication [*cp*. 22 40, 46].

        cp. 12 40, 46.

---

cp. 7 27, 28; 8 14; 9 29, 30.

§ 222. **The Parable of the Talents**

[*Cp*. Matt. 24 45-51: Luke 12 41-48; 16 10-12]

Matt. 25 14-30

14 For *it is* as *when* a man, going into another   country [*cp*. 21 33], *cp*. 18 23; 22 2 *ff*.; 25 34, 40.

called   his own [1] servants,

and delivered unto them his goods. **15** And unto one he gave   five talents [*cp*. 18 24],   to another two, to another one; to each according to his several ability;

Mark 13 **34** *It is* as *when* a man, sojourning in another   country [*cp*. 12 1],

        having left his house, and given authority to his   [1] servants,   to each one his work, commanded also the porter to watch.

[1] Gr. *bondservants*.

Luke 19 12-27

12 He said therefore,   A certain nobleman went into a far [*cp*. 15 13] country [*cp*. 20 9], to receive for himself a kingdom, and to return.   **13** And he called   ten [1] servants of his,

        and gave them ten [2] pounds,

        and said unto them, Trade ye *herewith* till I come.

---

cp. 21 22, 23.

and he went on his journey [cp. 21 33].

cp. 12 1.

cp. 20 9.
14 But his citizens hated him, and sent an ambassage [cp. 14 32] after him, saying, We will not that this man reign over us.

16 Straightway he that received the five talents went and traded with them, and made other five talents. **17** In like manner he also that *received* the two gained other two. **18** But he that received the one went away and digged in the earth, and hid his lord's [cp. 18 25, *etc.*] money. **19** Now after a long time the lord of those [1] servants [cp. 18 27; 24 50] cometh,

and maketh a reckoning with them [cp. 18 23].
20 And he that received the five talents came and brought other five talents, saying, Lord, thou deliveredst unto me five talents: lo, I have gained other five talents. **21** His lord said unto him, Well done, good and faithful [cp. 24 45] [2] servant: thou hast been faithful over a few things, I will set thee over [cp. 24 47 *and* 45] many things: enter [cp. 7 13; *etc.*] thou into the joy of thy lord. **22** And he also that *received* the two talents came and said, Lord, thou deliveredst unto me two talents: lo, I have gained other two talents. **23** His lord said unto him, Well done, good and faithful [cp. 24 45] [2] servant; thou hast been faithful over a few things, I will set thee over [cp. 24 47 *and* 45] many things: enter [cp. 7 13; *etc.*] thou into the joy of thy lord. **24** And he also that had received the one talent came and said, Lord, I knew thee that thou art a hard man, reaping where thou didst not sow, and gathering where thou didst not scatter: **25** and I was afraid, and went away and hid thy talent in the earth: lo, thou hast thine own. **26** But his lord answered and said unto him, Thou wicked [cp. 18 32: *also* 24 48] and slothful [2] servant, thou knewest that I reap where I sowed not, and gather where I did not scatter; **27** thou oughtest therefore to have put my money to the bankers, and at my coming I should have received back mine own with interest.
cp. 16 28; 26 73; 27 47.
28 Take ye away therefore the talent from him, and give it unto him that hath the ten talents [cp. 21 43].

cp. 9 43; *etc.*

cp. 9 43; *etc.*

cp. 9 1; 11 5; 14 47, 69, 70; 15 35, 39.

15 And it came to pass, when he [cp. 12 46] was come back again, having received the kingdom, that he commanded these [1] servants, unto whom he had given the money, to be called to him, that he might know what they had gained by trading. 16 And the first came before him, saying, Lord, thy pound hath made ten pounds more. 17 And he said unto him, Well done, thou good [cp. 12 42] [3] servant: because thou wast found faithful in a very little [cp. 16 10: *also* 12 26], have thou authority over [cp. 12 44 *and* 42] ten cities. cp. 13 24; *etc.*
18 And the second came, saying, Thy pound, Lord, hath made five pounds. 19 And he said unto him also,
cp. 12 42.
Be thou also over [cp. 12 44 *and* 42] five cities.
cp. 13 24; *etc.*
20 And [4] another came, saying, Lord, behold, *here is* thy pound, which I kept laid up in a napkin: 21 for I feared thee, because thou art an austere man: thou takest up that thou layedst not down, and reapest that thou didst not sow.

22 He saith unto him, Out of thine own mouth will I judge thee, thou wicked [3] servant. Thou knewest that I am an austere man, taking up that I laid not down, and reaping that I did not sow; 23 then wherefore gavest thou not my money into the bank, and [5] I at my coming should have required it with interest? 24 And he said unto them that stood by [cp. 9 27], Take away from him the pound, and give it unto him that hath the ten pounds. 25 And they said unto him,

cp. 3 5; 10 1, 2, 9: *and* 15 11; 17 13.

cp. 3 5; 10 1, 2, 9: *and* 15 11; 17 13.

cp. 12 29.

29 For unto every one that hath shall be given, and he shall have abundance: but from him that hath not, even that which he hath shall be taken away.

Matt. 13 **12** For whosoever hath, to him shall be given, and he shall have abundance: but whosoever hath not, from him shall be taken away even that which he hath.

Mark 4 **25** For he that hath, to him shall be given: and he that hath not, from him shall be taken away even that which he hath.

30 And cast ye out the unprofitable [1] servant into the outer darkness [cp. 8 12; 22 13]:

there shall be the weeping and gnashing of teeth [cp. 8 12; 13 42, 50; 22 13; 24 51].

Lord, he hath ten pounds. **26** I say unto you, that unto every one that hath shall be given;

but from him that hath not, even that which he hath shall be taken away from him.

Luke 8 **18** For whosoever hath, to him shall be given;

and whosoever hath not, from him shall be taken away even that which he [6] thinketh he hath.

cp. 17 10.

27 Howbeit these mine enemies, which would not that I should reign over them, bring hither, and slay them before me.

cp. 13 28.

[1] Gr. bondservants.   [2] Gr. bondservant.

[1] Gr. bondservants.
[2] *Mina*, here translated a pound, is equal to one hundred drachmas. See ch. 15 8.
[3] Gr. bondservant.   [4] Gr. *the other.*
[5] Or, *I should have gone and required*
[6] Or, *seemeth to have*

§ 223. The Parable of the Sheep and the Goats

Matt. 25 31-46

31 But when the Son of man shall come in his glory [cp. 16 27; 24 30; 26 64], and all the angels with him [cp. 16 27: *also* 13 41, 49; 24 31], then shall he sit on the throne of his glory [cp. 19 28]: **32** and before him shall be gathered all the nations: and he shall separate them one from another [cp. 3 12; 13 30, 47-50: *also* 22 10], as the shepherd separateth the sheep from the [1] goats: **33** and he shall set the sheep on his right hand, but the [1] goats on the left. **34** Then shall the King [cp. 18 23; 22 2, 7, 11, 13; 25 40] say [cp. 7 23] unto them on his right hand, Come, ye blessed of my Father, inherit the kingdom prepared [cp. 20 23] for you from the foundation of the world [cp. 13 35]: **35** for I was an hungred, and ye gave me meat: I was thirsty, and ye gave me drink: I was a stranger, and ye took me in; **36** naked, and ye clothed me: I was sick, and ye visited me: I was in prison, and ye came unto me. **37** Then shall the righteous answer him, saying, Lord, when saw we thee an hungred, and fed thee? or athirst, and gave thee drink? **38** And when saw we thee a stranger, and took thee in? or naked, and clothed thee? **39** And when saw we thee sick, or in prison, and came unto thee? **40** And the King [see verse 34 above] shall answer and say unto them, Verily I say unto you, Inasmuch as ye did it unto one of these my brethren, *even* these least, ye did it unto me [cp. 10 40-42]. **41** Then shall he say [cp. 7 23] also unto them on the left hand, [2] Depart from me [cp. 7 23], ye cursed, into the eternal fire [cp. 18 8 *and* 25 46: *also* 3 12; 5 22; 13 42, 50; 18 9: *and* 5 29, 30; 10 28; 23 33] which is prepared for the devil and his angels: **42** for I was an hungred, and ye gave me no meat: I was thirsty, and ye gave me no drink: **43** I was a stranger, and ye took me not in; naked, and ye clothed me not; sick, and in prison, and ye visited me not. **44** Then shall they also answer, saying, Lord, when saw we thee an hungred, or athirst, or a stranger, or naked, or sick, or in prison, and did not minister unto thee? **45** Then shall he answer them, saying, Verily I say unto you, Inasmuch as ye did it not unto one of these least, ye did it not unto me. **46** And these shall go away into eternal punishment [see verse 41 above]: but the righteous into eternal life [cp. 19 16, 29].

cp. 8 38; 13 26, 27; 14 62: *also* 10 37.

cp. 9 26; 21 27: *also* 12 8, 9; and 9 32; 24 26. cp. 3 17.

cp. 1 14; 2 11; 12 41; 17 5, 22, 24.

cp. 19 12, 15, 27: *and* 13 27.

cp. 10 40.   cp. 11 50.   cp. 17 24.

cp. 19 12, 15, 27.

cp. 9 41.   cp. 13 27.
             cp. 13 27.
cp. 9 43, 45, 47.   cp. 3 17: *also* 12 5.   cp. 15 6.

cp. 3 29.   cp. 5 29.
cp. 10 17, 30.   cp. 10 25; 18 18, 30: *also* 16 9.   cp. 3 15; *etc.*

[1] Gr, *kids.*   [2] Or. *Depart from me under a curse*

(iv) Summary (§ 224)

§ 224. The Jerusalem Ministry in Retrospect

	Mark 11 19	Luke 21 37-38	
cp. 26 55: also 21 23. cp. 21 17; 26 30. cp. 24 3; 26 30.	cp. 14 49: also 12 35. 19 And [1] every evening [2] he went forth out [cp. 11 11; 14 26] of the city. cp. 13 3; 14 26. cp. 12 37.	37 And every day he was teaching in the temple [cp. 19 47; 22 53: also 20 1]; and every night he went out [cp. 22 39], and lodged in the mount that is called the mount of Olives [cp. 22 39]. 38 And all the people came early in the morning to him in the temple, to hear him [cp. 19 48].	cp. 18 20: also 7 28; 8 20. cp. 18 1-2. cp. 8 1. cp. 8 2.

[1] Gr. whenever evening came.
[2] Some ancient authorities read they.

F. The Passion and Resurrection (§§ 225-259)

(i) The Prologue to the Passion (§§ 225-228)

§ 225. The Plot to destroy Jesus

Matt. 26 1-5	Mark 14 1-2	Luke 22 1-2	John 11 55, 47-53
1 And it came to pass, when Jesus had finished all these words [cp. 7 28; 11 1; 13 53; 19 1], he said unto his disciples, 2 Ye know that after two days the passover cp. 26 17. cometh,		cp. 7 1.	
	1 Now after two days was *the feast of* the passover and the un-leavened bread [cp. 14 12]:	1 Now the feast of un-leavened bread [cp. 22 7] drew nigh, which is called the Passover.	55 Now the passover of the Jews was at hand.
and the Son of man is delivered up to be crucified [cp. 16 21; 17 12, 22-23; 20 18-19: also 20 28; 26 24, 25].	cp. 8 31; 9 12, 31; 10 33-34: also 10 45; 14 21, 41.	cp. 9 22, 44; 18 31-33; 24 7: also 13 32-33; 17 25; 22 22.	cp. 2 19; 3 14; 12 32-33.
3 Then were gathered together the chief priests, and the elders of the people, unto the court [cp. 26 57, 58: also 26 69: *and* John 18 15]	and the chief priests and the scribes cp. 14 53, 54: also 14 66.	2 And the chief priests and the scribes cp. 22 55.	47 The chief priests therefore and the Pharisees gathered a council, and said, What do we? for this man doeth many signs. 48 If we let him thus alone, all men will believe on him: and the Romans will come and take away both our place and our nation. 49 But a certain one of them,
of the high priest, who was called Caiaphas [cp. 26 57];		cp. 3 2.	Caiaphas [cp. 18 13, 14, 24, 28], being high priest that year, said unto them, Ye know nothing at all, 50 nor do ye take account that it is expedient for you that one man should die for the people, and that the whole nation perish not. 51 Now this he said not of himself: but being high priest that year, he pro-phesied that Jesus should die for the nation [cp. 10 11, 15, 17]; 52 and not
cp. 20 28.	cp. 10 45.		

cp. 8 11; 10 18; 21 31, 41, 43; 22 7-10; 24 14; 26 13; 28 19. cp. 5 9: also 5 45; and 8 12; 13 38.	cp. 12 9; 13 10; 14 9; 16 15.	cp. 2 30-32; 3 6; 13 29; 14 21-24; 20 16; 24 47. cp. 20 36: also 6 35; 16 8.	for the nation only [cp. 10 16], but that he might also gather together into one the children of God [cp. 1 12: also 12 36] that are scattered abroad. 53 So from that day forth they took counsel that they might
4 and they took counsel together that they might take Jesus by subtilty, and kill him [cp. 12 14; 21 46; 27 1: also 22 15; and 12 10]. 5 But they said, Not during the feast, lest a tumult [cp. 27 24] arise among the people [cp. 21 26, 46: so 14 5].	sought how they might take him with subtilty, and kill him [cp. 3 6; 11 18; 12 12: also 12 13; and 3 2]: 2 for they said, Not during the feast, lest haply there shall be a tumult of the people [cp. 11 18, 32; 12 12].	sought how they might put him to death [cp. 6 11; 19 47; 20 19, 20: also 11 53-54; and 6 7]; for they feared the people [cp. 19 48; 20 6, 19].	put him to death [cp. 5 16, 18; 7 30, 32: also 8 6].

§ 226. The Anointing in Bethany

Matt. 26 6-13	Mark 14 3-9	Luke 7 36-50	John 12 1-8
		36 And one of the Pharisees desired him that he would eat [cp. 7 34] with him. And he entered into the Pharisee's house,	
6 Now when Jesus was in Bethany, in the house of Simon the leper,	3 And while he was in Bethany in the house of Simon the leper,	cp. 7 40, 43, 44.	1 Jesus therefore six days before the passover came to Bethany, where Lazarus was, whom Jesus raised from the dead. 2 So they made him a supper there: and Martha served; but Lazarus was one of them that sat at meat with him.
	as he sat at meat,	cp. 10 40. and sat down to meat [cp. 11 37; 14 1].	
7 there came unto him a woman	there came a woman	37 And behold, a woman which was in the city, a sinner [cp. 7 34]; and when she knew that he was sitting at meat in the Pharisee's house, she	3 Mary therefore
having 1 an alabaster cruse of exceeding precious ointment, and she poured it upon his head, as he sat at meat.	having 1 an alabaster cruse of ointment of 2 spikenard very costly; and she brake the cruse, and poured it over his head.	brought 1 an alabaster cruse of ointment,	took a pound of ointment of 1 spikenard, very precious,
		38 and standing behind at his feet [cp. 8 35; 10 39], weeping, she began to wet his feet with her tears, and wiped them with the hair of her head, and 2 kissed his feet, and anointed them with the ointment. 39 Now when the Pharisee	and anointed the feet of Jesus, and wiped his feet with her hair: and the house was filled with the odour of the ointment. 4 But Judas Iscariot, one of his disciples, which should betray him,
8 But when the disciples saw it, they had indignation, saying,	4 But there were some that had indignation among themselves, saying,	which had bidden him saw it, he spake within himself [cp. 11 38], saying,	saith

To what purpose is this waste ? **9** For this *ointment* might have been sold for much, and given to the poor. *cp.* 15 23 ; 19 13.	To what purpose hath this waste of the ointment been made ? **5** For this ointment might have been sold for above three hundred ¹pence, and given to the poor. And they murmured against her [*cp.* 10 13].	*cp.* 18 15.	**5** Why was not this ointment sold for three hundred ² pence, and given to the poor?

			6 Now this he said, not because he cared for the poor ; but because he was a thief, and having the ³ bag [*cp.* 13 29] ⁴ took away what was put therein. **7** Jesus therefore *cp.* 5 6; 6 15. said,
10 But Jesus perceiving it [*cp.* 12 15 ; 16 8 ; 22 18] said unto them, Why trouble ye the woman ? for she hath wrought a good work upon me. *cp.* 19 14.	**6** But Jesus *cp.* 8 17. said, Let her alone ; why trouble ye her ? she hath wrought a good work on me. *cp.* 10 14.	*cp.* 18 16.	
11 For ye have the poor always with you ; but me ye have not always. **12** For in that she ² poured this ointment upon my body, she did it to prepare me for burial. **13** Verily I say unto you, Wheresoever ³ this gospel [*cp.* 4 23 ; 9 35 ; 24 14] shall be preached in the whole world [*cp.* 24 14 : *also* 8 11 ; 10 18 ; 21 31, 41, 43 ; 22 7-10 ; 28 19], that also which this woman hath done shall be spoken of for a memorial of her.	**7** For ye have the poor always with you, and whensover ye will ye can do them good : but me ye have not always. **8** She hath done what she could : she hath anointed my body aforehand for the burying. **9** And verily I say unto you, Wheresoever the gospel [*cp.* 1 1, 14, 15 ; 8 35 ; 10 29 ; 13 10 ; 16 15] shall be preached throughout the whole world [*cp.* 13 10 : *also* 12 9 ; 16 15], that also which this woman hath done shall be spoken of for a memorial of her.	*cp.* 2 30-32 ; 3 6 ; *etc.*	**5** Suffer her to keep it against the day of my burying. **8** For the poor ye have always with you ; but me ye have not always. *cp.* 10 16 ; 11 52.

¹ Or, *a flask*   ² Gr. *cast.*
³ Or, *these good tidings*

¹ Or, *a flask*
² Gr. *pistic nard*, pistic being perhaps a local name. Others take it to mean *genuine* ; others, *liquid.*
³ See marginal note on Matt. 18 28.

¹ See marginal note on Mark 14 3.
² See marginal note on Matt. 18 28.
³ Or, *box*
⁴ Or, *carried what was put therein*
⁵ Or, *Let her alone : it was that she might keep it*

cp. 13 57 ; 21 11, 46.	*cp.* 6 4, 15.	This man, if he were ³ a prophet [*cp.* 4 24 ; 7 16 ; 13 33 ; 24 19], would have perceived who and what manner of woman this is which toucheth [*cp.* 6 19 ; 8 44 : Matt. 9 20 ; 14 36 : Mark 3 10 ; 5 27 ; 6 56 : John 20 17] him, that she is a sinner [*cp.* 5 30 ; 15 2 ; 19 7]. **40** And Jesus answering said unto him, Simon, I have somewhat to say unto thee. And he saith, ⁴ Master, say on. **41** A certain lender had two debtors : the one owed five hundred ⁵ pence, and the other fifty. **42** When they had not *wherewith* to pay, he forgave them both. Which of them therefore will love him most ? **43** Simon answered and said, He, I suppose, to whom he forgave the most. And he said unto him, Thou hast rightly judged [*cp.* 10 28]. **44** And turning [*cp.* 7 9 ; 9 55 ; 10 23 ; 14 25 ; 22 61 ; 23 28] to the woman, he said unto Simon, Seest thou this woman ? I entered into thine house, thou gavest me no water for my feet : but she hath wetted my feet with her tears, and wiped them with her hair. **45** Thou gavest me no kiss : but she, since the time I came in, hath not ceased to ⁶ kiss my feet. **46** My head with oil thou didst not anoint : but she hath anointed my feet with ointment. **47** Wherefore I say unto thee, Her sins, which are many, are forgiven ; for she loved much : but to whom little is forgiven, *the same* loveth little [*cp.* 5 32 ; 7 29, 30 ; 15 7, 10 ; 18 14 ; 19 10]. **48** And he said unto her, Thy sins are forgiven [*cp.* 5 20]. **49** And they that sat at meat with him began to say ⁷ within themselves, Who is this [*cp.* 5 21 : *also* 4 36 ; 8 25 ; 9 9] that even forgiveth sins ? **50** And he said unto the woman, Thy faith hath saved thee [*cp.* 8 48 ; 17 19 ; 18 42] ; go in peace [*cp.* 8 48].	*cp.* 4 19, 44 ; 6 14 ; 7 40 ; 9 17.
cp. 9 11 ; 11 19. *cp.* 26 6.	*cp.* 2 16. *cp.* 14 3.		
cp. 18 23-34. *cp.* 18 25.			
cp. 9 22 ; 16 23.	*cp.* 5 30 ; 8 33.		*cp.* 1 38.
cp. 9 13 ; 21 31.	*cp.* 2 17.		
cp. 9 2.	*cp.* 2 5.		
cp. 8 27 ; 21 10.	*cp.* 1 27 ; 2 7 ; 4 41.		*cp.* 5 12 : *also* 12 34.
cp. 9 22.	*cp.* 5 34 ; 10 52.		

¹ Or, *a flask*   ² Gr. *kissed much.*
³ Some ancient authorities read *the prophet.* See John 1 21, 25.   ⁴ Or, *Teacher*
⁵ See footnote on Matt. 18 28.   ⁶ Gr. *kiss much.*   ⁷ Or, *among*

§ 227. The Treachery of Judas

Matt. 26 14-16	**Mark 14** 10-11	**Luke 22** 3-6	
14 Then one of the twelve, who was called Judas Iscariot,	**10** And Judas Iscariot, [1] he that was one of the twelve, went away unto the chief priests,	**3** And Satan [*cp.* 22 31] entered into Judas who was called Iscariot, being of the number of the twelve. **4** And he went away, and communed with the chief priests and captains [*cp.* 22 52], how he might deliver him unto them.	*cp.* 13 2, 27.
went unto the chief priests,			
15 and said, What are ye willing to give me, and I will deliver him unto you? And they	that he might deliver him unto them. **11** And they, when they heard it, were glad, and promised to give him money.	**5** And they were glad, and covenanted to give him money.	
weighed unto him thirty pieces of silver [*cp.* 27 3].			
16 And from that time he sought opportunity to deliver him *unto them.*	And he sought how he might conveniently deliver him *unto them.*	**6** And he consented, and sought opportunity to deliver him unto them [1] in the absence of the multitude [*cp.* 22 2].	
cp. 26 5.	*cp.* 14 2.		

Matt. 26 15 : *cp.* Zech. 11 12.

[1] Gr. *the one of the twelve.*

[1] Or, *without tumult*

§ 228. The Preparation for the Passover

Matt. 26 17-19	**Mark 14** 12-16	**Luke 22** 7-13	
17 Now on the first *day of* unleavened bread	**12** And on the first day of unleavened bread, when they sacrificed the passover [*cp.* 14 1],	**7** And the day of unleavened bread came, on which the passover [*cp.* 22 1] must be sacrificed.	
cp. 26 1.	his disciples		
the disciples came [*cp.* 5 1; 13 10, 36; 14 15; 15 12, 23; 17 19; 18 1; 24 1, 3] to Jesus, saying, Where wilt thou that we make ready for thee to eat the passover?	*cp.* 6 35.	*cp.* 9 12.	
	say unto him, Where wilt thou that we go and make ready that thou mayest eat the passover? **13** And he sendeth two [*cp.* 11 1: *also* 6 7] of his disciples, and saith unto them, Go	**8** And he sent [*cp.* 19 29: *also* 10 1] Peter and John, saying, Go and make ready for us the passover, that we may eat. **9** And they said unto him, Where wilt thou that we make ready? **10** And he said unto them, Behold, when ye are entered into the city, there shall meet you a man bearing a pitcher of water; follow him into the house whereinto he goeth.	
cp. 21 1.			
18 And he said, Go			
into the city	into the city, and there shall meet you a man bearing a pitcher of water: follow him; **14** and wheresoever he shall enter in,		
to such a man, and say unto him,	say to the goodman of the house, The [1] Master saith,	**11** And ye shall say unto the goodman of the house, The [1] Master saith unto thee,	*cp.* 11 28.
The [1] Master saith, My time is at hand [*cp.* 26 45];	[*cp.* 14 41: *also* 14 35] Where is my guest-chamber, where I shall eat the passover with my disciples?	[*cp.* 22 14] Where is the guest-chamber, where I shall eat the passover with my disciples?	*cp.* 12 23; 13 1; 17 1: *also* 12 27: *and* 2 4; 7 6, 8, 30; 8 20.
I keep the passover at thy house with my disciples.	**15** And he will himself shew you a large upper room furnished *and* ready: and there make ready for us. **16** And	**12** And he will shew you a large upper room furnished: there make ready. **13** And	
19 And			

the disciples did as Jesus appointed them [*cp.* 21 6]; and they made ready the passover.	the disciples went forth, and came into the city, and found as he had said unto them: and they made ready the passover.	they went, and found as he had said unto them [*cp.* 19 32]: and they made ready the passover.
¹ Or, *Teacher*	¹ Or, *Teacher*	¹ Or, *Teacher*

(ii) In the Upper Room (§§ 229-234)

§ 229. **The Prophecy of the Betrayal** (Matt. and Mark)

Matt. 26 20-25	**Mark 14** 17-21	**Luke 22** 14 (21-23)	John 13 21, 18-19, 22-30
20 Now when even [*cp.* 26 45: *also* 26 18] was come, he was sitting at meat *cp.* 10 2. with the twelve ¹ disciples; **21** and as they were eating [*cp.* 26 26], he said, Verily I say unto you, that one of you shall betray me.	**17** And when it was evening [*cp.* 14 35, 41] he cometh with the twelve. **18** And as they ¹ sat *cp.* 6 30. and were eating [*cp.* 14 22], Jesus said, Verily I say unto you, One of you shall betray me, *even*	**14** And when the hour [*cp.* 22 53] was come, he sat down, and the apostles[*cp.* 6 13; 9 10; 17 5; 24 10] with him. **21** But behold, the hand of him that betrayeth me	*cp.* 12 23, 27; 13 1; 17 1: *also* 2 4; 7 6, 8, 30; 8 20. **21** When Jesus had thus said, he was troubled in the spirit, and testified, and said, Verily, verily, I say unto you, that one of you shall betray me. . . . **18** I speak not of you all: I know whom I ¹ have chosen [*cp.* 6 70]: but that the scripture may be fulfilled, He that eateth ² my bread lifted up his heel against me. **19** From henceforth I tell you before it come to pass, that, when it is come to pass, ye may believe that ³ I am *he*. . . . **22** The disciples looked [*cp.* 16 6, 20, 22] one on another, doubting of whom he spake. **23** There was at the table reclining in Jesus' bosom one of his disciples, whom Jesus loved. **24** Simon Peter therefore beckoneth to him, and saith unto him, Tell *us* who it is of whom he speaketh. **25** He leaning back, as he was, on Jesus' breast saith unto him, Lord, who is it? **26** Jesus therefore answereth, He it is, for whom I shall dip the sop, and give it him.
verse 24	*verse* 21 he that eateth with me.	*verse* 22 is with me on the table.	
22 And they were exceeding sorrowful [*cp.* 17 23; 18 31: *also* 26 37], and began	**19** They began to be sorrowful, and	*cp.* 22 45.	
to say unto him every one, Is it I, Lord? **23** And he answered and said, He that dipped his hand with me in the dish, the same shall betray me.	to say unto him one by one, Is it I? **20** And he said unto them, *It is* one of the twelve, he that dippeth with me in the dish.	*verse* 23	*verse* 18 *cp.* 2 19, 22; 3 14; 12 32, 33: *also* 5 39; 15 25; 17 12.
24 The Son of man goeth, even as it is written of him [*cp.* 16 21-23; 17 12, 22-23; 20 17-19, 28; 26 2, 45: *also* 26 12, 18; *and* 21 42; 26 31, 54, 56]: but woe [*cp.* 18 7: *also* 23 13 *ff.*] unto that man through whom the Son of man is be-	**21** For the Son of man goeth, even as it is written of him [*cp.* 8 31-33; 9 12, 30-32; 10 32-34, 45; 14 41: *also* 14 8; *and* 12 10; 14 27, 49]: but woe unto that man through whom the Son of man is be-	**22** For the Son of man indeed goeth, as it hath been determined[*cp.* 9 22, 43-45; 13 32-33; 17 25; 18 31-34; 24 7, 44: *also* 20 17; 22 37; 24 25-27, 46]: but woe [*cp.* 17 1: *also* 11 42 *ff.*] unto that man through whom he is be-	

trayed ! good were it ² for that man if he had not been born.

verse 22

25 And

Judas, which betrayed him, answered and said, Is it I, Rabbi [*cp.* 26 49: *also* 23 7, 8] ? He saith unto him, Thou has said [*cp.* 26 64: *also* 27 11].

¹ Many authorities, some ancient, omit *disciples*.
² Gr. *for him if that man*.

---

trayed ! good were it ² for that man if he had not been born.

verse 19

cp. 9 5; 11 21; 14 45: *also* 10 51.
cp. 15 2.

¹ Gr. *reclined*.
² Gr. *for him if that man*.

---

trayed !

23 And they began to question among themselves, which of them it was that should do this thing.

cp. 23 3 : *also* 22 70.

cp. 22 3.

---

verse 22

So when he had dipped the sop, he taketh and giveth it to Judas, *the son* of Simon Iscariot.

cp. 1 38, 49; *etc.*: *also* 20 16.
cp. 18 37.

27 And after the sop, then entered Satan into him. Jesus therefore saith unto him,

---

That thou doest, do quickly. **28** Now no man at the table knew for what intent he spake this unto him. **29** For some thought, because Judas had the ⁴ bag, that Jesus said unto him, Buy what things we have need of for the feast ; or, that he should give something to the poor. **30** He then having received the sop went out straightway : and it was night.

¹ Or, *chose*
² Many ancient authorities read *his bread with me*.
³ Or, *I am*   ⁴ Or, *box*

§ 230. The Institution of the Eucharist

[*Cp.* John 6 48-59]

Matt. 26 26-29	Mark 14 22-25	Luke 22 15-20	1 Corinthians 11 23-25
26 And as they were eating [*cp.* 26 21], Jesus	**22** And as they were eating [*cp.* 14 18], he	**15** And	
		he said unto them, With desire I have desired to eat this passover with you before I suffer : **16** for I say unto you, I will not eat [*cp.* 22 30: *also* 13 29; 14 15] it, until it be fulfilled in the kingdom of God. **17** And he received a cup, and when he had given thanks [*cp. verse* 19], he said, Take [*cp.* Matt. 26 26 *and* Mark 14 22] this, and divide it among yourselves : **18** for I say unto you, I will not drink [*cp.* 22 30: *also* 13 29; 14 15] from henceforth [*cp.* 1 48; 5 10; 12 52; 22 69] of the fruit of the vine, until the kingdom of God shall come. **19** And he took	
cp. 15 36; 26 27.	*cp.* 8 6; 14 23.	*cp.* 6 11.	
verse 29	*verse* 25		
¹ bread, and [*cp.* 15 36; 26 27] blessed [*cp.* 14 19], and brake it; and he gave to the disciples,	¹ bread, and when he had [*cp.* 8 6; 14 23] blessed [*cp.* 6 41; 8 7], he brake it, and gave to them,	¹ bread, and when he had given thanks [*cp. verse* 17], [*cp.* 9 16; 24 30] he brake it, and gave to them,	**23** For I received of the Lord that which also I delivered unto you, how that the Lord Jesus in the night in which he was betrayed took bread ; **24** and when he had given thanks, he brake it,
		cp. 6 11.	

Matt.

and said, Take, eat; this is my body.

27 And he took ² a cup, and gave thanks [*cp.* 15 36], and gave to them, saying, Drink ye all of it; **28** for this is my blood of ³ the ⁴ covenant, which is shed for many [*cp.* 20 28] unto remission of sins. **29** But I say unto you, I will not drink [*cp.* 8 11] henceforth [*cp.* 23 39; 26 64] of this fruit of the vine, until that day [*cp.* 7 22; 24 36] when I drink it new with you in my Father's [*cp.* 13 43] kingdom.

¹ Or, *a loaf*
² Some ancient authorities read *the cup.*
³ Or, *the testament*
⁴ Many ancient authorities insert *new.*

Mark.

and said, Take ye: this is my body.

23 And he took a cup, and when he had given thanks [*cp.* 8 6], he gave to them: and they all drank of it. **24** And he said unto them, This is my blood of ² the ³ covenant, which is shed for many [*cp.* 10 45]. *cp.* 1 4. **25** Verily I say unto you, I will no more drink of the fruit of the vine, until that day [*cp.* 13 32] when I drink it new in the kingdom of God.

¹ Or, *a loaf*
² Or, *the testament*
³ Some ancient authorities insert *new.*

Luke.

saying [*cp. verse* 17], This is my body ² which is given for you: this do in remembrance of me. **20** And the cup in like manner after supper,

cp. verses 17 *and* 19.

saying, This cup is the new ³ covenant in my blood, *even* that which is poured out for you. *cp.* 3 3: *also* 1 77; 24 47.

verse 18; *cp.* 16. *cp.* 10 12; 17 31; 21 34.

¹ Or, *a loaf*
² Some ancient authorities omit *which is given for you ... which is poured out for you.*
³ Or, *testament*

cp. 6 11.

cp. 13 19; 14 7.

cp. 14 20; 16 23, 26.

and said, This is my body, which ¹ is for you: this do in remembrance of me. **25** In like manner also the cup, after supper, saying, This cup is the new ² covenant in my blood:

this do, as oft as ye drink *it*, in remembrance of me.

¹ Many ancient authorities read *is broken for you.*
² Or, *testament*

Matt. 26 28 ‖ Mark 14 24 ‖ Luke 22 20 ; *cp.* Is. 52 15 ; 53 4-6, 8, 11-12.

§ 231. **The Prophecy of the Betrayal** (Luke)

Matt. 26 20-25	Mark 14 17-21	Luke 22 (14) 21-23	John 13 21, 18-19, 22-30
20 Now when even [*cp.* 26 45: *also* 26 18] was come, he was sitting at meat *cp.* 10 2. with the twelve ¹ disciples; **21** and as they were eating [*cp.* 26 26], he said, Verily I say unto you, that one of you shall betray me.	**17** And when it was evening [*cp.* 14 35, 41] he cometh with the twelve. **18** And as they ¹ sat *cp.* 6 30. and were eating [*cp.* 14 22], Jesus said, Verily I say unto you, One of you shall betray me, *even*	**14** And when the hour [*cp.* 22 53] was come, he sat down, and the apostles [*cp.* 6 13; 9 10 17 5; 24 10] with him.	*cp.* 12 23, 27; 13 1; 17 1: *also* 2 4; 7 6, 8, 30; 8 20.
verse 24	*verse* 21 he that eateth with me.	**21** But behold, the hand of him that betrayeth me *verse* 22 is with me on the table.	**21** When Jesus had thus said, he was troubled in the spirit, and testified, and said, Verily, verily, I say unto you, that one of you shall betray me. . . . **18** I speak not of you all: I know whom I ¹ have chosen [*cp.* 6 70]: but that the scripture may be fulfilled, He that eateth ² my bread lifted up his heel against me. **19** From henceforth I tell you before it come to pass, that, when it is come to pass, ye may believe that ³ I am *he*. . . . **22** The disciples looked [*cp.* 16 6, 20, 22] one on another, doubting of whom he spake. **23** There was at
22 And they were exceeding sorrowful [*cp.* 17 23; 18 31: *also* 26 37], **and** began	**19** They began to be sorrowful, and	*cp.* 22 45.	

the table reclining in Jesus' bosom one of his disciples, whom Jesus loved. **24** Simon Peter therefore beckoneth to him, and saith unto him, Tell *us* who it is of whom he speaketh. **25** He leaning back, as he was, on Jesus' breast saith unto him,

Lord, who is it? **26** Jesus therefore answereth,

He it is, for whom
I shall   dip

the sop, and give it him.

---

to say   one,
Is it I, Lord? **23** And he
answered and
said,

He that dipped his hand with me in the dish,

the same shall betray me. **24** The Son of man goeth, even as it is written of him [*cp.* 16 21-23; 17 12, 22-23; 20 17-19,28; 26 2,45: *also* 26 12, 18; *and* 21 42; 26 31, 54, 56]: but woe [*cp.* 18 7: *also* 23 13 *ff.*] unto that man through whom the Son of man is betrayed! good were it [2] for that man if he had not been born.

verse 22

25 And

Judas,
which betrayed him, answered and said, Is it I, Rabbi [*cp.* 26 49: *also* 23 7, 8]? He saith unto him, Thou hast said [*cp.* 26 64: *also* 27 11].

[1] Many authorities, some ancient, omit *disciples*.
[2] Gr. *for him if that man*.

---

to say
Is it I? **20** And he

said unto them, *It is* one of the twelve, he that dippeth with me in the dish.

21 For the Son of man goeth, even as it is written of him [*cp.* 8 31-33; 9 12, 30-32; 10 32-34,45; 14 41: *also* 14 8; *and* 12 10; 14 27,49]: but woe   unto that man through whom the Son of man is betrayed! good were it [2] for that man if he had not been born.

verse 19

cp. 9 5; 11 21; 14 45: *also* 10 51.
cp. 15 2.

[1] Gr. *reclined.*
[2] Gr. *for him if that man.*

---

verse 23

22 For the Son of man indeed goeth, as it hath been determined [*cp.* 9 22, 43-45; 13 32-33; 17 25; 18 31-34; 24 7, 44: *also* 20 17; 22 37; 24 25-27, 46]: but woe [*cp.* 17 1: *also* 11 42 *ff.*] unto that man through whom he   is betrayed!

23 And they began to question among themselves, which of them it was that should do this thing.

cp. 23 3: *also* 22 70.

cp. 22 3.

---

verse 18
cp. 2 19, 22; 3 14; 12 32, 33: *also* 5 39; 15 25
17 12.

verse 22

So when he had dipped the sop, he taketh and giveth it to Judas, *the son* of Simon Iscariot.

cp. 1 38, 49; *etc.*: *also* 20 16.
cp. 18 37.

27 And after the sop, then entered Satan into him. Jesus therefore saith unto him, That thou doest, do quickly. **28** Now no man at the table knew for what intent he spake this unto him. **29** For some thought, because Judas had the [4] bag, that Jesus said unto him, Buy what things we have need of for the feast; or, that he should give something to the poor. **30** He then having received the sop went out straightway: and it was night.

[1] Or, *chose*   [2] Many ancient authorities read *his bread with me*.
[3] Or, *I am*   [4] Or, *box*

---

§ 232. Rivalry among the Disciples and Sayings of Rebuke: the Necessity and Rewards of Service: the Prophecy of Peter's Denial (Luke)

[*Cp.* Matt. 18 1-5: Mark 9 33-37: Luke 9 46-48]
[*Cp.* Matt. 10 16-42; 16 24-28: Mark 8 34-9 1; 13 9-13: Luke 9 23-27; 21 12-19:
John 12 26; 14 2-3; 15 18-21; 16 2-3, 33]

Matt. 20 24-28; 23 11; 19 27-29; 26 33-35

cp. 18 1.

Mark 10 41-45; 9 35; 10 28-30; 14 29-31

cp. 9 33-34.

Luke 22 24-34

24 And there arose also a contention among them [*cp.* 9 46], which of them is accounted to be [1] greatest.

204   Matt. 26 29 (p. 202): 26 30 (p. 206) — Mark 14 25 (p. 202): 14 26 (p. 206) — **Luke 22 25-30**

20 24 And when the ten heard it, they   were moved with indignation concerning the two brethren.   **25** But Jesus called them unto him, and said,   Ye know that
the rulers of the Gentiles lord it over them, and their great ones exercise authority over them.

26 Not
so shall it be among you : but whosoever would become great among you shall be   your [1] minister ; **27** and whosoever would be first among you shall be your [2] servant :

23 11 But   he that   is [3] greatest among you shall be
your [4] servant.

20 28 even as the Son of man came [*cp.* 18 11] not to be ministered unto, but to minister,
and to give his life a ransom for many [*cp.* 26 28]. **19 27** Then answered Peter [*cp.* 14 28 ; 15 15 ; 16 22 ; 17 4 ; 18 21 ; 26 33 : *also* 16 16 ; 17 24]   and said unto him, Lo, we have left all,
and
followed thee [*cp.* 4 20, 22 ; 9 9] ; what then shall we have ? **28** And Jesus said unto them, Verily I say unto you, that ye
which have followed me,
in the regeneration when the Son of man shall sit on the throne of his glory [*cp.* 25 31 : *also* 16 27],

cp. 8 11 ; 26 29.

[*cp.* 16 28 ; 20 21]   ye also shall sit upon twelve thrones, judging the twelve tribes of Israel. **29** And every one   that hath left houses,
or brethren, or sisters,
or father, or mother, [5] or children [*cp.* 10 37], or lands, for my name's sake [*cp.* 10 22 ; 24 9 : *also* 5 11 ; 10 18, 39 ; 16 25],
and for the [*cp.* 4 23 ; 9 35 ; 24 14 ; 26 13.

shall

---

10 41 And when the ten heard it, they began to be moved with indignation concerning James and John.   **42** And Jesus called them to him, and saith unto them, Ye know that they which are accounted to rule over the Gentiles lord it over them ; and their great ones exercise authority over them.

43 But   it is not so   among you : but whosoever would become great   among you, shall be   your [1] minister : **44** and whosoever would be first among you, shall be   [2] servant of all.

9 35 If any man would be first,   he shall be last of all, and minister of all.

10 45 For verily the Son of man came   not to be ministered unto, but to minister,
and to give his life a ransom for many [*cp.* 14 24]. **10 28** Peter [*cp.* 8 32 ; 9 5 ; 11 21 ; 14 29 : *also* 8 29]
began to say unto him, Lo, we have left all,
and have followed thee [*cp.* 1 18, 20 ; 2 14].

29 Jesus said, Verily I say unto you,

cp. 10 37 : *also* 8 38.

cp. 14 25.

There is no man that hath left house,
or brethren, or sisters, or mother, or father,
or children,   or lands, for my   sake [*cp.* 8 35 ; 13 9 : *also* 13 13], and for the gospel's sake [*cp.* 8 35 : *also* 1 1, 14, 15 ; 13 10 ; 14 9 ; 16 15],

30 but he shall

---

25 And he said unto them,

The kings of the Gentiles have lordship over them ; and they that have authority over them are called Benefactors. **26** But ye *shall* not *be* so :
but he that   is the greater among you, let him become as the younger ;   and he that is chief, as he that doth serve.
9 48 For   he that   is [2] least among you all, the same is great.

27 For whether is greater, he that [3] sitteth at meat, or he that serveth ? is not he that [3] sitteth at meat [*cp.* 17 7, 8] ? but   I am in the midst [*cp.* 9 55 ; 19 10]

of you as he that serveth [*cp.* 12 37].

18 28 And   Peter [*cp* 8 45 ; 9 33 ; 12 41 : *also* 5 8 ; 9 20]
said, Lo, we have left [*cp.* 5 11, 28 ; 14 33] [4] our own, and followed thee [*cp.* 5 11, 28].

29 And he said unto them, Verily I say unto you, **28** But ye are they which have continued with me in my temptations [*cp.* 4 13 ; 8 13] ;

[*cp.* 9 26, 32 ; 24 26] **29** and [5] I appoint unto you a kingdom, even as my Father appointed unto me, **30** that ye may eat and drink at my table [*cp.* 13 29 ; 14 15 ; 22 16, 18] in my kingdom [*cp.* 23 42] ;   and ye shall sit on thrones judging the twelve tribes of Israel.
There is no man that hath left house, or wife [*cp.* 14 26], or brethren,   or parents,
or children [*cp.* 14 26],

cp. 6 22 ; 9 24 ; 21 12, 17.

for the kingdom of God's sake,   **30** who shall not

---

cp. John 13 2-17.

cp. 10 11, 15, 17 ; 11 51, 52.

cp. 13 36, 37 ; 21 21 : *also* 6 68.

cp. 1 14 ; 2 11 ; 12 41 ; 17 5, 22, 24.

cp. Jo 13 36-1

cp. 18 36.

cp. 15 21.

receive [6] a hundredfold [*cp.* 13 8, 23 : *and* 6 33],	receive a hundredfold [*cp.* 4 8, 20, *and* 24]	receive [*cp.* 8 8] manifold more [*cp.* 12 31] in this time,	
	now in this time, houses, and brethren, and sisters, and mothers, and children, and lands, with persecutions [*cp.* 4 17]; and in the [3] world to come eternal life [*cp.* 10 17].	and in the [6] world to come eternal life [*cp.* 18 18: *also* 10 25].	

cp. 13 21. and [*cp.* 12 32] shall inherit eternal life [*cp.* 19 16: *also* 25 46].			*cp.* 3 15; *etc.*
Matt. 26 33 But Peter [*cp.* 14 28 ; 15 15 ; 16 22 ; 17 4 ; 18 21 ; 19 27 : *also* 16 16 ; 17 24] answered and said unto him,	Mark 14 29 But Peter [*cp.* 8 32 ; 9 5 ; 10 28 ; 11 21 : *also* 8 29]	*cp.* 8 45 ; 9 33 ; 12 41 ; 18 28 : *also* 5 8 ; 9 20.	John 13 36 Simon Peter [*cp.* 21 21 : *also* 6 68]
If all shall be [7] offended in thee, I will never be [7] offended.	said unto him, Although all shall be [4] offended, yet will not I.		saith unto him, Lord, whither goest thou ?

			Jesus answered, Whither I go, thou canst not follow me now ; but thou shalt follow afterwards [*cp.* 21 18-19].
cp. 16 17 ; 17 25.	*cp.* 14 37.	**31** Simon, Simon, behold, Satan [*cp.* 22 3] [7] asked to have you, that he might sift you as wheat: **32** but I made supplication for thee, that thy faith [*cp.* 8 25 ; 12 28 ; 17 5, 6: *also* 24 11, 12, 38, 41 : *and* 24 25] fail not: and do thou, when once thou hast turned again, stablish thy brethren. **33** And he said unto him, Lord,	*cp.* 1 42 ; 21 15, 16, 17.
cp. 8 26 ; 14 31 ; 16 8 ; 17 20 ; 21 21 ; 28 17.	*cp.* 4 40 ; 11 22 ; 16 11, 13, 14.		*cp.* 3 12 ; 6 64 ; 14 10 20 25, 27.
cp. 16 18-19.		with thee I am ready to go both to prison and to death. **34** And he said,	*cp.* 21 15-17. 37 Peter saith unto him, Lord, why cannot I follow thee even now ? I will lay down my life for thee. 38 Jesus answereth, Wilt thou lay down thy life for me ? Verily, verily, I say unto thee,

verse 35 34 Jesus said unto him,	*verse* 31 30 And Jesus saith unto him,		
Verily I say unto thee, that this night, before the cock crow,	Verily I say unto thee, that thou to-day, *even* this night, before the cock crow twice [*cp.* 14 68, 72],	I tell thee, Peter, the cock shall not crow this day, until thou shalt thrice deny that thou knowest [*cp.* 22 57, 60] me [*cp.* 22 61].	The cock shall not crow, till thou hast denied
thou shalt deny *cp.* 26 70, 72, 74. me thrice [*cp.* 26 75]. 35 Peter saith unto him,	shalt deny *cp.* 14 68, 71. me thrice [*cp.* 14 72]. 31 But he spake exceed-		me thrice [*cp.* 18 27].
Even if I must die with thee, *yet* will I not deny thee. Likewise also said all the disciples.	ing vehemently, If I must die with thee, I will not deny thee. And in like manner also said they all.	*verse* 33	*verse* 37

[1] Or, *servant*   [2] Gr. *bondservant.*
[3] Gr. *greater.*   [4] Or, *minister*
[5] Many ancient authorities add *or wife* : as in Luke 18 29.
[6] Some ancient authorities read *manifold.*
[7] Gr. *caused to stumble.*

[1] Or, *servant*
[2] Gr. *bondservant.*
[3] Or, *age*
[4] Gr. *caused to stumble.*

[1] Gr. *greater.*
[2] Gr. *lesser.*   [3] Gr. *reclineth.*
[4] Or, *our own homes*
[5] Or, *I appoint unto you, even as my Father appointed unto me a kingdom, that ye may eat and drink &c.*
[6] Or, *age*
[7] Or, *obtained you by asking*

Matt. 20 28 ‖ Mark 10 45 : *cp.* Is. 52 15 ; 53 4-6, 8, 11, 12.

§ 233. **Reflection on the Designs of Providence**

		Luke 22 35-38

Luke 22 35-38

cp. 10 10.

cp. 19 21.   cp. 10 21.

cp. 21 42;   cp. 9 12; 12
26 24, 31,   10; 14 21,
54, 56.   27, 49.
cp. 26 51.   cp. 14 47.

35 And he said unto them, When I sent you forth without purse, and wallet, and shoes [cp. 10 4], lacked ye anything? And they said, Nothing. **36** And he said unto them, But now, he that hath a purse, let him take it, and likewise a wallet: ¹ and he that hath none, let him sell [cp. 12 33; 18 22] his cloke, and buy a sword. **37** For I say unto you, that this which is written must be fulfilled [cp. 18 31; 20 17; 24 25-27, 44-46: also 12 50; and 13 32] in me, And he was reckoned with transgressors: for that which concerneth me hath ² fulfilment. **38** And they said, Lord, behold, here are two swords [cp. 22 49, 50: John 18 10]. And he said unto them, It is enough.

cp. 5 39; 13
18; 15 25;
17 12: also
4 34; 5
36; 17 4;
19 28, 30.

¹ Or, and he that hath no sword, let him sell his cloke, and buy one.
² Gr. end.

Luke 22 37 = Is. 53 12.

§ 234. **The Concluding Hymn and Departure to the Mount of Olives**

Matt. 26 30	**Mark 14** 26	**Luke 22** 39	John 18 1

30 And when they had sung a hymn,   they went out [cp. 21 17]
 	
     unto the mount of Olives [cp. 24 3].
	26 And when they had sung a hymn, they went out [cp. 11 11, 19]
	
	     unto the mount of Olives [cp. 13 3].
		39 And
		     he came out, and went, [cp. 21 37] as his custom was [cp. 21 37 : also 4 16 ; and 1 9; 2 42], unto the mount of Olives [cp. 21 37]; and the disciples also followed him.
			1 When Jesus had spoken these words, he went forth
			
			cp. 18 2.
			
			cp. 8 1. with his disciples over the ¹ brook ² Kidron.
			
			¹ Or, ravine Gr. winter-torrent.
			² Or, of the Cedars

(iii) On the Way to Gethsemane (§ 235)

§ 235. **Prophecies of the Flight of the Disciples, of the Resurrection, and of Peter's Denial**
(Matt. and Mark)

Matt. 26 31-35	**Mark 14** 27-31	Luke 22 31-34	John 16 32; 13 36-38
31 Then saith Jesus unto them, All ye shall be ¹ offended [cp. 11 6; 13 57; 15 12: also 13 21; 24 10] in me this night [cp. verse 34]: for it is written [cp. 21 42; 26 24, 54, 56], I will smite the shepherd, and the sheep [cp. 9 36; 10 6; 15 24] of the flock shall be scattered abroad [cp. 26 56].	**27** And Jesus saith unto them, All ye shall be ¹ offended [cp. 6 3: also 4 17]: for it is written [cp. 9 12; 12 10; 14 21, 49], I will smite the shepherd, and the sheep [cp. 6 34] shall be scattered abroad [cp. 14 50].	cp. 7 23. cp. 18 31; 20 17; 22 37; 24 25-27, 44-46.	16 **32** Behold, the hour cometh, yea, is come, cp. 6 61: also 16 1. cp. 5 39; 13 18; 15 25; 17 12. cp. 10 11-16. that ye shall be scattered, every man to his own, and shall leave me alone [cp. 8 16, 29]. cp. 2 19-22.
32 But after I am raised up [cp. 16 21; 17 9, 23; 20 19], I will go before you into Galilee [cp. 28 7]. **33** But Peter [cp. 14 28; 15 15; 16 22; 17 4; 18 21; 19 27: also 16 16; 17 24] answered and said unto him,	**28** Howbeit, after I am raised up [cp. 8 31; 9 9, 31; 10 34], I will go before you into Galilee [cp. 16 7]. **29** But Peter [cp. 8 32; 9 5; 10 28; 11 21: also 8 29] said unto him,	cp. 9 22; 13 32; 18 33; 24 7, 26, 46. cp. 8 45; 9 33; 12 41; 18 28: also 5 8; 9 20.	13 **36** Simon Peter [cp. 21 21: also 6 68] saith unto him, Lord, whither goest

Matt.	Mark	Luke	John
If all shall be [1] offended in thee, I will never be [1] offended.	Although all shall be [1] offended, yet will not I.		thou?
			Jesus answered, Whither I go, thou canst not follow me now ; but thou shalt follow afterwards [*cp.* 21 18-19].
cp. 16 17; 17 25.	*cp.* 14 37.	31 Simon, Simon, behold, Satan [*cp.* 22 3] [1]asked to have you, that he might sift you as wheat : 32 but I made supplication for thee, that thy faith [*cp.* 8 25 ; 12 28 ; 17 5, 6 : *also* 24 11, 12, 38, 41 : *and* 24 25] fail not : and do	*cp.* 1 42; 21 15, 16, 17.
cp. 8 26; 14 31; 16 8; 17 20; 21 21; 28 17.	*cp.* 4 40; 11 22; 16 11, 13, 14.	thou, when once thou hast turned again, stablish thy brethren. 33 And he said unto him, Lord,	*cp.* 3 12; 6 64; 14 10; 20 25, 27.
cp. 16 18-19.		with thee I am ready to go both to prison and to death. 34 And he said,	*cp.* 21 15-17. 37 Peter saith unto him, Lord, why cannot I follow thee even now ? I will lay down my life for thee. 38 Jesus answereth,
verse 35 34 Jesus said unto him, Verily I say unto thee, that this night, before the cock crow, thou shalt deny	*verse* 31 30 And Jesus saith unto him, Verily I say unto thee, that thou to-day, *even* this night, before the cock crow twice [*cp.* 14 68, 72], shalt deny	I tell thee, Peter, the cock shall not crow this day, until thou shalt thrice deny that thou knowest [*cp.* 22 57, 60]	Wilt thou lay down thy life for me ? Verily, verily, I say unto thee, The cock shall not crow, till thou hast denied
cp. 26 70, 72, 74. me thrice [*cp.* 26 75]. 35 Peter saith unto him, Even if I must die with thee, *yet* will I not deny thee. Likewise also said all the disciples.	*cp.* 14 68, 71. me thrice [*cp.* 14 72]. 31 But he spake exceedingly vehemently, If I must die with thee, I will not deny thee. And in like manner also said they all.	me [*cp.* 22 61]. *verse* 33	me thrice [*cp.* 18 27]. *verse* 37
[1] Gr. *caused to stumble.*	[1] Gr. *caused to stumble.*	[1] Or, *obtained you by asking*	

Matt. 26 31 ‖ Mark 14 27 = Zech. 13 7.

(iv) In Gethsemane (§§ 236-238)

§ 236. **The Agony**

Matt. 26 36-46	**Mark 14** 32-42	**Luke 22** 40-46	**John 18** 1 ; 12 27 ; 14 31
cp. 26 30.	*cp.* 14 26.	*cp.* 22 39.	18 1 When Jesus had spoken these words, he went forth with his disciples over the [1] brook [2] Kidron, where was a garden, into the which he entered, himself and his disciples. *cp.* 18 2.
36 Then cometh Jesus with them unto [1] a place called Gethsemane, and saith unto his disciples, Sit ye here, while I go yonder and pray.	32 And they come unto [1]a place which was named Gethsemane : and he saith unto his disciples, Sit ye here, while I pray.	40 And when he was at the place, he said unto them, Pray that ye enter not into temptation [*cp. verse* 46].	
37 And he took with him Peter and the two sons of Zebedee [*cp.* 17 1],	33 And he taketh with him Peter and James and John [*cp.* 1 29; 5 37;	*cp.* 8 51; 9 28.	

and began to
be sorrowful [*cp. verse* 38:
also 17 23; 18 31; 26 22]
and sore troubled.
38 Then saith he unto
them, My soul
is exceeding sorrowful,
even unto death: abide
ye here, and watch [*cp.*
24 42; 25 13; 26 41]
with me.
    39 And he went
forward a little,
        and
fell on his face, and
prayed [*cp.* 14 23; 19 13;
26 36, 42, 44: *also* 11 25],

cp. 26 45: *also* 26 18.

      saying,
O my Father [*cp. verse* 42
and 11 25, 26: *also* 6 9],
if   it be possible,
      cp. 19 26.
let   this cup [*cp.* 20
22, 23] pass away from
me: nevertheless, not as I
will, but as thou wilt
[*cp. verse* 42 *and* 6 10: *also*
7 21; 12 50; 21 31].

cp. 4 11; 26 53.

40 And
       he cometh
unto the disciples, and
findeth them sleeping [*cp.*
verse 43: *also* 25 5], [*cp.*
verse 38: *also* 17 23; 26 22]
and saith unto Peter,
    cp. 16 17; 17 25.
What, could ye not
watch with me one hour?
41 ² Watch [*cp. verse* 38]
and pray,
that ye enter not into
temptation [*cp.* 6 13]:
    the spirit indeed
is willing, but the flesh
is weak.   **42** Again
a second time he went
away, and prayed, saying
[*verse* 44],   O my
Father [*cp. verse* 39], if
this cannot pass away,
except I drink it, thy
will be done [*cp. verse*
39]. **43** And   he

9 2; 13 3], and began to
be greatly amazed,

and sore troubled.
34 And he saith unto
them, My soul
is exceeding sorrowful
even unto death: abide
ye here, and watch [*cp.*
13 33, 35, 37; 14 38].

    35 And he went
forward a little,
        and
fell on the ground, and
prayed [*cp.* 1 35; 6 46;
14 32, 39]

that, if it were possible,

          the hour
[*cp. verse* 41]

    might pass away
from him.

36 And he said, Abba,
    Father,

all things are possible
unto thee [*cp.* 10 27];
remove this cup [*cp.* 10
38, 39]   from
me: howbeit not what I
will, but what thou wilt
[*cp.* 3 35].

cp. 1 13.

37 And
       he cometh,
       and
findeth them sleeping [*cp.*
verse 40: *also* 13 36], [*cp.*
verse 34: *also* 14 19]
and saith unto Peter,
Simon, sleepest thou?
    couldest thou not
watch   one hour?
38 ² Watch [*cp. verse* 34]
    and pray [*cp.* 13 33],
that ye enter not into
temptation:
    the spirit indeed
is willing, but the flesh
is weak. **39** And again
       he went
away, and prayed, saying
the same words.

40 And again he

cp. 12 37; 21 36.

41 And he was
parted from them about
a stone's cast; and he
    kneeled down and
prayed [*cp.* 3 21; 5 16;
6 12; 9 18, 28, 29; 11
1; 22 44: *also* 10 21],

cp. 22 14, 53.

42 saying,
    Father [*cp.* 10 21,
22; 23 34, 46: *also* 11 2],
if thou be willing,
    cp. 1 37; 18 27.
remove this cup
       from
me: nevertheless not my
will, but thine, be done.

43 ¹ And there appeared
unto him an angel from
heaven, strengthening
him. **44** And being in
an agony he prayed more
earnestly: and his sweat
became as it were great
drops of blood falling
down upon the ground.
45 And when he rose up
from his prayer, he came
unto the disciples, and
found them sleeping [*cp.*
9 32]   for
sorrow,
46 and said unto them,
[*cp.* 22 31] Why sleep ye?

    cp. 12 37; 21 36.
rise and pray [*cp.* 21 36],
that ye enter not into
temptation [*cp. verse* 40
and 11 4].

cp. verse 42.

12 27 Now is my sou
    troubled;

       and what shall
I say?

cp. 11 41; 12 27-28;
    17 1-26.

Father [*cp.* 11 41; 12 28;
17 1, 5, 11, 21, 24, 25],
save me from this ³ hour
[*cp.* 12 23; 13 1; 17 1:
also 2 4; 7 6, 8, 30;
8 20].
    But for this cause,
came I unto this hour.

cp. 18 11.

cp. 4 34; 5 30; 6 38;
    7 17; 9 31.

cp. 1 51; 12 29.

cp. 16 6, 20, 22.

cp. 1 42; 21 15, 16, 17.

came again and found them sleeping [*cp. verse* 40], for their eyes were heavy.	came, and found them sleeping [*cp. verse* 37], for their eyes were very heavy; and they wist not what to answer him [*cp.* 9 6]. **41** And he	*cp. verse* 45. *cp.* 9 32. *cp.* 9 33.	
44 And he left them again, and went away, and prayed a third time, saying again the same words. **45** Then cometh he to the disciples, and saith unto them, Sleep on now, and take your rest: behold, the hour [*cp.* 26 18] is at hand, and the Son of man is betrayed into the hands of sinners [*cp.* 17 22-23; 20 18-19; 26 2: *also* 16 21; 17 12; 26 24]. **46** Arise, let us be going: behold, he is at hand that betrayeth me.	*verse* 39 cometh the third time, and saith unto them, Sleep on now, and take your rest: it is enough; the hour [*cp. verse* 35] is come; behold, the Son of man is betrayed into the hands of sinners [*cp.* 9 31; 10 33: *also* 8 31; 9 12; 14 21]. **42** Arise, let us be going: behold, he that betrayeth me is at hand.	*cp.* 22 14, 53. *cp.* 9 44; 18 31-33; 24 7; *also* 9 22; 13 32-33; 17 25; 22 22.	*cp.* 12 23, 27; 13 1; 17 1: *also* 2 4; 7 6, 8, 30; 8 20. 14 31 Arise, let us go hence.

[1] Gr. *an enclosed piece of ground.*
[2] Or, *Watch ye, and pray that ye enter not*

[1] Gr. *an enclosed piece of ground.*
[2] Or, *Watch ye, and pray that ye enter not*

[1] Many ancient authorities omit ver. 43, 44.

[1] Or, *ravine*   Gr. *winter-torrent.*
[2] Or, *of the Cedars*
[3] Or, *hour?*

§ 237. The Arrest

Matt. 26 47-56	**Mark 14** 43-50	**Luke 22** 47-53	**John 18** 2-11, 20
cp. 26 36.	*cp.* 14 32.	*cp.* 22 40.	**2** Now Judas also, which betrayed him, knew the place: for Jesus oft-times resorted thither with his disciples.
47 And while he yet spake [*cp.* 12 46; 17 5], lo, Judas, one of the twelve, came, and with him a great multitude with swords and staves, from the chief priests and elders of the people.	**43** And straightway, while he yet spake [*cp.* 5 35], cometh Judas, one of the twelve, and with him a multitude with swords and staves, from the chief priests and the scribes and the elders.	**47** While he yet spake [*cp.* 8 49; 22 60], behold, a multitude, and he that was called Judas, one of the twelve, went before them; *verse* 52	**3** Judas then, having received the [1] band *of soldiers,* and officers from the chief priests and the Pharisees, cometh thither with lanterns and torches and weapons. **4** Jesus therefore, knowing all the things that were coming upon him, went forth, and saith unto them, Whom seek ye? **5** They answered him, Jesus of Nazareth [*cp. verse* 7: *also* 1 45; 19 19]. Jesus saith unto them, I am *he.* And Judas also, which betrayed him, was standing with them.
cp. 2 23; 26 71: *also* 21 11.	*cp.* 1 24; 10 47; 14 67; 16 6.	*cp.* 4 34; 18 37; 24 19.	
48 Now he that betrayed him gave them a sign, saying, Whomsoever I shall kiss, that is he: take him. **49** And straightway he came to Jesus, and said, Hail	**44** Now he that betrayed him had given them a token, saying, Whomsoever I shall kiss, that is he; take him, and lead him away safely. **45** And when he was come, straightway he came to him, and saith,	and he drew near unto Jesus	

[Matthew column]

[cp. 27 29; 28 9], Rabbi; and ¹ kissed him. **50** And Jesus said unto him,

Friend [cp. 20 13; 22 12], *do* that for which thou art come.

Then they came and laid hands on Jesus, and took him. **51** And behold, one of them that were with [cp. 16 28; 27 47: *also* 26 73] Jesus

stretched out his hand, and drew his sword, and smote the ² servant of the high priest, and struck off his [cp. 5 29, 30, 39; 27 29] ear.

52 Then saith Jesus unto him,

cp. 8 3, 15; 9 18, 25, 29; 14 31; 17 7; 19 13, 15; 20 34: *also* 9 20; 14 36.

Put up again thy sword into its place: cp. 26 39: *also* 20 22, 23.

for all they that take the sword shall perish with the sword. **53** Or thinkest thou that I cannot beseech my Father, and he shall even now send me more than twelve legions of angels [cp. 4 11] ? **54** How then should the scriptures be fulfilled. that thus it must be [cp. *verse* 56] ? **55** In that hour [cp. 18 1] said Jesus to the multitudes,

verse 47

Are ye come out as against a robber with swords and

[Mark column]

[cp. 15 18] **Rabbi;** and ¹ kissed him.

46 And they laid hands on him, and took him. **47** But a certain one of them that stood by [cp. 9 1; 11 5; 15 35: *also* 14 69, 70; 15 39]

drew his sword, and smote the ² servant of the high priest, and struck off his ear.

48 And Jesus answered

cp. 1 31, 41; 5 23, 41; 6 2, 5; 7 33; 8 22, 23, 25; 9 27; 10 13, 16: *also* 3 10; 5 27; 6 56.

cp. 14 36: *also* 10 38, 39.

cp. 1 13.

and said unto them,

verse 43

Are ye come out, as against a robber, with swords and

[Luke column]

cp. 1 28.

to kiss him. **48** But Jesus said unto him, Judas, betrayest thou the Son of man with a kiss ?

49 And when they that were about him saw what would follow, they said, Lord, shall we smite with the sword ?

50 And a certain one of them cp. 9 27: *also* 19 24.

cp. 22 36, 38.

smote the ¹ servant of the high priest, and struck off his right [cp. 6 6] ear.

51 But Jesus answered and said, Suffer ye thus far. And he touched [cp. 4 40; 5 13; 7 14; 8 54; 13 13; 14 4; 18 15: *also* 6 19; 7 39; 8 44] his ear, and healed [cp. 6 19; 9 2, 11, 42; 14 4] him.

cp. 22 42.

52 And cp. 7 21; 10 21; 13 31. Jesus said unto the chief priests, and captains [cp. 22 4] of the temple, and elders, which were come against him, Are ye come out, as against a robber, with swords and

[John column]

cp. 19 3.

cp. 13 27. **6** When therefore he said unto them, I am *he*, they went backward, and fell to the ground. **7** Again therefore he asked them, Whom seek ye ? And they said, Jesus of Nazareth [cp. *verse* 5]. **8** Jesus answered, I told you that I am *he* : if therefore ye seek me, let these go their way : **9** that the word might be fulfilled which he spake, Of those whom thou hast given me I lost not one.

10 Simon Peter therefore cp. 12 29.

having a sword

drew it, and struck the high priest's ²servant, and cut off his right ear. Now the ² servant's name was Malchus. **11** Jesus therefore said unto Peter,

cp. 9 6: *also* 20 17.

Put up the sword into the sheath : the cup which the Father hath given me, shall I not drink it ?

cp. 1 51; 12 29.

20 Jesus answered him,

verse 3

staves to seize me ?	staves to seize me ?	staves ? *cp.* 22 54.	*cp.* 18 12. I have spoken openly to the world ; I ever taught
I sat daily in the temple [*cp.* 21 23] teaching, and ye took me not.	**49** I was daily with you in the temple [*cp.* 12 35] teaching, and ye took me not :	**53** When I was daily with you in the temple [*cp.* 19 47 ; 20 1 ; 21 37], ye stretched not forth your hands against me : but this is your hour [*cp.* 22 14], and the power of darkness.	in ³ synagogues, and in the temple [*cp.* 7 28 ; 8 20], where all the Jews come together ; and in secret spake I nothing.
56 But all this is *cp.* 26 18, 45.	but *this is cp.* 14 35, 41.		*cp.* 12 23, 27 ; 13 1 ; 17 1 : *also* 2 4 ; 7 6, 8, 30 ; 8 20.
come to pass, that the scriptures of the prophets might be fulfilled [*cp. verse* 54: *also* 21 42 ; 26 24, 31]. Then all the disciples left him, and fled [*cp.* 26 31].	*done* that the scriptures might be fulfilled [*cp.* 9 12 ; 12 10 ; 14 21, 27]. **50** And they all left him, and fled [*cp.* 14 27].	*cp.* 18 31 ; 20 17 ; 22 37 ; 24 25-27, 44-46.	*cp.* 5 39 ; 13 18 ; 15 25 ; 17 12. *cp.* 16 32 : *also* 8 16, 29.
¹ Gr. *kissed him much.* ² Gr. *bondservant.*	¹ Gr. *kissed him much.* ² Gr. *bondservant.*	¹ Gr. *bondservant.*	¹ Or, *cohort* ² Gr. *bondservant.* ³ Gr. *synagogue.*

§ 238. The Young Man who escaped

Mark 14 51-52

51 And a certain young man followed with him, having a linen cloth cast about him, over *his* naked *body* : and they lay hold on him ; **52** but he left the linen cloth, and fled naked.

(v) The Trial (§§ 239-249)

§ 239. Jesus led to the High Priest's House

Matt. 26 57-58	**Mark 14** 53-54	**Luke 22** 54-55	John 18 12-13, 24, 15-16, 1
57 And they that had taken Jesus led him away	**53** And they *cp.* 14 48 *and* Matt. 26 55. led Jesus away	**54** And they seized him, and led him *away*,	**12** So the ¹ band and the ² chief captain, and the officers of the Jews, seized Jesus and bound him, **13** and led him to Annas first ; for he was father in law to Caiaphas, which was high priest that year. . . . **24** Annas therefore sent him bound unto Caiaphas [*cp.* 11 49] the high priest. . . .
the house of Caiaphas [*cp.* 26 3] the high priest, where	the high priest : and there come together with him all the chief priests and the elders and the scribes.	*cp.* 3 2. and brought him into *cp.* 3 2. the high priest's house. *cp.* 22 66.	
the scribes and the elders were gathered together [*cp.* 26 3]. **58** But Peter followed him afar off,	**54** And Peter had followed him afar off,	But Peter followed afar off.	**15** And Simon Peter followed Jesus, and *so did* another disciple. Now that disciple was known unto the high priest, and entered in with Jesus into the court of the high priest ; **16** but Peter was standing at the door without. So the other disciple, which was known unto the high priest, went out and spake unto her that kept
unto the court [*cp.* 26 3, 69] of the high priest,			

Matt.	Mark	Luke	John
and entered in,	even within, into the court [cp. 14 66: *also* 15 16] of the high priest;		the door, and brought in Peter .... **18** Now the ³ servants and the officers were standing *there*, having made ⁴ a fire of coals; for it was cold; and they were warming themselves: and Peter also was with them, standing and warming himself [cp. 18 25].
and sat with the officers,	and he was sitting with the officers, and warming himself [cp. 14 67] in the light *of the fire*.	**55** And when they had kindled a fire in the midst of the court, and had sat down together, Peter sat in the midst of them. cp. 22 56.	
to see the end.			

¹ Or, *cohort*
² Or, *military tribune* Gr. *chiliarch.*
³ Gr. *bondservants.*
⁴ Gr. *a fire of charcoal.*

§ 240. **Peter's Denial** (Luke)

Matt. 26 69-75	Mark 14 66-72	Luke 22 56-62	John 18 17, 25-27
69 Now Peter was sitting without in the court [cp. 26 58]: and a maid	**66** And as Peter was beneath in the court [cp. 14 54], there cometh one of the maids of the high priest;	cp. 22 55. **56** And a certain maid	cp. 18 15. **17** The maid therefore that kept the door
came unto him, saying, Thou also wast with cp. verse 71. Jesus the Galilæan.	**67** and seeing Peter cp. 14 54. warming himself [cp. 14 54], she looked upon him, and saith, Thou also wast with the Nazarene [cp. 1 24; 10 47; 16 6], *even* Jesus. cp. verse 70.	seeing him as he sat in the light *of the fire*, and looking stedfastly upon him, said, This man also was with him. [cp. 4 34; 18 37; 24 19] cp. verse 59.	cp. 18 18, 25. saith un to Peter Art thou also *one* of cp. 18 5, 7; 19 19: *also* 1 45. this man's disciples? He saith,
70 But he denied before them all, saying, I know not what thou sayest. **71** And when he was gone out into the porch,	**68** But he denied, saying, ¹ I neither know, nor understand what thou sayest: and he went out into the ² porch; ³ and the cock crew, **69** And	**57** But he denied, saying, Woman, I know him not.	I am not.
another *maid* saw him, and saith unto them that were there, This man also was with Jesus the Nazarene [cp. 2 23: *also* 21 11].	cp. 14 54, 67. the maid saw him, and began again to say to them that stood by [cp. verse 70], This is *one* of them. cp. verse 67.	**58** And after a little while another saw him, and said, Thou also art *one* of them. cp. 4 34; 18 37; 24 19.	**25** Now Simon Peter was standing and warming himself [cp. 18 18] They said therefore unto him, Art thou also *one* of his disciples? cp. 18 5, 7; 19 19: *also* 1 45.
72 And again he denied with an oath, I know not the man. **73** And after a little while	**70** But he again denied it. And after a little while again	But Peter said, Man, I am not. **59** And after the space of about one hour	He denied, and said, I am not.
they that stood by [cp. 16 28; 27 47]	they that stood by [cp. 9 1; 11 5; 14 47, 69; 15 35, 39]	cp. 9 27; 19 24.	cp. 12 29. **26** One of the ¹ servants of the high priest, being a kinsman or him whose ear Peter cut off,
came and said to Peter, Of a truth thou also art	said to Peter, Of a truth thou art	another confidently affirmed, saying, Of a truth this man also was with him:	saith,

Matt.

one of them ;
[cp. verse 69] for thy speech bewrayeth thee.

74 Then began he to curse and to swear, I know not the man. And straightway
cp. 12 46 ; 17 5 ; 26 47.
the cock crew.

cp. 9 22 ; 16 23.

75 And Peter remembered the word which Jesus had said, Before the cock crow, thou shalt deny me thrice [cp. 26 34]. And he went out, and wept bitterly.

Mark.

one of them; for thou art a Galilæan.

71 But he began to curse, and to swear, I know not this man of whom ye speak. **72** And straightway
cp. 5 35 ; 14 43.
the second time the cock crew.
cp. 16 19, 20.

cp. 5 30 ; 8 33.

And Peter called to mind the word, how that Jesus said unto him, Before the cock crow twice [cp. 14 68, 72], thou shalt deny me thrice [cp. 14 30]. ⁴ And when he thought thereon, he wept.

1 Or, I neither know, nor understand: thou, what sayest thou ?
2 Gr. forecourt.
3 Many ancient authorities omit and the cock crew.
4 Or, And he began to weep.

Luke.

for he is a Galilæan.

60 But Peter said, Man, I know not what thou sayest. And immediately, while he yet spake [cp. 8 49; 22 47], the cock crew. **61** And the Lord [cp. 7 13, 19; 10 1, 39, 41; 11 39; 12 42; 13 15; 17 5, 6; 18 6; 19 8; 24 3, 34] turned [cp. 7 9, 44; 9 55; 10 23; 14 25; 23 28], and looked upon Peter. And Peter remembered [cp. 24 6, 8] the word of the Lord, how that he said unto him, Before the cock crow this day, thou shalt deny me thrice [cp. 22 34]. **62** And he went out, and wept bitterly.

John.

Did not I see thee in the garden with him ? **27** Peter therefore denied again : and straightway the cock crew.
cp. 4 1 ; 6 23 ; 11 2 ; 20 2, 18, 20, 25 ; 21 7, 12.

cp. 1 38.

cp. 2 22 ; 12 16.

cp. 13 38.

1 Gr. bondservants.

§ 241. The Mockery in the High Priest's House (Luke)

[Cp. Matt. 27 27-31 ‖ Mark 15 16-20 ‖ John 19 2-3; Matt. 27 39-44 ‖ Mark 15 29-32 ‖ Luke 23 35-39; Luke 23 11: also Matt. 20 19 ‖ Mark 10 34 ‖ Luke 18 32]

Matt. 26 67-68

cp. 27 29, 31, 41 : also 20 19.

67 Then did they spit [cp. 27 30] in his face and buffet him : and some smote him ¹ with the palms of their hands, **68** saying, Prophesy unto us, thou Christ [cp. 27 17, 22 : also 26 63 : and 16 16]: who is he that struck thee ?

1 Or, with rods

Mark 14 65

65 And some
cp. 15 20, 31 : also 10 34.

began to spit [cp. 15 19 : also 10 34] on him, and to cover his face, and to buffet him,

and to say unto him, Prophesy :
cp. 15 32 : also 14 61 : and 8 29.

and the officers received him with ¹ blows of their hands.

1 Or, strokes of rods

Luke 22 63-65

63 And the men that held ¹ Jesus mocked [cp. 23 11, 35, 36 : also 18 32] him, and beat him.
cp. 18 32.

64 And they blindfolded him,

and asked him, saying, Prophesy :
cp. 23 35, 39 : also 22 67 ; 23 2 : and 9 20.
who is he that struck thee ?

65 And many other [cp. 3 18] things spake they against him, reviling him.

1 Gr. him.

John 18 22-23

22 And when he had said this,

cp. 19 3.

cp. 1 41 ; 4 25, 26, 29 ; 7 26, 41 ; 9 22 ; 10 24 ; 11 27.

one of the officers standing by struck Jesus ¹ with his hand [cp. 19 3], saying, Answerest thou the high priest so ? **23** Jesus answered him, If I have spoken evil, bear witness of the evil : but if well, why smitest thou me ?

1 Or, with a rod

§ 242. **Jesus before the Council**

Matt. 26 59-68	**Mark 14** 55-65	**Luke 22** 66-71 (63-64)	John 18 19-23 ; 2 18-19 ; 10 24-25 ; 1 51
cp. 27 1.	*cp.* 15 1.	**66** And as soon as it was day, the assembly of the elders of the people was gathered together, both chief priests and scribes; and they led him away into their council,	*cp.* 18 28.
cp. 26 57.	*cp.* 14 53.		
59 Now the chief priests and the whole council sought false witness against Jesus, that they might put him to death; **60** and they found it not, though many false witnesses came.	**55** Now the chief priests and the whole council sought witness against Jesus to put him to death; and found it not. **56** For many bare false witness against him, and their witness agreed not together. **57** And there stood up certain, and bare false witness against him, saying, **58** We heard him say,		*cp.* 10 25 (*below*).
But afterward came two, **61** and said, This man said, I am able to destroy the [1] temple of God, and to build it in three days [*cp.* 27 40: *also* 12 40; 16 21; 17 23; 20 19; 27 63, 64].	I will destroy this [1] temple that is made with hands, and in three days [*cp.* 15 29: *also* 8 31; 9 31; 10 34] I will build another made without hands. **59** And not even so did their witness agree together.	*cp.* 9 22; 13 32; 18 33; 24 7, 21, 46.	**2 18** The Jews therefore answered and said unto him, What sign shewest thou unto us, seeing that thou doest these things ? **19** Jesus answered and said unto them, Destroy this [1] temple, and in three days I will raise it up.
62 And the high priest stood up, and said unto him, Answerest thou nothing ? what is it which these witness against thee ? **63** But Jesus held his peace. *cp.* 27 12, 14: *also* 15 23.	**60** And the high priest stood up in the midst, and asked Jesus, saying, Answerest thou nothing ? what is it which these witness against thee ? **61** But he held his peace, and answered nothing [*cp.* 15 5].	*cp.* 23 9.	**18 19** The high priest therefore asked Jesus of his disciples, and of his teaching. *cp.* 19 10. **20** Jesus answered [*cp.* 19 9] him, I have spoken openly to the world ; I ever taught in [2] synagogues, and in the temple [*cp.* 7 28; 8 20], where all the Jews come together ; and in secret spake I nothing. **21** Why askest thou me ? ask them that have heard *me*, what I spake unto them : behold, these know the things which I said.
cp. 26 55: *also* 21 23.	*cp.* 14 49: *also* 12 35.	*cp.* 22 53: *also* 19 47; 20 1; 21 37.	
			10 24 The Jews therefore came round about him, and said unto him, How long dost thou hold us in suspense ?
And the high priest said unto him, I adjure thee by the living [*cp.* 16 16] God, that thou tell us whether thou be the Christ [*cp.* 16 16: *also* 26 68; 27 17,22],	Again the high priest asked him, and saith unto him, *cp.* 5 7. Art thou the Christ [*cp.* 8 29: *also* 15 32],	saying, **67** If thou art the Christ [*cp.* 9 20: *also* 23 2, 35, 39], tell us. But he said unto them, If I tell you, ye will not believe :	If thou art the Christ [*cp.* 1 41 ; 4 25, 26, 29 ; 7 26, 41 ; 9 22 ; 11 27], tell us plainly. **25** Jesus answered them, I told you, and ye believe not : the works that I do in my Father's name,

cp. verses 59 *and* 60.

cp. verses 55 *and* 56.

68 and if I ask *you*, ye will not answer. **69** But from henceforth [*cp.* 1 48; 5 10; 12 52; 22 18] shall the Son of man be seated at the right hand of the power of God.

these bear witness of me.

verse 64

verse 62

70 And they all said, Art thou then the Son of God [*cp.* 1 35; 4 3, 9, 41; 8 28: *also* 3 22; 9 35]?

the Son of God [*cp.* 4 3, 6; 8 29: 14 33; 16 16; 27 40, 43, 54: *also* 3 17; 17 5]. **64** Jesus saith unto him, Thou hast said [*cp.* 26 25: *also* 27 11]: [*cp.* 24 5] nevertheless I say unto you, Henceforth [*cp.* 23 39; 26 29] ye shall see [*cp.* 16 28]

the Son of the Blessed? [*cp.* 1 1; 3 11; 5 7; 15 39: *also* 1 11; 9 7] **62** And Jesus said, *cp.* 15 2. I am [*cp.* 13 6]: and ye shall see [*cp.* 9 1]

And he said unto them, *cp.* 23 3. ¹ Ye say that I am [*cp.* 21 8].

cp. 9 27.

cp. 10 36: *also* 1 34; *etc.*

1 51 And he saith unto him, *cp.* 18 37. *cp.* 8 24, 28; 13 19. Verily, verily, I say unto you, *cp.* 13 19; 14 7. Ye shall see the heaven opened, and the angels of God ascending and descending upon the Son of man.

the Son of man sitting at the right hand of power, and coming on the clouds of heaven [*cp.* 16 27-28; 24 30-31; 25 31]. **65** Then the high priest rent his garments, saying, He hath spoken blasphemy [*cp.* 9 3]: what further need have we of witnesses? behold, now ye have heard the blasphemy: **66** what think ye [*cp.* 17 25; 18 12; 21 28; 22 17, 42]? They answered and said, He is ² worthy of death. **67** Then *cp.* 27 29, 31, 41: *also* 20 19. did they spit [*cp.* 27 30] in his face and buffet him: and some smote him ³ with the palms of their hands, **68** saying, Prophesy unto us, thou Christ [*cp.* 27 17, 22: *also* 26 63: *and* 16 16]: who is he that struck thee?

the Son of man sitting at the right hand of power [*cp.* 16 19], and coming with the clouds of heaven [*cp.* 8 38; 13 26-27]. **63** And the high priest rent his clothes, and saith, *cp.* 2 7. What further need have we of witnesses? **64** Ye have heard the blasphemy: what think ye? And they all condemned him to be ² worthy of death. **65** And some *cp.* 15 20, 31: *also* 10 34. began to spit [*cp.* 15 19: *also* 10 34] on him, and to cover his face, and to buffet him, and to say unto him, Prophesy: *cp.* 15 32: *also* 14 61: *and* 8 29. and the officers received him with ³ blows of their hands.

verse 69

cp. 9 26; 21 27.

71 And they said, *cp.* 5 21. What further need have we of witness? for we ourselves have heard from his own mouth.

63 And the men that held ² *Jesus* mocked [*cp.* 23 11, 35, 36: *also* 18 32] him, and beat him. *cp.* 18 32. **64** And they blindfolded him, and asked him, saying, Prophesy: [*cp.* 23 35, 39: *also* 22 67; 23 2: *and* 9 20] who is he that struck thee?

18 22 And when he had said this, *cp.* 10 33, 36.

cp. 11 56.

cp. 19 3.

cp. 1 41; 4 25, 26, 29; 7 26, 41; 9 22; 10 24; 11 27. one of the officers standing by struck Jesus ³ with his hand [*cp.* 19 3], saying, Answerest thou the high priest so? 23 Jesus answered him, If I have spoken evil, bear witness of the evil: but if well, why smitest thou me?

---

¹ Or, *sanctuary*: as in ch. 23 35; 27 5.   ¹ Or, *sanctuary*   ² Gr. *liable to.*   ¹ Or, *Ye say it, because I am.*   ¹ Or, *sanctuary*   ² Gr. *synagogue.*
² Gr. *liable to.*   ³ Or, *with rods*   ³ Or, *strokes of rods*   ² Gr. *him.*   ³ Or, *with a rod*

Mark 14 59: *cp.* Num. 35 30.   Matt. 26 64 ‖ Mark 14 62 ‖ Luke 22 69: *cp.* Ps. 110 1 *and* Dan. 7 13.

§ 243. **Peter's Denial** (Matt. and Mark)

Matt. 26 69-75	**Mark 14** 66-72	Luke 22 56-62	John 18 17, 25-27
69 Now Peter was sitting without in the court [*cp.* 26 58] : and a maid	**66** And as Peter was beneath in the court [*cp.* 14 54], there cometh one of the maids of the high priest; **67** and seeing Peter *cp.* 14 54. warming himself [*cp.* 14 54], she looked upon him, and saith,	*cp.* 22 55. 56 And a certain maid seeing him as he sat in the light *of the fire,* and looking stedfastly upon him, said,	*cp.* 18 15. **17** The maid therefore that kept the door *cp.* 18 18, 25.
came unto him, saying, Thou also wast with *cp. verse* 71. Jesus the Galilæan. **70** But he denied before them all, saying, I know not what thou sayest. **71** And when he was gone out into the porch,	Thou also wast with the Nazarene [*cp.* 1 24; 10 47; 16 6], *even* Jesus. *cp. verse* 70. **68** But he denied, saying, ¹ I neither know, nor understand what thou sayest : and he went out into the ² porch; ³ and the cock crew. **69** And	This man also was with him. [*cp.* 4 34; 18 37; 24 19] *cp. verse* 59. **57** But he denied, saying, Woman, I know him not.	saith unto Peter, Art thou also *one* of *cp.* 18 5, 7; 19 19: *also* 1 45. this man's disciples ? He saith, I am not.
another *maid* saw him, and saith unto them that were there, This man also was with Jesus the Nazarene [*cp.* 2 23: *also* 21 11]. **72** And again he denied with an oath, I know not the man. **73** And after a little while	*cp.* 14 54, 67. the maid saw him, and began again to say to them that stood by [*cp. verse* 70], This is *one* of them. *cp. verse* 67. **70** But he again denied it.	**58** And after a little while another saw him, and said, Thou also art *one* of them. *cp.* 4 34; 18 37; 24 19. But Peter	**25** Now Simon Peter was standing and warming himself [*cp.* 18 18]. They said therefore unto him, Art thou also *one* of his disciples ? *cp.* 18 5, 7; 19 19: *also* 1 45. He denied, and said, I am not.
they that stood by [*cp.* 16 28; 27 47]	And after a little while again they that stood by [*cp.* 9 1; 11 5; 14 47, 69; 15 35, 39]	said, Man, I am not. **59** And after the space of about one hour *cp.* 9 27; 19 24.	*cp.* 12 29. **26** One of the ¹ servants of the high priest, being a kinsman of him whose ear Peter cut off,
came and said to Peter, Of a truth thou also art *one* of them ; [*cp. verse* 69] for thy speech bewrayeth thee.	said to Peter, Of a truth thou art *one* of them ; for thou art a Galilæan.	another confidently affirmed, saying, Of a truth this man also was with him : for he is a Galilæan.	saith, Did not I see thee in the garden with him ? **27** Peter therefore
74 Then began he to curse and to swear, I know not the man. And straightway *cp.* 12 46; 17 5; 26 47. the cock crew.	**71** But he began to curse, and to swear, I know not this man of whom ye speak. **72** And straightway *cp.* 5 35; 14 43. the second time the cock crew. *cp.* 16 19, 20.	**60** But Peter said, Man, I know not what thou sayest. And immediately, while he yet spake [*cp.* 8 49; 22 47], the cock crew. **61** And the Lord [*cp.* 7 13, 19; 10 1, 39, 41; 11 39; 12 42; 13 15; 17 5, 6; 18 6; 19 8; 24 3, 34] turned	denied again : and straightway the cock crew. *cp.* 4 1; 6 23; 11 2; 20 2, 18, 20, 25; 21 7, 12.

cp. 9 22 ; 16 23.	*cp.* 5 30 ; 8 33.	[*cp.* 7 9, 44 ; 9 55 ; 10 23 ; 14 25 ; 23 28], and looked upon Peter. And Peter remembered [*cp.* 24 6, 8] the word of the Lord, how that he said unto him, Before the cock crow this day,	*cp.* 1 38.

75 And Peter remembered the word which Jesus had said, Before the cock crow, thou shalt deny me thrice [*cp.* 26 34]. And he went out, and wept bitterly.

And Peter called to mind the word, how that Jesus said unto him, Before the cock crow twice [*cp.* 14 68, 72], thou shalt deny me thrice [*cp.* 14 30]. [4] And when he thought thereon, he wept.

thou shalt deny me thrice [*cp.* 22 34]. **62** And he went out, and wept bitterly.

cp. 2 22 ; 12 16.

cp. 13 38.

[1] Or, *I neither know, nor understand : thou, what sayest thou ?*
[2] Gr. *forecourt.*
[3] Many ancient authorities omit *and the cock crew.*
[4] Or, *And he began to weep.*

[1] Gr, *bondservants.*

§ 244. **Jesus brought to Pilate**

Matt. 27 1-2	**Mark 15** 1	**Luke 23** 1	John 18 28
1 Now when morning was come, all the chief priests and the elders of the people took counsel [*cp.* 12 14 ; 22 15 ; 27 7 ; 28 12] against Jesus to put him to death : **2** and they bound him, and led him away, and delivered him up to Pilate the governor [*cp.* 27 11, 14, 15, 21, 27 ; 28 14]. *cp.* 27 27.	**1** And straightway in the morning the chief priests with the elders and scribes, and the whole council, held a consultation [*cp.* 3 6], and bound Jesus, and carried him away, and delivered him up to Pilate. *cp.* 15 16.	**1** And *cp.* 22 66. the whole company of them rose up, and brought him before Pilate. *cp.* 20 20.	28 They lead Jesus therefore from Caiaphas into the [1] palace [*cp.* 18 33 ; 19 9] and it was early . . . [1] Gr. *Praetorium.*

§ 245. **The Death of Judas**

Matt. 27 3-10

3 Then Judas, which betrayed him, when he saw that he was condemned, repented himself, and brought back the thirty pieces of silver to the chief priests and elders, **4** saying, I have sinned in that I betrayed [1] innocent [*cp.* 27 24] blood. But they said, What is that to us ? see thou *to it* [*cp.* 27 24]. **5** And he cast down the pieces of silver into the sanctuary, and departed ; and he went away and hanged himself. **6** And the chief priests took the pieces of silver, and said, It is not lawful to put them into the [2] treasury, since it is the price of blood. **7** And they took counsel [*cp.* 12 14 ; 22 15 ; 27 1 ; 28 12], and bought with them the potter's field, to bury strangers in.

cp. 3 6 ; 15 1.

cp. 21 22, 23.

8 Wherefore that field was called, The field of blood, unto this day [*cp.* 11 23 ; 28 15]. **9** Then was fulfilled that which was spoken [3] by Jeremiah the prophet, saying, And [4] they took the thirty pieces of silver, the price of him that was priced, [5] whom *certain* of the

Acts 1 18 Now this man obtained a field with the reward of his iniquity ; and falling headlong, he burst asunder in the midst, and all his bowels gushed out. 19 And it became known to all the dwellers at Jerusalem ; insomuch that in their language that field was called Akeldama, that is, The field of blood.

children of Israel did price; **10** and ⁶ they gave them for the potter's field, as the Lord appointed me.

¹ Many ancient authorities read *righteous.*
² Gr. *corbanas,* that is, *sacred treasury.* Compare Mark 7 11.
³ Or, *through*   ⁴ Or, *I took*
⁵ Or, *whom they priced on the part of the sons of Israel*
⁶ Some ancient authorities read *I gave.*

Matt. 27 6 : *cp.* Deut. 23 18 ?   Matt. 27 7 : *cp.* Jer. 19 11.   Matt. 27 9-10 : Zech. 11 12-13—*cp.* Jer. 32 6-15 : *also* 18 1-12 ; 19 1-13.

§ 246. Jesus before Pilate (i)

Matt. 27 11-14	Mark 15 2-5	Luke 23 2-7	John 18 28-38 ; 19 8-10
			18 28 And they themselves entered not into the ¹palace, that they might not be defiled, but might eat the passover. **29** Pilate therefore went out unto them, and saith, What accusation bring ye against this man ? **30** They answered and said unto him, If this man
verse 12	*verse* 3	**2** And they began to accuse him, saying, We found this man perverting [*cp.* 23 14] our nation, and forbidding to give	
cp. 22 15-22.	*cp.* 12 13-17.	tribute [*cp.* 20 20-26] to Cæsar, and saying that he himself is ¹ Christ	*cp.* 19 12.
cp. 26 63-64: *also* 26 68; 27 17, 22 : *and* 16 16.	*cp.* 14 61-62: *also* 15 32: *and* 8 29.	[*cp.* 22 67: *also* 23 35, 39: *and* 9 20] a king [*cp. verse* 3].	*cp.* 4 25, 26 : *also* 1 41 ; 4 29 ; 7 26, 41 ; 9 22 ; 11 27. were not

an evil-doer, we should not have delivered him up unto thee. **31** Pilate therefore said unto them, Take him yourselves, and judge him according to your law. The Jews said unto him, It is not lawful for us to put any man to death : **32** that the word of Jesus might be fulfilled, which he spake, signifying by what manner of death he should die. **33** Pilate therefore entered again into the ¹ palace, and called Jesus,

		cp. 20 20.	
11 Now Jesus stood before the governor [*cp.* 27 2, 14, 15, 21, 27; 28 14]: and the governor asked him, saying, Art thou the King of the Jews [*cp.* 2 2; 27 29, 37: *also* 27 42: *and* 21 5] ?	**2** And Pilate asked him, Art thou the King of the Jews [*cp.* 15 9, 12, 18, 26: *also* 15 32] ?	**3** And Pilate asked him, saying, Art thou the King of the Jews [*cp.* 23 37, 38: *and* 19 38] ?	and said unto him, Art thou the King of the Jews [*cp.* 18 39 ; 19 3, 19, 21 : *also* 1 49 ; 12 13 : *and*

6 15 ; 12 15 ; 18 37 ; 19 12, 14, 15] ? **34** Jesus answered, Sayest thou this of thyself, or did others tell it thee concerning me ? **35** Pilate answered, Am I a Jew ? Thine own nation and the chief priests delivered thee unto me : what hast thou done ? **36** Jesus answered, My kingdom is not of this world : if my kingdom were of this world, then would my ² servants fight, that I should not be delivered to the Jews : but now is my kingdom not from hence. **37** Pilate therefore said unto him, Art thou a king then ?

And Jesus said unto him, Thou sayest [*cp.* 26 25, 64].	And he answering saith unto him, Thou sayest.	And he answered him and said, Thou sayest [*cp.* 22 70].	Jesus answered,

³ Thou sayest that I am a king. To this end have I been born, and to this end am I come into the world, that I should bear witness unto the truth. Every one that is of the truth heareth my voice. **38** Pilate saith unto him, What is truth ? And when he had said this, he went out again unto the Jews, and saith unto them,

		4 And Pilate said unto the chief priests and the multitudes, I find no fault [*cp.* 23 14, 22] in this	I find no crime [*cp.* 19 4, 6] in him.
cp. 27 24. **12** And when he was accused by the chief priests and elders,	**3** And the chief priests accused him of many things. *cp.* 15 11.	man. **5** But they were the more urgent, *cp.* 23 2, 10. saying, He stirreth up the people, teaching throughout all Judæa, and beginning	*cp.* 18 29, 30.

Matthew	Mark	Luke	John
he answered nothing [cp. 26 63; 27 14: also 15 23].	cp. 14 61; 15 5.	from Galilee even unto this place. cp. 23 9. **6** But when Pilate heard it,	cp. 19 9.
13 Then saith Pilate unto him,	**4** And Pilate again asked him, saying,	he asked whether the man were a Galilæan.	19 8 When Pilate therefore heard this saying, he was the more afraid; **9** and he entered into the ¹ palace again, and saith unto Jesus, Whence art thou?
Hearest thou not how many things they witness against thee? **14** And he gave him no answer [cp. 26 63; 27 12: also 15 23], not even to one word: insomuch that the governor [cp. verse 11; etc.] marvelled greatly.	Answerest thou nothing? behold how many things they accuse thee of. **5** But Jesus no more answered [cp. 14 61] anything; insomuch that Pilate marvelled.	cp. 23 9.	But Jesus gave him no answer.
		7 And when he knew that he was of Herod's jurisdiction, he sent him unto Herod, who himself also was at Jerusalem in these days.	**10** Pilate therefore saith unto him, Speakest thou not unto me? knowest thou not that I have ⁴ power to release thee, and have ⁴ power to crucify thee?
		¹ Or, *an anointed king*	¹ Gr. *Praetorium.* ² Or, *officers* ³ Or, *Thou sayest* it, *because I am a king.* ⁴ Or, *authority*

§ 247. Jesus before Herod

Luke 23 8-12

Matthew	Mark	Luke	John
cp. 26 63; 27 12, 14: *also* 15 23. cp. 26 67-68; 27 27-31, 39-44: *also* 20 19.	cp. 14 61; 15 5. cp. 14 65; 15 16-20, 29-32: *also* 10 34.	**8** Now when Herod saw Jesus, he was exceeding glad: for he was of a long time desirous to see him [cp. 9 9], because he had heard concerning him [cp. 9 7, 9]; and he hoped to see some ¹ miracle done by him. **9** And he questioned him in many words; but he answered him nothing. **10** And the chief priests and the scribes stood, vehemently accusing him [cp. 23 2, 5: Matt. 27 12: Mark 15 3: John 18 29, 30]. **11** And Herod with his soldiers set him at nought, and mocked [cp. 22 63-65; 23 35-39: *also* 18 32] him, and arraying him in gorgeous apparel [cp. Matt. 27 28: Mark 15 17: John 19 2] sent him back to Pilate. **12** And Herod and Pilate became friends with each other that very day: for before they were at enmity between themselves. ¹ Gr. *sign.*	cp. 19 9. cp. 19 2-3.

§ 248. Jesus before Pilate (ii)

Matt. 27 15-26	Mark 15 6-15	Luke 23 13-25	John 18 39-40; 19 1, 4-6, 12-16
15 Now at ¹ the feast the governor [cp. 27 2, 11, 14, 21, 27; 28 14] was wont to release unto the multitude one prisoner,	**6** Now at ¹ the feast he used to release unto them one prisoner,	cp. 20 20.	18 39 But ye have a custom, that I should release unto you one at the pass-

whom they would.
16 And they had
then a notable prisoner,
called Barabbas.

17 When there-
fore they were gathered
together,

Pilate said
unto them,

cp. 27 24.

cp. verse 26.

Whom will ye
that I release
unto you?
cp. 2 2; 27 11, 29, 37:
also 27 42: and 21 5.

Barabbas,
or Jesus which is called
Christ [cp. 1 16; 27 22:
also 26 63, 64, 68: and
16 16]? **18** For he knew
that for envy they
had de-
livered him up. **19** And
while he was sitting on
the judgement-seat, his
wife sent unto him, say-
ing, Have thou nothing to
do with that righteous
man [cp. verse 24]: for
I have suffered many
things this day in a dream
[cp. 1 20; 2 12, 13, 19, 22]
because of him. **20** Now
the chief priests and the
elders persuaded the mul-
titudes that they should
ask for Barabbas,
and destroy
Jesus. **21** But the governor [cp. verse 15] answered
and said unto them,
Whether of the twain will
ye that I release unto
you? And they

said,

Barabbas.

---

whom they asked of
him. **7** And there was
one
called Barabbas, *lying*
bound with them that
had made insurrection,
men who in the insur-
rection had committed
murder. **8** And the
multitude went up and
began to ask him *to do* as
he was wont to do unto
them. **9** And Pilate
answered them, saying,

cp. verse 15.

Will ye
that I release
unto you the King of the
Jews [cp. 15 2, 12, 18,
26: also 15 32]?

cp. 14 61, 62; 15 32: and
8 29.
10 For he per-
ceived that for envy the
chief priests had de-
livered him up.

11 But
the chief priests
stirred up the mul-
titude, that he should
rather release Barabbas
unto them.

---

verse 19

13 And
Pilate called
together the chief priests
and the rulers and the
people, **14** and
said
unto them, Ye brought
unto me this man, as
one that perverteth [cp.
23 2] the people: and
behold, I, hav-
ing examined him before
you, found no fault [cp.
23 4, 22] in this man
touching those things
whereof ye accuse him:
15 no, nor yet Herod:
for he sent him back
unto us; and behold,
nothing worthy of death
hath been done by him.
16 I will therefore chastise him, and release him
[cp. verse 22].[1]

cp. 23 3, 37, 38: and 19
38; 23 2.

cp. 22 67; 23 2, 35, 39:
and 9 20.

cp. 23 47.

cp. 23 5.

18 But they cried
out all together,
saying, Away
with this man,
and release unto us
Barabbas: **19** one
who for a certain insur-

---

over.

cp. 18 40.

19 4 And
Pilate went out again,

and
saith
unto them, Behold, I bring
him out
to you,
that
ye may know that I

find no crime [cp.
18 38; 19 6] in him.
5 Jesus therefore came out,
wearing the crown of
thorns and the purple
garment. And *Pilate*
saith unto them, Behold,
the man [cp. 19 14]!

cp. 19 1.

18 39 b Will ye
therefore that I release
unto you the King of the
Jews [cp. 18 33; 19 3, 19,
21: also 1 49; 12 13:
and 6 15; 12 15; 18 37;
19 12, 14, 15]?

cp. 4 25, 26: also 1 41;
4 29; 7 26, 41; 9 22;
11 27.

18 40 They cried
out there-
fore again, saying, [cp. 19
15] Not this man, but

Barabbas. Now Barabbas

Matthew

22 Pilate
saith
unto them, What then shall I do unto Jesus which is called

Christ [cp. verse 17]?

They all say, Let him be crucified.
23 And he said,

Why, what evil hath he done?

cp. 27 24.

cp. verse 26.

cp. 23 2.
cp. 27 62. | cp. 15 42. | cp. 23 54.
cp. 27 45. | cp. 15 33. | cp. 23 44.

But they cried out exceedingly, saying,
Let him be crucified.

24 So when Pilate saw that he prevailed nothing, but rather that a tumult [cp. 26 5] was arising, he took water, and washed his hands before the multitude, saying, I am innocent [cp. 27 4] [2] of the blood of this righteous man [cp. verse 19]: see ye to it [cp. 27 4]. 25 And all the people answered and said, His blood be on us, and on our children.

26 Then released he unto them Barabbas:

but
Jesus he
scourged and delivered

Mark

verse 7
12 And Pilate again answered and said unto them, What then shall I do unto him whom ye call the King of the Jews [cp. verse 9]?

13 And they cried out again, Crucify him.
14 And Pilate said unto them, Why, what evil hath he done?

cp. verse 15.

But they cried out exceedingly,

Crucify him.

15 And Pilate,

wishing to content the multitude,

released unto them Barabbas,

and delivered Jesus, when he had scourged

Luke

rection made in the city, and for murder, was cast into prison. 20 And Pilate spake unto them again,

desiring to release Jesus; 21 but they shouted, saying, Crucify, crucify him. 22 And he said unto them the third time, Why, what evil hath this man done [cp. 23 41]?

I have found no cause [cp. 23 4, 14] of death in him: I will therefore chastise him and release him [cp. verse 16].
cp. verse 20.

23 But they were instant with loud voices, asking that he might
cp. 23 18.
be crucified.

And their voices prevailed. 24 And Pilate

cp. 23 47.

gave sentence that what they asked for should be done. 25 And he released him that for insurrection and murder had been cast into prison, whom they asked for; but Jesus
cp. verse 16 and 22.
he delivered up

John

was a robber.

cp. 19 12.
19 6 When therefore the chief priests and the officers saw him, they cried out, saying, Crucify him, crucify him. Pilate saith unto them,

Take him yourselves, and crucify him: for I find no crime [cp. 18 38; 19 4] in him. . . .
cp. 19 1.
12 Upon this Pilate sought to release him: but the Jews cried out, saying, If thou release this man, thou art not Cæsar's friend: every one that maketh himself a king [1] speaketh against Cæsar. 13 When Pilate therefore heard these words, he brought Jesus out, and sat down on the judgement-seat at a place called The Pavement, but in Hebrew, Gabbatha. 14 Now it was the Preparation [cp. 19 31, 42] of the passover: it was about the sixth hour. And he saith unto the Jews, Behold, your King [cp. 19 5]! 15 They therefore cried out,

Away with him, away with him, crucify him. Pilate saith unto them, Shall I crucify your King? The chief priests answered, We have no king but Cæsar.

19 1 Then Pilate therefore took Jesus, and scourged him. . . . 16 Then therefore he delivered him

to be crucified.	him, to be crucified.	to their will.	unto them to be crucified.

1 Or, *a feast*
2 Some ancient authorities read *of this blood : see ye &c.*

1 Or, *a feast*

1 Many ancient authorities insert ver. 17 *Now he must needs release unto them at the feast one* prisoner. Others add the same words after ver. 19.

1 Or, *opposeth Caesar*

Matt. 27 24 : *cp.* Deut. 21 6-9 ; Susanna 46.

§ 249. The Mockery in the Prætorium

[*Cp.* Matt. 26 67-68 ‖ Mark 14 65 ‖ Luke 22 63-65; Matt. 27 39-44 ‖ Mark 15 29-32 ‖ Luke 23 35-39; Luke 23 11 : *also* Matt. 20 19 ‖ Mark 10 34 ‖ Luke 18 32]

Matt. 27 27-31	Mark 15 16-20		John 19 2-3
27 Then the soldiers of the governor [*cp.* 27 1, *etc.*] took Jesus into *cp.* 26 3, 58, 69. the 1 palace, and gathered unto him the whole 2 band. **28** And they 3 stripped him, and put on him a scarlet robe. **29** And they plaited a crown of thorns and put it upon his head, and a reed in his right [*cp.* 5 29, 30, 39] hand ; and they kneeled down before him, and mocked [*cp.* 27 31, 41 : *also* 20 19] him, saying, Hail, King of the Jews [*cp.* 2 2; 27 11, 37: *also* 27 42 : *and* 21 5] ! **30** And they *cp.* 26 67. spat [*cp.* 26 67] upon him, and took the reed and smote him on the head. **31** And when they had mocked [*cp.* 27 29, 41: *also* 20 19] him, they took off from him the robe, and put on him his garments, and led him away to crucify him.	**16** And the soldiers led him away within the court [*cp.* 14 54, 66], which is the 1 Prætorium ; and they call together the whole 2 band. **17** And they clothe him with purple, and plaiting a crown of thorns, they put it on him ; **18** and they *cp.* 15 20, 31 : *also* 10 34. began to salute him, Hail, King of the Jews [*cp.* 15 2, 9, 12, 26: *also* 15 32] ! **19** And they smote his head with a reed, [*cp.* 14 65] and did spit [*cp.* 14 65: *also* 10 34] upon him, and bowing their knees worshipped him. **20** And when they had mocked [*cp.* 15 31: *also* 10 34] him, they took off from him the purple, and put on him his garments. And they lead him out to crucify him.	*cp.* 20 20. *cp.* 22 55. *cp.* 23 11. *cp.* 6 6; 22 50. *cp.* 22 63; 23 11, 35, 36: *also* 18 32. *cp.* 23 3, 37, 38: *and* 19 38; 23 2. *cp.* 18 32. *cp.* 22 63; 23 11, 35, 36: *also* 18 32. *cp.* 23 26.	2 And the soldiers *cp.* 18 15. *cp.* 18 28, 33 ; 19 9. plaited a crown of thorns, and put it on his head, and arrayed him in a purple garment ; *cp.* 18 10. **3** and they came unto him, and said, Hail, King of the Jews [*cp.* 18 33, 39 ; 19 19, 21 : *also* 1 49 ; 12 13 : *and* 6 15 ; 12 15 ; 18 37 ; 19 12, 14, 15] ! and they struck him 1 with their hands [*cp.* 18 22]. *cp.* 19 16b.

1 Gr. *Prætorium.* See Mark 15 16.
2 Or, *cohort*
3 Some ancient authorities read *clothed.*

1 Or, *palace*   2 Or, *cohort*

1 Or, *with rods*

(vi) On the Way to Golgotha (§§ 250-252)

§ 250. Simon of Cyrene compelled to bear the Cross

Matt 27 32	Mark 15 21	Luke 23 26	John 19 16-17
cp. 27 31.	*cp.* 15 20.	**26** And when they led him away,	
32 And as they came out, they found a man of Cyrene, Simon by name :	**21** And they 1 compel one passing by, Simon of Cyrene, coming from the country, the father of Alexander	they laid hold upon one Simon of Cyrene, coming from the country,	16 They took Jesus therefore : 17 and he went out,

him they [1] compelled to go *with them*,	and Rufus, to go *with them*,	and laid on him the cross, to bear it after Jesus.	bearing for
that he might bear his cross.	that he might bear his cross.		
[1] Gr. *impressed*.	[1] Gr. *impress*.	the cross himself.	

§ 251. A Lament over the Daughters of Jerusalem

[*Cp*. Matt. 23 37-39 ‖ Luke 13 34-35 : *also* Luke 19 41-44 *and* 21 20]

Luke 23 27-31

cp. 9 22; 16 23.	cp. 5 30; 8 33.	**27** And there followed him a great multitude of the people [*cp*. 23 35, 48], and of women who bewailed and lamented him. **28** But Jesus turning [*cp*. 7 9, 44; 9 55; 10 23; 14 25; 22 61] unto them said, Daughters of Jerusalem, weep not [*cp*. 7 13; 8 52] for me, but weep for yourselves [*cp*. 19 41], and for your children. **29** For behold, the days are coming [*cp*. 5 35; 17 22; 19 43; 21 6], in which they shall say, Blessed are the barren, and the wombs that never bare, and the breasts that never gave suck. **30** Then shall they begin to say to the mountains, Fall on us; and to the hills, Cover us. **31** For if they do these things in the green tree, what shall be done in the dry ?	cp. 1 38.
cp. 9 15.	cp. 2 20.		

Luke 23 30 : Hos. 10 8.

§ 252. Two Malefactors led out with Jesus

Luke 23 32

cp. 27 38.	cp. 15 27.	**32** And there were also two others, malefactors, led with him to be put to death [*cp*. 23 33].	cp. 19 18.

(vii) On Golgotha (§§ 253-255)

§ 253. The Crucifixion

Matt. **27** 33-44	Mark **15** 22-32	Luke **23** 33-38	John **19** 16-18, 23-24, 19-22
			16 They took Jesus therefore : **17** and he went out, bearing the cross for himself,
33 And when they were come unto a place called Golgotha, that is to say, The place of a skull,	**22** And they bring him unto the place Golgotha, which is, being interpreted, The place of a skull.	**33** And when they came unto the place which is called [1] The skull,	unto the place called The place of a skull, which is called in Hebrew Golgotha ;
34 they gave him wine to drink mingled with gall [*cp*. 27 48]: and when he had tasted it, he would not drink. **35** And when they had crucified him, *verse 38*	**23** And they offered him wine mingled with myrrh [*cp*. 15 36]: but he received it not. **24** And they crucify him, *verse 27*	*verse 36* there they crucified him, and the malefactors, one on the right hand and the other on the left. **34** [2]And Jesus said, Father [*cp*. 10 21, 22; 22 42; 23 46: *also* 11 2], forgive them [*cp*. 6 28]; for they know not what they do. And	cp. 19 29-30. **18** where they crucified him, and with him two others, on either side one, and Jesus in the midst. cp. 11 41 ; 12 27, 28 ; 17 1, 5, 11, 21, 24, 25.
cp. 11 25, 26; 26 39, 42: *also* 6 9. cp. 5 44. they	cp. 14 36. and		**23** The soldiers therefore, when they had crucified Jesus

parted his garments among them,	part his garments among them,	parting his garments among them,	took his garments, and made four parts, to every soldier a part; and also the ¹ coat: now the ¹ coat was without seam, woven from the top throughout. **24** They said therefore one to another, Let us not rend it, but cast lots for it, whose it shall be:
casting lots:	casting lots upon them, what each should take.	they cast lots.	that the scripture might be fulfilled, which saith, They parted my garments among them, And upon my vesture did they cast lots. These things therefore the soldiers did.
	25 And it was the third hour, and they crucified him.	*cp. verse 35.*	
36 and they sat and watched [*cp.* 27 54] him there.			**19** And Pilate wrote a title also, and put it on the cross.
37 And they set up over his head his accusation written, THIS IS JESUS THE KING OF THE JEWS [*cp.* 2 2; 27 11, 29: *also* 27 42: *and* 21 5].	**26** And the superscription of his accusation was written over, THE KING OF THE JEWS [*cp.* 15 2, 9, 12, 18: *also* 15 32].	*verse* 38	And there was written JESUS OF NAZARETH, THE KING OF THE JEWS [*cp.* 18 33, 39; 19 3, 21: *also* 1 49; 12 13: *and* 6 15; 12 15; 18 37

19 12, 14, 15].   **20** This title therefore read many of the Jews: ² for the place where Jesus was crucified was nigh to the city: and it was written in Hebrew, *and* in Latin, *and* in Greek.   **21** The chief priests of the Jews therefore said to Pilate, Write not, The King of the Jews; but, that he said, I am King of the Jews.   **22** Pilate answered, What I have written I have written.

38 Then are there crucified with him two robbers, one on the right hand, and one on the left. *cp. verse 36.*	**27** And with him they crucify two robbers; one on his right hand, and one on his left.¹	*verse* 33	*verse* 18
		35 And the people stood beholding [*cp.* 23 27, 48].	
39 And they that passed by railed on him, wagging their heads, **40** and saying, Thou that destroyest the ¹ temple, and buildest it in three days [*cp.* 26 61: *also* 12 40; 16 21; 17 23; 20 19; 27 63, 64], save thyself: if thou art the Son of God [*cp.* 4 3, 6: *also* 8 29; 14 33; 16 16; 26 63; 27 43, 54: *and* 3 17; 17 5], come down from the cross. **41** In like manner also the chief priests mocking *him*, with the scribes and elders, said, **42** He saved others; ² himself he cannot save. *cp.* 26 68; 27 17, 22: *also* 26 63: *and* 16 16.	**29** And they that passed by railed on him, wagging their heads, and saying, Ha! thou that destroyest the ² temple, and buildest it in three days [*cp.* 14 58: *also* 8 31; 9 31; 10 34], **30** save thyself, *cp.* 1 1; 3 11; 5 7; 15 39: *and* 1 11; 9 7. and come down from the cross. **31** In like manner also the chief priests mocking *him* among themselves with the scribes said, He saved others; ³ himself he cannot save. **32** Let the Christ, [*cp.* 14 61: *and* 8 29],	*cp.* 9 22; 13 32; 18 33; 24 7, 21, 46. *verse* 37 *cp.* 4 3, 9: *also* 1 35; 4 41; 8 28; 22 70: *and* 3 22; 9 35. And the rulers also scoffed [*cp.* 16 14] at him, saying, He saved others; let him save himself, if this is the Christ [*cp.* 23 39: *also* 22 67; 23 2: *and* 9 20] of God [*cp.* 9 20], his chosen [*cp.* 9 35].	*cp.* 2 19. *cp.* 1 34; *etc.* *cp.* 1 41; 4 25, 26, 29; 7 26, 41; 9 22; 10 24; 11 27.
He is the King of Israel	the King of Israel		

Cp. Matt. 26 67-68 ‖ Mark 14 65 ‖ Luke 22 63-65   Matt. 27 27-31 ‖
Mark 15 16-20 ‖ John 19 2-3; Luke 23 11: *also* Matt. 20 19 ‖
Mark 10 34 ‖ Luke 18 32.

[left vertical margin]
Cp. Matt. 26 67-68 ‖ Mark 14 65 ‖ Luke 22 63-65; Matt. 27 27-31 ‖ Mark 15 16-20 ‖ John 19 2-3; Luke 23 11: also Matt. 20 19 ‖ Mark 10 34 ‖ Luke 18 32.

[*cp. verse* 37, *etc.*]; let him now come down from the cross, and we will believe on him. **43** He trusteth on God; let him deliver him now, if he desireth him: for he said, I am the Son of God [*cp.* 26 63, 64: *also* 4 3, 6; 8 29; 14 33; 16 16; 27 40, 54: *and* 3 17; 17 5].	[*cp. verse* 26, *etc.*], now come down from the cross, that we may see and believe.	*cp. verse* 38, *etc.*	*cp.* 1 49; 12 13: *and* 19 19; *etc.*
	cp. 1 1; 3 11; 5 7; 15 39: *and* 1 11; 9 7.	*cp.* 22 70: *also* 1 35; 4 3, 9, 41; 8 28: *and* 3 22; 9 35.	*cp.* 1 34; *etc.*
verse 34: *cp.* 27 48.	*verse* 23: *cp.* 15 36.	**36** And the soldiers also mocked him, coming to him, offering him vinegar, **37** and saying, If thou art the King of the Jews [*see below*], save thyself [*cp.* 23 39: *also* 4 23]. **38** And there was also a superscription over him, THIS IS THE KING OF THE JEWS [*cp.* 23 3, 37: *and* 19 38; 23 2].	*cp.* 19 29-30.
verse 40	*verse* 30		
verse 37	*verse* 26		*verse* 19
44 And the robbers also that were crucified with him cast upon him the same reproach.	And they that were crucified with him reproached him.	23 39.	

¹ Or, *sanctuary*
² Or, *can he not save himself?*

¹ Many ancient authorities insert ver. 28 *And the scripture was fulfilled, which saith, And he was reckoned with transgressors.* See Luke 22 37.
² Or, *sanctuary*
³ Or, *can he not save himself?*

¹ According to the Latin, *Calvary*, which has the same meaning.
² Some ancient authorities omit *And Jesus said, Father, forgive them; for they know not what they do.*

¹ Or, *tunic*
² Or, *for the place of the city where Jesus was crucified was nigh at hand*

Matt. 27 34 ‖ Mark 15 23 ‖ Luke 23 36: *cp.* Ps. 69 21.   Luke 23 34: *cp.* Is. 53 12.   Matt. 27 35 ‖ Mark 15 24 ‖ Luke 23 34 ‖ John 19 23-24: *cp.* Ps. 22 18.   Matt. 27 36: *cp.* Ps. 22 17.   Matt. 27 38 ‖ Mark 15 27 ‖ Luke 23 33 ‖ John 19 18: *cp.* Is. 53 12.   Luke 23 35: *cp.* Ps. 22 17.   Matt. 27 39-44 ‖ Mark 15 29-32 ‖ Luke 23 35-39: *cp.* Ps. 22 6-8.   Matt. 27 43: Ps. 22 8   *cp.* Wisd. 2 13, 16-18.

§ 254. The Penitent Malefactor

Luke 23 39-43

27 44 *cp.* 27 40.	15 32 *cp.* 15 30.	**39** And one of the malefactors which were hanged railed on him, saying, Art not thou the Christ? save thyself [*cp.* 23 37: *also* 4 23] and us. **40** But the other answered, and rebuking him said, Dost thou not even fear God, seeing thou art in the same condemnation? **41** And we indeed justly; for we receive the due reward of our deeds: but this man hath done nothing amiss [*cp.* 23 22]. **42** And he said, Jesus, remember me when thou comest ¹ in thy kingdom [*cp.* 22 29, 30]. **43** And he said unto him, Verily I say unto thee, To-day shalt thou be with me in Paradise.
cp. 16 28; 20 21.		

[rightmost column] *cp.* 18 36.

¹ Some ancient authorities read *into thy kingdom*.

Luke 23 43: *cp.* Is. 53 12.

§ 255. The Death of Jesus

Matt. 27 45-56	Mark 15 33-41	Luke 23 44-49	John 19 28-30, 25-27
45 Now from the sixth hour there was darkness over all the ¹ land until the ninth hour.	**33** And when the sixth hour was come, there was darkness over the whole ¹ land until the ninth hour.	**44** And it was now about the sixth hour, and a darkness came over the whole ¹ land until the ninth hour, **45** ² the sun's light failing: and the veil of the ³ temple was rent in the midst. **46** ⁴ And when	*cp.* 19 14.
verse 51 **46** And about	*verse* 38 **34** And		**28** After this

the ninth hour Jesus	at the ninth hour Jesus	Jesus	Jesus, knowing that all things are now finished, that the scripture might be accomplished,
cried with a loud voice, saying, Eli, Eli, lama sabachthani? that is, My God, my God, ² why hast thou forsaken me?	cried with a loud voice, Eloi, Eloi, lama sabachthani? which is, being interpreted, My God, my God, ² why hast thou forsaken me?	had cried with a loud voice,	saith, I thirst.
47 And some of them that stood there [cp. 16 28: also 26 73], when they heard it, said, This man calleth Elijah.	**35** And some of them that stood by [cp. 9 1; 11 5: also 14 47, 69, 70; 15 39], when they heard it, said, Behold, he calleth Elijah.	cp. 9 27: also 19 24.	cp. 12 29.
48 And straightway one of them ran, and took a sponge, and filled it with vinegar [cp. 27 34], and put it on a reed, and gave him to drink. **49** And the rest said, Let be; let us see whether Elijah cometh to save him.³ **50** And Jesus	**36** And one ran, and filling a sponge full of vinegar [cp. 15 23], put it on a reed, and gave him to drink, saying, Let be; let us see whether Elijah cometh to take him down. **37** And Jesus	cp. 23 36.	**29** There was set there a vessel full of vinegar: so they put a sponge full of the vinegar upon hyssop, and brought it to his mouth.
cried again with a loud voice, cp. 11 25, 26; 26 39, 42: also 6 9.	uttered a loud voice cp. 14 36.	he said, Father [cp. 10 21, 22; 22 42; 23 34: also 11 2], into thy hands I commend my spirit: and having said this, he gave	**30** When Jesus therefore had received the vinegar, he said, cp. 11 41; 12 27, 28; 17 1, 5, 11, 21, 24 25.
and yielded up his spirit. **51** And behold, the veil of the ⁴ temple was rent in twain from the top to the bottom; and the earth did quake; and the rocks were rent; **52** and the tombs were opened; and many bodies of the saints that had fallen asleep were raised; **53** and coming forth out of the tombs after his resurrection they entered into the holy city [cp. 4 5] and appeared unto many. **54** Now the centurion,	and gave up the ghost. **38** And the veil of the ³ temple was rent in twain from the top to the bottom.	up the ghost. verse 45	It is finished: and he bowed his head, and gave up his spirit.
and they that were with him watching [cp. 27 36] Jesus, when they saw	**39** And when the centurion, which stood by [cp. verse 35] over against him,	**47** And when the centurion	
the earthquake, and the things that were done, feared [cp. 9 8; 17 6; 28 4, 8]	saw that he ⁴ so gave up the ghost,	saw	
exceedingly, cp. 9 8; 15 31: also 5 16.	cp. 4 41; 5 15, 33; 9 6, 32; 10 32; 16 8. he cp. 2 12.	what was done, cp. 1 12, 65; 2 9; 5 26; 7 16; 8 25, 35, 37, 47; 9 34, 45; 24 5, 37. he glorified God [cp. 2 20; 5 25, 26; 7 16; 13 13; 17 15; 18 43], saying, Certainly this was a righteous man. cp. 4 41: also 1 35; 4 3,	cp. 9 24.
saying, Truly this was ⁵ the Son of God [cp. 14 33; 16 16:	said, Truly this man was ⁵ the Son of God [cp. 3 11: also 1 1;		cp. 1 34; etc.

also 4 3, 6; 8 29; 26 63; 27 40, 43: *and* 3 17; 17 5].

5 7: *and* 1 11; 9 7].

9; 8 28; 22 70: *and* 3 22; 9 35.

48 And all the multitudes that came together to this sight [*cp.* 23 27, 35], when they beheld the things that were done, returned smiting their breasts [*cp.* 18 13]. **49** And all his acquaintance, and the women [*cp.* 8 2; 23 55; 24 1, 10, 22, 24] that followed with him from Galilee [*cp.* 23 55] stood afar off,

55 And many women were there

40 And there were also women

25 But there were

beholding from afar, which had followed Jesus from Galilee, ministering unto him:
56 among whom was

beholding from afar:

verse 41

among whom *were* both

cp. 8 3.
seeing these things.

standing

by the cross of Jesus

Mary Magdalene [*cp.* 27 61; 28 1], and Mary the mother of James and Joses [*cp.* 27 61; 28 1], and the mother [*cp.* 20 20] of the sons of Zebedee [*cp.* 20 20].

verse 55

Mary Magdalene [*cp.* 15 47; 16 1, 9], and Mary the mother of James the [6] less and of Joses [*cp.* 15 47; 16 1], and Salome [*cp.* 16 1];

cp. 8 2; 24 10.

cp. 24 10.

his mother, and his mother's sister, Mary the *wife* of Clopas, and Mary Magdalene [*cp.* 20 1, 18].

41 who, when he was in Galilee, followed him, and ministered unto him; and many other women which came up with him unto Jerusalem.

verse 49
cp. 8 3.

26 When Jesus therefore saw his mother, and the disciple standing by, whom he loved, he saith unto his mother, Woman, behold, thy son! **27** Then saith he to the disciple, Behold, thy mother! And from that hour the disciple took her unto his own *home.*

---

[1] Or, *earth*
[2] Or, *why didst thou forsake me?*
[3] Many ancient authorities add *And another took a spear and pierced his side, and there came out water and blood.* See John 19 34.
[4] Or, *sanctuary*
[5] Or, *a son of God*

[1] Or, *earth*
[2] Or, *why didst thou forsake me?*
[3] Or, *sanctuary*
[4] Many ancient authorities read *so cried out, and gave up the ghost.*
[5] Or, *a son of God*
[6] Gr. *little.*

[1] Or, *earth*
[2] Gr. *the sun failing.*
[3] Or, *sanctuary*
[4] Or, *And Jesus, crying with a loud voice, said*

Matt. 27 46 ‖ Mark 15 34: Ps. 22 1.　Matt. 27 48 ‖ Mark 15 36 ‖ John 19 29: *cp.* Ps. 69 21.　Luke 23 46: *cp.* Ps. 31 5.
Matt. 27 55 ‖ Mark 15 40 ‖ Luke 23 49: *cp.* Ps. 31 11; 88 8.

(viii) The Burial (§§ 256-257)

§ 256. **The Body of Jesus laid in the Tomb**

Matt. 27 57-61

Mark 15 42-47

Luke 23 50-56

John 19 31, 38-42

57 And when even was come,

cp. 27 62.

42 And when even was now come, because it was the Preparation, that is, the day before the sabbath,

verse 54

31 The Jews therefore, because it was the Preparation [*cp.* 19 14, 42], that the

Matt. 27 57-61

there came a rich man from Arimathæa, named Joseph,

who also himself was Jesus' disciple [cp. 13 52; 28 19]: **58** this man went to Pilate, and asked for the body of Jesus.

Then Pilate commanded it to be given up. **59** And Joseph

took the body,

and wrapped it in a clean linen cloth,

60 and laid it in his own new tomb, which he had hewn out in the rock:

and he rolled a great stone [cp. 27 66; 28 2] to the door of the tomb, and departed. cp. 27 62.

61 And cp. 27 55.

Mark 15 43-47

43 there came Joseph of Arimathæa, a councillor of honourable estate,

who also himself was looking for the kingdom of God;

and he boldly went in unto Pilate, and asked for the body of Jesus. **44** And Pilate marvelled if he were already dead: and calling unto him the centurion, he asked him whether he [1] had been any while dead. **45** And when he learned it of the centurion, he granted the corpse to Joseph. **46** And he bought a linen cloth, and taking him down,

cp. 16 1.

wound him in the linen cloth,

and laid him in a tomb which had been hewn out of a rock; and he rolled a [cp. 16 4] stone [cp. 16 3, 4] against the door of the tomb.

verse 42

47 And cp. 15 40.

Luke 23 50-55

50 And behold, a man named Joseph, who was a councillor, a good man and a righteous **51** (he had not consented to their counsel and deed), a man of Arimathæa, a city of the Jews, who was looking [cp. 2 25, 38] for the kingdom of God:

52 this man went to Pilate, and asked for the body of Jesus.

53 And he took it down,

cp. verse 56.

and wrapped it in a linen cloth,

and laid him in a tomb that was hewn in stone, where never man had yet lain [cp. 19 30].

cp. 24 2.

54 And it was the day of the Preparation, and the sabbath [1] drew on. **55** And the women [cp. 8 2; 23

[John]

bodies should not remain on the cross upon the sabbath (for the day of that sabbath was a high *day*), asked of Pilate that their legs might be broken, and *that* they might be taken away. . . . **38** And after these things

Joseph of Arimathæa,

being a disciple of Jesus, but secretly for fear of the Jews,

asked of Pilate that he might take away the body of Jesus:

cp. 19 33.

and Pilate gave *him* leave. He came therefore, and took away his body. **39** And there came also Nicodemus, he who at the first came to him by night [cp. 3 2; 7 50], bringing a [1] mixture of myrrh and aloes, about a hundred pound *weight*. **40** So they took the body of Jesus, and bound it in linen cloths with the spices, as the custom of the Jews is to bury. **41** Now in the place where he was crucified there was a garden; and in the garden a new tomb wherein was never man yet laid.

cp. 20 1.

42 There then because of the Jews' Preparation [cp. 19 14, 31] (for the tomb was nigh at hand) they laid Jesus.

cp. 27 55. Mary Magdalene [cp. 27 56; 28 1] was there, and the other Mary, cp. 27 56; 28 1. sitting over against the sepulchre.	cp. 15 41. Mary Magdalene [cp. 15 40; 16 1, 9] and Mary the *mother* of Joses [cp. 15 40; 16 1] beheld where he was laid. cp. 16 1.	49; 24 1, 10, 22, 24], which had come with him out of Galilee [cp. 23 49], cp. 8 2; 24 10. cp. 24 10. followed after, and beheld the tomb, and how his body was laid. **56** And they returned, and prepared spices [cp. 24 1], and ointments. And on the sabbath they rested according to the commandment.	cp. 19 25; 20 1, 18. cp. 19 25. cp. verses 39 *and* 40.
	[1] Many ancient authorities read *were already dead.*	[1] Gr. *began to dawn.*	[1] Some ancient authorities read *roll.*

Luke 23 56 (*cp.* John 19 31): Exod. 12 16; 20 9-10; Deut. 5 13-14.

§ 257. **The Posting of the Guard**

Matt. 27 62-66

62 Now on the morrow, which is *the day* after the Preparation, the chief priests and the Pharisees were gathered together unto Pilate, **63** saying, Sir, we remember that that deceiver said, while he was yet alive, After three days [Mark 8 31; 9 31; 10 34: *cp.* Matt. 16 21; 17 23; 20 19: *also* 12 40; 26 61; 27 40] I rise again [*cp.* 16 21; 17 9, 23; 20 19; 26 32]. **64** Command therefore that the sepulchre be made sure until the third day, lest haply his disciples come and steal him away [*cp.* 28 13], and say unto the people, He is risen from the dead [*cp.* 28 6, 7]: and the last error will be worse than the first. **65** Pilate said unto them, [1] Ye have a guard: go your way, [2] make it *as* sure as ye can. **66** So they went, and made the sepulchre sure, sealing the stone [*cp.* 27 60; 28 2], the guard being with them.	cp. 15 42. cp. 14 58; 15 29: *also* 8 31; 9 9, 31; 10 34; 14 28. cp. 16 6. cp. 15 46; 16 3, 4.	cp. 23 54. cp. 9 22; 13 32; 18 33: *also* 24 7, 21, 26, 46. cp. 24 6, 34. cp. 24 2.	cp. 19 14, 31, 42. cp. 2 19-22. cp. 20 1.
[1] Or, *Take a guard* [2] Gr. *make it sure, as ye know.*			

(ix) The Resurrection (§§ 258-259)

§ 258. **The Empty Tomb**

Matt. 28 1-10	Mark 16 1-8	Luke 24 1-12	John 20 1-18
1 Now late on the sabbath day,	**1** And when the sabbath was past, Mary Magdalene [cp. 15 40, 47; 16 9], and Mary the *mother* of James [cp. 15 40, 47], and Salome [cp. 15 40], bought spices, that they might come and anoint him.	*verse 10* cp. 23 56.	cp. 19 25. cp. 19 39, 40.
as it began to dawn toward the first *day* of the week, came Mary Magdalene [cp. 27 56, 61] and the other Mary [cp. 27 56, 61]	**2** And very early on the first *day* of the week, they come	**1** But on the first day of the week, at early dawn, they came	**1** Now on the first *day* of the week cometh Mary Magdalene [cp. 19 25; 20 18] cp. 19 25.
to see the sepulchre.	to the tomb when the sun was risen. cp. verse 1. **3** And	unto the tomb, bringing the spices [cp. 23 56] which they had prepared.	early, while it was yet dark, unto the tomb, cp. 19 39, 40.

they were saying among themselves, Who shall roll us away the stone [*cp.* 15 46; 16 4] from the door of the tomb?

2 And behold, there was a great earthquake; for an angel of the Lord descended from heaven, and came and rolled away the stone [*cp.* 27 60, 66], and sat upon it. **3** His appearance was as lightning, and his raiment white as snow [*cp.* 17 2]: **4** and for fear [*cp. verse* 8] of him the watchers did quake, and became as dead men.

cp. verse 5.

cp. verse 4.

cp. verse 12.

cp. verse 12.

cp. 9 26.   **4** and looking up, they see that the stone [*cp.* 15 46; 16 3] is rolled back:

2 And they found   the stone rolled away from the tomb.

and seeth the stone taken away from the tomb.

cp. 27 60.

for it was exceeding great. **5** And entering into the tomb,

3 And they entered in, and found not the body [*cp.* 24 23] [1] of the Lord [*cp.* 7 13, 19; 10 1, 39, 41; 11 39; 12 42; 13 15; 17 5, 6; 18 6; 19 8; 22 61; 24 34] Jesus. **4** And it came to pass, while they were perplexed thereabout, behold,

cp. verses 6-8.

cp. 4 1; 6 23; 11 2; 20 2, 18, 20, 25; 21 7, 12.

cp. 16 19, 20.

they saw a young man sitting on the right side, arrayed in a white [*cp.* 9 3] robe; and they were amazed [*cp.* 1 27; 2 12; 5 20, 42; 6 51; 7 37; 10 32; 15 5; 16 8: *also* 1 22; *etc.*].

two men [*cp.* 24 23] stood by them in dazzling [*cp.* 9 29] apparel: **5** and as they were   [*cp.* 5 9, 26; 8 25, 56; 9 43; 11 14; 24 12, 41: *also* 2 47, 48; *etc.*] affrighted [*cp.* 1 12, 65; 2 9; 5 26; 7 16; 8 25, 35, 37, 47; 9 34, 45; 24 37], and bowed down their faces to the earth, they

cp. verse 3.

cp. verse 12.

cp. 8 27; 9 33; 12 23; 15 31; 21 20; 27 14: *also* 7 28; *etc.*

cp. 7 15, 21, 46.

cp. 9 8; 17 6; 27 54; 28 4, 8.

cp. 4 41; 5 15, 33; 9 6, 32; 10 32; 16 8.

5 And the angel answered and said unto the women,   Fear not ye: for I know that ye seek Jesus, [*cp.* 2 23; 26 71: *also* 21 11] which hath been crucified.

6 And he saith unto them,   Be not amazed: ye seek Jesus, the Nazarene [*cp.* 1 24; 10 47; 14 67], which hath been crucified:

said unto them,

cp. verses 12 and 13.

cp. 4 34; 18 37; 24 19.

cp. 18 5, 7; 19 19: *also* 1 45.

6 He is not here; for he is risen,   even as he said.

he is risen; he is not here:

Why seek ye [2] the living among the dead?   **6** [3] He is not here, but is risen: remember [*cp. verse* 8] how he spake unto you when he was yet

cp. verse 7.

Come,   see the place [1] where the Lord lay.   **7** And go quickly, and tell his disciples,   He is risen from the dead [*cp.* 27 64]; and lo, he goeth before you into Galilee [*cp.* 26 32]; there shall ye see him [*cp. verse* 10]:

behold, the place where they laid him! **7** But go,   tell his disciples and Peter,

He goeth before you into Galilee [*cp.* 14 28]: there shall ye see him

cp. 24 34.

in Galilee,

lo, I have told you.
cp. verse 6.

cp. 26 45.
cp. 20 19: *also* 23 34.

cp. 16 21; *etc.*

cp. 26 75.

8 And they departed quickly from the tomb

with fear [*cp. verse* 4: *also* 9 8; 17 6; 27 54] and great joy, and ran to bring his disciples word. **9** And behold, Jesus met them, saying, All hail [*cp.* 26 49; 27 29]. And they came and took hold of his feet, and worshipped him [*cp.* 2 11; 8 2; 9 18; 14 33; 15 25; 20 20; 28 17: *also* 17 14]. **10** Then saith Jesus unto them, Fear not [*cp.* 14 27; 17 7]: go tell my brethren that they depart into Galilee, and there shall they see me [*cp. verse* 7 *and* 28 16-20].

verse 1

cp. 27 55.

cp. 10 2.

cp. 28 17.

---

as he said unto you.

cp. 14 41.

cp. 8 31; *etc.*

cp. 14 72.

8 And they went out, and fled from the tomb; for trembling and astonishment [*cp. verse* 5] had come upon them: and they said nothing to any one; for they were afraid [*cp.* 4 41; 5 15, 33; 9 6, 32; 10 32].

cp. 15 18.

cp. 5 6: *also* 1 40; 3 11; 5 22, 33; 7 25; 10 17.

cp. 6 50.

cp. verse 7.

cp. 16 10.

verse 1

cp. 15 40-41.

cp. 6 30.

cp. 16 11, 13, 14.

---

7 saying that the Son of man must be delivered up into the hands of sinful men, and be crucified, and the third day rise again [*cp.* 9 22, 43-44; 18 31-33: *also* 13 32, 33; 17 25; 22 22: *and* 24 26, 44, 46]. **8** And they remembered [*cp.* 22 61] his words, **9** and returned 4 from the tomb,

cp. 1 12, 65; 2 9; 5 26; 7 16; 8 25; *etc.*
cp. 24 41, 52.

cp. 1 28.

cp. 24 52: *also* 5 8, 12; 8 28, 41, 47; 17 16.

and told all these things [*cp. verses* 10 *and* 23] to the eleven, and to all the rest. **10** Now they were Mary Magdalene [*cp.* 8 2], and Joanna [*cp.* 8 3], and Mary the *mother* of James: and the other women [*cp.* 8 2, 3; 23 49, 55; 24 22, 24] with them told these things unto the apostles [*cp.* 6 13; 9 10; 17 5; 22 14].
see verse 3.

11 And these words appeared in their sight as idle talk; and they disbelieved [*cp.* 24 38, 41: *also* 24 25] them. **12** 5 But Peter arose,

and ran

---

cp. 2 19-22; 3 14; 12 32-33.

cp. 2 22; 12 16.

cp. 20 20: *also* 16 22.
2 She runneth therefore,

cp. 19 3.

cp. 9 38: *also* 11 32; 18 6.

cp. 6 20.
cp. verse 17.

and cometh to Simon Peter, and to the other disciple, whom Jesus loved,

cp. verse 18.

cp. 19 25.

cp. 19 25.
and

saith unto them,

They have taken away the Lord [*cp.* 4 1; 6 23; 11 2; 20 18, 20, 25; 21 7, 12] out of the tomb, and we know not where they have laid him.

cp. 20 25.

3 Peter therefore went forth, and the other disciple, and they went toward the tomb. **4** And they ran both together: and the other

unto the tomb; and stooping and looking in, he seeth the linen cloths

disciple outran Peter, and came first to the tomb; 5 and stooping and looking in, he seeth the linen cloths lying; yet entered he not in. 6 Simon Peter therefore also cometh, following him, and entered into the tomb; and he beholdeth the linen cloths lying, 7 and the napkin, that was upon his head, not lying with the linen cloths, but rolled up in a place by itself. 8 Then entered in therefore the other disciple also, which came first to the tomb, and he saw, and believed. 9 For as yet they knew not the scripture, that he must rise again from the dead. 10 So the disciples went away again unto their own home.

cp. verse 5.   *cp. verse 3.*

by themselves; *cp. verse 3.*

cp. verse 5.

he ⁶ departed to his home, wondering at that which was come to pass [*cp. verse 5*].

11 But Mary was standing without at the tomb weeping: so, as she wept, she stooped and looked into the tomb; 12 and she beholdeth two angels in white sitting, one at the head, and one at the feet, where the body of Jesus had lain. 13 And they say unto her, Woman, why weepest thou? She saith unto them, Because they have taken away my Lord, and I know not where they have laid him. 14 When she had thus said, she turned herself back, and

cp. 28 2, 3, 5.   *cp. 16 5.*   *cp. 24 4.*

¹ Many ancient authorities read *where he lay.*

¹ Some ancient authorities omit *of the Lord Jesus.*
² Gr. *him that liveth.*
³ Some ancient authorities omit *He is not here, but is risen.*
⁴ Some ancient authorities omit *from the tomb.*
⁵ Some ancient authorities omit ver. 12.
⁶ Or, *departed, wondering with himself*

cp. 16 9.

cp. 28 10.
cp. 28 8.   *cp. 16 10.*   *cp. 24 9, 10, 23.*

beholdeth Jesus standing, and knew not that it was Jesus. 15 Jesus saith unto her, Woman, why weepest thou? whom seekest thou? She, supposing him to be the gardener, saith unto him, Sir, if thou hast borne him hence, tell me where thou hast laid him, and I will take him away. 16 Jesus saith unto her, Mary. She turneth herself, and saith unto him in Hebrew, Rabboni; which is to say, ¹ Master. 17 Jesus saith to her, ² Touch me not; for I am not yet ascended unto the Father: but go unto my brethren, and say to them, I ascend unto my Father and your Father, and my God and your God. 18 Mary Magdalene cometh and telleth the disciples, I have seen the Lord; and *how that* he had said these things unto her.

¹ Or, *Teacher*   ² Or, *Take not hold on me*

§ 259. The Report of the Guard

Matt. 28 11-15

11 Now while they were going, behold, some of the guard came into the city, and told unto the chief priests all the things that were come to pass. 12 And when they were assembled with the elders, and had taken counsel [*cp.* 12 14; 22 15; 27 1, 7], they gave large money unto the soldiers, 13 saying, Say ye, His disciples came by night, and stole him away [*cp.* 27 64] while we slept. 14 And if this ¹ come to the governor's [*cp.* 27 2, 11, 14, 15, 21, 27] ears, we will persuade him, and rid you of care. 15 So they took the money, and did as they were taught: and this saying was spread abroad among the Jews, *and continueth* until this day [*cp.* 11 23; 27 8].

cp. 3 6; 15 1.   *cp.* 20 20.

¹ Or, *come to a hearing before the governor*

G. The Appearances after the Resurrection and the Commissioning of the Eleven
(§§ 260-268).

(i) The Appearance and Commission according to Matthew (§ 260)

§ 260. **To the Eleven on the Mount in Galilee**

Matt. **28** 16-20	Mark 16 15-16	Luke 24 46-49	John 20 21-23
16 But the eleven disciples went into Galilee, unto the mountain [*cp.* 5 1; 14 23; 15 29; 17 1: *also* 24 3] where Jesus had appointed them [*cp.* 28 10]. **17** And when they saw him, they worshipped *him* [*cp.* 2 11; 8 2; 9 18; 14 33; 15 25; 20 20; 28 9: *also* 17 14]: but some doubted [*cp.* 14 31]. **18** And Jesus came to them and spake unto them, saying,	*cp.* 3 13; 6 46; 9 2: *also* 13 3. *cp.* 5 6: *also* 1 40; 3 11; 5 22, 33; 7 25; 10 17. *cp.* 16 11, 13, 14. **15** And he said unto them,	*cp.* 6 12; 9 28. *cp.* 24 52: *also* 5 8, 12; 8 28, 41, 47; 17 16. *cp.* 24 11, 38, 41. **46** And he said unto them, Thus it is written [*cp.* 24 26: *also* 18 31-33; 20 17; 22 37: *and* 9 22, etc.], that the Christ should suffer, and rise again from the dead the third day;	*cp.* 6 3, 15. *cp.* 9 38: *also* 11 32; 18 6. *cp.* 20 25. **21** Jesus therefore said to them again, Peace *be* unto you: *cp.* 5 39; 13 18; 15 25; 17 12.
All authority [*cp.* 7 29; 9 6, 8; 21 23-27: *also* 11 27] hath been given unto me in heaven and on earth. *cp.* 26 28.	*cp.* 1 22, 27; 2 10; 11 27-33. *cp.* 1 4.	*cp.* 4 32, 36; 5 24; 20 1-8: *also* 10 22. **47** and that repentance [1] and remission of sins [*cp.* 1 77; 3 3] should be preached in his name [*cp.* 9 48, 49; 10 17; 21 8]	*cp.* 5 27; 17 2: *also* 3 35; 13 3.
[*cp. verse* 19: *also* 7 22; 18 5, 20; 24 5] **19** Go ye therefore, and make disciples [*cp.* 13 52; 27 57] of all the nations [*cp.* 24 14; 26 13: *also* 8 11; 10 18; 21 31, 41-43; 22 7-10], *cp.* 4 23; 9 35; 24 14; 26 13.	[*cp.* 16 17: *also* 9 37, 38, 39; 13 6] Go ye into all the world, and *cp.* 13 10; 14 9: *also* 12 9. preach the gospel [*cp.* 1 1, 14, 15; 8 35; 10 29; 13 10; 14 9] to the whole creation [*cp.* 10 6; 13 19].	unto all the [2] nations [*cp.* 2 30-32; 3 6: *also* 13 29; 14 21-24; 20 16],	*cp.* 14 13, 14, 26; 15 16; 16 23, 24, 26. *cp.* 10 16; 11 52.
baptizing them into the name of the Father and of the Son and of the Holy Ghost:	**16** He that believeth and is baptized shall be saved; but he that disbelieveth shall be condemned.	beginning from Jerusalem. *cp. verse* 47.	
20 teaching them to observe all things whatsoever I commanded you:		**48** Ye are witnesses of these things. **49** And behold, I send forth the promise of my Father upon you: but tarry ye in the city,	*cp.* 14 15, 23. *cp.* 15 27. as the Father hath sent me, even so send I *cp.* 14 16, 26 15 26; 16 7. you.

			until ye be clothed with power [*cp.* 1 17, 35 ; 4 14, 36 ; 5 17 ; 6 19 ; 8 46 ; 9 1] from on high [*cp.* 1 78].	
	cp. 5 30.			**22** And when he had said this, he breathed on them, and saith unto them, Receive ye the ¹ Holy Ghost : **23** whose soever sins ye forgive, they are forgiven unto them ; whose soever *sins* ye retain, they are retained.
cp. 16 19 ; 18 18.				*cp.* 14 23.
and lo, I am with you [*cp.* 1 23] ¹ alway [*cp.* 18 20], even unto ² the end of the world [*cp.* 13 39, 40, 49 ; 24 3]. Gr. *all the days.* ² Or, *the consummation of the age*			¹ Some ancient authorities read *unto.* ² Or, *nations. Beginning from Jerusalem, ye are witnesses*	¹ Or, *Holy Spirit*

(ii) The Appearances and Commission according to Luke (§§ 261-264)

§ 261. **The Appearance to Two Disciples on the Way to Emmaus**

	Mark 16 12-13	Luke 24 13-35	
	12 And after these things he was manifested in another form unto two of them, as they walked, on their way into the country.	**13** And behold, two of them were going that very day to a village named Emmaus, which was threescore furlongs from Jerusalem. **14** And they communed with each other of all these things which had happened. **15** And it came to pass, while they communed and questioned together, that Jesus himself drew near, and went with them. **16** But their eyes were holden that they should not know him. **17** And he said unto them, ¹ What communications are these that ye have one with another, as ye walk ? And they stood still, looking sad. **18** And one of them, named Cleopas, answering said unto him, ² Dost thou alone sojourn in Jerusalem and not know the things which are come to pass there in these days ? **19** And he said unto them, What things ? And they said unto him, The things concerning Jesus of Nazareth [*cp.* 4 34 ; 18 37], which was a prophet [*cp.* 4 24 ; 7 16, 39 ; 13 33] mighty in deed and word before God and all the people : **20** and how the chief priests and our rulers delivered him up to be condemned to death, and crucified him. **21** But we hoped that it was he which should redeem [*cp.* 1 68 ; 2 38 ; 21 28] Israel. Yea and beside all this, it is now the third day [*cp.* 9 22 ; 13 32 ; 18 33 ; 24 7, 46] since these things came to pass. **22** Moreover certain women of our company amazed us, having been early at the tomb ; **23** and when they found not his body [*cp.* 24 3], they came, saying, that they had also seen a vision of angels, which said that he was alive [*cp.* 24 4-10]. **24** And certain of them that were with us went to the tomb, and found it even so as the women had said : but him they saw not [*cp.* 24 11, 12]. **25** And he said unto them, O foolish men, and slow of heart to believe [*cp.* 24 11, 38, 41] ³ in all that the prophets have spoken ! **26** Behoved it not the Christ to suffer these things [*cp.* 24 46: *also* 18 31-33 ; 20 17 ; 22 37: *and* 9 22, 44 ; 13 32, 33 ; 17 25 ; 22 22 ; 24 7], and to enter [*cp.* 11 52 ; 13 24 ; 18 17, 24, 25] into his glory [*cp.* 9 26, 32: *and* John 1 14 ; 2 11 ; 12 41 ; 17 5, 22, 24] ? **27** And beginning from Moses and from all the prophets [*cp.* 16 29, 31], he interpreted to them in all the scriptures the things concerning himself [*cp.* 24 44]. **28** And they drew nigh unto the village, whither they were going : and he made as though he would go further. **29** And they constrained him, saying, Abide with us : for it is toward evening, and the day is now far spent [*cp.* 9 12]. And he went in to abide with	
cp. 2 23 ; *etc.* *cp.* 13 57 ; 21 11, 46.	*cp.* 1 24 ; *etc.* *cp.* 6 4, 15.		*cp.* 20 14 ; 21 4. *cp.* 18 5 ; *etc.* *cp.* 4 19, 44 ; 6 14 ; 7 40 ; 9 17.
cp. 16 21 ; *etc.*	*cp.* 8 31 ; *etc.*		*cp.* 2 19.
cp. 28 5-8.	*cp.* 16 5-7.		*cp.* 20 11-18.
cp. 28 17.	*cp.* 16 11, 13, 14.		*cp.* 20 3-10. *cp.* 20 25, 27.
cp. 26 24 ; *etc.*	*cp.* 14 21 ; *etc.*		
cp. 5 20 ; *etc.* *cp.* 19 28 ; 25 31.	*cp.* 9 43 ; *etc.* *cp.* 10 37.		*cp.* 3 5 ; 10 1, 2, 9. *cp.* 1 45 ; 5 46.
cp. 14 15.	*cp.* 6 35.		

Matt.	Mark	Mark	Luke	John
cp. 14 19; 15 36; 26 26.	cp. 6 41; 8 6; 14 22.		them. **30** And it came to pass, when he had sat down with them to meat, he took the ⁴ bread, and blessed it, and brake, and gave to them [cp. 9 16; 22 19]. **31** And their eyes were opened, and they knew him; and he vanished out of their sight. **32** And they said one to another, Was not our heart burning within us, while he spake to us in the way, while he opened to us the scriptures [cp. 24 45]?	cp. 6 11.
		13 And they went away	**33** And they rose up that very hour, and returned to Jerusalem, and found the eleven gathered together, and them that were with them,	
		cp. 16 19, 20.	**34** saying, The Lord [cp. 7 13, 19; 10 1, 39, 41; 11 39; 12 42; 13 15; 17 5, 6; 18 6; 19 8; 22 61; 24 3]	cp. 4 1; 6 23; 11 2; 20 2, 18, 20, 25; 21 7, 12.
cp. 27 64; 28 6, 7.		cp. 16 6.	is risen [cp. 24 6] indeed, and hath appeared to Simon. **35** And they	
		told it and	rehearsed the things *that happened* in the way, and how he was known of them in the breaking of the bread.	
cp. 28 17.		unto the rest : neither believed they them [cp. 16 11, 14].	cp. 24 11, 38, 41: *also* 24 25.	cp. 20 25.

¹ Gr. *What words are these that ye exchange one with another.*
² Or, *Dost thou sojourn alone in Jerusalem, and knowest thou not the things*
³ Or, *after*   ⁴ Or, *loaf*

§ 262. The Appearance to the Eleven in Jerusalem

Matt.	Mark	Mark 16 14	Luke 24 36-43	John 20 19-20
		14 And afterward	**36** And as they spake these things,	19 When therefore it was evening, on that day, the first *day* of the week, and when the doors were shut where the disciples were, for fear of the Jews, Jesus
		he was manifested unto the eleven themselves as they sat at meat;	he himself	
cp. 9 8; 17 6; 27 54; 28 4, 8. cp. 14 26.	cp. 4 41; 5 15, 33; 9 6, 32; 10 32; 16 8. cp. 6 49.		stood in the midst of them, ¹ and saith unto them, Peace *be* unto you. **37** But they were terrified and affrighted [cp. 1 12, 65; 2 9; 5 26; 7 16; 8 25, 35, 37, 47; 9 34, 45; 24 5], and supposed that they beheld a spirit. **38** And he said unto them,	came and stood in the midst, and saith unto them, Peace *be* unto you.
cp. 28 17: *also* 13 58. cp. 19 8.		and he upbraided them with their unbelief [cp. 16 11, 13 : *also* 6 6] and hardness of heart [cp. 6 52; 8 17: *also* 3 5; 10 5], because they believed not them which had seen him after he was risen.		cp. 20 25, 27. cp. 12 40.
cp. 28 17.			Why are ye troubled? and wherefore do reasonings arise in your heart [cp. 24 11, 41: *also* 25]? **39** See my hands and my feet, that it is I myself: handle me, and see; for a spirit hath not flesh and bones, as ye behold me having. **40** ² And when he had said this, he shewed them his hands and his feet.	cp. 20 25, 27. cp. 20 27. 20 And when he had said this, he shewed unto them his hands and his side. The disciples therefore were
cp. 28 17. cp. 28 8.	cp. 16 11, 13, 14.		**41** And while they still disbelieved [cp. 24 11, 38: *also* 24 25] for joy [cp. 24 52],	cp. 20 25, 27. glad [cp. 16 22],

| | | and wondered, he said unto them, Have ye here anything to eat? **42** And they gave him a piece of a broiled fish.[3] **43** And he took it, and did eat before them. | when they saw the Lord.

cp. 21 5. |

[1] Some ancient authorities omit *and saith unto them, Peace* be unto you.
[2] Some ancient authorities omit ver. 40.
[3] Many ancient authorities add *and a honeycomb.*

§ 263. The Commission to the Eleven in Jerusalem

Matt. 28 18-20	Mark 16 15-16	Luke 24 44-49	John 20 21-23
18 And Jesus came to them and spake unto them, saying,	**15** And he said unto them,	**44** And he said unto them, These are my words which I spake unto you, while I was yet with you, how that all things must needs be fulfilled, which are written in the law of Moses, and the prophets, and the psalms [*cp.* 16 29, 31; 24 27: *also* 20 42], concerning me [*cp.* 24 27]. **45** Then opened he their mind, that they might understand the scriptures [*cp.* 24 32]; **46** and he said unto them, Thus it is written	**21** Jesus therefore said to them again, Peace *be* unto you : *cp.* 14 25 ; 16 4. *cp.* 1 45 ; 5 46.
cp. 21 42 ; 26 24, 31, 54, 56 : *also* 16 21 ; *etc.*	*cp.* 9 12 ; 12 10 ; 14 21, 27, 49 : *also* 8 31 ; *etc.*	[*cp.* 24 26 : *also* 18 31-33; 20 17; 22 37 : *and* 9 22 ; *etc.*], that the Christ should suffer, and rise again from the dead the third day;	*cp.* 5 39; 13 18; 15 25; 17 12.
All authority [*cp.* 7 29 ; 9 6, 8 ; 21 23-27 : *also* 11 27] hath been given unto me in heaven and on earth. *cp.* 26 28.	*cp.* 1 22, 27 ; 2 10 ; 11 27-33. *cp.* 1 4.	*cp.* 4 32, 36 ; 5 24; 20 1-8: *also* 10 22.	*cp.* 5 27; 17 2: *also* 3 35; 13 3.
[*cp. verse* 19: *also* 7 22 ; 18 5, 20 ; 24 5] **19** Go ye therefore, and make disciples [*cp.* 13 52 ; 27 57] of all the nations [*cp.* 24 14 ; 26 13: *also* 8 11; 10 18; 21 31, 41-43 ; 22 7-10], *cp.* 4 23 ; 9 35 ; 24 14 ; 26 13.	[*cp.* 16 17 : *also* 9 37, 38, 39 ; 13 6] Go ye into all the world, and *cp.* 13 10 ; 14 9: *also* 12 9. preach the gospel [*cp.* 1 1, 14, 15 ; 8 35 ; 10 29; 13 10; 14 9] to the whole creation [*cp.* 10 6 ; 13 19].	**47** and that repentance [1] and remission of sins [*cp.* 1 77; 3 3] should be preached in his name [*cp.* 9 48, 49; 10 17; 21 8] unto all the [2] nations [*cp.* 2 30-32; 3 6: *also* 13 29; 14 21-24; 20 16],	*cp.* 14 13, 14, 26; 15 16; 16 23, 24, 26. *cp.* 10 16 ; 11 52.
baptizing them into the name of the Father and of the Son and of the Holy Ghost :	**16** He that believeth and is baptized shall be saved ; but he that disbelieveth	beginning from Jerusalem. *cp. verse* 47.	

20 teaching them to observe all things whatsoever
I commanded you :

shall be condemned.

cp. 5 30.

cp. 16 19 ; 18 18.

and lo, I am with
you [cp. 1 23] [1] alway [cp.
18 20], even unto [2] the end
of the world [cp. 13 39, 40,
49 ; 24 3].

[1] Gr. *all the days.*
[2] Or, *the consummation of the age*

cp. 14 15, 23.

48 Ye
are witnesses of these
things. **49** And behold,

cp. 15 27.

I send forth the
promise of my Father
upon you : but tarry ye
in the city, until ye be
clothed with power [cp.
1 17, 35 ; 4 14, 36 ; 5
17 ; 6 19 ; 8 46 ; 9 1]
from on high [cp. 1 78].

as the Father hath sent me,
even so send I
cp. 14 16, 26   15 26 ; 16 7.
you.

22 And when he had said
this, he breathed on them,
and saith unto them, Re-
ceive ye the [1] Holy Ghost :
23 whoso ever sins ye
forgive, they are forgiven
unto them ; whoso ever
sins ye retain, they are
retained.

cp. 14 23.

[1] Some ancient authorities read
unto.
[2] Or, *nations. Beginning from
Jerusalem, ye are witnesses*

[1] Or, *Holy Spirit*

§ 264. **The Parting at Bethany**

	Mark 16 19-20	Luke 24 50-53	

| | **19** So then the Lord [cp. *verse* 20] Je-
sus, after he had spoken unto them, | **50** And he led them out until *they
were* over against Bethany : and he
lifted up his hands, and blessed them.
cp. 7 13, 19 ; 10 1, 39, 41 ; 11 39 ; *etc.* | cp. 4 1 ; 6
23 ; 11 2 ;
20 2, 18,
20, 25 ; 21
7, 12. |

cp. 28 17 :
also 2 11 ;
etc.
cp. 28 8.

was received up into heaven, and
sat down at the right hand of God.
cp. 5 6 : *also* 1 40 ; 3 11 ; 5 22, 33 ;
7 25 ; 10 17.

51 And it came to pass, while he
blessed them, he parted from them,
[1] and was carried up into heaven.

cp. 9 38 : *also*
11 32 ; 18 6.

52 And they [2] worshipped him [cp. 5
8, 12 ; 8 28, 41, 47 ; 17 16], and
returned to Jerusalem with great joy
[cp. 24 41] : **53** and were continually
in the temple, blessing God [cp. 1 64 ;
2 28].

cp. 16 22 ; 20
20.

cp. 13 19-23.

20 And they went forth, and
preached everywhere, the Lord [*see
above*] working with them, and con-
firming the word [cp. 2 2 ; 4 14-20, 33]
by the signs that followed [cp. 16 17-
18]. Amen.

cp. 1 2 ; 4 32 ; 8 12-15 : *also* 5 1 ;
8 11, 21 ; 11 28.

cp. 4 41 ; 5
24, 38 ; *etc.*

[1] Some ancient authorities omit *and was carried up
into heaven.*
[2] Some ancient authorities omit *worshipped him,
and.*

(iii) The Appearances and Commission according to Mark (§§ 265-268)

§ 265. **The Appearance to Mary Magdalene**

Mark 16 9-11

cp. 28 1, 9,
10.

9 [1] Now when he was risen early on the first day of the week
[cp. 16 2], he appeared first to Mary Magdalene [cp. 16 1], from
whom he had cast out seven [2] devils. **10** She went and told

cp. 24 1, 10.
cp. 8 2.

cp. 20 1, 14-
17.

cp. 28 8.	them that had been with him, as they mourned and wept. **11** And they, when they heard that he was alive, and had been seen of her, disbelieved [*cp.* 16 13, 14].	*cp.* 24 9, 10, 23.	*cp.* 20 18.
cp. 28 17.		*cp.* 24 11, 38, 41 : *also* 25.	*cp.* 20 25, 27.

¹ The two oldest Greek manuscripts, and some other authorities, omit from ver. 9 to the end. Some other authorities have a different ending to the Gospel.
² Gr. *demons.*

§ 266. The Appearance to Two Disciples on their way into the Country

	Mark 16 12-13	Luke 24 13-35	
	12 And after these things he was manifested in another form unto two of them, as they walked, on their way into the country.	**13** And behold, two of them were going that very day to a village named Emmaus, which was threescore furlongs from Jerusalem. . . . . **33** And they rose up that very hour, and returned to Jerusalem, and found the eleven gathered together, and them that were with them, **34** saying, The Lord [*cp.* 7 13, 19 ; 10 1, 39, 41 ; 11 39 ; 12 42 ; 13 15 ; 17 5, 6 ; 18 6 ; 19 8 ; 22 61 ; 24 3] is risen [*cp.* 24 6] indeed, and hath appeared to Simon. **35** And they rehearsed the things *that happened* in the way, and how he was known of them in the breaking of the bread.	
	13 And they went away		*cp.* 4 1 ; 6 23 ; 11 2 ; 20 2, 18, 20, 25 ; 21 7, 12.
	cp. 16 19, 20.		
cp. 27 64 ; 28 6, 7.	*cp.* 16 6.		
	and told it		
cp. 28 17.	unto the rest : neither believed they them [*cp.* 16 11, 14].	*cp.* 24 11, 38, 41 : *also* 25.	*cp.* 20 25, 27.

§ 267. The Appearance and Commission to the Eleven as they sat at Meat

Matt. 28 18-20	**Mark 16** 14-18	Luke 24 36-49 10 17-19	John 20 19-23	John 20 26-29
18 And	**14** And afterward	**36** And as they spake these things,	**19** When therefore it was evening, on that day, the first *day* of the week, and when the doors were shut where the disciples were, for fear of the Jews,	**26** And after eight days again his disciples were within, and Thomas with them. Jesus
Jesus came to them	he was manifested unto the eleven themselves as they sat at meat;	he himself stood in the midst of them,	Jesus came and stood in the midst,	cometh, the doors being shut, and stood in the midst,
		¹ and saith unto them, Peace *be* unto you. **37** But they were terrified and affrighted [*cp.* 1 12, 65 ; 2 9 ; 5 26 ; 7 16 ; 8 25, 35, 37, 47 ; 9 34, 35 ; 24 5], and supposed that they beheld a spirit. **38** And he said unto them, Why are ye troubled? and wherefore do reasonings arise in your heart [*cp. verse* 41] ?	and saith unto them, Peace *be* unto you.	and said, Peace *be* unto you.
cp. 9 8 ; 17 6 ; 27 54 ; 28 4, 8.	*cp.* 4 41 ; 5 15, 33 ; 9 6, 32 ; 10 32 ; 16 8.			
cp. 14 26.	*cp.* 6 49. and he upbraided them			
				27 Then saith he to

39 See my hands and my feet, that it is I myself:

handle me, and see ; for a spirit hath not flesh and bones, as ye behold me having. 40 ²And when he had said this, he shewed them his hands and his feet.

Thomas, Reach hither thy finger, and see my hands ;

and reach *hither* thy hand, and put it into

20 And when he had said this, he shewed unto them his hands and his side. The disciples therefore [cp. 20 25]

cp. 28 17 : also 13 58.

with their unbelief [cp. 16 11, 13 : also 6 6] and hardness of heart [cp. 6 52 ; 8 17 : also 3 5 ; 10 5],

41 And while they still disbelieved [cp. 24 11, 38 : also 25]

my side : and be not faithless, but believing.

cp. 19 8.

cp. 28 8.

cp. 12 40.

for joy [cp. 24 52],

were glad [cp. 16 22], when they saw the Lord.

and wondered, he said unto them, Have ye here anything to eat ? 42 And they gave him a piece of a broiled fish.³ 43 And he took it, and did eat before them. . . .

cp. 21 5.

28 Thomas answered and said unto him, My Lord and my God. 29 Jesus saith unto him, Because thou hast seen me, ¹ thou hast believed : blessed *are* they that have not seen,

because they

believed not them which had seen him after he was risen.

and yet have believed.

and　　　spake unto them,　　saying, cp. 21 42 ; 26 24, 31, 54, 56 : also 16 21 ; etc.

15 And he　　　said unto them, cp. 9 12 ; 12 10 ; 14 21, 27, 49 : also 8 31 ; etc.

46 And he　　said unto them,　　Thus it is written [cp. 24 26 : also 18 31-33 ; 20 17 ; 22 37 : *and* 9 22 ; *etc.*], that the Christ should suffer, and rise again from the dead the third day ;

21 Jesus therefore said to them again, cp. 5 39 ; 13 18 ; 15 25 ; 17 12.

All authority [cp. 7 29 ; 9 6, 8 ; 21 23-27 : also 11 27] hath been given unto me in heaven and on earth.

cp. 1 22, 27 ; 2 10 ; 11 27-33.

cp. 4 32, 36 ; 5 24 ; 20 1-8 : also 10 22.

cp. 5 27 ; 17 2 ; *also* 3 35 ; 13 3.

47 and that repentance 4 and remission of sins [cp. 1 77 ; 3 3] should be preached in his name [cp. 9 48, 49 ; 10 17 ; 21 8]

cp. 26 28.

cp. verse 19 : also 7 22 ; 18 5, 20 ; 24 5.

cp. 1 4.

cp. verse 17 : also 9 37, 38, 39 ; 13 6.

cp. 14 13, 14, 26 ; 15 16 ; 16 23, 24, 26.

19 Go ye therefore, and make disciples [cp. 13 52 ; 27 57] of all the nations [cp. 24 14 ; 26 13 : also 8 11 ; 10 18 ; 21 31, 41-43 ; 22 7-10],
cp. 4 23 ; 9 35 ; 24 14 ; 26 13.

Go ye into all the world, and

cp. 13 10 ; 14 9 : also 12 9.

unto all the 5 nations [cp. 2 30-32 ; 3 6 : also 13 29 ; 14 21-24 ; 20 16],

cp. 10 16 ; 11 52.

preach the gospel [cp. 1 1, 14, 15 ; 8 35 ; 10 29 ; 13 10 ; 14 9] to the whole creation [cp. 10 6 ; 13 19].

16 He that believeth and is baptized

beginning from Jerusalem.

cp. *verse* 47.

baptizing them into the name of the Father and of the Son and

of the Holy Ghost :

20 teaching them to observe all things whatsoever I commanded you :

shall be saved; but he that disbelieveth shall be condemned.

48 Ye are witnesses of these things.   **49** And behold,

cp. 14 15, 23.

cp. 15 27.

Peace *be* unto you : as the Father hath sent me, even so send I
cp. 14 16, 26 ; 15 26 ; 16 7.
you.

I send forth the promise of my Father upon you : but tarry ye in the city, until ye be clothed with power [*cp.* 1 17, 35 ; 4 14, 36 ; 5 17 ; 6 19 ; 8 46 ; 9 1] from on high [*cp.* 1 78].

cp. 5 30.

22 And when he had said this, he breathed on them, and saith unto them, Receive ye the [2] Holy Ghost : 23 whose soever sins ye forgive, they are forgiven unto them ; whose soever *sins* ye retain, they are retained.
cp. 14 23.

cp. 16 19 ; 18 18.
and lo, I am with you [*cp.* 1 23] [1] alway [*cp.* 18 20], even unto [2] the end of the world [*cp.* 13 39, 40, 49 ; 24 3].

17 And these signs shall follow [*cp.* 16 20] them that believe :

10 **17** And the seventy returned with joy, saying,

cp. *verse* 19 : *also* 7 22; 18 5, 20 ; 24 5.

in my name [*cp.* 9 37, 38, 39 ; 13 6] shall they cast out [1] devils ; they shall speak with [2] new tongues ; **18** they shall

Lord, even the [6] devils are subject unto us in thy name [*cp.* 24 47 : *also* 9 48, 49 ; 21 8].

cp. 14 13, 14, 26 ; 15 16; 16 23, 24, 26.

18 And he said unto them, I beheld Satan fallen as lightning from heaven.   **19** Behold, I have given you authority [*cp.* 10 9 ; 9 1 : *also* 9 6, 40] to tread upon serpents and scorpions, and over all the power of the enemy : and nothing shall in any wise hurt you.

cp. 10 1, 8 : *also* 17 16.

[*cp.* 3 15 ; 6 7 : *also* 6 13; 9 18] take up serpents,

and if they drink any deadly   thing, it shall in no wise hurt them ; they shall lay hands on the sick, and they shall recover.

---

[1] Gr. *all the days.*
[2] Or, *the consummation of the age*

[1] Gr. *demons.*
[2] Some ancient authorities omit *new.*

[1] Some ancient authorities omit *and saith unto them, Peace be unto you.*
[2] Some ancient authorities omit ver. 40.
[3] Many ancient authorities add *and a honeycomb.*
[4] Some ancient authorities read *unto.*
[5] Or, *nations. Beginning from Jerusalem, ye are witnesses*
[6] Gr. *demons.*

[1] Or, *hast thou believed ?*
[2] Or, *Holy Spirit*

§ 268. The Reception into Heaven and the Mission which followed

	Mark 16 19-20	Luke 24 50-53	
	19 So then the Lord [*cp. verse 20*] Jesus, after he had spoken unto them,	*cp.* 7 13, 19 ; 10 1, 39, 41 ; 11 39 ; *etc.* 50 And he led them out until *they were* over against Bethany : and he lifted up his hands, and blessed them. 51 And it came to pass, while he blessed them, he parted from them, ¹ and was carried up into heaven.	*cp.* 4 1 ; 6 23 ; 11 2 ; 20 2, 18, 20, 25 ; 21 7, 12.
cp. 28 17: *also* 2 11 ; *etc.* *cp.* 28 8.	was received up into heaven, and sat down at the right hand of God. *cp.* 5 6: *also* 1 40; 3 11; 5 22, 33; 7 25; 10 17.	52 And they ² worshipped him [*cp.* 5 8, 12 ; 8 28, 41, 47 ; 17 16], and returned to Jerusalem with great joy [*cp.* 24 41]: 53 and were continually in the temple, blessing God [*cp.* 1 64 ; 2 28].	*cp.* 9 38: *also* 11 32; 18 6. *cp.* 16 22 ; 20 20.
cp. 13 19-23.	**20** And they went forth, and preached everywhere, the Lord [*see above*] working with them, and confirming the word [*cp.* 2 2 ; 4 14-20, 33] by the signs that followed [*cp.* 16 17-18]. Amen.	*cp.* 1 2 ; 4 32 ; 8 12-15 : *also* 5 1 ; 8 11, 21 ; 11 28.	*cp.* 4 41 ; 5 24, 38 ; *etc.*

¹ Some ancient authorities omit *and was carried up into heaven.*
² Some ancient authorities omit *worshipped him, and.*

INDEX OF JOHANNINE PARALLELS
printed in the text in full

INDEX TO SECTION HEADINGS

PART II

THE GOSPEL ACCORDING TO ST. JOHN
WITH THE
SYNOPTIC PARALLELS

PART II

TABLE OF CONTENTS

§		John	Matt.	Mark	Luke	Page

§		John	Matt.	Mark	Luke	Page

A. The Preparation for the Ministry (§§ 1-5)

(i) The Prologue (§ 1)

§ 1. The Incarnation of the Word and the Mission of John the Baptist

John 1 1-18

1 IN the beginning was the Word, and the Word was with God [*cp.* 17 5, 24: *also verse* 18 *and* 17 11], and the Word was God. 2 The same was in the beginning with God. 3 All things were made [1]by him [*cp. verse* 10]; and without him [2]was not anything made that hath been made. 4 In him was life [*cp.* 5 26; 6 57; 11 25; 14 6: *also* 3 15; *etc.*]; and the life was the light [*cp.* 8 12; 9 5; 12 35, 46: *also* 3 19] of men. 5 And the light shineth in the darkness [*cp.* 8 12; 12 35, 46]; and the darkness [3]apprehended it not [*cp.* 12 35: *also* 3 19-20]. 6 There came a man, sent from God [*cp.* 1 33; 3 28], whose name was John. 7 The same came for witness [*cp. verse* 15: *also* 1 19-36; 3 26-36; 5 33-36; 10 41], that he might bear witness of the light, that all might believe through him. 8 He was not the light [*cp.* 5 35], but *came* that he might bear witness of the light. 9 [4]There was the true [*cp.* 6 32; 15 1: *also* 6 55: *and* 17 3] light, *even the light* which lighteth [5]every man, coming into the world [*cp.* 3 19; 12 46: *also* 6 14; 9 39; 10 36; 11 27; 16 28; 17 18; 18 37: *and* 12 35]. 10 He was in the world, and the world was made [1]by him [*cp. verse* 3], and the world knew him not [*cp.* 1 26, 31, 33; 8 19; 14 9; 16 3: *also* 20 14; 21 4: *and* 8 55; 14 17; 17 25]. 11 He came unto [6]his own [*cp.* 8 44; 15 19; 16 32; 19 27], and they that were his own [*cp.* 13 1] received him not [*cp.* 5 43: *also* 3 11, 32: *and* 4 44]. 12 But as many as received him, to them gave he the right to become children of God [*cp.* 11 52: *also* 12 36], *even* to them that believe on his name [*cp.* 2 23; 3 18]: 13 which were [7]born [*cp.* 3 3, 5-7], not of [8]blood, nor of the will of the flesh, nor of the will of man, but of God. 14 And the Word became flesh [*cp.* 6 51], and [9]dwelt among us (and we beheld his glory [*cp.* 2 11; 12 41; 17 5, 22, 24], glory as of [10]the only begotten [*cp. verse* 18 *and* 3 16, 18] from the Father [*cp.* 5 44; 6 46; 7 29; 9 16, 33; 16 27, 28; 17 8]), full of grace [*cp. verse* 17] and truth [*cp. verse* 17: *also* 5 33; 8 32; 14 6; 18 37]. 15 John beareth witness [*cp. verse* 7: *also* 1 19-36; *etc.*] of him, and crieth, saying, [11]This was he of whom I said, He that cometh [*cp.* 1 27; 3 31; 6 14; 11 27; 12 13] after me is become before me: for he was [12]before me [*cp.* 1 26-27, 30; 3 26-30]. 16 For of his fulness we all received, and grace for grace. 17 For the law was given [1]by Moses [*cp.* 7 19: *also* 1 45; 7 23; 8 5]; grace [*cp. verse* 14] and truth [*cp. verse* 14: *also* 5 33; 8 32; 14 6; 18 37] came [1] by Jesus Christ. 18 No man hath seen God at any time [*cp.* 5 37; 6 46: *also* 14 7-9]; [13]the only begotten [*cp. verse* 14: *also* 3 16, 18] Son, which is in the bosom of the Father [*cp. verse* 1 *and* 17 5, 24: *also* 17 11: *and* 6 46; 7 29; 8 19; 10 15], he hath declared *him* [*cp.* 3 11, 32; 8 26, 40; 15 15; 17 6, 25-26].

cp. 3 1.	*cp.* 1 4.	*cp.* 3 2-3.
		cp. 18 28.
cp. 13 53-58; 21 37-39. *cp.* 5 9: *also* 8 12; 13 38: *and* 5 45	*cp.* 6 1-6; 12 6-8.	*cp.* 4 16-30; 20 13-15. *cp.* 20 36: *also* 6 35; 16 8.
cp. 19 28; 25 31.	*cp.* 10 37.	*cp.* 9 26, 32; 24 26.
cp. 3 17; 12 18; 17 5.	*cp.* 1 11; 9 7; 12 6.	*cp.* 3 22; 9 35; 20 13.
cp. 3 11; 11 3; 21 9; 23 39. *cp.* 3 11.	*cp.* 11 9. *cp.* 1 7-8.	*cp.* 7 19, 20; 13 35; 19 38. *cp.* 3 16.
cp. 3 17; 12 18; 17 5. *cp.* 11 27.	*cp.* 1 11; 9 7; 12 6.	*cp.* 3 22; 9 35; 20 13. *cp.* 10 22.

[1] Or, *through*
[2] Or, *was not anything made. That which hath been made was life in him; and the life &c.*
[3] Or, *overcame.* See ch. 12 35 (Gr.).
[4] Or, *The true light, which lighteth every man, was coming*
[5] Or, *every man as he cometh*   [6] Gr. *his own things.*   [7] Or, *begotten*
[8] Gr. *bloods.*   [9] Gr. *tabernacled.*   [10] Or, *an only begotten from a father*
[11] Some ancient authorities read (*this was he that said*).
[12] Gr. *first in regard of me.*   [13] Many very ancient authorities read *God only begotten.*

(ii) The Witness of John the Baptist (§§ 2-3)

§ 2. **John's Witness concerning himself and his Relationship to the Christ**

[*Cp.* Matt. 3 14; Luke 1 41-44; John 1 15, 29-34, 35-36; 3 26-36: *also* Matt. 11 2-19; 17 10-13; 21 24-32; Mark 9 11-13; 11 29-33; Luke 7 18-35; 16 16; 20 3-8; John 1 1-8; 5 33-36; 10 41; Acts 1 5; 11 16; 18 25; 19 1-7.]

John **1** 19-28	Matt. 3 3, 11	Mark 1 2-3, 7-8	Luke 3 15, 4, 16	Acts 13 25
19 And this is the witness of John, when the Jews sent unto him from Jerusalem [*cp.* 5 33] priests and Levites to ask him, Who art thou [*cp.* 8 25; 21 12]? **20** And he confessed, and denied not; and he confessed, I am not the Christ [*cp.* 3 28: *also* 1 8]. **21** And they asked him, What then? Art thou Elijah? And he saith, I am not. Art thou the prophet [*cp.* 6 14; 7 40]? And he answered, No. **22** They said therefore unto him, Who art thou? that we may give an answer to them that sent us. What sayest thou of thyself? **23** He said, I am			**15** And as the people were in expectation, and all men reasoned in their hearts concerning John, whether haply he were the Christ;	**25** And as John was fulfilling his course, he said, What suppose ye that I am? I am not *he*.
	cp. 3 4; 11 10, 14; 17 10–13.	*cp.* 1 2, 6; 9 11-13.	*cp.* 1 17, 76; 7 27.	
	3 For this is he that was spoken of [1]by Isaiah the prophet, saying, 11 10	**2** Even as it is written [1]in Isaiah the prophet, Behold, I send my messenger before thy face, Who shall prepare thy way;	**4** as it is written in the book of the words of Isaiah the prophet, 7 27	
the voice of one crying in the wilderness, Make straight the way of the Lord,	The voice of one crying in the wilderness, Make ye ready the way of the Lord, Make his paths straight.	**3** The voice of one crying in the wilderness, Make ye ready the way of the Lord, Make his paths straight.	The voice of one crying in the wilderness, Make ye ready the way of the Lord, Make his paths straight.	
as said Isaiah the prophet. **24** [1]And they had been sent from the Pharisees [*cp.* 5 33]. **25** And they asked him, and said unto him, Why then baptizest thou, if thou art not the Christ, neither Elijah, neither the prophet? **26** John answered them, saying, I baptize [2]with water [*cp.* 1 31, 33]:	*cp.* 3 6, 7. **11** I indeed baptize you [2]with water unto repentance:	*cp.* 1 4. **7** And he preached, saying,	*cp.* 3 7. **16** John answered, saying unto them all, I indeed baptize you with water;	

in the midst of you standeth one whom ye know not [*cp.* 1 10, 31, 33; 8 19; 14 9; 16 3: *also* 20 14; 21 4: *and* 8 55; 14 17; 17 25], **27** *even* he that cometh [*cp.* 1 15, 30; 3 31; 6 14; 11 27; 12 13] after me,

the latchet of whose shoe I am not worthy to unloose.

cp. 1 33.
28 These things were done in [3]Bethany beyond Jordan, where John was baptizing [*cp.* 3 26; 10 40: *also* 3 23].

but he that cometh [*cp.* 11 3; 21 9; 23 39] after me is mightier than I, whose shoes I am not [3]worthy to bear:

he shall baptize you [2]with the Holy Ghost and *with* fire.

cp. 3 1, 6.

There cometh [*cp.* 11 9] after me he that is mightier than I, the latchet of whose shoes I am not [2]worthy to stoop down and unloose. **8** I baptized you [3]with water; but he shall baptize you [3]with the [4]Holy Ghost.

cp. 1 4-5.

but there cometh [*cp.* 7 19, 20; 13 35; 19 38] he that is mightier than I, the latchet of whose shoes I am not [1]worthy to unloose:

he shall baptize you [2]with the Holy Ghost and *with* fire.

cp. 3 3.

But behold, there cometh one after me, the shoes of whose feet I am not worthy to unloose.

cp. 11 16: *also* 1 5; 19 6.

---

[1] Or, *And* certain *had been sent from among the Pharisees.*
[2] Or, *in*
[3] Many ancient authorities read *Bethabarah*, some, *Betharabah.*

[1] Or, *through*
[2] Or, *in*
[3] Gr. *sufficient.*

[1] Some ancient authorities read *in the prophets.*
[2] Gr. *sufficient.*
[3] Or, *in*
[4] Or, *Holy Spirit* : and so throughout this book.

[1] Gr. *sufficient.*
[2] Or, *in.*

John 1 21: *cp.* Mal. 4 5 *and* Deut. 18 15.　　Mark 1 2 = Exod. 23 30; Mal. 3 1.
John 1 23 || Matt. 3 3 || Mark 1 3 || Luke 3 4 = Is. 40 3.

§ 3. John bears Witness to Jesus

John 1 29-34

29 On the morrow [*cp.* 1 35, 43; 2 1: *also* 6 22; 12 12] he seeth Jesus coming unto him, and saith, Behold, the Lamb of God [*cp.* 1 36], which [1]taketh away the sin of the world [3 16-17; 4 42; 12 47]! **30** This is he of whom I said, After me cometh a man which is become before me: for he was [2]before me [*cp.* 1 15, 26-27; 3 26-30]. **31** And I knew him not [*cp.* 1 10, 26, 33; 8 19; 14 9; 16 3: *also* 8 55; 14 17; 17 25]; but that he should be made manifest [*cp.* 2 11; 3 21; 7 4; 9 3; 17 6; 21 1, 14: *also* 14 21, 22] to Israel, for this cause came I baptizing [3]with water [*cp.* 1 26, 33]. **32** And John bare witness, saying,

cp. 27 62.

cp. 11 12.

cp. 16 12, 14.

Matt. 3 13-17

13 Then cometh Jesus from Galilee to the Jordan unto John, to be baptized of him. **14** But John would have hindered him, saying, I have need to be baptized of thee, and comest thou to me? **15** But Jesus answering said unto him, Suffer [1]*it* now: for thus it becometh us to fulfil all righteousness [*cp.* 5 6, 10, 20; 6 1, 33; 21 32]. Then he suffereth him.

Mark 1 9-11

9 And it came to pass in those days, that Jesus came from Nazareth of Galilee, and was baptized of John

Luke 3 21-22

21 Now it came to pass, when all the people were baptized,

John	Matthew	Mark	Luke
cp. 11 41-42; 12 27-28; 17 1-26.	**16** And Jesus, when he was baptized, cp. 14 23; 19 13; 26 36, 39, 42, 44: also 11 25-26. went up straightway from the water: and lo,	[1]in the Jordan. **10** And cp. 1 35; 6 46; 14 32, 35, 39. straightway coming up out of the water,	that, Jesus also having been baptized, and praying [cp. 5 16; 6 12; 9 18, 28, 29; 11 1; 22 41, 44: also 10 21],
I have beheld the Spirit descending as a dove out of heaven; and it abode upon him.	the heavens were opened, [2]unto him, and he saw the Spirit of God descending as a dove, and coming upon him;	he saw the heavens rent asunder, and the Spirit as a dove descending	the heaven was opened, **22** and the Holy Ghost descended in a bodily form, as a dove,
cp. 12 28.	**17** and lo, a voice out of the heavens [cp. 17 5],	upon him: **11** and a voice came out of the heavens [cp. 9 7],	upon him, and a voice came out of heaven [cp. 9 35],
verse 34	saying, [3]This is my beloved Son [cp. 12 18; 17 5:	Thou art my beloved Son [cp. 9 7; 12 6:	Thou art my beloved Son [cp. 9 35; 20 13:
cp. 1 14, 18; 3 16, 18: also 1 34, 49; etc.	also 4 3; etc.], in whom I am well pleased [cp. 17 5: also 11 26; 12 18].	also 1 1; etc.], in thee I am well pleased.	also 1 35; etc.]; in thee I am well pleased [cp. 2 14; 10 21; 12 32].
33 And I knew him not [cp. verse 31]: but he that sent me [cp. 1 6; 3 28] to baptize [3]with water [cp. 1 26, 31], he said unto me, Upon whomsoever thou shalt see the Spirit descending, and abiding upon him, the same is he that baptizeth [3]with the Holy Spirit. **34** And I have seen, and have borne witness that this is the Son of God [cp. 1 49; 3 18; 5 25; 9 35; 10 36; 11 4, 27; 19 7; 20 31: also 1 18; 3 16-17, 35-36; etc.].	cp. 3 11. verse 17 cp. 4 3, 6; 8 29; 14 33; 16 16; 26 63; 27 40, 43, 54: also 3 17; 17 5.	cp. 1 8. verse 11 cp. 1 1; 3 11; 5 7; 15 39: also 1 11; 9 7.	cp. 3 16. verse 22 cp. 1 35; 4 3, 9, 41; 8 28; 22 70: also 3 22; 9 35.
[1] Or, beareth the sin [2] Gr. first in regard of me. [3] Or, in	[1] Or, me [2] Some ancient authorities omit unto him. [3] Or, This is my Son; my beloved in whom I am well pleased. See ch. 12 18.	[1] Gr. into.	

John 1 29: cp. Is. 53 4, 7, 11-12.   John 1 32, 33 || Matt. 3 16 || Mark 1 10 || Luke 3 22: cp. Is. 11 2.
Matt. 3 17 || Mark 1 11 || Luke 3 22: cp. Ps. 2 7; Is. 42 1.

(iii) The First Disciples (§§ 4-5)

§ 4. Andrew, Simon, and One Other

John 1 35-42	Matt. 4 18-20; 16 16-18	Mark 1 16-18; 8 29	Luke 5 1-2, 10-11; 9 20
35 Again on the morrow [cp. 1 29, 43; 2 1: also 6 22; 12 12]	cp. 27 62.	cp. 11 12.	**5 1** Now it came to pass, while the multitude pressed upon him and heard the word of God,
John was standing, cp. 6 1; 21 1: also 6 16, etc.	**4 18** And walking by the sea of Galilee [cp. 15 29: also 8 24; etc.],	**1 16** And passing along by the sea of Galilee [cp. 7 31: also 2 13; etc.],	that he was standing by the lake of Gennesaret [cp. 5 2; 8 22, 23, 33]; **2** and
and two of his disciples [cp. 3 25; 4 1];	he saw two cp. 9 14; 11 2; 14 12. brethren, Simon who is called Peter [cp. 10 2; 16 16-18], and Andrew his brother,	he saw [cp. 2 14] cp. 2 18; 6 29. Simon cp. 3 16. and Andrew the brother of Simon	he saw two cp. 5 33; 7 18-19; 11 1. cp. 6 14. boats standing by the lake: but
verse 42			

John

cp. 1 43; 12 26; 21 19, 22.

36 and he looked upon Jesus as he walked, and saith, Behold, the Lamb of God [cp. 1 29]! **37** And the two disciples heard him speak, and

they   followed Jesus.
38 And Jesus turned, and beheld them following, and saith unto them, What seek ye [cp. 18 4, 7; 20 15: also 4 27]? And they said unto him, Rabbi [cp. 1 49; 3 2; 4 31; 6 25; 9 2; 11 8: also 20 16: and 3 26] (which is to say, being interpreted, ¹Master [cp. 20 16: also 8 4]), where abidest thou? **39** He saith unto them, Come, and ye shall see [cp. 1 46; 4 29; 11 34]. They came therefore and saw where he abode; and they abode with him that day: it was about the tenth hour [cp. 4 6, 52; 19 14]. **40** One of the two that heard John *speak*, and followed him, was Andrew [cp. 1 44; 6 8; 12 22], Simon Peter's [cp. 6 8, 68; *etc.*] brother. **41** He findeth first his own brother Simon, and saith unto him, We have found the Messiah [cp. 4 25] (which is, being interpreted, ²Christ [cp. 4 25, 29; 7 26, 41; 9 22; 10 24; 11 27: *also* 4 26, 42]). cp. 1 34, 49; 3 18; 5 25; 9 35; 10 36; 11 4, 27; 19 7; 20 31: *also* 1 18; *etc.*

42 He brought him unto Jesus. Jesus looked upon him, and said, Thou art Simon [cp. 21 15, 16, 17] the son of ³John [cp. 21 15, 16, 17]:

thou shalt be called Cephas (which is by interpretation, ⁴Peter). cp. 21 15-17.

¹ Or, *Teacher*   ² That is, *Anointed.*
³ Gr. *Joanes:* called in Matt. 16 17, *Jonah.*
⁴ That is, *Rock* or *Stone.*

Matt.

casting a net into the sea; for they were fishers. **19** And he saith unto them, Come ye after me [cp. 8 22; 9 9; 16 24; 19 21], and I will make you fishers of men.

20 And they straightway left the nets, and followed him [cp. 4 22; 9 9; 19 27]. cp. 9 22; 16 23.

cp. 26 25, 49: *also* 23 7, 8: *and* 8 19; *etc.*

cp. 4 18; 10 2.

16 16 And Simon Peter answered and said,

Thou art the Christ [cp. 26 63: *also* 26 68; 27 17, 22], the Son [cp. 4 3, 6; 8 29; 14 33; 26 63; 27 40, 43, 54: *also* 3 17; 17 5] of the living [cp. 26 63] God.

17 And Jesus answered and said unto him, Blessed art thou, Simon [cp. 17 25] Bar Jonah: for flesh and blood hath not revealed it unto thee [cp. 11 25], but my Father which is in heaven [cp. 5 16, 45; 6 1, 9; 7 11, 21; 10 32, 33; 12 50; 18 10, 14, 19: *also* 5 48; 6 14, 26, 32; 15 13; 18 35; 23 9]. **18** And I also say unto thee, that thou art [cp. 4 18; 10 2]

¹Peter, and upon this ²rock [cp. 7 24] I will build my church [cp. 18 17].

¹ Gr. *Petros.*   ² Gr. *petra.*

Mark

casting a net in the sea: for they were fishers. **17** And Jesus said unto them, Come ye after me [cp. 2 14; 8 34; 10 21], and I will make you to become fishers of men.

18 And straightway they left the nets, and followed him [cp. 1 20; 2 14; 10 28]. cp. 5 30; 8 33.

cp.9 5; 11 21; 14 45: *also* 10 51: *and* 4 38; *etc.*

cp.1 16, 29; 3 18; 13 3.

8 29 Peter answereth and saith him,

Thou art the Christ [cp. 14 61: *also* 15 32]. cp. 1 1; 3 11; 5 7; 15 39; *also* 1 11; 9 7.

cp. 14 37.

cp. 11 25, 26.

cp. 3 16.

Luke

the fishermen had gone out of them, and were washing their nets . . . . **10** And Jesus said unto Simon, Fear not; cp. 5 27; 9 23, 59; 18 22. from henceforth thou shalt ¹catch men.

11 And when they had brought their boats to land, they left all, and followed him [cp. 5 28; 18 28]. cp. 7 9, 44; 9 55; 10 23; 14 25; 22 61; 23 28.

cp. 7 40; *etc.*

cp. 6 14. cp. 5 8.

9 20 And Peter answering said,

The Christ [cp. 22 67: *also* 23 2, 35, 39] cp. 1 35; 4 3, 9, 41; 8 28; 22 70: *also* 3 22; 9 35. of God [cp. 23 35].

cp. 22 31.

cp. 10 21.

cp. 11 13.

cp. 6 14.

cp. 6 48.
cp. 22 32.

¹ Gr. *take alive.*

§ 5. Philip and Nathanael

John 1 43-51

43 On the morrow [*cp.* 1 29, 35; 2 1; 6 22; 12 12] he was minded to go forth into Galilee [*cp.* 4 3, 43; 6 1], and he findeth Philip [*cp.* 6 5-7; 12 21-22; 14 8-9]: and Jesus saith unto him, Follow me [*cp.* 12 26; 21 19, 22]. **44** Now Philip was from Bethsaida [*cp.* 12 21], of the city of Andrew [*cp.* 1 40; 6 8; 12 22] and Peter. **45** Philip findeth Nathanael [*cp.* 21 2], and saith unto him, We have found him, of whom Moses in the law, and the prophets [*cp.* 5 46; 12 41], did write, Jesus of Nazareth [*cp.* 18 5, 7; 19 19], the son of Joseph [*cp.* 6 42]. **46** And Nathanael said unto him, Can any good thing come out of Nazareth [*cp.* 7 41, 52]? Philip saith unto him, Come and see [*cp.* 1 39; 4 29; 11 34]. **47** Jesus saw Nathanael coming to him, and saith of him, Behold, an Israelite indeed, in whom is no guile! **48** Nathanael saith unto him, Whence knowest thou me? Jesus answered and said unto him, Before Philip called thee, when thou wast under the fig tree, I saw thee [*cp.* 2 24, 25; 4 19, 29; 5 6, 42; 6 61, 64; 11 14; 13 11, 18; 16 19, 30; 18 4; 21 17]. **49** Nathanael answered him, Rabbi [*cp.* 1 38; 3 2; 4 31; 6 25; 9 2; 11 8: *also* 20 16: *and* 3 26],

thou art
cp. 10 24-25.

the Son of God [*cp.* 11 27: *also* 6 69; 20 28: *and* 1 34; 3 18; 5 25; 9 35; 11 4; *etc.*]; thou art King of Israel [*cp.* 12 13: *also* 18 33, 39; 19 3, 19, 21: *and* 6 15; 12 15; 18 37]. **50** Jesus answered and said unto him, Because I said unto thee, I saw thee underneath the fig tree, believest thou? thou shalt see greater things than these [*cp.* 5 20; 14 12]. **51** And he saith unto him,
Verily, verily, I say unto you,
Ye shall see the heaven

---

cp. 27 62.

cp. 10 3.

cp. 4 19; 8 22; 9 9; 16 24; 19 21.
cp. 11 21.

cp. 4 18; 10 2.

cp. 2 23; 26 71: *also* 21 11.
cp. 13 55.

cp. 9 4; 12 25; 16 8.

cp. 26 25, 49: *also* 23 7, 8.

Matt. 26 **63** And the high priest said unto him, I adjure thee by the living God, that thou tell us whether thou be the Christ,

verse 64

the Son of God [*cp.* 8 29; 14 33; 16 16; 27 54: *also* 4 3, 6; 27 40, 43: *and* 3 17; 17 5].
cp. 27 42: *also* 2 2; 27 11, 29, 37: *and* 21 5.

64 Jesus saith unto him, Thou hast said: nevertheless I say unto you, Henceforth ye shall see

---

cp. 11 12.

cp. 3 18.

cp. 1 17; 2 14; 8 34; 10 21.

cp. 6 45; 8 22.

cp. 1 16, 29; 3 18; 13 3.

cp. 1 24; 10 47; 14 67; 16 6.

cp. 2 8; 8 17.

cp. 9 5; 11 21; 14 45: *also* 10 51.

Mark 14 **61** Again the high priest asked him, and saith unto him,

Art thou the Christ,

verse 62

the Son of *cp.* 3 11; 5 7; 15 39: *also* 1 1: *and* 1 11; 9 7.
the Blessed? *cp.* 15 32: *also* 15 2, 9, 12, 18, 26.

62 And Jesus said,

I am: and

ye shall see

---

cp. 6 14.

cp. 5 27; 9 23, 59; 18 22.

cp. 10 13.

cp. 6 14.

cp. 16 29, 31; 24 27, 44.

cp. 4 34; 18 37; 24 19.
cp. 3 23; 4 22.

cp. 5 22; 6 8; 9 47; 11 17.

Luke 22 **67** If thou art the Christ, tell us. But he said unto them, If I tell you, ye will not believe: **68** and if I ask *you*, ye will not answer. **69** But from henceforth shall the Son of man be seated at the right hand of the power of God. **70** And they all said, Art thou then the Son of God [*cp.* 4 41; 8 28: *also* 1 35; 4 3, 9: *and* 3 22; 9 35]?

cp. 23 3, 37, 38: *also* 19 38; 23 2: *and* 1 33.

And he said unto them, [1]Ye say that I am.

opened, and the angels [cp. 12 29] of God ascending and descending upon the Son of man [cp. 6 62].	cp. 3 16. cp. 4 11; 26 53. the Son of man sitting at the right hand of power, and coming on the clouds of heaven.	cp. 1 10. cp. 1 13. the Son of man sitting at the right hand of power, and coming with the clouds of heaven.	cp. 3 21. cp. 22 43. *verse* 69

¹ Or, *Ye say it, because I am.*

John 1 47: *cp.* Ps. 32 2; Zeph. 3 13.   John 1 51: *cp.* Gen. 28 12.

B. The Ministry in Galilee, Samaria, and Judæa (§§ 6-48)

(i) In Galilee I (§§ 6-7)

§ 6. **The Marriage Feast at Cana**

John 2 1-11

1 And the third day [cp. 1 29, 35, 43] there was a marriage in Cana [cp. 4 46; 21 2] of Galilee; and the mother of Jesus was there: 2 and Jesus also was bidden, and his disciples, to the marriage. 3 And when the wine failed, the mother of Jesus saith unto him, They have no wine. 4 And Jesus saith unto her, Woman [cp. 19 26: *also* 4 21; 20 13, 15], what have I to do with thee? mine hour is not yet come [cp. 7 6, 8, 30; 8 20: *also* 12 23; 13 1; 17 1: *and* 12 27]. 5 His mother saith unto the servants, Whatsoever he saith unto you, do it. 6 Now there were six waterpots of stone set there after the Jews' manner of purifying [cp. 3 25], containing two or three firkins apiece. 7 Jesus saith unto them, Fill the waterpots with water. And they filled them up to the brim. 8 And he saith unto them, Draw out now, and bear unto the ¹ruler of the feast. And they bare it. 9 And when the ruler of the feast tasted the water ²now become wine [cp. 4 46], and knew not whence it was (but the servants which had drawn the water knew), the ruler of the feast calleth the bridegroom, 10 and saith unto him, Every man setteth on first the good wine; and when *men* have drunk freely, *then* that which is worse: thou hast kept the good wine until now. 11 This beginning of his signs [cp. 2 23; 3 2; 4 54; 6 2, 14, 26; 7 31; 9 16; 11 47; 12 18, 37; 20 30] did Jesus in Cana of Galilee, and manifested [cp. 1 31; 3 21; 7 4; 9 3; 17 6; 21 1, 14: *also* 14 21, 22] his glory [cp. 1 14; 12 41; 17 5, 22, 24]; and his disciples believed on him [cp. 2 23; 4 39, 41; 7 31; 8 30; 10 42; 11 45; 12 11, 42: *also* 3 16; 6 35; *etc.*].

cp. 15 28.
cp. 8 29.
cp. 26 18, 45.

cp. 1 24; 5 7.
cp. 14 35, 41.

cp. 7 3-4.

cp. 13 12.
cp. 4 34; 8 28.
cp. 22 14, 53.

cp. 5 39.

cp. 23 8.

cp. 16 12, 14.
cp. 10 37.
cp. 9 42.

cp. 19 28; 25 31.
cp. 18 6.

cp. 9 26; 32; 24 26.

¹ Or, *steward*   ² Or, *that it had become*

§ 7. **Jesus at Capernaum**

John 2 12

12 After this he went down to Capernaum, he, and his mother, and *his* brethren [cp. 7 3, 5, 10], and his disciples: and there they abode not many days.

cp. 4 13.
cp. 12 46-50; 13 55.

cp. 1 21.
cp. 3 31-35; 6 3.

cp. 4 23, 31.
cp. 8 19-21.

(ii) In Judæa I (§§ 8-13)

§ 8. The Cleansing of the Temple

[*Cp.* Mal. 3 1; Zech. 14 21]

John 2 13-22	Matt. 21 12-13; 26 60-61	Mark 11 15-17; 14 57-58	Luke 19 45-46
13 And the passover of the Jews was at hand [*cp.* 6 4; 11 55: *also* 5 1 *and* 7 2], and Jesus went up to Jerusalem [*cp.* 5 1; 7 10: *also* 7 14]. **14** And he found in the temple those that sold oxen and sheep and doves, and the changers of money sitting: **15** and he made a scourge of cords, and cast all out of the temple, both the sheep and the oxen; and he poured out the changers' money, and overthrew their tables; **16** and to them that sold the doves	21 **12** And Jesus entered into the temple ¹of God, and cast out all them that sold and bought in the temple, and overthrew the tables of the money-changers, and the seats of them that sold the doves;	11 **15** And they come to Jerusalem: and he entered into the temple, and began to cast out them that sold and them that bought in the temple, and overthrew the tables of the money-changers, and the seats of them that sold the doves; **16** and he would not suffer that any man should carry a vessel through the temple.	*cp.* 2 41. 19 **45** And he entered into the temple, and began to cast out them that sold,
he said, Take these things hence; make not my Father's house [*cp.* 14 2] a house of merchandise. **17** His disciples remembered that it was written, The zeal of thine house shall eat me up. **18** The Jews therefore answered and said unto him, What sign shewest thou unto us [*cp.* 6 30: *also* 4 48], seeing that thou doest these things [*cp.* 5 27; 17 2]?	**13** and he saith unto them, It is written, My house shall be called a house of prayer: but ye make it a den of robbers.	**17** And he taught, and said unto them, Is it not written, My house shall be called a house of prayer for all the nations? but ye have made it a den of robbers.	**46** saying unto them, It is written, And my house shall be a house of prayer: but ye have made it a den of robbers.
	cp. 12 38; 16 1.	*cp.* 8 11.	*cp.* 11 16.
	cp. 21 23: *also* 7 29; 9 6; 28 18.	*cp.* 11 28: *also* 1 22, 27; 2 10.	*cp.* 20 2: *also* 4 32, 36; 5 24.
19 Jesus answered and said unto them, Destroy this ¹temple, and in three days I will raise it up. **20** The Jews therefore said, Forty and six years was this ¹temple in building, and wilt thou raise it up in three days [*cp.* 8 57]?	**26 60** . . . But afterward came two, **61** and said, This man said, I am able to destroy the ²temple of God, and to build it in three days [*cp.* 27 40: *also* 12 40; 16 21; 17 23; 20 19; 27 63, 64].	**14 57** And there stood up certain, and bare false witness against him, saying, **58** We heard him say, I will destroy this ¹temple that is made with hands, and in three days [*cp.* 15 29: *also* 8 31; 9 31; 10 34]. I will build another made without hands.	*cp.* 9 22; 13 32; 18 33; 24 7, 21, 46.

John	Matt.	Mark	Luke
21 But he spake of the ¹temple of his body [*cp.* 10 18]. **22** When therefore he was raised from the dead, his disciples remembered [*cp.* 12 16: *also* 14 26; 16 4] that he spake this; and they believed the scripture [*cp.* 20 9], and the word which Jesus had said [*cp.* 3 14; 12 32—33].	*cp.* 26 75.	*cp.* 14 72.	*cp.* 24 6, 8: *also* 22 61.
			cp. 24 45-46.
	cp. 16 21-23; 17 9, 12, 22-23; 20 17-19, 28; 26 2, 32: *also* 26 12, 24.	*cp.* 8 31-33; 9 9, 12, 30-32; 10 32-34, 45; 14 28: *also* 14 8, 21.	*cp.* 9 22, 43-45; 13 32-33; 17 25; 18 31-34; 24 7: *also* 22 22.

¹ Or, *sanctuary*

¹ Many ancient authorities omit *of God*.
² Or, *sanctuary*

¹ Or, *sanctuary*

John 2 16 *and* Mark 11 16: *cp.* Zech. 14 21.   Matt. 21 13 || Mark 11 17 || Luke 19 46 = Is. 56 7: *cp.* Jer. 7 11.
John 2 17 = Ps. 69 9.

§ 9. Jesus in Jerusalem

John 2 23-25

John	Matt.	Mark	Luke
23 Now when he was in Jerusalem at the passover, during the feast, many [*cp.* 4 45] believed [*cp.* 2 11; 4 39, 41; 7 31; 8 30; 10 42; 11 45; 12 11, 42: *also* 3 16; 6 35; *etc.*] on his name [*cp.* 1 12; 3 18], beholding [*cp.* 6 2; 7 3; 11 45] his signs [*cp.* 2 11; 3 2; 4 54; 6 2, 14, 26; 7 31; 9 16; 11 47; 12 18, 37; 20 30] which he did. **24** But Jesus did not trust himself unto them, for that he knew all men [*cp.* 1 48; 2 25; 14 19, 29; 5 6, 42; 6 61, 64; 11 14; 13 11, 18; 16 19, 30; 18 4; 21 17], **25** and because he needed not that any one should bear witness concerning ¹man; for he himself knew what was in man [*see verse 24 above*].	*cp.* 18 6.	*cp.* 9 42.	
			cp. 23 8.
	cp. 9 4; 12 25; 16 8.	*cp.* 2 8; 8 17.	*cp.* 5 22; 6 8; 9 47; 11 17.

¹ Or, *a man; for . . . the man*

§ 10. Jesus and Nicodemus (i)

John 3 1-15

John	Matt.	Mark	Luke
1 Now there was a man of the Pharisees, named Nicodemus [*cp.* 7 50; 19 39], a ruler [*cp.* 7 26, 48; 12 42] of the Jews: **2** the same came unto him by night [*cp.* 9 22; 12 42], and said to him, Rabbi [*cp.* 1 38, 49; 4 31; 6 25; 9 2; 11 8: *also* 20 16: *and* 3 26], we know [*cp.* 4 42; 9 24, 29, 31; 16 30; 21 24] that thou art a teacher come from God: for no man can do these signs [*cp.* 2 11, 23; 4 54; *etc.*] that thou doest, except God be with him [*cp.* 9 16, 33; 10 21: *also* 5 36; 10 25]. **3** Jesus answered and said unto him, Verily, verily, I say unto thee, Except a man [*cp.* 3 5; 6 53; 8 24: *also* 13 8]	*cp.* 9 18.	*cp.* 5 22.	*cp.* 14 1; 18 18; 23 13, 35; 24 20: *also* 8 41; 13 14.
	cp. 26 25, 49: *also* 23 7, 8.	*cp.* 9 5; 11 21; 14 45: *also* 10 51.	
	cp. 22 16.	*cp.* 12 14.	*cp.* 20 21.
	Matt. 18 **3** Verily I say unto you, Except ye turn, and become	Mark 10 **15** Verily I say unto you, ever shall not receive (Whoso-)	Luke 18 **17** Verily I say unto you, ever shall not receive (Whoso-)

	Matt.	Mark	Luke
be born [*cp.* 1 12-13; 3 5-7] ¹anew, he cannot see [*cp.* 3 36] the kingdom of God. **4** Nicodemus saith unto him, How can a man be born when he is old [*cp.* 3 9; 6 42, 52; 8 33; 12 34: *also* 4 9; 6 60; 7 15]? can he enter a second time into his mother's womb, and be born? **5** Jesus answered, Verily, verily, I say unto thee, Except a man [*cp. verse* 3] be born [*cp.* 1 12-13; 3 3] of water and the Spirit, he cannot enter [*cp.* 10 1, 2, 9]	as little children,	the kingdom of God as a little child, *cp.* 9 1.	the kingdom of God as a little child, *cp.* 9 27.
into the kingdom of God.	ye shall in no wise enter [*cp.* 5 20; 7 21; 19 23, 24; 21 31; 23 13: *also* 7 13; 18 8, 9; 19 17; 25 21, 23] into the kingdom of heaven.	he shall in no wise enter [*cp.* 9 47; 10 23, 24, 25: *also* 9 43, 45] therein.	he shall in no wise enter [*cp.* 18 24, 25: *also* 11 52; 13 24; 24 26] therein.

6 That which is born of the flesh [*cp.* 1 13] is flesh; and that which is born of the Spirit is spirit [*cp.* 6 63]. **7** Marvel not [*cp.* 5 28] that I said unto thee, Ye must be born ¹anew. **8** ²The wind bloweth where it listeth, and thou hearest the voice thereof, but knowest not whence it cometh, and whither it goeth [*cp.* 8 14; *etc.*]: so is every one that is born of the Spirit. **9** Nicodemus answered and said unto him, How can these things be [*cp.* 3 4; 6 42, 52; 8 33; 12 34: *also* 4 9; 6 60; 7 15]? **10** Jesus answered and said unto him, Art thou the teacher of Israel, and understandest not these things [*cp.* 4 33; 8 27, 43; 10 6; 11 13; 12 16; 13 7, 28, 36; 14 5-10, 22; 16 17-18]? **11** Verily, verily, I say unto thee, We speak that we do know [*cp.* 4 22], and bear witness of that we have seen [*cp.* 3 32: *also* 1 18; 8 26, 40; 15 15: *and* 17 6, 26]; and ye receive not our witness [*cp.* 3 32: *also* 1 11; 5 43: *and* 12 37]. **12** If I told you earthly things, and ye believe not [*cp.* 6 64; 14 10; 20 27], how shall ye believe, if I tell you heavenly things? **13** And no man hath ascended into heaven, but he that descended out of heaven [*cp.* 3 31; 6 32-33, 38, 41-42, 50-51, 58: *also* 8 23], *even* the Son of man [*cp.* 6 62: *also* 20 17: *and* 1 51], ³which is in heaven. **14** And as Moses lifted up the serpent in the wilderness, even so must the Son of man be lifted up [*cp.* 8 28; 12 32-34: *also* 2 19-22]: **15** that whosoever ⁴believeth may in him have eternal life [*cp.* 3 16, 36; 5 24; 6 40, 47: *also* 11 25-26; 20 31: *and* 4 14, 36; *etc.*].

(verse)	Matt.	Mark	Luke
10-11	*cp.* 15 16; 16 8-12.	*cp.* 4 13; 6 52; 7 18; 8 17-21; 9 10, 32; 16 14.	*cp.* 2 50; 9 45; 18 34.
12-13	*cp.* 8 26; 14 31; 16 8; 17 20; 21 21; 28 17.	*cp.* 4 40; 11 22; 16 14.	*cp.* 8 25; 12 28; 17 5-6; 22 32; 24 25, 38.
14	*cp.* 16 21-23; *etc.*	*cp.* 8 31-33; *etc.*	*cp.* 9 22; *etc.*
15	*cp.* 19 16, 29; 25 46.	*cp.* 10 17, 30.	*cp.* 10 25; 18 18, 30.

¹ Or, *from above*   ² Or, *The Spirit breatheth*
³ Many ancient authorities omit *which is in heaven*.   ⁴ Or, *believeth in him may have*

John 3 8: *cp.* Eccl. 11 5.   John 3 13: *cp.* Deut. 30 12; Prov. 30 4.   John 3 14: *cp.* Num. 21 9; Wisd. 16 5-7.

§ 11. Jesus and Nicodemus (ii)

John 3 16-21

16 For God so loved the world, that he gave his only begotten [*cp. verse* 18 *and* 1 14, 18] Son, that whosoever believeth on him should not perish [*cp.* 10 28: *also* 17 12; 18 9: *and* 6 39], but have eternal life [*cp.* 3 15, 36; 5 24; 6 40, 47: *also* 11 25-26; 20 31: *and* 4 14, 36; *etc.*]. **17** For God sent not the Son into the world [*cp.* 10 36; 17 18: *also* 3 34; 5 38; 6 29; 17 3: *and* 1 9; 3 19; *etc.*] to judge the world [*cp.* 8 15; 12 47]; but that the world should be saved [*cp.* 12 47: *also* 4 42; 5 34; 10 9] through him. **18** He that believeth on him is not judged: he that believeth not hath been judged already [*cp.* 5 24: *also* 3 19; 12 31; 16 11: *and* 5 29; 12 48], because he hath not believed on the name [*cp.* 1 12: 2 23] of the

	Matt.	Mark	Luke
16	*cp.* 3 17; 12 18; 17 5.	*cp.* 1 11; 9 7; 12 6.	*cp.* 3 22; 9 35; 20 13.
16 (end)	*cp.* 19 16, 29; 25 46.	*cp.* 10 17, 30.	*cp.* 10 25; 18 18, 30.
18	*cp.* 1 21; 18 11: *also* 20 28.	*cp.* 10 45.	*cp.* 9 55; 19 10: *also* 2 11.

only begotten [*cp. verse* 16 *and* 1 14, 18] Son of God. **19** And this is the judgement, that the light is come into the world [*cp.* 1 9; 12 46: *also* 1 4, 5; 8 12; 9 5; 12 35-36: *and* 6 14; 9 39; 10 36; 11 27; 16 28; 17 18; 18 37], and men loved the darkness rather than the light; for their works were evil [*cp.* 7 7]. **20** For every one that ¹doeth ill hateth the light, and cometh not to the light [*cp.* 1 5], lest his works should be ²reproved. **21** But he that doeth the truth cometh to the light, that his works may be made manifest [*cp.* 1 31; 2 11; 7 4; 9 3; 17 6; 21 1, 14: *also* 14 21, 22], ³that they have been wrought in God [*cp.* 6 28-29; 9 3-4: *also* 10 25, 32, 37; 14 10: *and* 4 34; 5 36; 17 4: *and* 5 17; 7 21].

cp. 3 17; 12 18; 17 5.	*cp.* 1 11; 9 7; 12 6.	*cp.* 3 22; 9 35; 20 13.
	cp. 16 12, 14.	

¹ Or, *practiseth*   ² Or, *convicted*   ³ Or, *because*

§ 12. **John again bears Witness to Jesus** (i)

John 3 22-30

22 After these things came Jesus and his disciples into the land of Judæa; and there he tarried with them [*cp.* 11 54]; and baptized [*cp. verse* 26 *and* 4 1-2]. **23** And John also was baptizing in Ænon near to Salim [*cp. verse* 26: *and* 1 28; 10 40], because there ¹was much water there: and they came, and were baptized. **24** For John was not yet cast into prison. **25** There arose therefore a questioning on the part of John's disciples [*cp.* 1 35, 37; 4 1] with a Jew about purifying [*cp.* 2 6]. **26** And they came unto John, and said to him, Rabbi [*cp.* 1 38; *etc.*], he that was with thee beyond Jordan [*cp.* 1 28; 10 40: *also verse* 23], to whom thou hast borne witness [*cp.* 1 7, 8, 15, 19-36: *also* 5 33-36; 10 41], behold, the same baptizeth [*cp. verse* 22 *and* 4 1-2], and all men come to him [*cp.* 12 19]. **27** John answered and said, A man can receive nothing, except it have been given him [*cp.* 6 65; 19 11] from heaven. **28** Ye yourselves bear me witness, that I said, I am not the Christ [*cp.* 1 20: *also* 1 8], but, that I am sent [*cp.* 1 6, 33] before him [*cp.* 1 23, 27, 30]. **29** He that hath the bride is the bridegroom: but the friend of the bridegroom, which standeth and heareth him, rejoiceth greatly because of the bridegroom's voice: this my joy therefore is fulfilled [*cp.* 15 11; 16 24; 17 13]. **30** He must increase, but I must decrease.

cp. 2 6, 20, 21; 4 15; 10 15; 11 24.		
cp. 3 1, 6.	*cp.* 1 4-5.	*cp.* 3 3.
cp. 4 12; 11 2; 14 3.	*cp.* 1 14; 6 17.	*cp.* 3 20.
cp. 9 14; 11 2; 14 12.	*cp.* 2 18; 6 29.	*cp.* 5 33; 7 18, 19; 11 1.
cp. 3 1, 6.	*cp.* 1 4-5.	*cp.* 3 3.
cp. 21 25.	*cp.* 11 30.	*cp.* 20 4. *cp.* 3 15.
cp. 3 3, 11; 11 10.	*cp.* 1 2-3, 7.	*cp.* 1 17, 76; 3 4; *etc.*
cp. 9 15.	*cp.* 2 19.	*cp.* 5 34.
cp. 3 11.	*cp.* 1 7.	*cp.* 3 16.

¹ Gr. *were many waters.*

§ 13. **John again bears Witness to Jesus** (ii)

John 3 31-36

31 He that cometh [*cp.* 1 15, 27; 6 14; 11 27; 12 13: *also* 1 30] from above is above all: he that is of the earth is of the earth, and of the earth he speaketh: ¹he that cometh from heaven [*cp.* 3 13; 6 32-33, 38, 41-42, 50-51, 58: *also* 8 23] is above all. **32** What he hath seen and heard, of that he beareth witness [*cp.* 3 11: *also* 1 18; 8 26, 40; 15 15: *and* 17 6, 26]; and no man receiveth his witness [*cp.* 3 11: *also* 1 11; 5 43: *and* 12 37]. **33** He that hath received his witness hath set his seal [*cp.* 6 27] to *this*, that God is true [*cp.* 7 28; 8 26: *also* 17 17]. **34** For he whom God hath sent [*cp.* 5 38; 6 29; 10 36; 17 3: *also* 3 17; *etc.*] speaketh the words of God [*cp.* 8 26, 47; 12 47-50; 14 10; 17 8, 14: *also* 6 63, 68]: for he giveth not the Spirit [*cp.* 7 39: *also* 1 33; 20 22] by measure. **35** The Father loveth the Son [*cp.* 5 20; 10 17; 15 9-10; 17 23, 24, 26], and hath given all things into his hand [*cp.* 5 27; 13 3; 17 2: *also* Matt. 9 6, 8; 11 27; 28 18: Mark 2 10: Luke 5 24; 10 22]. **36** He that believeth on the Son hath eternal life [*cp.* 3 15, 16; 5 24; 6 40, 47: *also* 11 25-26; 20 31: *and* 4 14, 36; *etc.*]; but he that ²obeyeth not the Son shall not see [*cp.* 3 3] life, but the wrath of God abideth on him.

cp. 3 11; 11 3; 21 9; 23 39.	*cp.* 11 9; *also* 1 7.	*cp.* 7 19, 20; 13 35; 19 38; *also* 3 16.
		cp. 11 13.
cp. 3 17; 17 5.	*cp.* 1 11; 9 7; 12 6.	*cp.* 3 22; 20 13.
cp. 19 16, 29; 25 46.	*cp.* 10 17, 30.	*cp.* 10 25; 18 18, 30.

¹ Some ancient authorities read *he that cometh from heaven beareth witness of what he hath seen and heard.*   ² Or, *believeth not*

John 3 34: *cp.* Ezek. 4 11, 16.

(iii) In Samaria (§§ 14–16)

§ 14. **Jesus and a Samaritan Woman**

John 4 1-26	Matt. 4 12	Mark 1 14	Luke 4 14
1 When therefore the Lord [*cp.* 6 23; 11 2; 20 2, 18, 20, 25; 21 7, 12] knew how that the Pharisees had heard that Jesus was making and baptizing [*cp.* 3 22, 26] more disciples than John **2** (although Jesus himself baptized not, but his disciples), [*cp.* 3 24] **3** he left Judæa, and departed again	**12** Now when he heard that John was delivered up [*cp.* 11 2; 14 3], he withdrew	**14** Now after *cp.* 16 19, 20. **that John** was delivered up [*cp.* 6 17], Jesus came	**14** And *cp.* 7 13, 19; 10 1, 39, 41; 11 39; 12 42; 13 15; 17 5, 6; 18 6; 19 8; 22 61; 24 3, 34. *cp.* 3 19-20. Jesus returned in the power of the Spirit

into Galliee [*cp.* 4 47, 54: *also* 1 43; 6 1]. **4** And he must needs pass through Samaria. **5** So he cometh to a city of Samaria, called Sychar, near to the parcel of ground that Jacob gave to his son Joseph: **6** and Jacob's [1]well was there. Jesus therefore, being wearied with his journey, sat [2]thus [*cp.* 13 25] by the [1]well. It was about the sixth hour [*cp.* 1 39; 4 52; 19 14]. **7** There cometh a woman of Samaria to draw water: Jesus saith unto her, Give me to drink. **8** For his disciples were gone away into the city to buy food. **9** The Samaritan woman therefore saith unto him, How is it [*cp.* 6 60; 7 15: *also* 3 4, 9; 6 42, 52; 8 33; 12 34] that thou, being a Jew, askest drink of me, which am a Samaritan woman? ([3]For Jews have no dealings with Samaritans [*cp.* 8 48].) **10** Jesus answered and said unto her, If thou knewest the gift of God, and who it is that saith to thee, Give me to drink; thou wouldest have asked of him, and he would have given thee living water [*cp.* 7 38]. **11** The woman saith unto him, [4]Sir, thou hast nothing to draw with, and the well is deep: from whence then hast thou that living water? **12** Art thou greater than our father [*cp.* 8 53] Jacob, which gave us the well, and drank thereof himself, and his sons, and his cattle? **13** Jesus answered and said unto her, Every one that drinketh of this water shall thirst again: **14** but whosoever drinketh of the water that I shall give him shall never thirst [*cp.* 6 35: *also* 7 37]; but the water that I shall give him [*cp.* 6 27, 51] shall become in him a well of water springing up unto eternal life. **15** The woman saith unto him, [4]Sir, give me [*cp.* 6 34] this water, that I thirst not, neither come all the way hither to draw. **16** Jesus saith unto her, Go, call thy husband, and come hither. **17** The woman answered and said unto him, I have no husband. Jesus saith unto her, Thou saidst well, I have no husband: **18** for thou hast had five husbands; and he whom thou now hast is not thy husband: this hast thou said truly. **19** The woman saith unto him, [4]Sir, I perceive that thou art a prophet [*cp.* 1 48; 2 24, 25; 4 29; 5 6, 42; 6 61, 64; 11 14; 13 11, 18; 16 19, 30; 18 4; 21 17: *also* 4 44; 6 14; 7 40; 9 17]. **20** Our fathers worshipped in this mountain; and ye say, that in Jerusalem is the place [*cp.* 11 48] where men ought to worship. **21** Jesus saith unto her, Woman, believe me, the hour cometh [*cp.* 4 23; 5 25, 28; 16 2, 25, 32], when neither in this mountain, nor in Jerusalem, shall ye worship the Father. **22** Ye worship that which ye know not: we worship that which we know [*cp.* 3 11]: for salvation is from the Jews. **23** But the hour cometh [*cp. verse* 21 *above*], and now is [*cp.* 5 25; 16 32], when the true worshippers shall worship the Father in spirit and truth: [5]for such doth the Father seek to be his worshippers. **24** [6]God is a Spirit [*cp.* 3 6]: and they that worship him must worship in spirit and truth. **25** The woman saith unto him, I know that Messiah [*cp.* 1 41] cometh (which is called Christ [*cp.* 1 41]): when he is come [*cp.* 7 27, 31], he will declare unto us

Column cross-references (lower section):

	Matt.	Mark	Luke
			cp. 17 11.
			cp. 9 52, 56; 10 38.
		cp. 4 36.	
	cp. 10 5.		*cp.* 9 52-53.
	cp. 9 4; 12 25; 16 8: *also* 13 57; 21 11, 46.	*cp.* 2 8; 8 17: *also* 6 4, 15.	*cp.* 5 22; 6 8; 9 47; 11 17: *also* 4 24; 7 16, 39; 13 33; 24 19.
	cp. 2 4-6.		*cp.* 1 69, 71, 77; 2 30; 19 9: *also* 3 6.
	cp. 1 16; 27 17, 22.		

all things [*cp.* 16 13-15]. **26** Jesus saith unto her, I that speak unto thee [*cp.* 9 37] am *he* [*cp.* 10 24–25: *also* 1 41; 4 29; 7 26, 41; 9 22; 11 27: *and* 4 42].

cp. 26 63-64: *also* 16 16: *and* 26 68; 27 17, 22.	*cp.* 14 61-62: *also* 8 29: *and* 15 32.	*cp.* 22 67-68: *also* 9 20: *and* 23 2, 35,39.

[1] Gr. *spring:* and so in ver. 14; but not in ver. 11, 12.   [2] Or, *as he was*
[3] Some ancient authorities omit *For Jews have no dealings with Samaritans.*
[4] Or, *Lord*   [5] Or, *for such the Father also seeketh*   [6] Or, *God is spirit*

John 4 5, 6, 12: *cp.* Gen. 33 19, 48 22; Josh. 24 32.

§ 15. Discourse with the Disciples

John 4 27-38

27 And upon this came his disciples; and they marvelled that he was speaking with a woman; yet no man said, What seekest thou [*cp.* 1 38; 18 4, 7; 20 15]? or, Why speakest thou with her [*cp.* 21 12]? **28** So the woman left her waterpot, and went away into the city, and saith to the men, **29** Come, see [*cp.* 1 39, 46; 11 34] a man, which told me all things that *ever* I did [*cp.* 4 17-19: *also* 4 39]: can this be the Christ [*cp.* 4 25]? **30** They went out of the city, and were coming to him. **31** In the mean while the disciples prayed him, saying, Rabbi [*cp.* 1 38, 49; 3 2; 6 25; 9 2; 11 8: *also* 20 16: *and* 3 26], eat. **32** But he said unto them, I have meat to eat that ye know not. **33** The disciples therefore said one to another, Hath any man brought him *aught* to eat [*cp.* 3 10; 8 27, 43; 10 6; 11 13; 12 16; 13 7, 28, 36; 14 5-10, 22; 16 17-18]? **34** Jesus saith unto them, My meat [*cp.* Matt. 4 4; Luke 4 4] is to do the will of him that sent me [*cp.* 5 30; 6 38: *also* 7 17; 9 31], and to accomplish his work [*cp.* 5 36; 17 4: *also* 19 28, 30: *and* 10 25, 32, 37; 14 10: *and* 3 21; 6 28-29; 9 3-4: *and* 5 17; 7 21]. **35** Say not ye, There are yet four months, and *then* cometh the harvest? behold, I say unto you, Lift up your eyes, and look on the fields, that they are [1]white already unto harvest. **36** He that reapeth receiveth wages, and gathereth fruit unto life eternal; that he that soweth and he that reapeth may rejoice together. **37** For herein is the saying true, One soweth, and another reapeth. **38** I sent you to reap that whereon ye have not laboured: others have laboured, and ye are entered into their labour.

cp. 26 25, 49: *also* 23 7, 8.	*cp.* 9 5; 11 21; 14 45: *also* 10 51.	
cp. 15 16; 16 8-12.	*cp.* 4 13; 6 52; 7 18; *etc.*	*cp.* 2 50; 9 45; 18 34.
cp. 7 21; 12 50; 21 31: *also* 6 10; 26 39, 42.	*cp.* 3 35: *also* 14 36.	*cp.* 22 42. *cp.* 12 50; 18 31; 22 37: *also* 13 32: *and* 2 49.
cp. 9 37. *cp.* 10 10. *cp.* 13 3, 18, 37.	*cp.* 4 3, 14.	*cp.* 10 2. *cp.* 10 7. *cp.* 8 5.
cp. 9 38.		*cp.* 10 2.

[1] Or, *white unto harvest. Already he that reapeth &c.*

John 4 36: *cp.* Ps. 126 5-6; Is. 9 3.   John 4 37: *cp.* Job 31 8; Mic. 6 15.

§ 16. Many of the Samaritans believe

John 4 39-42

39 And from that city many of the Samaritans believed on him [*cp.* 2 11, 23; 7 31; 8 30; 10 42; 11 45; 12 11, 42: *also* 7 48] because of the word of the woman [*cp.* 17 20], who testified, He told me all things that *ever* I did [*cp.* 4 29: *also* 4 17-19]. **40** So when the Samaritans came unto him, they besought him to abide with them: and he abode there two days [*cp.* 4 43]. **41** And many more believed because of his word [*cp.* 5 24; 8 31, 37, 43, 51, 52; 12 48; 14 23, 24; 15 3, 20: *also* 5 38; 8 55; 14 24; 17 6, 14, 17,20]; **42** and they said to the woman, Now we believe, not because of thy speaking: for we have heard for ourselves, and know [*cp.* 3 2; 9 24, 29, 31; 16 30; 21 24] that this is indeed the Saviour of the world [*cp.* 3 16-17; 5 34: 10 9; 12 47: *also* 1 29].

cp. 18 6.	*cp.* 9 42.	*cp.* 17 16: *also* 9 56; 10 33.
cp. 13 19-23.	*cp.* 2 2; 4 14-20, 33; 16 20.	*cp.* 4 32: *also* 1 2; 5 1; 8 11; *etc.*
cp. 22 16. *cp.* 1 21: *also* 18 11: *and* 20 28.	*cp.* 12 14. *cp.* 10 45.	*cp.* 20 21. *cp.* 2 11: *also* 9 55; 19 10.

(iv) In Galilee II (§§ 17-18)

§ 17. The Galilæans receive Jesus

John **4** 43-45	Matt. 13 57; 4 12	Mark 6 4; 1 14	Luke 4 24; 4 14-15
43 And after the two days [*cp.* 4 40] he went forth from thence into Galilee. **44** For Jesus himself testified, that a prophet [*cp.* 4 19; 6 14; 7 40; 9 17] hath no honour in his own country [*cp.* 1 11; 5 43: *also* 3 11, 32]. **45** So when *cp.* 3 24. he came into Galilee, the Galilæans received him, having seen all the things that he did in Jerusalem at the feast [*cp.* 2 23]: for they also went unto the feast. *cp.* 18 20.	13 **57** But Jesus said unto them, A prophet [*cp.* 21 11, 46] is not without honour, save in his own country, and in his own house. 4 **12** Now when he heard that John was delivered up [*cp.* 11 2; 14 3], he withdrew into Galilee. *cp.* 4 24: *also* 9 26. *cp.* 4 23; 9 35.	6 **4** And Jesus said unto them, A prophet [*cp.* 6 15] is not without honour, save in his own country, and among his own kin, and in his own house. 1 **14** Now after that John was delivered up [*cp.* 6 17], Jesus came into Galilee. *cp.* 1 28. *cp.* 1 39.	4 **24** And he said, Verily I say unto you, No prophet [*cp.* 7 16, 39; 13 33; 24 19] is acceptable in his own country. 4 **14** And *cp.* 3 19-20. Jesus returned in the power of the Spirit into Galilee: and a fame went out concerning him through all the region round about [*cp.* 4 37; 5 15; 7 17]. **15** And he taught in their synagogues [*cp.* 4 44], being glorified of all.

§ 18. The Healing of a Nobleman's Son

John **4** 46-54	Matt. 8 5-13		Luke 7 1-10; 13 28-30
46 He came therefore again unto Cana [*cp.* 2 1: *also* 21 2] of Galilee, where he made the water wine [*cp.* 2 9]. And there was a certain ¹nobleman, whose son was sick at Capernaum. *verse* 47 **47** When he heard that Jesus was come out of Judæa into Galilee [*cp.* 4 3, 54: *also* 1 43; 6 1], he went unto him, and besought *him* that he would come down, and heal his son: for he was at the point of death. **48** Jesus therefore said unto him, Except ye see signs and wonders, ye will in no wise believe [*cp.*	**5** And when he was entered into Capernaum, there came unto him a centurion, beseeching him, *cp.* 24 24. *cp.* 12 38; 16 1.	*cp.* 13 22. *cp.* 8 11.	**7 1** After he had ended all his sayings in the ears of the people, he entered into Capernaum. **2** And a certain centurion's ¹servant, who was ²dear unto him, was sick and at the point of death [*cp.* 8 42]. **3** And when he heard concerning Jesus, he sent unto him elders of the Jews, asking him that he would come and save his ¹servant. *verse* 2 *cp.* 11 16.

2 18; 6 30].

49 The ¹nobleman saith unto him, ²Sir, come down ere my child die [*cp.* 11 21, 32].

6 and saying,

Lord, my ¹servant lieth in the house sick of the palsy [*cp.* 4 24; 9 2 *ff.*], grievously tormented [*cp.* 4 24].

cp. 2 3*ff.*

cp. 5 18*ff.*

4 And they, when they came to Jesus, besought him earnestly, saying, He is worthy that thou shouldest do this for him: 5 for he loveth our nation, and himself built us our synagogue.

6 And Jesus went with them. And when he was now not far from the house, the centurion sent friends to him, saying unto him, Lord, trouble [*cp.* 8 49] not thyself: for I am not ³worthy that thou shouldest come under my roof: 7 wherefore neither thought I myself worthy to come unto thee: but ⁴say the word [*cp.* 4 35, 39; 5 13, 24; 6 10; 7 14; 8 29, 32, 48, 54; 9 42; 13 12; 17 14; 18 42], and my ⁵servant shall be healed. 8 For I also am a man set under authority, having under myself soldiers: and I say to this one, Go, and he goeth; and to another, Come, and he cometh; and to my ¹servant, Do this, and he doeth it. 9 And when Jesus heard these things, he marvelled at him, and turned [*cp.* 7 44; 9 55; 10 23; 14 25; 22 61; 23 28] and said unto the multitude that followed him,   I say unto you, I have not found so great faith, no, not in Israel.

7 And he saith unto him, I will come and heal him. 8 And   the centurion answered and said,   Lord,   I am not ²worthy that thou shouldest come under my roof: but only say ³the word [*cp.* 8 16: *also* 8 3, 13, 32; 9 6, 22, 29; 12 13; 15 28; 17 7, 18], and my ¹servant shall be healed. 9 For I also am a man ⁴under authority, having under myself soldiers: and I say to this one, Go, and he goeth; and to another, Come, and he cometh; and to my ⁵servant, Do this, and he doeth it. 10 And when Jesus heard it,   he marvelled,

cp. 5 35.

cp. 1 25, 41; 2 11; 3 5; 5 8, 34, 41; 7 29, 34; 9 25; 10 52.

cp. 4 50; 5 8; 9 7; 11 43.

cp. 1 38.

cp. 9 22; 16 23.

and said to them   that followed,   Verily I say unto you, ⁶I have not found so great faith, no, not in Israel. 11 And I say unto you, that many shall come from the east and the west, and shall ⁷sit down [*cp.* 26 29]

cp. 5 30; 8 33.

cp. 14 25.

with Abraham, and Isaac, and Jacob,   in the kingdom of heaven [*cp.* 21 31, 41, 43; 22 7-10: *also* 10 18; 24 14; 26 13; 28 19]:

cp. 10 16; 11 52.

cp. 12 36: *also* 1 12; 11 52.

12 but the sons of the kingdom [*cp.* 13 38: *also* 5 9, 45] shall be cast forth into the outer darkness [*cp.* 22 13; 25 30]: there shall be the weeping and gnashing of teeth [*cp.* 13 42, 50; 22 13; 24 51; 25 30].

cp. 12 9; 13 10; 14 9; 16 15.

cp. 14 15; 22 16, 18, 30.

13 28 There shall be the weeping and gnashing of teeth, when ye shall see Abraham, and Isaac, and Jacob, and all the prophets, in the kingdom of God [*cp.* 14 21-24; 20 16: *also* 2 30-32; 3 6; 24 47],   and yourselves

cp. 6 35; 16 8; 20 36.

cast forth

without.

29 And they shall come from the east and west, and from the north and south, and shall ⁶sit down in the kingdom of God. 30 And behold, there are last which shall be first, and there are first which shall be last.

cp. 19 30; 20 16.

cp. 10 31.

50 Jesus saith unto him,   Go thy way; thy son liveth. The man believed   the word that Jesus spake unto him, and he went his way.

13 And Jesus said unto the centurion, Go thy way;   as thou hast believed, *so* be it done unto thee [*cp.* 9 29; 15 28].

cp. 7 29.

51 And as he was now going down, his ³servants met him, saying, that his son   lived.   *verse* 53
52 So he inquired of them the hour when he began to amend. They said therefore unto him, Yesterday at the seventh hour [*cp.* 1 39; 4 6; 19 14] the fever

cp. 7 30.

7 **10** And they that were sent, returning to the house,

And the ¹servant was healed   in that hour [*cp.* 9 22; 15 28; 17 18].

found
the ¹servant   whole.

left him. **53** So the father knew that *it was* at that hour in which Jesus said unto him, Thy son liveth: and himself believed, and his whole house. **54** This is again the second sign that Jesus did [*cp.* 2 11], having come out of Judæa into Galilee [*cp.* 4 3, 47: *also* 1 43; 6 1].	*cp.* 8 15. *verse* 13	*cp.* 1 31.	*cp.* 4 39.

[1] Or, *king's officer*   [2] Or, *Lord*
[3] Gr. *bondservants.*

[1] Or, *boy*   [2] Gr. *sufficient.*
[3] Gr. *with a word.*
[4] Some ancient authorities insert *set*: as in Luke 7 8.
[5] Gr. *bondservant.*
[6] Many ancient authorities read *With no man in Israel have I found so great faith.*
[7] Gr. *recline.*

[1] Gr. *bondservant.*
[2] Or, *precious to him* Or, *honourable with him*
[3] Gr. *sufficient.*
[4] Gr. *say with a word.*
[5] Or, *boy*   [6] Gr. *recline.*

(v) In Judæa II (§§ 19-23)

§ 19. **Jesus goes up to Jerusalem**

John 5 1

1 After these things there was [1]a feast of the Jews [*cp.* 6 4; 7 2: *also* 2 13; 11 55]; and Jesus went up to Jerusalem [*cp.* 2 13; 7 10: *also* 7 14].

[1] Many ancient authorities read *the feast.*

§ 20. **The Healing of a Sick Man at the Pool of Bethesda**

John 5 2-9a

John	Matt.	Mark	Luke
2 Now there is in Jerusalem by the sheep *gate* a pool, which is called in Hebrew [1]Bethesda, having five porches. **3** In these lay a multitude of them that were sick, blind, halt, withered[2]. **5** And a certain man was there, which had been thirty and eight years in his infirmity. **6** When Jesus saw him lying, and knew [*cp.* 6 15: *also* 1 48; 2 24, 25; 4 19, 29; 5 42; 6 61, 64; 11 14; 13 11, 18; 16 19, 30; 18 4; 21 17] that he had been now a long time *in that case*, he saith unto him, Wouldest thou be made whole? **7** The sick man answered him, [3]Sir, I have no man, when the water is troubled [*cp. verse* 4], to put me into the pool: but while I am coming, another steppeth down before me.	*cp.* 14 35. *cp.* 12 15; 16 8; 22 18; 26 10: *also* 9 4; 12 25.	*cp.* 6 55. *cp.* 8 17: *also* 2 8.	*cp.* 13 11. *cp.* 5 22; 6 8; 9 47; 11 17.
	Matt. 9 5-7	**Mark 2** 9-12	**Luke 5** 23-25
	5 For whether is easier, to say, Thy sins are forgiven; or to say, Arise, and walk? **6** But that ye may know that the Son of man hath [1]power [*cp.* 7 29; 21 23 *ff.*; 28 18] on earth to forgive sins (then saith he to the sick of the palsy),	**9** Whether is easier, to say to the sick of the palsy, Thy sins are forgiven; or to say, Arise, and take up thy bed, and walk? **10** But that ye may know that the Son of man hath [1]power [*cp.* 1 22, 27; 11 28 *ff.*] on earth to forgive sins (he saith to the sick of the palsy), **11** I say unto thee, Arise [*cp.* 3 3; 5 41; 10 49],	**23** Whether is easier, to say, Thy sins are forgiven thee; or to say, Arise and walk? **24** But that ye may know that the Son of man hath [1]power [*cp.* 4 32, 36; 20 2 *ff.*] on earth to forgive sins (he said unto him that was palsied), I say unto thee, Arise [*cp.* 6 8; 7 14; 8 54], and take up thy couch, and go
verse 8 *cp.* 5 27; 17 2. **8** Jesus saith unto him, Arise, take up thy bed, and walk.	Arise, and take up thy bed, and go	take up thy bed, and go	

John	Matt	Mark	Luke
9 And straightway the man was made whole, and took up his bed and walked. *cp.* 9 24.	unto thy house. 7 And he arose, and departed to his house. *cp.* 5 16; 9 8; 15 31.	unto thy house. 12 And he arose, and straightway took up the bed, and went forth before them all. *cp.* 2 12.	unto thy house. 25 And immediately he rose up before them, and took up that whereon he lay, and departed to his house, glorifying God [*cp.* 2 20; 5 26; 7 16; 13 13; 17 15, 18; 18 43; 23 47].
1 Some ancient authorities read *Bethsaida*, others, *Bethzatha*. 2 Many ancient authorities insert, wholly or in part, *waiting for the moving of the water: 4 for an angel of the Lord went down at certain seasons into the pool, and troubled the water: whosoever then first after the troubling of the water stepped in was made whole, with whatsoever disease he was holden.* 3 Or, *Lord*	1 Or, *authority*	1 Or, *authority*	1 Or, *authority*

John 5 2: *cp.* Neh. 3 1, 32; 12 39.

§ 21. Consequent Controversy about Observance of the Sabbath

[*Cp.* Matt. 12 9-14 || Mark 3 1-6 || Luke 6 6-11; Luke 13 10-17, 14 1-6; John 7 21-24, 9 1-34: *also* Matt. 12 1-8 || Mark 2 23-28 || Luke 6 1-5]

John 5 9b-18

John	Matt	Mark	Luke
Now it was the sabbath on that day [*cp.* 9 14]. 10 So the Jews said unto him that was cured, It is the sabbath, and it is not lawful for thee to take up thy bed. 11 But he answered them, He that made me whole [*cp. verse* 15 *and* 7 23], the same said unto me, Take up thy bed, and walk. 12 They asked him, Who is the man [*cp.* 12 34] that said unto thee, Take up *thy bed*, and walk? 13 But he that was healed wist not who it was: for Jesus had conveyed himself away [*cp.* 6 15], a multitude being in the place. 14 Afterward Jesus findeth him in the temple, and said unto him, Behold, thou art made whole: sin no more [*cp.* 8 11], lest a worse thing befall thee. 15 The man went away, and told the Jews that it was Jesus which had made him whole [*cp. verse* 11 *and* 7 23]. 16 And for this cause did the Jews persecute Jesus [*cp. verse* 18: *also* 15 20], because he did these things on the sabbath [*cp. verse* 18: *also* 7 23; 9 16]. 17 But Jesus answered them, My Father worketh even until now, and I work [*cp.* 7 21: *also* 4 34; 5 36; 17 4: *and* 10 25, 32, 37; 14 10: *and* 3 21; 6 28-29; 9 3-4]. 18 For this cause therefore the Jews sought the more to kill him [*cp.* 7 1, 19, 25; 8 37, 40: *also* 11 53: *and* 7 30, 32, 44; 10 39; 11 57: *and* 5 16], because he not only brake the sabbath [*cp. verse* 16: *also* 7 23; 9 16], but also called God his own Father, making himself [*cp.* 8 53; 10 33; 19 7, 12] equal with God [*cp.* 10 33, 36; 19 7].	*cp.* 12 2: *also* 12 10, 12. *cp.* 8 27; 21 10. *cp.* 12 14; 26 4; 27 1: *also* 21 46. *cp.* 26 63-64.	*cp.* 2 24: *also* 3 4. *cp.* 1 27; 2 7; 4 41. *cp.* 11 18: *also* 3 6; 14 1: *and* 12 12. *cp.* 14 61-62.	*cp.* 6 2: *also* 6 9; 14 3. *cp.* 4 36; 5 21; 7 49; 8 25; 9 9. *cp.* 19 47: *also* 22 2: *and* 20 19: *and* 6 11. *cp.* 22 70.

John 5 18: *cp* Wisd. 2 16-20.

§ 22. A Discourse of Jesus (i)

John 5 19-29

19 Jesus therefore answered and said unto them,
　Verily, verily, I say unto you, The Son can do nothing of himself [*cp.* 5 30; 8 28: *also* 5 31; 7 17, 28; 8 13, 14, 18, 42, 54; 10 18; 12 49; 14 10: *and* 16 13], but what he seeth the Father doing: for what things soever he doeth, these the Son also doeth in like manner [*cp.* 12 45; 14 9-11; 15 24: *also* 10 30; 17 11, 22]. 20 For

the Father loveth the Son [*cp.* 3 35; 10 17; 15 9-10; 17 23, 24, 26], and sheweth him all things that himself doeth: and greater works than these [*cp.* 1 50; 14 12] will he shew him, that ye may marvel. **21** For as the Father raiseth the dead and quickeneth them, even so the Son also quickeneth whom he will [*cp.* 6 39, 40, 44, 54; 11 25-26]. **22** For neither doth the Father judge any man, but he hath given all judgement unto the Son [*cp.* 5 27; 9 39: *also* 8 26: *and* 3 17; 12 47]; **23** that all may honour the Son, even as they honour the Father [*cp.* 8 49]. He that honoureth not the Son honoureth not the Father which sent him [*cp.* 12 44-45; 13 20: *also* 15 23]. **24** Verily, verily, I say unto you, He that heareth my word [*cp.* 8 43: *also* 4 41; 8 31, 37, 51, 52; 12 48; 14 23, 24; 15 3, 20: *and* 5 38; 8 55; 14 24; 17 6, 14, 17, 20], and believeth him that sent me, hath eternal life [*cp.* 3 15, 16, 36; 6 40, 47: *also* 11 25-26; 20 31: *and* 4 14, 36; *etc.*: Matt. 19 16, 29; 25 46: Mark 10 17, 30: Luke 10 25; 18 18, 30], and cometh not into judgement [*cp.* 3 18-19: *also* 12 31; 16 11: *and* 5 29; 12 48], but hath passed out of death into life [*cp.* 6 50, 51, 58; 8 51; 10 28; 11 25-26]. **25** Verily, verily, I say unto you, The hour cometh [*cp.* 4 21, 23; 5 28; 16 2, 25, 32], and now is [*cp.* 4 23; 16 32], when the dead shall hear the voice of the Son of God [*cp.* 5 28; 10 16, 27; 18 37: *also* 11 43-44]; and they that hear shall live. **26** For as the Father hath life in himself [*cp.* 6 57], even so gave he to the Son also to have life in himself [*cp.* 1 4; 6 57; 11 25; 14 6: *also* 3 15; *etc*: *and* 10 18]: **27** and he gave him authority [*cp.* 3 35; 13 3; 17 2: *also* 10 18] to execute judgement, because he is [1] the Son of man [*cp.* 5 22; 9 39: *also* 8 26: *and* 3 17; 12 47]. **28** Marvel not [*cp.* 3 7] at this: for the hour cometh [*cp. verse* 25], in which all that are in the tombs shall hear his voice [*cp. verse* 25], **29** and shall come forth [*cp.* 11 43-44]; they that have done good, unto the resurrection of life; and they that have [2] done ill, unto the resurrection of judgement [*cp.* 12 48].

cp. 3 17; 17 5.	*cp.* 1 11; 9 7; 12 6.		*cp.* 3 22; 20 13.
cp. 16 27; 25 31-46.			
cp. 10 40.	*cp.* 9 37.		*cp.* 9 48; 10 16.
cp. 13 19-23.	*cp.* 2 2; 4 14-20, 33; 16 20.		*cp.* 4 32: *also* 1 2; 8 12-15: *and* 5 1; 8 11, 21; 11 28.
cp. 16 16; 26 63.			
cp. 9 6, 8; 11 27; 28 18.	*cp.* 2 10.		*cp.* 5 24; 10 22.
cp. 16 27; 25 31-46.			
cp. 25 46.			

[1] Or, *a son of man*   [2] Or, *practised*

John 5 29: *cp.* Is. 26 19; Dan. 12 2.

§ 23. **A Discourse of Jesus** (ii)

John 5 30-47

30 I can of myself do nothing [*cp.* 5 19; 8 28: *also* 5 31; 7 17, 28; 8 13, 14, 18, 42, 54; 10 18; 12 49; 14 10: *and* 16 13]: as I hear, I judge: and my judgement is righteous [*cp.* 8 16: *also* 7 24]; because I seek not mine own will [*cp.* 6 38], but the will of him that sent me [*cp.* 4 34; 6 38: *also* 7 17; 9 31]. **31** If I bear witness of myself [*cp.* 8 13, 14, 18: *also* 5 19, 30; 7 17; *etc.*], my witness is not true [*cp.* 8 13, 14: *also* 19 35; 21 24]. **32** It is another that beareth witness of me [*cp. verse* 37 *and* 8 18]; and I know that the witness which he witnesseth of me is true. **33** Ye have sent unto John [*cp.* 1 19, 24], and he hath borne witness unto the truth [*cp.* 1 7, 8, 15, 19-36; 3 26-36; 10 41: *also* 18 37]. **34** But the witness which I receive is not from man [*cp. verse* 41]: howbeit I say these things, that ye may be saved [*cp.* 3 16-17; 10 9; 12 47: *also* 4 42]. **35** He was the lamp [*cp.* 1 8] that burneth and shineth: and ye were willing to rejoice for a season in his light. **36** But the witness which I have is greater than *that of* John: for the works which the Father hath given me to accomplish [*cp.* 4 34; 17 4: *also* 19 28, 30: *and* 10 25, 32, 37; 14 10: *and* 3 21; 6 28-29; 9 3-4: *and* 5 17; 7 21], the very works that I do, bear witness of me [*cp.* 10 25: *also* 3 2; 9 16, 33; 10 21], that the Father hath sent me. **37** And the Father which sent me, he hath borne witness of me [*cp.* 8 18: *also* 5 32]. Ye have neither heard his voice at any time, nor seen his form [*cp.* 1 18; 6 46: *also* 14 7-9]. **38** And ye have not his word [*cp.* 8 55; 14 24; 17 6, 14, 17, 20: *also* 5 24; 8 31; *etc.*] abiding in you: for whom he sent [*cp.* 3 34; 6 29; 10 36; 17 3: *also* 3 17; *etc.*], him ye believe not. **39** [1] Ye search the

cp. 7 21; 12 50; 21 31: *also* 6 10; 26 39, 42.	*cp.* 3 35: *also* 14 36.	*cp.* 22 42.
cp. 1 21: *also* 18 11: *and* 20 28.	*cp.* 10 45.	*cp.* 2 11: *also* 9 55; 19 10.
		cp. 12 50; 18 31; 22 37: *also* 13 32: *and* 2 49 *mg.*
		cp. 5 1; 8 11, 21; 11 28.

scriptures, because ye think that in them ye have eternal life; and these are they which bear witness [cp. 13 18; 15 25; 17 12] of me; **40** and ye will not come to me [cp. 6 35, 37, 44, 45, 65; 7 37], that ye may have life [cp. 1 4; 10 10; etc.]. **41** I receive not glory from men [cp. verse 34]. **42** But I know you [cp. 1 48; 2 24, 25; 5 6; 6 15, 61, 64; 13 11, 18; 16 19, 30; 18 4; 21 17: also 4 19, 29; 11 14], that ye have not the love of God [cp. Luke 11 42: also Matt. 22 37; Mark 12 30, 33; Luke 10 27] in yourselves. **43** I am come in my Father's name[cp. 10 25: also 12 13: and 17 12], and ye receive me not [cp. 1 11: also 3 11, 32: and 4 44]: if another shall come in his own name, him ye will receive. **44** How can ye believe [cp. 12 39], which receive glory one of another, and the glory that *cometh* from 2the only [cp. 17 3] God ye seek not [cp. 12 43: also 1 14; 6 46; 7 29; 9 16, 33; 16 27, 28; 17 8]? **45** Think not that I will accuse you to the Father: there is one that accuseth you, *even* Moses, on whom ye have set your hope [cp. 9 28-29]. **46** For if ye believed Moses, ye would believe me; for he wrote of me [cp. 1 45]. **47** But if ye believe not his writings, how shall ye believe my words?

cp. 21 42; etc. cp. 11 28.	cp. 9 12; etc.	cp. 18 31; etc.
cp. 9 4; 12 15, 25; 16 8; 22 18; 26 10.	cp. 2 8; 8 17.	cp. 5 22; 6 8; 9 47; 11 17.
cp. 21 9; 23 39.	cp. 11 9.	cp. 13 35; 19 38.
cp. 24 4-5, 24.	cp. 13 5-6, 22.	cp. 21 8.
		cp. 24 27, 44. cp. 16 31.

1 Or, *Search the scriptures*   2 Some ancient authorities read *the only* one.

John 5 35: *cp.* Ecclus. 48 1.   John 5 37: *cp.* Deut. 4 12, 15.

(vi) In Galilee III (§§ 24-31)

§ 24. The Feeding of the Five Thousand

[*Cp.* Matt. 15 32-39: Mark 8 1-10]

John 6 1-14	Matt. 14 13-21	Mark 6 30-44	Luke 9 10-17
		30 And the apostles gather themselves together unto Jesus; and they told him all things, whatsoever they had done, and whatsoever they had taught.	**10** And the apostles, when they were returned, declared unto him what things they had done.
1 After these things Jesus	**13** Now when Jesus		
	heard *it*,	**31** And he saith unto them, Come ye yourselves apart [cp. 4 10, 34; 9 2, 28; 13 3] into a desert place, and rest a while. For there were many coming and going, and they had no leisure so much as to eat [cp. 3 20].	And he took them, cp. 10 23.
	cp. 17 1, 19; 20 17; 24 3.		
went away	he withdrew [cp. 8 18] from thence in a boat, to a desert place apart [*see above*]:	**32** And they went away [cp. 1 35, 45] in the boat to a desert place apart [*see above*]. cp. 6 45; 8 22.	and withdrew [cp. 4 42; 5 16] apart [*see above*] to a city called Bethsaida.
cp. 1 44; 12 21. to the other side of the sea [cp. 6 16, etc.] of Galilee, which is *the sea* of Tiberias [cp. 21 1]. **2** And a great multitude	cp. 4 18; 15 29: also 8 24; etc.	cp. 1 16; 7 31: also 2 13; etc.	cp. 5 1, 2; 8 22, 23, 33.
followed him,	and when the multitudes heard there-of, they followed him 1on foot from the cities.	**33** And *the people* saw them going, and many knew *them*, and they ran there together 1on foot from all the cities, and outwent them.	**11** But the multitudes perceiving it followed him:
	14 And he came forth, and saw a great multitude, and he had compassion on them [cp. 9 36; 15 32: also 20 34],	**34** And he came forth and saw a great multitude, and he had compassion on them [cp. 8 2: also 1 41], because	and he welcomed them [cp. 7 13: and 10 33; 15 20],

John	Matthew	Mark	Luke
cp. 10 11-16.	cp. 9 36: also 10 6; 15 24; 26 31.	they were as sheep not having a shepherd [cp. 14 27]: and he began to teach them many things.	and spake to them of the kingdom of God, and them that had need of healing he healed [cp. 6 19; 9 2, 42; 14 4; 22 51].
	and healed		
because they beheld [cp. 2 23; 7 3; 11 45] the signs [cp. 2 11, 23; 3 2; 4 54; 6 14, 26; 7 31; 9 16; 11 47; 12 18, 37; 20 30] which he did on them that were sick. **3** And Jesus went up into the mountain [cp. 6 15], and there he sat with his disciples. **4** Now the passover, the feast of the Jews [cp. 5 1; 7 2: also 2 13; 11 55], was at hand. **5** Jesus therefore lifting up his eyes, and seeing that a great multitude cometh unto him, saith unto Philip [cp. 1 43-48; 12 21-22; 14 8-9],	their sick. cp. 5 1; 14 23; 15 29; 17 1; 28 16. cp. 15 29: also 5 1; 24 3.	cp. 3 13; 6 46; 9 2. cp. 13 3.	cp. 6 12; 9 28.
	cp. 3 7; 5 1; 8 18; 9 36.		cp. 6 20.
	cp. 10 3.	cp. 3 18.	cp. 6 14.
	15 And when even was come, the disciples came to him, saying, The place is desert, and the time is already past; send the multitudes away [cp. 15 23], that they may go into the villages,	**35** And when the day was now far spent, his disciples came unto him, and said, The place is desert, and the day is now far spent: **36** send them away, that they may go into the country and villages round about, and buy themselves somewhat to eat.	**12** And the day began to wear away; and the twelve came, and said unto him, Send the multitude away, that they may go into the villages and country round about, and lodge, and get victuals:
Whence are we to buy ¹bread, that these may eat? **6** And this he said to prove him: for he himself knew what he would do.	and buy themselves food.		
	16 But Jesus said unto them, They have no need to go away; give ye them to eat. **17** And they say unto him,	**37** But he answered and said unto them, Give ye them to eat. And they say unto him, Shall we go and buy two hundred ²pennyworth of bread,	for we are here in a desert place. **13** But he said unto them, Give ye them to eat. And they said,
7 Philip answered him, Two hundred ²pennyworth of ¹bread is not sufficient [cp. 14 8] for them, that every one may take a little.		and give them to eat? **38** And he saith unto them, How many loaves have ye [cp. 8 5]? go and see. And when they knew,	
	cp. 15 34.		
8 One of his disciples, Andrew [cp. 1 40, 44; 12 22] Simon Peter's [cp. 1 40; 6 68; etc.] brother, saith unto him, **9** There is a lad here, which hath	cp. 14 18; 10 2. cp. 16 16.	cp. 1 16, 29; 3 18; 13 3. they say,	cp. 6 14. cp. 5 8.
five barley loaves, and two fishes [cp. verse 11; and 21 9, 10, 13]: but what are these among so many?	We have here but five loaves, and two fishes.	Five, and two fishes.	We have no more than five loaves and two fishes; except we should go and buy food for all this people.

Column 1 (John)

verse 10

10 Jesus said,

Make the people sit down.

Now there was much grass in the place. So the men sat down, in number about five thousand. 11 Jesus therefore took the loaves;
and
cp. 11 41; 17 1.

having given thanks [*cp.* 6 23],
he distributed

to them that were set down; likewise [*cp.* 21 13] also of the fishes [*cp. verse* 9: *and* 21 9, 10, 13] as much as they would. 12 And when they were filled, he saith unto his disciples, Gather up the broken pieces which remain over, that nothing be lost. 13 So they gathered them up, and filled twelve baskets with broken pieces from the five barley loaves, which remained over unto them that had eaten.

verse 10

14 When therefore the people saw the ³sign [*cp.* 6 2] which he did, they said, This is [*cp.* 1 34; 4 29, 42; 7 41] of a truth the prophet [*cp.* 7 40: *also* 1 21, 25: *and* 4 19, 44; 9 17] that cometh [*cp.* 1 15, 27; 3 31; 11 27; 12 13: *also* 1 30] into the world [*cp.* 11 27: *also* 1 9; 3 19; 9 39; 10 36; 12 46; 16 28; 17 18; 18 37].

¹ Gr. *loaves.*
² See marginal note on Matt. 18 28.
³ Some ancient authorities read *signs.*

Column 2 (Matt.)

verse 21

18 And he said,
Bring them hither to me [*cp.* 17 17]. 19 And he commanded the multitudes to ²sit down

on the grass;

verse 21

and he took the five loaves, and the two fishes, and looking up to heaven, he blessed [*cp.* 26 26: *also* 15 36; 26 27], and brake
and gave the loaves to the disciples, and the disciples to the multitudes.

20 And they did all eat, and were filled:

and they took up

that which remained over of the broken pieces, twelve baskets full. 21 And they that did eat were about five thousand men, beside women and children [*cp.* 15 38].

cp. 12 23; 14 2; 21 11; 27 54: *also* 8 27; 21 10.

cp. 13 57; 21 11, 46.

cp. 3 11; 11 3; 21 9; 23 39.

¹ Or, *by land*
² Gr. *recline.*

Column 3 (Mark)

verse 44

39 And he commanded them that all should ³sit down by companies

upon the green grass. 40 And they

sat down in ranks, by hundreds, and by fifties.

verse 44

41 And he took the five loaves and the two fishes, and looking up to heaven [*cp.* 7 34], he blessed [*cp.* 8 7; 14 22: *also* 8 6; 14 23],
and brake the loaves; and he gave to the disciples to set before them;

and the two fishes divided he among them all. 42 And they did all eat, and were filled.

43 And they took up

broken pieces, twelve basketfuls, and also of the fishes. 44 And they that ate the loaves were five thousand men.

cp. 6 15; 15 39: *also* 2 7; 4 41: *and* 1 27.

cp. 6 4, 15.

cp. 11 9: *also* 1 7.

¹ Or, *by land*
² See marginal note on Matt. 18 28.
³ Gr. *recline.*

Column 4 (Luke)

14 For they were about five thousand men. And he said unto his disciples,

Make them ¹sit down in companies, about fifty each.

15 And they did so, and made them all ¹sit down.

verse 14

16 And he took the five loaves and the two fishes, and looking up to heaven, he blessed [*cp.* 24 30: *also* 22 17, 19] them, and brake; and gave to the disciples to set before the multitude.

17 And they did eat, and were all filled:

and there was taken up

that which remained over to them of broken pieces, twelve baskets.

verse 14

cp. 23 47: *also* 5 21; 7 49; 8 25; 9 9: *and* 4 36.

cp. 4 24; 7 16, 39; 13 33; 24 19.

cp. 7 19, 20; 13 35; 19 38: *also* 3 16.

¹ Gr. *recline.*

John 6 14: *cp.* Deut. 18 15.

§ 25. **Jesus walks on the Water**

[*Cp*. Matt. 8 23-27: Mark 4 35-41: Luke 8 22-25]

John 6 15-21	Matt. 14 22-33	Mark 6 45-52	
15 Jesus therefore perceiving [*cp*. 5 6] that they were about to come and take him by force, to make him king [*cp*. 12 12-15],	*cp*. 12 15; 16 8; 22 18; 26 10.	*cp*. 8 17.	
	cp. 21 9. **22** And straightway he constrained the disciples to enter into the boat, and to go before him unto the other side [*cp*. 8 18],	*cp*. 11 9-10. **45** And straightway he constrained his disciples to enter into the boat, and to go before *him* unto the other side [*cp*. 4 35] to Bethsaida [*cp*. 8 22], while he himself sendeth	*cp*. 19 37-38. *cp*. 8 22. *cp*. 9 10.
with-drew again into the mountain [*cp*. 6 3: *also* 5 13] himself alone.	till he should send the multitudes away. **23** And after he had sent the multitudes away, he went up into the mountain [*cp*. 5 1; 15 29; 17 1; 28 16] apart to pray [*cp*. 19 13; 26 36, 39, 42, 44: *and* 11 25]:	the multitude away. **46** And after he had taken leave of them, he departed into the mountain [*cp*. 3 13; 9 2]	*cp*. 6 12; 9 28: *also* 3 21; 5 16; 9 18, 29; 11 1; 22 41, 44: *and* 10 21.
cp. 11 41; 12 27-28; 17 1 *ff*. **16** And when evening came, his disciples went down unto the sea; **17** and they entered into a boat, and were going over the sea into Capernaum.	and when even was come,	to pray [*cp*. 1 35; 14 32, 35, 39]. **47** And when even was come,	
And it was now dark, and Jesus had not yet come to them. **18** And the sea was rising by reason of a great wind that blew. **19** When therefore they had rowed about five and twenty or thirty furlongs,	he was there alone. **24** But the boat [1]was now in the midst of the sea, dis-tressed by the waves; for the wind was contrary. **25** And	the boat was in the midst of the sea, and he alone on the land. **48** And seeing them distressed in rowing, for the wind was contrary unto them,	
they behold Jesus walking on the sea, and drawing nigh unto the boat:	in the fourth watch of the night he came unto them, walking upon the sea. **26** And when the disciples saw him walking on the sea,	about the fourth watch of the night he cometh unto them, walking on the sea; and he would have passed by them: **49** but they, when they saw him walking on the sea,	
and they were afraid. **20** But he saith unto them, *cp*. 16 33. It is I; be not afraid. *cp*. 13 36, 37; 21 21: *also* 6 68.	they were troubled, saying, It is an apparition; and they cried out for fear. **27** But straightway Jesus spake unto them, saying, Be of good cheer [*cp*. 9 2, 22]; it is I; be not afraid [*cp*. 17 7; 28 10]. **28** And Peter [*cp*. 15 15; 16 22; 17 4; 18 21; 19 27; 26 33: *also* 16 16; 17 24] answered him and said, Lord, if it be thou, bid me come unto thee upon the waters. **29** And he said, Come. And Peter went down from the boat, and walked upon the waters, [2]to come to Jesus. **30** But when he saw the wind[3], he was afraid; and beginning to sink, he cried out, saying, Lord, save me [*cp*. 8 25]. **31** And immediately Jesus stretched forth his hand, and	supposed that it was an apparition, and cried out: **50** for they all saw him, and were troubled. But he straightway spake with them, and saith unto them, Be of good cheer [*cp*. 10 49]: it is I; be not afraid. *cp*. 8 32; 9 5; 10 28; 11 21; 14 29: *also* 8 29.	*cp*. 24 37. *cp*. 8 45; 9 33; 12 41; 18 28: *also* 5 8; 9 20.
cp. 21 7.			

cp. 3 12; 6 64; 14 10; 20 27.

21 They were willing therefor to receive him into the boat: and straightway the boat was at the land whither they were going.

---

took hold of him, and saith unto him, O thou of little faith [*cp.* 6 30; 8 26; 16 8: *also* 17 20], wherefore didst thou doubt [*cp.* 21 21; 28 17]? **32** And when they were gone up into the boat, the wind ceased.

cp. 14 34.

33 And they that were in the boat worshipped him, saying, Of a truth thou art the Son of God.

cp. 4 40; 11 22; 16 14.

cp. 11 23; 16 14.   **51** And he went up unto them into the boat; and the wind ceased [*cp.* 4 39]:

cp. 6 53.

and they were sore amazed in themselves; **52** for they understood not concerning the loaves, but their heart was hardened.

cp. 12 28: also 8 25; 17 5, 6; 22 32; 24 25, 38.

¹ Some ancient authorities read *was many furlongs distant from the land*.
² Some ancient authorities read *and came*.
³ Many ancient authorities add *strong*.

§ 26. Jesus the Bread of Life (i)

John 6 22-40

22 On the morrow [*cp.* 1 29, 35, 43; 12 12] the multitude which stood on the other side of the sea saw that there was none other ¹boat [*cp.* 21 8] there, save one, and that Jesus entered not with his disciples into the boat, but that his disciples went away alone **23** (howbeit there came ²boats from Tiberias nigh unto the place where they ate the bread after the Lord [*cp.* 4 1; 11 2; 20 2, 18, 20, 25; 21 7, 12] had given thanks [*cp.* 6 11]): **24** when the multitude therefore saw that Jesus was not there, neither his disciples, they themselves got into the ²boats, and came to Capernaum, seeking Jesus. **25** And when they found him on the other side of the sea, they said unto him, Rabbi [*cp.* 1 38, 49; 3 2; 4 31; 9 2; 11 8: *also* 20 16: *and* 3 26], when camest thou hither? **26** Jesus answered them and said, Verily, verily I say unto you, Ye seek me, not because ye saw signs [*cp.* 2 11, 23; 3 2; 4 54; 6 2, 14; *etc.*], but because ye ate of the loaves, and were filled. **27** Work not for the meat which perisheth, but for the meat which abideth unto eternal life, which the Son of man shall give unto you [*cp.* 4 14; 6 51]: for him the Father, *even* God, hath sealed [*cp.* 3 33]. **28** They said therefore unto him, What must we do, that we may work the works of God [*cp.* 3 21; 9 3-4: *also* 10 25, 32, 37; 14 10: *and* 4 34; 5 36; 17 4: *and* 5 17; 7 21]? **29** Jesus answered and said unto them, This is the work of God, that ye believe on him whom ³he hath sent [*cp.* 3 34; 5 38; 10 36; 17 3: *also* 3 17; *etc.*]. **30** They said therefore unto him, What then doest thou for a sign [*cp.* 2 18: *also* 4 48], that we may see, and believe thee? what workest thou? **31** Our fathers ate the manna in the wilderness [*cp.* 6 49]; as it is written, He gave them bread out of heaven to eat. **32** Jesus therefore said unto them, Verily, verily, I say unto you, It was not Moses that gave you the bread out of heaven; but my Father giveth you the true [*cp.* 6 55: *also* 1 9; 15 1: *and* 17 3] bread out of heaven. **33** For the bread of God is that which cometh down out of heaven [*cp. verse* 38 *below*], and giveth life unto the world. **34** They said therefore unto him, Lord, evermore give us [*cp.* 4 15] this bread. **35** Jesus said unto them, I am the bread of life [*cp.* 6 48: *also* 6 51: *and* 6 41, 51, 58]: he that cometh to me [*cp.* 5 40; 6 37, 44, 45, 65; 7 37] shall not hunger, and he that believeth on me shall never thirst [*cp.* 4 14: *also* 7 37]. **36** But I said unto you, that ye have seen me, and yet believe not [*cp.* 10 25; 12 37: *also* 1 11; 3 11, 32; 5 43]. **37** All that which the Father giveth me [*cp.* 10 29; 17 2, 6, 9, 11, 12, 24; 18 9] shall come unto

Cross-references:

cp. 27 62. | cp. 11 12.
| cp. 3 9.
| cp. 16 19, 20. | cp. 7 13, 19; 10 1, 39, 41; *etc.*

cp. 26 25, 49: *also* 23 7, 8. | cp. 9 5; 11 21; 14 45: *also* 10 51.

cp. 19 16. | cp. 10 17. | cp. 3 10, 12, 14; 10 25; 18 18.

cp. 12 38; 16 1. | cp. 8 11. | cp. 11 16.

cp. 11 28.

me [cp. verse 35 above]; and him that cometh to me I will in no wise cast out. **38** For I am come down from heaven [cp. 3 13, 31; 6 42; 8 23: also 6 32-33, 41, 50, 58], not to do mine own will [cp. 5 30], but the will of him that sent me [cp. 4 34; 5 30: also 7 17; 9 31]. **39** And this is the will of him that sent me, that of all that which he hath given me [cp. verse 37 above] I should lose nothing [cp. 17 12; 18 9: also 3 16; 10 28], but should raise it up at the last day [cp. 6 40, 44, 54: also 11 24: and 5 21; 11 25: and 12 48]. **40** For this is the will of my Father, that every one that beholdeth the Son [cp. 6 62: also 12 45; 14 19; 16 10, 16, 17, 19: and 14 17], and believeth on him, should have eternal life [cp. 3 15, 16, 36; 5 24; 6 47: also 11 25-26; 20 31: and 4 14, 36; etc.]; and [4]I will raise him up at the last day [cp. verse 39 above].	cp. 11 28. cp. 7 21; 12 50; 21 31: also 6 10; 26 39, 42. cp. 18 14. cp. 19 16, 29; 25 46.	cp. 3 35: also 14 36. cp. 10 17, 30.	cp. 22 42. cp. 15 6. cp. 10 25; 18 18, 30.

[1] Gr. *little boat*.   [2] Gr. *little boats*.   [3] Or, *he sent*   [4] Or, *that I should raise him up*

John 6 27: cp. Is. 55 2: and Ezek. 9 4.   John 6 31: Neh. 9 15; Ps. 78 24; Ps. 105 40: cp. Exod. 16 15: also Num. 11 7-9.

§ 27. **Jesus the Bread of Life** (ii)

John 6 41-51	Matt. 13 53-57	Mark 6 1-3	Luke 4 16, 21-22, 28
41 The Jews therefore murmured [cp. 6 43, 61; 7 12, 32] concerning him,			
	53 And it came to pass, when Jesus had finished these parables, he departed thence. **54** And coming into his own country [cp. 9 1: also 4 13]	**1** And he went out from thence; and he cometh into his own country; and his disciples follow him. **2** And when the sabbath was come, he began to teach in the synagogue:	**16** And he came to Nazareth, where he had been brought up: and he entered, as his custom was, into the synagogue on the sabbath day, and stood up to read. . . . **21** And he began to say unto them, To-day hath this scripture been fulfilled in your ears. **22** And all bare him witness, and
cp. 1 11.			
cp. 6 59: also 18 20.	he taught them in their synagogue,		
	cp. 4 17.	cp. 1 15.	
cp. 7 15, 21, 46.	insomuch that they were astonished [cp. 7 28; 19 25; 22 22, 33: also 8 27; 9 33; 12 23; 15 31; 21 20; 27 14],	[1]many hearing him were astonished [cp. 1 22, 27; 10 24, 26; 11 18; 12 17: also 2 12; 5 20, 42; 6 51; 7 37; 10 32; 15 5; 16 8],	wondered [cp. 2 47, 48; 4 32, 36; 20 26: also 5 9, 26; 8 25, 56; 9 43; 11 14; 24 12, 41] at the words of grace which proceeded out of his mouth:
because he said, I am the bread which came down out of heaven [cp. verses 50, 51, and 58: also 6 35, 48, 51: and 3 13, 31; 6 38, 42; 8 23]. **42** And they said,	and said, Whence hath this man [cp. verse 56] this wisdom,	saying, Whence hath this man these things? and, What is the wisdom that is given unto this man, and *what mean* such [2]mighty works wrought by his hands [cp. 1 31, 41; 5 23, 41; 6 5; 7 33; 8 22, 23, 25; 9 27: and 10 13, 16]?	and they said,
cp. 9 6.	and these [1]mighty works? cp. 8 3, 15; 9 18, 25, 29; 20 34: also 14 31; 17 7; 19 13, 15.		cp. 4 40; 5 13; 7 14; 8 54; 13 13; 14 4; 22 51: also 18 15.
Is not this Jesus, the son of Joseph [cp. 1 45], whose father and mother we know [cp. 7 27, 28: also 8 14, 19; 9 29, 30]?	**55** Is not this the carpenter's son? is not his mother called	**3** Is not this the carpenter, the son of	Is not this Joseph's son [cp. 3 23]?

	Matt.	Mark	Luke
	Mary? and his brethren, James, and Joseph, and Simon, and Judas? **56** And his sisters, are they not all with us? Whence then hath this man all these things?	Mary, and brother of James, and Joses, and Judas, and Simon? and are not his sisters here with us? *verse 2*	
how doth he now say [*cp.* 3 4, 9; 6 52; 8 33; 12 34: *also* 4 9; 6 60; 7 15], I am come down out of heaven [*cp.* 6 38]? *cp.* 6 61: *also* 16 1.	**57** And they were ²offended [*cp.* 11 6; 15 12; 26 31, 33: *also* 13 21; 24 10] in him.	And they were ³offended [*cp.* 14 27, 29: *also* 4 17] in him.	**28** And they were *cp.* 7 23. all filled with wrath in the syna- gogue, as they heard these things. . . .
	¹ Gr. *powers.* ² Gr. *caused to stumble.*	¹ Some ancient authorities in- sert *the.* ² Gr. *powers.* ³ Gr. *caused to stumble.*	

43 Jesus answered and said unto them, Murmur [*cp. verse* 41 *above*] not among yourselves. **44** No man can come to me [*cp.* 5 40; 6 35, 37, 45, 65; 7 37], except the Father which sent me draw him [*cp.* 6 65: *also* 12 32]: and I will raise him up in the last day [*cp.* 6 39, 40, 54: *also* 11 24: *and* 5 21; 11 25: *and* 12 48]. **45** It is written in the prophets, And they shall all be taught of God. Every one that hath heard from the Father, and hath learned, cometh unto me [*cp. verse* 44 *above*]. **46** Not that any man hath seen the Father [*cp.* 1 18; 5 37: *also* 14 7-9], save he which is from God [*cp.* 1 14; 5 44; 7 29; 9 16, 33; 16 27, 28; 17 8], he hath seen the Father [*cp.* 1 18; 7 29; 8 19; 10 15; 17 25-26]. **47** Verily, verily, I say unto you, He that believth hath eternal life [*cp.* 3 15, 16, 36; 5 24; 6 40: *also* 11 25-26; 20 31: *and* 4 14, 36; *etc.*]. **48** I am the bread of life [*cp.* 6 35: *also* 6 51: *and* 6 41, 51, 58]. **49** Your fathers did eat the manna in the wilderness [*cp.* 6 31], and they died. **50** This is the bread which cometh down out of heaven [*cp.* 6 58], that a man may eat thereof, and not die [*cp.* 6 51, 58: *also* 5 24; 8 51; 10 28; 11 25-26]. **51** I am the living bread [*cp.* 6 35, 48] which came down out of heaven [*cp.* 6 41, 50, 58: *also* 3 13, 31; 6 38, 42; 8 23]: if any man eat of this bread, he shall live for ever [*cp. verse* 50 *above*]: yea and the bread which I will give [*cp.* 4 14; 6 27] is my flesh, for the life of the world.

	Matt.	Mark	Luke
(v. 44)	*cp.* 11 28.		
(v. 46)	*cp.* 11 28.		
(v. 47)	*cp.* 11 27. *cp.* 19 16, 29; 25 46.	*cp.* 10 17, 30.	*cp.* 10 22. *cp.* 10 25; 18 18, 30.

John 6 45: Is. 54 13.

§ 28. **Jesus the Bread of Life** (iii)

John 6 52-59

52 The Jews therefore strove one with another [*cp.* 7 12, 40-43; 9 16; 10 19-21], saying, How can this man give us his flesh [*cp.* 1 14] to eat [*cp.* 3 4, 9; 6 42; 8 33; 12 34: *also* 4 9; 6 60; 7 15]? **53** Jesus therefore said unto them, Verily, verily, I say unto you, Except ye [*cp.* 3 3, 5; 8 24: *also* 13 8] eat the flesh of the Son of man and drink his blood, ye have not life in yourselves. **54** He that eateth my flesh and drinketh my blood hath eternal life; and I will raise him up at the last day [*cp.* 6 39, 40, 44: *also* 11 24: *and* 5 21; 11 25: *and* 12 48]. **55** For my flesh is ¹meat indeed [*cp.* 6 32: *also* 1 9; 15 1: *and* 17 3], and my blood is ²drink indeed. **56** He that eateth my flesh and drinketh my blood abideth in me [*cp.* 15 4, 5, 7: *also* 8 31: *and* 14 20; 17 21, 23, 26], and I in him. **57** As the living Father [*cp.* 5 26] sent me, and I live because of the Father [*cp.* 5 26]; so he that eateth me, he also shall live be- cause of me [*cp.* 1 4; 11 25; 14 6: *also* 3 15; *etc.*]. **58** This is the bread which came down out of heaven [*cp.* 6 50]: not as the

	Matt.	Mark	Luke
(v. 57)	*cp.* 16 16; 26 63.		

fathers did eat, and died: he that eateth this bread shall live for ever [*cp.* 6 50, 51: *also* 5 24; 8 51; 10 28; 11 25-26]. **59** These things said he in [3]the synagogue [*cp.* 18 20], as he taught in Capernaum.   *cp.* 13 54.   *cp.* 6 2.   *cp.* 4 16.

[1] Gr. *true meat.*   [2] Gr. *true drink.*   [3] Or, *a synagogue*

§ 29. Many Disciples hesitate

John 6 60-65			
60 Many therefore of his disciples, when they heard *this*, said, This is a hard saying; who can [*cp.* 4 9; 7 15: *also* 3 4, 9; 6 42, 52; 8 33; 12 34] hear [1]it [*cp.* 16 12, 25]? **61** But Jesus knowing in himself [*cp.* 1 48; 2 24, 25; 5 6, 42; 6 64; 13 11, 18; 16 19, 30; 18 4; 21 17: *also* 4 19, 29; 11 14] that his disciples murmured [*cp.* 6 41, 43; 7 12, 32] at this, said unto them, Doth this cause you to stumble [*cp.* 16 1]? **62** *What* then if ye should behold the Son of man [*cp.* 6 40: *also* 12 45; 14 19; 16 10, 16, 17, 19: *and* 14 17] ascending where he was before [*cp.* 3 13: *also* 20 17: *and* 1 51]? **63** It is the spirit that quickeneth; the flesh profiteth nothing [*cp.* 3 6]: the words that I have spoken unto you are spirit, and are life [*cp.* 6 68; 12 50: *also* 3 34; 8 26, 47; 12 47-50; 14 10; 17 8, 14]. **64** But there are some of you that believe not. For Jesus knew [*cp. verse* 61] from the beginning [*cp.* 15 27; 16 4: *also* 8 44] who they were that believed not [*cp.* 3 12; 14 10; 20 27], and who it was that should betray him [*cp.* 13 11, 21: *also* 6 71; 12 4; 18 2, 5: *and* 13 2]. **65** And he said, For this cause have I said unto you [*cp.* 6 44], that no man can come unto me [*cp.* 5 40; 6 35, 37, 44, 45; 7 37], except it be given unto him [*cp.* 3 27; 19 11] of the Father.	*cp.* 11 15; 13 9, 43: *also* 19 11, 12: *and* 13 34. *cp.* 9 4; 12 25; 16 8. *cp.* 11 6; 13 57; 15 12; 26 31, 33: *also* 13 21; 24 10. *cp.* 26 64. *cp.* 8 26; 14 31; 16 8; 17 20; 21 21; 28 17. *cp.* 26 21: *also* 10 4; 26 25, 46, 48; 27 3: *and* 26 23, 24. *cp.* 11 28.	*cp.* 4 33: *also* 4 9, 23; 7 16: *and* 4 34. *cp.* 2 8; 8 17. *cp.* 6 3; 14 27, 29; *also* 4 17. *cp.* 14 62. *cp.* 4 40; 11 22; 16 14. *cp.* 14 18: *also* 3 19; 14 42, 44: *and* 14 21.	*cp.* 8 8; 14 35. *cp.* 5 22; 6 8; 9 47; 11 17. *cp.* 7 23. *cp.* 22 69. *cp.* 1 2. *cp.* 8 25; 12 28; 17 5-6; 22 32; 24 25, 38. *cp.* 22 21: *and* 22 22.

[1] Or, *him*

§ 30. **Some go back: Peter's Confession**

John 6 66-71	Matt. 16 13-16	Mark 8 27-29	Luke 9 18-20
66 Upon this many of his disciples went back [*cp.* 6 60, 64], and walked no more with him. **67** Jesus said therefore unto the twelve, Would ye also go away?			
	13 Now when Jesus came into the parts of Cæsarea Philippi,	**27** And Jesus went forth, and his disciples, into the villages of Cæsarea Philippi: and in the way	**18** And it came to pass, as he was praying [*cp.* 3 21; 5 16; 6 12; 9 28, 29; 11 1; 22 41, 44: *also* 10 21] alone, the disciples were with him: and he asked
cp. 11 41; 12 27-28; 17 1-26.	*cp.* 14 23; 19 13; 26 36, 39, 42, 44: *also* 11 25.	*cp.* 1 35; 6 46, 47; 14 32, 35, 39.	
	he asked his disciples, saying, Who do men say [1]that the Son of man is? **14** And they said [*cp.* 14 2], Some *say* John the Baptist; some, Elijah: and others, Jeremiah, or one of the prophets. **15** He saith unto them, But who say ye that I am? **16** And Simon	he asked his disciples, saying unto them, Who do men say that I am? **28** And they told him, saying [*cp.* 6 14, 15], John the Baptist: and others, Elijah; but others, One of the prophets.	them, saying, Who do the multitudes say that I am? **19** And they answering said [*cp.* 9 7, 8], John the Baptist; but others *say*, Elijah; and others, that one of the old prophets is risen again.
68 Simon [*cp.* 1 40; 6 8; 13 6, 36; *etc.*] Peter [*cp.* 13 36-37; 21 21]	[*cp.* 4 18; 10 2] Peter [*cp.* 14 28; 15 15; 16 22; 17 4; 18 21; 19 27; 26 33: *also* 17 24] answered and said,	**29** And he asked them, But who say ye that I am? Peter [*cp.* 8 32; 9 5; 10 28; 11 21; 14 29]	**20** And he said unto them, But who say ye that I am? And *cp.* 5 8. Peter [*cp.* 8 45; 9 33; 12 41; 18 28]
answered him, Lord, to whom shall we go? thou [1]hast the words of eternal life [*cp.* 6 63; 12 50: *also* 3 34; 8 26, 47; 12 47-50; 14 10; 17 8, 14]. **69** And we have believed and know [*cp.* 9 38; 11 27; 16 30: *also* 16 27; 17 8: *and* 20 31] that thou art the Holy One *cp.* 1 41; 4 25, 26, 29; 7 26, 41; 9 22; 10 24; 11 27. *cp.* 1 34; *etc.*		answereth and saith unto him,	answering said,
of [*cp.* 6 57: *also* 5 26] God.	Thou art the Christ [*cp.* 26 63: *also* 26 68; 27 17, 22], the Son [*cp.* 4 3, 6; 8 29; 14 33; 26 63; 27 40, 43, 54: *also* 3 17; 17 5] of the living [*cp.* 26 63] God.	*cp.* 1 24. Thou art the Christ [*cp.* 14 61: *also* 15 32]. *cp.* 1 1; 3 11; 5 7; 15 39: *also* 1 11; 9 7.	*cp.* 4 34. The Christ [*cp.* 22 67: *also* 23 2, 35, 39] *cp.* 1 35; 4 3, 9, 41; 8 28; 22 70: *also* 3 22; 9 35. of God [*cp.* 23 35].
70 Jesus answered them, Did not I choose you [*cp.* 13 18; 15 16, 19] the twelve, and one of you is a devil [*cp.* 13 2, 27]?		*cp.* 3 14.	*cp.* 6 13.
			cp. 22 3.
71 Now he spake of Judas *the son* of Simon Iscariot [*cp.* 13 26: *also* 13 2: *and* 12 4; 14 22], for he it was that should betray him [*cp.* 6 64; 12 4; 13 11; 18 2, 5: *also* 13 2, 21], *being* one of the twelve [*cp.* 20 24].	*cp.* 10 4; 26 14. *cp.* 10 4; 26 25, 46, 48; 27 3: *also* 26 21, 23, 24. *cp.* 26 14, 47.	*cp.* 3 19; 14 10. *cp.* 3 19; 14 42, 44: *also* 14 18, 21. *cp.* 14 10, 20, 43.	*cp.* 6 16; 22 3. *cp.* 22 21, 22. *cp.* 22 47.

[1] Or, *hast words*

[1] Many ancient authorities read *that I the Son of man am.* See Mark 8 27; Luke 9 18.

§ 31. **Jesus remains in Galilee**

John 7 1-9

1 And after these things Jesus walked in Galilee: for he would not walk in Judæa, because the Jews sought to kill him [*cp.* 5 18; 7 19, 25; 8 37, 40: *also* 11 53: *and* 7 30, 32, 44; 10 39; 11 57: *and* 5 16]. **2** Now the feast of the Jews [*cp.* 5 1; 6 4: *also* 2 13; 11 55], the feast of tabernacles, was at hand. **3** His brethren [*cp.* 2 12; 7 5, 10] therefore said unto him, Depart hence, and go into Judæa, that thy disciples also may behold [*cp.* 2 23; 6 2; 11 45] thy works which thou doest. **4** For no man doeth anything in secret [*cp.* 7 10: *also* 18 20], [1]and himself seeketh to be known openly [*cp.* 7 13, 26; 10 24: *also* 11 14, 54; 16 25, 29; 18 20]. If thou doest these things, manifest thyself [*cp.* 1 31; 2 11; 3 21; 9 3; 17 6; 21 1, 14: *also* 14 21, 22] to the world [*cp.* 14 22]. **5** For even his brethren [*see verse* 3 *above*] did not believe on him. **6** Jesus therefore saith unto them, My time is not yet come [*cp. verse* 8: *also* 2 4; 7 30; 8 20: *and* 12 23, 27; 13 1; 17 1]; but your time is alway ready. **7** The world cannot hate you [*cp.* 15 18, 19; 17 14]; but me it hateth [*cp.* 15 18, 24], because I testify of it, that its works are evil [*cp.* 3 19]. **8** Go ye up unto the feast: I go not up [2]yet unto this feast; because my time is not yet fulfilled [*cp. verse* 6]. **9** And having said these things unto them, he abode *still* in Galilee.

[1] Some ancient authorities read *and seeketh it to be known openly.*
[2] Many ancient authorities omit *yet.*

cp. 12 14; 21 46; 26 4; 27 1.	*cp.* 3 6; 11 18; 12 12; 14 1.	*cp.* 6 11; 19 47; 20 19; 22 2.
cp. 12 46-50; 13 55.	*cp.* 3 31-35; 6 3.	*cp.* 8 19-21.
	cp. 8 32.	
	cp. 16 12, 14.	
cp. 13 57-58.	*cp.* 6 3-6.	
cp. 26 18: *also* 26 45.	*cp.* 14 35, 41.	*cp.* 22 14: *also* 22 53.
cp. 10 22; 24 9.	*cp.* 13 13.	*cp.* 1 71; 6 22, 27; 21 17.

(vii) In Judæa III (§§ 32-47)

§ 32. **Jesus goes up to Jerusalem for the Feast of Tabernacles**

John 7 10-13

10 But when his brethren [*cp.* 2 12; 7 3, 5] were gone up unto the feast, then went he also up [*cp.* 2 13; 5 1: *also* 7 14], not publicly, but as it were in secret [*cp.* 7 4: *also* 18 20]. **11** The Jews therefore sought him [*cp.* 11 56] at the feast, and said, Where is he [*cp.* 9 12: *also* 8 10]? **12** And there was much murmuring [*cp.* 6 41, 43, 61; 7 32] among the multitudes concerning him [*cp.* 6 52; 7 40-43; 9 16; 10 19-21]: some said, He is a good man; others said, Not so, but he leadeth the multitude astray [*cp.* 7 47]. **13** Howbeit no man spake openly [*cp.* 7 4, 26; 10 24: *also* 11 14, 54; 16 25, 29; 18 20] of him for fear of the Jews [*cp.* 19 38; 20 19: *also* 9 22: *and* 12 42].

cp. 12 46-50; 13 55.	*cp.* 3 31-35; 6 3.	*cp.* 8 19-21.
	cp. 8 32.	*cp.* 23 2, 14.

§ 33. **Jesus teaches in the Temple during the Feast**

John 7 14-24

14 But when it was now the midst of the feast Jesus went up into the temple [*cp.* 2 13-14: *also* 5 14; 10 23], and taught [*cp.* 7 28; 8 2, 20; 18 20]. **15** The Jews therefore marvelled [*cp. verse* 21: *also* 7 46], saying, How knoweth [*cp.* 4 9; 6 60: *also* 3 4, 9; 6 42, 52; 8 33; 12 34] this man letters, having never learned? **16** Jesus therefore answered them, and said, My teaching is not mine [*cp.* 14 24: *also* 3 34; 8 26, 28, 38, 40; 12 49; 14 10; 15 15], but his that sent me. **17** If any man willeth to do his will [*cp.* 9 31: *also* 4 34; 5 30; 6 38], he shall know of the teaching, whether it be of God, or *whether* I speak from myself [*cp.* 12 49; 14 10: *also* 5 19, 30; 8 28: *and* 7 28; 8 42: *and* 16 13]. **18** He that speaketh from

cp. 21 12: *also* 21 23; 26 55.	*cp.* 11 11, 15: *also* 11 27; 12 35; 14 49.	*cp.* 19 45: *also* 19 47; 20 1; 21 37; 22 53.	
cp. 7 28; 13 54; 19 25; 22 22, 33: *also* 8 27; *etc.*	*cp.* 1 22, 27; 6 2; 10 24, 26; 11 18; 12 17: *also* 2 12; *etc.*	*cp.* 2 47; 4 22, 32, 36; 20 26: *also* 5 9; *etc.*	
cp. 7 21; 12 50; 21 31: *also* 6 10; 26 39, 42.	*cp.* 3 35: *also* 14 36.	*cp.* 22 42.	

himself seeketh his own glory [*cp.* 8 50: *also* 5 44]: but he that seeketh the glory of him that sent him, the same is true, and no unrighteousness is in him. **19** Did not Moses give you the law [*cp.* 1 17: *also* 1 45; 7 23; 8 5], and *yet* none of you doeth the law? Why seek ye to kill me [*cp.* 5 18; 7 1, 25; *etc.*]? **20** The multitude answered, Thou hast a [1]devil [*cp.* 8 48, 52; 10 20]: who seeketh to kill thee? **21** Jesus answered and said unto them, I did one work [*cp.* 5 17: *also* 4 34; 5 36; 17 4: *and* 10 25, 32, 37; 14 10: *and* 3 21; 6 28-29; 9 3-4], and ye all [2]marvel [*cp. verse* 15]. **22** For this cause hath Moses given you circumcision (not that it is of Moses, but of the fathers); and on the sabbath ye circumcise a man. **23** If a man receiveth circumcision on the sabbath, that the law of Moses may not be broken; are ye wroth with me, because I made a man every whit whole [*cp.* 5 11, 15] on the sabbath [*cp.* 5 16, 18; 9 16]? **24** Judge not according to appearance, but judge righteous judgement [*cp.* 5 30: *also* 8 16].

	cp. 12 14; *etc.* *cp.* 9 34; 10 25; 12 24.	*cp.* 11 18; *etc.* *cp.* 3 22.	*cp.* 19 47; *etc.* *cp.* 11 15, 18.
	cp. 12 5.		
	cp. 12 11-12.	*cp.* 3 4.	*cp.* 6 9; 13 15-16; 14 5.
			cp. 12 57.

[1] Gr. *demon.*   [2] Or, *marvel because of this. Moses hath given you circumcision*

John 7 22: *cp.* Lev. 12 3 *and* Gen. 17 9-14.   John 7 24: *cp.* Deut. 1 16-17; 16 18-19.

§ 34. Questioning among the People about who Jesus is provokes an Attempt by the Chief Priests and Pharisees to arrest Him

John 7 25-36

25 Some therefore of them of Jerusalem said, Is not this he whom they seek to kill [*cp.* 5 18; 7 1, 19; *etc.*]? **26** And lo, he speaketh openly [*cp.* 7 4, 13; 10 24: *also* 11 14, 54; 16 25, 29; 18 20], and they say nothing unto him. Can it be that the rulers [*cp.* 3 1; 7 48; 12 42] indeed know that this is the Christ [*cp.* 1 41; 4 25, 29; 7 41; 9 22; 10 24; 11 27: *also* 4 26, 42: Matt. 16 16; 26 63: *also* 26 68; 27 17, 22: Mark 8 29; 14 61: *also* 15 32: Luke 9 20; 22 67: *also* 23 2, 35, 39]? **27** Howbeit we know this man whence he is [*cp.* 6 42: *also* 8 14, 19; 9 29, 30: *and* 19 9]: but when the Christ cometh [*cp.* 4 25; 7 31], no one knoweth whence he is. **28** Jesus therefore cried in the temple, teaching [*cp.* 7 14; 8 2, 20; 18 20] and saying, Ye both know me, and know whence I am; and I am not come of myself [*cp.* 8 42: *also* 5 19, 30; 8 28: *and* 7 17; 12 49; 14 10; *etc.*: *and* 16 13], but he that sent me is true [*cp.* 8 26: *also* 3 33: *and* 17 17], whom ye know not [*cp.* 8 19, 55; 15 21; 16 3; 17 25: *also* 4 22]. **29** I know him [*cp.* 8 55; 10 15; 17 25: *also* 1 18; 6 46; 8 19]; because I am from him [*cp.* 1 14; 5 44; 6 46; 9 16, 33; 16 27, 28; 17 8], and he sent me. **30** They sought therefore to take him [*cp. verse* 32; 7 44; 10 39; 11 57: *also* 5 18; 7 1, 19, 25; 8 37, 40; 11 53: *and* 5 16]: and no man laid his hand on him [*cp.* 7 44; 8 20], because his hour was not yet come [*cp.* 2 4; 7 6, 8; 8 20: *also* 12 23; 13 1; 17 1: *and* 12 27]. **31** But of the multitude many believed on him [*cp.* 2 11, 23; 4 39, 41; 8 30; 10 42; 11 45; 12 11, 42: *also* 7 48]; and they said, When the Christ shall come [*cp.* 4 25; 7 27], will he do more signs [*cp.* 2 11, 23; 3 2; *etc.*] than those which this man hath done? **32** The Pharisees heard the multitude murmuring these things concerning him [*cp.* 7 12: *also* 6 41, 43, 61: *and* 6 52; 7 40-43; 9 16; 10 19-21]; and the chief priests and the Pharisees sent officers [*cp.* 7 45, 46] to take him [*cp. verse* 30]. **33** Jesus therefore said, Yet a little while [*cp.* 12 35; 13 33; 14 19; 16 16-19] am I with you, and I go unto him that sent me [*cp.* 16 5: *also* 14 12, 28; 16 10, 17, 28: *and* 17 11, 13: *and* 20 17: *and* 13 1, 3]. **34** Ye shall seek me [*cp.* 7 36; 8 21; 13 33], and shall not find me: and where I am [*cp.* 7 36; 12 26; 14 3; 17 24], ye cannot come [*cp.* 7 36; 8 21, 22; 13 33: *also* 13 36]. **35** The Jews therefore said among themselves, Whither will this man go [*cp.* 8 14; *etc.*] that we shall not find him [*cp.* 8 22]? will he go unto the Dispersion [1]among the Greeks [*cp.* 12 20], and teach the Greeks? **36** What is this word that he said, Ye shall seek me, and shall not find me: and where I am, ye cannot come?

	cp. 12 14; *etc.*	*cp.* 11 18; *etc.* *cp.* 8 32.	*cp.* 19 47; *etc.*
	cp. 9 18.	*cp.* 5 22.	*cp.* 14 1; 18 18; 23 13, 35; 24 20: *also* 8 41; 13 14.
	cp. 13 55-56.	*cp.* 6 3.	*cp.* 4 22: *also* 13 25, 27.
	cp. 21 23; 26 55.	*cp.* 11 27; 12 35; 14 49.	*cp.* 19 47; 20 1; 21 37; 22 53.
	cp. 11 27.		*cp.* 10 22.
	cp. 21 46; *etc.*	*cp.* 12 12; *etc.*	*cp.* 20 19; *etc.*
	cp. 26 18, 45.	*cp.* 14 35, 41.	*cp.* 22 14, 53.
	cp. 18 6.	*cp.* 9 42.	
	cp. 21 46: *also* 12 14; 26 4; 27 1.	*cp.* 12 12: *also* 3 6; 11 18; 14 1.	*cp.* 20 19: *also* 19 47; 22 2: *and* 6 11.
		cp. 7 26.	

[1] Gr. *of.*

§ 35. Jesus's Teaching on the Last Day of the Feast leads to a Division among the People

John 7 37-44

37 Now on the last day, the great *day* of the feast, Jesus stood and cried, saying, If any man thirst [*cp.* 4 14; 6 35], let him come unto me [*cp.* 5 40; 6 35, 37, 44, 45, 65], and drink. **38** He that believeth on me, as the scripture hath said, out of his belly shall flow rivers of living water [*cp.* 4 10: *also* 19 34]. **39** But this spake he of the Spirit, which they that believed on him were to receive [*cp.* 20 22: *also* 14 17, 26; 15 26; 16 13: *and* 14 16; 16 7: *and* 1 33; 3 34]: [1]for the Spirit was not yet *given*; because Jesus was not yet glorified [*cp.* 12 16, 23; 13 31: *also* 11 4; 17 10: *and* 17 1 *ff.*]. **40** *Some* of the multitude therefore, when they heard these words, said, This is of a truth the prophet [*cp.* 6 14: *also* 1 21, 25: *and* 4 19, 44; 9 17]. **41** Others said, This is the Christ [*cp.* 1 41; 4 25, 29; 7 26; 9 22; 10 24; 11 27: *also* 4 26, 42: Matt. 16 16; 26 63: *also* 26 68; 27 17, 22: Mark 8 29; 14 61: *also* 15 32: Luke 9 20; 22 67: *also* 23 2, 35, 39]. But some said, What, doth the Christ come out of Galilee [*cp.* 7 52: *also* 1 46]? **42** Hath not the scripture said that the Christ cometh of the seed of David, and from Bethlehem, the village where David was? **43** So there arose a division in the multitude because of him [*cp.* 9 16; 10 19-21: *also* 6 52; 7 12]. **44** And some of them would have taken him [*cp.* 7 30, 32; 10 39; 11 57: *also* 5 18; 7 1, 19, 25; 8 37, 40; 11 53: *and* 5 16]; but no man laid hands on him [*cp.* 7 30; 8 20].	*cp.* 5 6. *cp.* 11 28. *cp.* 13 57; 21 11, 46. *cp.* 1 1; 22 42. *cp.* 2 4-6. *cp.* 21 46: *also* 12 14; 26 4; 27 1.	*cp.* 6 4, 15. *cp.* 12 35. *cp.* 12 12: *also* 3 6; 11 18; 14 1.	*cp.* 24 49: *also* 11 13. *cp.* 4 24; 7 16, 39; 13 33; 24 19. *cp.* 20 41. *cp.* 2 4. *cp.* 20 19: *also* 19 47; 22 2: *and* 6 11.

[1] Some ancient authorities read *for the Holy Spirit was not yet given.*

John 7 37: *cp.* Lev. 23 36; Num. 29 35: *also* Neh. 8 18: *and* Is. 55 1.   John 7 38: *cp.* Is. 12 3; Ezek. 47 1?   John 7 40: *cp.* Deut. 18 15.   John 7 42: *cp.* Is. 11 1: *also* Mic. 5 2: *and* 1 Sam. 16 1.

§ 36. The Attempt at Arrest fails

John 7 45-52

45 The officers [*cp.* 7 32] therefore came to the chief priests and Pharisees; and they said unto them, Why did ye not bring him? **46** The officers answered, Never man so spake [*cp.* 7 15, 21]. **47** The Pharisees therefore answered them, Are ye also led astray [*cp.* 7 12]? **48** Hath any of the rulers [*cp.* 3 1; 7 26; 12 42] believed on him, or of the Pharisees? **49** But this multitude which knoweth not the law are accursed. **50** Nicodemus saith unto them (he that came to him before [*cp.* 3 1 *ff.*; 19 39], being one of them), **51** Doth our law [*cp.* 19 7: *also* 8 17; 10 34; 15 25; 18 31] judge a man, except it first hear from himself and know what he doeth? **52** They answered and said unto him, Art thou also of Galilee? Search, and [1]see that out of Galilee [*cp.* 7 41: *also* 1 46] ariseth no prophet.	*cp.* 7 28; 13 54; etc. *cp.* 9 18.	*cp.* 1 22, 27; etc. *cp.* 5 22.	*cp.* 2 47; 4 22; etc. *cp.* 14 1; 18 18; 23 13, 35; 24 20; *also* 8 41; 13 14.

[1] Or, *see: for out of Galilee &c.*

John 7 51: *cp.* Deut. 1 16: *also* 17 6; 19 15.

§ 37. Jesus is questioned about a Woman taken in Adultery

John 7 53 - 8 11

53 [1][And they went every man unto his own house: **8 1** but Jesus went [*cp.* 18 1] unto the mount of Olives. **2** And early in the morning he came again into the temple, and all the people came	*cp.* 26 30: *also* 21 17: *and* 24 3.	*cp.* 14 26: *also* 11 11, 19: *and* 13 3.	*cp.* 21 37; 22 39. *cp.* 21 38.

unto him; and he sat down, and taught them [*cp.* 7 14, 28; 8 20; 18 20]. **3** And the scribes and the Pharisees bring a woman taken in adultery; and having set her in the midst, **4** they say unto him, ²Master, this woman hath been taken in adultery, in the very act. **5** Now in the law [*cp.* 1 17, 45; 7 19, 23] Moses commanded us to stone such: what then sayest thou of her? **6** And this they said,³ tempting him, that they might have *whereof* to accuse him. But Jesus stooped down, and with his finger wrote on the ground. **7** But when they continued asking him, he lifted up himself, and said unto them, He that is without sin among you, let him first cast a stone at her. **8** And again he stooped down, and with his finger wrote on the ground. **9** And they, when they heard it, went out one by one, beginning from the eldest, *even* unto the last: and Jesus was left alone, and the woman, where she was, in the midst. **10** And Jesus lifted up himself, and said unto her, Woman, where are they [*cp.* 7 11; 9 12]? did no man condemn thee? **11** And she said, No man, Lord. And Jesus said, Neither do I condemn thee: go thy way; from henceforth sin no more [*cp.* 5 14].]

cp. 21 23; 26 55.	*cp.* 11 27; 12 35; 14 49.	*cp.* 19 47; 20 1; 21 37; 22 53.
cp. 16 1; *etc.* *cp.* 12 10; 22 15.	*cp.* 8 11; *etc.* *cp.* 3 2; 12 13.	*cp.* 10 25; *etc.* *cp.* 6 7; 11 53-54; 20 20.
cp. 7 3-4.		*cp.* 6 41-42.

¹ Most of the ancient authorities omit John 7 53-8 11. Those which contain it vary much from each other. ² Or, *Teacher* ³ Or, *trying*

John 8 5: Lev. 20 10; Deut. 22 22-24: *cp.* Ezek. 16 38, 40. John 8 7: *cp.* Deut. 17 7.

§ 38. **Jesus the Light of the World**

John 8 12-20

12 Again therefore Jesus spake unto them, saying, I am the light of the world [*cp.* 9 5; 12 46: *also* 1 4, 5, 9; 3 19; 12 35-36]: he that followeth me [*cp.* 10 27: *also* 10 4: *and* 1 43; 12 26; 21 19, 22] shall not walk in the darkness [*cp.* 12 35: *also* 1 5; 12 46: *and* 11 10], but shall have the light of life [*cp.* 1 4]. **13** The Pharisees therefore said unto him, Thou bearest witness of thyself [*cp.* 5 31; 8 14, 18: *also* 5 19, 30; 7 17; *etc.*]; thy witness is not true [*cp.* 5 31, 32; 8 14: *also* 19 35; 21 24]. **14** Jesus answered and said unto them, Even if I bear witness of myself, my witness is true [*cp. verse* 13 *above*]; for I know whence I came [*cp.* 7 27, 28; 9 29, 30; 19 9: *also* 3 8], and whither I go [*cp.* 8 21, 22; 13 33, 36; 14 4: *also* 7 35; 13 36; 14 5; 16 5: *and* 3 8; 12 35]; but ye know not whence I come, or whither I go [*cp.* 9 29, 30; 19 9: *also* 6 42; 7 27, 28: *and* 3 8]. **15** Ye judge after the flesh; I judge no man [*cp.* 12 47: *also* 3 17]. **16** Yea and if I judge, my judgement is true [*cp.* 5 30: *also* 7 24]; for I am not alone [*cp.* 8 29; 16 32], but I and the Father that sent me. **17** Yea and in your law [*cp.* 10 34; 18 31: *also* 15 25: *and* 7 51; 19 7] it is written, that the witness of two men is true. **18** I am he that beareth witness of myself [*cp. verse* 13 *above*], and the Father that sent me beareth witness of me [*cp.* 5 37: *also* 5 32]. **19** They said therefore unto him, Where is thy Father? Jesus answered, Ye know neither me [*cp.* 16 3 *and verse* 14 *above*], nor my Father [*cp.* 7 28; 8 55; 15 21; 16 3; 17 25: *also* 4 22]: if ye knew me, ye would know my Father also [*cp.* 14 7]. **20** These words spake he in the treasury, as he taught in the temple [*cp.* 7 14, 28; 8 2; 18 20]: and no man took him [*cp.* 7 30, 44]; because his hour was not yet come [*cp.* 2 4; 7 6, 8, 30: *also* 12 23; 13 1; 17 1: *and* 12 27].

cp. 5 14. *cp.* 16 24; *etc.*	*cp.* 8 34; *etc.*	*cp.* 9 23; *etc.*
		cp. 13 25, 27.
cp. 26 56.	*cp.* 14 50.	
cp. 18 16.		
cp. 21 23; 26 55. *cp.* 26 18, 45.	*cp.* 11 27; 12 35; 14 49. *cp.* 14 35, 41.	*cp.* 19 47; 20 1; *etc.* *cp.* 22 14, 53.

John 8 17: Deut. 19 15; *cp.* Deut. 17 6 *and* Num. 35 30.

§ 39. **Further Teaching of Jesus about who He is**

John 8 21-30

21 He said therefore again unto them, I go away [*cp.* 14 28: *also* 7 33; 14 2, 3; *etc.*], and ye shall seek me [*cp.* 7 34, 36; 13 33], and shall die in your sin: whither I go [*cp.* 8 14, 22; 13 33, 36; 14 4: *also* 7 35; 13 36; 14 5: *and* 3 8; 12 35], ye cannot come [*cp.* 7 34, 36; 8 22; 13 33: *also* 13 36]. **22** The Jews therefore said, Will he kill himself, that he saith, Whither I go, ye cannot come [*cp.* 7 35]? **23** And he said unto them, Ye are from beneath; I am from above [*cp.* 3 31: *also* 3 13; 6 32-33, 38, 41-42, 50-51, 58]: ye are of this world; I am not of this world [*cp.* 17 14, 16: *also* 18 36: *and* 15 19]. **24** I said therefore unto you, that ye shall die in your sins [*cp. verse* 21 *above*]: for except ye [*cp.* 3 3, 5; 6 53: *also* 13 8] believe that [1]I am *he* [*cp. verse* 28 *below and* 13 19: *also* 8 58], ye shall die in your sins [*cp.* 16 9]. **25** They said therefore unto him, Who art thou [*cp.* 1 19; 21 12]? Jesus said unto them, [2]Even that which I have also spoken unto you from the beginning. **26** I have many things to speak [*cp.* 16 12: *also* 14 30] and to judge concerning you [*cp.* 5 22, 27: *also* 9 39: *and* 3 17; 12 47]: howbeit he that sent me is true [*cp.* 7 28: *also* 3 33: *and* 17 17]; and the things which I heard from him [*cp.* 3 34; 7 16; 8 28, 38, 40; 12 49, 50; 14 10, 24; 15 15], these speak I [3]unto the world [*cp.* 3 34; 8 47; 12 47-50; 14 10; 17 8, 14: *also* 6 63, 68: *and* 18 20]. **27** They perceived not [*cp.* 3 10; 4 33; 8 43; 10 6; 11 13; 12 16; 13 7, 28, 36; 14 5-10, 22; 16 17-18] that he spake to them of the Father. **28** Jesus therefore said, When ye have lifted up the Son of man [*cp.* 3 14; 12 32-34: *also* 2 19-22], then shall ye know that [4]I am *he* [*cp. verse* 24 *above and* 13 19: *also* 8 58], and *that* I do nothing of myself [*cp.* 5 19, 30: *also* 5 31; 7 17, 28; 8 13, 14, 18, 42, 54; 10 18; 12 49; 14 10: *and* 16 13], but as the Father taught me [*cp.* 3 34; 7 16; 8 26, 38, 40; 12 49, 50; 14 10, 24; 15 15], I speak these things. **29** And he that sent me is with me; he hath not left me alone [*cp.* 8 16; 16 32]; for I do always the things that are pleasing to him. **30** As he spake these things, many believed on him [*cp.* 2 11, 23; 4 39, 41; 7 31; 10 42; 11 45; 12 11, 42: *also* 7 48].

	cp. 13 6; 14 62.	*cp.* 21 8; 22 70.
cp. 15 16; 16 8-12.	*cp.* 4 13; 6 52; 7 18; 8 17-21; *etc.*	*cp.* 2 50; 9 45; 18 34.
cp. 16 21-23; *etc.*	*cp.* 8 31-33; *etc.*: *and* 13 6; 14 62.	*cp.* 9 22; *etc.*: *and* 21 8; 22 70.
cp. 26 56.	*cp.* 14 50.	
cp. 18 6.	*cp.* 9 42.	

[1] Or, *I am* [2] Or, How is it *that I even speak to you at all?* [3] Gr. *into.* [4] Or, *I am* Or, *I am* he: *and I do*

§ 40. **Jesus, Abraham, and Abraham's Seed**

John 8 31-59

31 Jesus therefore said to those Jews which had believed him [*cp.* 8 30], If ye abide in [*cp.* 6 56; 15 4, 5, 7: *also* 17 21] my word [*cp.* 4 41; 5 24; 8 37, 43, 51, 52; 12 48; 14 23, 24; 15 3, 20: *also* 5 38; 8 55; 14 24; 17 6, 14, 17, 20], *then* are ye truly my disciples [*cp.* 13 35; 15 8]; **32** and ye shall know the truth [*cp.* 1 14, 17; 5 33; 14 6; 18 37], and the truth shall make you free. **33** They answered unto him, We be Abraham's seed [*cp. vv.* 37, 39, 53, *below*], and have never yet been in bondage to any man: how sayest thou [*cp.* 12 34: *also* 14 9: *and* 3 4, 9; 6 42, 52, 60: *and* 4 9; 7 15], Ye shall be made free? **34** Jesus answered them, Verily, verily, I say unto you, Every one that committeth sin is the bond-servant of sin. **35** And the bondservant abideth not in the house for ever: the son abideth for ever. **36** If therefore the Son shall make you free, ye shall be free indeed. **37** I know that ye are Abraham's seed [*cp. verse* 33 *above*]; yet ye seek to kill me [*cp.* 5 18; 7 1, 19, 25; 8 40: *also* 11 53: *and* 7 30, 32, 44; 10 39; 11 57: *and* 5 16], because my word [*cp. verse* 31 *above*] [1]hath not free course in you. **38** I speak the things which I have seen with [2]*my* Father [*cp.* 3 34; 7 16; 8 26, 28, 40; 12 49, 50; 14 10, 24; 15 15]: and ye also do the things which ye heard from *your* father. **39** They answered and said unto him, Our father is Abraham [*cp. verse*

cp. 13 19-23.	*cp.* 2 2; 4 14-20, 33; 16 20.	*cp.* 4 32; *etc.*
		cp. 14 26, 27, 33.
cp. 3 9.		*cp.* 3 8; 13 16; 16 24, 30; 19 9.
cp. 3 9.		*cp.* 3 8; *etc.*
cp. 12 14; *etc.*	*cp.* 11 18; *etc.*	*cp.* 19 47; *etc.*
cp. 19 11, 12.		
cp. 3 9.		*cp.* 3 8; *etc.*

33 *above*]. Jesus saith unto them, If ye ³were Abraham's children, ⁴ye would do the works of Abraham. **40** But now ye seek to kill me [*cp. verse* 37 *above*], a man that hath told you the truth, which I heard from God [*cp. verse* 38 *above*]: this did not Abraham. **41** Ye do the works of your father. They said unto him, We were not born of fornication; we have one Father, *even* God. **42** Jesus said unto them, If God were your Father, ye would love me: for I came forth and am come from God [*cp.* 16 28: *also* 13 3; 16 27, 30; 17 8]; for neither have I come of myself [*cp.* 7 28: *also* 5 19, 30; 8 28: *and* 7 17; 12 49; 14 10; *etc.*: *and* 16 13], but he sent me. **43** Why do ye not ⁵understand my speech [*cp.* 3 10; 4 33; 8 27; 10 6; 11 13; 12 16; 13 7, 28, 36; 14 5-10, 22; 16 17-18]? *Even* because ye cannot hear my word [*cp.* 5 24 *and verse* 31 *above*]. **44** Ye are of *your* father the devil, and the lusts of your father it is your will to do. He was a murderer from the beginning, and ⁶stood not in the truth, because there is no truth in him. ⁷When he speaketh a lie, he speaketh of his own [*cp.* 1 11; 13 1; 15 19; 16 32; 19 27]: for he is a liar, and the father thereof. **45** But because I say the truth, ye believe me not. **46** Which of you convicteth me of sin [*cp.* 16 8]? If I say truth, why do ye not believe me? **47** He that is of God heareth the words of God [*cp.* 3 34; 8 26; 12 47-50; 14 10; 17 8, 14: *also* 6 63, 68]: for this cause ye hear *them* not, because ye are not of God. **48** The Jews answered and said unto him, Say we not well that thou art a Samaritan [*cp.* 4 9], and hast a ⁸devil [*cp.* 7 20; 8 52; 10 20]? **49** Jesus answered, I have not a ⁸devil; but I honour my Father [*cp.* 5 23], and ye dishonour me. **50** But I seek not mine own glory [*cp.* 7 18: *also* 5 44: *and verse* 54 *below*]: there is one that seeketh and judgeth. **51** Verily, verily, I say unto you, If a man keep my word [*cp. verse* 52 *below and* 14 23, 24; 15 20: *also verse* 31 *above*: *and* 14 15, 21; 15 10], he shall never see death [*cp.* 5 24; 6 50, 51, 58; 10 28; 11 25-26]. **52** The Jews said unto him, Now we know that thou hast a ⁸devil [*cp. verse* 48 *above*]. Abraham is dead, and the prophets; and thou sayest, If a man keep my word, he shall never taste of death. **53** Art thou greater than our father [*cp.* 4 12: *also vv.* 33, 37, 39, *above*] Abraham, which is dead? and the prophets are dead: whom makest thou thyself [*cp.* 5 18; 10 33; 19 7, 12: *also* 1 22]? **54** Jesus answered, If I glorify myself [*cp. verse* 50 *above*: *also* 5 31; 8 13, 14, 18; *etc.*], my glory is nothing: it is my Father that glorifieth me [*cp.* 13 32; 16 14; 17 1, 5: *also* 7 39; *etc.*]; of whom ye say, that he is your God [*cp. verse* 41 *above*]; **55** and ye have not known him [*cp.* 7 28; 8 19; 15 21; 16 3; 17 25: *also* 4 22]: but I know him [*cp.* 7 29; 10 15; 17 25: *also* 1 18; 6 46; 8 19]; and if I should say, I know him not, I shall be like unto you, a liar: but I know him, and keep his word [*cp.* 5 38; 14 24; 17 6, 14, 17, 20: *also* 5 24; 8 31; *etc.*]. **56** Your father Abraham rejoiced ⁹to see my day; and he saw it, and was glad. **57** The Jews therefore said unto him, Thou art not yet fifty years old [*cp.* 2 20], and hast thou seen Abraham? **58** Jesus said unto them, Verily, verily, I say unto you, Before Abraham ¹⁰was, I am [*cp.* 17 5, 24: *also* 1 1, 2, 18: *and* 8 24, 28; 13 19]. **59** They took up stones therefore to cast at him [*cp.* 10 31; 11 8]: but Jesus ¹¹hid himself, and went out of the temple [*cp.* 10 39: *also* 12 36].¹²	*cp.* 12 14; *etc.* *cp.* 15 16; 16 8-12. *cp.* 13 19-23. *cp.* 19 4. *cp.* 10 5: *and* 9 34; 10 25; 12 24. *cp.* 9 34; 10 25; 12 24. *cp.* 16 28. *cp.* 3 9. *cp.* 11 27. *cp.* 13 19-23.	*cp.* 11 18; *etc.* *cp.* 1 38. *cp.* 4 13; 6 52; *etc.* *cp.* 2 2; *etc.* *cp.* 3 22. *cp.* 3 22. *cp.* 9 1. *cp.* 2 2; *etc.* *cp.* 13 6; 14 62.	*cp.* 19 47; *etc.* *cp.* 2 50; 9 45; 18 34. *cp.* 4 32: *also* 1 2; *etc.* *cp.* 18 28. *cp.* 9 52-53: *and* 11 15, 18. *cp.* 2 26. *cp.* 11 15, 18. *cp.* 9 27. *cp.* 3 8; *etc.* *cp.* 10 22. *cp.* 5 1; 8 11, 21; *etc.* *cp.* 17 22; *etc.* *cp.* 3 23. *cp.* 21 8; 22 70. *cp.* 4 30.

¹ Or, *hath no place in you*   ² Or, *the Father: do ye also therefore the things which ye heard from the Father.*   ³ Gr. *are.*   ⁴ Some ancient authorities read *ye do the works of Abraham.*   ⁵ Or, *know*   ⁶ Some ancient authorities read *standeth.*   ⁷ Or, *When one speaketh a lie, he speaketh of his own: for his father also is a liar.*   ⁸ Gr. *demon.*   ⁹ Or, *that he should see*   ¹⁰ Gr. *was born.*   ¹¹ Or, *was hidden, and went &c.*   ¹² Many ancient authorities add *and going through the midst of them went his way and so passed by.*

John 8 35: *cp.* Gen. 21 10.   John 8 41: *cp.* Deut. 32 6; Is. 63 16; 64 8; Mal. 2 10.   John 8 44: *cp.* Wisd. 2 24.   John 8 49: *cp.* Exod. 20 12; Deut. 5 16.   John 8 52; *cp.* Zech. 1 5.   John 8 58: *cp.* Exod. 3 14.

§ 41. A Blind Beggar receives his Sight

[*Cp.* Matt. 9 27-31; 12 22; 15 30-31; 20 29-34; 21 14: Mark 8 22-26; 10 46-52: Luke 7 21; 18 35-43]

John 9 1-12

1 And as he passed by, he saw a man blind from his birth. **2** And his disciples asked him, saying, Rabbi [*cp.* 1 38, 49; 3 2; 4 31; 6 25; 11 8: *also* 20 16: *and* 3 26], who did sin, this man, or his parents, that he should be born blind [*cp.* 9 34]? **3** Jesus answered, Neither did this man sin, nor his parents: but [*cp.* 11 4] that the works of God [*cp. verse* 4 *below*] should be made manifest in him [*cp.* 1 31; 2 11; 3 21; 7 4; 17 6; 21 1, 14: *also* 14 21, 22]. **4** We must work the works of him that sent me [*cp.* 3 21; 6 28-29: *also* 10 25, 32, 37; 14 10: *and* 4 34; 5 36; 17 4: *and* 5 17; 7 21], while it is day [*cp.* 11 9; 12 35]: the night cometh [*cp.* 11 10: *also* 13 30], when no man can work. **5** When I am in the world, I am the light of the world [*cp.* 8 12; 12 46: *also* 1 4, 5, 9; 3 19; 12 35-36]. **6** When he had thus spoken, he spat on the ground [*cp.* 18 6], and made clay of the spittle, [1]and anointed [*cp.* 20 17] his eyes with the clay, **7** and said unto him [*cp.* 4 50; 5 8; 11 43], Go, wash in the pool of Siloam (which is by interpretation, Sent). He went away therefore, and washed, and came seeing. **8** The neighbours therefore, and they which saw him aforetime, that he was a beggar, said, Is not this he that sat and begged? **9** Others said, It is he: others said, No, but he is like him. He said, I am *he*. **10** They said therefore unto him, How then were thine eyes opened? **11** He answered, The man that is called Jesus made clay, and anointed mine eyes, and said unto me, Go to Siloam, and wash: so I went away and washed, and I received sight. **12** And they said unto him, Where is he [*cp.* 7 11: *also* 8 10]? He saith, I know not.

[1] Or, *and with the clay thereof anointed* his *eyes*

cp. 26 25, 49: *also* 23 7, 8.	*cp.* 9 5; 11 21; 14 45: *also* 10 51.	*cp.* 13 1-5.
	cp. 16 12, 14.	
cp. 5 14.	*cp.* 7 33; 8 23.	
cp. 9 29; *etc.*	*cp.* 8 25; *etc.*	*cp.* 4 40; *etc.*
cp. 8 8; *etc.*	*cp.* 10 52; *etc.*	*cp.* 18 42; *etc.*
		cp. 13 4.
	cp. 10 46.	*cp.* 18 35.
cp. 11 5; 20 34.	*cp.* 10 51-52.	*cp.* 7 22; 18 41-43.

John 9 2: *cp.* Exod. 20 5; 34 7; Num. 14 18; Deut. 5 9.   John 9 7, 11: *cp.* II Kings 5 10, 14-15: *also* Neh. 3 15; Is. 8 6.

§ 42. The Pharisees object

[*Cp.* Matt. 12 9-14 ‖ Mark 3 1-6 ‖ Luke 6 6-11; Luke 13 10-17, 14 1-6; John 5 1-18, 7 21-24: *also* Matt. 12 1-8 ‖ Mark 2 23-28 ‖ Luke 6 1-5]

John 9 13-34

13 They bring to the Pharisees him that aforetime was blind. **14** Now it was the sabbath on the day [*cp.* 5 9] when Jesus made the clay, and opened his eyes. **15** Again therefore the Pharisees also asked him how he received his sight. And he said unto them, He put clay upon mine eyes, and I washed, and do see. **16** Some therefore of the Pharisees said, This man is not from God [*cp. verse* 33 *and* 6 46: *also* 1 14; 5 44; 7 29; 16 27, 28; 17 8], because he keepeth not the sabbath [*cp.* 5 16, 18; 7 23]. But others said, How can a man that is a sinner [*cp. vv.* 24, 25, 31] do such signs [*cp. verse* 33: *also* 3 2; 10 21: *and* 5 36; 10 25]? And there was a division among them [*cp.* 7 40-43; 10 19-21: *also* 6 52; 7 12]. **17** They say therefore unto the blind man again, What sayest thou of him, in that he opened thine eyes? And he said, He is a prophet [*cp.* 4 19, 44; 6 14; 7 40]. **18** The Jews therefore did not believe concerning him, that he had been blind, and had received his sight, until they called the parents of him that had received his sight, **19** and asked them, saying, Is this your son, who ye say was born blind? how then doth he now see? **20** His parents answered and said, We know that this is our son, and that he was born blind: **21** but how he now seeth, we know not; or who opened his eyes, we know not: ask him; he is of age

cp. 9 11, 13; 11 19; 26 45.	*cp.* 2 16, 17; 14 41.	*cp.* 5 8, 30, 32; 6 32, 33, 34; 7 34, 37, 39; 15 1, 2; *etc.*
cp. 13 57; 21 11, 46.	*cp.* 6 4, 15.	*cp.* 4 24; 7 16, 39; 13 33; 24 19.

[cp. verse 23 below]; he shall speak for himself. **22** These things said his parents, because they feared the Jews [cp. 7 13; 19 38; 20 19: also 12 42]: for the Jews had agreed already, that if any man should confess him to be Christ [cp. 1 41; 4 25, 26, 29, 42; 7 26, 41; 10 24, 25; 11 27: also 3 2; 12 42], he should be put out of the synagogue [cp. 12 42; 16 2]. **23** Therefore said his parents, He is of age; ask him [cp. verse 21 above]. **24** So they called a second time the man that was blind, and said unto him, Give glory to God: we know [cp. vv. 29 and 31: also 3 2; 4 42; 16 30; 21 24; Matt. 22 16; Mark 12 14; Luke 20 21] that this man is a sinner [cp. vv. 16, 25, and 31]. **25** He therefore answered, Whether he be a sinner, I know not: one thing I know, that, whereas I was blind, now I see. **26** They said therefore unto him, What did he to thee? how opened he thine eyes? **27** He answered them, I told you even now [cp. verse 15], and ye did not hear: wherefore would ye hear it again? would ye also become his disciples? **28** And they reviled him, and said, Thou art his disciple; but we are disciples of Moses [cp. 5 45]. **29** We know [cp. vv. 24 and 31: also 3 2; 4 42; 16 30; 21 24] that God hath spoken unto Moses: but as for this man, we know not whence he is [cp. 8 14, 19; 19 9: also 6 42; 7 27, 28]. **30** The man answered and said unto them, Why, herein is the marvel, that ye know not whence he is, and yet he opened mine eyes. **31** We know [cp. vv. 24 and 29: also 3 2; 4 42; 16 30; 21 24] that God heareth not sinners [cp. vv. 16, 24, 25, above]: but if any man be a worshipper of God, and do his will [cp. 7 17: also 4 34; 5 30; 6 38], him he heareth. **32** Since the world began it was never heard that any one opened the eyes of a man born blind. **33** If this man were not from God [cp. verse 16 and 6 46: also 1 14; 5 44; 7 29; 16 27, 28; 17 8], he could do nothing [cp. verse 16: also 3 2; 10 21: and 5 36; 10 25]. **34** They answered and said unto him, Thou wast altogether born in sins [cp. 9 2], and dost thou teach us? And they cast him out.

verse			
22–23	cp. 16 16: also 26 63, 68; 27 17, 22.	cp. 8 29: also 14 61-62; 15 32.	cp. 9 20: also 22 67; 23 2, 35, 39.
24	cp. 5 16; 9 8; 15 31.	cp. 2 12.	cp. 17 18: also 2 20; 5 25, 26; 7 16; 13 13; 17 15; 18 43; 23 47.
29	cp. 22 16.	cp. 12 14.	cp. 20 21. cp. 13 25, 27.
31	cp. 22 16.	cp. 12 14.	cp. 20 21.
32	cp. 7 21; 12 50; 21 31: also 6 10; 26 39, 42.	cp. 3 35: also 14 36.	cp. 22 42.

John 9 24: cp. Josh. 7 19; Jer. 13 16: also I Sam. 6 5; Is. 42 12.   John 9 31: cp. Job 27 9; Ps. 66 18; Prov. 28 9; Is. 1 15: also Ps. 34 15-16; 145 18-20; Prov. 15 29.

§ 43. Jesus answers the Pharisees

John 9 35-41

35 Jesus heard that they had cast him out; and finding him, he said, Dost thou believe on ¹the Son of God? **36** He answered and said, And who is he, Lord, that I may believe on him? **37** Jesus said unto him, Thou hast both seen him, and he it is that speaketh with thee [cp. 4 26].

38 And he said, Lord, I believe [cp. 6 69; 11 27; 16 30: also 16 27; 17 8; 20 31]. And he worshipped him [cp. 11 32; 18 6]. **39** And Jesus said, For judgement came I [cp. 5 22, 27: also 8 26: and 3 17; 12 47] into this world [cp. 12 46; 16 28; 18 37: also 1 9; 3 19; 6 14; 11 27: and 3 17; 10 36; 17 18], that they which see not may see; and that they which see may become blind. **40** Those of the Pharisees which were with him heard these things, and said unto him, Are we also blind? **41** Jesus said unto them, If ye were blind, ye would have no sin [cp. 15 22, 24]: but now ye say, We see: your sin remaineth.

¹ Many ancient authorities read the Son of man.

verse			
38 (believe)	cp. 16 16.	cp. 9 24: also 8 29.	cp. 9 20.
38 (worshipped)	cp. 2 11; 8 2; 9 18; 14 33; 15 25; 20 20; 28 9, 17: also 17 14.	cp. 5 6: also 1 40; 3 11; 5 22, 33; 7 25; 10 17.	cp. 24 52: also 5 8, 12; 8 28, 41, 47; 17 16.
39 (see not)	cp. 11 5.		cp. 4 18: also 7 22.
39 (become blind)	cp. 13 13.	cp. 4 12.	cp. 8 10.
41	cp. 15 14; 23 16, 17, 19, 24, 26.		cp. 6 39.

John 9 39: cp. Is. 29 18; 35 5; 42 16: and 6 9-10.

§ 44. The Parable of the Shepherd

[*Cp.* Matt. 18 12-13 ‖ Luke 15 3-7]

John 10 1-6

1 Verily, verily, I say unto you, He that entereth not by the door into the fold of the sheep, but climbeth up some other way, the same is a thief and a robber. 2 But he that entereth in [*cp. verse* 1 *above and* 10 9: *also* 3 5] by the door is ¹the shepherd of the sheep. 3 To him the porter openeth; and the sheep hear his voice: and he calleth his own sheep by name, and leadeth them out. 4 When he hath put forth all his own, he goeth before them, and the sheep follow him [*cp.* 10 27]: for they know his voice [*cp.* 10 14: *also* 10 16, 27]. 5 And a stranger will they not follow, but will flee from him: for they know not the voice of strangers. 6 This ²parable [*cp.* 16 25, 29] spake Jesus unto them: but they understood not what things they were which he spake unto them [*cp.* 12 16: *also* 3 10; 4 33; 8 27, 43; 11 13; 13 7, 28, 36; 14 5-10, 22; 16 17-18].

cp. 5 20; 7 21; 18 3; 19 23, 24; 21 31; 23 13: *also* 7 13; 18 8, 9; 19 17; 25 21, 23.

cp. 9 47; 10 15, 23, 24, 25: *also* 9 43, 45.

cp. 18 17, 24, 25: *also* 11 52; 13 24; 24 26.

cp. 15 16; 16 8-12.

cp. 4 13; 6 52; 7 18; 8 17-21; 9 10, 32; 16 14.

cp. 2 50; 9 45; 18 34.

¹ Or, *a shepherd*   ² Or, *proverb*

§ 45. Jesus the Good Shepherd

John 10 7-18

7 Jesus therefore said unto them again, Verily, verily, I say unto you, I am the door of the sheep. 8 All that came before me are thieves and robbers: but the sheep did not hear them. 9 I am the door: by me if any man enter in [*cp.* 10 1, 2: *also* 3 5], he shall be saved [*cp.* 3 16-17; 5 34; 12 47: *also* 4 42], and shall go in and go out, and shall find pasture. 10 The thief cometh not, but that he may steal, and kill, and destroy: I came that they may have life [*cp.* 1 4; 5 40; *etc.*], and may ¹have *it* abundantly.

cp. 5 20; *etc.* *cp.* 1 21: *also* 18 11: *and* 20 28.

cp. 9 47; *etc.* *cp.* 10 45.

cp. 18 17; *etc.* *cp.* 2 11: *also* 9 55; 19 10.

11 I am the good shepherd [*cp. verse* 14 *below and* 21 15-17]: the good shepherd layeth down his life [*cp. vv.* 15 *and* 17 *below*: *also* 13 37, 38; 15 13: *and* 11 51-52] for the sheep.

cp. 9 36: *also* 10 6; 15 24: *and* 26 31.

cp. 6 34: *and* 14 27.

cp. 20 28: *also* 26 28.

cp. 10 45: *also* 14 24.

12 He that is a hireling, and not a shepherd, whose own the sheep are not, beholdeth the wolf coming, and leaveth the sheep, and fleeth, and the wolf snatcheth them [*cp.* 10 28, 29], and scattereth *them* [*cp.* 16 32]: 13 *he fleeth* because he is a hireling, and careth not for the sheep. 14 I am the good shepherd [*cp. verse* 11 *above and* 21 15-17]; and I know mine own [*cp.* 10 27: *also* 16 14, 15; 17 10], and mine own know me [*cp.* 10 4: *also* 10 16, 27], 15 even as the Father knoweth me, and I know the Father [*cp.* 7 29; 8 55; 17 25: *also* 1 18; 6 46; 8 19]; and I lay down my life [*cp. verses* 11 *and* 17] for the sheep. 16 And other sheep I have, which are not of this fold [*cp.* 11 52]: them also I must ²bring, and they shall hear my voice [*cp.* 10 27: *also* 10 4: *and* 5 25, 28; 18 37]; and ³they shall become one flock [*cp.* 11 52; 17 11, 21, 22, 23: *also* 12 32], one shepherd. 17 Therefore doth the Father love me [*cp.* 3 35; 5 20; 15 9-10; 17 23, 24, 26], because I lay down my life [*cp. vv.* 11 *and* 15 *above*], that I may take it again. 18 No one ⁴taketh it away from me, but I lay it down of myself [*cp.* 5 19, 30, 31; 7 17; *etc.*]. I have ⁵power [*cp.* 5 27; 17 2] to lay it down, and I have ⁵power to take it again [*cp.* 2 19, 21: *also* 5 26: *and* 5 27]. This commandment received I from my Father [*cp.* 12 49; 14 31: *also* 15 10].

cp. 26 31.

cp. 14 27.

cp. 9 36: *also* 10 6; 15 24: *and* 26 31.

cp. 11 27.

cp. 6 34: *and* 14 27.

cp. 10 22.

cp. 8 11; 10 18; 21 31, 41, 43; 22 7-10; *etc.*

cp. 12 9; 13 10; 14 9; 16 15.

cp. 2 30-32; 36; 13 29; 14 21-24; *etc.*

cp. 3 17; 17 5.

cp. 1 11; 9 7; 12 6.

cp. 3 22; 20 13.

cp. 28 18.

¹ Or, *have abundance*   ² Or, *lead*   ³ Or, *there shall be one flock*   ⁴ Some ancient authorities read *took it away.*   ⁵ Or, *right*

John 10 8, 10, 12-13: *cp.* Jer. 23 1-2; Ezek. 34 1-6; Zech. 11 16-17.   John 10 9: *cp.* Ps. 23 2; Ezek. 34 14. John 10 11: *cp.* Ps. 23 1-6; Is. 40 11; Ezek. 34 11-12, 23.   John 10 16: *cp.* Ezek. 34 11-13, 23; 37 24.

§ 46. The Jews are again divided

John 10 19-21

19 There arose a division again among the Jews [*cp.* 7 40-43; 9 16: *also* 6 52; 7 12] because of these words. **20** And many of them said, He hath a [1]devil [*cp.* 7 20; 8 48, 52], and is mad; why hear ye him? **21** Others said, These are not the sayings of one possessed with a [1]devil. Can a [1]devil open the eyes of the blind [*cp.* 3 2; 9 16, 33: *also* 5 36; 10 25]?	*cp.* 9 34; 10 25; 12 24.	*cp.* 3 22: *and* 3 21.	*cp.* 11 15, 18.

[1] Gr. *demon.*

§ 47. At the Feast of the Dedication

John 10 22-39	Matt. 26 63	Mark 14 61	Luke 22 66-68
22 [1]And it was the feast of the dedication at Jerusalem: it was winter; **23** and Jesus was walking in the temple in Solomon's porch. **24** The Jews therefore came round about him, and said unto him, How long dost thou hold us in suspense?			**66** And as soon as it was day, the assembly of the elders of the people was gathered together, both chief priest and scribes; and they led him away into their council, saying,

If thou art the Christ [*cp.* 1 41; 4 25, 26, 29; 7 26, 41; 9 22; 11 27], tell us plainly [*cp.* 7 4, 13, 26: *also* 11 14, 54; 16 25, 29; 18 20]. **25** Jesus answered them, I told you, and ye believe not [*cp.* 6 36; 12 37: *also* 1 11; *etc.*]:	And the high priest said unto him,
	
	I adjure thee by the living [*cp.* 16 16] God, that thou tell us whether thou be the Christ [*cp.* 16 16: *also* 26 68; 27 17, 22].
		Again the high priest asked him, and saith unto him,
		
		Art thou the Christ [*cp.* 8 29: *also* 15 32]?
		    cp. 8 32.
			67 If thou art the Christ [*cp.* 9 20: *also* 23 2, 35, 39] tell us.
			
			But he said unto them, If I tell you, ye will not believe:
			      68 and if I ask you, ye will not answer.

the works [*cp. vv.* 32, 37, *and* 14 10: *also* 4 34; 5 36; 17 4: *and* 3 21; 6 28-29; 9 3-4: *and* 10 38; 14 11: *and* 5 17; 7 21; 15 24] that I do in my Father's name [*cp.* 5 43: *also* 12 13: *and* 17 12], these bear witness of me [*cp.* 5 36: *also* 3 2; 9 16, 33; 10 21]. **26** But ye believe not, because ye are not of my sheep. **27** My sheep hear my voice [*cp.* 10 16: *also* 10 4: *and* 5 25, 28; 18 37], and I know them [*cp.* 10 14], and they follow me [*cp.* 10 4: *also* 8 12: *and* 1 43; 12 26; 21 19, 22]: **28** and I give unto them eternal life [*cp.* 17 2: *also* 3 15, 16, 36; 5 24; 6 40; *etc.*: *and* 8 51; 11 25-26]; and they shall never perish [*cp.* 3 16: *also* 17 12; 18 9: *and* 6 39], and no one shall snatch them [*cp.* 10 12] out of my hand. **29** [2]My Father, which hath given *them* unto me [*cp.* 6 37, 39; 17 2, 6, 9, 11, 12, 24; 18 9], is greater [*cp.* 14 28] than all; and no one is able to snatch [3]*them* [*cp.* 10 12] out of the Father's hand. **30** I and the Father are one [*cp.* 17 11, 22: *also* 5 19, 12 45; 14 9-11; 15 24]. **31** The Jews took up stones again to stone him [*cp.* 8 59; 11 8]. **32** Jesus answered them, Many good works have I shewed you from the Father [*cp. vv.* 25, 37, *and* 38]; for which of those works do ye stone me? **33** The Jews answered him, For a good work we stone thee not, but for blasphemy [*cp. verse* 36]; and because that thou, being a man, makest thyself [*cp.* 5 18; 8 53; 19 7, 12] God [*cp. verse* 36: *also* 5 17, 18: *and* 19 7]. **34** Jesus answered them, Is it not written in your law [*cp.* 8 17; 18 31: *also* 15 25: *and* 7 51; 19 7], I said, Ye are gods? **35** If he called them gods, unto whom the word of God came (and the scripture cannot be broken), **36** say ye of him, whom the Father [4]sanctified [*cp.* 17 17, 19] and sent into the world [*cp.* 3 17; 17 18: *also* 3 34; 5 38; *etc.*: *and* 1 9; 3 19; *etc.*], Thou blasphemest [*cp. verse* 33]; because I said, I am *the* Son of God [*cp. verse* 33: *also* 5 17, 18: *and* 19 7]?	*cp.* 16 24; *etc.* *cp.* 9 3; 26 65. *cp.* 26 63-64. *cp.* 5 17-19. *see above.* *see above.*	*cp.* 8 34; *etc.* *cp.* 2 7; 14 64. *cp.* 14 61-62. *see above.* *see above.*	*cp.* 9 23; *etc.* *cp.* 5 21. *cp.* 22 70. *cp.* 16 17. *see above.* *see above.*

37 If I do not the works of my Father [*cp. vv.* 25, 32, *and* 38], believe me not. **38** But if I do them, though ye believe not me, believe the works [*cp.* 14 11: *also vv.* 25, 32, 37, *above; etc.*]: that ye may know and understand that the Father is in me, and I in the Father [*cp.* 14 10, 11; 17 21: *also* 14 20; 17 23]. **39** They sought again to take him [*cp.* 7 30, 32, 44; 11 57: *also* 5 18; 7 1, 19,. 25; 8 37, 40; 11 53: *and* 5 16]: and he went forth out of their hand [*cp.* 8 59: *also* 12 36: Luke 4 30].	*cp.* 21 46: *also* 12 14; 26 4; 27 1.	*cp.* 12 12: *also* 3 6; 11 18; 14 1.	*cp.* 20 19: *also* 19 47; 22 2: *and* 6 11.

¹ Some ancient authorities read *At that time was the feast.*   ² Some ancient authorities read *That which my Father hath given unto me.*   ³ Or, aught   ⁴ Or, *consecrated*

John 10 22: *cp.* I Macc. 4 59.   John 10 33: *cp.* Lev. 24 16.   John 10 34 = Ps. 82 6.

(viii) Beyond Jordan (§ 48)

§ 48. **Many acknowledge that John's Witness to Jesus was true**

John 10 40-42

40 And he went away again beyond Jordan into the place where John was at the first baptizing [*cp.* 1 28: 3 26: *also* 3 23]; and there he abode. **41** And many came unto him; and they said, John indeed did no sign: but all things whatsoever John spake of this man were true [*cp.* 1 7, 15, 29-34; 3 27-36; 5 33]. **42** And many believed on him there [*cp.* 2 11, 23; 4 39, 41; 7 31; 8 30; 11 45; 12 11, 42: *also* 7 48].	*cp.* 19 1. *cp.* 3 1, 6. *cp.* 18 6.	*cp.* 10 1. *cp.* 1 4-5. *cp.* 9 42.	*cp.* 3 3.

C. The Passion and Resurrection (§§ 49-85)

(i) The Prologue to the Passion (§§ 49-59)

§ 49. **Mary and Martha appeal to Jesus to come and help Lazarus**

John 11 1-16

1 Now a certain man was sick, Lazarus of Bethany [*cp.* 12 1], of the village of Mary and her sister Martha. **2** And it was that Mary which anointed the Lord [*cp.* 4 1; 6 23; 20 2, 18, 20, 25; 21 7, 12] with ointment, and wiped his feet with her hair [*cp.* 12 3], whose brother Lazarus was sick. **3** The sisters therefore sent unto him, saying, Lord, behold, he whom thou lovest [*cp. verses* 5 *and* 36] is sick. **4** But when Jesus heard it, he said, This sickness is not unto death, but [*cp.* 9 3] for the glory of God [*cp.* 11 40], that the Son of God may be glorified thereby [*cp.* 12 23; 13 31: *also* 7 39; 12 16; 17 10: *and* 8 54; 13 32; 16 14; 17 1 *ff.*]. **5** Now Jesus loved [*cp. verses* 3 *and* 36] Martha, and her sister, and Lazarus. **6** When therefore he heard that he was sick, he abode at that time two days in the place where he was. **7** Then after this he saith to the disciples, Let us go into Judæa again. **8** The disciples say unto him, Rabbi [*cp.* 1 38, 49; 3 2; 4 31; 6 25; 9 2: *also* 20 16: *and* 3 26], the Jews were but now seeking to stone thee [*cp.* 10 31: *also* 8 59]; and goest thou thither again? **9** Jesus answered, Are there not twelve hours in the day? If a man walk in the day [*cp.* 9 4; 12 35], he stumbleth not, because he seeth the light of this world. **10** But if a man walk in the night [*cp.* 8 12; 12 35: *also* 9 4; 13 30], he stumbleth, because the light is not in him. **11** These things spake he: and after this he saith unto them, Our friend Lazarus is fallen asleep; but I go, that I may awake him out of sleep. **12** The disciples therefore said unto him, Lord, if he is fallen asleep, he will ¹recover. **13** Now Jesus had spoken	*cp.* 26 25, 49: *also* 23 7, 8. *cp.* 9 24.	*cp.* 16 19, 20. *cp.* 9 5; 11 21; 14 45: *also* 10 51. *cp.* 5 39.	*cp.* 10 38, 39. *cp.* 7 13, 19; 10 1, 39, 41; 11 39; 12 42; 13 15; 17 5, 6; 18 6; 19 8; 22 61; 24 34: *also* 24 3. *cp.* 8 52.

of his death: but they thought [*cp.* 3 10; 4 33; 8 27, 43; 10 6; 12 16; 13 7, 28, 36; 14 5-10, 22; 16 17-18] that he spake of taking rest in sleep. **14** Then Jesus therefore said unto them plainly [*cp.* 7 4, 13, 26; 10 24; 11 54; 16 25, 29; 18 20: *and* Mark 8 32], Lazarus is dead [*cp.* 1 48; 2 24, 25; 4 19, 29; 5 6, 42; 6 61, 64; 13 11, 18; 16 19, 30; 18 4; 21 17]. **15** And I am glad for your sakes that I was not there, to the intent ye may believe [*cp.* 13 19; 14 29: *also* 19 35; 20 31: *and* 11 42]; nevertheless let us go unto him. **16** Thomas [*cp.* 14 5; 20 24, 26-29; 21 2] therefore, who is called [2]Didymus [*cp.* 20 24; 21 2], said unto his fellow-disciples, Let us also go, that we may die with him [*cp.* 13 37].

[1] Gr. *be saved.*   [2] That is, *Twin.*

cp. 15 16; 16 8-12.	*cp.*4 13; 6 52; 7 18; 8 17-21; 9 10, 32; 16 14.	*cp.*2 50; 9 45; 18 34.
cp. 9 4; 12 25; 16 8.	*cp.* 2 8; 8 17.	*cp.* 5 22; 6 8; 9 47; 11 17.
cp. 10 3.	*cp.* 3 18.	*cp.* 6 15.
cp. 26 35.	*cp.* 14 31.	*cp.* 22 33.

§ 50. **The Raising of Lazarus**

John 11 17-44

17 So when Jesus came, he found that he had been in the tomb four days already [*cp. verse* 39]. **18** Now Bethany was nigh unto Jerusalem, about fifteen furlongs off; **19** and many of the Jews [*cp.* 11 45] had come to Martha and Mary, to console them concerning their brother [*cp. verse* 31]. **20** Martha therefore, when she heard that Jesus was coming, went and met him: but Mary still sat in the house. **21** Martha therefore said unto Jesus, Lord, if thou hadst been here, my brother had not died [*cp. verse* 32: *also* 4 49]. **22** And even now I know that, whatsoever thou shalt ask of God, God will give thee. **23** Jesus saith unto her, Thy brother shall rise again. **24** Martha saith unto him, I know that he shall rise again in the resurrection at the last day [*cp.* 6 39, 40, 44, 54; 12 48]. **25** Jesus said unto her, I am the resurrection [*cp.* 5 21; 6 39, 40, 44, 54], and the life [*cp.* 14 6: *also* 1 4; 5 26; 6 57]: he that believeth on me, though he die, yet shall he live: **26** and whosoever liveth and believeth on me shall never die [*cp.* 3 15, 16, 36; 5 24; 6 40, 47; 20 31: *also* 6 50, 51, 54, 58; 8 51; 10 28]. Believest thou this? **27** She saith unto him, Yea, Lord: I have believed [*cp.* 6 69; 9 38; 16 30: *also* 16 27; 17 8: *and* 20 31] that thou art the Christ [*cp.* 1 41; 4 25, 26, 29; 7 26, 41; 9 22; 10 24; 20 31], the Son of God [*cp.* 1 34, 49: *also* 3 18; 5 25; 9 35; 10 36; 11 4; 19 7: *and* 1 18; 3 16-17, 35-36; *etc.*: *and* 20 31], *even* he that cometh [*cp.* 1 15, 27; 3 31; 6 14; 12 13: *also* 1 30]

		cp. 10 39.

into the world. **28** And when she had said this, she went away, and called Mary [1]her sister secretly, saying, The [2]Master [*cp.* 13 13, 14: *also* 1 38; *etc.*] is here, and calleth thee. **29** And she, when she heard it, arose quickly, and went unto him. **30** (Now Jesus was not yet come into the village, but was still in the place where Martha met him.) **31** The Jews then which were with her in the house, and were comforting her [*cp. verse* 19], when they saw Mary, that she rose up quickly and went out, followed her, supposing that she was going unto the tomb to [3]weep there. **32** Mary therefore, when she came where Jesus was, and saw him, fell down [*cp.* 18 6: *also* 9 38] at his feet, saying unto him, Lord, if thou hadst been here, my brother had not died [*cp. verse* 21: *also* 4 49]. **33** When Jesus therefore saw her [4]weeping, and the Jews *also* [4]weeping which came with her, he [5]groaned in the spirit, and [6]was troubled [*cp.* 12 27; 13 21: *also* 14 1, 27], **34** and said, Where have ye laid him? They say unto him, Lord, come and see [*cp.* 1 39, 46; 4 29]. **35** Jesus wept. **36** The Jews therefore said, Behold how he loved him [*cp.* 11 3, 5]! **37** But some of them said, Could not this man, which opened the eyes of him that was blind [*cp.* 9

cp. 16 16: *also* 26 63, 68; 27, 17, 22.	*cp.* 8 29: *also* 14 61; 15 32.	*cp.* 9 20: *also* 22 67; 23 2, 35, 39.
cp. 4 3, 6; 8 29; 14 33; 16 16; 26 63; 27 40, 43, 54: *also* 3 17; 17 5.	*cp.* 1 1; 3 11; 5 7; 15 39: *also* 1 11; 9 7.	*cp.* 1 35; 4 3, 9, 41; 8 28; 22 70: *also* 3 22; 9 35.
cp. 3 11; 11 3; 21 9; 23 39.	*cp.* 11 9: *also* 1 7.	*cp.* 7 19, 20; 13 35; 19 38: *also* 3 16.
cp. 26 18.	*cp.* 14 14.	*cp.* 22 11.
cp. 2 11: *also* 17 14: *and* 8 2; 9 18; 14 33; 15 25; 20 20; 28 9, 17.	*cp.* 3 11; 5 22, 33; 7 25: *also* 1 40; 10 17; *and* 5 6.	*cp.* 5 8, 12; 8 28, 41, 47; 17 16: *also* 24 52.

6-7], have caused that this man also should not die? **38** Jesus therefore again [7]groaning in himself cometh to the tomb. Now it was a cave, and a stone lay [8]against it. **39** Jesus saith, Take ye away the stone. Martha, the sister of him that was dead, saith unto him, Lord, by this time he stinketh: for he hath been *dead* four days [*cp. verse* 17]. **40** Jesus saith unto her, Said I not unto thee [*cp. verses* 25 *and* 26], that, if thou believedst, thou shouldest see the glory of God [*cp.* 11 4]? **41** So they took away the stone.

And Jesus lifted up his eyes [*cp.* 17 1], and said, Father [*cp.* 12 27, 28; 17 1, 5, 11, 21, 24, 25], I thank thee that thou heardest me. **42** And I knew that thou hearest me always: but because of the multitude which standeth around [*cp.* 12 29] I said it, that they may believe [*cp.* 11 15; 13 19; 14 29; 19 35; 20 31] that thou didst send me [*cp.* 17 8, 21 : *also* 17 25 : *and* 5 36, 38; 6 29 : *and* 3 17, 34; *etc.*]. **43** And when he had thus spoken, he cried with a loud voice [*cp.* 4 50; 5 8], Lazarus, come forth [*cp.* 5 28]. **44** He that was dead came forth [*cp.* 5 29], bound hand and foot with [9]grave-clothes [*cp.* 19 40]; and his face was bound about with a napkin [*cp.* 20 7]. Jesus saith unto them, Loose him, and let him go.

cp. 14 19. *cp.* 11 25, 26; 26 39, 42: *also* 14 23; 19 13; 26 36, 39, 42, 44: *and* 6 9.	*cp.* 6 41; 7 34. *cp.* 14 36: *also* 1 35; 6 46; 14 32, 35, 39.	*cp.* 9 16. *cp.* 10 21, 22; 22 42; 23 34, 46: *also* 3 21; 5 16; 6 12; 9 18; *etc.*: *and* 11 2.
cp. 16 28; 27 47: *also* 26 73.	*cp.* 9 1; 11 5; 14 47; 15 35: *also* 14 69, 70; 15 39.	*cp.* 9 27; 19 24.
cp. 8 8, 13; *etc.*	*cp.* 10 52; *etc.*	*cp.* 18 42; *etc.*

[1] Or, *her sister, saying secretly*   [2] Or, *Teacher*   [3] Gr. *wail.*   [4] Gr. *wailing.*
[5] Or, *was moved with indignation in the spirit*   [6] Gr. *troubled himself.*   [7] Or, *being moved with indignation in himself*   [8] Or, *upon*   [9] Or, *grave-bands*

§ 51. A Report is made to the Pharisees

John 11 45-46

45 Many therefore of the Jews [*cp.* 11 19], which came to Mary and beheld [1]that which he did [*cp.* 2 23; 6 2; 7 3], believed on him [*cp.* 12 11: *also* 2 11, 23; 4 39, 41; 7 31; 8 30; 10 42; 12 42: *and* 7 48]. **46** But some of them went away to the Pharisees, and told them the things which Jesus had done.

cp. 18 6.	*cp.* 9 42.	

[1] Many ancient authorities read *the things which he did.*

§ 52. The Plot to destroy Jesus

John 11 47-53	Matt. 26 1-5	Mark 14 1-2	Luke 22 1-2
	1 And it came to pass, when Jesus had finished all these words, he said unto his disciples, **2** Ye know that after two days		
cp. 11 55.	the passover *cp.* 26 17. cometh,	**1** Now after two days was *the feast of* the passover and the unleavened bread [*cp.* 14 12]:	**1** Now the feast of unleavened bread [*cp.* 22 7] drew nigh, which is called the Passover.
cp. 2 19; 3 14; 12 32-33.	and the Son of man is delivered up to be crucified [*cp.* 16 21; 17 12, 22-23; 20 18-19: *also* 20 28; 26 24, 25]. **3** Then were gathered together the chief priests,	*cp.* 8 31; 9 12, 31; 10 33-34: *also* 10 45; 14 21, 41.	*cp.* 9 22, 44; 18 31-33; 24 7: *also* 13 32-33; 17 25; 22 22.
47 The chief priests therefore and the Pharisees gathered a council, and said, What	and the elders of the people, unto the court [*cp.* 26 57, 58: *also*	and the chief priests and the scribes *cp.* 14 53, 54: *also* 14 66.	**2** And the chief priests and the scribes *cp.* 22 55.

do we? for this man doeth many signs. **48** If we let him thus alone, all men will believe on him [*cp.* 12 19]: and the Romans will come and take away both our place [*cp.* 4 20] and our nation. **49** But a certain one of them,	26 69: *and* John 18 15]		
	cp. 21 46: *also verse 5 below.*	*cp.* 11 18; 12 12: *also verse 2 below.*	*cp.* 19 48; 20 19: *also verse 2 below.*
	of the high priest, who was called Caiaphas [*cp.* 26 57];		
Caiaphas [*cp.* 18 13, 14, 24, 28], being high priest that year [*cp. verse* 51 *below and* 18 13], said unto them, Ye know nothing at all, **50** nor do ye take account that it is expedient [*cp.* 16 7; 18 14] for you that one man should die for the people [*cp.* 18 14], and that the whole nation perish not. **51** Now this he said not of himself: but being high priest that year [*cp. verse* 49 *above and* 18 13], he prophesied that Jesus should die for the nation [*cp.* 10 11, 15, 17]; **52** and			*cp.* 3 2.
not for the nation only [*cp.* 10 16], but that he might also gather together into one [*cp.* 10 16; 17 11, 21, 22, 23: *also* 12 32] the children of God [*cp.* 1 12: *also* 12 36] that are scattered abroad. **53** So from that day forth	*cp.* 20 28. *cp.* 8 11; 10 18; 21 31, 41, 43; 22 7-10; 24 14; 26 13; 28 19.	*cp.* 10 45. *cp.* 12 9; 13 10; 14 9; 16 15.	*cp.* 2 30-32; 3 6; 13 29; 14 21-24; 20 16; 24 47.
	cp. 5 9: *also* 5 45: *and* 8 12; 13 38.		*cp.* 20 36: *also* 6 35; 16 8.
they took counsel that they might	**4** and they took counsel together that they might take Jesus by subtilty, and kill him [*cp.* 12 14; 21 46; 27 1: *also* 22 15: *and* 12 10].	sought how they might take him with subtilty, and kill him [*cp.* 3 6; 11 18; 12 12: *also* 12 13: *and* 3 2]:	sought how they might
put him to death [*cp.* 5 18; 7 1, 19, 25; 8 37, 40: *also* 5 16; 7 30, 32, 44; 10 39; 11 57].	**5** But they said, Not during the feast, lest a tumult arise among the people.	**2** for they said, Not during the feast, lest haply there shall be a tumult of the people.	put him to death [*cp.* 6 11; 19 47; 20 19, 20: *also* 11 53-54: *and* 6 7]; for they feared the people.

§ 53. Jesus withdraws

John 11 54-57

54 Jesus therefore walked no more openly [*cp.* 7 4, 13, 26; 10 24; 11 14; 16 25, 29; 18 20] among the Jews, but departed thence into the country near to the wilderness, into a city called Ephraim; and there he tarried with the disciples [*cp.* 3 22]. **55** Now the passover of the Jews was at hand [*cp.* 2 13; 6 4: *also* 5 1; 7 2]: and many went up to Jerusalem out of the country before the passover, to purify themselves [*cp.* 18 28]. **56** They sought therefore for Jesus [*cp.* 7 11], and spake one with another, as they stood in the temple, What think ye? That he will not come to the feast? **57** Now the chief priests and the Pharisees had given commandment, that, if any man knew where he was, he should shew it, that they might take him [*cp.* 7 30, 32, 44; 10 39: *also* 5 18; 7 1, 19, 25; 8 37, 40; 11 53: *and* 5 16].	*cp.* 17 25; 18 12; 21 28; 22 17, 42; 26 66.	*cp.* 8 32.	

John 11 55: *cp.* II Chron. 30 17: *also* Num. 9 6.

§ 54. **The Anointing in Bethany**

John **12** 1-8	Matt. 26 6-13	Mark 14 3-9	Luke 7 36-50
1 Jesus therefore six days before the passover [cp. 13 1] came to Bethany [cp. 11 1],	**6** Now when Jesus was in Bethany, in the house of Simon the leper,	**3** And while he was in Bethany [cp. 11 1] in the house of Simon the leper,	cp. 19 29. cp. 7 40, 43, 44. **36** And one of the Pharisees desired him that he would eat [cp. 7 34] with him. And he entered into the Pharisee's house,
where Lazarus was, whom Jesus raised from the dead. **2** So they made him a supper there: and Martha served; but Lazarus was one of them that sat at meat with him. **3** Mary therefore			cp. 10 40.
	as he sat at meat, there came a woman	as he sat at meat, there came a woman	and sat down to meat [cp. 11 37; 14 1]. **37** And behold, a woman which was in the city, a sinner [cp. 7 34]; and when she knew that he was sitting at meat in the Pharisee's house, she brought [1]an alabaster cruse of ointment,
took a pound of ointment of [1]spikenard, very precious,	having [1]an alabaster cruse of exceeding precious ointment, and she poured it upon his head, as he sat at meat.	having [1]an alabaster cruse of ointment of [2]spikenard very costly; *and* she brake the cruse, and poured it over his head.	
and anointed the feet of Jesus, and wiped his feet with her hair [cp. 11 2]: and the house was filled with the odour of the ointment. **4** But Judas Iscariot [cp. 14 22: *also* 6 71; 13 2, 26], one of his disciples, which should betray him [cp. 6 64, 71; 13 11; 18 2, 5: *also* 13 2, 21],	**8** But cp. 10 4; 26 14. when the disciples cp. 10 4; 26 25, 46, 48; 27 3: *also* 26 21, 23, 24.	**4** But cp. 3 19; 14 10. there were some cp. 3 19; 14 42, 44: *also* 14 18, 21.	**38** and standing behind at his feet [cp. 8 35; 10 39], weeping, she began to wet his feet with her tears, and wiped them with the hair of her head, and [2]kissed his feet, and anointed them with the ointment. **39** Now cp. 6 16; 22 3. cp. 22 21, 22. when the Pharisee which had bidden him
saith,	saw it, they had indignation, saying,	they had indignation among themselves, *saying,*	saw it, he spake within himself [cp. 11 38], saying,
	To what purpose is this waste?	To what purpose hath this waste of the ointment been made? **5** For this	
5 Why was not this ointment sold for three hundred [2]pence, and given to the poor [cp. 13 29]? **6** Now this he said, not because he cared for the poor; but because he was a thief, and having the [3]bag [cp.	**9** For this ointment might have been sold for much, and given to the poor. cp. 15 23; 19 13.	ointment might have been sold for above three hundred [3]pence, and given to the poor. And they murmured against her [cp. 10 13].	cp. 18 15.

John

13 29] [4]took away what was
put therein. **7** Jesus therefore
cp. 5 6; 6 15.
said,

[5]Suffer her to keep it against
the day of my burying. **8** For
the poor ye have always
with you;

but me ye have not always.

cp. 10 16; 11 52.

[1] See marginal note on Mark 14 3.
[2] See marginal note on Matt. 18 28.
[3] Or, *box*
[4] Or, *carried what was put therein*
[5] Or, *Let her alone:* it was *that she might keep it*

Matthew

10 But Jesus
perceiving it [*cp.* 12 15; 16 8;
22 18] said unto them,
Why trouble ye
the woman? for she hath
wrought a good work upon me.
cp. 19 14.
11 For
ye have the poor always
with you;

but me ye have not always.
12 For in that
she [2]poured this ointment
upon my body, she
did it to prepare me for
burial. **13** Verily I say
unto you, Wheresoever [3]this
gospel [*cp.* 4 23; 9 35; 24 14]
shall
be preached in the
whole world [*cp.* 24 14: *also*
8 11; 10 18; 21 31, 41, 43;
22 7-10; 28 19], that also
which this woman hath done
shall be spoken of for a memorial
of her.

[1] Or, *a flask*
[2] Gr. *cast.*
[3] Or, *these good tidings*

Mark

6 But Jesus
cp. 8 17.
said, Let
her alone; why trouble ye
her? she hath
wrought a good work on me.
cp. 10 14.
7 For
ye have the poor always
with you, and whensoever ye
will ye can do them good:
but me ye have not always.
8 She hath done what she
could: she hath anointed
my body aforehand
for the
burying. **9** And verily I say
unto you, Wheresoever the
gospel [*cp.* 1 1, 14, 15; 8 35;
10 29; 13 10; 16 15] shall
be preached throughout the
whole world [*cp.* 13 10: *also*
12 9; 16 15],
that also
which this woman hath done
shall be spoken of for a memorial
of her.

[1] Or, *a flask*
[2] Gr. *pistic nard,* pistic being perhaps a local name. Others take it to mean *genuine*; others, *liquid.*
[3] See marginal note on Matt. 18 28.

Luke

cp. 18 16.

cp. 2 30-32;
3 6; *etc.*

John: *cp.* 4 19, 44; 6 14; 7 40; 9 17. — *cp.* 1 38. — *cp.* 5 12: *also* 12 34.

Matthew: *cp.* 13 57; 21 11, 46. — *cp.* 9 11; 11 19. — *cp.* 26 6. — *cp.* 18 23-34. — *cp.* 18 25. — *cp*, 9 22; 16 23. — *cp.* 9 2. — *cp.* 8 27; 21 10. — *cp.* 9 22.

Mark: *cp.* 6 4, 15. — *cp.* 2 16. — *cp.* 14 3. — *cp.* 5 30; 8 33. — *cp.* 2 5. — *cp.* 1 27; 2 7; 4 41. — *cp.* 5 34; 10 52.

Luke:

This man, if he were [3]a prophet [*cp.* 4 24; 7 16; 13 33; 24 19], would have
perceived who and what manner of woman this is which toucheth him,
that she is a sinner [*cp.* 5 30; 15 2; 19 7]. **40** And Jesus answering said unto
him, Simon, I have somewhat to say unto thee. And he saith, [4]Master, say
on. **41** A certain lender had two debtors: the one owed five hundred [5]pence,
and the other fifty. **42** When they had not *wherewith* to pay, he forgave
them both. Which of them therefore will love him most? **43** Simon answered and said, He, I suppose, to whom he forgave the most. And he said
unto him, Thou hast rightly judged [*cp.* 10 28]. **44** And turning [*cp.* 7 9;
9 55; 10 23; 14 25; 22 61; 23 28] to the woman, he said unto Simon, Seest
thou this woman? I entered into thine house, thou gavest me no water for
my feet: but she hath wetted my feet with her tears, and wiped them with
her hair. **45** Thou gavest me no kiss: but she, since the time I came in, hath
not ceased to [6]kiss my feet. **46** My head with oil thou didst not anoint: but
she hath anointed my feet with ointment. **47** Wherefore I say unto thee,
Her sins, which are many, are forgiven; for she loved much: but to whom
little is forgiven, *the same* loveth little. **48** And he said unto her, Thy sins are
forgiven [*cp.* 5 20]. **49** And they that sat at meat with him began to say
[7]within themselves, Who is this [*cp.* 5 21: *also* 4 36; 8 25; 9 9] that even
forgiveth sins? **50** And he said unto the woman, Thy faith hath saved thee
[*cp.* 8 48; 17 19; 18 42]; go in peace [*cp.* 8 48].

[1] Or, *a flask* [2] Gr. *kissed much.* [3] Some ancient authorities read *the prophet.* See John 1 21, 25. [4] Or, *Teacher* [5] See footnote on Matt. 18 28. [6] Gr. *kiss much.* [7] Or, *among*

§ 55. The Common People come to see both Jesus and Lazarus

John 12 9-11

9 The common people therefore of the Jews learned that he was there: and they came, not for Jesus' sake only, but that they might see Lazarus also, whom he had raised from the dead [*cp.* 12 17-19]. **10** But the chief priests took counsel that they might put Lazarus also to death; **11** because that by reason of him many of the Jews went away, and believed on Jesus [*cp.* 11 45: *also* 2 11, 23; 4 39, 41; 7 31; 8 30; 10 42; 12 42: *and* 7 48].

cp. 18 6.   *cp.* 9 42.   *cp.* 16 31.

§ 56. The Triumphal Entry

John 12 12-19	Matt. 21 1-11	Mark 11 1-11	Luke 19 29-40
12 On the morrow [*cp.* 1 29, 35, 43; 6 22] ¹a great	*cp.* 27 62.	*cp.* 11 12.	
	1 And when they drew nigh unto Jerusalem, and came unto Bethphage,	**1** And when they draw nigh unto Jerusalem, unto Bethphage and Bethany, at the mount	**29** And it came to pass, when he drew nigh unto Bethphage and Bethany, at the mount
cp. 12 1.	unto the mount of Olives, then Jesus sent two	of Olives, he sendeth two [*cp.* 14 13: *also* 6 7] of his disciples, **2** and saith	that is called *the mount* of Olives, he sent two [*cp.* 22 8: *also* 10 1] of
	disciples, **2** saying unto them, Go into the village that is over against you, and straightway	unto them, Go your way into the village that is over against you: and straightway as ye enter	the disciples, **30** saying, Go your way into the village over against *you;* in the which as ye enter
	ye shall find an ass tied, and a colt with her:	into it, ye shall find a colt tied, whereon no man	ye shall find a colt tied, whereon no man
cp. 19 41.	loose *them,* and bring *them* unto me. **3** And if any one say aught unto you,	ever yet sat; loose him, and bring him. **3** And if any one say unto you, Why do ye this?	ever yet sat [*cp.* 23 53]: loose him, and bring him. **31** And if any one ask you, Why do ye loose
	ye shall say, The Lord hath need of them; and straightway he will send them.	say ye, The Lord hath need of him; and straightway he ¹will send him ²back hither.	him? thus shall ye say, The Lord hath need of him.
	4 Now this is come to pass, that it might be fulfilled which was spoken ¹by the prophet, saying, **5** Tell ye the daughter of Zion,		
verse 15	Behold, thy King cometh unto thee, Meek, and riding upon an ass, And upon a colt the foal of an ass.		
	6 And the disciples went,	**4** And they went away, and found a colt tied at the door without in the open street; and they loose him. **5** And	**32** And they that were sent went away, and found even as he had said unto them [*cp.* 22 13]. **33** And as they were loosing the colt,
cp. 11 42; 12 29.	and did	certain of them that stood there [*cp.* 9 1; 14 47; 15 35: *also* 14 69, 70; 15 39] said unto them, What do	*cp.* 9 27: *also* 19 24. the owners thereof said unto them, Why
	cp. 16 28; 27 47: *also* 26 73.		

verse 14

multitude that had come to the feast, when they heard that Jesus was coming to Jerusalem,

13 took the branches of the palm trees,

and

went forth to meet him, and cried out,

verses 17 and 18

Hosanna:

Blessed *is* he that cometh [*cp.* 1 15, 27; 3 31; 6 14; 11 27: *also* 1 30] in the name [*cp.* 5 43; 10 25: *also* 17 12] of the Lord, even the King of Israel [*cp.* 1 49: *also* 18 33, 39; 19 3, 19, 21: *and* 6 15; 12 15; 18 37].

cp. 14 27; 16 33.

14 And Jesus, having found a young ass, sat thereon; as it is written, **15** Fear not, daughter of Zion: behold, thy King cometh, sitting on an ass's colt. **16** These things understood not his disciples [*cp.* 4 33; 11 13; 13 7, 28, 36; 14 5-10, 22; 16 17-18: *also* 3 10; 8 27, 43; 10 6] at the first: but when Jesus was glorified [*cp.* 7 39; 12 23; 13 31: *also* 11 4; 17 10: *and* 17 1 *ff.*],

---

even as Jesus appointed them [*cp.* 26 19],

7 and brought the ass, and the colt, and put on them their garments; and he sat thereon. **8** And the most part of the multitude

spread their garments in the way; and others cut branches from the trees, and spread them in the way. **9** And

the multitudes that went before him, and that followed, cried,

saying, Hosanna [*cp.* 21 15] to the son of David [*cp.* 1 1; 9 27; 12 23; 15 22; 20 30, 31; 21 15]: Blessed *is* he that cometh [*cp.* 3 11; 11 3]

in the name of the Lord [= 23 39]; *cp.* 27 42: *also* 2 2; 27 11, 29, 37: *and* 21 5.

cp. 5 9; 10 13.

Hosanna in the highest

verse 7

verses 4 and 5

cp. 15 16; 16 8-12.

---

ye, loosing the colt? **6** And they said unto them even as Jesus had said: and they let them go. **7** And they bring the colt unto Jesus, and cast on him their garments; and he sat upon him. **8** And

many

spread their garments upon the way; and others 3branches, which they had cut from the fields.

9 And

they that went before, and they that followed, cried,

Hosanna; *cp.* 10 47, 48.

Blessed *is* he that cometh [*cp.* 1 7]

in the name of the Lord: *cp.* 15 32: *also* 15 2, 9, 12, 18, 26.

10 Blessed *is* the kingdom that cometh, *the kingdom* of our father David: *cp.* 9 50.

Hosanna in the highest.

verse 7

cp. 4 13; 6 52; 7 18; 8 17-21; 9 10, 32: *also* 16 14.

---

loose ye the colt? **34** And they said, The Lord hath need of him.

35 And they brought him to Jesus: and they threw their garments upon the colt, and set Jesus thereon. **36** And

as he went, they spread their garments in the way.

37 And as he was now drawing nigh, *even* at the descent of the mount of Olives, the whole multitude of the disciples *cp.* 18 39.

began to rejoice and praise God [*cp.* 2 13, 20; 18 43] with a loud voice for all the 1mighty works which they had seen; **38** saying,

cp. 18 38, 39: *also* 1 32.

Blessed *is* the King [*see below*] that cometh [*cp.* 7 19, 20: *also* 3 16]

in the name of the Lord [= 13 35]: *cp.* 23 3, 37, 38: *also* 23 2: *and* 1 33.

peace [*cp.* 2 14: *also* 1 79; 2 29; 19 42] in heaven, and glory in the highest [*cp.* 2 14].

verse 35

cp. 9 45; 18 34: *also* 2 50.

then [cp. 13 7] remembered they that these things were written of him, and that they had done these things unto him [cp. 2 22: also 14 26; 16 4]. **17** The multitude therefore that was with him when he called Lazarus out of the tomb, and raised him from the dead, bare witness [cp. 12 9-11]. **18** For this cause also the multitude went and met him, for that they heard that he had done this sign [cp. 12 9-11].
19 The Pharisees therefore said

among themselves, ²Behold how ye prevail nothing: lo, the world is gone after him [cp. 11 48: also 3 26].

cp. 5 12: also 12 34.

cp. 4 19, 44; 6 14; 7 40; 9 17.
cp. 1 45; 18 5, 7; 19 19.

¹ Some ancient authorities read *the common people.*
² Or, *Ye behold*

---

cp. 26 75.

cp. 21 15-16.

cp. 21 46; 26 5.
10 And when he was come into Jerusalem, all the city was stirred, saying, Who is this [cp. 8 27]? **11** And the multitudes said, This is the prophet [cp. 13 57; 21 46], Jesus, from Nazareth [cp. 2 23; 26 71] of Galilee.

¹ Or, *through*

---

cp. 14 72.

cp. 11 18; 12 12; 14 2.
11 And   he entered into Jerusalem . . .

cp. 4 41: also 1 27.

cp. 6 4, 15.
cp. 1 24; 10 47; 14 67; 16 6.

¹ Gr. *sendeth.*
² Or, *again*
³ Gr. *layers of leaves.*

---

cp. 24 6, 8: also 22 61.

cp. 16 31.
verse 37

39 And some of the Pharisees from the multitude said unto him, ²Master, rebuke [cp. 18 39] thy disciples. **40** And he answered and said, I tell you that, if these shall hold their peace [cp. 18 39], the stones will cry out [cp. 18 39].

cp. 19 48; 20 19; 22 2.

cp. 5 21; 7 49; 8 25; 9 9: also 4 36.
cp. 4 24; 7 16, 39; 13 33; 24 19.
cp. 4 34; 18 37; 24 19.

¹ Gr. *powers.*
² Or, *Teacher*

Matt. 21 5: cp. Is. 62 11.   John 12 13: cp. I Macc. 13 51.   John 12 13 || Matt. 21 9 || Mark 11 9 || Luke 19 38: cp. Ps. 118 25-26.   John 12 15 || Matt. 21 5 = Zech. 9 9.

§ 57. Certain Greeks wish to see Jesus

John 12 20-36a

20 Now there were certain Greeks [cp. 7 35] among those that went up to worship at the feast: **21** these therefore came to Philip [cp. 1 43-48; 6 5-7; 14 8-9], which was of Bethsaida [cp. 1 44] of Galilee, and asked him, saying, Sir, we would see Jesus. **22** Philip cometh and telleth Andrew [cp. 1 40, 44; 6 8]: Andrew cometh, and Philip, and they tell Jesus. **23** And Jesus answereth them, saying, The hour is come [cp. 13 1; 17 1: also 12 27: and 2 4; 7 6, 8, 30; 8 20], that the Son of man should be glorified [cp. 7 39; 12 16; 13 31: also 11 4; 17 10: and 17 1 ff.]. **24** Verily, verily, I say unto you, Except a grain of wheat fall into the earth and die, it abideth by itself alone; but if it die, it beareth much fruit.

	Matt.	Mark	Luke
		cp. 7 26.	
	cp. 10 3.	cp. 3 18.	cp. 6 14.
	cp. 11 21.	cp. 6 45; 8 22.	cp. 10 13.
			cp. 9 9; 19 3.
	cp. 4 18; 10 2.	cp. 1 16, 29; 3 18; 13 3.	cp. 6 14.
	cp. 26 45: also 26 18.	cp. 14 41: also 14 35.	cp. 22 14: also 22 53.

cp. *verse 25.*

Matt. 10 **37** He that loveth   father or mother   more than me is not worthy of me; and he that loveth son or daughter
cp. 19 27-29.

cp. 10 28-30.

Luke 14 **26** If any man cometh unto me, and hateth not his own father, and mother, and wife [cp. 18 29],   and   children, and brethren, and sisters [cp. 18 28-30],

[Matt., top] more
than me is not worthy of me.
cp. 8 18-22.
38 And he that doth not take his
cross and follow after me, is not worthy
of me.

[Luke, top] yea, and his own life also,
he can-
not be my disciple [*cp.* 9 57-62].
27 Whosoever doth not bear his own
cross, and come after me,
cannot be my disciple.

[John]

25 He that
loveth his ¹life
loseth it; and he that
hateth [*cp.* Luke 14 26
above] his ¹life
in this world shall
keep it unto life eternal.
26 If any man
serve me,
let him

follow
me [*cp.* 1 43; 21 19, 22];
and where I am [*cp.* 7 34,
36; 14 3; 17 24], there
shall also my servant be
[*cp.* 14 3; 17 24]: if any
man serve me, him will

cp. 15 21.

the
Father honour.

27 Now is my soul
troubled [*cp.* 11 33; 13 21: *also* 14 1,
27];

and what shall
I say?

cp. 11 41; 12 27-28; 17
1-26.

Father [*cp.* 11 41; 12 28;
17 1, 5, 11, 21, 24, 25],
save me from this ²hour
[*cp.* 12 23; 13 1; 17 1: *also*
2 4; 7 6, 8, 30; 8 20].
But for this cause
[*cp.* 18 37] came I unto
this hour.
28 Father [*see above*],

cp. 18 11.

cp. 4 34; 5 30; 6 38;
7 17; 9 31.
glorify thy name. There
came therefore a voice out
of heaven, *saying*, I have
both glorified it, and will
glorify it again. 29 The

[Matt.]

39 He that
¹findeth his ²life shall
lose it; and he that
³loseth
his ²life for my sake
[*see below*] shall
find it.
Matt. 16 24 If any man
would come after
me, let him deny him-
self, and take up his
cross, and follow
me [*cp.* 4 19; 8 22; 9 9:
19 21].

25 For whosoever would
save his ²life shall lose
it: and whosoever shall
lose his ²life for my
sake [*cp.* 5 11; 10 18, 39:
also 10 22; 19 29; 24 9]

shall find it.
26 38 Then saith he unto
them, My soul
is exceeding sorrowful,

even unto death: abide
ye here, and watch [*cp.*
24 42; 25 13; 26 41]
with me.

39 And he went
forward a little,
and
fell on his face, and
prayed [*cp.* 14 23; 19 13;
26 36, 42, 44: *also* 11 25],

cp. 11 25, 26; 26 39, 42: *also*
6 9.

cp. 26 45: *also* 26 18.

saying,
O my Father [*see above*],
if it be possible,
cp. 19 26.
let this cup [*cp.* 20
22, 23] pass away from
me: nevertheless, not as I
will, but as thou wilt
[*cp.* 26 42 *and* 6 10: *also*
7 21; 12 50; 21 31].

cp. 3 17; 17 5.

[Mark]

Mark 8 34 If any man
would come after
me, let him deny him-
self, and take up his
cross, and follow
me [*cp.* 1 17; 2 14; 10 21].

35 For whosoever would
save his ¹life shall lose
it; and whosoever shall
lose his ¹life for my
sake [*cp.* 10 29; 13 9;
also 13 13] and the
gospel's [*cp.* 10 29]
shall save it.
14 34 And he saith unto
them, My soul
is exceeding sorrowful

even unto death: abide
ye here, and watch [*cp.*
13 33, 35, 37; 14 38].

35 And he went
forward a little,
and
fell on the ground, and
prayed [*cp.* 1 35; 6 46;
14 32, 39]
that, if it were possible,
cp. 14 36.

the hour
[*cp.* 14 41]
might pass away
from him.

36 And he said, Abba,
Father [*see above*],
all things are possible
unto thee [*cp.* 10 27];
remove this cup [*cp.* 10
38, 39] from
me: howbeit not what I
will, but what thou wilt
[*cp.* 3 35].

cp. 1 11; 9 7.

[Luke]

Luke 17 33 Whosoever shall
seek to gain his ¹life shall
lose it: but whosoever shall
lose
his ¹life
shall
²preserve it.
Luke 9 23 If any man
would come after
me, let him deny him-
self, and take up his
cross daily, and follow
me [*cp.* 5 27; 9 59; 18 22].

24 For whosoever would
save his ¹life shall lose
it; but whosoever shall
lose his ¹life for my
sake [*cp.* 6 22; 18 29;
21 12, 17], the
same shall save it.

cp. 12 50.

cp. 12 37; 21 36.

22 41 And he was
parted from them about
a stone's cast; and he
kneeled down and
prayed [*cp.* 3 21; 5 16; 6 12; 9
18, 28, 29; 11 1; 22 44: *also*
10 21],

cp. 10 21, 22; 22 42; 23 34,
46: *also* 11 2.

cp. 22 14, 53.

42 saying,
Father [*see above*],
if thou be willing,
cp. 1 37; 18 27.
remove this cup
from
me: nevertheless not my
will, but thine,

be done.

cp. 3 22; 9 35.

multitude therefore, that stood by [*cp.* 11 42], and heard it, said that it had thundered: others said,	*cp.* 16 28; 27 47: *also* 26 73.	*cp.* 9 1; 11 5; 14 47; 15 35: *also* 14 69, 70; 15 39.	*cp.* 9 27; 19 24.
An angel [*cp.* 1 51]	*cp.* 4 11; 26 53.	*cp.* 1 13.	**43** [3]And there appeared unto him an angel from heaven, strengthening him.
hath spoken to him. **30** Jesus answered and said, This voice hath not come for my sake, but for your sakes. **31** Now is [3]the judgement of this world [*cp.* 3 18, 19: 5 24; 16 11: *and* 5 29; 12 48]: now shall the prince of this world [*cp.* 16 11: *also* 14 30] be cast out. **32** And I, if I be lifted up [*cp.* 3 14; 8 28] [4]from the earth, will draw [*cp.* 6 44] all men [*cp.* 10 16; 11 52; 17 11, 21, 22, 23] unto myself [*cp.* 14 3: *also* 14 21].	*cp.* 8 11; 10 18; 21 31, 41, 43; 22 7-10; 24 14; 26 13; 28 19.	*cp.* 12 9; 13 10; 14 9; 16 15.	*cp.* 10 18. *cp.* 2 30-32; 3 6; 13 29; 14 21-24; 20 16; 24 47.
33 But this he said, signifying by what manner of death he should die [*cp.* 18 32: *also* 21 19: *and* 2 19-22; 3 14; 8 28]. **34** The multitude therefore answered him, We have heard out of the law that the Christ abideth for ever: and how sayest thou [*cp.* 8 33: *also* 14 9: *and* 3 4, 9; 6 42, 52, 60: *and* 4 9; 7 15], The Son of man must be lifted up?	*cp.* 16 21-23; 17 9, 12, 22-23; 20 17-19, 28; 26 2, 24, 32.	*cp.* 8 31-33; 9 9, 12, 30-32; 10 32-34, 45; 14 21, 28.	*cp.* 9 22, 43-45; 13 32-33; 17 25; 18 31-34; 22 22; 24 7.
	[1] Or, *found* [2] Or, *soul* [3] Or, *lost*	[1] Or, *soul*	[1] Or, *soul* [2] Gr. *save it alive.* [3] Many ancient authorities omit ver. 43, 44.
who is this Son of man[*cp.* 5 12]? **35** Jesus therefore said unto them, Yet a little while [*cp.* 7 33; 13 33; 14 19; 16 16-19] is the light [5]among you. Walk while ye have the light [*cp.* 9 4; 11 9], that darkness overtake you not [*cp.* 1 5: *also* 3 19-20]: and he that walketh in the darkness [*cp.* 8 12: *also* 1 5; 12 46: *and* 11 10] knoweth not whither he goeth [*cp.* 8 14; *etc.*]. **36** While ye have the light [*cp.* 1 4, 5, 9; 8 12; 9 5; 12 46: *also* 3 19], believe on the light, that ye may become sons of light [*cp.* 1 12; 11 52].	*cp.* 8 27; 21 10. *cp.* 5 9, 45; 8 12; 13 38.	*cp.* 4 41: *also* 1 27.	*cp.* 5 21; 7 49; 8 25; 9 9: *also* 4 36. *cp.* 16 8: *also* 6 35; 20 36.

[1] Or, *soul*   [2] Or, *hour?*   [3] Or, *a judgement*   [4] Or, *out of*   [5] Or, *in*

John 12 34: *cp.* Pss. 89 4 *and* 110 4; Is. 9 7; Ezek. 37 25.

§ 58. **Jesus again withdraws**

John 12 36b-43

These things spake Jesus [*cp.* 17 1], and he departed and [1]hid himself from them [*cp.* 8 59; 10 39]. **37** But though he had done so many signs before them, yet they believed not on him [*cp.* 6 36; 10 25: *also* 1 11; 3 11, 32; 5 43]: **38** that the word of Isaiah the prophet might be fulfilled, which he spake,
Lord, who hath believed our report?
And to whom hath the arm of the Lord been revealed?
39 For this cause they could not believe [*cp.* 5 44], for that Isaiah said again,
40 He hath blinded their eyes, and he hardened their heart;
  Lest they should see with their eyes, and perceive with their heart,
  And should turn,
			cp. 4 30.

	cp. 13 15. *cp.* 19 8.	*cp.* 3 5; 10 5: *also* 6 52; 8 17; 16 14.	

And I should heal them.

41 These things said Isaiah, because he saw his glory [*cp.* 1 14; 2 11; 17 5, 22, 24]; and he spake of him [*cp.* 1 45: *also* Luke 24 27, 44]. **42** Nevertheless even of the rulers [*cp.* 3 1; 7 26, 48] many believed on him [*cp.* 7 48: *also* 2 11, 23; 4 39, 41; 7 31; 8 30; 10 42; 11 45]; but because of the Pharisees [*cp.* 7 13; 9 22; 19 38; 20 19] they did not confess ²it [*cp.* 9 22: *also* 3 2], lest they should be put out of the synagogue [*cp.* 9 22; 16 2]: **43** for they loved the glory of men more than the glory of God [*cp.* 5 44].

cp. 19 28; 25 31.	*cp.* 10 37.	*cp.* 9 26, 32; 24 26.
cp. 9 18.	*cp.* 5 22.	*cp.* 14 1; 18 18; 23 13, 35; 24 20: *also* 8 41; 13 14.

¹ Or, *was hidden from them*   ² Or, *him*

John 12 38 = Is. 53 1.   John 12 40 = Is. 6 10.   John 12 41: *cp.* Is. 6 1, 5.

§ 59. **Jesus the Father's Agent**

John **12** 44-50	Matt. 18 5; 10 40	Mark 9 37	Luke 9 48; 10 16
44 And Jesus cried and said, He that believeth on me, believeth not on me, but on him that sent me [*cp.* 14 1]. **45** And he that beholdeth me [*cp.* 14 19; 16 10, 16, 17, 19: *also* 6 40, 62] beholdeth him that sent me [*cp.* 14 9-11; 15 24: *also* 10 30; 17 11. 22: *and* 5 19].			
	18 **5** And whoso shall receive one such little child in my name [*cp.* 18 20; 24 5: *also* 7 22] receiveth me.	9 **37** Whosoever shall receive one of such little children in my name [*cp.* 9 38, 39; 13 6; 16 17], receiveth me: and whosoever receiveth me, receiveth not me, but him that sent me.	9 **48** Whosoever shall receive this little child in my name [*cp.* 9 49; 10 17; 21 8; 24 47] receiveth me: and whosoever shall receive me receiveth him that sent me.
cp. 14 13, 14, 26; 15 16; 16 23, 24, 26.			
13 **20** He that receiveth whomsoever I send receiveth me; and he that receiveth me receiveth him that sent me. **46** I am come a light into the world [*cp.* 8 12; 9 5: *also* 1 4, 5, 9; 3 19; 12 35-36: *and* 9 39; 16 28; 18 37: *and* 6 14; 11 27], that whosoever believeth on me may not abide in the darkness [*cp.* 8 12; 9 5: *also* 1 5: *and* 11 10]. **47** And if any man hear my sayings, and keep them not, I judge him not [*cp.* 8 15: *also* 3 17]: for I came not to judge the world, but to save the world [*cp.* 3 17: *also* 4 42; 5 34; 10 9].	10 **40** He that receiveth you receiveth me, and he that receiveth me receiveth him that sent me.		
	cp. 7 26.		*cp.* 6 49.
	cp. 1 21; 18 11: *also* 20 28.	*cp.* 10 45.	*cp.* 9 55; 19 10: *also* 2 11. 10 **16** He that heareth you heareth me; and he that rejecteth you rejecteth me; and he that rejecteth me rejecteth him that sent me.
48 He that rejecteth me [*cp.* 15 23: *also* 5 23], and receiveth not my sayings, hath one that judgeth him: the word that I spake [*cp.* 4 41; 5 24; 8 31, 37, 43, 51, 52; 14 23, 24; 15 3, 20: *also* 5 38; *etc.*],	*cp.* 13 19-23.	*cp.* 2 2; 4 33: *also* 4 14-20; 16 20.	*cp.* 4 32, 36: *also* 1 2; 8 12-15: *and* 5 1; 8 11, 21; 11 28.

the same shall judge him [*cp.* 5 28-29] in the last day [*cp.* 6 39, 40, 44, 54; 11 24]. **49** For I spake not from myself [*cp.* 14 10: *also* 7 17: *and* 5 19, 30; 8 28: *and* 7 28; 8 42: *and* 16 13]; but the Father which sent me, he hath given me a commandment [*cp.* 10 18; 14 31: *also* 15 10], what I should say, and what I should speak. **50** And I know that his commandment is life eternal: the things therefore which I speak, even as the Father hath said unto me, so I speak [*cp.* 3 34; 7 16; 8 26, 28, 38, 40; 14 24: *also* 15 15; 17 8, 14].

(ii) At Supper before the Passover (§§ 60-70)

§ 60. **Jesus washes the Disciples' Feet**

John 13 1-11

1 Now before the feast of the passover [*cp.* 12 1], Jesus knowing that his hour was come [*cp.* 12 23; 17 1: *also* 12 27: *and* 2 4; 7 6, 8, 30; 8 20] that he should depart out of this world unto the Father [*cp.* 14 12, 28; 16 10, 17, 28: *also* 7 33; 16 5: *and* 17 11, 13: *and* 20 17: *and verse* 3 *below*], having loved his own [*cp.* 1 11: *also* 8 44; 15 19; 16 32; 19 27: *and* 13 34; 15 9, 12] which were in the world, he loved them ¹unto the end. **2** And during supper, the devil [*cp.* 13 27: *also* 6 70] having already put into the heart of Judas Iscariot [*cp.* 6 71; 12 4; 13 26; 14 22], Simon's *son* [*cp.* 6 71; 13 26], to betray him [*see verse* 11 *below*], **3** *Jesus*, knowing that the Father had given all things into his hands [*cp.* 3 35; 5 27; 17 2], and that he came forth from God [*cp.* 8 42; 16 27, 28, 30; 17 8], and goeth unto God [*see verse* 1 *above*], **4** riseth from supper, and layeth aside his garments; and he took a towel, and girded himself. **5** Then he poureth water into the bason, and began to wash the disciples' feet, and to wipe them with the towel wherewith he was girded. **6** So he cometh to Simon Peter. He saith unto him, Lord, dost thou wash my feet? **7** Jesus answered and said unto him, What I do thou knowest not now [*cp.* 13 12; 15 15: *also* 4 33; 11 13; 12 16; 13 28, 36; 14 5-10, 22; 16 17-18: *and* 3 10; 8 27, 43; 10 6]; but thou shalt understand hereafter [*cp.* 13 36]. **8** Peter saith unto him, Thou shalt never wash my feet. Jesus answered him, If I [*cp.* 3 3, 5; 6 53; 8 24] wash thee not, thou hast no part with me. **9** Simon Peter saith unto him, Lord, not my feet only, but also my hands and my head. **10** Jesus saith to him, He that is bathed needeth not ²save to wash his feet, but is clean every whit: and ye are clean [*cp.* 15 3], but not all [*cp. verse* 11 *below and* 13 18]. **11** For he	*cp.* 26 45: *also* 26 18. *cp.* 10 4; 26 14. *cp.* 9 6, 8; 11 27; 28 18. *cp.* 15 16; 16 8-12.	*cp.* 14 41: *also* 14 35. *cp.* 3 19; 14 10. *cp.* 2 10. *cp.* 4 13; 6 52; 7 18; 8 17-21; 9 10, 32: *also* 16 14.	*cp.* 22 14: *also* 22 53. *cp.* 18 28. *cp.* 22 3. *cp.* 6 16; 22 3. *cp.* 5 24; 10 22. *cp.* 12 37; 17 8. *cp.* 22 26-27: *also* 12 37: 17 8. *cp.* 9 45; 18 34: *also* 2 50.
knew [*cp.* 1 48; 2 24, 25; 5 6, 42; 6 61, 64; 13 18; 16 19, 30; 18 4; 21 17: *also* 4 19, 29; 11 14] him that should betray him [*cp.* 6 64; 13 21: *also* 6 71; 12 4; 18 2, 5: *and* 13 2]; therefore said he, Ye are not all clean [*cp. verse* 10 *above and* 13 18].	*cp.* 9 4; 12 25; 16 8. *cp.* 26 21: *also* 10 4; 26 25, 46, 48; 27 3: *and* 26 23, 24.	*cp.* 2 8; 8 17. *cp.* 14 18: *also* 3 19; 14 42, 44: *and* 14 21.	*cp.* 5 22; 6 8; 9 47; 11 17. *cp.* 22 21: *and* 22 22.

¹ Or, *to the uttermost*   ² Some ancient authorities omit *save*, and *his feet*.

§ 61. The Foot-washing explained

[*Cp.* Luke 22 24-27]

John 13 12-20

12 So when he had washed their feet, and taken his garments, and ¹sat down again, he said unto them, Know ye what I have done to you [*cp.* 13 7: *also* 15 15]? **13** Ye call me, ²Master [*cp.* 1 38; 8 4; 11 28; 20 16: *also* 1 49; *etc.*], and, Lord: and ye say well; for so I am. **14** If I then, the Lord and the ²Master, have washed your feet, ye also ought to wash one another's feet. **15** For I have given you an example, that ye also should do as I have done to you. **16** Verily, verily, I say unto you,

cp. 8 19; *etc.*: *and* 7 21.

cp. 4 38; *etc.*

cp. 7 40; *etc.*: *and* 6 46.

cp. 11 29.

John 15 20	Matt. 10 24-25		Luke 6 40

A ³servant is not greater than his lord; neither ⁴one that is sent greater than he that sent him.

20 Remember the word that I said unto you,

A ¹servant is not greater than his lord.

24 A disciple is not above his ¹master, nor a ²servant above his lord.

40 The disciple is not above his ¹master:

25 It is enough for the disciple that he be as his ¹master, and the ²servant as his lord. If they have called the master of the house ³Beelzebub [*cp.* 9 34; 12 24], how much more *shall they call* them of his household!

but every one when he is perfected shall be as his ¹master.

If they persecuted me, they will also persecute you; if they kept my word, they will keep yours also.

cp. 7 20; 8 48, 52; 10 20.

cp. 3 22.

cp. 11 15, 18.

¹ Gr. *bondservant.*

¹ Or, *teacher*
² Gr. *bondservant.*
³ Gr. *Beelzebul.*

¹ Or, *teacher*

17 If ye know these things, blessed are ye if ye do them. **18** I speak not of you all [*cp.* 13 10, 11]: I know [*cp.* 1 48; 2 24, 25; 5 6, 42; 6 61, 64; 13 11; 16 19, 30; 18 4; 21 17: *also* 4 19, 29; 11 14] whom I ⁵have chosen [*cp.* 6 70; 15 16, 19]: but that the scripture may be fulfilled,

cp. 24 46.

cp. 12 37, 43: *also* 11 28.

cp. 9 4; 12 25; 16 8.

cp. 2 8; 8 17.

cp. 5 22; 6 8; 9 47; 11 17.

cp. 2 19, 22; 3 14; 12 32, 33: *also* 5 39; 15 25; 17 12.

cp. 3 14.

cp. 6 13.

Matt. 26 **24** The Son of man goeth, even as it is written of him [*cp.* 16 21-23; 17 12, 22-23; 20 17-19, 28; 26 2, 45: *also* 26 12, 18: *and* 21 42; 26 31, 54, 56]: but woe [*cp.* 18 7: *also* 23 13 *ff.*] unto that man through whom the Son of man is betrayed! . . . **21** And as they were eating, he said, Verily I say unto you, that one of you shall betray me.

Mark 14 **21** For the Son of man goeth, even as it is written of him [*cp.* 8 31-33; 9 12, 30-32; 10 32-34, 45; 14 41: *also* 14 8: *and* 12 10; 14 27, 49]: but woe unto that man through whom the Son of man is betrayed! . . . **18** And as they ¹sat and were eating, Jesus said, Verily I say unto you, One of you shall betray me, *even* he that eateth with me.

Luke 22 **22** For the Son of man indeed goeth, as it hath been determined [*cp.* 9 22, 43-45; 13 32-33; 17 25; 18 31-34; 24 7, 44: *also* 20 17; 22 37; 24 25-27, 46]: but woe [*cp.* 17 1: *also* 11 42 *ff.*] unto that man through whom he is betrayed! . . .

cp. 13 21.

He that eateth ⁶my bread lifted up his heel against me [*cp.* 5 39; 15 25; 17 12].

cp. 21 42; 26 24, 31, 54, 56.

cp. 9 12; 12 10; 14 21, 27, 49.

21 But behold, the hand of him that betrayeth me is with me on the table.

cp. 18 31; 20 17; 22 37; 24 25-27, 44-46.

19 From henceforth [*cp.* 14 7] I tell you before it come to pass [*cp.* 14 29: *also* 16 4], that, when it is come to pass, ye may believe [*cp.* 14 29: *also* 11 15: *and* 19 35; 20 31: *and* 11 42] that [7]I am *he* [*cp.* 8 24, 28: *also* 8 58]. **20** Verily, verily, I say unto you,
 	
He that receiveth whomsoever I send receiveth me; and he that receiveth me receiveth him that sent me [*cp.* 12 44-48: *also* 5 23: *and* 15 23].
	cp. 23 39; 26 29, 64.
	
	cp. 24 25.
	
	Matt. 10 **40** He that receiveth you
	   receiveth me, and he that receiveth me receiveth him that sent me.
	
	Matt. 18 **5** And whoso shall receive one such little child in my name receiveth me.
		cp. 13 23.
		
		cp. 13 6; 14 62.
		
		Mark 9 **37** Whosoever shall receive one of such little children in my name, receiveth me: and whoso-ever receiveth me, receiveth not me, but him that sent me.
			cp. 21 8; 22 70.
			
			Luke 10 **16** He that heareth you heareth me; and he that rejecteth you
			   rejecteth me; and he that rejecteth me rejecteth him that sent me.
			
			Luke 9 **48** Whosoever shall receive this little child in my name receiveth me: and whoso-ever shall receive me receiveth him that sent me.

[1] Gr. *reclined.*   [2] Or, *Teacher*
[3] Gr. *bondservant.*
[4] Gr. *an apostle.*   [5] Or, *chose*
[6] Many ancient authorities read *his bread with me.*   [7] Or, *I am*

[1] Gr. *reclined.*

John 13 18 = Ps. 41 9.

§ 62. **The Prophecy of the Betrayal**

John 13 21-30	Matt. 26 20-25	Mark 14 17-21	Luke 22 14, 21-23
21 When Jesus had thus said, he was troubled [*cp.* 11 33; 12 27: *also* 14 1, 27] in the spirit, and testified, *cp.* 12 23, 27: 13 1; 17 1: *also* 2 4; 7 6, 8, 30; 8 20. and said, Verily, verily, I say unto you, that one of you shall betray me [*cp.* 6 64; 13 11]. *cp.* 13 18. **22** The disciples looked *cp.* 16 6, 20, 22. one on another, doubting of whom he spake. **23** There was at the table reclining in Jesus' bosom one of his disciples, whom Jesus loved [*cp.* 19 26; 20 2; 21 7, 20: *also* 11 36]. **24** Simon Peter therefore beckoneth to him, and saith unto him, Tell *us* who it is of whom he speaketh.	**20** Now when even [*cp.* 26 45: *also* 26 18] was come, he was sitting at meat *cp.* 10 2. with the twelve [1]disciples; **21** and as they were eating [*cp.* 26 26], he said, Verily I say unto you, that one of you shall betray me. **22** And they were exceeding sorrowful [*cp.* 17 23; 18 31: *also* 26 37], and began	**17** And when it was evening [*cp.* 14 35, 41] he cometh with the twelve. **18** And as they [1]sat *cp.* 6 30. and were eating [*cp.* 14 22], Jesus said, Verily I say unto you, One of you shall betray me, *even* he that eateth with me. **19** They began to be sorrowful, and	**14** And when the hour [*cp.* 22 53] was come, he sat down, and the apostles [*cp.* 6 13; 9 10; 17 5; 24 10] with him. . . . **21** But behold, the hand of him that betrayeth me is with me on the table. *cp.* 22 45.

25 He leaning back [*cp.* 21 20], as he was [*cp.* 4 6], on Jesus' breast saith unto him,
Lord, who is it? **26** Jesus therefore answereth,
He it is,
for whom
I shall   dip
the sop, and give it him.
cp. 13 18.

cp. 2 19, 22; 3 14; 12 32, 33: *also* 5 39; 15 25; 17 12.

verse 22
So when he had dipped the sop, he taketh and giveth it to Judas, *the son* of Simon Iscariot [*cp.* 6 71: *also* 13 2: *and* 12 4; 14 22].

cp. 1 38, 49; *etc.*: *also* 20 16.

cp. 18 37.
27 And after the sop, then entered Satan [*cp.* 13 2: *also* 6 70] into him. Jesus therefore saith unto him, That thou doest, do quickly. **28** Now no man at the table knew for what intent he spake this unto him [*cp.* 4 33; 11 13; 12 16; 13 7, 36; 14 5-10, 22; 16 17-18: *also* 3 10; 8 27, 43; 10 6]. **29** For some thought, because Judas had the ¹bag [*cp.* 12 6], that Jesus said unto him, Buy what things we have need of for the feast; or, that he should give something to the poor [*cp.* 12 5]. **30** He then having received the sop went out straightway: and it was night [*cp.* 9 4; 11 10: *also* 12 35].

¹ Or, *box*

---

to say unto him every one,
Is it I, Lord? **23** And he answered and said,

He that dipped his hand with me in the dish,
the same shall betray me. **24** The Son of man goeth, even as it is written of him [*cp.* 16 21-23; 17 12, 22-23; 20 17-19, 28; 26 2, 45: *also* 26 12, 18: *and* 21 42; 26 31, 54, 56]: but woe [*cp.* 18 7: *also* 23 13 *ff.*] unto that man through whom the Son of man is betrayed! good were it ²for that man if he had not been born.

verse 22
25 And

Judas,
cp. 10 4; 26 14.
which betrayed him, answered and said, Is it I, Rabbi [*cp.* 26 49: *also* 23 7, 8]? He saith unto him, Thou has said [*cp.* 26 64: *also* 27 11].

¹ Many authorities, some ancient, omit *disciples*.
² Gr. *for him if that man.*

---

cp. 4 36.
to say unto him one by one,
Is it I? **20** And he
said unto them, *It is* one of the twelve,
he that dippeth with me in the dish.

21 For the Son of man goeth, even as it is written of him [*cp.* 8 31-33; 9 12, 30-32; 10 32-34, 45; 14 41: *also* 14 8: *and* 12 10; 14 27, 49]: but woe unto that man through whom the Son of man is betrayed! good were it ²for that man if he had not been born.

verse 19

cp. 3 19; 14 10.

cp. 9 5; 11 21; 14 45: *also* 10 51.
cp. 15 2.

¹ Gr. *reclined.*
² Gr. *for him if that man.*

---

verse 23

22 For the Son of man indeed goeth, as it hath been determined [*cp.* 9 22, 43-45; 13 32-33; 17 25; 18 31-34; 24 7, 44: *also* 20 17; 22 37; 24 25-27, 46]: but woe [*cp.* 17 1: *also* 11 42 *ff.*] unto that man through whom he is betrayed!

23 And they began to question among themselves, which of them it was that should do this thing.

cp. 6 16; 22 3.

cp. 23 3: *also* 22 70.

cp. 22 3.

---

cp. 26 50.
cp. 15 16; 16 8-12.

cp. 4 13; 6 52; 7 18; 8 17-21; 9 10,32:*also* 16 14.

cp. 9 45; 18 34: *also* 2 50.

Mark 14 18 || Luke 22 21: *cp.* Ps.41 9.

§ 63. **A New Commandment of Love**

John 13 31-35

31 When therefore he was gone out, Jesus saith, Now ¹is the Son of man glorified [*cp.* 7 39; 12 16, 23: *also* 11 4; 17 10: *and* 17 1*ff.*], and God ¹is glorified in him [*cp.* 14 13: *also* 15 8]; **32** and God shall glorify him in himself, and straightway shall he glorify him [*cp.* 8 54; 16 14; 17 1, 5: *also* 7 39; *etc.*]. **33** Little children, yet a little while [*cp.* 7 33; 12 35; 14 19; 16 16-19] I am with you. Ye shall seek me [*cp.* 7 34, 36; 8 21]: and as I said unto the Jews, Whither I go [*cp.* 8 14, 21, 22; 13 36; 14 4: *also* 7 35; 13 36; 14 5;

			cp. 14 26, 27, 33.
16 5: *and* 3 8; 12 35], ye cannot come [*cp.* 7 34, 36; 8 21, 22: *also* 13 36]; so now I say unto you. **34** A new commandment I give unto you [*cp.* 15 12: *also* 14 15, 21; 15 10], that ye love one another [*cp. verse* 35 *below and* 15 12, 17]; [2]even as I have loved you [*cp.* 15 12: *also* 13 1; 15 9], that ye also love one another. **35** By this shall all men know that ye are my disciples [*cp.* 8 31; 15 8], if ye have love one to another [*cp. verse* 34 *above and* 15 12, 17].			

[1] Or, *was*   [2] Or, *even as I loved you, that ye also may love one another*

§ 64. **The Prophecy of Peter's Denial**

[*For* John 13 36-14 4 *cp.* Matt. 19 27-29 ‖ Mark 10 28-30 ‖ Luke 18 28-30 *and* 22 28-30]

John 13 36-38	Matt. 26 33-35	Mark 14 29-31	Luke 22 31-34
36 Simon Peter [*cp.* 21 21: *also* 6 68]	**33** But Peter [*cp.* 14 28; 15 15; 16 22; 17 4; 18 21; 19 27: *also* 16 16; 17 24] answered and said unto him,	**29** But Peter [*cp.* 8 32; 9 5; 10 28; 11 21: *also* 8 29] said unto him,	*cp.* 8 45; 9 33; 12 41; 18 28: *also* 5 8; 9 20.
saith unto him, Lord, whither goest thou [*cp.* 16 5: *also* 4 33; 11 13; 12 16; 13 7, 28; 14 5-10, 22; 16 17-18: *and* 3 10; 8 27, 43; 10 6]?	*cp.* 15 16; 16 8-12.	*cp.* 4 13; 6 52; 7 18; 8 17-21; 9 10, 32: *also* 16 14.	*cp.* 9 45; 18 34: *also* 2 50.
	If all shall be [1]offended in thee, I will never be offended.	Although all shall be [1]offended, yet will not I.	
Jesus answered, Whither I go [*cp.* 8 14, 21, 22; 13 33; 14 4: *also* 7 35; 14 5; 16 5: *and* 3 8; 12 35], thou canst not follow me now [*cp.* 7 34, 36; 8 21, 22; 13 33]; but thou shalt follow afterwards [*cp.* 13 7: *also* 21 18-19]. *cp.* 1 42; 21 15, 16, 17.	*cp.* 16 17; 17 25.	*cp.* 14 37.	**31** Simon, Simon, behold, Satan [*cp.* 22 3] [1]asked to have you, that he might sift you as wheat: **32** but I made supplication for thee, that thy faith [*cp.* 8 25; 12 28; 17 5, 6: *also* 24 11, 12, 38, 41: *and* 24 25] fail not: and do thou, when once thou hast turned again, stablish thy brethren. **33** And he said unto him, Lord,
cp. 3 12; 6 64; 14 10; 20 25, 27.	*cp.* 8 26; 14 31; 16 8; 17 20; 21 21; 28 17.	*cp.* 4 40; 11 22; 16 11, 13, 14.	
cp. 21 15-17. **37** Peter saith unto him, Lord, why cannot I follow thee even now? I will lay down my life [*cp.* 10 11, 15, 17; 15 13] for thee [*cp.* 11 16].	*cp.* 16 18-19.		with thee I am ready to go both to prison and to death.
38 Jesus answereth, Wilt thou lay down thy life for me? Verily, verily, I say unto thee,	*verse* 35 **34** Jesus said unto him, Verily I say unto thee, that	*verse* 31 **30** And Jesus saith unto him, Verily I say unto thee, that thou to-day,	**34** And he said, I tell thee, Peter,
The cock shall not crow,	this night, before the cock crow,	*even* this night, before the cock crow twice [*cp.* 14 68, 72],	the cock shall not crow this
till thou hast denied	thou shalt deny	shalt deny	day, until thou shalt thrice deny that thou

cp. 18 17, 25, 27.	*cp.* 26 70, 72, 74.	*cp.* 14 68, 70, 71.	knowest [*cp.* 22 57, 58, 60]
me thrice [*cp.* 18 27].	me thrice [*cp.* 26 75].	me thrice [*cp.* 14 72].	me [*cp.* 22 61].
	35 Peter saith into him,	**31** But he spake exceed-	
	Even if	ing vehemently, If	
verse 37	I must die with thee, *yet*	I must die with thee,	*verse* 33
	will I not deny thee.	I will not deny thee.	
	Likewise also	And in like manner also	
	said all the disciples.	said they all.	
¹ Gr. *caused to stumble.*	¹ Gr. *caused to stumble.*	¹ Or, *obtained you by asking*	

§ 65. Jesus the Way, the Truth, and the Life: The Promise of the Spirit

[*For* John 13 36-14 4 *cp.* Matt. 19 27-29 ‖ Mark 10 28-30 ‖ Luke 18 28-30 *and* 22 28-30]

John 14 1-24

1 Let not your heart be troubled [*cp.* 14 27: *also* 11 33; 12 27; 13 21]: ¹ye believe in God, believe also in me [*cp.* 12 44]. **2** In my Father's house [*cp.* 2 16] are many ²mansions; if it were not so, I would have told you; for I go to prepare a place for you. **3** And if I go and prepare a place for you, I come again [*cp.* 14 28: *also verse* 18 *below: and* 21 22, 23], and will receive you unto myself [*cp.* 12 32]; that where I am [*cp.* 7 34, 36; 12 26; 17 24], *there* ye may be also [*cp.* 17 24: *also* 12 26]. **4** ³And whither I go [*cp.* 8 14, 21, 22; 13 33, 36: *also* 7 35; 13 36; 14 5; 16 5: *and* 3 8; 12 35], ye know the way. **5** Thomas [*cp.* 11 16; 20 24, 26-29; 21 2] saith unto him, Lord, we know not whither thou goest; how know we the way [*cp. vv.* 8 *and* 22 *below*; 4 33; 11 13; 12 16; 13 7, 36; 16 17-18: *also* 3 10; 8 27, 43; 10 6]? **6** Jesus saith him, I am the way, and the truth [*cp.* 1 14, 17; 5 33; 8 32; 18 37], and the life [*cp.* 11 25: *also* 1 4; 5 26; 6 57: *and* 3 15; *etc.*]: no one cometh unto the Father, but ⁴by me. **7** If ye had known me, ye would have known my Father also [*cp.* 8 19]: from hence-forth [*cp.* 13 19] ye know him, and have seen him. **8** Philip [*cp.* 1 43-48; 6 5-7; 12 21-22] saith unto him, Lord, shew us the Father, and it sufficeth [*cp.* 6 7] us. **9** Jesus saith unto him, Have I been so long time with you, and dost thou not know me [*cp.* 1 10, 26, 31, 33; 8 19; 16 3: *also* 20 14; 21 4: *and* 8 55; 14 17; 17 25], Philip? he that hath seen me hath seen the Father [*cp.* 12 45; 15 24: *also* 10 30; 17 11, 22: *and* 5 19]; how sayest thou [*cp.* 8 33; 12 34], Shew us the Father? **10** Believest thou not [*cp.* 3 12; 6 64; 20 27] that I am in the Father, and the Father in me [*cp. verse* 11; 10 38; 17 21: *also* 14 20; 17 23]? the words that I say unto you [*cp.* 3 34; 8 26, 47; 12 47-50; 17 8, 14: *also* 6 63, 68] I speak not from myself [*cp.* 12 49: *also* 7 17: *and* 5 19, 30; 8 28: *and* 7 28; 8 42: *and* 16 13: *see also verse* 24 *below*]: but the Father abiding in me doeth his works [*cp.* 10 25, 32, 37: *also* 4 34; 5 36; 17 4: *and* 3 21; 6 28-29; 9 3-4: *and* 10 38; 14 11: *and* 5 17; 7 21; 15 24]. **11** Believe me that I am in the Father, and the Father in me: or else believe me for the very works' sake. **12** Verily, verily, I say unto you, He that believeth on me, the works that I do shall he do also; and greater *works* than these [*cp.* 1 50; 5 20] shall he do; because I go unto the Father [*cp.* 14 28; 16 10, 17, 28: *also* 7 33; 16 5: *and* 17 11, 13: *and* 20 17: *and* 13 1, 3].

	cp. 10 3.	*cp.* 3 18.	*cp.* 6 15.
	cp. 15 16; 16 8-12.	*cp.* 4 13; 6 52; 7 18; 8 17-21; 9 10, 32: *also* 16 14.	*cp.* 9 45; 18 34: *also* 2 50.
	cp. 23 39; 26 29, 64.		
	cp. 10 3.	*cp.* 31 8.	*cp.* 6 14.
	cp. 17 17.	*cp.* 9 19.	*cp.* 9 41.
	cp. 8 26; 14 31; 16 8; 17 20; 21 21; 28 17.	*cp.* 4 40; 11 22; 16 14.	*cp.* 8 25; 12 28; 17 5-6; 22 32; 24 25, 38.

John 15 16; 16 23-24	Matt. 21 22; 7 7	Mark 11 24	Luke 11 9
13 And whatsoever ye shall ask in my name [*cp. verse* 14 *below*; 16 23, 24, 26: *also* 14 26],	**15 16** . . . that whatsoever ye shall ask of the Father in my name,	**21 22** And all things, whatsoever ye shall ask in *cp.* 18 5, 20; 24 5: *also* 7 22.	**11 24** All things whatsoever ye *cp.* 9 37, 38, 39; 13 6; 16 17.	All things whatsoever ye *cp.* 9 48, 49; 10 17; 21 8; 24 47.
		prayer, believing,	pray and ask for, believe that ye have received them, and	
that will I do, that the Father may be	he may give it you.	ye shall receive.	ye shall have them.	

glorified in the Son [*cp.*13 31: *also* 15 8].

14 If ye shall ask
⁵me anything

in my name, that
will I do.

                    15 7 Ask
whatsoever ye will,
and it shall be done
unto you.

16 23 If ye shall ask anything of the Father, he will give it you in my name.	*cp.* 18 19.		
24 Hitherto have ye asked nothing in my name: ask,			
7 7 Ask,		**11 9** Ask,	
and ye shall receive.	and it shall be given you; seek, and ye shall find; knock, and it shall be opened unto you.	and it shall be given you; seek, and ye shall find; knock, and it shall be opened unto you.	

                    15 If ye
love me, ye will keep my commandments [*cp. verse* 21 *and* 15
10: *also* 13 34; 15 12: *and* 8 51, 52; 14 23, 24; 15 20].
16 And I will ⁶pray the Father [*cp.* 16 26: *also* 17 9, 15, 20], and
he shall give you another ⁷Comforter [*cp.* 14 26; 15 26; 16 7],
that he may be with you for ever, **17** *even* the Spirit of truth [*cp.*
15 26; 16 13]: whom the world cannot receive; for it beholdeth
him not, neither knoweth him: ye know him; for he abideth with
you, and shall be in you. **18** I will not leave you ⁸desolate: I come
unto you [*cp. verse 3 above and* 14 28: *also* 21 22, 23]. **19** Yet a little
while [*cp.* 7 33; 12 35; 13 33; 16 16-19], and the world beholdeth me no more; but ye behold me [*cp.* 12 45; 16 10, 16, 17,
19: *also* 6 40, 62]: because I live, ⁹ye shall live also. **20** In that
day [*cp.* 16 23, 26] ye shall know that I am in my Father [*cp.
verse* 10 *above*], and ye in me, and I in you [*cp.* 17 21, 23, 26:
also 6 56; 15 4, 5, 7]. **21** He that hath my commandments, and
keepeth them [*cp. verse* 15 *above*], he it is that loveth me [*cp. verse* 15
and 15 10: *also* 13 34; 15 12]: and he that loveth me shall be
loved of my Father [*cp. verse* 23 *below*; 16 27; 17 23: *also* 21 15-
17], and I will love him, and will manifest myself [*cp.* 7 4, 21 1,
14: *also* 1 31; 2 11; 3 21; 9 3; 17 6] unto him. **22** Judas (not
Iscariot) saith unto him, Lord, what is come to pass that thou
wilt manifest thyself unto us, and not unto the world [*cp.* 7 4: *also
verse* 5 *above*]? **23** Jesus answered and said unto him, If a man
love me, he will keep my word [*cp.* 8 51, 52; 15 20: *also verse* 24
below: *and* 14 15, 21; 15 10]: and my Father will love him [*cp.
verse* 21 *above*], and we will come unto him, and make our abode
with him. **24** He that loveth me not keepeth not my words [*cp.
verse* 23 *above*: *also* 4 41; 5 24; 8 31, 37, 43, 51, 52; 12 48; 15 3,
20]: and the word [*cp.* 5 38; 8 55; 17 6, 14, 17, 20] which ye
hear is not mine, but the Father's who sent me [*cp.* 7 16: *also* 3
34; 8 26, 28, 38, 40; 12 49, 50; 14 10; 15 15].

The marginal cross-references (reading top to bottom in the outer columns):

cp. 28 20.			
			cp. 24 49.
cp. 7 22; 24 36: *also* 26 29.	*cp.* 13 32: *also* 14 25.	*cp.* 10 12; 17 31; 21 34.	
	cp. 16 12, 14.	*cp.* 6 16: *also* Acts 1 13.	
cp. 28 20.			

¹ Or, *believe in God*   ² Or, *abiding-places*   ³ Many ancient authorities read *And whither I go ye know, and the way ye know.*
⁴ Or, *through*   ⁵ Many ancient authorities omit *me.*   ⁶ Gr. *make request of.*   ⁷ Or, *Advocate* Or, *Helper* Gr. *Paraclete.*   ⁸ Or, *orphans*   ⁹ Or, *and ye shall live*

§ 66. **The Gift of Peace**

John 14 25-31

25 These things have I
spoken unto you [*cp.* 15
11; 16 1, 4, 6, 25, 33],
while *yet* abiding with you
[*cp.* 16 4]. **26** But the
¹Comforter [*cp.* 14 16; 15
26; 16 7], *even* the Holy
Spirit, whom the Father
will send [*cp.* 15 26: *also* 14
16: *and* 16 7] in my name
[*cp.* 14 13, 14; 15 16; 16

			cp. 24 44.
			cp. 24 49.
cp. 18 5, 20; 24 5: *also* 7 22.	*cp.* 9 37, 38, 39; 13 6; 16 17.	*cp.* 9 48, 49; 10 17; 21 8; 24 47.	

23, 24, 26], he shall teach you all things [cp. 15 26; 16 13], and bring to your remembrance [cp. 16 4: also 2 22; 12 16] all that I said unto you. **27** Peace I leave with you; my peace I give unto you [cp. 16 33: also 20 19, 21, 26]: not as the world giveth, give I unto you. Let not your heart be troubled [cp. 14 1: also 11 33; 12 27; 13 21], neither let it be fearful. **28** Ye heard how I said to you, I go away [cp. 8 21: also 7 33; etc.], and I come unto you [cp. 14 3, 18: also 21 22, 23]. If ye loved me, ye would have rejoiced, because I go unto the Father [cp. 14 12; 16 10, 17, 28: also 7 33; 16 5: and 17 11, 13: and 20 17: and 13 1, 3]: for the Father is greater [cp. 10 29] than I. **29** And now I have told you before it come to pass [cp. 13 19: also 16 4], that, when it is come to pass, ye may believe [cp. 13 19: also 11 15: and 19 35; 20 31: and 11 42]. **30** I will no more speak much with you [cp. 8 26; 16 12], for the prince of the world [cp. 12 31; 16 11] cometh: and he hath nothing in me; **31** but that the world may know [cp. 17 23: also 17 21] that I love the Father, and as the Father gave me commandment [cp. 10 18; 12 49: also 15 10], even so I do.

Matthew	Mark	Luke
cp. 10 19, 20.	cp. 13 11.	cp. 12 11, 12.
cp. 26 75.	cp. 14 72.	cp. 22 61: also 24 6, 8.
cp. 5 9; 10 13.	cp. 9 50.	cp. 1 79; 2 14, 29; 10 6; 19 38: also 24 36.
cp. 24 25.	cp. 13 23.	

cp. 12 23, 27; 13 1; 17 1: also 2 4; 7 6, 8, 30; 8 20.

Arise, let us go hence.

John	Matthew	Mark	Luke
	Matt. 26 **44** And he left them again, and went away, and prayed a third time, saying again the same words. **45** Then cometh he to the disciples, and saith unto them, Sleep on now, and take your rest: behold, the hour [cp. 26 18] is at hand, and the Son of man is betrayed into the hands of sinners. **46** Arise, let us be going: behold, he	Mark 14 **41** And he cometh the third time, and saith unto them, Sleep on now, and take your rest: it is enough; the hour [cp. 14 35] is come; behold, the Son of man is betrayed into the hands of sinners. **42** Arise, let us be going: behold, he that betrayeth me is at hand.	cp. 22 14, 53.
	is at hand that betrayeth me.		

1 Or, *Advocate* Or, *Helper* Gr. *Paraclete.*

§ 67. Jesus the True Vine

John 15 1-27

1 I am the true [cp. 1 9; 6 32: also 6 55; 17 3] vine, and my Father is the husbandman. **2** Every branch in me that beareth not fruit, he taketh it away [cp. verse 6 below]: and every *branch* that beareth fruit, he cleanseth it, that it may bear more fruit. **3** Already ye are clean [cp. 13 10] because of the word which I have spoken unto you [cp. 4 41; 5 24; 8 31, 37, 43, 51, 52; 12 48; 14 23, 24; 15 20: also 5 38; etc.]. **4** Abide in me, and I in you [cp. verses 5, 7, and 6 56: also 8 31: and 14 20; 17 21, 23, 26]. As the branch cannot bear fruit [cp. verses 5, 8, and 16] of itself, except it abide in the vine; so neither can ye, except ye abide in me. **5** I am the vine, ye are the branches: He that abideth in me, and I in him [cp. verses 4 and 7], the same beareth much fruit [cp. verses 4, 8, and 16]: for apart from me ye can do nothing. **6** If a man abide not in me, he is cast forth as a branch, and is withered; and they gather them, and cast them into the fire, and they are burned. **7** If ye abide in me, and my words abide in you [cp. verses 4 and 5 above], ask [cp. verse 16 below]

Matthew	Mark	Luke
cp. 3 10; 7 19.		cp. 3 9; 13 7, 9.
cp. 13 23.	cp. 4 20.	cp. 8 15.
cp. 13 23.	cp. 4 20.	cp. 8 15.
cp. 3 10; 7 19: also 3 12; 5 22, 29; etc.	cp. 9 43, 45, 47.	cp. 3 9: also 3 17; 12 5.

whatsoever ye will, and it shall be done unto you. **8** Herein [1]is my Father glorified [*cp.* 13 31; 14 13], [2]that ye bear much fruit [*cp. verses* 4, 5, *and* 16]; and *so* shall ye be my disciples [*cp.* 8 31; 13 35]. **9** Even as the Father hath loved me [*cp.* 3 35; 5 20; 10 17; 17 23, 24, 26], I also have loved you [*cp.* 13 1, 34; 15 12]: abide ye in my love. **10** If ye keep my commandments [*cp.* 14 15, 21: *also* 13 34; 15 12: *and* 8 51, 52; 14 23, 24; 15 20], ye shall abide in my love; even as I have kept my Father's commandments [*cp.* 10 18; 12 49; 14 31], and abide in his love. **11** These things have I spoken unto you [*cp.* 14 25; 16 1, 4, 6, 25, 33], that my joy may be in you, and *that* your joy may be fulfilled [*cp.* 3 29; 16 24; 17 13]. **12** This is my commandment [*cp. verse* 17 *below and* 13 34: *also* 14 15, 21; 15 10], that ye love one another [*cp. verse* 17 *below and* 13 34, 35], even as I have loved you [*cp.* 13 34: *also* 13 1; 15 9]. **13** Greater love hath no man than this, that a man lay down his life [*cp.* 10 11, 15, 17; 13 37, 38] for his friends. **14** Ye are my friends, if ye do the things which I command you. **15** No longer do I call you [3]servants; for the [4]servant knoweth not [*cp.* 13 7, 12] what his lord doeth: but I have called you friends; for all things that I heard from my Father I have made known unto you [*cp.* 14 24; 17 8, 14: *also* 3 34; 7 16; 8 26, 28, 38, 40; 12 49, 50]. **16** Ye did not choose me, but I chose you, and appointed you, that ye should go and bear fruit, and *that* your fruit should abide: that

(Matt.)	(Mark)	(Luke)
cp. 13 23.	*cp.* 4 20.	*cp.* 8 15. / *cp.* 14 26; *etc.*
cp. 3 17; 17 5.	*cp.* 1 11; 9 7; 12 6.	*cp.* 3 22; 20 13.
cp. 28 20.		
cp. 25 21, 23.		
cp. 12 50.	*cp.* 3 35.	*cp.* 12 4: *also* 8 21.

(John 15 column continues): whatsoever ye shall ask of the Father in my name [*cp.* 14 13, 14; 16 23, 24, 26: *also* 14 26], he may give it you.

16 23 If ye shall ask anything of the Father, he will give it you in my name. **24** Hitherto have ye asked nothing in my name: ask, and ye shall receive.

John 14 13-14; 15 7	Matt. 21 22; 7 7	Mark 11 24	Luke 11 9
cp. 15 19: *also* 6 70; 13 18.		*cp.* 3 14.	*cp.* 6 13.
cp. 15 4, 5, 8.	*cp.* 13 23.	*cp.* 4 20.	*cp.* 8 15.
14 13 And whatsoever ye shall ask in my name,	**21 22** And all things, whatsoever ye shall ask	**11 24** All things whatsoever ye	
	cp. 18 5, 20; 24 5: *also* 7 22.	*cp.* 9 37, 38, 39; 13 6; 16 17.	*cp.* 9 48, 49; 10 17; 21 8; 24 47.
	in prayer, believing,	pray and ask for, believe that ye have received them, and ye shall have them.	
that will I do, that the Father may be glorified in the Son.	ye shall receive.		
14 If ye shall ask [1]me anything in my name, that will I do.	*cp.* 18 19.		
15 7 Ask whatsoever ye will, and it shall be done unto you.	**7 7** Ask, and it shall be given you; seek, and ye shall find; knock, and it shall be opened unto you.		**11 9** Ask, and it shall be given you; seek, and ye shall find; knock, and it shall be opened unto you.

[1] Many ancient authorities omit *me*.

17 These things I command you [*cp. verse* 12 *above and* 13 34: *also* 14 15, 21; 15 10], that ye may love one another [*cp. verse* 12 *above and* 13 34, 35]. **18** If the world hateth you [*cp.* 17 14: *also* 7 7], [5]ye know that it hath hated me [*cp.* 7 7; 15 24] before *it hated* you. **19** If ye were of the world, the world would love its own [*cp* 1 11; 8 44; 16 32; 19 27]: but because ye are not of the world [*cp.* 8 23; 17 14, 16; 18 36], but I chose you [*cp. verse* 16 *above: also* 6 70; 13 18] out of the world, therefore the world hateth you. **20** Remember the word that I said unto you,

	Matt.	Mark	Luke
	cp. 10 22; 24 9.	*cp.* 13 13.	*cp.* 1 71; 6 22, 27; 21 17. / *cp.* 18 28.
		cp. 3 14.	*cp.* 6 13.

John 13 16	Matt. 10 24-25		Luke 6 40
16 Verily, verily, I say unto you,	**24** A disciple is not above		**40** The disciple is not above

A [4]servant is not greater than his lord.	A [1]servant is not greater than his lord; neither [2]one that is sent greater than he that sent him.	his [1]master, nor a [2]servant above his lord.		his [1]master:
		25 It is enough for the disciple that he be as his [1]master, and the [2]servant as his lord. If they have		but everyone when he is perfected shall be as his [1]master.
If they persecuted me [*cp.* 5 16, 18],		called the master of the house [3]Beelzebub [*cp.* 9 34; 12 24], how much more *shall they call* them of his household!		
	cp. 7 20; 8 48, 52; 10 20.		*cp.* 3 22.	*cp.* 11 15, 18.
they will also persecute you; if they have kept my word [*cp.* 8 51, 52; 14 23, 24: *also* 14 15, 21; 15 10: *and* 4 41; 5 24; 8 31; *etc.*], they will keep yours also. **21** But all these things will they do [*cp.* 16 3] unto you for my name's sake, because they know not [*cp.* 7 28; 8 19, 55; 16 3; 17 25: *also* 4 22] him that sent me. **22** If I had not come and spoken unto them, they had not had sin [*cp. verse* 24 *below and* 9 41]: but now they have no excuse for their sin.		*cp.* 5 11; 10 23: *also* 23 34.		*cp.* 21 12: *also* 11 50.
		cp. 10 22; 19 29; 24 9: *also* 5 11; 10 18, 39; 16 25.	*cp.* 13 13: *also* 8 35; 10 29; 13 9.	*cp.* 21 12, 17: *also* 6 22; 9 24: *and* 18 29.
	[1] Gr. *bondservant.* [2] Gr. *an apostle.*	[1] Or, *teacher* [2] Gr. *bondservant.* [3] Gr. *Beelzebul.*		[1] Or, *teacher*

23 He that hateth me hateth my Father also [*cp.* 5 23; 12 44-45; 13 20]. **24** If I had not done among them the works [*cp.* 10 25, 32, 37, 38; 14 10, 11: *also* 3 21; 4 34; 5 36; *etc.*] which none other did, they had not had sin [*cp. verse* 24 *above and* 9 41]: but now have they both seen and hated [*cp. verse* 18 *above*] both me and my Father [*cp.* 12 45; 14 9-11: *also* 10 30; 17 11, 22: *and* 5 19]. **25** But *this cometh to pass*, that the word may be fulfilled that is written in their law [*cp.* 7 51; 8 17; 10 34; 18 31: *also* 19 7], They hated me without a cause. **26** But when the [6]Comforter [*cp.* 14 16, 26; 16 7] is come, whom I will send unto you from the Father [*cp.* 14 26: *also* 14 16: *and* 16 7], *even the Spirit of truth* [*cp.* 14 17; 16 13], which [7]proceedeth from the Father, he shall bear witness of me: **27** [8]and ye also bear witness [*cp.* 19 35; 21 24], because ye have been with me from the beginning [*cp.* 6 64; 16 4: *also* 8 44].	*cp.* 10 40.	*cp.* 9 37.	*cp.* 9 48; 10 16. *cp.* 24 49. *cp.* 24 48. *cp.* 1 2.

[1] Or, *was*   [2] Many ancient authorities read *that ye bear much fruit, and be my disciples.* [3] Gr. *bondservants.*   [4] Gr. *bondservant.*   [5] Or, *know ye*   [6] Or, *Advocate* Or, *Helper* Gr. *Paraclete.*   [7] Or, *goeth forth from*   [8] Or, *and bear ye also witness*

John 15 1: *cp.* Jer. 2 21.   John 15 6: *cp.* Ezek. 15 4; 19 12.   John 15 25 = Pss. 35 19 *and* 69 4.

§ 68. The Spirit will guide the Disciples into all the Truth: Their Sorrow will be turned into Joy

John 16 1-24

1 These things have I spoken unto you [*cp.* 14 25; 15 11; 16 4, 6, 25, 33], that ye should not be made to stumble [*cp.* 6 61]. **2** They shall put you out of the synagogues [*cp.* 9 22, 12 42]: yea, the hour cometh [*cp.* 4 21, 23; 5 25, 28; 16 25, 32], that whosoever killeth you shall think that he offereth service unto God. **3** And these things will they do [*cp.* 15 21], because they have not known the Father [*cp.* 7 28; 8 19, 55; 15 21; 17 25: *also* 4 22], nor me [*cp.* 1 10, 26, 31, 33; 8 19; 14 9: *also* 20 14; 21 4: *and* 8 55; 14 17; 17 25]. **4** But these things have I spoken unto you [*cp. verse* 1 *above*], that when their hour is come, ye may remember them [*cp.* 14 26: *also* 2 22; 12 16], how that I told you [*cp.* 13 19; 14 29]. And these things I said not unto you from the beginning [*cp.* 6 64; 15 27: *also* 8 44], because I was with you [14 25]. **5** But now I go unto him that sent me [*cp.* 7 33: *also* 14 12, 28; 16 10, 17, 28: *and* 17 11, 13: *and* 20 17: *and* 13 1, 3]; and none of you asketh me, Whither goest thou [*cp.* 13 36: *also* 8 14; *etc.*]? **6** But because I have spoken these things unto you [*cp. verse* 1 *above*], sorrow hath filled your heart [*cp. verses* 20 *and* 22]. **7** Nevertheless I tell you the truth; It is expedient [*cp.* 11 50, 18 14] for you that I go away: for if I go not away, the [1]Comforter [*cp.* 14 16, 26; 15 26] will not come unto you; but if I go, I will send him unto you [*cp.* 15 26: *also* 14 16, 26]. **8** And he, when he is come, will convict the world in respect of sin [*cp.* 8 46], and of righteousness, and of judgement: **9** of sin, because they believe not on me [*cp.* 8 24]; **10** of righteousness, because I go to the Father [*cp.* 14 12, 28; 16 17, 28: *also* 7 33; 16 5: *and* 17 11, 13: *and* 20 17: *and* 13 1, 3], and ye behold me no more [*cp. verses* 16, 17, 19, *and* 14 19: *also* 12 45: *and* 6 40, 62: *and* 14 17]; **11** of judgement, because the prince of this world [*cp.* 12 31: *also* 14 30] hath been judged [*cp.* 3 18, 19; 5 24; 12 31: *and* 5 29; 12 48]. **12** I have yet many things to say unto you [*cp.* 8 26: *also* 14 30], but ye cannot bear them now [*cp.* 16 25: *also* 6 60]. **13** Howbeit when he, the Spirit of truth [*cp.* 14 17; 15 26], is come, he shall guide you into all the truth: for he shall not speak from himself [*cp.* 5 19, 30; 8 28: *also* 7 17; 12 49; 14 10: *and* 8 42]; but what things soever he shall hear, *these* shall he speak: and he shall declare unto you [*cp. verses* 14 *and* 15 *and* 4 25] the things that are to come [*cp.* 14 26]. **14** He shall glorify me [*cp.* 8 54; 13 32; 17 1, 5: *also* 7 39; *etc.*]: for he shall take of mine [*cp.* 10 14; 16 15; 17 10], and shall declare *it* unto you. **15** All things whatsoever the Father hath are mine: therefore said I, that he taketh of mine, and shall declare *it* unto you. **16** A little while [*cp.* 7 33; 12 35; 13 33; 14 19], and ye behold me no more [*cp. verse* 10 *above*]; and again a little while, and ye shall see me [*cp. verse* 22 *below*]. **17** *Some* of his disciples therefore said one to another [*cp.* 4 33; 11 13; 12 16; 13 7, 28, 36; 14 5-10, 22: *also* 3 10; 8 27, 43; 10 6], What is this that he saith unto us, A little while, and ye behold me not; and again a little while, and ye shall see me: and, Because I go to the Father [*cp. verse* 10 *above*]? **18** They said therefore, What is this that he saith, A little while? We know not what he saith. **19** Jesus perceived [*cp.* 1 48; 2 24, 25; 5 6, 42; 6 61, 64; 13 11, 18; 16 30; 18 4; 21 17: *also* 4 19, 29; 11 14] that they were desirous to ask him, and he said unto them, Do ye inquire among yourselves concerning this, that I said, A little while, and ye behold me not, and again a little while, and ye shall see me? **20** Verily, verily, I say unto you, that ye shall weep and lament, but the world shall rejoice: ye shall be sorrowful [*cp. verses* 6 *and* 22], but your sorrow shall be turned into joy. **21** A woman when she is in travail hath sorrow, because her hour is come: but when she is delivered of the child, she remembereth no more the anguish, for the joy that a man is born into the world. **22** And ye therefore now have sorrow [*cp. verses* 6 *and* 20 *above*]: but I will see

cp. 11 6; 13 21, 57; 15 12; *etc.*	*cp.* 4 17; 6 3; 14 27, 29.	*cp.* 7 23.
cp. 10 17-21; 24 9.	*cp.* 13 9-12.	*cp.* 21 12-16: *also* 12 11.
cp. 26 75: *also* 24 25.	*cp.* 14 72: *also* 13 23.	*cp.* 22 61: *also* 24 6, 8.
		cp. 24 44.
cp. 17 23: *also* 26 22, 37.	*cp.* 14 19.	*cp.* 22 45.
		cp. 24 49.
		cp. 10 18.
cp. 15 16; 16 8-12.	*cp.* 4 13; 6 52; 7 18; 8 17-21; 9 10, 32: *also* 16 14.	*cp.* 9 45; 18 34: *also* 2 50.
cp. 9 40; 12 25; 16 8.	*cp.* 2 8; 8 17.	*cp.* 5 22; 6 8; 9 47; 11 17.
cp. 9 15.	*cp.* 2 20; 16 10.	*cp.* 5 35.
cp. 5 4.		*cp.* 6 21.
see above.	*see above.*	*see above.*

	John 14 13-14; 15 7	Matt. 21 22; 7 7	Mark 11 24	Luke 11 9
you again [*cp. verse* 16 *above*], and your heart shall rejoice, and your joy [*cp.* 20 20] no one taketh away from you. **23** And in that day [*cp.* 14 20; 16 26] ye shall [2]ask me nothing. Verily, verily, I say unto you, 15 **16** . . . that whatsoever ye shall ask of the Father in my name,		*cp.* 28 8. *cp.* 7 22; 24 36: *also* 26 29.	*cp.* 13 32: *also* 14 25.	*cp.* 24 41, 52. *cp.* 10 12; 17 31; 21 34.
	14 **13** And whatsoever ye shall ask in my name,	21 **22** And all things, whatsoever ye shall ask in prayer, believing ye shall receive.	11 **24** All things whatsoever ye pray and ask for, believe that ye have received them, and ye shall have them.	
he may give it you.	that will I do, that the Father may be glorified in the Son. **14** If ye shall ask [1]me anything			
If ye shall ask anything of the Father, he will give it you in my name [*cp.* 14 13, 14; 15 16; 16 24, 26: *also* 14 26]. **24** Hitherto have ye asked nothing in my name:	in my name, that will I do.	*cp.* 18 19. *cp.* 18 5, 20; 24 5: *also* 7 22.	*cp.* 9 37, 38, 39; 13 6; 16 17.	*cp.* 9 48, 49; 10 17; 21 8; 24 47.
ask, and ye shall receive,	15 **7** Ask whatsoever ye will, and it shall be done unto you.	7 **7** Ask, and it shall be given you; seek, and ye shall find; knock, and it shall be opened unto you.		11 **9** Ask, and it shall be given you; seek, and ye shall find; knock, and it shall be opened unto you.
that your joy may be fulfilled [*cp.* 3 29; 15 11; 17 13].		*cp.* 25 21, 23.		

[1] Or, *Advocate* Or, *Helper* Gr. *Paraclete.*
[2] Or, *ask me no question*

[1] Many ancient authorities omit *me.*

John 16 20: *cp.* Jer. 31 13.   John 16 21: *cp.* Is. 26 17.   John 16 22: *cp.* Is. 66 14.

§ 69. The Prophecy of the Flight of the Disciples

John 16 25-33

25 These things have I spoken unto you [*cp.* 14 25; 15 11; 16 1, 4, 6, 33] in [1]proverbs [*cp. verse* 29 *below and* 10 6]: the hour cometh [*cp.* 4 21, 23; 5 25, 28; 16 2, 32], when I shall no more speak unto you in [1]proverbs, but shall tell you plainly [*cp.* 10 24; 11 14, 54; 16 29; 18 20: *also* 7 4, 13, 26] of the Father. **26** In that day [*cp.* 14 20; 16 23] ye shall ask in my name [*cp.* 14 13, 14; 15 16; 16 23, 24: *also* 14 26]: and I say not unto you, that I will [2]pray the Father [*cp.* 14 16: *also* 17 9, 15, 20] for you; **27** for the Father himself loveth you [*cp.* 14 21, 23; 17 23], because ye have loved me [*cp.* 14 21, 23; 17 23: *also* 21 15-17], and have believed [*cp. verse* 30 *below*] that I came forth from the Father [*cp.* 8 42; 13 3; 16 28, 30: *also* 1 14; 5 44; 7 29; 9 16; 33, 17 8]. **28** I came out from the Father, and am come into the world [*cp.* 9 39; 12 46; 18 37: *also* 1 9; 3 19; 6 14; 11 27: *and* 3 17; 10 36; 17 18]: again, I leave the world, and go unto the Father [*cp.* 14 12, 28; 16 10, 17: *also* 7 33; 16 5: *and* 17 11, 13: *and* 20 17: *and* 13 1, 3]. **29** His disciples say, Lo, now speakest thou plainly [*cp. verse* 25 *above*],	*cp.* 13 34. *cp.* 7 22; *etc.: and* 8 5; *etc.*	*cp.* 8 32: *also* 4 33-34. *cp.* 13 32; *etc.: and* 9 37; *etc.* *cp.* 1 38. *cp.* 8 32.	*cp.* 10 12; *etc.: and* 9 48; *etc.*

John	Matt.	Mark	Luke
and speakest no [3]proverb [*cp. verse* 25 *above*]. **30** Now know we [*cp.* 3 2; 4 42; 9 24, 29, 31; 21 24: *also* 17 7] that thou knowest all things [*cp.* 21 17: *also* 2 24, 25: *and* 1 48; 4 19, 29; 5 6, 42; 6 61, 64; 11 14; 13 11, 18; 16 19; 18 4], and needest not that any man should ask thee: by this we believe [*cp.* 6 69; 9 38; 11 27: *also* 16 27; 17 8; *and* 20 31] that thou camest forth from God [*cp. verse* 27 *above*].	*cp.* 22 16; *also* 9 4; 12 25; 16 8.	*cp.* 4 34. *cp.* 12 14: *also* 2 8; 8 17.	*cp.* 20 21: *also* 5 22; 6 8; 9 47; 11 17.

John	Matt. 26 31	Mark 14 27	Luke
31 Jesus answered them, Do ye now believe? *cp.* 6 61: *also* 16 1.	Then saith Jesus unto them, All ye shall be [1]offended [*cp.* 11 6; 13 57; 15 12: *also* 13 21; 24 10] in me this night:	And Jesus saith unto them, All ye shall be [1]offended [*cp.* 6 3: *also* 4 17]:	*cp.* 7 23.
32 Behold, the hour cometh [*cp. verse* 25 *above*], yea, is come [*cp.* 4 23; 5 25], that ye	for it is written, I will smite the shepherd,	for it is written, I will smite the shepherd,	
cp. 10 11-16.	and the sheep [*cp.* 9 36; 10 6; 15 24] of the flock	and the sheep [*cp.* 6 34]	
shall be scattered,	shall be scattered abroad.	shall be scattered abroad.	
every man to his own [*cp.* 19 27: *also* 1 11; 8 44; 13 1; 15 19], and shall leave me alone:			*cp.* 18 28.
and *yet* I am not alone [*cp.* 8 16, 29], because the Father is with me.	*cp.* 26 56.	*cp.* 14 50.	
33 These things have I spoken unto you [*cp. verse* 25 *above*], that in me ye may have peace [*cp.* 14 27: *also* 20 19, 21, 26].	*cp.* 5 9; 10 13.	*cp.* 9 50.	*cp.* 1 79; 2 14, 29; 10 6; 19 38: *also* 24 36.
In the world ye have tribulation: but be of good cheer; I have overcome the world.	*cp.* 9 2, 22; 14 27.	*cp.* 6 50; 10 49.	
[1] Or, *parables* [2] Gr. *make request of.* [3] Or, *parable*	[1] Gr. *caused to stumble.*	[1] Gr. *caused to stumble.*	

Matt. 26 31 ‖ Mark 14 27 = Zech. 13 7.

§ 70. The High Priestly Prayer

John 17 1-26	Matt.	Mark	Luke
1 These things spake Jesus [*cp.* 12 36]; and lifting up his eyes to heaven [*cp.* 11 41], he said, Father [*cp. verses* 5, 11, 21, 24, 25, *and* 11 41; 12 27, 28],	*cp.* 14 19. *cp.* 11 25, 26; 26 39, 42: *also* 14 23; *etc.*: *and* 6 9.	*cp.* 6 41; 7 34. *cp.* 14 36: *also* 1 35; *etc.*	*cp.* 9 16. *cp.* 10 21, 22; 22 42; 23 34, 46: *also* 3 21; *etc.*: *and* 11 2.
the hour is come [*cp.* 12 23; 13 1: *also* 12 27: *and* 2 4; 7 6, 8, 30; 8 20]; glorify thy Son [*cp. verse* 5 *and* 8 54; 13 32; 16 14], that the Son may glorify thee [*cp. verse* 4 *below*]:	*cp.* 26 45: *also* 26 18.	*cp.* 14 41: *also* 14 35.	*cp.* 22 14: *also* 22 53.
2 even as thou gavest him authority [*cp.* 3 35; 5 27; 13 3: *also* 10 18] over all flesh, that whatsoever thou hast given him [*cp. verses* 6, 9, 11, 12, 24, *and* 6 37, 39; 10 29; 18 9], to them he should give eternal life [*cp.* 10 28: *also* 3 15, 16; *etc.*]. **3** And this is life eternal, that they should know thee the only [*cp.* 5 44] true [*cp.* 1 9; 6 32; 15 1: *also* 6 55] God, and him whom thou didst send, *even* Jesus Christ. **4** I glorified thee [*cp. verse* 1 *above*] on the earth, having accomplished the work [*cp.* 4 34; 5 36: *also* 19 28, 30: *and* 10 25, 32, 37; 14 10:	*cp.* 9 6, 8; 11 27; 28 18.	*cp.* 2 10.	*cp.* 5 24; 10 22. *cp.* 12 50; 13

and 3 21; 6 28-29; 9 3-4: and 5 17; 7 21] which thou hast given me to do. **5** And now, O Father [*cp. verse 1 above*], glorify thou me [*cp. verse 1 above*] with thine own self with the glory [*cp. verses 22 and 24 and 1 14; 2 11; 12 41*] which I had with thee before the world was [*cp. verse 24 and 1 1, 2, 18; 8 58*]. **6** I manifested [*cp. 1 31; 2 11; 3 21; 7 4; 9 3; 21 1, 14: also 14 21, 22*] thy name [*cp. verse 26: and 1 18; 3 11, 32; 8 26, 40; 15 15*] unto the men whom thou gavest me [*cp. verse 2 above*] out of the world: thine they were, and thou gavest them to me; and they have kept thy word [*cp. 8 55: also 5 38; 14 24; 17 14, 17: and 5 24; 8 31; etc.*]. **7** Now they know [*cp. 16 30*] that all things whatsoever thou hast given me are from thee: **8** for the words which thou gavest me [*cp. 3 34; 8 26; 12 49, 50; 14 10*] I have given unto them [*cp. verse 14 and 14 24; 15 15: also 3 34; 7 16; 8 26, 28, 38, 40; 12 49, 50*]; and they received *them*, and knew of a truth that I came forth from thee [*cp. 8 42; 13 3; 16 27, 28, 30: also 1 14; 5 44; 7 29; 9 16, 33*], and they believed [*cp. 16 27, 30: also 6 69; 9 38; 11 27; 20 31*] that thou didst send me [*cp. verses 21, 25, and 11 42: also 5 36, 38; 6 29: and 3 17, 34; etc.*]. **9** I ¹pray [*cp. verses 15 and 20; 14 16; 16 26*] for them: I ¹pray not for the world, but for those whom thou hast given me [*cp. verse 2 above*]; for they are thine: **10** and all things that are mine are thine, and thine are mine [*cp. 10 14; 16 14, 15*]: and I am glorified [*cp. 7 39; 12 16, 23; 13 31: also 11 4*] in them. **11** And I am no more in the world, and these are in the world, and I come to thee [*cp. verse 13: also 7 33; 13 1, 3; 14 12, 28; 16 5, 10, 17, 28: and 20 17*]. Holy Father [*cp. verse 1 above*], keep them in thy name [*cp. verse 12 and 5 43; 10 25: also 12 13*] which thou hast given me [*cp. verse 2 above*], that they may be one [*cp. verses 21, 22, 23 and 10 16; 11 52: also 12 32*], even as we *are* [*cp. verse 22 and 10 30: also 5 19; 12 45; 14 9-11; 15 24*]. **12** While I was with them, I kept them in thy name which thou hast given me [*cp. verse 2 above*]: and I guarded them, and not one of them perished [*cp. 18 9: also 3 16; 10 28: and 6 39*], but the son of perdition; that the scripture might be fulfilled. **13** But now I come to thee [*cp. verse 11 above*]; and these things I speak in the world, that they may have my joy fulfilled [*cp. 3 29; 15 11; 16 24*] in themselves. **14** I have given them thy word [*cp. verse 8 above*]; and the world hated them [*cp. 15 18, 19: also 7 7*], because they are not of the world [*cp. verse 16 and 15 19*], even as I am not of the world [*cp. verse 16 and 8 23: also 18 36: and 15 19*]. **15** I ¹pray [*cp. verses 9 and 20*] not that thou shouldest take them ²from the world, but that thou shouldest keep them ²from ³the evil *one*. **16** They are not of the world, even as I am not of the world [*cp. verse 14 above*]. **17** ⁴Sanctify them [*cp. verse 19 and 10 36*] in the truth: thy word is truth [*cp. 3 33; 7 28; 8 26*]. **18** As thou didst send me into the world [*cp. 3 17; 10 36: also 3 34; 5 38; etc.: and 1 9; 3 19; etc.*], even so sent I them into the world [*cp. 20 21*]. **19** And for their sakes I ⁴sanctify myself [*cp. verse 17 and 10 36*], that they themselves also may be sanctified in truth. **20** Neither for these only do I ¹pray [*cp. verses 9 and 15*], but for them also that believe on me through their word [*cp. 4 39*]; **21** that they may all be one[*cp. verses 11, 22, 23*]; even as thou, Father [*cp. verse 1 above*], *art* in me, and I in thee [*cp. verse 23 and 10 38; 14 10, 11, 20*], that they also may be in us [*cp. verses 23, 26, and 14 20: also 6 56; 15 4-7: and 8 31*]: that the world may believe [*cp. 14 31; 17 23*] that thou didst send me [*cp. verses 8 and 25*]. **22** And the glory [*cp. verses 5 and 24*] which thou hast given me I have given unto them; that they may be one [*cp. verses 11, 21, 23*], even as we *are* one [*cp. verse 11*]; **23** I in them, and thou in me [*cp. verses 21 and 26*], that they may be perfected into one [*cp. verse 11, 21, 22*]; that the world may know [*cp. 14 31: also 17 21*] that thou didst send me, and lovedst them [*cp. 14 21, 23; 16 27*], even as thou lovedst me [*cp. verses 24 and 26 below: also 3 35; 5 20; 10 17; 15 9*]. **24** Father [*cp. verse 1 above*], ⁵that which thou hast given me, I will that, where I am [*cp. 7 34, 36; 12 26; 14 3*], they also may be [*cp. 14 3: also 12 26*] with me; that they may behold my glory [*cp. verses 5 and 22*], which thou hast given me [*cp. verse 2 above*]: for thou lovedst me [*cp. verses 23 and 26*] before the foundation of the world [*cp. verse 5 and 1 1, 2, 18; 8 58*]. **25** O righteous Father [*cp. verse 1 above*], the world knew

		cp. 9 32; 18 31; 22 37.
cp. 19 28; 25 31.	*cp.* 10 37.	*cp.* 9 26, 32; 24 26.
cp. 11 27.	*cp.* 16 12, 14.	*cp.* 10 22.
	cp. 1 38.	
cp. 25 21, 23.		
cp. 10 22; 24 9.	*cp.* 13 13.	*cp.* 1 71; 6 22, 27; 21 17.
cp. 5 37, 39; 6 13; 13 19, 38.		
cp. 28 19-20.	*cp.* 16 15.	*cp.* 24 47-49.
cp. 3 17; 17 5.	*cp.* 1 11; 9 7; 12 6.	*cp.* 3 22; 20 13.
cp. 13 35; 25 34.		*cp.* 11 50.

thee not [*cp.* 7 28; 8 19, 55; 15 21; 16 3: *also* 4 22], but I knew thee [*cp.* 7 29; 8 55; 10 15: *also* 1 18; 6 46; 8 19]; and these knew that thou didst send me [*cp. verses* 8 *and* 21]; **26** and I made known unto them thy name [*cp. verse* 6 *above*], and will make it known; that the love wherewith thou lovedst me [*cp. verses* 23 *and* 24] may be in them, and I in them [*cp. verses* 21 *and* 23].	*cp.* 11 27.		*cp.* 10 22.

¹ Gr. *make request.*   ² Gr. *out of.*   ³ Or, *evil*   ⁴ Or, *Consecrate*   ⁵ Many ancient authorities read *those whom.*

John 17 8, 26: *cp.* Ps. 22 22.   John 17 12: *cp.* Is. 34 16 *and* Ps. 109 8.   John 17 17: *cp.* II Sam. 7 28 *and* Ps 119 160.

(iii) In the Garden (§ 71)

§ 71. **The Arrest**

John 18 1-11	Matt. 26 30, 36, 47-54	Mark 14 26, 32, 43-47	Luke 22 39-40, 47-51
1 When Jesus had spoken these words, he went forth *cp. verse* 2.	**30** And when they had sung a hymn, they went out [*cp.* 21 17] unto the mount of Olives.	**26** And when they had sung a hymn, they went out [*cp.* 11 11, 19] unto the mount of Olives.	**39** And he came out, and went, [*cp.* 21 37] as his custom was [*cp.* 21 37: *also* 4 16: *and* 1 9; 2 42], unto the mount of Olives; and the disciples also followed him.
with his disciples over the ¹brook ²Kidron, where was a garden [*cp.* 18 26: *also* 19 41], into the which he entered, himself and his disciples. **2** Now Judas also, which betrayed him [*cp. verse* 5 *and* 6 64, 71; 13 11: *also* 13 2, 21], knew the place:	**36** Then cometh Jesus with them unto *cp.* 10 4; 26 25, 46, 48; 27 3: *also* 26 21, 23, 24. ¹a place called Geth-semane, . . .	**32** And they come unto *cp.* 3 19; 14 42, 44: *also* 14 18, 21. ¹a place which was named Geth-semane: . . .	**40** And when he was at *cp.* 21 21, 22. the place . . .
for Jesus oft-times resorted thither with his disciples.	**47** And while he yet spake, lo, Judas, one of the twelve, came, and with him a great multitude with swords and staves, from the chief priests and elders of the people.	**43** And straight-way, while he yet spake, co-meth Judas, one of the twelve, and with him a multitude with swords and staves, from the chief priests and the scribes and the elders.	**47** While he yet spake, be-hold, a multitude, and he that was called Judas, one of the twelve, went before them; *cp.* 22 52.
3 Judas then, having received the ³band *of soldiers*, and officers from the chief priests and the Pharisees, cometh thither with lan-terns and torches and weapons. **4** Jesus there-fore, knowing [*cp.* 1 48; 2 24, 25; 5 6, 42; 6 61, 64; 13 11, 18; 16 19, 30; 21 17: *also* 4 19, 29; 11 14] all the things that were com-ing upon him, went forth, and saith unto them, Whom seek ye [*cp. verse* 7 *and* 20 15: *also* 1 38: *and* 4 27]? **5** They answered him, Jesus of Nazareth [*cp. verse* 7 *and* 1 45; 19 19]. Jesus saith unto them, I	*cp.* 9 4; 12 25; 16 8. *cp.* 2 23; 26 71: *also* 21 11.	*cp.* 2 8; 8 17. *cp.* 1 24; 10 47; 14 67; 16 6.	*cp.* 5 22; 6 8; 9 47; 11 17. *cp.* 4 34; 18 37; 24 19.

am *he*. And Judas also, which betrayed him [*cp. verse 2 above*], was standing with them.

cp. 19 3.

cp. 13 27.
6 When therefore he said unto them, I am *he*, they went backward, and fell [*cp.* 11 32: *also* 9 38] to the ground [*cp.* 9 6]. **7** Again therefore he asked them, Whom seek ye [*cp. verse 4 above*]? And they said, Jesus of Nazareth [*cp. verse 5*]. **8** Jesus answered, I told you that I am *he*: if therefore ye seek me, let these go their way: **9** that the word might be fulfilled which he spake, Of those whom thou hast given me [*cp.* 6 37, 39; 10 29; 17 2, 6, 9, 11, 12, 24] I lost not one [*cp.* 17 12: *also* 6 39; 10 28: *and* 3 16].

10 Simon Peter therefore
cp. 11 42; 12 29.

having a sword

drew it,   and struck
          the high
priest's [4]servant, and cut off his right
          ear. Now the [4]servant's   name   was Malchus.
11 Jesus therefore
said unto Peter,
Put   up   the
sword into the sheath: the cup which the Father hath given me, shall I not drink it?

---

48 Now he that betrayed him

gave them a sign, saying, Whomsoever I shall kiss, that is he: take him.
49 And

straightway he came to Jesus, and said, Hail [*cp.* 27 29; 28 9], Rabbi; and [2]kissed him. **50** And Jesus   said   unto   him,

Friend [*cp.* 20 13; 22 12], *do* that for which thou art come.

cp. 2 11: *also* 17 14: *and* 8 2; 9 18; 14 33; 15 25; 20 20; 28 9, 17.

cp. 2 23; *etc.*

Then they came and laid hands on Jesus, and took him. **51** And behold, one of them that were with [*cp.* 16 28; 27 47: *also* 26 73] Jesus

stretched out his hand, and drew his sword, and smote the [3]servant of the high priest,   and struck off his   [*cp.* 5 29, 30, 39; 27 29] ear.

52 Then saith
Jesus
unto him,
Put up again thy sword into its place:
cp. 26 39: *also* 20 22, 23.

for all they that take the sword shall perish with the sword. **53** Or thinkest thou that I cannot beseech my Father, and he shall even now send me more

---

44 Now he that betrayed him

had given them a token, saying, Whomsoever I shall kiss, that is he; take him, and lead him away safely. **45** And when he was come, straightway he came to him, and saith, [*cp.* 15 18]   Rabbi; and [2]kissed him.

cp. 3 11; 5 22, 33; 7 25: *also* 1 40; 10 17: *and* 5 6.

cp. 1 24; *etc.*

46 And they laid hands on him, and took him. **47** But a certain one of them that stood by [*cp.* 9 1; 11 5; 15 35: *also* 14 69, 70; 15 39]

drew his sword, and smote the [3]servant of the high priest,   and struck off his
          ear.

cp. 14 36: *also* 10 38, 39.

---

and

he drew near unto Jesus
cp. 1 28.
to kiss him. **48** But Jesus   said   unto   him, Judas, betrayest thou the Son of man with a kiss?

cp. 5 8, 12; 8 28, 41, 47; 17 16: *also* 24 52.

cp. 4 34; *etc.*

49 And when they that were about him saw what would follow, they said, Lord, shall we smite   with   the   sword?

50 And a certain one of them *cp.* 9 27: *also* 19 24.

cp. 22 26, 38.

smote the [1]servant of the high priest,   and struck off his right [*cp.* 6 6] ear.

51 But
Jesus   answered
and said,   Suffer
ye thus far.

cp. 22 42.

cp. 1 51; 12 29.	than twelve legions of angels [*cp.* 4 11]? **54** How then should the scriptures be fulfilled, that thus it must be?	*cp.* 1 13.	*cp.* 22 43.
			And he touched his ear, and healed him.
[1] Or, *ravine* Gr. *winter-torrent.* [2] Or, *of the Cedars* [3] Or, *cohort* [4] Gr. *bondservant.*	[1] Gr. *an enclosed piece of ground.* [2] Gr. *kissed him much.* [3] Gr. *bondservant.*	[1] Gr. *an enclosed piece of ground.* [2] Gr. *kissed him much.* [3] Gr. *bondservant.*	[1] Gr. *bondservant.*

(iv) The Trial (§§ 72-79)

§ 72. **Jesus led to Annas**

John 18 12-14	Matt. 26 57	Mark 14 53	Luke 22 54
12 So the [1]band and the [2]chief captain, and the officers of the Jews, seized Jesus and bound him [*cp.* 18 24], **13** and led him to Annas [*cp.* 18 24] first; *cp.* 18 24. for he was father in law to Caiaphas [*cp.* 11 49; 18 24, 28], which was high priest that year [*cp.* 11 49, 51]. **14** Now Caiaphas was he which gave counsel to the Jews, that it was expedient [*cp.* 11 50; 16 7] that one man should die for the people [*cp.* 11 50]. [1] Or, *cohort* [2] Or, *military tribune* Gr. *chiliarch.*	**57** And they that had taken Jesus [*cp.* 27 2] led him away to *the house of* Caiaphas [*cp.* 26 3] the high priest.	**53** And they [*cp.* 15 1] led Jesus away to the high priest.	**54** And they seized him, and led him *away,* [*cp.* 3 2] and brought him into the high priest's house. *cp.* 3 2.

§ 73. **Peter's Denial** (i)

John 18 15-18	Matt. 26 58, 69-71	Mark 14 54, 66-68	Luke 22 54, 56-57, 55
15 And Simon Peter followed Jesus, and *so did* another disciple [*verse* 16 *and* 20 2, 3, 4, 8]. Now that disciple was known unto the high priest, and entered in with Jesus into the court of the high priest; **16** but Peter was standing at the door without. So the other disciple, which was known unto the high priest, went out and spake unto her that kept the door, and brought in Peter. *cp. verse* 15.	**58** But Peter followed him afar off, unto the court [*cp.* 26 3, 69] of the high priest, and entered in, . . . **69** Now Peter was sitting without in the court [*cp.* 26 3, 58]:	**54** And Peter had followed him afar off, even within, into the court [*cp. verse* 66; *also* 15 16] of the high priest, . . . **66** And as Peter was beneath in the court [*cp. verse* 54], there	**54** But Peter followed afar off. *cp. verse* 55.

17 The maid therefore that kept the door

cp. 18 18, 25.

saith unto Peter, Art thou also *one* of cp. 18 5, 7; 19 19: *also* 1 45.

this man's disciples? He saith, I am not.

18 Now the 1servants and the officers were standing *there*, having made 2a fire of coals [cp. 21 9]; for it was cold; and they were warming themselves: and Peter also was with them, standing and warming himself [cp. 18 25].

1 Gr. *bondservants.*
2 Gr. *a fire of charcoal.*

---

and a maid came unto him, saying, Thou also wast with cp. 26 71. Jesus the Galilaean. **70** But he denied before them all, saying, I know not what thou sayest. **71** And when he was gone out into the porch . . .

58 . . . and sat with the officers,

to see the end.

---

cometh one of the maids of the high priest;

67 and seeing Peter cp. verse 54. warming himself [cp. verse 54], she looked upon him, and saith, Thou also wast with the Nazarene [cp. 1 24; 10 47; 16 6], *even* Jesus. cp. 14 70. **68** But he denied, saying, 1I neither know, nor understand what thou sayest: and he went out into the 2porch; 3and the cock crew.

54 . . . and he was sitting with the officers, and warming himself [cp. verse 67] in the light *of the fire.*

1 Or, *I neither know, nor understand: thou, what sayest thou?*
2 Gr. *forecourt.*
3 Many ancient authorities omit *and the cock crew.*

---

56 And a certain maid seeing him as he sat in the light *of the fire,* and looking stedfastly upon him, said, This man also was with him. [cp. 4 34; 18 37; 24 19] cp. 22 59. **57** But he denied, saying, Woman, I know him not.

55 And when they had kindled a fire in the midst of the court, and had sat down together, Peter sat in the midst of them.

cp. verse 56.

§ 74. Jesus before Annas

John 18 19-24

19 The high priest therefore asked Jesus of his disciples, and of his teaching. cp. 19 10.

cp. 19 9.

20 Jesus answered him,

I have spoken openly [cp. 7 4, 13, 26; 10 24; 11 14, 54; 16 25, 29] to the world [cp. 8 26]; I ever taught in 1synagogues [cp. 6 59], and in the

---

Matt. 26 62-63, 55, 67-68, 57

62 And the high priest stood up, and said unto him, Answerest thou nothing? what is it which these witness against thee? **63** But Jesus held his peace. cp. 27 12, 14: *also* 15 23.

55 In that hour said Jesus to the multitudes,

Are ye come out as against a robber with swords and staves to seize me?

I sat daily cp. 4 23; 9 35; 13 54. in the

Mark 14 60-61, 48-49, 65, 53

60 And the high priest stood up in the midst, and asked Jesus, saying, Answerest thou nothing? what is it which these witness against thee? **61** But he held his peace, and answered nothing [cp. 15 5]. . . . **48** And Jesus answered and said unto them,

Are ye come out, as against a robber, with swords and staves to seize me? cp. 8 32.

49 I was daily with you [cp. 1 21, 39; 6 2] in the

Luke 22 52-53, 63-65, 54

cp. 23 9.

52 And Jesus said unto the chief priests, and captains of the temple, and elders, which were come against him, Are ye come out, as against a robber, with swords and staves?

53 When I was daily with you [cp. 4 15, 16, 44; 6 6; 13 10] in the

temple [*cp.* 7 14, 28; 8 2, 20], where all the Jews come together; and in secret [*cp.* 7 4, 10] spake I nothing.	temple [*cp.* 21 23]	temple [*cp.* 11 27; 12 35]	temple [*cp.* 19 47; 20 1; 21 37],
	teaching, and ye took me not.	teaching, and ye took me not.	ye stretched not forth your hands against me.
21 Why askest thou me? ask them that have heard *me*, what I spake unto them: behold, these know the things which I said. **22** And when he had said this,	*cp.* 27 29, 31, 41: *also* 20 19.	**65** And some *cp.* 15 20, 31: *also* 10 34.	**63** And the men that held [1]*Jesus* mocked [*cp.* 23 11, 35, 36: *also* 18 32] him, and beat him. *cp.* 18 32.
cp. 19 3.	**67** Then did they spit [*cp.* 27 30] in his face and buffet him: and some smote him [1]with the palms of their hands, **68** saying, Prophesy unto us, thou Christ [*cp.* 27 17, 22: *also* 26 63: *and* 16 16]: who is he that struck thee?	began to spit [*cp.* 15 19: *also* 10 34] on him, and to cover his face, and to buffet him, and to say unto him, Prophesy: *cp.* 15 32: *also* 14 61: *and* 8 29.	**64** And they blindfolded him, and asked him, saying, Prophesy: *cp.* 23 35, 39: *also* 22 67; 23 2: *and* 9 20. who is he that struck thee?
cp. 1 41; 4 25, 26, 29; 7 26, 41; 9 22; 10 24; 11 27.			
one of the officers standing by struck Jesus [2]with his hand [*cp.* 19 3], saying, Answerest thou the high priest so? **23** Jesus answered him, If I have spoken evil, bear witness of the evil: but if well, why smitest thou me?		and the officers received him with [1]blows of their hands.	**65** And many other [*cp.* 3 18] things spake they against him, reviling him. . . .
18 12 So the [3]band and the [4]chief captain, and the officers of the Jews, seized Jesus and bound him, **13** and led him to Annas first; for he was father in law to Caiaphas, which was high priest that year. . . . **24** Annas therefore sent him bound unto Caiaphas [*cp.* 18 13, 14, 28: *and* 11 49] the high priest.	**57** And they that had taken Jesus led him away to *the house of* Caiaphas [*cp.* 26 3] the high priest.	**53** And they led Jesus away to the high priest.	**54** And they seized him, and led him *away,* *cp.* 3 2. and brought him into *cp.* 3 2. the high priest's house.
[1] Gr. *synagogue.* [2] Or, *with a rod* [3] Or, *cohort* [4] Or, *military tribune* Gr. *chiliarch.*	[1] Or, *with rods*	[1] Or, *strokes of rods*	[1] Gr. *him.*

John 18 20: *cp.* Is. 45 19; 48 16.

§ 75. Peter's Denial (ii)

John 18 25-27	Matt. 26 71-74	Mark 14 69-72	Luke 22 58-60
25 Now Simon Peter was standing and warming himself [*cp.* 18 18].		*cp.* 14 54, 67.	
	71 . . . another	**69** And the	**58** And after a little while another

They said therefore unto him, Art thou also *one* of his disciples? *cp.* 18 5, 7; 19 19: *also* 1 45.	*maid* saw him, and saith unto them that were there, This man also was with Jesus the Nazarene [*cp.* 2 23: *also* 21 11]. **72** And	maid saw him, and began again to say to them that stood by [*cp. verse* 70], This is *one* of them.	saw him, and said, Thou also art *one* of them. *cp.* 4 34; 18 37; 24 19.
He denied and said, I am not.	again he denied with an oath, I know not the man. **73** And after a little while	*cp.* 14 67. **70** But he again denied it. And after a little while again	But Peter said, Man, I am not. **59** And after the space of about one hour
cp. 11 42; 12 29. **26** One of the ¹servants of the high priest, being a kinsman of him whose ear Peter cut off, saith,	they that stood by [*cp.* 16 28; 27 47]	they that stood by [*cp.* 9 1; 11 5; 14 47, 69; 15 35, 39]	*cp.* 9 27; 19 24.
Did not I see thee in the garden [*cp.* 18 1: *also* 19 41] with him? **27** Peter therefore	came and said to Peter, Of a truth thou also art *one* of them; [*cp.* 26 69] for thy speech bewrayeth thee.	said to Peter, Of a truth thou art *one* of them; for thou art a Galilæan.	another confidently affirmed, saying, Of a truth this man also was with him: for he is a Galilæan.
denied again: and straightway the cock crew [*cp.* 13 38].	**74** Then began he to curse and to swear, I know not the man. And straightway the cock crew [*cp.* 26 34].	**71** But he began to curse, and to swear, I know not this man of whom ye speak. **72** And straightway the second time [*cp.* 14 68] the cock crew [*cp.* 14 30].	**60** But Peter said, Man, I know not what thou sayest. And immediately, while he yet spake, the cock crew [*cp.* 22 34].

¹ Gr. *bondservants.*

§ 76. **Jesus led to Pilate**

John 18 28-32	Matt. 27 1-2	Mark 15 1	Luke 23 1-2
28 They *cp.* 18 12, 24. lead Jesus therefore from Caiaphas [*cp.* 18 13, 14, 24: *and* 11 49] into the ¹palace [*cp.* 18 33; 19 9]: and it was early; and they themselves entered not into the ¹palace, that they might not be defiled [*cp.* 11 55], but might eat the passover. **29** Pilate therefore went out [*cp.* 18 38;	**1** Now when morning was come, all the chief priests and the elders of the people took counsel [*cp.* 12 14; 22 15; 27 7; 28 12] against Jesus to put him to death: **2** and they bound him, and led him away, *cp.* 26 3, 57. and delivered him up to Pilate the governor [*cp.* 27 11, 14, 15, 21, 27; 28 14]. *cp.* 27 27.	**1** And straightway in the morning the chief priests with the elders and scribes, and the whole council, held a consultation [*cp.* 3 6], and bound Jesus, and carried him away, and delivered him up to Pilate. *cp.* 15 16.	**1** And *cp.* 22 66. the whole company of them rose up, *cp.* 3 2. and brought him before Pilate. *cp.* 20 20.

John	Matt.	Mark	Luke
19 4] unto them, and saith, What accusation bring ye against this man? **30** They answered and said unto him, If this man *cp.* 7 12: *also* 7 47.	*cp.* 27 12.	*cp.* 15 3.	**2** And they began to accuse him, saying, We found this man perverting [*cp.* 23 14] our nation, and forbidding to give tribute [*cp.* 20 20-26] to Cæsar, and saying that he himself is ¹Christ [*cp.* 22 67: *also* 23 35, 39: *and* 9 20] a king [*cp.* 23 3].
cp. 19 12.	*cp.* 22 15-22.	*cp.* 12 13-17.	
cp. 4 25, 26: *also* 1 41; 4 29; 7 26, 41; 9 22; 11 27.	*cp.* 26 63-64: *also* 26 68; 27 17, 22: *and* 16 16.	*cp.* 14 61-62: *also* 15 32: *and* 8 29.	

were not an evil-doer, we should not have delivered him up unto thee. **31** Pilate therefore said unto them, Take him yourselves [*cp.* 19 6], and judge him according to your law [*cp.* 8 17; 10 34: *also* 7 51; 15 25: *and* 19 7]. The Jews said unto him, It is not lawful for us to put any man to death: **32** that the word of Jesus might be fulfilled, which he spake, signifying by what manner of death he should die [*cp.* 12 33: *also* 21 19: *and* 2 19-22; 3 14; 8 28].

¹ Gr. *Prætorium.*

¹ Or, *an anointed king*

John 18 28: *cp.* Num. 9 6.

§ 77. Jesus before Pilate

John 18 33-38a	Matt. 27 11	Mark 15 2	Luke 23 3
33 Pilate therefore entered again into the ¹palace [*cp.* 18 28; 19 9], and called Jesus,	*cp.* 27 27.	*cp.* 15 16.	*cp.* 20 20.
and said unto him, Art thou the King of the Jews [*cp.* 18 39; 19 3, 19, 21: *also* 1 49; 12 13: *and* 6 15; 12 15; 18 37; 19 12, 14, 15]?	**11** Now Jesus stood before the governor [*cp.* 27 2, 14, 15, 21, 27; 28 14]: and the governor asked him, saying, Art thou the King of the Jews [*cp.* 2 2; 27 29, 37: *also* 27 42: *and* 21 5]?	**2** And Pilate asked him, Art thou the King of the Jews [*cp.* 15 9, 12, 18, 26: *also* 15 32]?	**3** And Pilate asked him, saying, Art thou the King of the Jews [*cp.* 23 37, 38: *and* 19 38; 23 2]?

34 Jesus answered, Sayest thou this of thyself, or did others tell it thee concerning me? **35** Pilate answered, Am I a Jew? Thine own nation and the chief priests delivered thee unto me: what hast thou done? **36** Jesus answered, My kingdom is not of this world [*cp.* 8 23; 17 14, 16: *also* 15 19]: if my kingdom were of this world, then would my ²servants fight, that I should not be delivered to the Jews: but now is my kingdom not from hence. **37** Pilate therefore said unto him, Art thou a king then? Jesus answered,

		Mark *cp.* 16 28; 20 21.	Luke *cp.* 22 29, 30; 23 42.

³Thou sayest that I am a king.

	And Jesus said unto him, Thou sayest [*cp.* 26 25, 64].	And he answering saith unto him, Thou sayest.	And he answered him and said, Thou sayest [*cp.* 22 70].

To this end [*cp.* 12 27] have I been born, and to this end am I come into the world [*cp.* 9 39; 12 46; 16 28: *also* 1 9; 3 19; 6 14; 11 27: *and* 3 17; 10 36; 17 18], that I should bear witness unto the truth [*cp.* 5 33: *also* 1 14, 17; 8 32; 14 6]. Every one that is of the truth heareth my voice [*cp.* 10 16, 27: *also* 5 25, 28]. **38** Pilate saith unto him, What is truth?

¹ Gr. *Prætorium.*
² Or, *officers*: as in ver. 3, 12, 18, 22.
³ Or, *Thou sayest* it, *because I am a king.*

§ 78. **Who should be released?**

John 18 38b-40	Matt. 27 15-21	Mark 15 6-11	Luke 23 4, 13-14, 16, 18-19
38b And when he had said this, he went out again [*cp*. 18 29; 19 4] unto the Jews, and saith unto them, I find no crime [*cp*. 19 4, 6] in him.	*cp*. 27 24. **15** Now at [1]the feast the governor [*cp*. 27 2, 11, 14, 21, 27; 28 14] was wont to release unto the multitude one prisoner, whom they would. **16** And they had then a notable prisoner, called Barabbas.	**6** Now at [1]the feast he used to release unto them one prisoner, whom they asked of him. **7** And there was one called Barabbas, *lying* bound with them that had made insurrection, men who in the insurrection had committed murder. **8** And the multitude went up and began to ask him *to do* as he was wont to do unto them. **9** And Pilate answered them, saying,	**4** And Pilate said unto the chief priests and the multitudes, I find no fault [*cp*. 23 14, 22] in this man. *cp*. 20 20. *verse* 19 **13** And Pilate called together the chief priests and the rulers and the people, **14** and said unto them, Ye. . . . . **16** I will therefore chastise him, and release him [*cp*. 23 22].[1]
39 But ye have a custom, that I should release unto you, one at the passover: *cp*. 19 1. will ye therefore that I release unto you the King of the Jews [*cp*. 18 33; 19 3, 19, 21: *also* 1 49; 12 13: *and* 6 15; 12 15; 18 37; 19 12, 14, 15]? *cp*. 4 25, 26: *also* 1 41; 4 29; 7 26, 41; 9 22; 11 27.	**17** When therefore they were gathered together, Pilate said unto them, *cp*. 27 26. Whom will ye that I release unto you? *cp*. 2 2; 27 11, 29, 37: *also* 27 42: *and* 21 5. Barabbas, or Jesus which is called Christ [*cp*. 1 16; 27 22: *also* 26 63, 64, 68: *and* 16 16]? **18** For he knew that for envy they had delivered him up. **19** And while he was sitting on the judgement-seat, his wife sent unto him, saying, Have thou nothing to do with that righteous man [*cp*. 27 24]: for I have suffered many things this day in a dream because of him. **20** Now the chief priests and the elders persuaded the multitudes that they should ask for Barabbas, and destroy Jesus. **21** But the governor [*cp. verse* 15] answered and said unto them, Whether of the twain will ye that I release unto you? And they said,	*cp*. 15 15. Will ye that I release unto you the King of the Jews [*cp*. 15 2, 12, 18, 26: *also* 15 32]? *cp*. 14 61, 62; 15 32: *and* 8 29. **10** For he perceived that for envy the chief priests had delivered him up. **11** But the chief priests stirred up the multitude, that he should rather release Barabbas unto them.	*cp*. 23 3, 37, 38: *and* 19 38; 23 2. *cp*. 22 67; 23 2, 35, 39: *and* 9 20. *cp*. 23 47. *cp*. 23 5.
40 They cried out therefore again, saying, [*cp*. 19	said,		**18** But they cried out all together, saying, Away

15] Not this man, but Barabbas. Now Barabbas	Barabbas.		with this man, and release unto us Barabbas: **19** one who for a certain insurrection made in the city, and for murder, was cast into prison.
		verse 7	
was a robber.			
	¹ Or, *a feast*	¹ Or, *a feast*	¹ Many ancient authorities insert ver. 17 *Now he must needs release unto them at the feast one prisoner.* Others add the same words after ver. 19.

§ 79. Jesus is scourged, mocked, and delivered to be crucified

John 19 1-16a	Matt. 27 27-30, 22-23, 13-14, 23-26	Mark 15 16-19, 12-14, 4-5, 14-15	Luke 23 13-14, 20-22, 6, 23-25
1 Then Pilate therefore took Jesus, and scourged him. **2** And the soldiers	*cp.* 27 26. **27** Then the soldiers of the governor [*cp.* 27 2, 11, 14, 15, 21; 28 14] took Jesus into	*cp.* 15 15. **16** And the soldiers led him away within the court [*cp.* 14 54, 66], which is the ¹Prætorium; and they call together the whole ²band. **17** And they clothe	*cp.* 23 16, 22. *cp.* 20 20. *cp.* 22 55.
cp. 18 15. *cp.* 18 28, 33; 19 9.	*cp.* 26 3, 58, 69. the ¹palace, and gathered unto him the whole ²band. **28** And they ³stripped him, and put on him a scarlet robe. **29** And they plaited a crown of thorns and put it upon his head,	him with purple, and plaiting a crown of thorns, they put it on him;	*cp.* 23 11.
plaited a crown of thorns, and put it on his head, and arrayed him in a purple garment; *cp.* 18 10. **3** and they came unto him,	and a reed in his right [*cp.* 5 29, 30, 39] hand; and they kneeled down before him, and mocked [*cp.* 27 31, 41: *also* 20 19] him,		*cp.* 23 11. *cp.* 6 6; 22 50.
and said, Hail, King of the Jews [*cp.* 18 33, 39; 19 19, 21: *also* 1 49; 12 13: *and* 6 15; 12 15; 18 37; 19 12, 14, 15]! and they struck him ¹with their hands [*cp.* 18 22].	saying, Hail, King of the Jews [*cp.* 2 2; 27 11, 37: *also* 27 42: *and* 21 5]!	**18** and they began to salute him, Hail, King of the Jews [*cp.* 15 2, 9, 12, 26: *also* 15 32]!	*cp.* 22 63; 23 11, 35, 36: *also* 18 32. *cp.* 23 3, 37, 38: *and* 19 38; 23 2.
	30 And they *cp.* 26 67. spat [*cp.* 26 67] upon him, and took the reed and smote him on the head.	**19** And they smote his head with a reed, [*cp.* 14 65] and did spit [*cp.* 14 65: *also* 10 34] upon him, and bowing their knees worshipped him.	*cp.* 18 32.
4 And Pilate went out again [*cp.* 18 29, 38], and saith unto them, Behold, I bring him out to you, that ye may know that I find no crime [*cp.* 18 38; 19 6] in him.	*cp.* 27 24.		**13** And Pilate called together the chief priests and the rulers and the people, **14** and said unto them, Ye brought unto me this man, as one that perverteth [*cp.* 23 2] the people: and behold, I, having examined him before you, found no fault [*cp.* 23 4, 22] in this man touching those things whereof ye accuse him.
5 Jesus therefore came out, wearing the crown of thorns and the purple			

[John]

garment. And *Pilate* saith unto them, Behold, the man [*cp. verse* 14]!

cp. verse 12.
6 When therefore the chief priests and the officers saw him, they cried out, saying, Crucify *him*, crucify *him*. Pilate saith unto them,

Take him yourselves [*cp.* 18 31], and crucify him: for I find no crime [*cp.* 18 38; 19 4] in him.
cp. verse 1.
7 The Jews answered him, We have a law [*cp.* 7 51: *also* 8 17; 10 34; 15 25; 18 31], and by that law he ought to die, because he made himself the Son of God [*cp.* 5 17, 18; 10 33, 36: *also* 8 53; 19 12]. 8 When Pilate therefore heard this saying, he was the more afraid; 9 and he entered into the 2palace again, and saith unto Jesus, Whence art thou [*cp.* 7 27, 28; 8 14; 9 29, 30]?

But Jesus gave him no answer.

10 Pilate therefore saith unto him, Speakest thou not unto me? knowest thou not that I have 3power to release thee, and have 3power to crucify thee? 11 Jesus answered him, Thou wouldest have no 3power against me, except it were given thee [*cp.* 3 27; 6 65] from above: therefore he that delivered me unto thee hath greater sin. 12 Upon this Pilate sought to release him: but the Jews cried out, saying, If thou release this man, thou art not Cæsar's friend: every one that maketh himself [*cp. verse* 7 above] a king 4speaketh against Cæsar. 13 When Pilate therefore heard these words, he brought Jesus out, and sat down on the judgement-seat at a place called The Pavement, but in Hebrew, Gabbatha. 14 Now it was the Preparation [*cp.* 19 31, 42] of the passover: it was about the sixth hour [*cp.* 4 6: *also* 1 39: *and* 4 52]. And he saith unto the Jews, Behold, your King [*cp. verse* 5]! 15 They therefore cried out,

[Matthew]

22 Pilate saith unto them, What then shall I do unto Jesus which is called Christ [*cp.* 27 17]?

They all say, Let him be crucified.
23 And he said, Why, what evil hath he done? . . .

cp. 27 24.

cp. 27 26.

cp. 26 63-64.

13 Then saith Pilate unto him,

Hearest thou not how many things they witness against thee? 14 And he gave him no answer [*cp.* 26 63; 27 12: *also* 15 23], not even to one word: insomuch that the governor [*cp.* 27 2, 11, 15; *etc.*] marvelled greatly.

cp. 26 62.

cp. 27 19.

cp. 27 62.
cp. 27 45.

23 . . . But they cried out exceedingly,

[Mark]

12 And Pilate again answered and said unto them, What then shall I do unto him whom ye call the King of the Jews [*cp.* 15 9]?
13 And they cried out again, Crucify him.
14 And Pilate said unto them, Why, what evil hath he done? . . .

cp. 15 15.

cp. 14 61-62.

4 And Pilate again asked him, saying,

Answerest thou nothing? behold how many things they accuse thee of. 5 But Jesus no more answered [*cp.* 14 61] anything; insomuch that Pilate marvelled.

cp. 14 60.

cp. 15 42.
cp. 15 33.

14 . . . But they cried out exceedingly,

[Luke]

20 And Pilate spake unto them again,

desiring to release Jesus; 21 but they shouted, saying, Crucify, crucify him. 22 And he said unto them the third time, Why, what evil hath this man done [*cp.* 23 41]? I have found no cause [*cp.* 23 4, 14] of death in him: I will therefore chastise him and release him [*cp.* 23 16].

cp. 22 70.

6 But when Pilate heard it, he asked

cp. 13 25, 27.
whether the man were a Galilæan.

cp. 23 9.

cp. 23 20.
cp. 23 2.

cp. 23 54.
cp. 23 44.

23 But they were instant with

John 19

Away with *him*, away with *him*, crucify him. Pilate saith unto them, Shall I crucify your King? The chief priests answered, We have no king but Cæsar.

16 Then therefore he delivered him *cp. verse 1.* unto them to be crucified.

1 Or, *with rods*
2 Gr. *Prætorium.*
3 Or, *authority*
4 Or, *opposeth Caesar*

Matt. 27

saying, Let him be crucified.

24 So when Pilate saw that he prevailed nothing, but rather that a tumult [*cp.* 26 5] was arising, he took water, and washed his hands before the multitude, saying, I am innocent [*cp.* 27 4] 4of the blood of this righteous man [*cp.* 27 19]: see ye *to it* [*cp.* 27 4]. **25** And all the people answered and said, His blood *be* on us, and on our children.

26 Then released he unto them Barabbas: but Jesus he scourged and delivered to be crucified.

1 Gr. *Prætorium.* See Mark 15 16.
2 Or, *cohort*
3 Some ancient authorities read *clothed.*
4 Some ancient authorities read *of this blood: see ye &c.*

Mark 15

Crucify him.

15 And Pilate,

wishing to content the multitude,

released unto them Barabbas,

and delivered Jesus, when he had scourged him, to be crucified.

1 Or, *palace*
2 Or, *cohort*

Luke 23

loud voices, asking that *cp.* 23 18. he might be crucified.

And their voices prevailed. **24** And Pilate

cp. 23 47.

gave sentence that what they asked for should be done. **25** And he released him that for insurrection and murder had been cast into prison, whom they asked for; but Jesus he delivered up *cp.* 23 16, 22. to their will.

John 19 7: *cp.* Lev. 24 16.

(v) On Golgotha (§§ 80-83)

§ 80. The Crucifixion

John 19 16b-22	Matt. 27 32-35, 38, 37	Mark 15 21-24, 27, 26	Luke 23 26, 32-33a, 36, 33b, 38

John 19 16b-22

Jesus **17** and   **16b** They took therefore: he went out,

the cross himself,   bearing for

Matt. 27 32-35, 38, 37

cp. 27 31.

32 And as they came out, they found a man of Cyrene, Simon by name:

him they 1compelled to go *with them,*

that he might bear his cross.

Mark 15 21-24, 27, 26

cp. 15 20.

21 And they 1compel one passing by, Simon of Cyrene, coming from the country, the father of Alexander and Rufus, to go *with them,*

that he might bear his cross.

Luke 23 26, 32-33a, 36, 33b, 38

26 And when they led him away,

they laid hold upon one Simon of Cyrene, coming from the country,

and laid on him the cross, to bear it after Jesus. **32** And there were also two others, male-

unto the place called The place of a skull, which is called in Hebrew Golgotha:	**33** And when they were come unto a place called Golgotha, that is to say, The place of a skull,	**22** And they bring him unto the place Golgotha, which is, being interpreted, The place of a skull.	factors, led with him to be put to death. **33** And when they came unto the place which is called [1]The skull, . . .
cp. 19 29-30.	**34** they gave him wine to drink mingled with gall [*cp.* 27 48]: and when he had tasted it, he would not drink. **35** And when they had crucified him, . . .	**23** And they offered him wine mingled with myrrh [*cp.* 15 36]: but he received it not. **24** And they crucify him, . . .	**36** And the soldiers also mocked him, coming to him, offering him vinegar.
18 where they crucified him, and with him two others, on either side one,	**38** Then are there crucified with him two robbers, one on the right hand, and one on the left.	**27** And with him they crucify two robbers; one on his right hand, and one on his left.	**33b** there they crucified him, and the malefactors, one on the right hand and the other on the left.
and Jesus in the midst. **19** And Pilate wrote a title also, and put it on the cross. And there was written, JESUS OF NAZARETH [*cp.* 1 45; 18 5, 7], THE KING OF THE JEWS [*cp.* 18 33, 39; 19 3, 21: *also* 1 49; 12 13: *and* 6 15; 12 15; 18 37; 19 12, 14, 15]. **20** This title therefore read many of the Jews: [1]for the place where Jesus was crucified was nigh to	**37** And they set up over his head his accusation written, THIS IS JESUS *cp.* 2 23; 26 71: *also* 21 11. THE KING OF THE JEWS [*cp.* 2 2; 27 11, 29: *also* 27 42: *and* 21 5].	**26** And the superscription of his accusation was written over, *cp.* 1 24; 10 47; 14 67; 16 6. THE KING OF THE JEWS [*cp.* 15 2, 9, 12, 18: *also* 15 32].	**38** And there was also a superscription over him, THIS IS *cp.* 4 34; 18 37; 24 19. THE KING OF THE JEWS [*cp.* 23 3, 37: *and* 19 38; 23 2].
	[1] Gr. *impressed.*	[1] Gr. *impress.*	[1] According to the Latin, *Calvary*, which has the same meaning.

the city: and it was written in Hebrew, *and* in Latin, *and* in Greek.
21 The chief priests of the Jews therefore said to Pilate, Write not, The King of the Jews; but, that he said, I am King of the Jews.
22 Pilate answered, What I have written I have written.

[1] Or, *for the place of the city where Jesus was crucified was nigh at hand*

§ 81. The Garments of Jesus parted among the Soldiers: His Mother committed to the Disciple whom He loved

John 19 23-27	Matt. 27 35, 55-56	Mark 15 24, 40-41	Luke 23 34, 49
23 The soldiers therefore, when they had crucified Jesus, took his garments, and made four parts, to every soldier a part; and also the [1]coat: now the [1]coat was without seam, woven from the top throughout. **24** They said therefore one to another, Let us not rend it, but cast lots for it, whose it shall be: that the scripture might be fulfilled, which saith, They parted my gar-	**35** And when they had crucified him, they parted his garments among them, *cp.* 5 40. casting lots.	**24** And they crucify him, and part his garments among them, casting lots upon them, what each should take.	**34** And parting his garments among them, *cp.* 6 29. they cast lots.

John	Matt.	Mark	Luke
ments among them, And upon my vesture did they cast lots. These things therefore the soldiers did. **25** But there were	**55** And many women were there	**40** And there were also women	**49** And all his acquaintance, and the women [cp. 8 2; 23 55; 24 1, 10, 22, 24] that followed with him from Galilee [cp. 23 55[stood afar off,
standing by the cross of Jesus	beholding from afar, which had followed Jesus from Galilee, ministering unto him:	beholding from afar: *verse 41*	cp. 8 3. seeing these things.
	56 among whom was	among whom *were* both	
his mother, and his mother's sister, Mary the *wife* of Clopas, and Mary Magdalene [cp. 20 1, 18].	Mary Magdalene [cp, 27 61; 28 1], and Mary the mother of James and Joses [cp. 27 61; 28 1], and the mother [cp. 20 20] of the sons of Zebedee [cp. 20 20].	Mary Magdalene [cp. 15 47; 16 1, 9], and Mary the mother of James the [1]less and of Joses [cp. 15 47; 16 1], and Salome [cp. 16 1];	cp. 8 2; 24 10. cp. 24 10.
	verse 55	**41** who, when he was in Galilee, followed him, and ministered unto him; and many other women which came up with him unto Jerusalem.	*verse 49* cp. 8 3.
		[1] Gr. *little*.	
26 When Jesus therefore saw his mother, and the disciple standing by, whom he loved [cp. 13 23; 20 2; 21 7, 20: *also* 11 36], he saith unto his mother, Woman [cp. 2 4: *also* 4 21; 20 13, 15], behold, thy son! **27** Then saith he to the disciple, Behold, thy mother! And from that hour the disciple took her unto his own [cp. 16 32: *also* 1 11; 8 44; 13 1; 15 19] home.	cp. 15 28.		cp. 13 12. cp. 18 28.

[1] Or, *tunic*

John 19 24 = Ps. 22 18.

§ 82. The Death of Jesus

John 19 28-30	Matt. 27 45-51	Mark 15 33-38	Luke 23 44-46
cp. 19 14.	**45** Now from the sixth hour there was darkness over all the [1]land until the ninth hour.	**33** And when the sixth hour was come, there was darkness over the whole [1]land until the ninth hour.	**44** And it was now about the sixth hour, and a darkness came over the whole [1]land until the ninth hour, **45** [2]the sun's light failing: and the veil of the [3]temple was rent in the midst. **46** [4]And when Jesus
28 After this Jesus, knowing that all things are now finished [cp. *verse* 30 *and* 4 34; 5 36: 17 4], that the scripture might be accomplished, saith,	*verse 51* **46** And about the ninth hour Jesus	*verse 38* **34** And at the ninth hour Jesus	cp. 12 50; 18 31; 22 37: *also* 13 32.
	cried with a loud voice, saying, Eli, Eli, lama sabachthani? that is, My God, my	cried with a loud voice, Eloi, Eloi, lama sabachthani? which is, being interpreted, My God, my	had cried with a loud voice,

John	Matt.	Mark	Luke
I thirst.	God, [2]why hast thou forsaken me? **47** And some of them that stood there when they heard it, said, This man calleth Elijah.	God, [2]why hast thou forsaken me? **35** And some of them that stood by, when they heard it, said, Behold, he calleth Elijah.	
29 There was set there a vessel full of vinegar: so they put a sponge full of the vinegar upon hyssop, and brought it to his mouth.	**48** And straightway one of them ran, and took a sponge, and filled it with vinegar [*cp.* 27 34], and put it on a reed, and gave him to drink. **49** And the rest said, Let be; let us see whether Elijah cometh to save him.[3]	**36** And one ran, and filling a sponge full of vingear [*cp.* 15 23], put it on a reed, and gave him to drink, saying, Let be; let us see whether Elijah cometh to take him down.	*cp.* 23 36.
30 When Jesus therefore had received the vinegar, he said,	**50** And Jesus cried again with a loud voice,	**37** And Jesus uttered a loud voice,	he said, Father into thy hands I commend my spirit [*cp.* 12 50; 18 31; 22 37: *also* 13 32]:
It is finished [*cp. verse* 28 *and* 4 34; 5 36; 17 4]: and he bowed his head, and gave up his spirit.	and yielded up his spirit. **51** And behold, the veil of the [4]temple was rent in twain from the top to the bottom; and the earth did quake; . . .	and gave up the ghost. **38** And the veil of the [3]temple was rent in twain from the top to the bottom.	and having said this, he gave up the ghost. *verse* 45
	[1] Or, *earth* [2] Or, *why didst thou forsake me?* [3] Many ancient authorities add *And another took a spear and pierced his side, and there came out water and blood.* See John 19 34. [4] Or, *sanctuary*	[1] Or, *earth* [2] Or, *why didst thou forsake me?* [3] Or, *sanctuary*	[1] Or, *earth* [2] Gr. *the sun failing.* [3] Or, *sanctuary* [4] Or, *And Jesus, crying with a loud voice, said*

John 19 28-29 ‖ Matt. 27 48 ‖ Mark 15 36 (‖ Luke 23 36): Ps. 69 21.

§ 83. One of the Soldiers pierces the Side of Jesus with a Spear

John 19 31-37	Matt. 27 57	Mark 15 42	
31 The Jews therefore, because it was the Preparation [*cp.* 19 14, 42], that the bodies	**57** And when even was come, . . . *cp.* 27 62.	**42** And when even was now come, because it was the Preparation, that is, the day before the sabbath, . . .	*cp.* 23 54.
should not remain on the cross upon the sabbath (for the day of that sabbath was a high *day*), asked of Pilate that their legs might be broken, and *that* they might be taken away. **32** The soldiers therefore came, and brake the legs of the first, and of the other which was crucified with him: **33** but when they came to Jesus, and saw that he was dead already, they brake not his legs:		*cp.* 15 44.	
34 howbeit one of the soldiers with a spear pierced his side [*cp.* 20 20, 25, 27], and straightway there came out blood and water [*cp.* 7 38]. **35** And he that hath seen hath borne witness [*cp.* 21 24: *also* 15 27], and his witness is true [*cp.* 21 24: *also* 5 31, 32; 8 13, 14]: and he knoweth that he saith true, that ye also may believe [*cp.* 20 31: *also* 11 15; 13 29; 14 29: *and* 11 42]. **36** For these things came to pass, that the scripture might be fulfilled, A bone of him shall not be [1]broken. **37** And again another scripture saith, They shall look on him whom they pierced.			*cp.* 24 48.

[1] Or, *crushed*

John 19 31: *cp.* Deut. 21 23 *and* Exod. 12 16. John 19 36: Exod. 12 46; Num. 9 12; Ps. 34 20.
John 19 37 = Zech. 12 10.

(vi) The Burial (§ 84)

§ 84. **The Body of Jesus laid in the Tomb**

John 19 38-42	Matt. 27 57-60	Mark 15 42-46	Luke 23 50-54
38 And after these things	**57** And when even was now come,	**42** And when even was now come, because it was the Preparation, that is, the day before the sabbath,	
verse 42	*cp.* 27 62.	**43** there came	*verse* 54
	there came a rich man from Arimathæa, named Joseph,		**50** And behold, a man named
Joseph of Arimathæa,		Joseph of Arimathæa, a councillor of honourable estate,	Joseph, who was a councillor,
			a good man and a righteous **51** (he had not consented to their counsel and deed),
	who also himself	who also himself was looking for the kingdom of God;	*a man* of Arimathæa, a city of the Jews, who was looking for [*cp.* 2 25, 38] the kingdom of God:
being a disciple of Jesus, but secretly for fear of the Jews [*cp.* 7 13; 20 19: *also* 9 22: *and* 12 42],	was Jesus' disciple:		
asked of Pilate that he might take away the body of Jesus:	**58** this man went to Pilate, and asked for the body of Jesus.	and he boldly went in unto Pilate, and asked for the body of Jesus.	**52** this man went to Pilate, and asked for the body of Jesus.
cp. 19 33.		**44** And Pilate marvelled if he were already dead: and calling unto him the centurion, he asked him whether he [1]had been any while dead. **45** And when he learned it of the centurion, he	
and	Then Pilate commanded it to be given up. **59** And Joseph	granted the corpse to Joseph. **46** And he	
Pilate gave *him* leave. He came therefore, and took away his body.	took the body,	he bought a linen cloth, and taking him down,	**53** And he took it down,
39 And there came also Nicodemus, he who at the first came to him by night [*cp.* 3 1-2; 7 50], bringing a [1]mixture of myrrh and aloes, about a hundred pound *weight*. **40** So they took the body of Jesus, and bound it [*cp.* 11 44] in linen cloths [*cp.* 20 5, 6, 7: *and* Luke 24 12] with the spices, as the custom of the Jews is to bury. **41** Now in the place where he was crucified there was a garden [*cp.* 20 1, 5: *also* 18 1, 26]; and in the garden a new tomb		*cp.* 16 1.	*cp.* 23 56.
	and wrapped it in a clean linen cloth,	wound him in the linen cloth,	and wrapped it in a linen cloth,
wherein was never man yet laid.	**60** and laid it in his own new tomb, which he had hewn out in the rock:	and laid him in a tomb which had been hewn out of a rock; *cp.* 11 2.	and laid him in a tomb that was hewn in stone, where never man had yet lain [*cp.* 19 30].
cp. 20 1.	and he rolled a great stone [*cp.* 27 66; 28 2] to the	and he rolled a [*cp.* 16 4] stone [*cp.* 16 3, 4] against the	*cp.* 24 2.

John	Matt.	Mark	Luke
42 There then because of the Jews' Preparation [cp. 19 14, 31] (for the tomb was nigh at hand) they laid Jesus.	door of the tomb, and departed. cp. 27 62.	door of the tomb. verse 42	**54** And it was the day of the Preparation, and the sabbath ¹drew on.

¹ Some ancient authorities read *roll*.   ¹ Many ancient authorities read *were already dead*.   ¹ Gr. *began to dawn*.

John 19 39: *cp.* Ps. 45 8; Song 4 14.

(vii) The Resurrection (§ 85)

§ 85. The Empty Tomb

John 20 1-10	Matt. 28 1-8	Mark 16 1-8	Luke 24 1-12
	1 Now late on the sabbath day,	**1** And when the sabbath was past, Mary Magdalene [cp. 15 40, 47; 16 9], and Mary the *mother* of James [cp. 15 40, 47], and Salome [cp. 15 40], bought spices, that they might come and anoint him.	
cp. 19 25.			verse 10
cp. 19 39, 40.			cp. 23 56.
1 Now on the first *day* of the week [cp. 20 19] cometh Mary Magdalene [cp. 19 25; 20 18] cp. 19 25. early, while it was yet dark, unto the tomb,	as it began to dawn toward the first *day* of the week, came Mary Magdalene [cp. 27 56, 61] and the other Mary [cp. 27 56, 61] to see the sepulchre.	**2** And very early on the first day of the week, they come to the tomb when the sun was risen. cp. verse 1.	**1** But on the first day of the week, at early dawn, they came unto the tomb, bringing the spices [cp. 23 56] which they had prepared.
cp. 19 39, 40.		**3** And they were saying among themselves, Who shall roll us away the stone [cp. 15 46; 16 4] from the door of the tomb?	
cp. 20 12.	**2** And behold, there was a great earthquake; for an angel of the Lord descended from heaven, and came and rolled away the stone [cp. 27 60, 66], and sat upon it. **3** His appearance was as lightning, and his raiment white as snow [cp. 17 2]: **4** and		
cp. 20 12.	for fear [cp. *verse* 8] of him the watchers did quake, and became as dead men.	cp. verse 5.	cp. verse 4.
and seeth the stone taken away from the tomb.	cp. 27 60, 66; 28 2.	[cp. 9 26]. **4** and looking up, they see that the stone [cp. 15 46; 16 3] is rolled back: for it was exceeding great. **5** And	**2** And they found the stone rolled away from the tomb.
cp. vv. 6-8.	cp. 27 60.	entering into the tomb, cp. 16 19.	**3** And they entered in, and found not the body [cp. 24 23] ¹of the Lord Jesus. **4** And it came to pass, while they were per-

cp. 20 12.

cp. 20 12.
cp. 7 15, 21, 46.

cp. 20 13.

cp 18 5, 7; 19 19; *also* 1 45.

cp. 2 19-22; 3 14; 12 32-33.
cp. 2 22; 12 16.

cp. 20 20: *also* 16 22.

---

cp. verse 3.
cp. 8 27; 9 33; 12 23; 15 31; 21 20; 27 14: *also* 7 28; *etc.*

cp. 9 8; 17 6; 27 54; 28 4, 8.

5 And
the angel answered and said unto
the women, Fear
not ye: for I know that ye seek
Jesus, [*cp.* 2 23; 26 71:
also 21 11] which hath been crucified.
6 He
is not here; for he is risen,
even as he said.
Come,
see the place [1]where the Lord
lay. **7** And go quickly, and
tell his disciples, He is
risen from the dead [*cp.* 27 64]; and
lo, he goeth before you into
Galilee [*cp.* 26 32]; there shall ye
see him [*cp.* 28 10]: lo, I have told
you. *cp. verse* 6.

cp. 26 45.
cp. 20 19: *also* 23 34.
cp. 16 21; *etc.*

cp. 26 75.
8 And they
departed quickly from the tomb

with fear [*cp. verse* 4:
also 9 8; 17 6; 27 54] and great joy,
and ran to bring his disciples word.

[1] Many ancient authorities read *where he lay.*

---

they
saw a young man
sitting on the right side, arrayed
in a white [*cp.* 9 3] robe;
and they were amazed [*cp.* 1
27; 2 12; 5 20, 42; 6 51; 7 37; 10
32; 15 5; 16 8: *also* 1 22; *etc.*].
cp. 4 41; 5 15, 33; 9 6, 32; 10 32;
16 8.

6 And
he saith unto
them, Be not amazed:
ye seek
Jesus, the Nazarene [*cp.* 1 24; 10
47; 14 67], which hath been crucified:
he is risen; he
is not here:
cp. verse 7.

behold, the place where they
laid him! **7** But go,
tell his disciples and Peter,

He goeth before you into
Galilee [*cp.* 14 28]: there shall ye
see him
as he said unto you.

cp. 14 41.

cp. 8 31; *etc.*

cp. 14 72.
8 And they
went out, and fled from the tomb;
for trembling and astonishment
[*cp. verse* 5] had come upon them:
and they said nothing to any one;
for they were afraid [*cp.* 4 41; 5
15, 33; 9 6, 32; 10 32].

---

plexed thereabout, behold,
two men [*cp.* 24 23]
stood by them
in dazzling [*cp.* 9 29] apparel:
5 and as they were [*cp.* 5
9, 26; 8 25, 56; 9 43; 11 14; 24
12, 41: *also* 2 47, 48; *etc.*] affrighted [*cp.* 1 12, 65; 2 9; 5 26;
7 16; 8 25, 35, 37, 47; 9 34, 45;
24 37], and bowed down their
faces to the earth,
they said unto
them,

cp. 4 34; 18 37; 24 19.

Why seek ye [2]the living
among the dead? **6** [3]He
is not here, but is risen: remember [*cp. verse* 8] how he spake
unto you when he was yet

cp. 24 34.
in
Galilee,

7 saying
that the Son of man must be
delivered up into the hands of
sinful men, and be crucified, and
the third day rise again [*cp.* 9 22,
43-44; 18 31-33: *also* 13 32, 33;
17 25; 22 22: *and* 24 26, 44, 46].
8 And they remembered [*cp.* 22
61] his words, **9** and
returned [4]from the tomb,

cp. 1 12, 65; 2 9; 5 26; 7 16; *etc.*
cp. 24 41, 52.

---

2 She runneth therefore, and cometh
to Simon Peter, and to the other
disciple [*cp. verses* 3, 4, 8, *and* 18 15,
16], whom Jesus loved [*cp.* 13 23; 19
26; 21 7, 20: *also* 11 36],
cp. 20 18.

cp. 19 25.
cp. 19 25.

and saith
unto them, They have taken
away the Lord [*cp.* 4 1; 6 23; 11 2;
20 18, 20, 25; 21 7, 12] out of the
tomb, and we know not where they
have laid him [*cp.* 20 13].

cp. 20 25.
3 Peter
therefore went forth, and the other
disciple, and they went toward the
tomb. **4** And they ran both together:
and the other disciple outran Peter,

---

verse 1

cp. 27 55.

cp. 28 17.

---

cp. 16 10.

verse 1

cp. 15 40-41.

cp. 16 19, 20.

cp. 16 11, 13, 14.

---

and told all
these things [*cp.* 24 10, 23] to the eleven,
and to all the rest. **10** Now they were
Mary Magdalene [*cp.* 8 2], and Joanna
[*cp.* 8 3], and Mary the *mother* of James: and
the other women [*cp.* 8 2, 3; 23 49, 55; 24 22,
24] with them told these things
unto the apostles.
cp. 7 13, 19; 10 1, 39, 41; 11 39; 12 42; 13 15;
17 5, 6; 18 6; 19 8; 22 61; 24 3, 34.

11 And
these words appeared in their sight as
idle talk; and they disbelieved [*cp.* 24
38, 41: *also* 24 25] them. **12** [5]But Peter
arose,

and ran

John	Matthew	Mark	Luke
and came first to the tomb; **5** and stooping and looking in, he seeth the linen cloths [*cp. verses* 6, 7, *and* 19 40] lying; yet entered he not in. **6** Simon Peter therefore also cometh, following him, and entered into the tomb; and he beholdeth the linen cloths lying, **7** and the napkin [*cp.* 11 44], that was upon his head, not lying with the linen cloths, but rolled up in a place by itself. **8** Then entered in therefore the other disciple also, which came first to the tomb, and he saw, and believed. **9** For as yet they knew not the scripture, that he must rise again from the dead [*cp.* 2 22: *also* 2 19–22]. **10** So the disciples went away again unto their own home.	*cp.* 27 59.	*cp.* 15 46.	unto the tomb; and stooping and looking in, he seeth the linen cloths [*cp.* 23 53]
		cp. verse 5.	*cp. verse* 3.
		cp. verse 5.	by themselves;
			cp. verse 3.
	cp. 22 29: *and* 16 21; *etc.*	*cp.* 12 24: *and* 8 31; *etc.*	*cp.* 24 46: *also* 9 22; *etc.*
			and he ⁶departed to his home, wondering at that which was come to pass [*cp. verse* 5].

¹ Some ancient authorities omit *of the Lord Jesus.*
² Gr. *him that liveth.*
³ Some ancient authorities omit *He is not here, but is risen.*
⁴ Some ancient authorities omit *from the tomb.*
⁵ Some ancient authorities omit *ver.* 12.
⁶ Or, *departed, wondering with himself*

D. The Appearances after the Resurrection and the Commissioning of the Disciples (§§ 86-92)

(i) The Appearances in Jerusalem (§§ 86-90)

§ 86. **The Appearance to Mary Magdalene**

John 20 11-18

John	Matthew (Matt. 28 9-10)	Mark	Luke
11 But Mary was standing without at the tomb weeping: so, as she wept, she stooped and looked into the tomb; **12** and she beholdeth two angels in white sitting, one at the head, and one at the feet, where the body of Jesus had lain. **13** And they say unto her, Woman, why weepest thou [*cp. verse* 15 *below*]? She saith unto them, Because they have taken away my Lord, and I know not where they have laid him [*cp.* 20 2].	*cp.* 28 2, 3, 5: *also* 17 2.	*cp.* 16 5: *also* 9 3.	*cp.* 24 4: *also* 9 29.
		cp. 5 39.	*cp.* 7 13; 8 52; 23 28.
14 When she had thus said, she turned herself back, and beholdeth Jesus standing, and knew not that it was Jesus [*cp.* 21 4]. **15** Jesus saith unto her, Woman, why weepest thou [*cp. verse* 13 *above*]? whom seekest thou [*cp.* 18 4, 7: *also* 1 38; 4 27]?	**9** And behold, Jesus met them, saying,	*cp.* 16 9.	*cp.* 24 16.
cp. 19 3.		*cp.* 5 39.	*cp.* 7 13; 8 52; 23 28.
cp. verse 17.	All hail [*cp.* 26 49; 27 29]. And they came and took hold of his feet, and worshipped	*cp.* 15 18.	*cp.* 1 28.
cp. 9 38: *also* 11 32; 18 6.	him [*cp.* 2 11; 8 2; 9 18; 14 33; 15 25; 20 20; 28 17: *also* 17 14].	*cp.* 5 6: *also* 1 40; 3 11; *etc.*	*cp.* 24 52: *also* 5 8, 12; 8 28; *etc.*
She, supposing him to be the gardener [*cp.* 19 41], saith unto him, Sir, if thou hast borne him hence, tell me where thou has laid him, and I will take him away. **16** Jesus saith unto her, Mary. She turneth herself, and saith unto him in Hebrew, Rabboni [*cp.* 1 38, 49; 3 2; 4 31; 6 25; 9 2; 11 8: *also* 3 26]; which is to say, ¹Master. **17** Jesus saith to [*cp.* 6 20] her ²Touch me not; for I am not yet ascended unto the Father: but go unto my brethren,	*cp.* 26 25, 49: *also* 23 7, 8.	*cp.* 10 51: *and* 9 5; 11 21; 14 45.	
	10 Then saith Jesus unto them, Fear not [*cp.* 14 27; 17 7]:	*cp.* 6 50.	
	cp. verse 9.		
	go tell my brethren		

and say to them, I ascend [*cp.* 6 62: *also* 3 13]
unto my Father and your Father [*cp.* 13 1;
14 12, 28; 16 10, 17, 28], and my God and
your God [*cp.* 13 3: *also* 7 33; 16 5: *and*
17 11, 13].

	that they depart into Galilee, and there shall they see me [*cp.* 28 7 *and* 16-20].		
18 Mary Magdalene cometh and telleth the disciples, I have seen the Lord [*cp.* 20 25: *also* 4 1; 6 23; 11 2; 20 2, 20; 21 7, 12]; and *how that* he had said these things unto her.	*cp.* 28 8.	*cp.* 16 10. *cp.* 16 19, 20.	*cp.* 24 9, *etc.* *cp.* 7 13, 19; 10 1; *etc.*

¹ Or, *Teacher*
² Or, *Take not hold on me*

§ 87. The First Appearance to the Disciples and their Commissioning

John 20 19-23		Mark 16 14-16	Luke 24 36-49
19 When therefore it was evening, on that day, the first *day* of the week [*cp.* 20 1], and when the doors were shut [*cp.* 20 26] where the disciples were, for fear of the Jews [*cp.* 7 13; 19 38: *also* 9 22: *and* 12 42], Jesus		**14** And afterward he was manifested unto the eleven themselves as they sat at meat;	**36** And as they spake these things, he himself
came and stood in the midst [*cp.* 20 26], and saith unto them, Peace *be* unto you [*cp.* 20 21, 26: *also* 14 27].	*cp.* 9 8; 17 6; 27 54; 28 4, 8. *cp.* 14 26.	*cp.* 4 41; 5 15, 33; 9 6, 32; 10 32; 16 8. *cp.* 6 49.	stood in the midst of them, ¹and saith unto them, Peace *be* unto you.
			37 But they were terrified and affrighted [*cp.* 1 12, 65; 2 9; 5 26; 7 16; 8 25, 35, 37, 47; 9 34, 45; 24 5], and supposed that they beheld a spirit. **38** And he said unto them,
cp. 20 25, 27. *cp.* 12 40.	*cp.* 28 17: *also* 13 58. *cp.* 19 8.	and he upbraided them with their unbelief [*cp.* 16 11, 13: *also* 6 6] and hardness of heart [*cp.* 6 52; 8 17: *also* 3 5; 10 5], because they believed not them which had seen him after he was risen.	
cp. 20 25, 27. *cp.* 20 27.	*cp.* 28 17.		Why are ye troubled? and wherefore do reasonings arise in your heart [*cp.* 24 11, 41: *also* 25]? **39** See my hands and my feet, that it is I myself: handle me, and see; for a spirit hath not flesh and bones, as ye behold me having. **40** ²And when he had said this, he shewed them his hands and his feet.
20 And when he had said this, he shewed unto them his hands and his side [*cp.* 20 25, 27: *and* 19 34]. The disciples therefore were *cp.* 20 25, 27. glad [*cp.* 16 22], when they saw the Lord [*cp.* 4 1; 6 23; 11 2; 20 2, 25; 21 7, 12]. *cp.* 21 5.	*cp.* 28 17. *cp.* 28 8.	*cp.* 16 11, 13, 14. *cp.* 16 19, 20.	**41** And while they still disbelieved [*cp.* 24 11, 38: *also* 24 25] for joy [*cp.* 24 52], *cp.* 7 13, 19; 10 1, 39; *etc.* and wondered, he said unto them, Have ye here anything to eat? **42** And they gave him a piece of a broiled fish.³ **43** And he took it, and did eat before them. **44** And he
21 Jesus	Matt. 28 18-20 **18** And Jesus	**15** And he	

therefore
said to them
again, Peace *be* unto you
[*cp.* 20 19, 26: *also* 14 27]:

cp. 14 25; 16 4.

cp. 5 39.

cp. 5 27; 17 2: *also* 3 35;
13 3: *and* 10 18.

cp. verse 23.

cp. 14 13, 14, 26; 15 16;
16 23, 24, 26.

cp. 10 16; 11 52.

cp. 14 15, 23.

cp. 15 27.

cp. 14 16, 26; 15 26; 16 7.

as the Father hath sent me
[*cp.* 3 17, 34; 5 36-38; *etc.*],
even so send I you [*cp.* 17
18].

cp. 14 23.

22 And when he had said
this, he breathed on them,
and saith unto them, Re-
ceive ye the [1]Holy Ghost
[*cp.* 7 39: *also* 14 17, 26;
15 26; 16 13: *and* 14 16;
16 7: *and* 1 33; 3 34]:

---

came to them and
spake unto them, saying,

All authority [*cp.* 7 29; 9 6,
8; 21 23-27: *also* 11 27]
hath been given unto me
in heaven and on earth.

cp. 26 28.

[*cp.
verse* 19: *also* 7 22; 18 5, 20;
24 5] **19** Go ye therefore,
and
make disciples of all the
nations [*cp.* 24 14; 26 13:
also 8 11; 10 18; 21 31, 41-
43; 22 7-10],

baptizing
them into the name of the
Father and of the Son and
of the Holy Ghost:

20 teaching them to
observe all things whatsoever I commanded you:

and lo, I am with you [*cp.* 1
23] [1]alway [*cp.* 18 20], even
unto [2]the end of the world.

[1] Gr. *all the days.*
[2] Or, *the consummation of the age*

---

said unto them,

cp. 1 22, 27; 2 10; 11 27-33.

cp. 1 4.

[*cp.
16 17: *also* 9 37, 38, 39;
13 6] Go ye
into all the world, and

cp. 13 10; 14 9: *also* 12 9.

preach the gospel to
the whole creation
16 He that
believeth and is baptized

shall be
saved; but he that disbe-
lieveth shall be condem-
ned.

cp. 5 30.

---

said unto them,

These are my words which
I spake unto you, while I was
yet with you, how that all
things must needs be fulfilled, which are written in the
law of Moses, and the prophets, and the psalms, con-
cerning me. **45** Then opened he their mind, that they
might understand the scriptures [*cp.* 24 27, 32]; **46** and
he said unto them, Thus it
is written, that the Christ
should suffer, and rise again
from the dead the third day;
cp. 4 32, 36; 5 24; 20 1-8:
also 10 22.

47 and that repentance
[4]and remission of sins [*cp.*
1 77; 3 3] should be
preached in his name [*cp.*
9 48, 49; 10 17; 21 8]

unto all the
[5]nations [*cp.* 2 30-32; 3 6:
also 13 29; 14 21-24; 20 16],

beginning
from Jerusalem.

cp. verse 47.

48 Ye
are witnesses of these
things. **49** And behold,
I send forth the promise
of my Father upon you:

but tarry ye in the city,
until ye be clothed with
power [*cp.* 1 17, 35; 4 14,
36; 5 17; 6 19; 8 46; 9 1]
from on high [*cp.* 1 78].

[1] Some ancient authorities
omit *and saith unto them, Peace
be unto you.*
[2] Some ancient authorities
omit ver. 40.
[3] Many ancient authorities
add *and a honeycomb.*
[4] Some ancient authorities
read *unto.*
[5] Or, *nations. Beginning from
Jerusalem, ye are witnesses*

Matt. 16 **19** I will give   Matt. 18 **18** Verily I say

23 whose soever sins ye forgive, they are forgiven unto them; whose soever *sins* ye retain, they are retained.	unto thee the keys of the kingdom of heaven: and whatsoever thou shalt bind on earth shall be bound in heaven: and whatsoever thou shalt loose on earth shall be loosed in heaven.	unto you, What things soever ye shall bind on earth shall be bound in heaven: and what things soever ye shall loose on earth shall be loosed in heaven.		*cp.* 24 47.

[1] Or, *Holy Spirit*

§ 88. Thomas doubts

John 20 24-25

24 But Thomas [*cp.* 11 16; 14 5; 20 26-29; 21 2], one of the twelve, called [1]Didymus [*cp.* 11 16; 21 2], was not with them when Jesus came. **25** The other disciples therefore said unto him, We have seen the Lord [*cp.* 20 18: *also* 4 1; 6 23; 11 2; 20 2, 20; 21 7, 12]. But he said unto them, Except I shall see in his hands the print of the nails, and put my finger [*cp.* 20 27] into the print of the nails, and put my hand into his side [*cp.* 20 20, 27: *and* 19 34], I will not believe [*cp.* 20 27].	*cp.* 10 3. *cp.* 28 17.	*cp.* 3 18. *cp.* 16 19, 20. *cp.* 16 11, 13, 14.	*cp.* 6 15. *cp.* 7 13, 19; 10 1; *etc.* *cp.* 24 11, 25, 38, 41.

[1] That is, *Twin.*

§ 89. The Second Appearance to the Disciples: Thomas believes

John 20 26-29

26 And after eight days again his disciples were within, and Thomas [*cp.* 11 16; 14 5; 20 24-25; 21 2] with them. Jesus cometh, the doors being shut [*cp.* 20 19], and stood in the midst [*cp.*20 19], and said, Peace *be* unto you [*cp.* 20 19, 21: *also* 14 27]. **27** Then saith he to Thomas, Reach hither thy finger [*cp.* 20 25], and see my hands; and reach *hither* thy hand, and put it into my side [*cp.* 20 20, 25: *and* 19 34]: and be not faithless [*cp.* 20 25: *also* 3 12; 6 64; 14 10], but believing. **28** Thomas answered and said unto him, My Lord and my God. **29** Jesus saith unto him, Because thou hast seen me, [1]thou hast believed: blessed *are* they that have not seen, and *yet* have believed.	*cp.* 10 3. *cp.*28 17: *also* 6 30; 8 26; 14 31; 16 8: *and* 17 20; 21 21.	*cp.* 3 18. *cp.* 16 11, 13, 14: *also* 4 40; 11 22.	*cp.* 6 15. *cp.* 24 36. *cp.* 24 39. *cp.* 24 11, 25, 38, 41: *also* 8 25; 12 28; 17 5-6; 22 32.

[1] Or, *hast thou believed?*

§ 90. The Gospel has been written that others may believe

John 20 30-31

30 Many other signs therefore did Jesus [*cp.* 21 25: *also* 2 11; 4 54; *etc.*] in the presence of the disciples, which are not written in this book: **31** but these are written, that ye may believe [*cp.* 19 35: *also* 11 15; 13 19; 14 29: *and* 11 42: *and* 6 69; 9 38; 11 27; 16 27, 30; 17 8] that Jesus is the Christ [*cp.* 1 41; 4 25, 26, 29; 7 26, 41; 9 22; 10 24; 11 27], the Son of God [*cp.* 1 34, 49; 11 27: *also* 3 18; 5 25; 9 35; 10 36; 11 4; 19 7: *and* 1 18; 3 16-17, 35-36; *etc.*], and that believing ye may have life in his name [*cp.* 3 15, 16, 36; 5 24; 6 40, 47; 11 25-26].	*cp.* 16 16; 26 63, 68; 27 17, 22: *and* 4 3, 6; 8 29; 14 33; *etc.*	*cp.* 8 29; 14 61; 15 32; *and* 1 1; 3 11; 5 7; *etc.*	*cp.* 9 20; 22 67; 23 2, 35, 39: *and* 1 35; 4 3, 9, 41; *etc.*

(ii) The Final Appearance in Galilee (§§ 91-92)

§ 91. **Jesus is manifested through a miraculous Draught of Fishes**

John 21 1-14			Luke 5 1-11

John 21 1-14

1 After these things Jesus manifested himself [*cp. verse* 14: *also* 1 31; 2 11; 7 4; 14 21, 22: *and* 3 21; 9 3; 17 6] again to the disciples at the sea of Tiberias [*cp.* 6 1: *also* 6 16; *etc.*];

cp. 16 12, 14.

cp. 4 18; 15 29: *also* 8 24; *etc.*

cp. 1 16; 7 31: *also* 2 13; *etc.*

1 Now it came to pass, while the multitude pressed upon him and heard the word of God,

and he manifested *himself* on this wise. **2** There were together Simon Peter, and Thomas [*cp.* 11 16; 14 5; 20 24, 26-29] called [1]Didymus [*cp.* 11 16; 20 24], and Nathanael [*cp.* 1 45-51] of Cana in Galilee [*cp.* 2 1, 11; 4 46], and the *sons* of Zebedee, and two other of his disciples [*cp.* 1 35].
3 Simon Peter saith unto them, I go a fishing. They say unto him, We also come with thee. They went forth, and entered into the boat; and that night they took nothing. **4** But when day was now breaking,   Jesus stood on the beach:
        howbeit the disciples knew not that it was Jesus [*cp.* 20 14].

cp. 10 3.

cp. 3 18.

cp. 6 15.

verse 5
        that he   was standing by the lake of Gennesaret [*cp.* 5 2; 8 22, 23, 33];
cp. 24 16.
2 and he saw two boats standing by the lake: but the fishermen had gone out of them, and were washing their nets. **3** And he entered into one of the boats, which was Simon's, and asked him to put out a little from the land. And he sat down and taught the multitudes out of the boat. **4** And when he had left speaking, he
cp. 24 41.

5 Jesus therefore saith unto them, Children, have ye aught to eat? They answered him, No. **6** And he said unto them,
        Cast the net
on the right side of the boat, and ye shall find
verse 3

They cast therefore, and now they were not able to draw it for the   multitude of fishes.
verse 11

said unto Simon, Put out into the deep, and let down your nets for a draught.

5 And Simon answered and said, Master, we toiled all night, and took nothing: but at thy word I will let down the nets. **6** And when they had this done,

they inclosed a great multitude of fishes; and their nets were breaking; **7** and they beckoned unto their partners in the other boat, that they should come and help them. And they came, and filled both the boats, so that they began to sink.

7 That disciple therefore whom Jesus loved [*cp.* 13 23; 19 26; 20 2; 21 20: *also* 11 36] saith unto Peter, It is the Lord [*cp. verse* 12: *also* 4 1, 6 23; 11 2; 20 2, 18, 20, 25]. So when Simon Peter   heard that it was the Lord, he girt [*cp.* 21 18] his coat about him (for he was naked), and cast himself into the sea.

cp. 16 19, 20.

cp. 7 13, 19; 10 1; *etc.*
        8 But
Simon Peter, when he saw it,

cp. 14 28-29.

fell down at Jesus' knees, saying, Depart from me; for I am a sinful man, O Lord. **9** For he was amazed, and all that were with him,

8 But the other disciples came in the little boat [*cp.* 6 22] (for they were not far from the land, but about

cp. 3 9.

two hundred cubits off), dragging the net *full* of   fishes.

at the draught of the fishes which they had taken; **10** and so were also James and John, sons of Zebedee, which were partners with Simon. And Jesus said unto Simon, Fear not; from henceforth thou shalt [1]catch men. **11** And when they had brought their boats to land, they left all, and followed him [*cp.* 5 28; 18 28: *also* 5 27; 9 23, 59; 18 22].

          9 So when they got out upon   the land,
cp. 1 37: *also* 1 43; 12 26; 21 19, 22. they see [2]a fire of coals [*cp.* 18 18] there, and [3]fish [*cp. verses* 10, 13; *and* 6 9, 11] laid thereon, and [4]bread. **10** Jesus saith unto them, Bring of the fish [*cp. verses* 9, 13; *and* 6 9, 11] which ye have now taken. **11** Simon Peter therefore went [5]up, and drew the net to land, full of great fishes, a hundred and fifty and three: and for all there were so many, the net was not rent. **12** Jesus saith unto them, Come *and* break your fast. And none of the disciples durst inquire of him [*cp.* 4 27], Who art thou [*cp.* 1 19; 8 25]? knowing that it was the Lord [*cp. verse* 7 *above*]. **13** Jesus cometh, and taketh the [6]bread, and giveth them [*cp.* 6 11], and the fish [*cp. verses* 9, 10; *and* 6 9, 11] likewise [*cp.* 6 11]. **14** This is now the third time [*cp.* 20 19, 26] that Jesus was manifested [*cp. verse* 1] to the disciples, after that he was risen from the dead.

	cp. 4 20, 22; 9 9; 19 27; *also* 4 19; 8 22; 9 9; 16 24; 19 21.	*cp.* 1 18, 20; 2 14; 10 28: *also* 1 17; 2 14; 8 34; 10 21.		
cp. 14 19; 15 36; 26 26.	*cp.* 6 41; 8 6; 14 22. *cp.* 16 12, 14.	*cp.* 16 19, 20.	*verse 6* *cp.* 7 13, 19; *etc.* *cp.* 24 30: *also* 9 16; 22 19.	

[1] Gr. *take alive.*

[1] That is, *Twin.*   [2] Gr. *a fire of charcoal.*   [3] Or, *a fish*   [4] Or, *a loaf*
[5] Or, *aboard*   [6] Or, *loaf*

§ 92. The Commission to Peter and to the Disciple whom Jesus loved

John 21 15-23

15 So when they had broken their fast, Jesus saith to Simon Peter, Simon, *son of* [1]John [*cp. verses* 16, 17, *and* 1 42], [2]lovest thou me [*cp.* 14 21, 23; 16 27] more than these? He saith unto him, Yea, Lord; thou knowest that I [3]love thee. He saith unto him, Feed my lambs [*cp. verses* 16, 17: *also* 10 11-16, 26-27]. **16** He saith to him again a second time, Simon, *son of* [1]John, [2]lovest thou me? He saith unto him, Yea, Lord; thou knowest that I [3]love thee. He saith unto him, Tend my sheep. **17** He saith unto him the third time, Simon, *son of* [1]John, [3]lovest thou me? Peter was grieved because he said unto him the third time, [3]Lovest thou me? And he said unto him, Lord, thou knowest all things [*cp.* 16 30: *also* 2 24, 25: *and* 1 48; 4 19, 29; 5 6, 42; 6 61, 64; 11 14; 13 11, 18; 16 19; 18 4]; thou [4]knowest that I [3]love thee. Jesus saith unto him, Feed my sheep. **18** Verily, verily, I say unto thee, When thou wast young, thou girdedst thyself [*cp.* 21 7], and walkesdt whither thou wouldest: but when thou shalt be old, thou shalt stretch forth thy hands, and another shall gird thee, and carry thee whither thou wouldest not. **19** Now this he spake, signifying by what manner of death [*cp.* 12 33; 18 32] he should glorify God. And when he had spoken this, he saith unto him, Follow me [*cp. verse* 22 *below* and 13 36: *also* 1 43; 12 26]. **20** Peter, turning about, seeth the disciple whom Jesus loved [*cp.* 13 23; 19 26; 20 2; 21 7: *also* 11 36] following; which also leaned back on his breast [*cp.* 13 25] at the supper, and said, Lord, who is he that betrayeth thee [*cp.* 13 25]? **21** Peter [*cp.* 13 36: *also* 6 68] therefore seeing him saith to Jesus, Lord, [5]and what shall this man do? **22** Jesus saith unto him, If I will that he tarry till I come [*cp.* 14 3, 18, 28], what *is that* to thee [*cp. verse* 23 *below*]? follow thou me [*cp. verse* 19 *above*]. **23** This saying therefore went forth among the brethren, that that disciple should not die: yet Jesus said not unto him, that he should not die; but, If I will that he tarry till I come, what *is that* to thee [*cp. verse* 22 *above*]?

cp. 16 17: *also* 17 25.	*cp.* 14 37.	*cp* 22 31.
cp. 16 18, 19: *also* 9 36; 10 6; 15 24: *and* 26 31.	*cp.* 6 34: *and* 14 27.	*cp.* 22 32.
cp. 9 4; 12 25; 16 8.	*cp.* 2 8; 8 17.	*cp.* 5 22; 6 8; 9 47; 11 17.
cp. 4 19; 8 22; 9 9; 16 24; 19 21.	*cp.* 1 17; 2 14; 8 34; 10 21.	*cp.* 5 27; 9 23, 59; 18 22.
cp. 14 28; 15 15; *etc.* *cp.* 10 23; 16 28.	*cp.* 8 32; 9 5; *etc.*	*cp.* 8 45; 9 33; *etc.* *cp.* 19 13.
cp. 27 4.		

[1] Gr. *Joanes.* See ch. 1. 42, margin.   [2], [3] *Love* in these places represents two different Greek words.   [4] Or, *perceivest*   [5] Gr. *and this man, what?*

E. Concluding Notes (§§ 93-94)

§ 93. The Disciple whom Jesus loved is the Author of the Gospel

John 21 24

24 This is the disciple which beareth witness [*cp.* 19 35: *also* 15 27] of these things, and wrote these things: and we know [*cp.* 3 2; 4 42; 9 24, 29, 31; 16 30] that his witness is true [*cp.* 19 35: *also* 5 31, 32; 8 13, 14].	*cp.* 22 16.	*cp.* 12 14.	*cp.* 24 48. *cp.* 20 21.

§ 94. The Author of the Gospel has provided only a Selection from the available Material

John 21 25

25 And there are also many other things which Jesus did [*cp.* 20 30], the which if they should be written every one, I suppose that even the world itself would not contain the books that should be written.			

INDEX OF SYNOPTIC PARALLELS
printed in the text in full

MATTHEW

INDEX TO SECTION HEADINGS